The Coptic Encyclopedia

Editors and Consultants

The Coptic Encyclopedia

Aziz S. Atiya
EDITOR IN CHIEF

Volume 1

Macmillan Publishing Company
NEW YORK
Collier Macmillan Canada
TORONTO
Maxwell Macmillan International
NEW YORK · OXFORD · SINGAPORE · SYDNEY

Macmillan Publishing Company
866 Third Avenue, New York, NY 10022

Collier Macmillan Canada, Inc.
1200 Eglinton Avenue East, Suite 200, Don Mills, Ontario M3C 3N1

Library of Congress Catalog Card No.: 90-23448

Printed in the United States of America

printing number
1 2 3 4 5 6 7 8 9 10

Library of Congress Cataloging-in-Publication Data

The Coptic encyclopedia / Aziz S. Atiya, editor-in-chief.
p. cm.
Includes bibliographical references and index.
ISBN 0-02-897025-X (set)
1. Coptic Church—Dictionaries. 2. Copts—Dictionaries.
I. Atiya, Aziz S., 1898- .
BX130.5.C66 1991 90-23448
281′.7′03—dc20 CIP

The preparation of this volume was made possible in part by a grant from the National Endowment for the Humanities, an independent federal agency.

Photographs on pages 567, 736, 754, 755, 790, 791, 876–878, 1284, 1311, and 2168 are reproduced courtesy of the Metropolitan Museum of Art. Photography by the Egyptian Expedition.

Editorial and Production Staff

Philip Friedman
Publisher

Elly Dickason
Managing Editor

Sylvia Kanwischer Jonathan Wiener
Project Editors

Karin K. Vanderveer
Assistant Editor

Leland Lowther Elizabeth I. Wilson Susan C. Winslow
Copy-editors

Jonathan Aretakis Gretchen Gordon Helen Wallace
Proofreaders

Cynthia Crippen
Indexer

Matthew M. Kardovich
Production Manager

Contents

List of Articles

I

O

List of Contributors

Abd al-Rahim Abd al-Rahman Abd al-Rahim
Azhar University, Cairo
Bajuri, Shaykh Ibrāhīm, al-

Abdelsayyed, Rev. Gabriel
Coptic Orthodox Church of Saint Mark, Jersey City, N.J.
Anamnesis; Epiclesis; Migration: United States, Australia, Other Countries; Samuel; Shenouda III

Adams, Nettie K.
University of Kentucky
Nubian Textiles

Adams, William Y.
University of Kentucky
Abwāb, al-; 'Alwā; Axum; Ballana Kingdom and Culture; Banū al-Kanz; Baqṭ Treaty; Baṭn al-Ḥajar; Beja Tribes; Dongola; Dotawo; Faras; Faras Murals; Griffith, Francis Llewellyn; Ibn Ḥawqal; Ibn Salīm al-Aswānī; Jabal 'Addā; Julian, Evangelist; Kush, Empire of; Lālibalā; Longinus; Makouria; Menarti; Noba; Nobatia; Nobatia, Eparch of; Nubia; Nubia, Evangelization of; Nubia, Islamization of; Nubian Archaeology, Medieval; Nubian Ceramics; Nubian Christian Survivals; Nubian Church Art; Nubian Church Organization; Nubian Inscriptions, Medieval; Nubian Languages and Literature; Nubian Monasteries; Nubians; Philae; Qaṣr Ibrīm; Sai Island; Shibāb al-Dīn Aḥmad Nuwayrī; Soba; Tafa; Talmīs; Tamīt

Ahrens, Dieter
Staatliches Museum, Trier
Metrology, Coptic

Alcock, Anthony
Nuffield College, Oxford
Samuel of Qalamūn, Saint

Allouche, Adel
University of Pennsylvania
Umayyad Fleet, Coptic Contribution to

Altheim-Stiehl, Ruth
Westfälische Wilhelms-Universität, Munster
Persians in Egypt

As'ad, Maurice
Attorney, Cairo
Family Life, Coptic; Samuel

Athanasius, Archbishop
Coptic Church Bishopric, Banī Suef, Egypt
Women's Religious Communities

*Atiya, Aziz S.
University of Utah
'Abd al-Masīḥ Ṣalīb al-Masū'dī; Abilius, Saint; Abstinence; Abū al-Makārim; Abū Jirjah; Abū Ṣāliḥ the Armenian; Abū Shākir Ibn al-Rāhib; Achillas; Agrippinus; Ahl al-Dhimmah; Alexander I; Alexandria, Historic Churches in; Allberry, Charles Robert Cecil Austin; Amélineau, Emile Clément; Anastasius; Andronicus; Anianus; As'ad Abū al-Faraj Hibatallāh ibn al-'Assāl, al-; Assemani; Athanasius I; Athanasius II; Athanasius III; Awlād al-'Assāl; Ayyubid Dynasty and the Copts; Bardenhewer, Otto; Baronius, Cesare; Bible Text, Egyptian; Bollandists; Bouriant, Urbain; Budge, Ernest Alfred Thompson Wallis; Būlus al-Būshī; Butcher, Edith L.; Buṭrus al-Sidmantī; Catechetical School of Alexandria; Celadion, Saint; Cerdon, Saint; Chaîne, Marius Jean Joseph; Champollion, Jean François; Chassinat, Emile Gaston; Ciasca, Agostino; Clarke, Somers; Codex Alexandrinus; Codex Ephraemi Syri; Codex Sinaiticus; Codex Vaticanus; Covenant of 'Umar; Crusades, Copts and the; Curzon, Robert; Cyril I, Saint; Cyrus al-Muqawqas; Daressy, Georges Emile Jules; Dayr al-Amīr Tadrūs (Munā al-Amīr); Demetrius I; Dévaud, Eugène Victor; Dimyānah and Her Forty Virgins; Dionysius the Areopagite; Dionysius the Great; Drioton, (Chanoine) Etienne Marie Félix; Duchesne, Louis; Ecthesis; Erichsen, Wolja; Eucharistic Fast; Eumenius; Eusebius of Caesarea; Evelyn-White, Hugh Gerard; Fortescue, Adrian; Galtier, Emile Joseph; Gayet, Albert Jean Marie Philippe; Gospels, Synoptic; Groff, William N.; Guimet, Emile Etienne; Ḥabīb Jirjis; Hall, Henry Reginald Holland; Hardy, Edward R.; Ḥārit al-Rūm; Hauser, Walter; Hefele, Karl Joseph; Heraclas, Saint; Hesychian Bible; Hesychius; Hesychius of Alexandria; Heuser, Gustav; Higher Institute of Coptic Studies; Hyvernat, Henri Eugène Xavier Louis, Abbé; Ibn al-Biṭrīq, Sa'īd; Ibn Kabar; Ibn Mamātī; Ibn Sibā, Yuḥannā Ibn Abī Zakariyyā; Ibscher, Hugo; Ideler, Julius Ludwig; Isaac the Deacon; Isidhūrus; Jacob Baradaeus; Jerome, Saint; Jizyah; John XVII; John XVIII; John of Antioch; Julian, Saint; Junker, Hermann; Justus; Kharāj; Krall, Jakob; Labib Ḥabachi;

---

*Deceased.

Lefort, L. Théophile; Legrain, Georges; Lemm, Oskar Eduardovich von; Lenormant, Charles; Lepsius, Karl Richard; Le Quien, Michel; Letronne, Jean Antoine; Literature, Copto-Arabic; Makīn Ibn al-ʿAmīd, al-; Mallon, Marie Alexis; Mamluks and the Copts; Mansi, Giovanni Domenico; Manṣūr, ʿAbdallāh; Maqrīzī, Taqīy al-Dīn al-; Marcianus; Mariyyah the Copt; Mark I, Saint; Mark VII; Martyr, Feast of the; Martyrs, Coptic; Marucchi, Orazio; Maspero, Gaston Camille Charles; Maspero, Jean; Maximus, Saint; Michalowski, Kazimierz; Miedema, Rein; Migne, Jacques-Paul; Mīkhāʾīl Shārūbīm; Millet; Missionaries in India, Coptic; Monneret de Villard, Ugo; Muʾtaman Abū Isḥāq Ibrāhīm Ibn al-ʾAssāl; Munier, Adolphe Henri; Murray, Margaret Alice; Nawrūz; Neale, John Mason; Neander, Johann August Wilhelm; Origen; Origenist Controversies; Ottomans, Copts Under the; Parthey, Gustav Friedrich Constantin; Patriarchs, Dates and Succession of; Patrology; Paul the Black; Pellegrini, Astorre; Peter II; Peter III Mongus; Peter IV; Peyron, Amedeo Angelo Maria; Piankoff, F. Alexandre; Piehl, Karl Fredrik; Primus; Qaṣr al-Shamʿ; Quibell, James Edward; Ranke, Hermann; Renaudot, Eusèbe; Ricci, Seymour Montefiore Robert Rosso de; Rizq Agha; Rösch, Friedrich; Rossi, Francesco; Rufinus; Sacy, Antoine Isaac Sylvestre de; Saints, Coptic; Sāwīrus ibn al-Muqaffaʿ; Sayce, Archibald Henry; Schäfer, Heinrich; Schmidt, Carl; Sethe, Kurt Heinrich; Seyffarth, Gustavus; Shamm al-Nasim; Shukrallāh

Jirjis; Socrates; Sophia, Saint; Sozomen; Spiegelberg, Wilhelm; Steindorff, Georg; Stern, Ludwig; Ṣuqāʿi Faḍl Allāh Fakhr, al-; Synaxarion, Copto-Arabic; Synesius; Tattam, Henry; Theodoret; Theonas; Till, Walter Curt Franz Theodor Karl Alois; Timothy I, Saint; Tulunids and Ikhshids, Copts Under the; Ulphilas; Vigil; Yaʿqūb Nakhlah Rufaylah; Yūḥānnā; Yūḥānnā the Deacon; Zoega, Georg (Jorgen)

Attridge, Harold
University of Notre Dame

Tripartite Tractate

Auth, Susan
Newark Museum, New Jersey

Glass, Coptic

Baḥr, Samiraḥ
Capital Market Authority, Cairo

Coptic Congress of Asyūṭ; Egyptian Conference of Heliopolis; Modern Egypt, Copts in; Ummah al-Qibtiyah, al-

Ballet, Pascale
Institut français d'Archéologie orientale, Cairo

Ceramics, Coptic

Barnard, Leslie W.
University of Leeds

Antichrist; Apologist; Christology; Clement of Alexandria; Communicatio Idiomatum; Constantinople, Third Council of; Ephesus, First Council of; Iconoclasm

Basilios, Archbishop
Coptic Patriarchate, Jerusalem

Ablutions; Absolution; Advent; Agnus Dei; Alexandrian Theology; Alleluia; Altar Lights; Altar, Consecration of; Ambo; Angels; Anointing; Antimension; Antiphon; Apostles' Creed; Apostolic See; Apostolic Succession; Apostolic Tradition; Archangel; Archbishop; Archdeacon; Atonement; Baptism; Baptism, Liturgy of; Baptistery, Consecration of; Basilios II; Basilios III; Bishop; Bishops, Consecration of; Burial Rites and Practices; Candles; Canonical Hours, Book of; Canonization; Cantor; Catechumen; Catholicos; Celibacy, Clerical; Cherubim and Seraphim; Chorepiscopus; Chrism, Consecration of the; Chrismatory; Christ, Nature of; Church, Consecration of; Church, Laying the Cornerstone of; Communion; Communion Table; Compline; Concomitance; Confession and Penitence; Confirmation; Consecration; Consubstantiation; Cross, Sign of the; Cross, Veneration of the; Dayr al-Sulṭān; Deacon; Deacon and Archdeacon, Ordination of; Deaconess; Dead, Prayer for the; Digamy; Epiphany, Liturgy of the; Eucharist; Eucharistic Bread; Eucharistic Veils; Eucharistic Vessels and Instruments; Euchologion; Evangelist; Fasting; Feast; Feasts, Major, *articles on* Annunciation, Nativity, Epiphany, Palm Sunday, Easter; Forty-nine Martyrs of Scetis; Fraction; Genuflection; Gloria in Excelsis; Good Friday; Gregory the Illuminator, Saint; Guardian Angel; Hades; Hail Mary; Hands, Laying-on of; Heaven; Hegumenos; Hegumenos, Ordination of a; Hierarchy, Church; Holy Cross Day; Holy Land, Coptic Churches in the; Holy Saturday; Holy Week; Hosanna; Immaculate Conception; Immersion; Incarnation; Jerusalem, Coptic See of; Judgment, Last; Kiss of Peace; Kyrie Eleison; Lectionary; Liturgical Insignia; Liturgical Instruments; Liturgical Vestments; Martyrdom; Mass of the Catechumens; Mass of the Faithful; Matins, Liturgy of; Metropolitan; Nun; Offertory; Orientation Toward the East; Paradise; Patriarch, Consecration of; Penance; Priest, Ordination of; Priesthood; Provost; Rabitat al-Quds; Responsory; Theophilos I; Timotheos I, Archbishop of Jerusalem; Unction of the Sick, Holy Sacrament of; Vespers; Yacobus II

*Basta, Munir
Coptic Museum, Cairo
Coptic Museum; Girgis Mattha; Iqlādiyūs Labīb; Labib Ḥabachi; Yassa ʿAbd al-Masīḥ

Bates, Michael
American Numismatic Society, New York
Coinage in Egypt

Baumeister, Theofried
Mainz University
Abraham Persa; Acta Sanctorum; Apollonius and Philemon, Saints; Apostolic Fathers; Arianus, Saint; Cyprian the Magician; Hermas; Ignatius of Antioch, Saint; Martyrology; Panesneu, Saint; Panine and Paneu; Polycarp, Saint; Serapion, Saint; Til, Saint

Bayadi, S. al-
Inspector of Education, Cairo
Naguib Mahfouz

Behrens-Abuseif, Doris
University of Munich
Boutros Ghālī; British Occupation of Egypt; Coptic Reform Society; Political Parties, *article on* Nationalist Party

Benazeth, Dominique
Louvre Museum, Paris
Metalwork, Coptic; Mythological Subjects in Coptic Art, *articles on* Heracles, Nile Deity; Pen Cases; Symbols in Coptic Art, *articles on* Dolphin, Fish

Bestawros, Adel Azer
Attorney, Alexandria, Egypt
Community Council, Coptic; Waqf, Coptic

Bethge, Hans Gebhard
Humboldt-Universität, Mühlenbeck
On the Origin of the World

Bierbrier, M. L.
The British Museum, London
Barns, John Wintour Baldwin; Černý, Jaroslav; Dulaurier, Jean Paul Louis François Edouard Leuge; Kahle, Paul Eric; Marcel, Jean-Joseph; Muyser, Jacob Louis Lambert; Palanque, (Henri Amedée) Charles; Pococke, Richard; Rainer, Archduke; Turaev, Boris Alexandrovich; Wessely, Carl Franz Joseph; Worrell, William Hoyt

Bilaniuk, Petro B. T.
University of St. Michael's College, Toronto
Coptic Catholic Church; Coptic Relations with Rome; Florence, Copts at the Council of; Holy Spirit, Coptic Doctrine of the; Patriarch; Pope in the Coptic Church

Blanc-Ortolan, Monique
Musée des Arts décoratifs, Paris
Art, Coptic Influences on European; Art, Coptic and Irish

Böhlig, Alexander
University of Tübingen
Manichaeism

Boncenne, Catherine
Louvre Museum, Paris
Mythological Subjects in Coptic Art, *article on* Dionysus

Bonneau, Danielle
Paris
Karanis; Nilometer

Bouillet de Rozières, Marie-Françoise
Paris
Art Preservation

*Bourguet, Pierre du, S.J.
Louvre Museum, Paris
Art, Byzantine Influences on Coptic; Art, Coptic and Irish; Art, Historiography of Coptic; Art Survivals from Ancient Egypt; Bāwīṭ; Biblical Subjects in Coptic Art, *articles on* David at the Court of Saul, Demons, Jonah; Bone and Ivory Carving; Christian Subjects in Coptic Art, *overview article and articles on* Apostles and Evangelists, Baptism of Jesus, Bath of the Infant Jesus, Massacre of the Innocents, Orant, Parthian Horsemen, Shenute, Thecla; Clédat, Jean; Coptic Collections in Museums; Costume, Military; Cross, Triumph of the; Dating; Dayr Anbā Hadrā; Dayr al-Madīnah; Dayr al-Shuhadā' (Isnā); Ethiopian Art, Coptic Influences on; Hunting in Coptic Art; Illumination, Coptic; Magical Objects; Mythological Subjects in Coptic Art, *articles on* Aphrodite, Bellerophon and the Chimera, Dancers, Horus the Avenging Horseman, Leda, Nereids, Nilotic Scenes, The Seasons, The Three Graces; Portraiture, Coptic; Sauneron,

Serge; Simon, Jean; Statuary; Symbols in Coptic Art, *articles on* Conch Shell, Cross; Syrian Influences on Coptic Art; Textiles, Coptic, *articles on* Iconography of Woven Textiles, Iconography of Resist-Dyed Textiles; Warriors in Coptic Art; Wiesmann, Hermann

Braun, Hans
Martin Bodmer Foundation, Geneva-Cologny
Bodmer, Martin

Bresciani, Edda
Cairo
Madīnat Māḍī

Brown, S. Kent
Brigham Young University
Act of Peter; Apocalypse of Peter; Butler, Alfred Joshua; Discourse on the Eighth and Ninth; Evetts, Basil T.A.; Gospel of the Egyptians; Gospel of the Truth; Keimer, Ludwig; Ladeuze, Paulin; Ostracon; Plato's Republic; Prayer of Thanksgiving; Thunder, Perfect Mind

Cameron, Averil
King's College, London
Justin II; Procopius; Theodora

Carter, Lynn
Development planner, Peshawar, Pakistan
Press, Coptic

Castel, Georges
Institut français d'Archéologie orientale, Cairo
Dayr al-Fakhūrī; Dayr al-Shuhadā' (Isnā); Qurnat Mar'ī

Chiarelli, Leonard C.
University of Utah
Aqbāt, al-; Arsenal of Tunis

Cody, Aelred, O.S.B.
St. Meinrad Archabbey, Indiana
Anaphora of Saint Basil; Anaphora of Saint Cyril; Anaphora of Saint Gregory; Calendar, Coptic; Calendar, Gregorian; Calendar, Julian; Dayr Anbā Bishoi, Dayr al-Baramūs; Dayr al-Suryān; Doxology; Era of Martyrs; Eschatology; Evangeliary; Mark, Liturgy of Saint; Pascha; Paschal Controversy; Scetis

Coquin, Charlambia
Centre national de Recherches scientifiques, Paris
Church of Abū Sayfayn; Church of al-Mu'allaqah; Dayr Abū Sayfayn (Old Cairo)

Coquin, René-Georges
Ecole des Hautes Etudes, Paris
Abraham of Farshūt; Abraham and George of Scetis, Saints; Abraham of Minūf, Saint; Abydos; Agathon the Stylite, Saint; Akhmīm; Alexandra, Saint; Ammonius of Tūnah; Anastasia, Saint; Anastasius; Antinoopolis; Aphrodito; Apollo the Shepherd, Saint; Apostolic Constitutions; Aqfahṣ; 'Araj, al-; Atrīs; 'Ayn 'Amūr; Azarī; Bahjūrah; Bakhānis-Tmoushons; Banī Ḥasan and Speos Artemidos; Banī Kalb; Barsūm the Naked, Saint; Bāwīṭ; Brightman, Frank Edward; Būsh; Canon Law; Canons, Apostolic; Canons, Ecclesiastical; Canons of Clement; Canons of Epiphanius; Canons of Gregory of Nyssa; Canons of Hippolytus; Canons of Pseudo-Athanasius; Canons of Saint Basil; Canons of Saint John Chrysostom; Cell; Charisios; Claudius, Saint; Clysma; Constantine; Copres, Saint; Ctesippus of Enaton; Cyriacus; Damanhūr; Daniel and Moses; Dayr; Dayr Abīrūn; Dayr Abū Anūb, or Nūb; Dayr Abu al-Lif; Dayr Abū Bifām (Asyūṭ); Dayr Abū Bifām (Samālūt); Dayr Abu Bifam (Ṭimā); Dayr Abū Daraj; Dayr Abū Fānah; Dayr Abū Ḥalbānah; Dayr Abū Ḥinnis (Mallawi); Dayr Abū Isḥāq; Dayr Abū Maqrūfah and Dayr al-Janadlah; Dayr Abū al-Līf; Dayr Abū Mūsā; Dayr Abū Mūshā; Dayr Abū Sarabām; Dayr Abū Sayfayn (Qūṣ); Dayr Abū al-Sayfayn (Ṭamwayh); Dayr al-'Adawiyyah; Dayr al-'Adhrā' (Akhmīm); Dayr al-'Adhrā' (Asyūṭ); Dayr al-'Adhrā' (Bayad al-Naṣārā); Dayr al-'Adhrā' (Fayyūm); Dayr al-'Adhra-' (Samālūṭ); Dayr al-Aḥmar (Giza); Dayr al-Amīr Tadrūs (Jabal Abū Fūdah); Dayr al-Amīr Tadrūs (Luxor); Dayr Anbā Abshāy (Abū Tīj); Dayr Anbā Abshāy (Ṭūd); Dayr Anbā Anṭūniyūs; Dayr Anbā Bākhūm (Abydos); Dayr Anbā Bākhūm (Barjanūs-Minyā); Dayr Anbā Bākhūm (Madāmūd-Luxor); Dayr Anbā Bākhūm (Sawam'ah); Dayr Anbā Bīdābā; Dayr Anbā Bisādah; Dayr Anbā Bishoi (Suhāj); Dayr Anbā Būlā; Dayr Anbā Daryūs; Dayr Anbā Hadrā; Dayr Anbā Helias (Naqādah); Dayr Anbā Helias (Wādī al-Naṭrūn); Dayr Anbā Ḥiziqyāl; Dayr Anbā Palaemon; Dayr Anbā Pisentius; Dayr Anbā Ṣamū'īl of Qalamūn (Fayyūm); Dayr Anbā Sāwīrus; Dayr Anbā Shinūdah (Suhāj); Dayr Apa Anūb; Dayr Apa Hor (Minyā); Dayr Apa Hor (Qalyubiyyah); Dayr Apa Isḥāq; Dayr Apa Jeremiah (Saqqara); Dayr Apa Thomas; Dayr al-Arman; Dayr al-'Asal; Dayr Asfal al-Arḍ; Dayr al-'Askar; Dayr 'Atiyyah; Dayr al-'Awanah; Dayr al-'Azab; Dayr al-Bakhīt; Dayr al-Bala'yzah; Dayr

Bālūja; Dayr al-Ballāṣ; Dayr al-Barshah and Dayr al-Nakhlah; Dayr Bi'l-Ḥabash; Dayr al-Biṣrah; Dayr Buqṭur of Shū; Dayr al-Dīk; Dayr Durunkah; Dayr Ebifania; Dayr al-Fakhūrī; Dayr al-Ghanāyim; Dayr Ghubriyāl (Armant); Dayr al-Ḥadīd; Dayr al-Ḥājar (Dakhlah); Dayr al-Ḥammām; Dayr Harmīnā; Dayr al-Ikwah; Dayr al-ʿIẓām (Asyūṭ); Dayr al-Jabrāwī; Dayr al-Jarnūs; Dayr al-Jawlī; Dayr al-Juʿ; Dayr al-Khādīm; Dayr al-Khandaq; Dayr al-Kubāniyyah; Dayr al-Madīnah; Dayr al-Maghṭis; Dayr al-Majmaʿ; Dayr al-Malāk (Nag Hammadi); Dayr al-Malāk Mīkhā'īl; Dayr al-Malāk Mīkhā'īl (Akhmīm); Dayr al-Malāk Mīkhā'īl (Fayyūm); Dayr al-Malāk Mīkhā'īl (Idfū); Dayr al-Malāk Mīkhā'īl (Jirjā); Dayr al-Malāk Mīkhā'īl (Marāghah); Dayr al-Malāk Mīkhā'īl (Naqādah); Dayr al-Malāk Mīkhā'īl (Qamūlah); Dayr al-Malāk Mīkhā'īl (al-Rayramūn); Dayr Mār Buqṭur (Qamūlah); Dayr Mār Jirjis (Dimiqrāt); Dayr Mār Jirjis (Sidamant); Dayr Mār Jirjis al-Hadīdī; Dayr Mār Mīnā (Gharbiyyah); Dayr Mār Mīnā (Hiw-Nag Hammadi); Dayr Mār Mīnā (Jabal Abū Fudah); Dayr Mart Maryam; Dayr al-Maṭmar; Dayr Maṭrā; Dayr al-Maymah; Dayr al-Maymūn; Dayr al-Muḥarraq; Dayr al-Muḥarraqah; Dayr Muṣṭafā Kāshif; Dayr al-Muṭṭin; Dayr Nahyā; Dayr al-Nāmūs; Dayr al-Naṣārā (Antinoopolis); Dayr al-Naṣārā (Armant); Dayr al-Nasṭūr; Dayr Posidonios; Dayr al-Qaṣriyyah; Dayr Qibriyus; Dayr Qubbat al-Hawā; Dayr al-Qurqāṣ; Dayr al-Quṣayr (Jabal Abū Fūdah); Dayr al-Quṣayr (Ṭurah); Dayr Rīfah; Dayr al-Rūmāniyyah; Dayr al-Rūmī; Dayr al-Sabʿat Jibāl; Dayr al-Salīb; Dayr al-Sanad; Dayr al-Sanqūriyyah; Dayr al-Sāqiyah; Dayr al-Shahīd Philūthāwaus; Dayr Shahrān (Giza); Dayr al-Shalwīt; Dayr al-Shamʿ; Dayr al-Shuhadā' (Akhmīm); Dayr al-Shuhadā' (Isnā); Dayr Sitt Dimyānah; Dayr Sunbāṭ; Dayr Tāsā; Dayr al-Ṭīn; Dayr al-Ṭurfah; Dayr Yūḥannā; Dayr Yuḥannis; Dayr al-Zāwiyah; Desert Fathers; Diolkos; Dioscorus; Duwayr; Elias of Bishwāw, Saint; Elias of Samhūd, Saint; Encratite; Euphrosyna, Saint; Farshūṭ; Febronia, Saint; Hadrā of Aswan, Saint; Hadrā of Benhadab, Saint; Hamai of Kahyor, Saint; Ḥamīdāt, al-; Harmīnā, Saint; Hayz, al-; Hebbelynck, Adolphe; Hermitages, Theban; Ḥilwān; Hop of Ṭūkh, Apa; Hor (companion of Ambrosios); Hor, Apa; Hor of Abrahat, Saint; Idfā; Isaac of Qalamūn; Isaac, Disciple of Apollo; Jabal al-Silsilah; Jabal Khashm al-Quʿūd; Jabal al-Silsilah; Jabal Ṭarif; James, Saint; James of Scetis, Saint; Jeremiah, Saint; John, Saint; John, Hegumenos of Scetis; John Kāmā, Saint; John of Pake; Joseph; Joseph of Bishwāw, Saint; Joseph of Tsenti, Saint; Kellia, *article on* French Archaeological Activity; Kom al-Rāhib; Kuentz, Charles; Latson, Apa; Laura; Lectionary; Leroy, Jules; Macarius the Canonist; Macrobius, Saint; Malinine, Michel; Manasseh, Saint; Manqabad; Mark the Simple, Saint; Mary of Alexandria, Saint; Matthew the Poor, Saint; Meir; Menas; Menas, Saint; Menas of al-Ashmūnayn, Saint; Mīkhā'īl (bishop of Atrīb and Malīj); Mīkhā'īl (bishop of Damietta); Miṣā'īl, Saint; Monasteries in and Around Alexandria; Monasteries of the Beheirah Province; Monasteries in and Around Cairo; Monasteries in Cyprus; Monasteries in the Daqahliyvah Province; Monasteries of the Delta; Monasteries of the Eastern Desert; Monasteries of the Eastern Desert of the Delta and Sinai; Monasteries of the Fayyūm; Monasteries in the Gharbiyyah Province; Monasteries of the Lower Ṣaʿīd; Monasteries of the Middle Ṣaʿīd; Monasteries in the Minūfiyyah Province; Monasteries in the Qalyubiyyah Province; Monasteries in the Sharqiyyah Province; Monasteries of the Upper Ṣaʿīd; Monasteries of the Western Desert; Moses of Abydos; Murqus al-Antūnī; Nabdūnah; Naqīzah; Nicaea, Arabic Canons of; Nob, Apa; Nomocanons, Copto-Arabic; Octateuch of Clement; Onophrius, Saint; Palamon, Saint; Pamin, Saint; Paphnutius; Paphnutius, Saint; Patape; Patāsius, Saint; Patermuthius, Saint; Patriarchal Residences; Paul of Benhadab, Saint; Paul of Tamma, Saint; Pbow; Peiresc, Nicolas Claude de Fabri, Seigneur de; Peter the Presbyter, Saint; Peter of Scetis, Saint; Pharan; Philae; Phib, Saint; Phis, Saint; Pisentius, Saint; Pjol; Porcher, Ernest; Pseudo-Macarius, Homilies of; Pshoi, Saint; Pshoi of Scetis; Pshoi of Tūd; Psoï; Qurnat Marʿī; Raithou; Renaudin, Paul; Ṣaʿīd; Saint-Paul-Girard, Louis; Samuel of Benhadab, Saint; Ṣanabū; Sara, Saint; Seth; Seven Ascetics of Tūnah; Sharūnah; Shaykh Ḥasan, al-; Shaykh Ṣaʿīd, al-; Siwa; Synaxarion, Copto-Arabic; Synaxarion, Ethiopian; Synods, Letters of; Tabennēsē; Takinash; Tall al-ʿAmarnah; Tall Atrīb; Tamnuh; Ṭanbidā; Tbow; Theodora,

Saint; Theophilus; Tiḥna al-Jabal; Thomas, Saint; Timotheus, Saint; Tisserant, Eugène; Tuṭūn, Scriptoria of; Van Lantschoot, Arnold; Victor; Victor of Tabennēsē, Saint; Villecourt, Louis; Wādī al-Rayyān; Wādī Sarjah; Wiet, Gaston; Yuna (Jonas) of Armanat; Zenobios

Disuqi, Ali el-Din Hilal
Professor of Political Science, Cairo
Salāmah Mūsā

Devos, Paul, S.J.
Société des Bollandistes, Brussels
John of Lycopolis, Saint

Diebner, Bernd Jørg
University of Heidelberg
Hamburg Papyrus

Doresse, Jean
Centre national de Recherches scientifiques, Paris
Appendix, article on Cryptography

Dunn, Marilyn
University of Glasgow
Filioque

Effenberger, Arne
Staatliche Museen, Berlin
State Museum of Berlin

Emmel, Stephen
Beinecke Library, Yale University
Nag Hammadi Library

Esbroeck, Michel van
Pontifical Oriental Institute, Rome
Amphilochius of Iconium; Assumption; Athanasius of Clysma; Catena, Arabic Tradition of; Cosmas and Damian, Saints; Ephraem Syrus, Saint; Epimachus of Pelusium, Saint; Eusignius, Saint; Hilaria, Saint; John Colobos, Saint; Judas Cyriacus, Saint; Leontius of Tripoli, Saint; Maximus and Domitius; Melito of Sardis; Mercurius of Caesarea, Saint; Michael the Archangel, Saint; Philotheus of Antioch, Saint; Pidjimi, Saint; Proclus, Saint; Severian of Jabalah, Saint; Sophia, Saint; Theognosta, Saint; Three Hebrews in the Furnace; Victor

Evieux, Pierre
Centre national de Recherches scientifiques, Paris
Isidorus of Pelusium, Saint

Farag, Youssef
Opthalmologist, Hamburg
Labib, Subhi Yanni

Fiqi, Mustafa al-
Counselor, Cabinet of the President of Egypt
Makram Ebeid

Ferré, André
Institute for Arabic and Islamic Studies, Rome
Abū al-ʿAlāʾ Fahd Ibn Ibrahim; Abū al-Faḍl ʿĪsā Ibn Nasṭūrus; Fatimids and the Copts; Ḥākim Bi-Amr-Illāh Abū ʿAlī Manṣūr, al-

Flamm, Dominique
Costume, Civil

Forsyth, George H.
Kelsey Museum of Ancient and Medieval Archeology, Ann Arbor
Mount Sinai Monastery of Saint Catherine

Francia, Loretta del
University of Rome
Mythological Subjects in Coptic Art, *article on* Amazons; Symbols in Coptic Art, *article on* Alpha and Omega

Frantz-Murphy, Gladys
Iona College
Umayyads, Copts under the

Fraser, P. M.
All Souls College, Oxford
Alexandria, Christian and Medieval; Arab Conquest of Egypt; Archives of Papas; Basilios, Archive of; John of Nikiou

Frederick, Vincent
University of Utah
Abū al-Fakhr al-Masīḥī; Abū al-Khayr al-Rashid Ibn al-Ṭayyib; Athanasius; Butrus Sāwīrus al-Jamīl; Chronicon Orientale; Durr al-Thamīn, al-; Eliano, Giambattista; Farajallāh al-Akhmīmī; Ibn al-Dahīrī; Ibn Kātib Qayṣar; Ibrāhīm Ibn ʿAwn, the Nestorian; Jacob of Sarūj; John Sabas; Majmū Uṣūl al-Dīn; Misbāḥ al-Ẓulmah wa-Īdāḥ al-Khidmah; Moses; Murqus al-Mashriqī al-Mallāwanī; Murqus Ibn Qanbar; New Testament, Coptic Versions of the; Paul; Pseudo-Pisentius of Qifṭ; Tādrus al-Mashriqī; Wāḍih Ibn Rajāʾ, al-; Yūḥannā; Yūḥannā Ibn Sāwīrus

Frend, W. H. C.
University of Glasgow
Acacian Schism; Acephaloi; Agnoetae; Alexander of Lycopolis; Anathema; Anomoeans; Apion, Family of; Athanasian Creed; Basilides; Celsus; Chalcedon, Council of; Codex Theodosianus; Constantinople, First Council of; Constantinople, Second Council of; Cosmas Indicopleustes; Decius; Defensor Ecclesiae; Diocletian; Donatism; Ebionites; Ephesus, Second Council of; Ephesus, Third Council of; Eutyches;

Exoucontians; Gangra, Council of; Henoticon; Heracleon; Hexapla and Tetrapla; Homoeans; Hypostatic Union; Jovian; Julian; Julian the Apostate; Justin I; Leo I the Great; Monarchianism; Monenergism; Monophysitism; Monothelitism; Neocaesarea, Council of; Nero, Titus Claudius; Nubian Liturgy; Pelagianism; Philo of Alexandria; Philostorgius; Pulcheria; Sabellianism; Timothy Salofaciolus; Valerian; Zeno

Funk, Wolf-Peter
Laval University, Quebec
Appendix, article on Dialects, Morphology of

Gabra, Gawdat
Coptic Museum, Cairo
Hājir Idfū; Nabis; Patape; Pisentius, Saint

Garcin, Jean-Claude
Université de Provence, Aix-en-Provence
Qūṣ

Gascou, Jean
University of Strasbourg
Eikoston; Enaton, The; Lithazomenon and Saint Peter's Bridge; Metanoia, Monastery of the; Monasteries, Economic Activities of; Monasteries of the Lower Ṣaʿīd; Monasteries of the Middle Ṣaʿīd; Oktokaidekaton; Pempton; Rémondon, Roger

Gellens, Sam I.
Horace Mann School, Riverdale, N.Y.
Egypt, Islamization of

Ghali, Mirrit Boutros
Société d'Archéologie copte, Cairo
Abraam I; Bachatly, Charles; Burmester, Oswald Hugh Edward; Clerical College; Dayr Apa Phoibammon; Drescher, James Anthony Bede; Egyptian National Identity; Egyptian National Unity; Ethiopian Church Autocephaly; George Sobhy; Ḥannā Ṣalīb Saʿd; International Association for Coptic Studies; Kassa Asrate Stele; Murad Kamil; Murqus Simaykah; Omar Toussoun; Oriental Orthodox Churches; Press, Coptic; Sāmī Gabrā; Society of Coptic Archaeology; Yassa ʿAbd al-Masīḥ

Ghattas, Iskandar Guirguis
Court of Appeals, Cairo
Personal Status Law

Gignac, Francis T., S.J.
The Catholic University of America
Appendix, article on Phonology of the Greek of Egypt, Influence of Coptic on the

Girgis, Samir F.
Buchmann's Institute, Zurich
Exuperantius, Saint; Felix, Saint; Mauritius, Saint; Regula, Saint; Theban Legion; Ursus of Solothurn, Saint; Verena, Saint; Victor of Solothurn and Geneva, Saint

Godlewski, Wlodzimierz
Centre polonais d'Archéologie mediterranéenne, Heliopolis
Architectural Elements of Churches, *article on* Baptistery; Dayr Apa Phoibammon

Godron, Gerard
Université Paul Valéry, Montpellier
Healings in Coptic Literature

Goehring, James E.
Mary Washington College
Crosby Schøyen Codex

Graffin, François, S.J.
Institut catholique de Paris
Basset, René; Graffin, René; Nau, François-Nicolas; Patrologia Orientalis

Green, Henry A.
University of Miami
Paraphrase of Shem; Three Stelae of Seth

Greenfield, Jane
Yale University
Bookbinding

Gregorios, Bishop
Higher Institute of Coptic Studies, Cairo
Anbā Ruwayṣ; Apollinarianism; Feasts, Major, *articles on* Ascension, Pentecost; Feasts, Minor; Flight into Egypt; Marriage, *articles on* The Sacrament of Marriage, The Marriage Ceremony; Polycarp, Saint; Suriel, Archangel; Theotokos, Feasts of the; Virtues, the Twelve

Griggs, C. Wilfred
Brigham Young University
Carpocrates; Cerinthus; Chaldaean Oracles; Didascalia; Docetism; Heresy; Hermes Trismegistus; Homoiousion; Iamblichus; Lucian of Antioch; Patristics; Sarapion of Tmuis, Saint; Secret Gospel of Saint Mark; Valentinus

Grossmann, Peter
German Institute of Archaeology, Cairo
Abū Mīnā; Abūṣīr (Saqqara); Abūṣīr (Taposiris Magna); Abydos; ʿAlam Shaltūt; Altar; Altar-Board; ʿAmriyyah; Antinoopolis; Architectural Elements of Churches, *articles on* Aisle, Ambulatory, Apse, Atrium, Cancelli, Ceiling, Choir, Ciborium, Coffer, Colonnade, Crypt, Diaconicon, Dome, Gallery, Horseshoe Arch, Iconostasis,

Khūrus, Maqṣūrah, Naos, Narthex, Nave, Niche, Pastophorium, Pillar, Porch, Presbytery, Prothesis, Prothyron, Return Aisle, Roof, Sacristy, Saddleback Roof, Sanctuary, Synthronon, Tetraconch, Tribelon, Triconch, Triumphal Arch, Vault; Armant; Ashmūnayn, al-; Askinah; Aswan; Babylon; Bagawāt, al-; Bahīj; Baldachin; Balyana, al-; Basilica; Bayt al-ʿAjīn; Bayt al-Nisā'; Castrum; Church Architecture in Egypt; Cross-in-Square; Dandarah; Dayr Abū Fānah; Dayr Abū Ḥinnis; Dayr Abū Maqrūfah and Dayr al-Janadlah; Dayr Abū Mattā; Dayr al-ʿAdhrā' (Jabal al-Tayr); Dayr Anbā Anṭūniyūs; Dayr Anbā Bishoi (Scetis); Dayr Anbā Bishoi (Suhāj); Dayr Anbā Hadrā; Dayr Anbā Shinūdah (Suhāj); Dayr Anbā Ṣamū'īl of Qalamūn (Fayyūm); Dayr Apa Jeremiah (Saqqara); Dayr al-ʿAzab; Dayr al-Bakhīt; Dayr al-Bala'yzah; Dayr al-Banāt (Fayyūm); Dayr al-Barshah and Dayr al-Nakhlah; Dayr al-Biṣrah; Dayr al-Dīk; Dayr Epiphanius; Dayr al-Fakhūrī; Dayr al-Ḥammām; Dayr al-ʿIẓām (Asyūṭ); Dayr al-ʿIẓām (Cairo); Dayr al-Jabrāwī; Dayr al-Kubāniyyah; Dayr al-Majmaʿ; Dayr al-Malāk (Dakhlah Oasis); Dayr Mār Buqṭur (Qamūlah); Dayr al-Maṭmar; Dayr al-Maymūn; Dayr al-Misaykrah; Dayr al-Nāmūs; Dayr al-Naqlūn; Dayr al-Naṣārā (Antinoopolis): Dayr al-Naṣārā (Armant); Dayr al-Naṣārā (Asyūṭ); Dayr al-Qaṣiriyyah; Dayr Qubbat al-Hawā; Dayr al-Quṣayr; Dayr al-Rūmī; Dayr al-Sabʿat Jibāl; Dayr al-Ṣalīb; Dayr al-Shahīd Tadrus al-Muḥārib; Dayr al-Shuhadā' (Isnā); Dayr Simʿān; Dayr Sitt Dimyānah; Dayr al-Suryān; Elephantine; Enaton, The; Epiphany Tanks; Hawwārah; Hawwāriyyah; Hermitage; Ḥilwān; Ḥiṣn; Isnā; Karm al-Akhbāriyyah; Kaufmann, Carl Maria; Keep; Kellia, *article on* The Churches; Khirbat al-Filūsiyyah; Khizānah; Kom Namrūd; Kom Ombo; Laqqān; Luxor Temples, Churches in and Outside; Madamūd; Madīnat Hābū; Madīnat Māḍī; Makhūrah; Manqabād; Najʿ al-Ḥajar; Naqādah; Nubian Christian Architecture; Octagon-Domed Church; Parekklesia; Pbow; Qalʿat al-Bābayn; Qarārah; Qifṭ; Refectory; Ruzayqāt, al-; Shaykh ʿAbd al-Qurnah; Ṭūd; Umm al-Barakāt

Guillaumont, Antoine
Collège de France, Paris
Abbot; Ammonius of Kellia; Anachoresis; Antony of Egypt, Saint; Evagrius Ponticus; Hieracas of Leontopolis; Hilarion; Historia Monachorum in Aegypto; Kellia, *article on* History of the Site; Macarius Alexandrinus, Saint; Macarius the Egyptian, Saint; Mary the Egyptian, Saint; Monasticism, Egyptian; Nitria; Palladius; Paphnutius of Scetis, Saint; Paul the Simple, Saint; Paul of Thebes, Saint; Puech, Henri-Charles; Reclusion; Sara, Saint; Sarapion; Syncletica

*Guy, Jean Claude
Centre Sèvres, Paris
Cassian, Saint John

Habib, Samuel
Protestant minister, Cairo
Coptic Evangelical Church

Hägg, Tomas
University of Bergen, Norway
Greek Language in Christian Nubia

Haile, Getatchew
St. John's University, Collegeville, Minnesota
Ethiopian Heresies and Theological Controversies; Ethiopian Monasticism; Ethiopian Saints

Hamid, Raūf ʿAbbās
Cairo University
Muhammad ʿAlī Dynasty

Hanson, R. P. C.
Bishop of Winslow, England
Arianism; Homoousion; Hypostasis; Origen; Types

*Hardy, E. R.
Jesus College, Cambridge
Damian; Dioscorus II; Gaianus; John I; John II; Peter IV; Theodosius I; Timothy III

Hedrick, Charles W.
Southwest Missouri State University
Apocalypse of Adam; Apocalypse of James, Second

Heijer, Johannes den
University of Leiden
History of the Patriarchs of Alexandria; Mawhūb Ibn Manṣūr Ibn Mufarrij al-Iskandarānī

Heinen, Heinz
University of Trier
Alexandria in Late Antiquity; Annona; Army, Roman; Boule; Egypt, Roman and Byzantine Rule in; Eparchy; Greeks in Egypt; Greek Towns in Egypt; Pentapolis; Persecutions; Provincial Organization of Egypt; Roman Emperors in Egypt; Roman Travelers in Egypt; Taxation in Roman Egypt

Helderman, J.
Vrije Universiteit, Amsterdam
Ramshausen, Franciscus Wilhelm von

Hilal, Ibrahim Fahmy
Attorney, Cairo
Sarjiyūs Malatī

Hondelink, Hans
University of Leiden
Icons, Coptic

Ishak, Fayek
Lakehead University, Ontario
Dayr Yuḥannis Kama; Dayr Yuḥannis al-Qaṣīr (Wādī al-Naṭrūn); Liturgical Instruments; Virgin Mary, Apparition of the

Ishaq, Emile Maher
Clerical College, Cairo
Adām; Ankh; Awshiyah; Bishop, Translation of; Communion of the Sick; Coptic Language, Spoken; Coptologia; Dayr Abū Mūsā al-'Aswad; Difnār; Eucharistic Wine; Euchologion Stand; Festal Days, Monthly; Incense; Lectern; Lōbsh; Lord's Prayer; Metropolitan Sees; Mu'aqqab, al-; Paramone; Psalmodia; Sab'ah Wa-arba'ah; Sacrament; Sacrament, Reservation of the Blessed; Saturday; Shabehmōt; Sunday; Tafasīr; Theotokion; Trisagion; Wāham; Wāṭus; *Appendix, article on* Egyptian Arabic Vocabulary, Coptic Influence on

Janssens, Yvonne
Lycée royal de Charleroi, Belgium
Apocryphon of John; Gospel of Thomas; Trimorphic Protennoia

Jaquet, Jean
Institut français d'Archéologie orientale, Cairo
Karnak in the Christian Period

Johnson, David W., S.J.
The Catholic University of America
Macarius of Tkow, Saint; Nestorius

Johnstone, Penelope
Oriental Institute, Oxford
Abū al-Faḍl 'Īsā Ibn Naṣṭūrus; Abū Ḥulayqah; Ibn al-Biṭrīq, 'Īsā; Ibrāhīm Ibn 'Īsā; Muhadhdhab al-Dīn Abū Sa'īd Ibn Abī Sulaymān; Muwaffaq al-Dīn Abū Shākir Ibn Abī Sulaymān Dāwūd; Rashīd al-Dīn Abū Sa'īd

Jomier, Jacques
Catholic Institute, Toulouse
Dominicans in Egypt

Kakosy, Laszlo
Eötvös University, Budapest
Paganism and Christianity in Egypt

Karren, Stewart L.
Sandy, Utah
Asclepiades; Heraiscus; Horapollon

Kasser, Rodolphe
University of Geneva
Appendix, Foreword *and articles on* Alphabet in Coptic, Greek; Alphabets, Coptic; Alphabets, Old Coptic; 'Ayin; Bashmuric; Bodmer Papyri; Cryptophoneme; Dialect, Immigrant; Dialect, Sporadic; Dialect G (Basmuric or Mansuric); Dialect H (Hermopolitan or Ashmunic); Dialect I (Proto-Lycopolitan); Dialect P (Proto-Sahidic); Dialects, Coptic; Dialects, Grouping of: Dictionaries, Coptic; Djinkim; Fayyumic; Geography, Dialectal; Idiolect; Languages, Coptic; Memphitic; Mesodialect; Metadialect; Paleography; Phonology; Protodialect; Subdialects; Syllabication; Vocabulary, Copto-Greek; Vocabulary of Egyptian Origin, Autochthonous Coptic

Kelly, Joseph F.
John Carroll University
British Isles, Coptic Influences in the

Kiss, Zsolt
Center of Mediterranean Archaeology, Warsaw
Ampulla; Symbols in Coptic Art, *article on* Nimbus

Knezevich, Linda
Elmhurst, New York
Philoxenus of Mabbug; Severus of Antioch

Kolta, K. S.
Ludwig-Maximilians-Universität, Munich
Medicine, Coptic

Krause, Martin
Westfälische Wilhelms-Universität, Münster
Abraham of Hermonthis; Abraxas; Acta Alexandrinorum; Acts, Michigan Papyrus of; Akhmīm Fragments; Archives; Audientia Episcopalis; Balestri, Giuseppe; Bell, Harold Idris; Bible Manuscripts, Greek; Bilabel, Friedrich; Bishops, Biographies of; Bishops, Correspondence of; Bishops, Portraits of; Boeser, Pieter Adriaan Art; Borgia, Stefano; Breccia, A. Evaristo; Bruce, James; Brugsch, Heinrich Ferdinand Karl; Burkitt, Francis Crawford; Chairemon of Alexandria; Christodoros of Coptus; Clerical Instruction; Colophon; Coptological Studies; Coptology; Cramer, Maria; Crum, Walter Ewing; Defrocking of

Priests; Draguet, René; Erman, Adolf; Excommunication; Giamberardini, Gabriele; Graf, Georg; Graffiti; Grapow, Hermann; Grohmann, Adolf; Haase, Felix; Hengstenberg, Wilhelm; Horner, George W.; Huntington, Robert; Inscriptions; Interdict; International Congresses of Coptic Studies; Jablonski, Paul Ernst; Jernstedt, Petr Viktorovich; Johann Georg; Karabacek, Joseph von; Kenyon, Frederic George; Kircher, Athanasius; Kühnel, Ernst; La Croze-Veyssière, Mathurin; Lacau, Pierre; Lagarde, Paul Anton de; Legal Sources, Coptic; Liepoldt, Johannes; Libraries; Menas the Miracle Maker, Saint; Morenz, Siegfried; Mourning in Early Christian Times; Mummification; Mummy Labels; Nash Papyrus; Nonnos of Panopolis; O'Leary, De Lacy Evans; Obicini, Thomas; Olympiodoros of Thebes; Ordination, Clerical; Oriens Christianus; Pamprepios of Panopolis; Papyri, Coptic Literary; Papyri, Coptic Medical; Papyrus Collections; Papyrus Discoveries; Peeters, Paul; Penalization; Petersen, Theodore; Petraeus, Theodor; Pietro Delle Valle; Prosopography; Rückert, Friedrich; Schermann, Theodor; Schiller, A. Arthur; Scholtz, Christian; Schubart, Wilhelm; Schwartze, Moritz Gotthilf; Scriptorium; Stegemann, Viktor; Steinwenter, Artur; Strothmann, Rudolph; Strzygowski, Josef; Thompson, Henry Francis Herbert; Tischendorf, Konstantin von; Whittemore, Thomas; Wilcken, Ulrich; Wilke (Wilkius, Wilkins), David; Winstedt, Eric Otto; Wuide, Charles Godfrey; Wüstenfeld, Ferdinand; Zahn, Theodor von; Zosimus of Panopolis

Kuhn, K. H.
University of Durham, England
Besa; Coptic Testament of Isaac; Didache; Jeremiah, Apocryphon of; Paul of Thebes; Philosophy; Poetry; Shenute, Saint; Stephen of Hnēs

*Labib, Subhi Y.
Kiel University
Abraham, Saint; Alexander II; Amīn al-Dīn ʿAbdallāh Ibn Tāj al-Riyāsah al-Qibṭī; Badr al-Jamālī; Baghām Ibn Baqūrah al-Ṣawwāf; Benjamin II; Būlus al-Ḥabīs, Saint; Christodoulus; Cosmas I; Cosmas II; Cosmas III; Cyril II; Cyril III; Gabriel I; Gabriel II; Gabriel IV; Gabriel VIII; Hibat Allāh ʿAbd-allāh Ibn Saʿīd al-Dawlah al-Qibṭī; Ḥisbah; Ibn Qayyim al-Jawziyyah; Isaac, Saint; Jacob, Saint; John IV the Faster, Saint; John V; John VI; John VII; John VIII; John IX; John X; John XI; John XII; John XIII; John XIV; John XV; Kārimī Guild; Khā'īl I; Khā'īl II; Khā'īl III; Macarius I; Macarius II; Mark III, Saint; Mark IV; Mark V; Mark VI; Matthew I; Matthew II; Matthew III; Matthew IV; Michael IV; Michael V; Michael VI; Mīnā I; Mīnā II; Peter V; Philotheus; Political Parties; Semi-Arians; Shenute I; Shenute II; Simon I; Simon II, Saint; Theodorus, Saint; Theodosius II; Theophanes; Yūsāb I; Zacharias

Langen, Linda
University of Leiden
Icons, Coptic

Lewis, Suzanne
Stanford University
Mythological Subjects in Coptic Art, *article on* Thetis

Loebenstein, Helene
National Library, Vienna
Papyrus Collections

Louca, Anwar
University of Lyons
Chiftichi, Yuḥanna; Haraglī, Jean; Ilyās Buqṭur; Salippe Mikarius; Sīdārūs, Gabriel; Yaʿqūb, General

Lucchesi-Palli, Elisabetta
Art historian, Salzburg
Symbols in Coptic Art, *article on* Eagle

Luttikhuizen, Gerard P.
University of Groningen
Elkasites

MacCoull, Leslie S. B.
Society for Coptic Archeology, Cairo
Dioscorus of Aphrodito; Law, Coptic

Macomber, William
Brigham Young University
Ethiopian Liturgy

Makar, Ragai
University of Utah
Banī Suef; Mikhail, Kyriakos

Martin, Maurice, S.J.
College of the Holy Family, Cairo
Abydos; Antinoopolis; ʿAraj, al-; Atrīs; ʿAyn ʿAmūr; Azarī; Bahjūrah; Banī Ḥasan and Speos Artemidos; Banī Kalb; Bāwīṭ; Būsh; Clysma; Dayr Abīrūn; Dayr Abū Bifām (Asyūṭ); Dayr Abū Daraj; Dayr Abū Fānah; Dayr Abū Ḥinnis (Mallawi); Dayr Abū Isḥāq; Dayr Abū al-Līf; Dayr Abū Maqrufah and Dayr al-Janadlah; Dayr Abū Mūsā; Dayr Abū Mūshā; Dayr Abū Sarabām; Dayr Abū Sayfayn (Qūṣ); Dayr Abū al-Sayfayn

(Ṭamwayh); Dayr al-ʿAdwiyyah; Dayr al-Adhra (Akhmīm); Dayr al-ʿAdhrā' (Asyūṭ); Dayr al-ʿAdhrā' (Bayad al-Naṣārā); Dayr al-ʿAdhrā' (Samālūṭ); Dayr al-Aḥmar (Giza); Dayr al-Amīr Tadrūs (Jabal Abū Fūdah); Dayr al-Amīr Tadrūs (Luxor); Dayr Anbā Abshāy (Abū Tīj); Dayr Anbā Abshāy (Ṭūd); Dayr Anbā Anṭūniyūs; Dayr Anbā Bākhūm (Abydos); Dayr Anbā Bākhūm (Barjanūs-Minyā); Dayr Anbā Bākhūm (Madāmūd-Luxor); Dayr Anbā Bākhūm (Sawam'ah-Akhmīm); Dayr Anbā Bīḍābā; Dayr Anbā Bisādah; Dayr Anbā Bishoi (Suhāj); Dayr Anbā Būlā; Dayr Anbā Daryūs; Dayr Anbā Hadrā; Dayr Anbā Helias (Naqādah); Dayr Anbā Palaemon; Dayr Anbā Pisentius; Dayr Anbā Ṣamū'īl of Qalamūn (Fayyūm); Dayr Anbā Sāwīrus; Dayr Anbā Shinūdah (Suhāj); Dayr Apa Hor (Minyā); Dayr Apa Isḥāq; Dayr Apa Jeremiah (Saqqara); Dayr Apa Thomas; Dayr al-ʿAsal; Dayr Asfal al-Arḍ; Dayr al-ʿAskar; Dayr ʿAtiyyah; Dayr al-ʿAwanah; Dayr al-ʿAzab; Dayr al-Bakhīt; Dayr al-Ballās; Dayr Balūjā; Dayr al-Barshah and Dayr al-Nakhlah; Dayr al-Biṣrah; Dayr Buqṭur of Shū; Dayr al-Dīk; Dayr Durunkah; Dayr Ebifania; Dayr al-Fakhūrī; Dayr al-Ghanāyim; Dayr Ghubriyāl (Armant); Dayr al-Ḥadīd; Dayr al-Ḥājar (Dakhlah); Dayr al-Hammām; Dayr Harminā; Dayr al-Ikhwah; Dayr al-ʿIẓām (Asyūṭ); Dayr al-Jabrāwī; Dayr al-Jarnūs; Dayr al-Jawlī; Dayr al-Juʿ; Dayr al-Khādīm; Dayr al-Khandaq; Dayr al-Kubāniyyah; Dayr al-Madīnah; Dayr al-Malāk (Nag Hammadi); Dayr al-Malāk Mīkhā'īl (Akhmīm); Dayr al-Malāk Mīkhā'īl (Fayyūm); Dayr al-Malāk Mīkhā'īl (Idfū); Dayr al-Malāk Mīkhā'īl (Jirjā); Dayr al-Malāk Mīkhā'īl (Marāghah); Dayr al-Malāk Mīkhā'īl (Naqādah); Dayr al-Malāk Mīkhā'īl (al-Rayramūn); Dayr al-Malāk Mīkhā'īl (Qamūlah); Dayr al-Majmaʿ; Dayr Mār Buqṭur (Qamūlah); Dayr Mār Jirjis (Dimiqrāt); Dayr Mār Jirjis (Sidamant-Fayyūm); Dayr Mār Jirjis (Tura); Dayr Mār Jirjis al-Hadīdī; Dayr Mār Mīnā (Gharbiyyah); Dayr Mār Mīnā (Hiw-Nag Hammadi); Dayr Mār Mīnā (Jabal Abū Fudah); Dayr al-Maṭmar; Dayr Maṭrā; Dayr al-Maymūn; Dayr al-Muḥarraq; Dayr al-Muḥarraqah; Dayr Muṣṭafā Kāshif; Dayr al-Muṭṭin; Dayr Nahyā; Dayr al-Nāmūs; Dayr al-Naṣārā (Antinoopolis): Dayr al-Nasṭūr; Dayr Posidonios; Dayr al-Qaṣriyyah; Dayr Qibriyūs; Dayr Qubbat al-Hawā; Dayr al-Qurqāṣ; Dayr al-Quṣayr (Jabal Abū Fūdah); Dayr al-Quṣayr (Tūrah); Dayr Rīfah; Dayr al-Rūmāniyyah; Dayr al-Rūmī; Dayr al-Sabʿat Jibāl; Dayr al-Ṣalīb; Dayr al-Sanad; Dayr al-Sanqūriyyah; Dayr al-Sāqiyah; Dayr al-Shahīd Philūthāwaus; Dayr Shahrān (Giza); Dayr al-Shalwīt; Dayr al-Shamʿ; Dayr al-Shuhadā' (Akhmīm); Dayr al-Shuhadā' (Isnā); Dayr Sitt Dimyānah; Dayr Sunbāṭ; Dayr Tāsā; Dayr al-Ṭīn; Dayr al-Ṭurfah; Dayr Yūḥannā; Dayr Yuḥannis; Dayr al-Zāwiyah; Diolkos; Duwayr, al-; Farshūṭ; Ḥamīdāt, al-; Hayz, al-; Hermitages, Theban; Ḥilwān; Jabal al-Silsilah; Jabal Jarad; Jabal Khashm al-Quʿūd; Jabal Qattar (Eastern Desert); Jabal Ṭarif; Jesuits and the Coptic Church; Jullien, Michel Marie; Kom al-Rāhib; Manqabād; Meir; Monasteries in and Around Alexandria; Monasteries of the Beheirah Province; Monasteries in Cyprus; Monasteries in the Daqahliyyah Province; Monasteries of the Eastern Desert; Monasteries of the Eastern Desert of the Delta and Sinai; Monasteries of the Fayyūm; Monasteries in the Gharbiyyah Province; Monasteries in the Minūfiyyah Province; Monasteries in the Sharqiyyah Province; Naqīzah; Pbow; Philae; Pilgrims and Travelers in Christian Egypt; Qurnat Marʿī; Raithou; Ṣanabū; Shaykh Ḥasan, al-; Shaykh Ṣaʿīd, al-; Sicard, Claude; Siwa; Takinash; Tall al-ʿAmarnah; Tall Atrib; Ṭanbidā; Tiḥna al-Jabal; Vansleb, Johann-Michael; Wādī al-Rayyān; Wādī Sarjah

Mattā al-Miskīn
Saint Macarius Monastery, Cairo

Dayr Anbā Maqār (Wādī al-Naṭrūn)

McNally, Shela
University of Minnesota

Akhmīm; Dayr al-ʿAdhrā' (Akhmīm); Dayr Anbā Bisādah; Dayr al-Malāk Mīkhā'īl (Akhmīm); Dayr al-Malāk Mīkhā'īl (Najʿ al-Dayr); Dayr Mār Jirjis al-Hadīdī; Dayr Mār Tumās; Dayr al-Shuhadā' (Akhmīm)

Megally, Fuad
ʿAyn Sham University, Cairo

Accounts and Accounting, History of Coptic; Bashmuric Revolts; Benevolent Societies, Coptic; Chrism; Coptic Street; Egypt, Administrative Organization of; George, Saint; Manassā Yūḥannā; Monk; Muḥammad Ramzī; Numerical System, Coptic; Patriarchal Deputy; Priest, Ordination of; Subdeacon; Synod, Holy; Toponymy, Coptic; Waqʿat al-Kanāis; Waqʿat al-Naṣārā

Meinardus, Otto
German Bible Society, Ellerau
Asṭāsī al-Rūmī; Blessing; Cheirotonia; Christian Subjects in Coptic Art, *article on* Twenty-four Elders; Damrū; Dayr Abū Līfah; Dayr Anbā Anṭūniyūs; Dayr Anbā Būlā; Dayr al-Naqlūn; Sinjār; Twenty-four Elders

Messiha, Hishmat
Cairo University
Gospel Casket; Memnonia

Metcalf, William
American Numismatic Society, New York
Coinage in Egypt

Metzger, Bruce M.
Princeton Theological Seminary
Chester Beatty Biblical Papyri; Chester Beatty Coptic Papyri; New Testament, Coptic Versions of the

Meyer, Marvin W.
Chapman College
Allogenes; Asclepius 21–29; Hypsiphrone; Marsanes; Melchizedek; Thought of Norea; Wādī Shaykh 'Alī

Moftah, Ragheb
Higher Institute of Coptic Studies, Cairo
Music, Coptic, *articles on* Description of the Corpus and Present Musical Practice, Canticles, Oral Tradition, History, Cantors, Musical Instruments, Transcriptions in Western Notation

Moon, Beverly
Writer
Dialogue of the Savior; Gospel of Mary; Letter of Peter to Philip

Moorsel, Paul van
University of Leiden
Christ, Triumph of; Church Art; Christian Subjects in Coptic Art, *article on* Galactotrophousa; Dayr Anbā Anṭūniyūs

Morard, Françoise
University of Fribourg, Switzerland
Acts of the Apostles

Morfin-Gourdier, Nicole M. H.
Ecole du Louvre, Paris
Costume of the Religious

Motzki, Harald
University of Hamburg
Damanhūrī, Shaykh Ahmad, al-; Ibrāhīm al-Jawharī; Jirjis al-Jawharī; Kléber, Jean-Baptiste; Menou, Jacques François 'Abdallah; Mubāshirūn; Muhdī, Muḥammad al-

Müller, C. Detlef G.
Rheinische Friedrich-Wilhelms-Universität, Remagen
Agathon of Alexandria; Basil of Oxyrhynchus; Benjamin I, Saint; John III the Merciful; John of Parallos, Saint; Mark II, Saint; Physiologos; Pisentius, Saint; Romances; Zacharias, Saint

Murqus, Yuwakim Rizq
Cairo
Sudan, Copts in the

Musā, Anbā
Clerical College, Cairo
Youth Movements

Nagel, Peter
Martin Luther University, Halle
Old Testament, Coptic Translations of the; *Appendix, articles on* Akhmimic Dialect, Lycopolitan

Nāsīm, Sulaymān
Hilwan University, Cairo
Benevolent Societies, Coptic; Christian Religious Instruction in Egyptian Public Schools; Education, Coptic; Friends of the Bible; Mīkhā'īl Jirjīs, Mu'allim; Muyser, Jacob Louis Lambert

Nauerth, Claudia
University of Heidelberg
Biblical Subjects on Coptic Art, *article on* Joseph

Neyret, Clemence
Louvre Museum
Mythological Subjects in Coptic Art, *articles on* Apollo and Daphne, Daphne

Nigosian, S. A.
Victoria College, Toronto
Armenians and the Copts

Orlandi, Tito
University of Rome
Abbaton; Abgar; Acacius, Bishop of Caesarea; Agathonicus of Tarsus; Alexander I; Anastasius of Eucaita; Anatolius, Saint; Anub, Saint; Apaiule and Tolemaeus, Saints; Aphu; Apoli, Saint; Archelaus of Neapolis; Archellides, Saint; Ari, Saint; Ascla, Saint; Athanasius of Antioch; Bacheus; Basil of Oxyrhynchus; Besamon, Saint; Caetani, Leone; Calendologia; Camoul; Celestinus of Rome; Clement I, Saint; Cycle; Cyriacus and Julitta, Saints; Cyprian the Magician; Cyril of Jerusalem; Daniel of Scetis, Saint; Demetrius of Antioch; Dios, Saint; Epima, Saint; Eusebius, Saint; Eustathius and Theopista, Saints; Eustathius of Thrace; Evodius of Rome; Flavian of Ephesus; Gobidlaha, Dado, and Caxo, Saints; Gregory of Nazianzus, Saint; Gregory of Nyssa, Saint; Guidi, Ignazio;

Hagiography, Coptic; Heraclides, Saint; Herai, Saint; Herpaese and Julianus, Saints; Isaac of Typhre, Saint; Isidorus, Saint; James Intercisus, Saint; John the Faster, Saint; John Calybites; John Chrysostom; John of Mayuma; John the Presbyter; John of Shmun; John and Symeon; Joore; Justus, Saint; Krajon and Amun, Saints; Lacaron, Saint; Literature, Coptic; Macarius, Saint; Macrobius, Saint; Menas, Saint; Mui, Saint; Nabraha, Saint; Olympius, Saint; Paese and Tecla, Saints; Pantaleon, Saint; Philip of Anatolia; Pisura, Saint; Psote of Psoi, Saint; Sentences of Menandros; Shenufe, Saint; Ter and Erai, Saints; Teza, Emilio; Theodorus; Theodosius of Jerusalem; Theodotus of Ancyra; Theopistus of Alexandria; Tolemaus, Saint

Osborne, Eric Francis
Queens College, Melbourne
Pamphilus, Saint; Pantaenus; Plotinus; Subordinationism

Pagels, Elaine
Princeton University
Tripartite Tractate

Parlasca, Klaus
University of Erlangen, Nuremberg
Portraiture, Coptic

Parrott, Douglas M.
University of California, Riverside
Acts of Peter and the Twelve Apostles; Eugnostos the Blessed and Sophia of Jesus Christ

Partyka, Jan Stanislaw
Academy of Catholic Theology, Warsaw
Kellia, *article on* Epigraphy

Pearson, Birger A.
University of California, Santa Barbara
Eudoxia; Testimony of Truth

Peel, Malcolm L.
Coe College
Dayr Epiphanius; Treatise on the Resurrection

Pelsmaekers, Johnny
Catholic University, Louvain
Stela

Perez, Gonzalo Aranda
University of Navarra
Apocryphal Literature; Gabriel, Archangel; John the Baptist, Saint; Joseph the Carpenter; Raphael; Stephen, Saint

Petry, Carl F.
Northwestern University
Copts in Late Medieval Egypt

Pfister, Dominique
Costume, Civil

Poethke, Gunter
Staatliche Museen, Berlin
Codex; Codicology; Oxyrhynchus Papyri; Papyrology

Quaegebeur, Jan
Catholic University, Louvain
Appendix, articles on Greek Transcriptions, Old Coptic, Pre-Coptic

Quispel, Gilles
Rijksuniversiteit Utrecht
Gnosis; Gnosticism

Rassart-Debergh, Marguerite
Brussels
Biblical Subjects in Coptic Art, *articles on* Adam and Eve, Daniel in the Lion's Den, The Three Hebrews in the Furnace; Christian Subjects in Coptic Art, *articles on* Adoration of the Magi, Jeremiah, Nativity; Dayr Apa Jeremiah (Saqqara); Kellia, *article on* Paintings; Mareotis, Coptic Paintings at; Monastery Paintings, Coptic; Paintings, Coptic Mural

Regnault, Lucien
Abbey of Solesme, France
Achillas, Saint; Agathon, Saint; Ammonas, Saint; Apophthegmata Patrum; Arsenius of Scetis and Ṭurah, Saint; Barsanuphius, Saint; Bessarion, Saint; Isaac, Saint; Isaiah of Scetis, Saint; Isidorus of Scetis, Saint; John Colobos, Saint; Moses the Black, Saint; Pambo, Saint; Poemen, Saint; Silvanus of Scetis, Saint; Sisoēs; Theodorus of Pherme, Saint; Zacharias of Scetis

Rengstorf, Karl Heinrich
University of Münster
Josephus Flavius

Ricci, Lanfranco
Oriental Institute, Naples
Ethiopian Christian Literature

Rizq, Yūnān Labīb
'Ayn Sham University, Cairo
Cabinet, Egyptian; Consultative Council; Egyptian Ministry; Political Parties, *articles on* Republican Party, Nation's Party, Reform Party on Constitutional Principles, Egyptian Party, Egyptian Democratic Party, Wafd Party, Liberal Constitutional Party, Union Party, People's Party, Sa'dist Party, Wafdist Bloc; Sa'd Zaghlūl

Roberts, Colin Henderson
St. John's College, Oxford
Egerton Gospel; Fayyūm Gospel Fragment

Robertson, Marian
Utah State University
Laḥn; Music, Coptic, *articles on* Description of the Corpus and Present Musical Practice, Oral Tradition, Melody, History, Musical Instruments, Musicologists, Transcriptions in Western Notation, Nonliturgical Music

Robinson, Stephen E.
Brigham Young University
Hypostasis of the Archons; Second Treatise of the Great Seth

Roncaglia, Martiniano Pellegrino
Oriental Institute, Beirut
Arius; Didymus the Blind; Dioscorus I; Julian; Melchites and Copts; Nestorians and Copts; Theotokos

Roquet, G.
German Institute of Archaeology, Cairo
Bagawāt, al-; Hayz, al-; Jabal al-Ṭayr (Khargah)

Rosen-Ayalon, Myriam
Hebrew University, Jerusalem
Bookbinding; Illumination, Coptic; Islamic Influences on Coptic Art; Leather Bindings; Leatherwork, Coptic; Sassanid Influences on Coptic Art

Roy, Martha
Presbyterian Church, Cairo
Music, Coptic, *articles on* Description of the Corpus and Present Musical Practice, Canticles, Oral Tradition, History, Cantors, Musical Instruments, Musicologists, Transcriptions in Western Notation

Rutschowscaya, Marie-Hélène
Louvre Museum, Paris
Bourguet, Pierre du, S.J.; Christian Subjects in Coptic Art, *article on* Annunciation; Louvre Museum; Mythological Subjects in Coptic Art, *article on* Jason; Textiles, Coptic, *articles on* Types of Fibers, Manufacturing Techniques; Water Jugs and Stands; Woodwork, Coptic

Sadek, Ashraf
Le Monde Copte, *Paris*
Monde Copte, Le

Samir, Khalil, S.J.
Pontifical Oriental Institute, Rome
Ababius, Saint; Abāmūn of Tarnūṭ, Saint; Abāmūn of Ṭūkh, Saint; ʿAbdallāh; ʿAbdallāh Ibn Mūsā; ʿAbd al-ʿAzīz Ibn Sa'd al-Dīn; Abd al-Masīḥ (hegumenos); ʿAbd al-Masīḥ Ibn Isḥāq al-Kindī; ʿAbd al-Masīḥ al-Isrā'ilī; ʿAbd al-Masīḥ, Known as Ibn Nūḥ; Abīb Ibn Naṣr; Abrīm al-Qibṭī, Anbā; Abū al-Majd Ibn Yu'annis; Abū al-Mufaḍḍal Ibn Amīn al-Mulk; Abū al-Munā; Abū al-Munā; Abū al-Munā Ibn Nasīm al-Naqqāsh; Abū Isḥāq Ibn Faḍlallah; Abū Nasr Ibn Hārūn Ibn ʿAbd al-Masīh; Abū Sa'īd Ibn Sayyid al-Dār Ibn Abī al-Faḍl al-Masīḥi; Afthīmī al-Miṣrī; Agathon of Ḥomṣ; Agathon and His Brothers; Agāthūn Ibn Faṣīḥ al-Ṭūrsīna; Ahrūn Ibn Aʿyan al-Qass; ʿAlam Ṣalīb al-Ibnāsi, al-; Andrew of Crete; Anṭūniyūs Mulūkhiyyah; Apollonius and Philemon, Saints; Arsānī al-Miṣrī; Athanāsī al-Misrī; Bar Hebraeus; Barlām and Yuwāṣaf; Bisūrah al-Ḥarīrī; Book of Epact; Buṭrus; Buṭrus Ibn ʿAbd al-Sayyid; Buṭrus Ibn al-Khabbāz; Buṭrus Ibn Ṣahyūn al-Ghannāmī; Buṭrus Ibn Sālim al-Sunbāṭī; Caraccioli, Clement; Constantine; Fakhr al-Dawlah Abū al-Mufaḍḍal Ibn al-ʿAssāl; Fīs, Saint; Gabriel V; Gabriel VI; Gabriel VII; Ghubriyāl Ibn Fakhr al-Kafā'ah; Gregory II; Ḥasaballāh; Ibn al-Ṣā'igh; Ibrāhīm Ibn Sulaymān al-Najjār al-Mīrī; Isḥāq Ibn Ibrāhīm Ibn Nasṭās; Istifhām Baʿd al-Istibhām, al-; Jahshiyārī, Abū ʿAbd Allāh, al-; Jirji al-Simʿānī; Jirjis al-Jawharī al-Khanānī; Jirjis Ibn al-Qass Abī al-Mufaḍḍal; Jirjis Makramallāh al-Bahnasāwī; Kaysān Ibn ʿUthmān Ibn Kaysān; Makin Jirjis, al-; Makramallāh the Hegumenos; Manṣūr Ibn Sahlān Ibn Muqashshir; Marquṣ; Marqus al-Anṭūnī; Maximus the Confessor; Mīkhā'īl al-Baḥrāwī; Mīkhā'īl Ibn Buṭrus; Mīkhā'īl Ibn Ghāzī; Mīkhā'īl al-Miṣrī; Mīkhā'īl Ibn Ya'qūb ʿUbayd al-Miṣrī; Mufaḍḍal Ibn Mājid Ibn al-Bishr, al-; Mysteries of Greek Letters; Nasīm Abū Saʿd Ibn ʿAbd al-Sayyid; Nasṭās Ibn Jurayj; National Library, Paris, Arabic Manuscripts of Coptic Provenance in; Old Testament, Arabic Versions of the; Origen; Paul of Aigina; Pseudo-Cyril of Alexandria; Qusṭanṭīn Ibn Abī al-Maʿālī Ibn Abī al-Fatḥ Abū Al-Fatḥ; Sābā Yāsā; Ṣafī Ibn al-ʿAssāl, al-; Sahlān Ibn ʿUthmān Ibn Kaysān; Sālim Ibn Yūsuf al-Sibāʿī al-Itfāwī; Simʿān Ibn Abī Naṣr al-Ṭamada'i; Stephen the Theban; Tūmā Ibn al-Najīb Luṭfallāh; Victor; Victor of Shū, Saint; Yu'annis; Yūḥannā al-Ḥādhiq al-Qibṭī (Muʿallim); Yūḥannā al-Maqsī; Yuhannis Ibn Buqṭur al-Dimyāṭī; Yūsāb; Yūsūf Abū Daqn; Yūsuf al-Qibṭī

Sanders, James A.
School of Theology, Claremont, California
Scripture, Canon of the

Satzinger, Helmut Georg
University of Vienna

Appendix, articles on Old Coptic, Bohairic

Scanlon, George T.
American University, Cairo
Ceramics of the Late Coptic Period

Schenke, Hans Martin
Humboldt University, Berlin
Appendix, article on Mesokemic

Schoedel, William R.
University of Illinois
Apocalypse of James, First

Scopello, Madeleine
University of Strasbourg
Apocalypse of Paul; Authentikos Logos; Concept of Our Great Power; Exegesis on the Soul; Interpretation of Knowledge; Prayer of the Apostle Paul; Valentinian Exposition

Segelberg, Eric
Dalhousie University, Halifax, Nova Scotia
Gospel of Truth; Hippolytus

Severin, Hans-Georg
Staatliches Museum Preussisches Kulturbesitz, Berlin
Architectural Elements of Churches, *articles on* Cancelli, Column; Ashmūnayn, al-; Bāwīṭ; Dayr Anbā Bishoi (Suhāj); Dayr Anbā Shinūdah (Suhāj); Dayr Apa Jeremiah (Saqqara); Sculpture in Stone, Coptic

Shenouda III
Pope of Alexandria
Anchorite

Shepherd-Payer, Dorothy
Fort Meyers, Florida
Christian Subjects in Coptic Art, *article on* Virgin Enthroned

Shilaq, Ahmad Zakaria
'Ayn Sham University, Cairo
Political Thought in Modern Egypt

Shisha-Halevy, Ariel
Hebrew University, Jerusalem
Appendix, articles on Bohairic, Sahidic, Shenutean Idiom

Shoucri, Mounir
Physician, Alexandria, Egypt
Basilius; Cyril IV; Cyril V; Cyril VI; Dayr Abū Minā; Demetrius II; Ghālī; 'Iryān Jirjis Muftāḥ; John XIX; Macarius III; Malatī Yūsuf; Mār Minā Cultural Association; Mīkhā'īl 'Abd al-Sayyid; Patriarchal Election; Peter VII; Philūthāwus Ibrāhīm al-Baghdādī; Yūsāb II

Sieber, John
Luther College, Iowa
Zostrianus

Spanel, Donald B.
Brooklyn Museum, New York
Peter I; Phoibammon of Preht, Saint; Theophilus; Timothy II Aelurus

Stewart, Randall
University of Utah
Abū Tīj; Abūqīr; Abūṣīr Banā; Abūṣīr al-Malaq; Abyār; Aflāqah; Afrājūn, al-; Agharwah; Akhmīm; Anṣinā; Archon; Armant; Ashmūn; Ashmūn Ṭanāḥ; Asyūṭ; Atrīb; Awsīm; Babīj; Bahnasā, al-; Ballās, al-; Balyanā, al-; Banā; Banāwān, al-; Baramūn, al-; Barsanuphians; Bashbīsh; Bashmūr, al-; Basṭah; Batanūn, al-; Bilad; Bilbeis; Biljāy; Birmā; Būrah; Burullus, al-; Codex Justinianus; Colluthus; Constantine I; Dahlak; Dahshūr; Dalās; Damallū; Damanhūr al-Waḥsh; Daqādūs; Daqahlah; Dimayrah; Dinūshar; Dumyāṭ; Durunkah; Epistolography; Faramā; al-; Fayyūm, City of; Fīshah; Fuwwah; Giza; Gospel of Saint Mark; Hiw; Ibṭū; Idkū; Isnā; Iṭfīḥ; Jirjā; John of Ephesus; Justinian; Khandaq, al-; Khirbitah; Laqqānah; Libanius; Luxor; Maḥallah al-Kubrā, al-; Maḥallat Abū 'Alī; Maḥallat al-Amīr; Maḥallat Minūf; Malīj; Manṣūrah, al-; Marcellus; Mareotis; Marṣafā; Mashtūl; Maṣīl; Memphis; Minūf al-'Ulyah; Minyā; Nabarūh; Nag Hammadi; Naqādah; Nastaruh; Naucratis; Nikiou; Parchment; Pimandjoili; Qallīn; Qalyūb; Qays, al-; Qinā; Rashīd; Sakhā; Samannūd; Shanashā; Shuṭb; Sibirbāy; Sunbāṭ; Tanis; Tarnūṭ; Theodorus of Mopsuestia; Theodosians; Tinnis; Tirsā; Tmuis

Tafla, Bairu
University of Hamburg
Abun; Anointing of the Ethiopian Emperor; Eččagē; Ethiopian Orthodox Church; Haile Selassie I; Menelik II

Tedeschi, Salvatore
Rome
Ethiopian Prelates

Thompson, Deborah
Bangor, Maine
Mythological Subjects in Coptic Art, *article on* Pastoral Scenes

Timbie, Janet
Writer
Anthropomorphism; Melitian Schism; Melitius

Tóth, Margit
Society of Coptic Archeology, Cairo
Music, Coptic, *article on* Description of the Corpus and Present Musical Practice

Török, Laszlo
Hungarian Academy of Science, Budapest
ʿAbdallāh Nirqī; Ahnās

Torjesen, Karen
Claremont Graduate School, California
Nicaea, Council of; Nicene Creed

Tūkhī, Rushdī al-
Cairo
John XVI; Rūfā'īl al-Ṭūkhī

Turner, John D.
University of Nebraska
Book of Thomas the Contender

Vantini, Giovanni
Rev. Comboni Missionary Society, Khartoum
Sudan, Catholic Copts in the; Sudan, Coptic Evangelical Church in the

Veilleux, Armand
Monastery of the Holy Ghost, Conyers, Georgia
Cornelius; Horsiesios, Saint; Letter of Ammon; Monasticism, Pachomian; Pachomius, Saint; Pachomius the Younger; Palamon, Saint; Paphnutius of Pbow, Saint; Petronius, Saint; Souros; Theodorus of Alexandria, Saint; Theodorus of Tabennēsē, Saint

Verbeeck, Benedict
University of Trier
Greek Language; Pagarch; Prefect

Viaud, Gerard
Journalist, Cairo
Pilgrimages

Vycichl, Werner
University of Fribourg, Switzerland
Magic; Sullam, al-; *Appendix, articles on* Etymology; Vocabulary, African Contacts with Autochthonous Coptic; Vocabulary, Copto-Arabic; Vocabulary, Cuneiform Transcriptions of Prototypes of Autochthonous Coptic; Vocabulary of Semitic Origin, Autochthonous Coptic

Wagner, Guy
Institut français d'Archéologie orientale, Cairo
ʿAyn Murrah; Bagawāt, al-; Dayr, al-; Dūsh; Jabal Tafnīs; Qaṣr Nisīmah; Shams al-Dīn; Umm Dabadīb

Wassef, Cérès Wissa
Writer
Betrothal Customs; Birth Rites and Customs; Calendar and Agriculture; Calendar, Months of Coptic; Calendar, Seasons, and Coptic Liturgy; Funerary Customs; Marriage, *article on* Marriage Customs; Ramses Wissa Wassef; Wissa Wassef

Wild, Robert A., S.J.
Marquette University
Sentences of Sextus

Weidmann, Denis
Lausanne
Kellia, *article on* Swiss Archaeological Activity

Williams, Frank
University of Texas, El Paso
Apocryphon of John

Wilson, R. McL.
University of St. Andrews, Scotland
Gospel of Philip

Wipszycka, Ewa
University of Warsaw
Archimandrite; Confraternity; Deuterarios; Diaconia; Dikaion, Donation of Children; Oikonomos; Proestos; Textiles, Coptic, *article on* Organization of Production

Wissa, Myriam
Archaeologist, Paris
Ḥārit Zuwaylah

Yūsuf Khalil Yūsuf
National Center for Educational Research, Cairo
Christian Education in Egyptian Public Schools

*Zaki Yusef Saad
Egyptian Antiquities Service, Cairo
Dayr Abū Qarqūrah

Zandee, Jan
University of Amsterdam
Codex Jung; Teachings of Silvanus

Zeelst, L. van, O.F.M.
Franciscan Center of Oriental Christian Studies, Cairo
Franciscans in Egypt

Foreword

The Coptic Encyclopedia began as a dream. The visionary was Aziz Suryal Atiya, medievalist by profession and one of the founders of the University of Alexandria in 1942.

In 1952, Aziz Atiya resigned from the university and returned to Cairo to devote his time to writing. Shortly thereafter he was asked to join the Coptic Community Council, an organization supervising religious and secular church affairs. The church owned a building in Cairo with a large amphitheater for religious, cultural, and social services. In a meeting of the council in 1953, Dr. Atiya suggested the idea of establishing an institute for the study of the Coptic heritage, a field long neglected. He prevailed upon the church to assign a floor in the building to the institute, which became the Higher Institute of Coptic Studies. The idea was met with great enthusiasm, and donations of books from private libraries formed the nucleus for the new institute. A great asset to the institute close by was the Society of Coptic Archaeology founded by Mirrit Boutros Ghali, which holds a large specialized Coptic library.

With the Higher Institute of Coptic Studies established, a Coptic encyclopedia became a possibility. Accordingly, Dr. Atiya gathered around him a number of eminent Egyptologists and Coptologists, including Sami Gabra, Labib Habachi, and Murad Kamil. Others such as Ragheb Moftah and Isaac Fanous found a haven for their work in the institute. Dr. Atiya's thoughts never wavered from the concept of an encyclopedia, the possibility of which he continually advanced among his colleagues. Of them, Labib Habachi always showed great enthusiasm for the project.

In 1955 Dr. Atiya was invited to be a visiting professor at the University of Michigan at Ann Arbor for one year. Other universities and institutions prevailed upon him to extend his stay for short periods. It seemed as if fate kept him in the United States. His final assignment was at the University of Utah in 1959, where he established a Middle East Center. Realizing that his visit would be prolonged, he passed on the directorship of the Higher Institute of Coptic Studies to Sami Gabra. Even so, the dream of an encyclopedia persisted and, during each subsequent visit to Egypt, he would revive the idea with colleagues and enthusiasts.

By 1976, a Coptic encyclopedia seemed realizable. For the first time an International Congress of Coptic Studies convened in Cairo, sponsored by the Egyptian Antiquities Organization and UNESCO. Scholars from sixteen countries attended. His Holiness Pope Shenouda III made reference to an encyclopedia in his address to the Congress. During the meeting, the International Association for Coptic Studies (IACS) was created. The minutes of that congress led Dr. Atiya to names and addresses of persons involved in Coptic studies. He acted immediately by writing to them to solicit their assistance. The response was favorable, and most of them proposed topics in their own fields.

Encouraged, Dr. Atiya conducted a feasibility study, compiling a list of entries on various topics. At the same time, he explored ways to fund the project. The National Endowment for the Humanities (NEH) became the obvious source. Motivated by the number of articles in hand and by written commitments, Dr. Atiya submitted an application to the NEH in July 1977. NEH approved an outright award along with a matching funds grant, and the project of the *Coptic Encyclopedia* began officially in September 1979.

The search for matching funds became the first priority. The patriarch of the Coptic church, Pope Shenouda III, responded immediately. With funds in hand the work began, but the bulk of the matching funds were yet to be raised. Committees for that purpose were formed in America, Europe, and Egypt. Amin Fakry Abdelnour of Cairo took the lead in fund-raising. Hence, the first task, entirely financial, presented no major problems.

The next phase saw the selection of a committee to establish guidelines for the project. Contacts with international scholars resulted in a first meeting of consultants in March 1980. It was hosted by the Rockefeller Foundation at their Bellagio Study and Conference Center, Villa Serbelloni, Lake Como, Italy. During that first meeting the *Encyclopedia* began to take shape. An editorial board was formed, with each editor responsible for a particular area of study. At the end of the Bellagio session, it was agreed that the editorial board should meet again in September 1980 during the second International Congress of Coptic Studies in Rome. There, final guidelines were established. Three further editorial meetings were held in Switzerland in 1982, 1984, and 1985. These meetings allowed editors the opportunity to exchange ideas with each other, coordinate their work, or modify the list of entries.

Three editors died before the completion of the project: Subhi Y. Labib, Pierre du Bourguet, S.J., and Aziz S. Atiya. As stated by S. Kent Brown in announcing the loss of Dr. Atiya in the *Journal of the American Research Center:* "In light of both his untiring devotion to learning and, especially during the past eleven years, his complete attention to the encyclopedia project, it is perhaps fitting that the last brief illness, which claimed his life, overtook him as he sat at his desk laboring over his beloved Coptic Encyclopedia."

Thereafter, the academic work on the Encyclopedia needed very little to come to a close, and it became my responsibility to finish the work. With the help of the present director of the Middle East Center, Lee L. Bean, the *Coptic Encyclopedia* now finally sees the light.

The impact of the Coptic period of Egypt can be felt to the present day through survivals in the daily language of the people, the names of towns and villages in Upper and Lower Egypt, and the use of the Coptic agricultural calendar. In short, the Coptic heritage is shared by all Egyptians—regardless of their religious affiliation. Moreover, Coptic influence extended far beyond the boundaries of Egypt—to Europe and Asia—in Christendom's monastic orders, its illuminated manuscripts of the Bible, and its theological schools. Coptic Egypt has been a neglected phase of Egyptian history. It fell between the glamor of Pharaonic Egypt and the stupendous surge of Islam that swept the world, including Egypt. However, Coptic studies have acquired a renewed dynamism both with the discovery of the Nag Hammadi Codices in 1945 and through other discoveries, mainly from excavations and museum displays.

It is hoped that the publication of the *Coptic Encyclopedia* will shed more light on a period that started with the Christianization of Egypt by Saint Mark the Evangelist and continued for centuries after the Arab invasion of Egypt in the seventh century.

LOLA ATIYA

Preface

Four million according to the official census, and six million in the opinion of some unofficial contenders, the Copts are the purest descendants of the ancient Egyptians. They are sometimes dramatically, but not altogether correctly, described as the "modern sons of the pharaohs." Though it is difficult to define the exact genealogy of that Mediterranean race, there is no doubt that one cementing factor has kept their qualities as pure as can be expected. That factor is their religion and their church, in whose fold Copts have remained unperturbed throughout the centuries. The introduction of Christianity in Egypt was one of the most momentous events in the history of the country, and the ready acceptance of the new religion by the Egyptians calls for an inquiry into Egyptian history.

We must remember that Christianity was preached in the eternal city of Alexandria by Saint Mark, the author of the oldest known gospel. The astounding response to the new preaching and the spread of the new religion among the Copts was not a matter of chance. Ancient Egyptian mythology, strangely enough, prepared the way for the spread of the new gospel. The basic ideas in the Christian faith had parallels in Egyptian beliefs, and this took away the strangeness of Christianity from Egyptian minds. After all, the first monotheist in the annals of world history was Akhenaton in the fourteenth century B.C. Though unsuccessful at the time, this remained a potent precedent in Egyptian thought. The idea of the trinity found its double in every Egyptian nome or province that had its own triad. Most famous of all the triads is the one represented by the myth of Osiris, Isis, and Horus. The birth of a god from a virgin mother through a holy spirit was a common idea in ancient Egypt where the best representation of this principle is the birth of the bull god Apis from a virgin cow, in whose bosom the Ptah, father of all the gods, breathed his own spirit. Some pharaohs, such as Horemheb of the Twentieth Dynasty, claim descent from Osiris. The same pharaoh was anointed by washing with holy water for a spiritual rebirth, a ritual that finds its equivalent in the Christian baptism. Even the sign of the cross that Christians adopted as the symbol of eternal life had its counterpart in the ancient Egyptian *ankh,* a cross with a rounded head that was always found in the right hand of gods and pharaohs to attest their eternity.

The very foundation of the ancient religion and indeed all Egyptian civilization was centered on immortality and the reward of heaven or hell to the pious and the impious. The ancients upheld the doctrine of the resurrection of the body and consequently preserved the body or its likeness for the "Ka" or soul to return to it in the life beyond. This idea seems to be at the very root of all facets of ancient Egyptian culture. Pyramids and tombs, the glory of the ancients, were planned together with mummification for the protection of the dead. Sculpture and painting furnished a device for the "Ka" to identify its likeness and occupy it in case the mummy perished. Without identifying the ancient mythology with Christian doctrine, we must concede that that parallelism in thought paved the way for the acceptance of the new faith, for the purification of the late Egyptian debasement and corruption of the older mythology.

The Flight of the Holy Family to Egypt also played a role. Jesus who came as a mere infant returned to Palestine a young boy whose mind must have been exposed to the wisdom of the Egyptians. To the present day, the Copts cherish the thought that they gave refuge to Jesus the fugitive and follow the stations of the progress of the Holy Family in places of pilgrimage; churches have been constructed over some of them. People of all ages have followed in the steps of the Master through the Delta to Middle Egypt as far as the spot where the Monastery of the Virgin known as Dayr al-Muḥarraq still stands, continuously inhabited to this day.

The establishment of the Coptic church came to pass at the hands of Saint Mark the Evangelist, who became its first patriarch between A.D. 42, the year of his entry into Alexandria, and 68, the year of his martyrdom in the same city. His first convert was a cobbler named Anianus, who followed him in the episcopate of Alexandria. Since the Coptic mind had been ready for the acceptance of the new religion, it is no wonder that Christianity spread in Egypt with bewildering rapidity. The Copts, who refused to offer incense and libation to the imperial image as a common deity in those pagan days, were subjected to the severest persecution. The Copts cared little about their fate, and unlike many other Christians, they worshiped in the open and not in the catacombs, and in this way courageously sought the crown of martyrdom. So fierce was the wave of persecution in Egypt that the Copts decided to start their church calendar with the year of the accession of Emperor Diocletian (A.D. 284), during whose reign the massacre of the Christians is said to have reached its peak.

In spite of persecution the Catechetical School of Alexandria had become the natural successor to the brilliant ancient academy of learning known as the Museon. Thus for the first time in history did Christian theology have a scholarly home where men of learning began to systematize the hitherto amorphous Christian doctrines. Immortal names figure in the panel of its teachers, from Pantaenus to Clement, and from Origen to Didymus the Blind. All were men of tremendous learning, whose work still ranks high in all treatises on patrology. Origen, a true son of Egypt and its church, was perhaps the most prolific theologian of all time; an incredible five thousand books are ascribed to him. Whatever the truth of this contention, he is known to be the author of the first system of theology; the compiler of the Hexapla, including the whole text of the Bible in six ancient languages; and the commentator on almost all the books of the Old Testament.

The age of the church fathers abounds in saints whose great piety and untiring search for the Christian truths filled the entire community with that fire of the faith that can still illuminate the way for us. Some of these names are recited in every Coptic liturgy to this day. There is Demetrius, who led the Alexandrian populace in the battle for the extermination of paganism from that city, Athanasius the Apostolic, Arius the "arch-heretic," Saint Antony the Great, Saint Pachomius, Cyril the Great, Dioscorus, and others. Some of these men led the Christian world in the formative years of the ecumenical movement that Constantine the Great initiated in the Council of Nicaea (325). The bishop of Alexandria, Alexander, was accompanied to that council by a young deacon named Athanasius, who was the power behind the throne. Evidently it was he who composed the famous credo approved by the Nicene bishops as the basis of Christian dogma. Athanasius was destined to become patriarch of Alexandria at a time when the Arian heresy was rapidly spreading in the Christian world, and it fell to him to combat it.

This was also the age of monasticism. Begun by Paul the Hermit and Saint Antony the Great in the Eastern Desert, monastic rule was perfected by Saint Pachomius the Great in the Thebaid, while the societies of Macarius the Great and Macarius Alexandrinus in the wilderness of Mareotis and Nitria developed into ascetic and learned centers. Their settlements in the wilderness attracted pilgrims from the Byzantine empire and the rest of Europe. Saint Basil transplanted the rule of Pachomius to Greece, and John Cassian founded his famous monastery in southern France on a Coptic model. The vestiges of his influence are still seen in the Fort St. Victor in Marseilles and the monastery of the Ile de St. Honorat off the coast of Cannes.

This was equally the age of missionary endeavor. Wherever the Roman legionaries opened the way, Coptic missionaries followed in their trail to preach the faith and oftentimes earn the crown of martyrdom in distant lands. It was thus that the Coptic saints Felix, Exuperantius, and Regula, who appear on the arms of the city of Zurich, perished on the shores of the Limmat river and were buried under the Wasserkirche in the heart of that city. The Copts extended their message to many parts of Gaul. They are known even to have crossed the Channel to the British Isles long before the coming of Saint Augustine of Canterbury. The tombs of seven Coptic monks have been identified in Disert Aldith in County Donegal not far from Belfast at the northeastern tip of Ireland.

The fourth and fifth centuries were times of great religious turmoil that are marked by the Council of Nicaea in 325 and the Council of Chalcedon in 451. Between those two dates, the Coptic bishops championed the cause of orthodoxy against emerging heresies such as Arianism and Nestorianism. The leading role of Saint Cyril the Great at the Council of Ephesus in 431 was so overwhelming that the Western and Byzantine divines called the Coptic patriarchs Pharaohs of the Church. This did not sit well with the bishops of Byzantine and the West, where the prelates of Constantinople were in imperial favor and the bishops of Rome filled the imperial vacuum in the Eternal City. Thus we see a rising alliance against Egypt, which was regarded as a satellite province of the Byzantine empire. In this way, both the Roman and Byzantine bishops, backed by imperial power, united hands at Chalcedon in an attempt to humiliate Dioscorus, patriarch of Alexandria. It is a mistake to hold to the one-sided Western view that the issue was solely theological. The political background of the whole story of Coptic monophysitism versus the West's leaning toward diophysitism is not to be minimized.

Deposed and degraded, Dioscorus became the symbol of disaffection, and rising hatred begat new waves of persecutions of the Christians of the East by the Christians of the West. Two parallel lines of patriarchs arose in Alexandria: the one Melchite, Greek, and imperialist, the other native Egyptian, nationalist, and anti-Chalcedonian in profession. The one was appointed by the emperor and was seated on the throne of Alexandria by imperial arms; the other was elected by the Copts and became a patriarch errant among the Coptic monastic institutions of Egypt. Then Emperor Justinian, who was interested in a perfectly united theocracy, devised a new system of governance in Egypt, whereby the patriarch became the prefect of the country and the general of the armed forces. This irregular and totally unspiritual combination was intended to uproot "monophysitism" by brutal force. To this day the Copts remember diabolical persecutions of the Chalcedonian Patriarch-Prefect-General Cyrus on the eve of the Arab conquest of 639–642. They were reminiscent of the black days of Decius and Diocletian. At the time of the Arab invasion the Copts had already been so alienated from the mainstream of Western Christianity that they could do nothing but stand by and watch the edifice of imperial power crumble to the ground. Under Byzantine rule, the Copts had lost both political and religious independence. Indeed they had lost everything except self-respect and the tenacity to fight the persecution, rapacity, and brutality of the foreign legions. Under the Arabs, on the contrary, their church became the only official church. The native patriarch obtained considerable freedom to run the internal affairs of his people. This may help to elucidate the position of the Copts vis-à-vis the Arab conquest. They watched until their Greek oppressors were routed, and from that time the Copts were almost totally unknown by their co-religionists in the West.

The Copts' subsequent history under Arab rule was marked by further flight and endurance. The miracle of the survival of the Copts as a community through the ages may be ascribed to two main factors—the one internal and the other external. The internal factor may be summed up in their profound spirituality, which sustained their unflinching adherence to their church as a comprehensive way of life. The external factor was their acceptance as an integral part of the country by the Muslim rulers, who systematically employed them in the affairs and offices of state. With the emergence of democracy in modern times, the Copts' enfranchisement became complete.

AZIZ S. ATIYA

Acknowledgments

I know that Aziz Suryal Atiya would have wished to pen these lines himself, for he was well aware of the abundance of help and encouragement that came from many quarters in the long and arduous process of bringing this enterprise into being. It now becomes my duty to express that gratitude to all who contributed toward its achievement.

First and foremost, our thanks go to the National Endowment for the Humanities (NEH), which supported the *Coptic Encyclopedia* from 1979 to 1990. Their faith in the project was shown by an initial generous amount to start the funding for the project. The grants were based upon matching the NEH pledge dollar for dollar. Those engaged in the preparation of the *Encyclopedia* express appreciation for this support.

Two major benefactors have given generously of their own fortunes. They underwrote the NEH stipulation for matching funds: Mr. S. K. Roushdi of London, and a donor who wishes to remain anonymous, a request we reluctantly respect. Their philanthropy and encouragement we acknowledge with heartfelt thanks. Another benefactor was Wallace O. Tanner, a lawyer from Arizona.

His Holiness the patriarch of the Coptic Orthodox Church, Pope Shenouda III, gave his blessings and support before the work started and during its realization.

In a spirit of true ecumenism, the Church of Jesus Christ of Latter-day Saints presented us with a generous check toward the matching funds. Gifts also came from the Vatican, the World Council of Churches, and a number of Coptic churches outside Egypt.

Contributions were received from the embassy of the Arab Republic of Egypt in Washington, D.C., and the Ministry of Foreign Affairs in Egypt. We are particularly grateful for their support and for their official recognition that the *Coptic Encyclopedia* is an important link in the writing of the history of Egypt.

Copts and non-Copts in and outside Egypt supported the work done locally and abroad. The Egyptian fund was controlled by Mirrit Boutros Ghali, president of the Society of Coptic Archaeology, and Amin Fakhry Abdelnour, an international banker and an active fund-raiser for the *Encyclopedia*. Our sincere thanks to all of them.

This project could not have progressed without the support of the University of Utah through its former president, Dr. David Pierpont Gardner, and the present president, Dr. Chase N. Peterson.

Of great importance was the contribution of University of Utah personnel. We address our thanks to Dr. Khosrow Mostofi, former director of the Middle East Center, whose guidance and knowledge of federal grants helped us to implement and receive our first grant. Our thanks also to Dr. Lee L. Bean, present director of the Middle East Center, who has served as administrative consultant. He has given many hours of his time to the various requirements of the project, as has his assistant, Ellen Bartholomew. Support came from the Office of Sponsored Projects under the vice-president for research, Dr. James J. Brophy, including Richard H. Timpson, director; Joseph Vialpando, grant and contract administrator; and their assistants.

For eleven years the University of Utah has provided a home for the *Coptic Encyclopedia* in the Marriott Library. Roger Hansen, director of the University Libraries, generously placed at our disposal space for our offices and other resources of the library. We are grateful to him and to Ragai Makar, Middle East librarian, and to his assistant, Judy Jarrow.

Many of our articles were written in foreign languages and required the help of translators. R. McL. Wilson of St. Andrew's College, Scotland, remained with the *Encyclopedia* through the entire progression of the work. We express our thanks to him.

It would be impossible to acknowledge adequately all those who have assisted in the preparation of the *Encyclopedia*. We are not able to mention individually the great number of scholars who have contributed their special knowledge to the solution of particular problems, as well as the many institutions with which we have been happily associated.

To our staff, Dorothy Wiscombe, administrative assistant; Donna T. Smart, technical writer; Jolayne Bowen; Miriam Bushnell; and Lynne Wilburn, our thanks and appreciation for their patience and perseverance in dealing with an unusually difficult publication. We also wish to thank Randall Stewart, project researcher, who joined the *Encyclopedia* in its late stages.

Editorial board meetings were held at the Crêt Bérard Center in Puidoux, Switzerland. We address thanks to Pastor Deppierraz for placing these facilities at our disposal and to the efficient Monique Deppierraz and her staff, who provided living quarters in most pleasant surroundings, adequate working space, and equipment.

We thank Dr. Gawdat Gabra for authorizing the use of illustrations from the Coptic Museum collection.

Finally, I cannot conclude without expressing my own personal acknowledgment of the support and solidarity shown to me at a time when bereavement could have interrupted the progress of Aziz Suryal Atiya's long-cherished vision of a *Coptic Encyclopedia*.

LOLA ATIYA

Introduction

Most of the approximately 2,800 articles in the *Coptic Encyclopedia* are divided among four main areas: early Christian history, biographies of many saints and other important Coptic church figures, art and architecture, and archaeology. The geographical region covered in this work is present-day Egypt, Nubia (roughly modern-day Sudan), and Ethiopia.

The early history of the Coptic church is the early history of all Christians. Until the Council of Chalcedon in A.D. 451, when the Coptic church broke away from the rest of Christianity over the issue of monophysitism, Alexandria, with its famed Catechetical School, was a leading center of Christian learning. Origen was the most famous church father to come out of that school; there were many others. After 451, when the Copts no longer attended the ecumenical church councils, the West slowly forgot about the Christians in Egypt. They did not converge again until the time of the Crusades, when the Copts were treated as an enemy, a heretical sect to be driven from the holy places along with the Arabs.

Coptic history is still being unearthed today—literally. The many archaeological digs continue to bring to light the remains of old monasteries, papyri, and art objects from which we gain a better understanding of Coptic civilization. There are in the *Encyclopedia* over 400 entries for monasteries, ranging from those institutions that have been in existence since the beginning of monasticism, to the many ruins of monastery buildings, and to descriptions of monasteries known only from papyri. All these articles begin with "Dayr," the Arabic word for "house" and, by extension, monastery.

Volume 8 contains an appendix with articles on Coptic linguistics. Grouped together, and with an introduction by Rodolphe Kasser, these articles present all available knowledge about the origin of the Coptic language and its various subdialects, an invaluable resource for students of linguistics. Volume 8 also contains the extensive index for the first seven volumes.

No encyclopedia article can claim to be exhaustive. Therefore, almost all entries have a bibliography listing sources for further reading. Two types of references are not part of these bibliographies: classical texts, which can be found in a variety of modern editions; and modern works cited so frequently by the contributors to the *Encyclopedia* that they would have appeared in almost every bibliography (e.g., Georg Graf's *Geschichte der christlichen arabischen Literatur* and the many editions, in various languages, of the Synaxarion, the Coptic calendar of saints). These works can be found in the General Bibliography at the beginning of Volume 1.

The encyclopedia articles are linked by a comprehensive set of cross-references. When the reader encounters a word in small capital letters, that name or term is the subject of a separate entry. Thus in the sentence, "The founder of cenobitic monasticism was PACHOMIUS," the reader is alerted that there is a separate article on Pachomius. The reader will also find cross-references at the end of entries, such as "[*See also:* Monasticism, Pachomian]" at the end of the article on Theodorus of Tabennēsē. This system of cross-references allows the reader complete access to the information in the work.

Often, readers will attempt to find information and will be directed to another place in the encyclopedia. This set of so-called blind entries, arranged alphabetically throughout the *Encyclopedia* (such as "Adoration of the Magi. *See* Christian Subjects in Coptic Art"), direct the reader to the entry under which the desired information can be found.

A project such as the *Coptic Encyclopedia* is a major undertaking, requiring the cooperation of many people. I was very fortunate in working with Mrs. Lola Atiya, whose unfailing dedication and energy kept the project on schedule after her husband's death. Her two assistants, Donna Smart and Dorothy Wiscombe, know how much I owe them. If there will ever be a calendar of saints for editors, Donna and Dorothy will be the first to be canonized.

ELLY DICKASON
Managing Editor

General Bibliography

For frequently cited works the following abbreviations have been used:

CSCO	Corpus Scriptorum Christianorum Orientalium
CSEL	Corpus Scriptorum Ecclesiasticorum Latinorum
DCB	Dictionary of Christian Biography
ODCC	Oxford Dictionary of the Christian Church
PG	Patrologia Graeca
PL	Patrologia Latina
PO	Patrologia Orientalis

Abū al-Barakāt ibn Kabar. *Livre de la Lampe des Ténèbres et de l'Exposition (lumineuse) du Service (de l'Eglise)* (Lamp of Darkness), ed. and trans. L. Villecourt, E. Tisserant, and M. G. Wiet. Paris, 1928.

______. *Miṣbāḥ al-Ẓulmah fī Īḍāḥ al-Khidmah* (Luminary of Church Services). Repr. in part, Cairo, 1971.

Acta conciliorum oecumenicorum 2.1 (Home Synod of 448), ed. E. Schwartz. Berlin and Leipzig, 1933; 2.2 (Ephesus II), Berlin and Leipzig, 1932.

Acta Phileae. In *The Acts of the Christian Martyrs* 27, pp. 328–53, ed. and trans. H. Musurrillo. Oxford, 1972.

Apophthegmata Patrum. PG 65, cols. 71–440, ed. J. B. Cotelier. Paris, 1864.

Apophthegmata Patrum. Bibliothèque d'études coptes 6, ed. M. Chaine. Cairo, 1960.

Apostolical Canons, The: "The Canons of the Council of Trullo"; "The Canons of the Holy and Blessed Fathers Who Assembled at Neo Caesarea"; and "The Canons of 318 Holy Fathers Assembled in the City of Nice." In *A Select Library of the Nicene and Post-Nicene Fathers of the Christian Church,* 2nd ser., Vol. 14, ed. P. Schaff and H. Wace. Grand Rapids, Mich., 1956; repr. Grand Rapids, Mich., 1983. Originally published in 1894.

Athanasius, Saint. *Lettres festales et pastorales en copte.* CSCO 150–151, *Scriptores Coptici,* 19–20, ed. L.-T. Lefort. Louvain, 1955.

Basil the Great. *De Spiritu Sancto* 27.66. In *A Select Library of the Nicene and Post-Nicene Fathers of the Christian Church,* 2nd ser., Vol. 3, ed. P. Schaff and H. Wace. Grand Rapids, Mich., 1955.

Bibliotheca hagiographica graeca. Subsidia hagiographica 47, 3rd ed., Auctarium, ed. F. Halkin. Brussels, 1969.

Bibliothecae hagiographicae graecae, Novum auctarium. Subsidia hagiographica 65, ed. F. Halkin. Brussels, 1984.

Bibliotheca hagiographica latina, 2 vols. Subsidia hagiographica 6, ed. Société des Bollandistes. Brussels, 1898–1901; repr. 1949.

Bibliotheca hagiographica orientalis. Subsidia hagiographica 10, ed. P. Peeters. Brussels, 1910; repr. Profondeville, 1954.

Brooks, E. W., ed. and trans. *Vitae virorum apud Monophysitas celeberrimorum.* CSCO 7–8; *Scriptores Syri,* ser. 3, 25. Paris, 1907; *Scriptores Syri,* 7–8. Louvain, 1955.

Brooks, E. W.; I. Guidi; and I.-B. Chabot, eds. and trans. *Chronica minora II.* CSCO 1–6, *Scriptores Syri,* 4, pt. 3, "Chronicon miscellaneum ad annum domini 724 pertinens," pp. 61–119; pt. 4, "Chronicon anonymum, ad annum domini 846 pertinens," pp. 121–80. Paris, 1903–1905; repr. Louvain, 1960–1961.

Cassian, John. *De conlationes patrum.* Corpus Scriptorum Latinorum 13, ed. M. Petschenig. Vienna, 1888; Sources chrétiennes 42, 54, 64, ed. J.-C. Guy, Paris, 1955–1959; repr. New York, 1966. English trans. E. S. C. Gibson. In *The Nicene and Post-Nicene Fathers of the Christian Church,* 2nd ser., Vol. 11, pp. 161–641, ed. P. Schaff and H. Wace. Grand Rapids, Mich., 1955.

______. *Opera omnia,* ed. A. G. Atrebati. Paris, 1616; repr. PL 49–50. Paris, 1946.

______. *De institutis coenobiorum libri XII.* CSEL 17. Vienna, 1888; Sources chrétiennes 109, ed. J.-C. Guy. Paris, 1965.

Chabot, I.-B., ed. and trans. *Documenta ad origines Monophysitarum illustrandas.* CSCO 17, 103, *Scriptores Syri,* ser. 2, 37. Paris, 1907–1933; British Museum Manuscript [Vol. 17, 52], Paris and Leipzig, 1907–1952; repr. CSCO 15, 103, *Scriptores Syri,* 17, 52. Louvain, 1952–1962; repr. of 1907–1933 ed., Louvain, 1962–1965.

Chrysostom, John, Saint, Patriarch of Constantinople. *Admonitio.* PG 60. Montrouge, 1859.

______. *Interpretatio omnium epistolarum Paulinarum*

per homilias facta, Vol. 4, ed. J. H. Parker. Oxford, 1852.

The Churches and Monasteries of Egypt and Some Neighbouring Countries, Attributed to Abū Ṣāliḥ the Armenian, ed. and trans. B. T. A. Evetts, with notes by Alfred J. Butler. Oxford, 1895; repr. Oxford, 1969.

Clavis Patrum Graecorum, 5 vols. Vols. 1–4, ed. M. Geerard. Vol. 5, ed. M. Geerard and F. Glorie. Turnhout, 1983–1987.

Clement of Alexandria. *Stromata*, ed. O. Stählin. Leipzig, 1906; repr. Munich, 1936–1938; Nendeln, 1968. Books 1–6, Berlin, 1985; Books 7–8, Berlin, 1970.

———. *Stromata*, ed. C. A. Bernoulli and L. Früchtel. Basel, 1936.

———. *Stromata*, trans. M. Caster. Paris, 1951–.

———. *Stromata*. In *Ante-Nicene Fathers*, Vol. 2, ed. A. Roberts and J. Donaldson. Grand Rapids, Mich., 1956.

Constitutions of the Holy Apostles. In *The Ante-Nicene Fathers*, Vol. 7, ed. A. Roberts and J. Donaldson. Grand Rapids, Mich., 1951.

Cyril, Saint, Bishop of Jerusalem. *The Catechetical Lectures of S. Cyril*, trans. R. W. Church. Oxford and London, 1838; Oxford, 1845; 4th ed., Oxford and London, 1872 and 1885.

———. *Catechetical Lectures*. In *A Select Library of the Nicene and Post-Nicene Fathers of the Christian Church*, 2nd ser., Vol. 7. Grand Rapids, Mich., 1955; repr. 1983. Originally printed in 1894 by various publishers.

Cyprian, Saint, Bishop of Carthage. *De lapsis*. CSEL 3, pt. 1, pp. 235–64, ed. G. Hartel. Vienna, 1868.

———. *The Lapsed, the Unity of the Catholic Church*, trans. Maurice Bévenot. Westminster, Md., 1956, 1957.

———. *Letters*. CSEL 3, pt. 2, pp. 478–597, ed. G. Hartel. Vienna, 1871.

———. *Lettere scelte*, ed. Maria Gennaro. Catania, 1953.

———. *Letters*, trans. Sister Rose Bernard Donna. Washington, 1964.

———. *Le lettere*, ed. N. Marinangeli. Alba, 1979.

———. *The Letters of St. Cyprian of Carthage*, trans. G. W. Clarke. New York, 1984–(c.1989).

Al-Dasqūliyyah, ed. William Sulayman Qilādah. Cairo, 1979.

Didascalia Apostolorum. The Syriac version trans. and accompanied by the Verona Latin Fragments. Intro. and notes R. H. Connolly. Oxford, 1929; repr. 1969.

Elias. *Vita Johannis episcopi Tellae*, ed. and trans. E. W. Brooks. CSCO 8, *Scriptores Syri*, 8, pp. 21–60. Louvain, 1955.

Epiphanius, Saint, Bishop of Constantia in Cyprus. *Panarion*. Die griechischen-christlichen Schriftsteller der ersten drei Jahrhunderte 37, ed. K. Holl. Leipzig, 1937.

———. *Epiphanius II*. Panarion haeresies 34–64, ed. K. Holl. Berlin, 1980.

———. *Epiphanius III*. Panarion haeresies 65–80, ed. K. Holl. Berlin, 1985.

———. *The Panarion of Epiphanius of Salamis*, trans. F. Williams. Leiden and New York, 1987.

Eusebius [Pamphili], Bishop of Caesarea. *Chronica*. PG 19, cols. 99–598. Paris, 1857.

———. *Church History*. In *A Select Library of the Nicene and Post-Nicene Fathers of the Christian Church*, 2nd ser., Vol. 1. Grand Rapids, Mich., 1952.

———. *The Ecclesiastical History*, 2 vols. The Loeb Classical Library. English trans. K. Lake, J. E. L. Oulton, and H. J. Lawlor. Cambridge, Mass., and London, 1926–1932; repr. 1942–1949, 1953, 1957–1959; 1964–1965.

———. *The Ecclesiastical History and the Martyrs of Palestine*, ed. and trans. H. J. Lawlor and J. E. L. Oulton. London, New York, and Toronto, 1954.

———. *Histoire ecclésiastique*, 4 vols. Sources chrétiennes 31, 41, 55, 73, trans. G. Bardy. Paris, 1952–1971; 1984–; 3rd ed., Paris, 1987.

———. *Historia ecclesiastica*. PG 19–24. Montrouge, 1857.

———. *Historia eclesiástica*, 2 vols., ed. A. V. Delgado. Madrid, 1973.

———. *History of the Martyrs of Palestine*, ed. and trans. W. Cureton. London, Edinburgh, and Paris, 1861.

———. *Kirchengeschichte*, 2 vols., ed. P. Haeuser and H. A. Gartner. Munich, 1981.

———. *The Theophanis*, ed. and English trans. S. Lee. Cambridge, 1843.

———. *Die Theophanie*, ed. H. Gressmann. Leipzig, 1904.

———. *De vita Constantini*. Die griechischen christlichen Schriftsteller der ersten drei Jahrhunderte 7, ed. I. Z. Heikel. Leipzig, 1902.

———. *De vita Constantini*. Die griechischen christlichen Schriftsteller der ersten Jahrhunderte 54, ed. F. Winkelmann. Berlin, 1975.

Eutropius, Roman Historian. *Breviarium ab urbe condita*, ed. F. Ruehl. Leipzig, 1887; repr. 1897; Leipzig and Stuttgart, 1975; Stuttgart, 1985.

———. *Eutropi Breviarium ab urbe condita*. Monumenta Germaniae Historica Auctorum antiquissimorum 2, ed. H. Droysen. Munich, 1978.

Evagrius Scholasticus. *The Ecclesiastical History of Evagrius with the Scholis,* ed. J. Bidez and L. Parmentier. London, 1898; repr. Amsterdam, 1964; New York, 1979.

Facundus of Hermiana. *Pro defensione trium capitulorum* 12, 5. PL 67. Brepols and Turnhout, n. d.

Festugière, A.-J., ed. and trans. *Historia Monachorum in Aegypto* [attributed to Timothy Aelurus, Patriarch of Alexandria]. Subsidia hagiographica 53. Brussels, 1971.

Graf, G. *Geschichte der christlichen arabischen Literatur,* 5 vols. Vatican City, 1944, 1947, 1949, 1951, 1953.

Hippolytus, Antipope. *The Refutation of all Heresies.* In *Ante-Nicene Christian Library,* Vol. 6, pt. 1, ed. J. H. MacMahon and S. D. F. Salmond. Edinburgh, 1911.

______. *Refutatio omnium haeresium* VII.22 and X.18; 2 vols. Die griechischen-christlichen Schriftsteller der ersten drei Jahrhunderte, ed. P. Wendland. Leipzig, 1916; repr. Hildesheim, 1977.

______. *Refutatio,* ed. M. Marcovich. Berlin, 1986.

History of the Patriarchs of the Coptic Church. This work is available in several languages. We list here editions in Arabic, Latin, English, and German.

Kāmil Ṣāliḥ Nakhlah. *Kitāb Tarīkh wa-Jadāwil Baṭārikat al-Iskandariyyah al-Qibṭ.* Cairo, 1943.

Renaudot, E., ed. and trans. *Historia Patriarchum Alexandrinorum Jacobitarum.* Paris, 1713; repr. Brussels, 1969.

Sāwīrus ibn al-Muqaffa'. *History of the Patriarchs of the Coptic Church of Alexandria,* ed. and trans. B. T. A. Evetts. Vol. 1, pt. 1, PO 1.1. Paris, 1904; Vol. 1, pt. 2, PO 1.2. Paris, 1907; Vol. 1, pt. 3, PO 5. Paris, 1910; Vol. 1, pt. 4, PO 10.5. Paris, 1915.

______. *History of the Patriarchs of the Egyptian Church,* Vol. 2, pt. 1, trans. Yassa 'Abd al-Masīḥ and O. H. E. Burmester. Cairo, 1943. Vol. 2, pt. 2, trans. Aziz Suryal Atiya, Yassā 'Abd al-Masīḥ and O. H. E. Burmester. Cairo, 1948. Vol. 2, pt. 3, trans. Aziz Suryal Atiya, Yassā 'Abd al-Masīḥ, and O. H. E. Burmester. Cairo, 1959. Vol. 3, pt. 1, trans. Antoine Khater and O. H. E. Burmester. Cairo, 1968. Vol. 3, pts. 2 and 3, trans. Antoine Khater and O. H. E. Burmester. Cairo, 1970. Vol. 4, pt. 1, trans. Antoine Khater and O. H. E. Burmester. Cairo, 1974. Vol. 4, pt. 2, trans. Antoine Khater and O. H. E. Burmester. Cairo, 1974.

Seybold, C. F. *Alexandrinische Patriarchengeschichte von S. Marcus bis Michael I (61–767) nach der ältesten 1266 geschriebenen Handschrift.* Hamburg, 1912.

______, ed. *Severus Ben al-Moqaffa' Historia Patriarcharum Alexandrinorum.* CSCO 52, 59. *Scriptores arabici,* 8–9, ser. 3.1–2. Beirut and Paris, 1904–1910.

Ignatius. *Ad Philadelphen.* PG 5, cols. 817–840. Paris, 1894.

Irenaeus, Bishop of Lyons. *Adversus omnes haereses* 1.26.2. PG 7, cols. 433–1224. Paris, 1857.

______. *Adversus omnes haereses* 3.11.3. PG 7, cols. 879ff. Paris, 1857.

______. *Adversus omnes haereses,* ed. W. W. Harvey. London, 1965.

______. *Adversus haereses.* Sources chrétiennes 100, 152, 153, 210, 211, trans. A. Rousseau. Paris, 1965– (French, Latin, and Greek); Paris, 1984; 2nd ed. Paris, 1985.

Jerome, Saint. *Translatio Latinae Regulae Sancti Pachomii.* PL 23, cols. 65–90. Turnhout, n.d.

______. *De viris illustribus.* PL 23, cols. 631–766. Turnhout, n. d.

______. *De viris illustribus,* ed. C. A. Bernoulli. Freiburg im Breisgau and Leipzig, 1895; Frankfurt, 1968.

______. *De viris illustribus,* trans. E. C. Richardson. In *A Select Library of the Nicene and Post-Nicene Fathers of the Christian Church,* ser. 2, Vol. 6, ed. P. Schaff and H. Wace. Grand Rapids, Mich., 1954.

John of Biclar. *Chronica minora saec. IV, V, VI, VII.* Vol. 2, ed. T. Mommsen. Monumenta Germaniae Historica, Auctorum Antiquissimorum 11. Berlin, 1894; repr. Munich, 1981.

John of Ephesus. *Historiae ecclesiasticae, pars tertia,* ed. and Latin trans. W. Brooks. CSCO 105–106, *Scriptores Syri,* 54–55. Louvain, 1952.

______. *Lives of the Eastern Saints,* ed. and trans. E. W. Brooks. PO 17.1, 18.4, 19.2. Paris, 1923–1925; repr. Turnhout, 1974.

John, Bishop of Nikiou. *Chronique de Jean évêque de Nikiou.* Ethiopian text, H. Zotenberg. *Notices et extraits* 24 (1883):125–605.

______. *The Chronicle of John, Bishop of Nikiu,* ed. and trans. R. H. Charles from Zotenberg's Ethiopic text. London and Oxford, 1916; Amsterdam, 1981; repr. Cambridge, Mass., 1987.

John Rufus. *Plérophies: témoignages et révélations*

contre le Concile de Chalcédoine, ed. and French trans. F. Nau. PO 8.1. Paris, 1912. Also in Recueil de monographies 4. Turnhout, 1971.

John, Superieur de Monastère de Beith Aphthonia. *Vie de Sévère,* ed. and French trans. M.-A. Kugener. PO 2.3. Paris, 1907; repr. Turnhout, 1971.

Julian of Halicarnassus. *Fragmenta,* ed. R. Draguet. Louvain, 1924.

Justinian I, Emperor of the East. *Corpus juris civilis. Novellae constitutiones,* 2 vols., ed. C. E. Zachariae a Lingenthal. Leipzig, 1881.

Lactantius. *Divinae institutiones.* Sources chrêtiennes 204–205, 326, 337, ed. P. Monat. Paris, 1973–(1987).

———. *De mortibus persecutorum.* CSEL 27, ed. S. Brandt and G. Laubmann. Prague, Vienna, and Leipzig, 1897.

———. *De mortibus persecutorum,* 2 vols. Sources chrétiennes 39, ed. and trans. J. Moreau. Paris, 1954.

Leo. *Epistola.* PL 54, cols. 593–1213. Paris, 1846; Turnhout, n. d.

Liberatus of Carthage. *Breviarium causae Nestorianorum et Eutychianorum.* Acta Conciliorum Oecumenicorum 2.5, pp. 98–141, ed. E. Schwartz. Berlin, 1936. Also in PL 68, cols. 969–1050. Paris, 1847.

Maqrīzī, al-. *Macrizi's Geschichte der Copten,* ed. F. Wüstenfeld. Göttingen, 1845; repr. New York, 1879.

———. *Kitab al-Khiṭaṭ,* 2 vols. Edition Būlāq. Cairo, 1853.

———. *Al-Mawā'iẓ wa-al-I'tibār fī Dhikr al-Khiṭaṭ wa-al-Āthār,* 2 vols. Baghdad, 1970.

Michael I, Jacobite Patriarch of Antioch (Michael the Syrian). *Chronique de Michel le grand patriarche des syriens jacobites,* trans. Victor Langlois. Venice, 1868.

———. *Chronique,* 4 vols., ed. J.-B. Chabot. Paris, 1899–1910; repr. Brussels, 1963.

Nicephorus Callistus. *Historia ecclesiastica.* PG 145. Paris, 1904.

Origen. *Contra Celsum.* Die griechischen christlichen Schriftsteller der ersten drei Jahrhunderte 2 and 3, ed. P. Koetschau. Leipzig, 1899.

———. *Contra Celsum,* trans. into English H. Chadwick. New York and Cambridge, 1953, 1965; Cambridge, London, and New York, 1980.

———. *Contra Celsum.* Sources chrétiennes 132, 136, 147, 150, 227, trans. into French M. Borret. Paris, 1967–1976.

———. *Die Alēthēs Logos des Kelsos.* Beiträge zur Altertumswissenschaft 33, ed. R. Bader. Stuttgart and Berlin, 1940.

———. *Homiliae in Lucan.* PG 13, cols. 1801–1902. Paris, 1862.

———. *On First Principles,* trans. G. W. Butterworth. London, 1936; repr. Gloucester, Mass., 1973.

Oxyrhynchus Papyri, The, 51 vols., published by the Egypt Exploration Society in *Greco-Roman Memoirs,* ed. and trans. B. P. Grenfell and A. S. Hunt, London, 1898–; ed. J. R. Rea and N. Bartoli, London, 1900; ed. H. Zillicus, et al., Helsinki, 1979 (English and Greek).

Palladius. *The Lausiac History,* 2 vols., ed. D. C. Butler. Cambridge, 1898–1904; repr. Hildesheim, 1967.

Peter of Alexandria. *Apostolic Canons.* In *A Select Library of the Nicene and Post-Nicene Fathers of the Christian Church,* 2nd ser., Vol. 14. Grand Rapids, Mich., 1956.

Philoxenus [Mabbugensis], Bishop of Hierapolis. *Tractatus tres de Trinitate et incarnatione.* CSCO 9–10, *Scriptores Syri,* 9–10. Louvain, 1955.

———. *Lettre aux moines de Senoum.* CSCO 231–232, *Scriptores Syri,* 98–99, trans. A. de Halleux. Louvain, 1963.

Photius. *Bibliotheca* 109. PG 103, cols. 381ff. Paris, 1900.

Rufinus of Aquileia. *Historia monachorum in Aegypto.* PL 21, cols. 391–462. Turnhout, 1849.

———. *Historia monachorum, sive de vita sanctorum patrum,* ed. E. Schulz-Flügel. Berlin and New York, 1990.

Sacrorum conciliorum nova et amplissima collectio, 53 vols., ed. J. D. Mansi. Florence and Venice, 1759–1798; repr. Paris, 1901–1927; repr. Graz, 1960–1961.

Scriptores historiae Augustae, 2 vols., ed. E. Hohl. Leipzig, 1927; Leipzig, 1955–1971; ed. C. Samberger and W. Seyfarth. Leipzig, 1965.

Severus Sozopolitanus, Patriarch of Antioch. *Liber contra impium grammaticum.* CSCO 93–94, 101–102, 111–112. *Scriptores Syri,* ser. 4, 7 (text), 64–65 (trans.). Louvain, 1949.

———. *Le Philalèthe.* CSCO 133–134, *Scriptores Syri,* 68–69, ed. and trans. R. Hespel. Louvain, 1952.

———. *The Sixth Book of Select Letters of Severus, Patriarch of Antioch in the Syriac Version of Athanasius of Nisibis,* 2 vols. ed. and trans. E. W. Brooks. London, 1902–1904; Farnborough, 1969.

———. *A Collection of Letters of Severus of Antioch from Numerous Syriac Manuscripts.* PO 12.2, no. 58; 14.1, no. 67. Paris, 1919–1920; repr. Turnhout, 1973.

Simaykah, Murqus, and Yassa 'Abd al-Masīḥ. *Cata-*

logue of the Coptic and Arabic Manuscripts in the Coptic Museum, the Patriarchate, the Principal Churches of Cairo and Alexandria and the Monasteries of Egypt, 2 vols. Vol. 1, Cairo, 1939; Vol. 2, Cairo, 1942.

Simplicius Episcopus. *Epistulae.* In *Collectio Avellana,* ed. O. Guenther. CSEL 35, pt. 1. Prague and Leipzig, 1895.

Socrates Scholasticus. *Ecclesiastical History.* In *A Select Library of the Nicene and Post-Nicene Fathers of the Christian Church,* 2nd ser., Vol. 2, ed. P. Schaff and H. Wace. Grand Rapids, Mich., 1952.

______. *Historia ecclesiastica.* PG 67, cols. 33–842. Paris, 1964.

______. *A History of the Church in Seven Books.* London, 1844.

Sozomen. *Historia ecclesiastica.* Die griechischen christlichen Schriftsteller der ersten drei Jahrhunderte 50, ed. J. Bidez and G. C. Hansen. Berlin, 1960.

______. *A History of the Church in Nine Books.* London, 1846; ed. and trans. B. Grillet and G. Sabbah. Paris, 1983–.

Synaxarion. Following are a variety of editions, in several languages, of the calendar of saints.

'Abd al-Masīḥ Mikhā'il and Armāniyūs Ḥabashī Shaṭā al-Birmāwī. *Al-Sinaksār,* 2 vols. Cairo, 1935–1937.

Al-Sinaksār, 2 vols., comp. Buṭrus al-Jamīl, Bishop of Malīj; Mīkhā'īl, Bishop of Atrīb; Yuḥannā, Bishop of Burullus, and many more saintly fathers. Vol. 1, Cairo, 1978; Vol. 2, Cairo, 1972.

Basset, R., ed. and trans. *Le Synaxaire arabe-jacobite (rédaction copte).* PO 1.3, 3.3, 11.5, 16.3, 17.3, 20.5. Paris, 1907–1929; Turnhout, 1974–.

Budge, E. A. W., ed. and trans. *Mashafa sĕnĕksār* (The Book of the Saints of the Ethiopian Church), 4 vols. Cambridge, 1928.

Delehaye, H., ed. *Synaxarium ecclesiae Constantinoplitanae.* Brussels, 1902.

Forget, I., ed. and trans. *Synaxarium Alexandrinum* [attributed to Michael, Bishop of Atrib and Malij]. CSCO 47–49, 67, 78, 90. *Scriptores Arabici,* 3–5, 11–13. Louvain, 1953–1954. Reprint of Paris, 1911, ed.; *Scriptores Arabici,* ser. 8, 18–19. Beirut, 1905–1926.

Guidi, I., and S. Grébaut III. *Le Synaxaire éthiopien.* PO 9.4. Paris, 1912.

Malan, S. C., trans. *The Calendar of the Coptic Church.* London, 1873.

Wüstenfeld, F., ed. and trans. *Synaxarium, das ist heiliger Kalender der Coptischen Christen, aus dem arabischen übersetzt,* 2 vols. Gotha, 1879.

Tertullian. *Adversus Marcionen* III.8. PL 2, cols. 359ff. Paris, 1878; 2 vols., ed and trans. E. Evans. Oxford, 1972.

______. *Adversus Valentinianos* 27. PL 2, cols. 618ff. Paris, 1878; Padova, 1971; Sources chrétiennes 280–281, ed. J.-C. Fredouille. Paris, 1980–1981.

______. *Apologeticum.* Loeb Classical Library 250, ed. and trans. T. R. Glover. London and New York, 1931; repr. 1960; Cambridge, Mass., and London, 1984.

______. *De carne Christi* 5. PL 2, cols. 805ff. Paris, 1878; ed. and trans. C. Moreschini. Milan, 1984.

______. *De corona.* In *The Ante-Nicene Fathers,* Vol. 3, ed. A. Roberts and J. Donaldson. Repr. Grand Rapids, Mich., 1980; ed. and trans. P. A. Gramaglia. Rome, 1980.

______. *On Fasting.* In *The Ante-Nicene Fathers,* Vol. 4, ed. A. Roberts and J. Donaldson. Grand Rapids, Mich., 1951.

Theodoret, Bishop of Cyrrhus. *Kirchengeschichte,* 2nd ed. Die griechischen christlichen Schriftsteller der ersten drei Jahrhunderte 44, ed. L. Parmentier and F. Scheidweiler. Berlin, 1954.

______. *The Ecclesiastical History.* English Recusant Literature 287. Ilkley, 1976. Repr. of 1612 edition.

Theodorus Lector. *Historia ecclesiastica.* Die griechischen christlichen Schriftsteller der ersten drei Jahrhunderte 50, ed. J. Bidez and G. C. Hansen. Berlin, 1960.

Victor, Sextus Aurelius. *Liber de Caesaribus,* ed. F. Pichlmayr. Leipzig, 1911; repr. Leipzig, 1966; trans. B. T. Moss. Chapel Hill, N.C., 1942.

Zacharias, Bishop of Mytilene. *Historia ecclesiastica Zachariae rhetori vulgo adscripta.* CSCO 83–84, 87–88. *Scriptores Syri,* ser. 3, 5–6, ed. and Latin trans. E. W. Brooks, Paris, 1919–1924.

______. *The Syriac Chronicle Known as That of Zachariah of Mitylene,* trans. F. J. Hamilton and E. W. Brooks. London, 1899. New York, 1979.

Zacharias Scholasticus. *Sévère, Patriarche d'Antioche.* PO 2.1.3, ed. and French trans. M. A. Kugener. Paris, 1907; repr. Turnhout, 1971–.

Zosimus. *Historia nova,* ed. L. Mendelssohn. Leipzig, 1887; repr. Hildesheim, 1963.

______. *Historia nova; the Decline of Rome,* trans. J. J. Buchanan and H. T. Davis. San Antonio, Texas, 1967.

______. *Storia nuova,* ed. F. Conca. Milan, 1977.

______. *New History,* trans. R. T. Ridley. Canberra, 1982.

A

ABABIUS, SAINT, a monk of Scetis. The Copto-Arabic SYNAXARION by MĪKHĀ'ĪL, bishop of Atrīb and Malīj (about 1240), makes no mention of Saint Ababius. However, a fourteenth-century Arabic manuscript, copied in Syria, gives a long life of this saint. The manuscript attributes this life to JOHN COLOBOS (National Library, Paris, Arabe 259, fols. 57r–104v; Graf, 1947, p. 504).

This text is unique and as yet not translated. A translation of the incipit may be instructive: "O my brothers and you who love the living God, I now commence describing the virtues and the life of our father. The parents of this saint, Father Abābiyūs, were just and pious."

BIBLIOGRAPHY

Troupeau, G. *Catalogue des manuscrits arabes* [National Library], *Manuscrits chrétiens,* Vol. 1, no. 259, pp. 222–23. Paris, 1972.

KHALIL SAMIR, S.J.

ABĀMŪN OF TARNŪṬ, SAINT, a fourth-century martyr known only from the brief mention of him made by MĪKHĀ'ĪL, bishop of Atrīb and Malīj (c. 1240), in the Copto-Arabic SYNAXARION (feast day: 27 Abīb).

Tarnūṭ (with a nonemphatic initial T, contrary to the forms given by E. AMÉLINEAU, 1893, p. 493) is situated on the west branch of the Nile, where the road reaches it coming from Wādī al-Natrūn.

When Abāmūn was in Upper Egypt and saw how Christians were being martyred, he presented himself of his own free will to Arianus, governor of ANTINOOPOLIS, who had him tortured (blows, stringing-up, iron combs, and nails in his body). He then sent him to Alexandria, where many Christians, inspired by his example, offered themselves for martyrdom, including a girl named Theophila, who railed against the governor and his idols. She was cast into the fire, which failed to harm her, and was then beheaded. As for Abāmūn, his limbs were cut off and he was beheaded.

BIBLIOGRAPHY

Amélineau, E. *La Géographie de l'Egypte à l'époque copte.* Paris, 1893.

KHALIL SAMIR, S.J.

ABĀMŪN OF ṬŪKH, SAINT, martyr known only from the brief note dedicated to him by MĪKHĀ'ĪL, bishop of Atrīb and Malīj, around 1240, in the Copto-Arabic SYNAXARION (feast day: 13 Abīb).

He was from Ṭūkh in the diocese of Banā, known today as Abūsīr Banā (cf. E. AMÉLINEAU, 1893, pp. 84–85), a town situated about 10 miles (16 km) southeast of Mahallah al-Kubrā, in the province of al-Gharbiyyah. He was informed in a vision of the angel MICHAEL that he would suffer martyrdom at ANTINOOPOLIS. He therefore went there. The governor Eukhious made him suffer all kinds of tortures (the rack, fire, red-hot iron, flogging, furnace, flaying) and finally had him beheaded. Julius of Aqfahṣ (Kbehs) took his body, wrapped it in cloths, and had it carried to his homeland, as was the customary practice of this saint (Basset, p. 76, "He worked great miracles").

Mīkhā'īl, bishop of Atrīb and Malīj, adds an interesting detail: "His body is at present in the Ṣa'īd," which R. Basset mistakenly translated as "His body is *still* to-day in Upper Egypt" ("Son corps est encore aujourd'hui dans la Haute-Egypte"). This sentence was correctly translated by I. Forget (Vol. 2, p. 218, ll. 33–34) as "et illud corpus nunc in AEgypto superiore asservatur." In fact, his body had been carried to his homeland, that is, to Ṭūkh, and probably transferred to Upper Egypt at the beginning of the thirteen century. The indication is vague, typical of someone from the Delta, for whom the South is all simply "Ṣaʿīd Miṣr."

However, ABŪ ṢĀLIḤ THE ARMENIAN, at the beginning of the thirteenth century, records that one of the churches of al-Bahnasā was dedicated to Abamūn (with a short *a*) (cf. Abū Ṣāliḥ, fol. 73b, Arabic p. 93/8). Evetts, in a note (cf. English translation, p. 210), does not know whether this church is to be ascribed to Abāmūn of Ṭūkh or to his namesake of 27 Abīb.

There are several reasons to suppose that the dedication is to Abāmūn of Ṭūkh. The first is that Julius of Aqfahṣ, who was from this same region of al-Bahnasā, personally took care of this martyr and not of the other. The second is the information given in the Synaxarion that the martyr's body was at that time in the Ṣaʿīd, which entails a cult around a church. Finally, the Synaxarion states that he worked many miracles, and this, too, is always linked to the existence of a church dedicated to the martyr.

BIBLIOGRAPHY

Amélineau, E. *La Géographie de l'Egypte à l'époque copte,* pp. 84–85 (Banā) and 522–524 (Ṭūkh). Paris, 1893.

Delehaye, H. "Les Martyrs d'Egypte." *Analecta Bollandiana* 40 (1922):107.

KHALIL SAMIR, S.J.

ABARKAH. *See* Eucharistic Wine.

ʿABBĀS I. *See* Muḥammad ʿAlī Dynasty.

ʿABBĀS II. *See* Muḥammad ʿAlī Dynasty: Hilmi.

ABBASIDS AND COPTS. *See* Tulunids and Ikhshids, Copts Under the.

ABBATON. Abbaton occupies an important place in Coptic angelology as the angel of death. Two texts in particular give us details of him: a homily attributed to TIMOTHY I of Alexandria, *Enthronement of Abbaton,* and the *Apocalypse of Bartholomew.* (See APOCRYPHAL LITERATURE.)

According to the first text, the angel was originally called Muriel, and was given the task by God of collecting the earth used to form Adam. The angel was then nominated guardian. Everyone, both incarnate and bodiless beings, feared him, but by his prayers he obtained from God the promise that men who venerated him during their lifetime might be saved. An important role is also reserved for Abbaton on the day of the Last Judgment, as he will take the souls to the Josephat Valley.

According to the second text, he was present in the tomb of Christ at the moment of the Resurrection.

BIBLIOGRAPHY

Müller, C. D. G. *Die Engellehre der koptischen Kirche,* pp. 273–76. Wiesbaden, 1959.

TITO ORLANDI

ABBOT. In the ancient monastic sources (APOPHTHEGMATA PATRUM, HISTORIA MONACHORUM IN AEGYPTO, PALLADIUS' *Historia Lausiaca,* etc.), the name of a monk is generally preceded by the Greek word *abbas* or *abba,* the cognate of the Coptic *apa* (Sahidic) or *abba* (Bohairic), the Arabic *abā* or *anbā.* This is clearly the Aramaic and Syriac *ab* in its emphatic state, *abbā,* "father." (It is also attested, less frequently, in the feminine, in the form *ammas* or *amma,* corresponding to the Syriac *ʿem, ʿemmā, "mother.")*

The term is applied to the monk considered as a spiritual father, because endowed with charismata, as is shown by the apothegm Antony 31 in the *Apophthegmata Patrum* (85 B). One day, Antony receives a letter from the emperor Constantius II inviting him to come to Constantinople. "Must I go?" Antony asks his disciple Paul (probably PAUL THE SIMPLE). The latter replies, "If you go, you will be called Antony, but if you do not go, Abba Antony." If the monk remains in the desert, he is *abbā;* but if he goes into the world, he loses his qualities as *abbā,* that is, his charisma and spiritual authority. The story of Paul the Simple as it is related by Palladius (1904, Vol. 2, pp. 69–74) is also revealing in this respect: so long as Paul is a novice, he is simply "Paul," but when he has become a genuine ascetic, capable of working miracles, Antony calls him "Abba Paul."

This quality is not necessarily linked to a person's age. Thus, we read in the *Apophthegmata Patrum* (Poemen 61, 336 D) that the abbot Joseph is astonished to hear the abbot POEMEN call the young Agathon *abbā:* "He is still young; why do you call him *abbā?*" Poemen replies, "Because his mouth [that is, his words] makes one call him *abbā.*" This quality is also independent of any function in the community. In Chapter 34 of the *Historia lausiaca* (1904, Vol. 2, pp. 98–100), Palladius tells the story of a nun who, out of humility, passed herself off in a community of virgins as simpleminded and thus had contempt and ill treatment heaped upon her by her companions. One day a venerable anchorite came to visit them and asked to see this nun, whose holiness had been revealed to him in a vision. When she appeared, he said to them all, "It is you who are simpleminded, for she is our *amma,* yours and mine." Palladius adds, "It is in fact thus that those who are spiritual are called."

However, the usage became established—very rapidly it seems—of calling every monk *abbā* and every nun *amma.* Furthermore, when a monk comes to ask for a "word," or counsel, from an older monk or one whom he holds spiritually superior to himself, he addresses him deferentially as "Father." According to the Coptic lives of Pachomius, it seems that in the early Pachomian community, Pachomius was designated simply by the word *Apa* used as a proper noun (Lefort, 1943, pp. 375–76). Later, when the use of the word had become widespread and was applied to any monk, it was usual to designate the founder and superior of the community by saying "our father Pachomius" or "our father Apa Pachomius," and likewise for his successors, as in "our father Theodorus."

How can we explain this use of a word of Aramaic origin among the monks of Egypt? Following Reitzenstein (1916, p. 210), some have thought that it was due to an influence from Syria and the Syriac language. But we have no proof for any influence of Syrian monasticism on Coptic monasticism; moreover, the use of the word *abbā* as applied to the monks does not seem to be of Syriac origin. In that language it only appears in translations of Greek works, notably the *Apophthegmata Patrum,* in the *Paradise* of Enanisho (seventh century), and the word was retained thereafter largely to designate the superiors of monasteries. Thus, it appears more probable, as Hausherr asserts (1955, pp. 17–39), that this monastic use of the word *abbā* originates in the Scriptures, or more exactly the New Testament. As in Mark 14:36, Romans 8:15, and Galatians 4:6, the word was probably employed at first in the vocative, with a nuance at once of respect and of familiarity. In the New Testament the term (examined by Jeremias, 1966) is applied solely to God. The use that was made of it among the Egyptian monks is explained by the fact that the "spiritual father" was judged fit to direct or to counsel solely by virtue of the charisma that he had received from God. In a certain manner he participated in the divine paternity.

BIBLIOGRAPHY

Cotelier, J. B., ed. *Apophthegmata Patrum,* cols. 71A–440D. PG 65.

Hausherr, I. *Direction spirituelle en Orient autrefois.* Orientalia Christiana Analecta 144. Rome, 1955.

Jeremias, J. *Abba: Studien zur neutestamentlichen Theologie und Zeitgeschichte.* Göttingen, 1966.

Lefort, L. *Les Vies coptes de saint Pachôme et de ses premiers successeurs.* Bibliothèque du Muséon 16. Louvain, 1943.

Reitzenstein, R. *Historia Monachorum und Historia Lausiaca: Eine Studie zur Geschichte des Mönchtums und der frühchristlichen Begriffe Gnostiker und Pneumatiker.* Göttingen, 1916.

ANTOINE GUILLAUMONT

ʿABDALLĀH. A Coptic priest, ʿAbdallāh wrote in 1446–1447 that he had read an Arabo-Coptic manuscript transcribed in 1443 and containing principally the Psalter (National Library, Paris, Arabe 42). Folios 230v–31r include a note from him.

BIBLIOGRAPHY

Troupeau, G. *Catalogue des manuscrits arabes* [National Library], Vol. 1, *Manuscrits chrétiens,* pp. 31–32. Paris, 1972.

KHALIL SAMIR, S.J.

ʿABDALLĀH IBN MŪSĀ. ʿAbdallāh is known only from a note left in a manuscript (National Library, Paris, Arabe 107, fol. 126v), which states that he was a deacon and that the manuscript belonged to him. The manuscript was copied by a Copt and completed on 16 Kānūn II 1696 of the Greeks/A.D. 1385, suggesting that the copy was made in Syria. It contains the *Coptic Horologion* and the Song of the Three Young Men in the Furnace (fols. 1–132r), an anonymous commentary on John 20:17 (fols. 132–33), two pieces for the feast of the Epiphany (fols. 134–62), and the story of Job (fols. 162–88v).

BIBLIOGRAPHY

Slane, W. M. baron de. *Catalogue des manuscrits arabes de la Bibliothèque Nationale,* p. 25. Paris, 1883–1895

Troupeau, G. *Catalogue des manuscrits arabes de la Bibliothèque Nationale,* Vol. 1, pt. 1: *Manuscrits chrétiens,* p. 81. Paris, 1972.

KHALIL SAMIR, S.J.

ʿABDALLĀH NIRQĪ, the site of a medieval town and cemetery located in Egyptian Nubia on the west bank of the Nile, about 4 miles (6 km) to the east of the temple of Abu Simbel, now under the water of Lake Nasser. The name means "place of ʿAbdallāh," after the name of a local farmer in the time of the survey of U. Monneret de Villard (1921–1934). A partial excavation was made by a Dutch mission (director A. Klasens, 1962–1964, central church) and a Hungarian mission (director L. Castiglione, 1964, central part and western suburb, northern and southern church of Town A, a sector of Cemetery 249).

The earliest settlement consisted of poor houses in an irregular ground plan, and Ballana horizon pottery was discovered in the southern part of the center of Town A. In the central part and western suburb of the settlement, sudden growth occurred from the second half of the seventh century, with some building of substantial double houses, such as a longitudinal barrel-vaulted room divided into two parts. Occasionally there were small yards and housing for individual family units.

From the middle of the eighth century, unit houses were built. They were larger, mostly two-storied buildings with one larger transversal barrel-vaulted room occupying the whole width and three smaller vaulted rooms perpendicular to it. At that time a network of streets reached down to the river.

The central church, built around 700–750, contained the first painting in violet style (apse: Maria orant between apostles; walls: protection by Virgin, protection by archangel, standing figures of saints) (Jakobielski, 1982, pp. 154ff.) The southern church came slightly later.

Possibly in the early ninth century a citadel wall was erected around the central part including the central church. It was not for defensive purposes, however. Repainting of the central church in white and multicolored style took place from the early eleventh century onward. Protection scenes show an archangel, a saint, the Nativity, the Virgin, Saint Ann, Christ in tondo, Christ with book in a rectangular frame, Christ in *clipeus* (shield) between the four living creatures over a cross, the theophany of the cross, saints on horseback, a scene with a saint, and a "man in the jar" by the painter of Archangel Michael in the Faras cathedral, now in the Warsaw National Museum (Martens-Czarnecka, 1982, pp. 60ff.). Most of these well-preserved wall paintings are now found in the Coptic Museum in Old Cairo. The painting of the southern church in multicolored style is attributed to the eleventh century (saint on horseback, protection scene, bishop). The northern church is placed at the cemetery built in the late eleventh century. A gradual decline took place from the late eleventh to the early twelfth century. A collapse led to the rebuilding of the vaults of the southern church in the twelfth century, and the end of the settlement came in the late thirteenth century.

From the seventh to the ninth centuries a certain sector of Cemetery 249 was excavated. Small finds from the central church are now in the Antiquities Museum at Leiden. The Egyptian Department of the Museum of Fine Arts at Budapest conserves some artifacts from Town A and Cemetery 249, and there is one glass vessel (unpublished) in the Egyptian Museum, Cairo.

BIBLIOGRAPHY

Barkóczi, L., and Á. Salamon. "A. N. 1964. Archaeological Investigation of the Settlement Town A." *Acta Archaeologica Hungarica* 26 (1974):289–338.

Grossmann, P. *Mittelalterliche Langhauskuppelkirchen und verwandte Typen in Oberägypten.* Glückstadt, 1982.

Hajnóczi, G. "Architectural Characteristics of the Settlement and Buildings." *Acta Archaeologica Hungarica* 26 (1974):339–68.

Jakobielski, S. "Remarques sur la chronologie des peintures murales de Faras aux VIIIe et IXe siècles." *Nubia Christiana* 1 (1982):154ff.

Kákosy, L. "Cemetery 249 Burials." *Acta Archaeologica Hungarica* 26 (1974):103–117.

Martens-Czarnecka, M. "Les Eléments décoratifs sur les peintures de la Cathédrale de Faras." *Faras VII,* pp. 60ff. Warsaw, 1982.

Monneret de Villard, U. *La Nubia Medioevale,* Vol. 1, pp. 170ff. Cairo, 1935.

Moorsel, P. van; J. Jacquet; and H. Schneider. *The Central Church of Abdallah Nirqi.* Leiden, 1975.
Pósa, V. "Chemical Analysis of the Leather Finds." *Acta Archaeologica Hungarica* 27 (1975):155–56.
Smith, H. S. *Preliminary Reports of the Egypt Exploration Society's Nubian Survey.* Cairo, 1962.
Török, L. "Fragment eines spätantiken roten Tongefässes." *Mitteilungen Archaeologischen Instituts* (Budapest) 2 (1971):87–97.
______. "Finds with Inscriptions." *Acta Archaeologica Hungarica* 26 (1974):369–93.
______. "Fragments of Wall-Paintings." *Acta Archaeologica Hungarica* 26 (1974):395–403.
______. "Man in the Vessel—An Interpretation of a Nubian Fresco Representation." In *Nubia Récentes Recherches,* pp. 121–25. Warsaw, 1975.
______. "The Pottery Finds of the Settlement." *Acta Archaeologica Hungarica* 27 (1975):353ff.
Török, L., and I. Lengyel. "Bestimmung des einstigen Inhalts des Gefässes." *Mitteilungen Archaeologischen Instituts* (Budapest) 2 (1971):99–101.
______. "The Finds from the Excavation of the Hungarian Mission I, II." *Acta Archaeologica Hungarica* 27 (1975):119–53.

LÁSZLÓ TÖRÖK

ʿABD AL-ʿAZĪZ IBN SAʾD AL-DĪN. Probably a prominent Copt of the fourteenth or fifteenth century, he is known only from a note that states that a manuscript (National Library, Paris, Arabe 14, fol. A) belonged to him. This fourteenth-century Coptic manuscript contains the Arabic translation of the Pentateuch made by al-Ḥārith ibn Sinān ibn Sinbāṭ, a West Syrian translator of the ninth century, and well known to the Copts.

BIBLIOGRAPHY

Slane, W. M., baron de. *Catalogue des manuscrits arabes de la Bibliothèque Nationale,* p. 4. Paris, 1883–1895.
Troupeau, G. *Catalogue des manuscrits arabes de la Bibliothèque Nationale,* Vol. 1, pt. 1: *Manuscrits chrétiens,* pp. 18–19. Paris, 1972.

KHALIL SAMIR, S.J.

ʿABD AL-MASĪḤ. A manuscript of the Coptic Patriarchate, Cairo (Theology 290; Graf, no. 533; Simaykah, no. 333) contains a collection of 149 poems in simple literary Arabic on moral and religious subjects, composed by Anbā Bistawrah, known as al-Ḥarīrī (Graf, 1934, Vol. 4, p. 133). It was copied by Ibrāhīm ibn Sulaymān al-Najjār al-Mīrī in March 1709 for the *muʿallim* ʿAwaḍ al-Maḥallāwī, and was offered to the *hegumenos* ʿAbd al-Masīḥ.

He may be the same *hegumenos* (priest) who, during the reign of the 103rd patriarch, JOHN XVI (YU'ANNIS) (1676–1718), and in his patriarchal residence, copied a liturgical manuscript (Coptic Patriarchate, Cairo, Liturgy 15; Simaykah, no. 815; not in Graf) containing a lectionary in Coptic for the Sundays of the first six months of the year. This manuscript was restored in March 1715.

BIBLIOGRAPHY

Graf, G. *Catalogue de manuscrits arabes chrétiens conservés au Caire.* Studi e Testi 134, p. 200. Vatican City, 1934.

KHALIL SAMIR, S.J.

ʿABD AL-MASĪḤ IBN ISḤĀQ AL-KINDĪ. This pseudonym was used by a Nestorian author about 825 in defense of Christianity in reply to ʿAbdallāh ibn Ismāʿīl al-Hāshimī, the pseudonym of a Muslim author. This is one of the most important texts in Arabic Christian apologetic literature in reaction to Islam (analysis and bibliography are in Graf, 1944, Vol. 1, pp. 135–45).

Despite the importance of this text, it would appear that the Copts in the Middle Ages were not acquainted with it, although they possessed other, rare apologies, such as those of the Nestorians ʿAmmār al-Baṣrī (c. 820) and Ḥunayn ibn Isḥaq (d. 873), or that of the Melchite Qusṭā ibn Lūqā (d. c. 912). The Copts came to know this text only in the nineteenth century, and authors such as the *qummuṣ* SARJIYŪS (Sergius) were able to make use of it owing to the two editions made in Cairo (1885 and 1912) by the Society for Promoting Christian Knowledge.

KHALIL SAMIR, S.J.

ʿABD AL-MASĪḤ AL-ISRĀʾĪLI AL-RAQQĪ. The inscription in the title of the *Kitāb al-Istidlāl*—"Book of Dialectic, written by ʿAbd al-Masīḥ al-Isrāʾīlī al-Raqqī, who became a Christian at Miṣr thanks to ʿalā yadd Shaykh Manṣūr ibn Sahlān the physician" (Vatican Library, Arabic manuscript 145, fol. 114b)—reveals that ʿAbd al-Masīḥ was a Jew from Raqqah in Syria who was converted to Christianity in Egypt, probably before 969, the year Cairo was founded.

The physician who converted him was the famous Abū al-Fatḥ MANṢŪR IBN SAHLĀN IBN MUQASHSHIR, who practiced his art for many decades at the court of the Fatimid caliphs in Cairo, especially under al-ʿAzīz (975–996) and al-ḤĀKIM Bi-Amr Allāh (996–1021).

The *Book of Dialectic*, and especially its third and fifth sections, shows that ʿAbd al-Masīḥ was well versed not only in philosophy but also in mathematics.

Six treatises, contained in two manuscripts, have been attributed to ʿAbd al-Masīḥ. One of the manuscripts is in the Vatican Library (Arabic manuscript 145, copied in Egypt at the end of the thirteenth century); the other belonged to the heirs of Karkūr Ṣāʾigh, members of the Catholic Armenian community of Aleppo in the 1920s. It was described by Paul Sbath in his catalog. Unfortunately, this manuscript no longer exists.

In fact, the three treatises in the Vatican manuscript are not works of ʿAbd al-Masīḥ. The works ascribed to him follow:

1. The *Treatise on the Rational Soul* was attributed to ʿAbd al-Masīḥ by Joseph Simon ASSEMANI in his description of the Vatican manuscript 145, fol. 1a–28a, and in Sbath's description of the Aleppo manuscript (1938, p. 53, no. 410), which was repeated by Steinschneider (1877, p. 115). This treatise was actually the work of AWLĀD AL-ʿASSĀL (as shown by Graf, 1947, pp. 403f).

2. The *Brief Treatise on the Trinity* was also ascribed to ʿAbd al-Masīḥ by Assemani (1831, p. 271, col. 2), an observation followed by Steinschneider (p. 115). But it is in fact by al-ṢAFĪ IBN AL-ʿASSĀL (see Graf, 1947, p. 395, no. 4).

3. The *Proof of the Coming of Christ* was included in the Aleppo manuscript (Sbath, 1938, p. 53, no. 409), which most probably constitutes the first part of *The Book of Dialectic* (see below).

4. The *Refutation of the Jews* was also part of the Aleppo manuscript (Sbath, 1938, p. 53, no. 411).

5. The *Triumph of the Cross over Judaism and Paganism* is included in the Aleppo manuscript (Sbath, 1938, p. 53, no. 412).

6. For the now lost *Book of Dialectic*, the Vatican manuscript 145 has preserved a compendium *(mukhtaṣar)* with fol. 114b–22b (original Coptic numbering: 121b–29b). Any analysis of the work must be based on this compendium.

The *Kitāb al-Istidlāl* consists of an introduction and five parts. The introduction repeats the eight traditional *kephalaia* (headings) employed by the Alexandrian commentators on the works of Aristotle. These were used repeatedly throughout traditional Arab philosophy (by al-Fārābī, Yaḥya ibn ʿAdī, ʿAbdallāh ibn al-Ṭayyib, etc.). But only six of the eight *kephalaia* are found here: goal, usefulness, place, author, method, and divisions.

The first part deals with proofs concerning the coming of Christ, starting with prophecies in the Old Testament. The compiler of this material (probably Al-Ṣafī ibn al-ʿAssāl) did not summarize this initial segment. Instead, he indicated that sufficient information of this sort appeared in the two books of al-Kashkarī and al-Ruhāwī, doubtless works by the Nestorian priest Israel al-Kashkarī (Graf, 1947, pp. 155f.) and Taddāwus al-Ruhāwī, author of *The Book of the Master and of the Disciple* (Graf, 1947, p. 219, par. 1–2; p. 473, no. 9). These two books are mentioned by Abū al-Barakāt Ibn Kabar (d. 1324) in Chapter 7 of his *Miṣbāḥ al-Ẓulmah*, in a discussion of Nestorian authors (cf. Khalil Samir's edition, pp. 302–303, nos. 9–70).

The second part details the ways in which God is said to be substance by the Christians.

The third part is the best developed. The author explains the meaning of the Christian Trinity in seven different ways: by analogy with man (God is living, knowing, powerful); by analogy with geometry (the body is reality which is perfect, unified, and three-dimensional); by analogy with mathematics (the number three is the most perfect because it contains both an odd and an even number); by analogy with logic (gender, species, and individuality); through the testimony of the prophets in the Old Testament; through philosophy (the primary cause, the intellect, and the soul are the only three realities that are neither attainable through reason nor through the senses; they are the images of the Father, the Son, and the Holy Ghost; likewise, the Sabaeans venerate three altars, which are the world of the primary cause, the intellect, and the soul); and through the Gospel, because Christ and the Apostles are true. He then answers two objections: "Why limit oneself to only three hypostases?" and "If the eternal one joins the created, He becomes himself created."

The fourth part focuses on the Incarnation, employing two approaches: through prophecies of the Old Testament and through miracles. The compiler's summary does not do justice to this piece.

The fifth part responds to the question of why Christ did not prevent the Jews from killing him. If He was incapable, it means He was not God, and if He was capable and did not do so, then the Jews are not guilty. ʿAbd al-Masīḥ's answer rests on three premises: that God, in creating man, did so for man's own good; that God created men free and not constrained, an argument that sets predestination against divine foresight; and that though God sent prophets to one specific people, prophecy proved futile; He then became incarnate in order that all humanity might reach perfection. (Here is inserted a marginal gloss that should probably be attributed to Al-Ṣafī ibn al-ʿAssāl.)

He then offers two answers to the question of why Christ did not prevent His own death. If He had, He would not have acted fully as a man and would therefore not have served as an example for the human race. And if He had forced the Jews not to kill Him, he would have been limiting their free will, the very quality that makes them human.

The treatise ends with a beautiful prayer in rhymed prose.

BIBLIOGRAPHY

Assemani, J. S. *Scriptorum veterum nova collectio e vaticanis codicibus edita,* Vol. 4, pt. 1, pp. 271–72, ed. Angelo Mai. Rome, 1831. Description of Vatican Library, Arabic manuscript 145.

Sbath, P. *Al-Fihris. Catalogue de manuscrits arabes,* Vol. 1, p. 53, nos. 409–412. Cairo, 1938.

Steinschneider, M. *Polemische und apologetische Literatur in arabischer Sprache,* pp. 115–16, no. 91. Leipzig, 1877; reprint, Hildesheim, 1966.

______. *Die arabische Literatur der Juden. Ein Beitrag zur Literaturgeschichte der Araber grossenteils aus handschriftlichen Quellen.* Frankfurt, 1902; reprint, Hildesheim, 1964.

KHALIL SAMIR, S.J.

ʿABD AL-MASĪḤ, KNOWN AS IBN NŪḤ.

Everything known about this author comes from the Coptic encyclopedist Abū al-Barakāt IBN KABAR (d. 1324), who mentions him in his *Lamp of Darkness* at the end of Chapter 7 (Riedel, 1902, p. 666; Samir, 1971, p. 326; trans. Riedel, p. 703) as follows: *"Masāʾil wa-Ajwibah fī Maʿānī al-Iʿtiqād li-ʿAbd al-Masīḥ yuʿraf bi-Ibn Nūḥ"* (Questions and answers on the concepts of [Christian] dogma by ʿAbd al-Masīḥ, known as Ibn Nūḥ).

Although he mentions ʿAbd al-Masīḥ in the course of his text, Abū al-Barakāt does not include him in his special inventory. Consequently, it is impossible to determine where he came from and when he lived beyond Abū al-Barakāt's own time. One notes that he is mentioned in an appendix after the *Kitāb al-Barādīsūs,* that is, the *Lausiac History* of PALLADIUS. The reference to him in the *Lamp of Darkness,* however, shows that he was known by the Copts at the end of the thirteenth century.

BIBLIOGRAPHY

Riedel, W. ed. "Der Katalog der christlichen Schriften in arabischer Sprache von Abu'l Barakāt, herausgegeben und übersetzt." *Nachrichten der Gesellschaft der Wissenschaften zu Göttingen, Philologisch-historische Klasse,* Vol. 5. Berlin, 1902.

Samir, K., S. J., ed. *Miṣbāḥ al-Zulmah fī Iḍāḥ al-Khidmah, li-Shams al-Riyāsah Abī al Barakāt al-maʿrūf bi-Ibn Kabar.* Cairo, 1971.

KHALIL SAMIR, S.J.

ʿABD AL-MASĪḤ ṢALĪB AL-MASŪʿDĪ.

A monk at the monastery of the Virgin (DAYR AL-BARAMŪS in Wādī al-Naṭrūn), ʿAbd al-Masīḥ (1848–1935) was ordained a monk by his uncle, ʿAbd al-Masīḥ al-Kabīr, in 1874. His prolific writings covered linguistics, ritual, and history. He mastered Hebrew, Syriac, Greek, and Coptic. His best known work is his interpretation of the Epact, in the Arabic version of *al-Abukti* (reckoning of the derivation of feast days in the Coptic, Syrian, Armenian, and Greek churches).

His most significant works include *Kītāb al-Khulājī al-Muqaddas* (i.e., *Kitā al-Thalāth Quddāsāt;* The three masses, Cairo, 1903); *Kitāb al-Tuḥfah al-Saniyyah* (Theology, Cairo, 1925); *Kitāb al-Durrah al-Nafisah fī Ḥisābāt al-Kanīsah,* Cairo, 1926, a small and concise treatise on dates of the church developed in a much more detailed work of more than 617 pages entitled *Al-Tuḥfah al-Barāmūsiyyah fī Sharḥ wa-Tatimmat Qawāʿid Hisāb al-Abqaṭi lil-Kanīsah al-Qibṭiyyah al-Urthudhuksiyyah,* Cairo, 1925; *Kitāb al-Karmah* (Theology, Cairo, 1927); *Kitāb al-Asrār* (Coptic and Arabic terminology of the church defined, Cairo, 1926); and *Tuḥfat al-Sāʾilīn fī Dhikr Adyirat Ruhbān al-Miṣriyyīn* (On Coptic monasteries, Cairo, 1932).

He was summoned by Patriarch Cyril V to serve in the central administration of the church at the patriarchate in Cairo. He died at the age of eighty-seven in 1935.

AZIZ S. ATIYA

ABGAR,

king of Edessa in the first half of the first century (it would seem between 4 B.C. and A.D. 50) and the subject of a Christian legend found for the first time in Eusebius (*Historia ecclesiastica* 1.13.5–22). According to this version, Abgar, being ill, writes a letter to Jesus asking him to visit and cure him. Jesus rejects the request, but promises that after his ascension he will send a disciple to heal the king and to preach the gospel. Thaddeus, a disciple of Thomas, is, in fact, sent.

Eusebius says that he is giving the translation of a Syriac text. The legend is then found with certain variation in the so-called *Doctrina Addai,* a Syriac text that has survived complete in only one manuscript (Phillips, 1876). This text is late, but may be derived from the one used by Eusebius. The *Peregrinatio Aetheriae* asserts that Christ's original letter on parchment was conserved at Edessa.

A later addition to the legend speaks of Jesus' portrait, claiming that it was enclosed with the letter. In the Byzantine world the portrait aspect of the legend predominated, whereas in the more properly Eastern world, the text of the letter was more important and was used as a talisman to protect health and to assure personal safety.

The text of the letter is found in Coptic in a great number of manuscripts of every type (papyrus, parchment, shards, paper, and inscriptions) and from every era. A survey up to 1915 was made by Drioton, according to whom the use of the letter spread throughout Coptic circles after having originated in monasticism during the time of the Arian persecution, when Athanasius took refuge with the monks of the south.

BIBLIOGRAPHY

Drioton, E. "Un Apocryphe antiarien: la version copte de la Correspondence d'Abgar roi d'Edesse avec notre Seigneur." *Revue de l'Orient chrétien* 2 (1915):306–326, 337–73.

Giversen, S. "The Sahidic Version of the Letter of Abgar on a Wooden Tablet." *Acta Orientalia* 24 (1954):71–82.

Leclercq, H. "Abgar." In *Dictionnaire d'archéologie chrétienne et de liturgie,* Vol. 1, pp. 87–97. Paris, 1903.

Lipsius, R. A. *Die Edessenische Abgarsage.* Brunswick, West Germany, 1880.

Phillips, G., ed. *The Doctrine of Addai.* London, 1876.

TITO ORLANDI

ABĪB IBN NAṢR. A deacon in Cairo, Abīb worked as a copyist between 1756 and 1767, both in Coptic and in Arabic, for the archon NASĪM ABŪ SA'D IBN 'ABD AL-SAYYID and the priest al-Khazāyinī.

He is known from three manuscripts of the Coptic Museum of Cairo: (1) A large lectionary in Coptic for the month of Amshīr (Liturgy 317 [123 fols., 32 × 21 cm]; Graf, no. 689; Simaykah, Vol. 2, no. 228), completed on 1 Bashans A.M. 1472/7 May 1756, on commission from Nasīm abū Sa'd. The subscription (fol. 363) informs us that this lectionary is the third part of a lectionary for the second trimester of the Coptic year. (2) Another large lectionary in Arabic (Liturgy 320 [243 fols., 29.5 × 21 cm]; Graf, no. 691; Simaykah, Vol. 2, no. 232) for the weekdays of the first three months of the Coptic year (Tūt, Bābah, Hātūr), completed on 20 Ṭūbah A.M. 1474/26 January 1758, on commission from Nasīm abū Sa'd. (3) A smaller lectionary (Liturgy 52 [115 fols., 28 × 18 cm]; Graf, no. 70; Simaykah, Vol. 2, no. 236) in Arabic, for the fifty days following Easter. It was completed on 23 Baramhāt A.M. 1483/30 March 1767, on commission from the priest al-Khazāyinī, who bequeathed it to the Church of the Virgin of Ḥārit Zuwaylah.

BIBLIOGRAPHY

Graf, G. *Catalogue de manuscrits arabes chrétiens conservés au Caire.* Studi e Testi 134, 27 (no. 70), 254 (no. 689), and 255 (no. 691). Vatican City, 1934.

KHALIL SAMIR, S.J.

ABILIUS, SAINT, third patriarch of the See of Saint Mark (85–98) (feast day: 1 Tūt). According to the *Historia ecclesiastica* by EUSEBIUS OF CAESAREA, at the death of Patriarch Anianus, probably in 85, his suffragan bishops and priests from Egypt and the Pentapolis converged upon Alexandria, where they took counsel with the orthodox laity and, having cast lots, unanimously selected Abilius for his chastity and knowledge of Christ. He remained in office for thirteen years and nine months. He was laid to rest next to the remains of Saint Mark in the Church of Bucalis at Alexandria. Little is known about his reign.

AZIZ S. ATIYA

ABLUTION, cleansing by water. In pre-Christian times, ablution was a common practice. Pharaoh's daughter was washing in the river when she saw Moses in the basket among the reeds (Ex. 2). Ablution was also part of ritual purification in Jewish religious ceremonials. Washing of the hands and feet was prescribed by the Mosaic law on entering the sanctuary and when approaching the altar. Likewise, the seventy-two elders of the Septuagint had to wash their hands and purify themselves every morning before starting their work on the Bible.

In the Coptic church, ablution is an integral part of the eucharistic rite. The celebrating priest performs the service with clean hands and in clean clothes. Just as it is important to approach the Body and Blood of Christ with a heart cleansed and purified by penitence and a mind stripped of all worldly considerations, it is equally necessary to be physically and externally clean. The emphasis on washing the hands before communion arose from the fact that in the early centuries of Christianity a communicant had to spread his right hand over the left hand in the form of a cross, and the priest would place the Body in the middle of the palm.

The ewer and basin (see Liturgical Instruments) are kept in the northern corner of the altar, that is, to the right side, and the officiating priest has to wash his hands twice during the celebration of the liturgy.

The first is after the prayer of the Psalms, and before the prayer of the preparation of the altar. A deacon pours some water three times onto the priest's hands, who recites, at the first pouring, Psalm 51:7, "Purge me with hyssop, and I shall be clean; wash me, and I shall be whiter than snow"; at the second pouring, Psalm 51:8, "Fill me with joy and gladness; let the bones which thou hast broken rejoice"; and at the third pouring, Psalm 26:6, "I wash my hands in innocence, and go about thy altar, O Lord, singing aloud a song of thanksgiving." Then he wipes his hands with a clean towel.

The second occurs while the congregation recites the Creed in the same manner as the first. The priest washes his hands as a prelude to handling the Sacraments with his own hands. Then he faces the congregation and shakes the water gently off his hands as a gesture of admonition to those members of the congregation who are thinking of partaking of Holy Communion unworthily, and also acquitting himself personally from the responsibility for any unworthiness. It is as if the priest reminds them of the words of Saint Paul, "Whoever, therefore, eats the bread or drinks the cup of the Lord in an unworthy manner will be guilty of profaning the body and blood of the Lord" (1 Cor. 11:27). He then wipes his hands in a clean cloth.

If the patriarch is celebrating the liturgy, he is given precedence in washing his hands first, and is followed by the clergy according to rank.

When he has finished administering Holy Communion, the priest washes all the vessels—the chalice, paten, asterisk, and spoon—and drinks the water. He washes the paten a second and a third time and gives the deacons to drink. Then he washes his hands in the paten and drinks the water. If a second priest has assisted in the liturgy, he too washes his hands in the paten and drinks the water. A deacon then wipes the vessels and wraps them in the veils and mats, to be ready for use in the following liturgy.

Unlike other churches that use wine in ablution, only water is used in the Coptic church. The above procedure of ablution is similar to that followed in the Syrian Antioch liturgy and the Armenian liturgy. CYRIL OF JERUSALEM writes, "Ye saw the deacon who gave to the priest and to the elders surrounding the altar of God, water to wash their hands. . . . The washing of hands is a symbol of guiltlessness of sins" (*Catechetical Lectures* 8.11, 1838). It is a practice underlined by Saint JOHN CHRYSOSTOM, who says "Tell me, wouldst thou choose to draw near to the sacrifice with unwashen hands? I think not, but thou wouldst rather not draw near at all than with filthy hands. Wouldst thou, then, while thus careful in the little matter, draw near having a filthy soul?" (*Homily 3 in Epistolam ad Ephesios* 1.20–23). Likewise, Caesarius of Arles (470–542) says in one of his sermons, "If we are ashamed and afraid to touch the Eucharist with filthy hands, much more ought we to be afraid to receive the same Eucharist in a polluted soul" (*Sermon* 292.6, in *PL* 39, col. 2300).

BIBLIOGRAPHY

Caesarius of Arles. *Sermon* 292. In *PL* 39, cols. 2297–2301. Paris, 1841.

Creagh, J. T. "Ablutions of the Mass." In *New Schaff-Herzog Encyclopedia of Religious Knowledge*. New York and London, 1908–1912.

LeBrun, P. *Explication littérale, historique et dogmatique des prières et des cérémonies de la messe*. Paris, 1777.

ʿAbd-al-Masīḥ al-Masʿūdī. *Al-Khūlājī al-Muqaddas*. Cairo, 1902.

Maurice, V. "Ablutions de la messe." In *Dictionnaire de théologie catholique*. Paris, 1899–1961.

M'Clintock, J., and J. Strong. "Ablution." In *Cyclopedia of Biblical, Theological and Ecclesiastical Literature*, 12 vols. New York, 1867–1891.

Pétridès, S. "Ablutions." In *Dictionnaire d'archéologie chrétienne et de liturgie*, Vol. 1, cols. 103–222. Paris, 1907.

Scudamore, W. E. "Hands, washing of." In *Dictionary of Christian Antiquities*, 2 vols. London, 1875–1880.

Thalhofer, V. *Handbuch der katholischen Liturgik*, Vol. 2, pp. 291, 292. Freiburg-im-Breisgau, 1890.

Yūḥannā Salāmah. *Kitāb al-La'ālī' al-Nafīsah fī Sharḥ Ṭuqūs wa-Mu'taqadāt al-Kanīsah,* 2 vols. Cairo, 1909.

ARCHBISHOP BASILIOS

ABNUB. *See* Pilgrimages.

ABRAAM I, Saint, or Aphraam (1829–1914), bishop of the Fayyūm noted for his holiness and devotion to the poor (feast day: 3 Ba'ūnah). Bishop Abraam was born under the name of Būlus. According to the Copto-Arabic SYNAXARION, his birthplace was 'Izbat Jaldah in the district of Mallawī in the Minyā Province. He received his early education in the village scriptorium, where he read the Bible, memorized the Psalms, and practiced church singing. He was made deacon at his village church by Anbā Yūsāb, bishop of Ṣanabū.

At the age of nineteen he took the monastic vow at Dayr al-Muḥarraq near Asyūṭ, under the name of Būlus Ghubriyāl al-Muḥarraqī. There he remained for the next five years, during which he was elevated to the rank of HEGUMENOS. In the meantime, his monastic colleagues elected him head of their monastery. In this capacity, the monastery became a refuge for the poor people of the community, whom he aided unreservedly by the use of its income. In the long run, the monks became dissatisfied with his ways, which they considered as sheer dissipation of the fortunes of the monastery. They complained to Anbā Marcus, archbishop of Beheira and acting patriarchal deputy after the decease of Demetrius II, who decided to relieve him from the headship of al-Muḥarraq. Eventually, he moved to the monastery of Our Lady, known as DAYR AL-BARAMŪS in Wādī al-Naṭrūn. There, he concentrated on biblical studies and became closely acquainted with the head of that institution, John the Scribe (Yuḥannā al-Nāsikh) who later became Patriarch CYRIL V.

In 1881, Cyril V appointed him bishop of the Fayyūm, where he became identified as the father of the poor with whom he usually received his meals. When the patriarch offered him the title of metropolitan, he declined on the premise that the Bible mentioned only the titles of presbyter and bishop. His sanctity became known, and people of all faiths, including Muslims, came to seek his blessings. He gave all he possessed to the needy and conducted a strictly ascetic life. People spoke of his performance of miracles through prayer for the sick. At his death on 3 Ba'ūnah (10 June 1914) his funeral was followed by more than ten thousand people, including Muslims as well as Copts. His remains were deposited in the grave he had prepared for himself at DAYR AL-'AZAB in the Fayyūm, which became a pilgrimage place for his admirers.

MIRRIT B. GHALI

ABRAHAM, SAINT, sixty-second patriarch of the See of Saint Mark (975–978), who was a great reformer (feast day: 6 Kiyahk). Abraham was also known as Ephraem the Syrian, indicating his native origin, with the ascription Ibn Zar'ah always accompanying his name. He was a distinguished layman who made a large fortune in commerce that he used in charitable practices for the poor and the needy. He was a man of respectable stature with a flowing beard, which, according to the HISTORY OF THE PATRIARCHS, resembled the beard of the prophet Abraham in the Old Testament. He was highly regarded by the Islamic administration of Caliph al-Mu'izz, to whom he rendered many services through his import–export trade.

The story of Abraham's elevation to the dignity of the Coptic patriarchate in spite of the fact that he was not a clergyman is interesting. After the death of MĪNĀ II, his predecessor, the bishops, together with the clergy and the Coptic archons of Cairo, met in the Church of Saints Sergius and Bacchus in QAṢR AL-SHAM' in Old Cairo to deliberate on finding the person best fitted for patriarchal succession. While they were preparing for the performance of the liturgy, Abraham happened to enter the church for prayer, and one of the archons, noticing him, turned to one of the bishops and indicated that if he were looking for a candidate for the papacy, here was the man whom the Lord had sent for the solution to his problem. The whole group was impressed by the suggestion and immediately laid their hands on Abraham, who, in spite of his protests, was taken by force in iron fetters to Alexandria for consecration. He became one of the most significant patriarchs of the tenth century.

Immediately after his consecration, Abraham suppressed the practice of simony (CHEIROTONIA), which had been rampant during former patriarchates. Then he concentrated on reforming the morals of the Coptic archons, who kept many concubines in addition to their legal wives. He spared no effort to enforce the sanctity of marriage, even threatening to excommunicate all culprits.

Abraham was the contemporary of SĀWĪRUS IBN AL-MUQAFFAʿ, the famous author of the *History of the Patriarchs,* who accompanied the patriarch in most of his religious disputations with Jews and Muslims. Apparently al-Muʿizz sponsored such discussions, according to the chronicles of his reign as well as the *History of the Patriarchs.* Al-Muʿizz had a vizier or secretary by the name of Yaʿqūb ibn Killīs, an Islamized Jew, who looked with disfavor on his master's deference toward the patriarch and his leniency toward the Copts. In an attempt to turn al-Muʿizz from any favor toward the Christians, he proposed holding a discussion in the presence of the caliph between the patriarch and a learned Jewish friend by the name of Moses. Abraham came with Bishop Sāwīrus. In an argument in which Sāwīrus quoted the Old Testament and the Book of Isaiah, Abraham was able to silence his Jewish opponent.

The *History of the Patriarchs* (Vol. 2, pt. 2, pp. 94–97) details the famous parable of faith and the mustard seed. The Islamized Jewish vizier sought to embarrass the patriarch by informing the caliph that the Christian gospel claimed that faith the size of a mustard seed could move a mountain. The caliph wished the patriarch to prove the veracity of the parable; failure to do so would cause him to kill the Christians for this falsehood. The legend follows with an account of perpetual prayers and a dream in which the patriarch was directed toward a poor tanner, who happened to be the vehicle for moving the mountain. When the mountain was moved, the caliph was ready to grant any request by the patriarch. The conclusion of the legend is that the caliph sanctioned Abraham's church-building program. This included the restoration of the Church of Abū Sayfayn (Saint Mercurius), which had been destroyed by the mob in Old Cairo and used since as a storehouse for sugarcane. Further, the historic Church of al-Muʿallaqah in Old Cairo had suffered some wall damage and this was repaired without interference. Other churches were also restored or rebuilt with state subventions, if we believe the *History of the Patriarchs,* though it is more likely that Abraham used his own funds in the execution of these projects. And in Alexandria, the patriarch contributed 500 dinars in two successive years for the restoration of its churches.

When Abū al-Yumn ibn Quzmān ibn Mīnā, a Copt of great standing in al-Muʿizz's administration, was dispatched to Syria through the complicity of Ya'qūb ibn Killis, he left his accumulated fortune of 90,000 dinars in the custody of the patriarch, to use at his discretion. Though part of this was used to help the needy, we may assume that most of it must have been expended in church building and restoration.

Abraham spent his three and a half years in the papal office in constructive work for the community. He was aided by his wholesome relations with the Fatimid caliphate. His reign proved to be one of the finest periods in Coptic church history in the Middle Ages.

BIBLIOGRAPHY

Lane-Poole, S. *The Mohammadan Dynasties.* London, 1894.

______. *History of Egypt in the Middle Ages.* London, 1901.

SUBHI Y. LABIB

ABRAHAM OF FARSHŪṬ, a sixth-century abbot (feast day: 24 Ṭūbah). In addition to the SYNAXARION (Basset, 1916, p. 684; Forget, 1953–1954, 47–49, pp. 411–13 [text]; 78, pp. 401–05 [trans.]), which gives a brief résumé of his life, numerous Coptic folios (Campagnano, 1970, pp. 230–32, 239–41) contain the remains of two Encomia. Moreover, we have also in the life of MANASSEH, who was his cousin, a digression on Abraham's stay in Constantinople (pp. 230, 238).

Abraham was born at Farshūṭ, in the diocese of Diospolis Pârva (modern-day Hiww) in Upper Egypt. His parents, who were Christians and important among the inhabitants of this village, died when Abraham was twelve. The following year, he tried to convince his sister to preserve her virginity, but she did not let herself be persuaded. Abraham then went off to the monastery of PACHOMIUS, at that time under the direction of Pshintbahse. He devoted himself to the asceticism and exercises of the monastic state. On Pshintbahse's death, he was elected abbot to succeed him. But the emperor JUSTINIAN, wishing to gather the monks under the faith of CHALCEDON, sent a letter to the dux of the Thebaid some time after 535 ordering him to bring Abraham *manu militari* to Constantinople. Since the empress THEODORA, who took an active part in the protection of the Monophysites, died in 548, Abraham's stay in Constantinople is located between these two dates. Abraham set off with four brethren. "If only," says the narrator, "he had not taken them with him." This regret seems to indicate that Abraham's companions were not of the same opinion as he. When they arrived at court, Justinian summoned them and confronted Abraham with an alternative: either he would adopt the faith as expounded at the Council of Chalcedon or he would no longer be archimandrite of Pbow. Abraham flatly refused to subscribe to Chalcedon.

Theodora tried to intercede with Justinian, who remained inflexible. Abraham wrote of these events to his monks, saying that he preferred exile to a faith that he considered contrary to that of ATHANASIUS. It is probable, although the text does not speak of it, that Theodora succeeded in persuading him to leave for Egypt.

There were dissensions on this subject at Pbow, as the text leaves one to expect. But the partisans of Chalcedon won the day, thanks to the military support of Pancharis, the imperial envoy.

Driven from Pbow, Abraham founded a new monastery near his birthplace, Farshūṭ. It appears that the monks were few in number (the text speaks of two brethren who were with him). Gradually the number grew, obliging him to enlarge the construction. Pachomius, PETRONIUS, and SHENUTE appeared to him to announce his death and the name of his successor, THEOPHILUS.

Before his death he delivered to his monks long discourses in which he drew a parallel between the abundance of the monastery and their fidelity to the commandments of the Lord. He also founded a convent for nuns, to whom, as to his monks, he gave the rules of Shenute.

Abraham was a priest, as the Synaxarion mentions, and numerous miracles are related at the end of his encomium.

The folios of the second encomium indicate the number of the Pachomian communities at this period, twenty-four in the whole of Egypt. The text does not specify at what period Abraham died after being driven from Pbow. It appears from the Synaxarion that he often lived for periods as a hermit and then returned to his monastery.

BIBLIOGRAPHY

Campagnano, A. "Monaci egiziani fra V e VI secolo." *Vetera Christianorum* 15 (1978):223–46.

RENÉ-GEORGES COQUIN

ABRAHAM AND GEORGE OF SCETIS, SAINTS,

ABRAHAM AND GEORGE OF SCETIS, SAINTS, two seventh-century monks who shared a cell at Dayr Anbā Maqār for many years (feast days: 9 Ṭūbah and 18 Bashans, respectively). These two men, with Saint AGATHON THE STYLITE; Zacharias, bishop of Sā; Saint ISAAC (later patriarch of Alexandria); Saint MENAS, bishop of Tmuis; Epimachus of Arwāt; Saint ZACHARIAS, bishop of Sakhā; and Ptolemy, brought fame to Dayr Anbā Maqār (the Monastery of Saint Macarius) in Scetis. Abraham and George are always presented as inseparable companions, in contrast with the other disciples of JOHN, HEGUMENOS, a monk of Scetis. A joint biography was written by Zacharias, bishop of Sakhā, who was a monk at Scetis toward the end of their lives (National Library, Paris, Arabic 4888, fols. 175v–205v; summary in Evelyn-White, 1932, pp. 278–80; see also the Copto-Arabic SYNAXARION in Basset, PO 11, 1916, pp. 565–67; 16, 1922, pp. 393–95; and in Forget, CSCO 47–49, pp. 200–202; 67, pp. 126–218 [text]; 78, pp. 326–28; 90, pp. 126–27 [trans.]).

Abraham appears to have been born around 608. It seems that he is in fact the disciple of John the Hegumenos called Abraham of Phelbes (modern-day Bilbeis) in the story of the translation of the FORTY-NINE MARTYRS OF SCETIS (de Ricci and Winstedt, 1910, pp. 335, 349); this would indicate his place of origin. The Synaxarion relates that his mother was denounced to the Persians (who occupied Egypt from 616 to 628) and carried off into slavery, but the Arabic life speaks not of Persians but of "barbarians" during a raid in their district. After his father's death, Abraham refused the marriage that his mother proposed for him and, at age thirty-five, went off to Scetis, where he became a monk in the monastery of Saint Macarius under the direction of John the Hegumenos.

Later he went to the monastery of Anbā Orion, where he met George. The latter, whose place of birth is unknown, had at first been a shepherd but at the age of fourteen had become a monk in the monastery of Anbā Orion, the site of which is not known (Timm, 1984, pp. 671–72). He lived there for ten years and then went off into the desert. After two days' walking, in a vision he received the order to return to his monastery. He found himself at the monastery of DAYR AL-BARAMŪS, and from there he went back to his own monastery of Anbā Orion.

Abraham persuaded George to come with him to Scetis. George remained behind for some time to settle his affairs and then set off, became lost in the desert, and was miraculously transported to Scetis. The two friends installed themselves in the same cell (that is to say, a hermitage called Bajīj near Saint Macarius) belonging to John the Hegumenos. Both experienced apparitions of Jesus; they produced writings and exhortations, none of which, unfortunately, seems to have survived. One day during Lent they visited the future patriarch Isaac in the hermitage to which he had withdrawn. His disciples were numerous. Not long after John the Hegumenos died in 675, Abraham fell sick. His illness lasted eighteen years and he died at the age of eighty, around 693. George died after him, at the age of seventy-two.

Both their hermitage and their tombs were still in existence in the fourteenth century, when the desert was visited by the patriarchs at the time of the preparation of the chrism (see *Livre du chrême,* National Library, Paris, 100, fol. 58r; cf. Burmester, 1967, p. 220).

Abraham and George are called "the last great saints," because they seem to have been the last to lead the ancient hermit life as an end in itself, away from the ecclesiastical hierarchy.

BIBLIOGRAPHY

Burmester, O. H. E. *The Egyptian or Coptic Church.* Cairo, 1967.

Evelyn-White, H. G. *The Monasteries of the Wadi'n Natrūn,* Vol. 2, *The History of the Monasteries of Nitria and Scetis.* New York, 1932.

Ricci, S. de, and E. O. Winstedt. "Les Quarante-neuf vieillards de Scété." *Notices et extraits de manuscrits de la Bibliothèque nationale et autres bibliothèques* 39 (1910):323–58.

Timm. S. *Das christlich-koptische Ägypten in arabischer Zeit,* vols. 1–2. Wiesbaden, 1984.

RENÉ-GEORGES COQUIN

ABRAHAM OF HERMONTHIS

(late sixth century). Abraham is presented on a diptych (Crum, 1908) as the fourteenth bishop of Hermonthis. There is no mention of him in the SYNAXARION of the Coptic church. There are indeed no dates on the diptych, but we know that he was a contemporary of archbishop Damian of Alexandria (569–605). On the evidence of his portrait, painted on his accession to office, he was already old when he was consecrated bishop. On the evidence of his Greek testament (P. Lond. I 77) his father was called Sabinus, his mother Rebecca. We do not know when he became a monk, nor when he became abbot of Dayr Apa Phoibammon. While abbot of this monastery, excavated in 1948–1949 by the Société d'Archéologie copte, he was consecrated bishop of Hermonthis. Because of the remote situation of this monastery, 5 miles (8 km) from the Nile bank between Hermonthis and Madīnat Habu, he built another monastery before 590, at the instance of archbishop Damian, on the ground ceded by the town of Djeme in the former temple of Hatschepsut, the Dayr al-Bahri, also dedicated to Phoibammon. From this monastery, he officiated as bishop. He sent numerous communications to the Christians, both clerical and lay, of his diocese, and also received letters from the faithful under his charge. This correspondence shows us the duties and the activity of an Upper Egyptian bishop around 600, in a way not otherwise known to us to this extent. In the leadership of the Phoibammon monastery he was supported by his pupil, the priest Apa Victor, who became his successor as abbot. His successor as bishop was Moses.

BIBLIOGRAPHY

Crum, W. E. *Coptic Ostraca from the Collections of the Egypt Exploration Fund, the Cairo Museum and Others.* London, 1902.

______. "A Greek Diptych of the 7th Century." *Proceedings of the Society of Biblical Archaeology* 30 (1908):255–65; 30 (1909):288.

Krause, M. *Apa Abraham von Hermonthis. Ein oberägyptischer Bischof um 600,* 2 vols. Doctoral diss., Berlin, 1956.

______. "Die Beziehungen zwischen den beiden Phoibammon-Klöstern auf dem thebanischen Westufer." *Bulletin de la Société d'Archéologie copte* 27 (1985):31–44.

______. "Die Testamente der Äbte des Phoibammon-Klösters in Theben." *Mitteilungen des Deutschen Archäologischen Instituts Kairo* 25 (1969):57–67.

MARTIN KRAUSE

ABRAHAM OF MINŪF, SAINT,

a fourth-century monk and hermit (feast day: 30 Bābab), is known only from the SYNAXARION (Basset, 1904, p. 377; Forget, CSCO 47–49, p. 85 [text]; 78, p. 93 [trans.]). He was a native of Minūf in the Delta, born of Christian parents who held an important position in the world.

We do not know at what age he embraced the monastic life. The text says simply that "when he grew up, he went off to the land of Akhmīm, to join the great PACHOMIUS, who gave him the religious habit." He remained there twenty-three years. Then he asked to go and live as a hermit in a cavern, where he remained for sixteen years, leaving it only to receive communion every two or three years. He had at his service a secular brother who took the work of his hands, fishing nets, and sold them to buy beans for him, giving alms with the rest of the money.

When Abraham felt his death near, he sent for Apa Theodore, disciple of Pachomius; then he lay down facing the east. He was buried by the monks in the cemetery of the monastery. The mention of Theodore indicates that Abraham lived at the end of the fourth century.

Without the Synaxarion, we would not know that a Pachomian monk could become a hermit after spending some time in the cenobitic life.

RENÉ-GEORGES COQUIN

ABRAHAM PERSA. The Sahidic text published by E. O. Winstedt in *The Proceedings of the Society of Biblical Archaeology* (1908, with the variants of the two folios: W. E. Crum, 1905, No. 318 and G. Zoega, 1810, No. 222, from a copy by O. von Lemm) is probably part of an encomium. Among other things it deals with an Abraham in Mesopotamia, who was preserved from the fire of King Shapur (Sapor) by an angel of God. If the name Shapur were not here, on the basis of the context as a whole, one would inevitably think of the patriarch Abraham and the extrabiblical tale of his rescue from the fire of Nimrod. Crum refers to the Persian martyr Abraham, who met his death in the reign of Shapur II. Winstedt, who very clearly sees the difference between the Coptic text and the information on the Persian martyr and bishop of Arbela, remarks, "The Coptic writer may well have attributed to the Persian martyr sufferings similar to those which the patriarch was said to have endured at the hands of Nimrod, just as he refers David's words about the patriarch to the saint" (p. 233). There is also the possibility that the patriarch Abraham is intended, and that the Copt for some reason has given the name of Shapur, an enemy of the Christians, to Abraham's adversary.

BIBLIOGRAPHY

Crum, W. E. *Catalogue of the Coptic Manuscripts in the British Museum,* p. 141. London, 1905.
Delehaye, H. "Les Versions grecques des actes des martyrs persans sous Sapor II." In *Patrologia Orientalis,* Vol. 2, pp. 450–51.
Lucchesi, G. *Bibliotheca Sanctorum* 1 (1961):112ff.
Peeters, P. "Le Passionare d'Abiabène." *Analecta Bollandiana* 43 (1925):271–72.
Spadafora, F. *Bibliotheca Sanctorum* ser. 1 (1961): 89–106, esp. p. 98.
Winstedt, E. O. "Coptic Saints and Sinners I. Abraham." *The Proceedings of the Society of Biblical Archaeology* 30 (1908):231–37, 276–83 (on Zoega's *Catalogus Codicum* 222, see pp. 282ff).
Zoega, G. *Catalogus Codicum Copticorum Manu-Scriptorum qui in Museo Borgiano Veletris adservantur,* p. 548. Rome, 1810. Repr., Hildesheim, 1973.

THEOFRIED BAUMEISTER

ABRAHAM'S SACRIFICE OF ISAAC. *See* Biblical Subjects in Coptic Art.

ABRAXAS, also documented as Abrasax, a word with the numerical value of 365 ($\alpha = 1$, $\beta = 2$, $\rho = 100$, $\xi = 60$, $\sigma = 200$), which corresponds to the number of the days in a year. The name Abraxas designates a god who in the Gnosis of Basilides is Lord of the supernatural world. In addition, he appears in magical papyri and on amulets.

[*See also:* Basilides; Gnosis; Magic.]

BIBLIOGRAPHY

Dornseiff, F. *Das Alphabet in Mystik und Magie,* 2nd ed. Leipzig and Berlin, 1925.
Nilsson, M. P. *Geschichte der griechischen Religion,* Vol. 2, p. 617. Munich, 1961.

MARTIN KRAUSE

ABRĪM AL-QIBṬĪ, ANBĀ. Abrīm authored a history of the world from the time of creation until the year A.H. 614/A.D. 1216. The only known manuscript of this work belonged to ʿABD AL-MASĪḤ ṢALĪB AL-MASŪʿDĪ, a Coptic priest of Cairo. It is cited by Paul Sbath in both his manuscript catalogs (Sbath, 1938, 1939).

No Coptic bishop by the name of Abrīm is known. Graf suggested that the name might refer to a certain Afrīm, or Ephrem, but this does not help to identify him. One possible identification is Anba Abrā'ām, bishop of Nastarawayh, who was present both at the synod convened on 28 June 1240 under CYRIL III Ibn Laqlaq and at the ceremony of preparing the holy chrism in A.M. 973/A.D. 1257 (Munier, 1943). In the one manuscript, the name of this bishop is given as Abrām with only one *alif* (Sbath manuscript 1126; Sbath, 1934). Jacob Muyser (1944) has also suggested an equivalence between Abrām and Abrīm.

BIBLIOGRAPHY

Munier, H. *Recueil des listes épiscopales de l'église copte,* pp. 31 and 35. Cairo, 1943.

Muyser, J. "Contribution à l'étude des listes épiscopales de l'église copte." *Bulletin de la société d'Archéologie copte* 10 (1944):115–76, especially p. 156.

Sbath, P. *Bibliothèque de manuscrits Paul Sbath,* Vol. 3, p. 4. Cairo, 1934.

______. *Al-Fihris (Catalogue de manuscrits arabes),* Vol. 1, p. 7. Cairo, 1938.

______. "Manuscrits arabes d'auteurs coptes." *Bulletin de la Société d'Archéologie copte* 5 (1939): 159–73, especially p. 161.

KHALIL SAMIR, S. J.

ABSALIYYAH. *See* Music, Coptic: Description of the Corpus and Present Musical Practice.

ABSALMUDIYYAH. *See* Music, Coptic: Description of the Corpus and Present Musical Practice.

ABSOLUTION, the pronouncement of remission to the penitent, granting him release from the guilt of sin if he is truly contrite over his trespass, confesses to a priest, and promises not to revert to his former ways. The priest gives this absolution, not in his own name, but in the name of God, in accordance with the authority given to priesthood (Mt. 16:18, 18:18; Jn. 20:23). The prayer of absolution is said by the priest in his capacity as steward administering the church's holy sacraments.

Absolution is given: (1) when a penitent believer has shown genuine remorse following confession and carried out a course of penance; (2) at the end of the evening and morning offering of incense, and prior to the pronouncement of the blessing; (3) after the office of midnight prayer, when the prayer of the absolution of ministers is said; (4) in the course of liturgies celebrated at any time; (5) to every communicant following his confession; (6) in various church sacraments, such as Baptism, the Unction of the Sick, and Matrimony; (7) during other prayers performed by the church, such as the service of the foot-washing on Maundy Thursday, the blessing of the water, and genuflection (*sajdah*).

Formulas

In the Coptic church, as in other Eastern Orthodox churches, the priest follows the *precatory* method of absolution. After he has heard the penitent's confession, and read the appropriate prayer, his answer to the request of absolution is, "May God absolve you." That forgiveness of sins is the authority and grace of God alone is the firm position of the Coptic church based upon specific sources in Scripture. When David confessed to Nathan saying, "I have sinned against the Lord," Nathan's reply was, "The Lord also has put away your sin, you shall not die" (2 Sm. 12:13). Saint Paul, likewise, stresses unequivocally that the clergy are but servants of Christ and stewards of the mysteries of God (1 Cor. 14:1, 9:17, Ti. 1:7).

The Roman Catholic church used to adhere to this method in the past, but now it follows the *indicative* method of absolution, whereby the priest says in the vernacular to a penitent who requests absolution, "Ego absolvo te" ("I absolve you") instead of, as in the past, "Christus absolvit te" or "Deus absolvit te."

Prayers of Absolution

With the penitent kneeling before the entrance to the sanctuary, the confessor priest holds the cross and starts by saying the prayer of thanksgiving and Psalm 51, "Have mercy upon me, O God, according to Thy loving kindness," and the intercession for the sick, and, placing the cross on the penitent's head, he reads the three following absolution prayers that are addressed to God the Son:

> Yes Lord, the Lord who hath given authority unto us to tread upon serpents and scorpions and upon all the power of the enemy, crush his heads beneath our feet speedily and scatter before us his every design of wickedness that is directed against us, for Thou art King of us all, Christ, our God, and to Thee we send up the glory and the honor and the adoration, with Thy good Father and the Holy, life-giving, and consubstantial Spirit, now and at all times, and unto the age of all ages. Amen.

> Thou, Lord, who hast bowed the heavens, descended and become man for the salvation of mankind. Thou sittest upon the Cherubim and the Seraphim, and beholdest the lowly. We lift up the eyes of our hearts unto Thee, Lord, who forgiveth our iniquities and saveth our souls from corruption. We worship Thine unutterable compassion, and pray Thee to grant us Thy peace, for Thou hast granted everything unto us. Accept us, God

our Savior, for we know none other but Thee. Thy Holy Name we utter. Turn us, God, unto fear of Thee and desire of Thee. Be pleased that we abide in the enjoyment of Thy good things. Thy servant, [name], who has bowed his head beneath Thy hand, lift him in good conduct and adorn him with virtues. And may we all be worthy of Thy Kingdom of Heaven through the good-pleasure of God, Thy good Father, with Whom Thou art blessed with the Holy, Life-giving Spirit, Consubstantial with Thee, now and forever, and unto the age of all ages. Amen.

Master, Lord Jesus Christ, the Only-begotten Son and Word of God the Father, who hath severed every bond of our sins through His redeeming and life-giving sufferings, Who breathed into the faces of His holy disciples and pure apostles saying to them: "Receive the Holy Spirit, whosoever's sins you forgive they shall be forgiven, and whosoever's sins you withhold they shall be withheld." Now also, our Master, Thou hast given, through Thine holy apostles, grace to those who labour in the priesthood, in every age, in Thine holy church, to forgive sins upon the earth, and to bind and to loosen every bond of iniquity. Now also, we pray and entreat Thy goodness, O Lover of mankind, for Thy servant [name], and my weakness, we who bow our heads before Thy holy glory. Grant us Thy mercy, and loosen all the bonds of our sins, and, if we have committed any sin against Thee knowingly or unknowingly, or through anguish of heart, in deed, in word, or through faint heartedness, do Thou, the Master who knoweth the weakness of men, as a good God and lover of mankind, grant us the forgiveness of our sins. Bless us, purify us, absolve us, and absolve Thy servant [name]. Fill us with Thy fear, and guide us to Thy good Will, for Thou art our God. Glory, honor, dominion, and adoration are due to Thee with Thy good Father and the Holy Spirit. . . .

Absolution Prayers in the Liturgy

Whereas the aforementioned prayers are said silently, two other prayers are read aloud at certain places during the liturgy.

The first is the prayer of absolution of the ministers. At the conclusion of the offertory-consecratory prayer, all those ministering in the sanctuary go out with their faces looking to the east. Then the officiating priest (or high-priest) prays the following absolution:

May Thy servants, O Lord, ministering this day, the hegumenos, the priest, the deacons, the clergy, the congregation, and my own weakness, be absolved and blessed from the mouth of the Holy Trinity, the Father, the Son, and the Holy Spirit, from the mouth of the One Holy, Catholic, Apostolic Church, the mouths of the twelve apostles, of the beholder of God, Mark the Evangelist, the holy Apostle and Martyr, of the Patriarch Saint Severus, of our teacher Dioscorus, of Athanasius the Apostolic Saint, of Saint Peter the high-priest and seal of the Martyrs, of Saint John Chrysostom, Saint Cyril, Saint Basil, Saint Gregory, from the mouths of the three hundred and eighteen who met at Nicaea, the one hundred and fifty who met at Constantinople, and the two hundred who met at Ephesus, from the mouth of our honored high-priest and father [Anbā . . .] and his assistant in the apostolic ministry, our honored metropolitan [Bishop] and father [Anbā . . .], and from the mouth of my own weakness. For blessed and full of glory is Thy Holy Name, the Father, the Son, and the Holy Spirit, now and forever. . . .

The second is the prayer of absolution to the Father said after the fraction prayer, which is concluded by the Lord's Prayer:

Master, Lord God, the Almighty, healer of our souls, our bodies and our spirits, Thou hast said to our Father Peter, through the mouth of Thy Only-begotten Son our Lord, God, and Savior Jesus Christ, "Thou art Peter, and on this rock I build My Church, and the gates of hell shall not prevail against her. I will deliver the keys of the Kingdom of Heaven to thee, what thou bindst on earth shall be bound in heaven, and what thou loosest on earth shall be loosed in heaven." May, O lord, Thy servants, my fathers and brethren, and my own weakness, be absolved from my mouth, through Thy Holy Spirit, O good and lover of mankind. O God, who hast borne the sin of the world, vouchsafe to accept the repentance of Thy servants—as a light toward knowledge and remission of sins. For Thou art a kind and merciful God, forbearing, righteous, and compassionate. If we have sinned against Thee in word or in deed, do forgive us, for Thou art good and lover of mankind. Absolve us, O God, and absolve all Thy people [here the priest makes mention of the names of living and dead persons, and himself] of every sin, every curse, every ungratefulness, every false oath, every encounter with ungodly heretics. Bestow upon us, O Lord, a good mind and a power of understanding, to flee from every iniquity till the end, and to do those things which satisfy Thee every time. Write our names together with all the host of Thy Saints in the Kingdom of Heaven. In the Name of Jesus Christ, our Lord . . .

Observations

The absolution of ministers is designed to include, besides the clergy and deacons, the whole congregation. This is ample illustration of the importance that the Coptic church attaches to the presence and participation of the congregation during the service. They are not passive onlookers, but active partakers, forming an integral part of the service, and have their own responses to chant throughout the entire liturgy. The Eucharist, being the sacrament of the true Body of Christ, is also the sacrament of the church as a whole, with Christ at its head.

The Coptic rite is the only rite, with the exception of the fourth-century rite of North Africa, that includes the prayer of absolution to the Son, immediately after the fraction prayer, which is analogous to the inclusion of the prayer of absolution of ministers—with such comprehensive nature as we have seen above—right at the conclusion of the offering of the sacrificial Lamb.

The prayer of absolution of ministers is further evidence that a minister of the church, of whatever rank, may take part in the eucharistic service without obtaining proper absolution.

In the DIDACHE, which is the oldest eucharistic rite for Sunday services, dating to the first century, both confession and conciliation occur immediately before the partaking of Holy Communion, so as to guarantee absolute purity of the sacrifice.

BIBLIOGRAPHY

ʿAbd al-Masih al-Masʿūdī. *Al-Khūlājī al-Muqaddas.* Cairo, 1902.
ʿA Sulaymān. *Ṣalawāt al-Kanīsah.* Cairo, 1943.
Brightmann, L. E. W. *Liturgies Eastern and Western,* Vol. 1. Oxford, 1896.
Cabrol, F. "Absolution." In *Dictionnaire d'archéologie chrétienne et de liturgie,* Vol. 1. Paris, 1907.
Gregorios, Anbā. *Al-Qiyam al-Rūḥiyyah fī Sirr al-Tawbah.* Cairo, 1980.
Manqariyūs ʿAwaḍallah. *Manārat al- Aqdās fī Sharḥ Tuqūs al-Kanīsah al-Qibṭiyyah wa-al-Quddās.* Cairo, 1981.
Mattā al Miskīn. *Al-Ifkhāristiyyah.* Cairo, 1977.

ARCHBISHOP BASILIOS

ABSTINENCE, refraining from eating some or all kinds of food. Abstinence differs from orthodox fasting in that abstinence is not subject to the rules governing fasting. The practice, originally a form of penitence, dates from the Old Testament (Lv. 11), where elaborate prohibitionary rules were prescribed. These were later abrogated in the New Testament, but the early Coptic fathers voluntarily renewed the practice of abstinence with more vehemence as an individual demonstration of religious zeal. Saint ANTONY and his monks are said to have abstained from all manner of food except bread, salt, and water. Saint PACHOMIUS, though preserving this tradition, was more lenient, allowing the addition of a cabbage leaf to the cenobite's sustenance. Among Coptic ascetics, total abstinence until the rise of the first evening star was customary, especially during fast days. This practice was even intensified among certain heretical sects such as the Manichaeans and the Gnostics. Friday abstinence commemorates the Passion of Jesus, and Wednesday abstinence commemorates Job's suffering. Such practices were generally upheld by the fathers of the church, and some, such as Tertullian, extended the abstinence days to Saturday. Coptic Protestants, however, rejected abstinence and fasting altogether.

BIBLIOGRAPHY

Scudamore, W. E. "Fasting." In *Dictionary of Christian Antiquity,* Vol. 1, pp. 661–65. London, 1876.

AZIZ S. ATIYA

ABŪ. *See* Apa.

ABŪ AL-ʿALĀʾ FAHD IBN IBRAHIM. Abū al-ʿAlāʾ Fahd ibn Ibrahim first acted as Coptic secretary to Barjawān, tutor of the young caliph al-ḤĀKIM. Barjawān at that time was at the zenith of his power (in A.H. 387/A.D. 997). Fahd was given the honorary title of *al-raʾīs* (president). His office itself enabled him to have close contact with the caliph, especially during the *maẓālim* (oppressions) meetings. Fahd had no need to hide his religion because at that period Christians were not yet persecuted. In A.H. 388/A.D. 998 he was even officially present at the Coptic feast of Ghiṭās, and at Easter the same year he received presents from the caliph. When the great *qāḍī* Muḥammad ibn al-Nuʿmān died (Ṣafar 388), he was ordered to make an inventory of his possessions.

In 1000, restless under his tutorship, the caliph had Barjawān assassinated. Summoned to the palace during the night, Fahd had every reason to fear for his safety. But, on the contrary, the caliph reassured him and confirmed him in his charge of secretary, but henceforth in the service of Barjawān's successor, al-Ḥusayn ibn al-Jawhar, son of the celebrated general of al-Mu'izz. He was solemnly installed together with his new master, on 26 Jumādā I 390/4 May 1000. His power and authority appear to have aroused jealousy, for he was denounced to the caliph by two other functionaries, Maḥmūd al-Naḥwī and Ibn al-'Addās.

The HISTORY OF THE PATRIARCHS by SĀWĪRUS IBN AL-MUQAFFA' (Vol. 2, p. 123; trans., A. S. Atiya, 1943–1968, p. 186) relates that al-Ḥākim tried without success to get Fahd to convert to Islam, and so had him decapitated. This was on 8 Jumāda II 393/14 April 1003. His brother Abū al-Ghālib, leader of the *Dīwān al-Nafaqāt* (office of disbursement), hastened to bring the victim's possessions—which, it was said, amounted to 500,000 dinars—to the caliph. Al-Ḥākim had them distributed to his heirs saying, "We did not execute him because of his wealth." But Abū al-Ghālib was himself put to death shortly afterward.

Fahd's place was taken by a Muslim, 'Alī ibn 'Umar ibn al-'Addās; at the same time a number of Christian officials were imprisoned and their goods seized.

BIBLIOGRAPHY

Ibn al-Qalānisī. *Dhayl Tārīkh Dimashq,* ed. H. G. Amedroz, pp. 58–60. Leiden, 1908.

Ibn al-Ṣayrafī. "Al-Ishārah ilā man nāla al-Wizārah." *Bulletin de l'Institut français d'Archéologie orientale* 25 (1925):28 (95).

ANDRÉ FERRÉ

ABŪ AL-BARAKAT. *See* Ibn Kabar.

ABŪ AL-FAḌL 'ĪSĀ IBN NASṬŪRUS. Nothing is known of the life of this Christian before he became financial secretary during the caliphate of the Fatimid al-'Azīz, but he had probably been in the financial administration for some time and had risen gradually. Though he was a Christian, his name seems to indicate that ethnically he was not a Copt.

After the death of the vizier Ya'qūb ibn Killis (in A.H. 380/A.D. 991) we find him intervening in the Fatimid political scene in Syria. In fact, al-'Azīz the caliph was trying to take Aleppo from the Ḥamdānids and for that reason he had bribed general Bakjūr for his collaboration. But 'Īsā ibn Nasṭūrus, who disliked him, managed to have him betrayed and delivered into the hands of Ḥamdānid Sa'd al-Dawlah, who had him put to death (A.H. 381/A.D. 991).

In December 995, 'Īsā was given responsibility for the vizierate. Al-'Azīz then prepared a vast offensive to finally take the longed-for northern Syria. He had decided to attack by land and sea simultaneously, and the vizier was ordered to build up a war fleet. The work was well underway when, during the night of May 996, almost all the boats were destroyed by fire in the naval docks of al-Maqs, Cairo. The blame fell on the Greeks living in the neighborhood, and the vizier had a certain number of them executed or beaten. A fresh fleet was hastily prepared and attacked the port city of Anṭarṭūs unsuccessfully.

Muslim historians have certain reservations about 'Īsā. "He joined firmness to competence," says one of them; but he was suspected of favoring his fellow Christians by naming them to important posts and leaving aside the Muslims. He also appointed a Jew, Manashshā ibn Ibrāhīm, as delegate for the Syrian province. This caused a hardening of the Muslim opposition, which led to his destitution. His disgrace did not last long, however. The caliph's daughter, the famous Sitt al-Mulk, pleaded his cause with her father so that 'Īsā was reinstated, on condition that he give into Muslim hands the administrative posts due to them.

The caliph's sudden death on October 996 changed the vizier's destiny. Al-HĀKIM at first appointed him administrator of his personal possessions, but the Berber Kutāmah chieftains brought pressure to bear on him to replace 'Īsā by one of their own men. The vizier was arrested either on 25 February 996, or more likely 14 January 997. He was tortured to get money from him, then on 9 February he was led to al-Maqs on a donkey and beheaded. He saw in his own execution God's punishment for an unjust condemnation to death he had pronounced on a young man after the burning of the fleet.

A number of members of his family occupied important posts during al-Ḥākim's reign, particularly two of his sons. Zur'ah was *wāsiṭah* (mediator) from August 1011 to September 1012, with the title of al-Shāfī (healer). The caliph regretted not having been able to condemn him to death (he died from an illness). Ṣā'id occupied the same post from November 1018 to 13 April 1019, on which day he was executed by the caliph.

BIBLIOGRAPHY

Ibn al-Ṣayrafī. "Al-Ishārah ilā man Nāla al-Wizārah." *Bulletin de l'Institut français d'Archéologie orientale* 25 (1925):19–26, 87–94.

Ibn Ẓāfir. "Akhbar al-Duwal al-Munqaṭi'ah," ed. A. Ferré. *Bulletin de l'Institut français d'Archéologie orientale,* h.s., 12 (1972):40–41.

Nuwayrī, Aḥmad ibn 'Abd al-Wahhāb, al-. *Nihāyat al-Arab fī Funūn al-Adab.* Photostat of Leiden manuscript, Dār al-Kutūb. Cairo, no. 459, sect. 26, fol. 40a.

Silvestre de Sacy, Antoine Isaac, baron. *Chrestomathie arabe,* Vol. 1, pp. 94, 185, 187. Paris, 1806; 2nd ed., Paris, 1826–1827.

ANDRÉ FERRE

ABŪ AL-FAKHR AL-MASĪḤĪ, according to G. Graf (1947, pp. 435–36) author of the chronology for the oldest history of the *Chronicon orientale,* suggesting that he lived at the latest before the end of the thirteenth century. He was born a Jew and became a Christian (al-Masīḥī). There exists an exchange of letters between him and the Jew Abū al-'Alā' al-Ṣā'ij, the brother of Dāwūd al-Balāṭ, dating from the time at Abū al-Fakhr's conversion, in which difficult passages in the Gospels are explained and objections to Christian doctrine discussed.

There also is a chronological summary work, the *Book of Chronicles (Kitāb al-Tawārīkh)* in the British Museum (Arabic Supplement 34; 1789, following a 1594/5 copy) by an unknown author who used the *Chronicon orientale,* including the part due to Abū al-Fakhr, and the historical work of Sa'īd IBN AL-BIṬRĪQ, Agapius, Epiphanius, and others. In it there are time and dynasty tables up to the year 1257, and the popular time reckoning is brought into agreement with the Coptic (martyr) CALENDAR.

VINCENT FREDERICK

ABŪ ḤULAYQAH (Rashīd al-Dīn Abū al-Waḥsh ibn al-Fāris Abī al-Khayr ibn Abī Sulaymān Dāwūd ibn Abī al-Munā ibn Abī Fāna Abū Ḥulayqah; 1195–1277), physician. He spent his first seven or eight years in Edessa. One day his father introduced him to al-'Ādil (r. 1200–1218) and to his son al-Kāmil. The latter persuaded Rashīd al-Dīn's father to send the boy to Damascus to study medicine instead of carrying out his original intention of training him for a military career. He spent a year in Damascus, during which time he learned the *Aphorisms* and the *Prognostics* of Hippocrates. He went to Egypt in 1203 to work for al-Kāmil (1218–1238), and after his death, for his son al-Malik al-Ṣāliḥ Najm al-Dīn Ayyūb (1240–1249) and subsequently for Najm al-Dīn's son al-Mu'aẓẓam Tūrān Shāh (1249–1250).

After al-Mu'aẓẓam's death in 1250, Rashīd al-Dīn worked as a physician for al-Malik al-Ẓāhir Baybars (1260–1277). Toward the end of his life, Rashīd al-Dīn retired to a monastery, where he died in 1277.

Ibn Abī Uṣaybi'ah, his contemporary, met him several times and speaks of his great skill in all branches of the medical art, of his qualities of compassion and piety, and of several outstanding cures that he effected through his treatment. He manufactured a remedy inherited from the Greeks and held in great esteem throughout the Arab period as an antidote to poisons and the bite of venomous beasts or reptiles. This medicine was considered so effective that the sultan ordered that he should be provided with his own supply.

Rashīd al-Dīn composed poetry as well as medical works. The manuscript of his *Maqālah fī al-Ayārijāt* (Treatise on Hieras) was found in 1944 in Cairo, together with the manuscript of a work on melancholia.

BIBLIOGRAPHY

Ibn Abī Uṣaybi'ah. *'Uyūn al-Anba' fī Ṭabaqāt al-Aṭibbā',* pp. 590–98. Beirut, 1965.

Sbath, P. *Al-Fihris,* 2 vols. Cairo, 1938–1939.

Sbath, P., and C. D. Avierinos, eds. and trans. *Deux traités médicaux.* Textes arabes et études islamiques 10. Cairo, 1953.

Ullman, M. *Die Medizin im Islam.* Leiden, 1970.

PENELOPE JOHNSTONE

ABŪ ISḤĀQ IBN FAḌLALLĀH, tenth-century Coptic author and one of the first to write in Arabic. Abū Isḥāq left two works, composed in the year A.M. 641/A.D. 924–925. This is earlier than the work of SĀWĪRUS IBN AL-MUQAFFA', Coptic bishop of al-Ashmūnayn, who is generally considered the first Coptic author to write in Arabic.

The two works of Abū Isḥāq were contained in a single manuscript, which belonged to Armāniyūs

Ḥabashī Shattā al-Birmāwī around 1930. The present whereabouts of the manuscript is not known. Paul Sbath describes it (*al-Fihris,* nos. 2518 and 2519) as follows: (1) discourse on the Gospel verse: "Heaven and earth shall pass away, but my words shall never pass away" (Mk. 13:31); this treatise was composed in Cairo in 924–925; (2) treatise to announce what will happen at the end of time.

As can be seen from these descriptions, Abū Isḥāq was especially interested in questions concerning the end of the world and perhaps in the apocalyptic literature generally in vogue among the Copts at that time.

This author should be distinguished from his namesake Tāj al-Riyāsah Abū Isḥāq ibn Faḍlallāh, who translated the *Didascalia of the Apostles* from Coptic into Arabic in 1295.

BIBLIOGRAPHY

Sbath, P. *Al-Fihris (Catalogue de manuscrits arabes),* Vol. 3, Supplement, p. 9. Cairo, 1940.

KHALIL SAMIR, S. J.

ABŪ JIRJAH, the archdeacon, a noted seventh-century compiler of certain biographies of the Coptic patriarchs. He was a close friend and contemporary of SIMON I (689–701), forty-second in the line of succession to Saint Mark. He came originally from the town of Sakhā. His list comprises the lives of CYRIL I (412–444) to ALEXANDER II (705–730), that is, from the twenty-fourth to the forty-third patriarchs. His work was accomplished partly in the Monastery of Saint Macarius (see DAYR ANBĀ MAQĀR) in Wādī Habīb (Sāwīrus, 1907, Vol. 1, pt. 3, p. 91). Probably he was once nominated to succeed the fortieth patriarch, JOHN III (677–686), but his position was never upgraded beyond the rank of HEGUMENOS. Instead, Isaac of the Monastery of Saint Macarius was consecrated as the forty-first patriarch. Abū Jirjah was a contemporary of the Umayyad caliphs from ʿAbd al-Malik (685–705) to Hishām (724–743). The period he covered included the sensitive ecumenical age of CHALCEDON (451) and the upheaval caused by the ARAB CONQUEST OF EGYPT (641). As may be expected, the essential biographies in his list were those of his own contemporaries, that is, Simon I (Sāwīrus, 1907, Vol. 1, pt. 3, pp. 27–49) and Alexander II (pp. 50–83), as he was an eyewitness of the events of their reigns.

BIBLIOGRAPHY

Atiya, A. S. *History of Eastern Christianity.* Millwood, N.Y., 1980.
Eusebius of Caesarea. *Historia ecclesiastica.* 2 Vols., ed. and trans. K. Lake and J. E. L. Oulton, Books 2 and 3. Cambridge, Mass., and London, 1926–1932.
Kāmil Ṣāliḥ, Nakhlah. *Kitāb Tārīkh wa-Jadāwil Batārikat al-Iskandariyyah.* Cairo, 1943.
O'Leary, D. *The Saints of Egypt.* Amsterdam, 1974.
Roncaglia, M. *Histoire de l'église copte,* Vol. 1. Beirut, 1966 (6 vols. in progress).
Smith, W., and H. Wace. *Dictionary of Christian Biography,* 4 vols. New York, 1974.
Tillemont, L. S. N. *Mémoires pour servir à l'histoire écclesiastique,* Vol. 2. Paris, 1711.

AZIZ S. ATIYA

ABŪ AL-KHAYR AL-RASHĪD IBN AL-ṬAYYIB, thirteenth-century physician, priest, and author. The most significant, modern source of information on him is G. Graf's *Geschichte der christlichen arabischen Literatur* (1947, Vol. 2, pp. 344–48), from which the following data come.

His writings, largely in defense of Christianity, were composed in the period between 1204 and about 1245 at the latest. Among these is *Tiryāq al-ʿUqūl fī ʿIlm alʾUṣūl* (Theriac of the Understanding in the Science of the Fundamentals), a work he wrote at the instigation of the vizier Taqī al-Dīn. It was to serve as an "antidote" to Muslim polemicists. The twenty-four chapters of the principal dogmatic section discuss Christian teachings on the Trinity and Incarnation; the theology of the religions preceding Christianity, that is, the heathenism of "the philosophers," Zoroastrian dualism, and polytheism; the general resurrection, the reverence of images, baptism, and the Eucharist. A second part explains and justifies the Christian moral code. In the appended compendium of abstracts, the Jewish philosopher Maimonides (d. 1204) and the Muslim philosopher al-Rāzī (d. 1209) are cited among non-Christian writers.

Al-Muʾtaman Abū Isḥāq ibn al-ʿAssāl took an excerpt from the Tiryāq for his *Majmūʿ Uṣūl al-Dīn* (Compendium of the Principles of Religion) and introduced it with these words: "There is a treatise by the esteemed priest, the wise, respected, learned, and energetic administrator [al-ʿAlim wa-al-ʿĀmil] al-Rashīd Abū al-Khayr, the physician who assisted in the composition of this book—God keep him long among the living and preserve also that which results from his actions and teachings—from which I have taken the following."

The *Summa of the Beliefs* and a treatise are found in Vatican manuscripts adjoined to the *Tiryāq* where they are attributed to Abū al-Barakāt IBN KABAR. They are, however, from the pen of Ibn al-Ṭayyib. The *Summa [or the Most Important] of the beliefs of the Christian Faith and Refutation of the Islamic and Jewish Peoples from Their Own Principles and Fundamentals* was also written at the request of Muslim and Jewish friends. In it Ibn al-Ṭayyib explains the doctrine of the Trinity (in the preface) and demonstrates the messiahship of Christ (in three chapters). The quotations from church fathers (*Didascalia*, Irenaeus, Dionysius, Chrysostom) are taken from the anthology, *Confessions of the Fathers.* In a treatise Ibn al-Ṭayyib refutes fatalism and the erroneous doctrine of the temporality and the creation of the divine nature of Christ. He relies even more heavily on *Confessions of the Fathers* for quotations than he did in the *Summa.*

In the *Fihris* (Compendium) of Sbath are listed 131 sermons by Ibn al-Ṭayyib titled *Sermons for Sundays and Holidays,* and Abū al-Barakāt ibn Kabar cites "Sermons" among the written works of Ibn al-Ṭayyib. It is possible that the sermons mentioned by Ibn Kabar are to be identified with those listed in the *Fihris.* It is also possible that the sermons discussed in Sbath are to be found in the collection of eighty-seven sermons based on homilies on the Gospels by John Chrysostom that Abū al-Khayr arranged and assigned to specific days of the Coptic calendar (see Graf, Vol. 1, pp. 340–41).

BIBLIOGRAPHY

Al-Mu'taman Abū Isḥāq Ibrāhīm ibn al-ʿAssal. *Majmūʿ Uṣūl al-Dīn.* Cairo, 1908.

Sbath, P. *Al-Fihris* (Catalogue de manuscrits arabes). 3 vols in 2. Cairo, 1938–1940.

VINCENT FREDERICK

ABŪ AL-MAJD IBN ABI GHALIB. *See* Karimi.

ABŪ AL-MAJD IBN YU'ANNIS, a priest at Minyat Banī Khaṣīb (present-day Minyā), 150 miles (about 240 km) south of Cairo. When he lived is uncertain—he may have lived in either the twelfth or the thirteenth century—but he was dead in 1357 (cf. Vatican Library, Arabic manuscript 158, fol. 148r). He was a contemporary of Anbā Ghubriyāl (Gabriel), bishop of Qūṣ; however, information concerning this bishop is lacking, since the only bishops of Qūṣ attested in the Middle Ages are Badīr in 1086 and Mīnā in 1305 (cf. Munier, 1943, p. 29, l. 54, p. 37, l. 7). The opinion that he died in Diyār Bakr in A.D. 992 is treated below. (Although the name Yūnus is graphically possible, it is unlikely for an Upper Egyptian Copt.)

Abū al-Majd's name is linked to the *Commentary on the Creed,* which he composed at the request of Ghubriyāl, bishop of Qūṣ. The purpose was to reply to a Jew who criticized the Creed, saying: "Where did you get this text? And why have you inscribed it among the books of the church?" The commentary is composed almost exclusively of a series of texts from the Old Testament.

This text is quite different from other known commentaries on the Creed from the medieval Coptic church, and it cannot have drawn its inspiration from them. For example, the commentary by SĀWĪRUS IBN AL-MUQAFFAʿ, composed around 940, replies both to other Christian confessions (Melchites and Nestorians) and to the Muslims; it is thus philosophical and theological in character (text ed. L. Leroy, 1911, PO 6, pt. 4, pp. 523–91); cf. Abū al-Barakāt ibn Kabar, chap. 2 of his encyclopedia, PO 20, pt. 4, pp. 712–28; see also Samir, 1971, pp. 49–58). Another example is the commentary by Ibn Kabar himself, at the beginning of chapter 2 of his encyclopedia (Samir, 1971), composed circa 1310 (cf. PO 20, pt. 4, pp. 696–711; ed. Samir, 1971, pp. 40–48); here Ibn Kabar wishes to demonstrate that all the tenets come from scripture, but his quotations are drawn exclusively from the New Testament. Thus the three Coptic commentaries complement each other in a felicitous manner.

Abū al-Majd's text was evidently composed directly in Arabic. A study of the numerous biblical citations (especially from the prophets), comparing them with the existing Arabic versions, could help to date this commentary.

Only two manuscripts are known, of which only one is complete, in the Vatican Library (Arabic manuscript 158, fol. 148r–157), copied in 1357 by TŪMĀ IBN AL-NAJĪB LUṬFALLĀH AL-MAḤALLĪ. The other manuscript is also from the fourteenth century and of Egyptian provenance (National Library, Paris, Arabe 205, fols. 79v–84v). The last third of the commentary (corresponding to fol. 154r, l. 12, to fol.

157v, l., 22, of the Vatican manuscript) is now missing. The other ten manuscripts given in Graf (vol. 2, p. 450) do not refer to this text.

The following analysis of the commentary is based on the text (not yet published) in the Vatican manuscript. Not all the ninety-five citations have been identified. For each part of the text the "prophets" cited are indicated. In the manuscript neither the parts of the text nor the proper names nor the citations are distinguished from each other; the numbering here is arbitrary.

In the introduction (fols. 148r–49v), Abū al-Majd insists on the fact that the fathers of Nicaea did not compose the Creed on their own authority but that the Holy Spirit inspired them, being the 319th member present at the sessions of the council.

1. *We believe in one God:* he cites the Torah (2 quotations), Isaiah (2 quotations), Jeremiah, and the Gospel (2 quotations; these are the only quotations from the New Testament).
2. *The Father almighty, [Creator] of all things visible and invisible:* quotations from Zechariah (2), Nahum, and the books of Kings.
3. *And in one Lord Jesus Christ, the only-begotten, born of the Father before all ages:* quotations from Isaiah (2), David, Solomon (2), and Micah.
4. *Light of light, true God of true God, begotten not made:* quotations from Isaiah, Jeremiah, Isaiah, and David.
5. *For us, he came down from heaven:* quotations from David, Isaiah (3), Esdras, Jeremiah, David (2), an unnamed prophet, and Isaiah.
6. *He was incarnate of the Holy Spirit and the Virgin Mary:* quotations from Isaiah (2), Ezekiel (2), Nahum, Zephaniah, Zechariah, Daniel, and Isaiah (2).
7. *He suffered, was crucified, and was placed in the tomb:* quotations from Isaiah (4), Amos, Jonah, Zechariah (4), Joel, Jeremiah, Ezekiel, Daniel, Job, Esdras the priest, and David (3).
8. *He rose from the dead on the third day:* quotations from David (3), Isaiah (4), and Esdras the priest.
9. *He ascended into heaven and sits at the right of the Father in the heights:* quotations from David (3), Zechariah, and Daniel.
10. *He will come again in his glory to judge the living and the dead:* quotations from Isaiah (4), Solomon, David (2), Malachi, and Jeremiah.
11. *We believe in the Holy Spirit, the Lord, the giver of life, who spoke in the Prophets:* quotations from Isaiah (2), Joel, Jeremiah, and Ezekiel.
12. *And the confession of one baptism for the forgiveness of sins:* quotations from Isaiah and Ezekiel.
13. *We hope for the resurrection of the dead and the life of the world to come:* quotations from Isaiah (2), Ezekiel (very long), and Malachi.

Another commentary on the Creed is wrongly identified with Abū al-Majd. G. Graf, the only author to have mentioned Abū al-Majd (cf. Vol. 2, pp. 449–50), confused two similar but quite separate works. He identified Abū al-Majd's *Commentary* with another commentary attributed to Abū al-Majdalūs (Cheikho) or simply al-Majdalūs (Sbath, 1939; Mingana, 1934). Some consider this author to have been a Syro-Jacobite (cf. Graf, Vol. 4, p. 37, sec. 1); Mingana (1924, Vol. 1, col. 586) says the work is "for the use of the West Syrian Uniats"; while others (Mingana, Cheikho) assert that the author was a Melchite priest who died at Diyār Bakr (Diyarbekir) in 992.

However, when comparing the text of Abū al-Majdalūs' *Commentary* (given by the Milan manuscript) with the text of Abū al-Majd's *Commentary* (given by the Vatican manuscript), it is evident that the two texts are different, despite the fact that both quote many prophecies. What is more, Abū al-Majdalūs's *Commentary* is considerably longer, covering fifty large pages in the oldest complete manuscript (Oriental Library, Beirut 569a, dated 1452).

At the article "he was incarnate of the Holy Spirit and the Virgin Mary," Abū al-Majdalūs' *Commentary* cites several messianic witnesses from among pagan philosophers: the *Kitāb al-Asrār* attributed to Plato (cf. Graf, Vol. 1, p. 486, sec. 3); the *Kitāb al-'Ulūm al-'Ulwiyyah* and the *Letter to Alexander* attributed to Aristotle (cf. Graf, Vol. 1, p. 485, sec. 4); the *'Ilm al-Tanjīm* attributed to the philosopher Augustus (cf. Graf, Vol. 1, pp. 485, sec. 3, and 486, sec. 4); and a text attributed to a certain Yūniyūn or Yūthiyūn, depending upon the manuscripts, as yet unidentified.

Abū al-Majdalūs' *Commentary* is found most frequently in manuscripts of Syrian provenance; however, it could be of Coptic origin. In fact, the oldest known manuscript (not noted by Graf) (Ambrosian Library, Milan, I 10 Sup), is dated curiously 4 Tūt/1 Aylūl of the year A.M. [10]38 1 September A.D. 1321; its provenance is probably a Copt in Syria, where there were many Copts at this period.

Graf lists ten manuscripts of this text (cf. Vol. 2, p. 450, sec. 1); from these, of course, we must exclude the Vatican Arabic manuscript (158) and the Paris Arabic manuscript (205), which contain the authentic commentary of Abū al-Majd. To these should be added the Milan manuscript (cf. Löfgren and Traini, 1975–1981 pp. 8–9, no. 8); a manuscript in the Vatican (Arabic 148, fols. 28v–48v, copied in the sixteenth century and classified by Graf partly in Vol. 1, p. 485, sec. 1, and entirely in Vol. 4, p. 37, sec. 1); two Lebanese Melchite manuscripts, one at the Greek Orthodox Seminary of Balamand, (no. 32; A.H. 1109/A.D. 1697–1698), the other at Dayr al-Mukhalliṣ near Jūn (South Lebanon), which probably served as the model for Bacha's edition. Furthermore, the Mingana Syriac 481 (Western garshūnī, A.D. 1689, fols. 221v–25v) appears to contain a fragment of this commentary (cf. cols. 586 and 889 of the Mingana catalog, Vol. 1).

Abū al-Majd's *Commentary* was published in 1940 by Constantine Bacha, in Volume 7 of *Al-Risālah al-Mukhalliṣiyyah* in several issues, and reedited the same year in a small fascicule of thirty-five pages. Bacha based his edition on the manuscript of Dayr al-Shuwayr, which was the basis for the manuscript Louis Cheikho had had copied in 1897 (Beirut Oriental 569b). This manuscript of Dayr al-Shuwayr is no longer to be found there; it may be the uncoded manuscript of Dayr al-Mukhalliṣ, as several of Bacha's manuscripts passed to Dayr al-Mukhalliṣ after his death.

BIBLIOGRAPHY

Khalil Samir, S.J., ed. *Miṣbāḥ al-Ẓulmah fī Īḍaḥ al-Khidmah, li-Shams al-Riyāsah Abī al-Barakāt al-ma'rūf bi-Ibn Kabar.* Cairo, 1971.

Löfgren, O., and R. Traini. *Catalogue of the Arabic Manuscripts in the Biblioteca Ambrosiana.* Vicenza, 1975–1981.

Mingana, A. *Catalogue of the Arabic Manuscripts in the John Rylands Library.* Manchester, 1924, 1934.

Munier, H. *Recueil des listes épiscopales de l'église copte.* Cairo, 1943.

Sbath, P. "Manuscrits arabes d'auteurs coptes." *Bulletin de la Société d'Archéologie copte* 5 (1939):159–73.

KHALIL SAMIR, S.J.

ABŪ AL-MAKĀRIM. Al-Shaykh al-Mu'taman Abū al-Makārim Sa'd-Allāh Jirjis ibn Mas'ūd was a priest of the Coptic church with the title of *qummuṣ* (HEGUMENOS) who lived in the thirteenth century. He is best known as the author of the famous work entitled *Tārīkh al-Kanā'is wa-al-Adyirah* (History of Churches and Monasteries), which he is known to have written between the years A.M. 893–920/A.D. 117–1204. This work was first published by B. T. A. Evetts (1895) and ascribed wrongly to Abu Ṣāliḥ the Armenian, under whose name the anonymous manuscript appeared as owner and not author. This is the manuscript in the National Library, Paris, which was bought for three piasters by J. M. VANSLEB during his journey in Egypt in 1674. The discovery of other manuscripts with the name of the real author rectified the ascription. The same work was edited by the monk Samuel al-Suryānī (1984) of DAYR AL-SURYĀN in Wādī al-Naṭrūn on the basis of a manuscript supplied to him by Anbā Yū'annis, bishop of the Gharbiyyah province, where the authorship of that work is elucidated beyond all doubt. The new text has appeared in five parts. This new edition is merely a reproduction of the editor's handwritten text with marginal indications of the original folios.

This work is one of the most important sources on Coptic churches and monasteries as they stood in the thirteenth century. The value of the work extends to the general historical background of these religious institutions and throws a great deal of light on the geography of medieval Egypt. The author enumerates the churches in the property ownership register of Cairo divided into various quarters including ḤĀRĪT ZUWAYLAH, Ḥārit al-Rūm, DAYR AL-KHANDAQ, Shubrā, Maṭariyyah, and other districts. He then devotes whole sections to Lower Egypt, to Alexandria and neighboring regions, and to Upper Egypt, where he groups its provinces in several chapters. He devotes one chapter to the route of the Holy Family in Egypt. The author also supplements the work with a number of chapters on the churches and monasteries of Nubia, Abyssinia, Africa, India, and Yemen. A special part is devoted to the churches and monasteries of Sinai, Jerusalem and Palestine, Mesopotamia, Antioch, Ephesus, Constantinople, Rome, and Corinth. Most of the latter sections were omitted from the Paris manuscript. They appear here in a rather repetitious form which needs organization in a special study.

BIBLIOGRAPHY

Suryanis S. al-, ed. *Tārīkh al-Kanā'is wa-al-Adyirah fī al-Qarn al Thānī 'Ashar al-Milādī by Abū al-Makārim,* 5 pts. Cairo, 1984.

AZIZ S. ATIYA

ABŪ MĪNĀ, a pilgrimage center in the Libyan desert where the tomb of Saint MENAS THE MIRACLE MAKER was venerated from the fourth century on. It was about 28 miles (46 km) southwest of Alexandria, near Lake Mareotis. The settlement consisted of a civil area and an ecclesiastical area, which included Menas' tomb, a market and accommodations for pilgrims, and a great tripartite complex—the Martyr Church, the Great Basilica, and the baptistery. There were also the North Basilica and, nearby, the East Church in a group of hermits' dwellings. These structures, now in ruins, are described below.

The ancient name of the site has not come down to us. Despite its considerable area, which is partially surrounded by a fortification wall that was once quite high, it was not a municipality in the legal sense. No bishop was ever in residence there. According to legends and literary sources, which go back only to the seventh century and attribute too early a date to everything that took place, the body of Menas, the martyr who died in the persecution, under DIOCLETIAN, was buried in an insignificant site in the Libyan desert. The tomb itself was forgotten; it was first rediscovered decades later through a number of miraculous incidents. The rediscovery prompted the setting up of a small memorial structure that is said to have had the form of a tetrapylon.

The first pilgrim church, as the legends tell, was established under the emperor Jovian about 363. In the time of his successor, Valens, the transfer of the bones of Menas to the crypt was carried out. At the request of THEOPHILUS, patriarch of Alexandria, a second church was built by the emperor Arcadius in the early fifth century. It expanded upon the old church, but the work was delayed to such an extent that the building was completed only under TIMOTHY II AELURUS, patriarch of Alexandria in the late fifth century.

Under the emperor Zeno, a start was made on extending the settlement. He provided the necessary land, erected hostels for pilgrims, and established a garrison. Furthermore, he is reputed to have completed the pilgrim's way from Lake MAREOTIS. All these assumptions, however, are based on very weak grounds and are without archaeological confirmation.

The Tomb of the Martyr

Beneath the Martyr Church, which constitutes the principal sanctuary of Abū Mīnā, lies an ancient hypogeum (underground burial chamber) whose most important (though not oldest) tomb forms an arcosolium (arched niche) venerated as the burial place of Saint Menas. Leading from the hypogeum are two galleries with several lateral burial chambers, unfortunately robbed of all their original artifacts. The original entrance consisted of a shaft situated to the north of the tomb in the area of a small dome-shaped hall that was built later. An incomplete extension of the same shaft was found in a slightly displaced position immediately beneath the tomb of Menas. These shafts fell out of use when the formal veneration of Menas was established in the hypogeum. A proper staircase was cut with horizontal corridors. At the same time the entrances to the older galleries were moved. Later, new tomb chambers were established along the corridors, two of which have been preserved in the southeast corner of what is now the eastern staircase.

The cult of Menas was first practiced in the hypogeum. In the first half of the sixth century, when the ground level of the Martyr Church took its final shape above the tomb, the below-ground area of the cult was once more thoroughly reorganized, at the expense of the neighboring tombs, which were now rendered inaccessible. The level of the remaining area was lowered about 4 feet (1.2 m), and a small domed chamber (*confessio*) for the pilgrims' use and occasional liturgies was arranged in front of the tomb of Menas. To cope with the flow of pilgrims, it was further necessary to separate the entrance from the exit by building another staircase, which made it possible to circumambulate the tomb.

The Settlement

It may be considered certain that the hypogeum under the Martyr Church belonged to an older settlement. Several more tombs were located in the area of the baptistery. The precise site of this older settlement, however, has not yet been identified. Nevertheless, in the course of investigations in the Great Basilica, several sections of older houses were discovered that might have belonged to the marginal quarters of this early settlement. The settlement developed considerably as the cult of Menas grew and contributed substantially to the prosperity of the region. The most conspicuous part of the settlement is a partially walled ecclesiastical area containing a large, rectangular pilgrim's court in the center, near which are set the Martyr Church on the south side and the *xenodochia* (guests' houses) on the north side. The access to this pilgrim's court consists of a long processional way flanked on both sides with colonnades behind which lay shops, storerooms, and public buildings such as two public bathhouses and a large building with a peristyle. A covered market was situated in the western region. At the south side of the church is a semicircular court surrounded by a colonnade, which gave access to a number of rooms. Since the rooms are nearly equidistant from the crypt with the tomb of the saint, they probably served as rest chambers for sick visitors.

The civil and residential parts of the settlement are situated outside the ecclesiastical area and for the most part consist of ordinary mud-brick houses. Occasionally, however, the houses are impressively large. When the processional way was extended to the north, it passed through the northern part of this area, and a number of stone buildings were erected on both sides of the street.

At the end of the sixth century measures were taken to surround the whole settlement with a fortification wall. A long section of this wall with several towers and two gates was found in the north and northwest parts of the settlement. It seems, however, that the wall was never completed. There is no evidence of monastery buildings within the settlement, nor are there even rudimentary accommodations for monks. Traces of a small group of hermits were found in the neighborhood of the East Church.

The Martyr Church

The Martyr Church erected over the tomb of Menas is the most important building of the pilgrim center. Here the cult began in earnest, and here the last great church was built after many destructions in the ninth century. Archaeologically, it is possible to distinguish five phases of construction indicated by drastic alterations.

The first building was a very small rectangular structure of undressed stones put up about the end of the fourth century. It was no larger than a walled sarcophagus and was probably intended as a cenotaph.

At the beginning of the fifth century this structure was enclosed in a small building made of mud

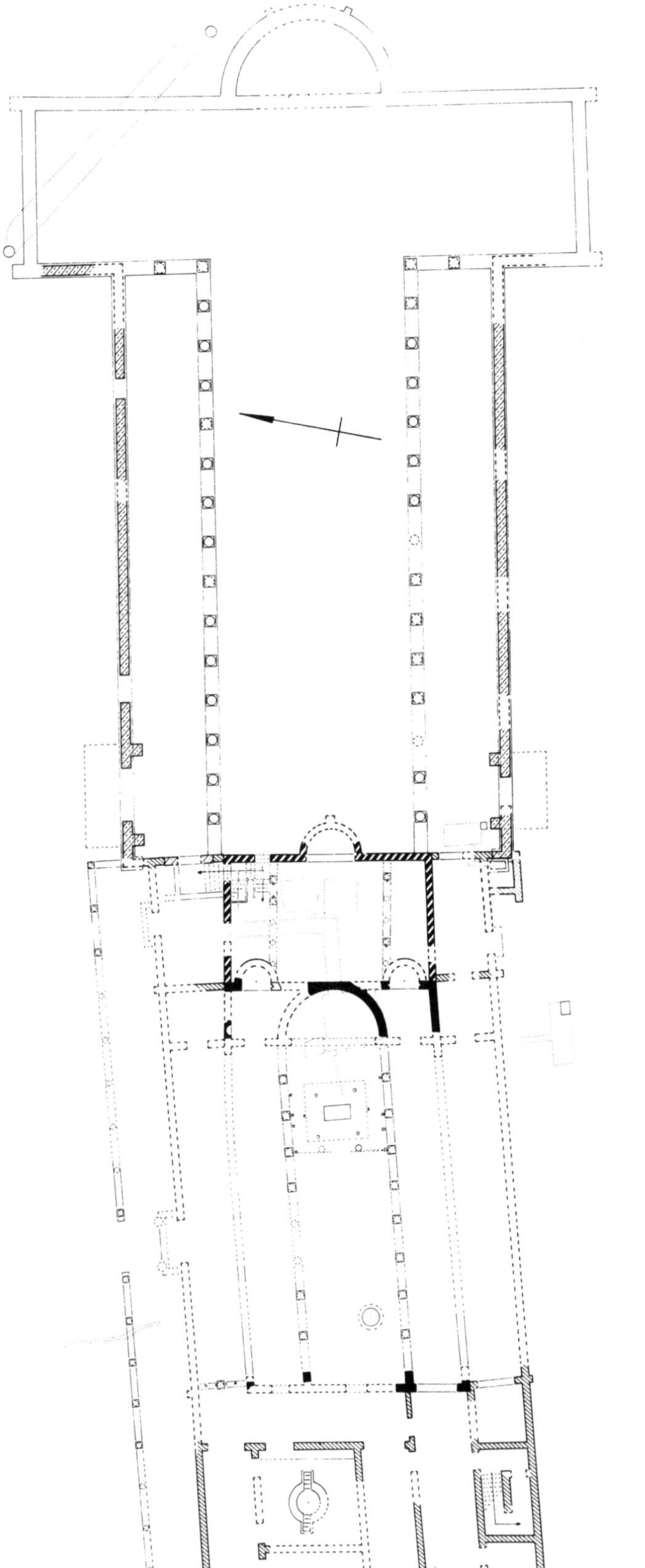

Plan of the tomb church and the Great Basilica at Abū Mīnā, fifth century. *Courtesy Peter Grossmann.*

brick that allowed freedom of access on three sides. Only the west wall lay directly in front of the cenotaph. Unfortunately, only a few sections of the west wall and the extension of the south wall of this mud-brick building have been preserved. Everything else was destroyed by later construction on the same site.

In a third phase that cannot be fixed before the second quarter of the fifth century, the two structures were replaced by a new building in the form of a basilica with a nave and two aisles. It had the customary tripartite division of the sanctuary with an apse and adjoining rooms on both sides. However, it had no return aisle along the western end. A little later it seems that a baptistery was added to this building. As further extensions on the other sides indicate, this basilica was in operation for a comparatively lengthy period. It appears that later it was changed into a basilica with a nave and four aisles. In connection with further extensions to the martyr's crypt, an annex with a nave and two aisles and an apse was attached, in whose northeast corner the older entry to the crypt was accommodated.

Near the end of the fifth century the decision was made to transform anew the whole structure of the building and to add new buildings, a process that lasted several decades. Everything was to be on a much larger scale than before. The Great Basilica was erected first. Then in the sixth century the baptistery in the Martyr Church was renovated. After the completion of the Great Basilica and the baptistery, the reconstruction of the Martyr Church started at the time of Justinian, after 528. In this fourth phase the earlier basilica with its annexes was replaced by a large tetraconch construction (having a semicircular room on each side) with a slightly elongated ground plan and a rectangular outer form. It was openly joined to the narthex (entrance area) of the Great Basilica. Its interior was richly decorated with mosaics and polychrome marble incrustation on the walls. This fine church was destroyed sometime during the seventh century, probably during the Persian invasion in 619. It would appear from archaeological finds that the church as well as all the other buildings in Abū Mīnā suffered mostly by fire. After this only very provisional repairs were made.

With the Arab conquest in 639–641 the whole pilgrimage center came into the hands of the Coptic church, and apparently the majority of the population emigrated from the site. The rebuilding of the church, however, took place only in the eighth

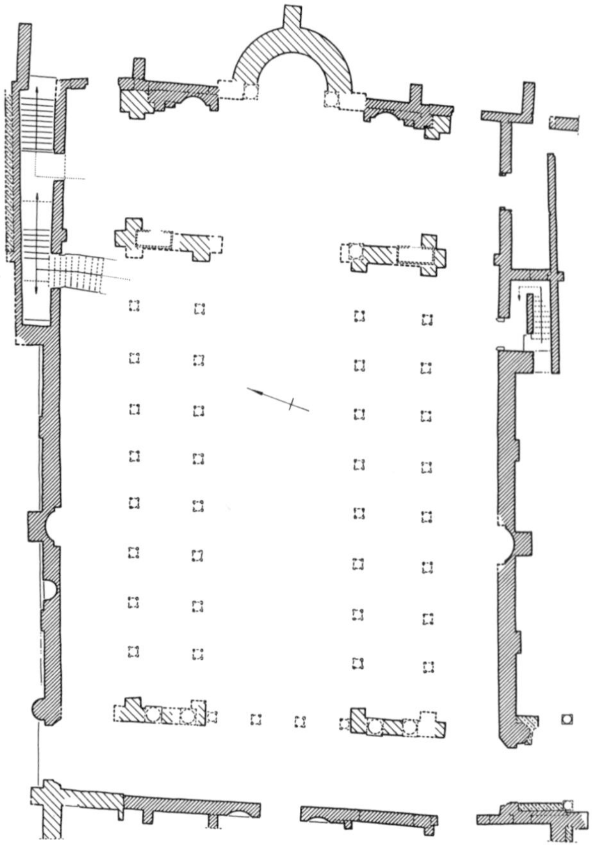

Plan of the eighth-century tomb church at Abū Mīnā. *Courtesy Peter Grossmann.*

century and is mentioned for the first time in the life of Patriarch MICHAEL I (Sāwirūs, 1910, pp. 119–32). It represents the last really large church, not only of Abū Mīnā but of the whole of Egypt. It was built as a basilica with a nave and four aisles and a compartmented narthex, all fitted between the outer walls of the old tetraconch church. The *khūrus* (room between the sanctuary and the rest of the church) customary for that period occupied the area of the narthex of the Great Basilica, while in the broad opening to the nave of the Great Basilica a relatively small apse was placed. Special features are the open compartments of the outer side sections of the *khūrus*. They have separate access from the outer aisles.

The Great Basilica

The Great Basilica was founded when the cult of Saint Menas was already flourishing. Begun about the end of the fifth century, it formed the first part of a richly designed renovation of the whole church complex of the site. It was east of the Martyr

Church, attached directly to the still functioning east annex of that church in its basilica stage, and it had the shape of a transept basilica. Two phases of building can be recognized. In the first it had a nave and three aisles and a one-aisled transept.

During the second phase, the single-aisled transept was transformed into one with three aisles. In this transformation the foundations of the outer walls were used as stylobates (foundations) for the new rows of columns. The apse jutted out farther to the east at this time. The rooms adjacent to the apse, which constitute a regular feature of Egyptian church building, were first added during the second stage of construction and covered the whole length of the transept. Likewise, in the west of the church a narthex was added later, probably in association with the construction of the tetraconch phase of the Martyr Church. On each of the two narrow sides (east and west) the narthex was provided with a conch, or semicircular exedra (extension), with columns. The western front consisted of a row of columns that merged with the columns in the east conch of the Martyr Church. Other structures—courtyards, additional devotional rooms, storehouses, and shops—were attached at the south side of the Great Basilica, although they are no longer immediately connected to it.

The Baptistery

The baptistery, the third and last part of the great tripartite church complex at Abū Mīnā, is situated west of the Martyr Church. It appears to have been rebuilt several times. In its first phase it consisted of a rather narrow annex of the Martyr Church in its small-basilica phase. In connection with the lateral extensions on all sides of the latter, a spacious, multiroomed baptistery was erected lying on the same axis that already included the lateral extensions of the basilica. Its main constituent was a square room with a piscina (font) in the center, in addition to an area that may be called a narthex. The function of the remaining rooms is uncertain. Even before the Martyr Church entered into its tetraconch phase, the baptistery was rebuilt again, and extensions were made to the south and west. The square central room was replaced by an octagon covered with a dome that enclosed semicircular niches in the diagonal corners. A second apsidal room, also containing a piscina and thus sharing a function similar to that of the octagon, was added to the west side. On the extended south side, a small courtyard took the place of the original rooms. The last building activity in the area of the baptistery falls within the period of the eighth century, when extensive protective measures were carried out on the cupola of the octagon, which threatened to collapse. Extra small rooms were erected on the north side.

Other Buildings

The North Basilica, whose construction is defined with extraordinary clarity, is situated in the north of the settlement beyond the walled ecclesiastical area. It has a ground plan with a nave and two aisles, the traditional tripartite sanctuary, and a return aisle on the west. The staircase at the southern end of the return aisle originally extended as a rectangular component part outside to the south of the body of the church. Later the church was furnished with additional outbuildings, some of which belonged to the original project, although they were constructed only later. The most important of these

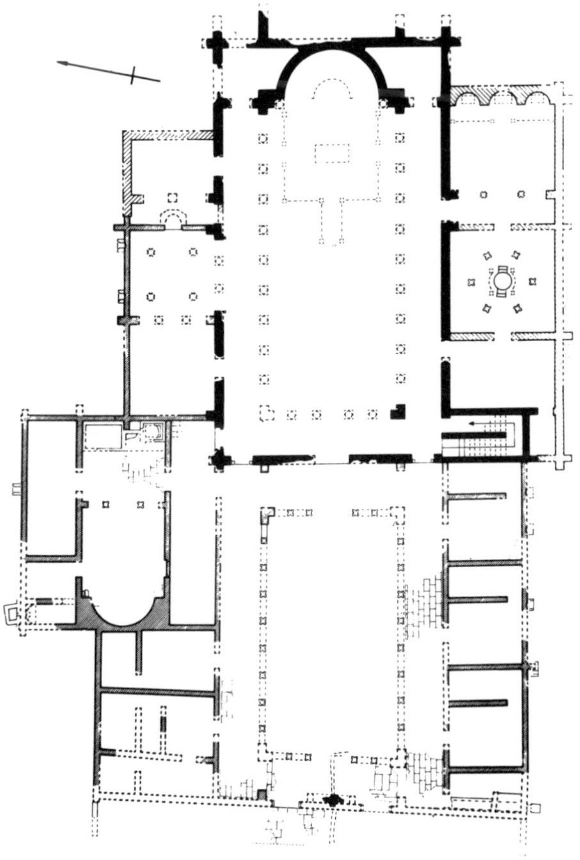

Plan of the North Basilica at Abū Mīnā. *Courtesy Peter Grossmann.*

is the atrium in the west, which is more of a residential courtyard bordered by rooms on both sides with a small triclinium (dining room) in the northeast corner. To the newer buildings not contained in the original plan of the church belong the baptistery on the south side and a devotional room with three apses in the east. On the basis of pottery finds, the North Basilica can be dated to the first half of the sixth century.

The East Church is situated about 1 mile (1.6 km) from Abū Mīnā and belongs, like the Martyr Church in its later stage, to the tetraconch type. In contrast

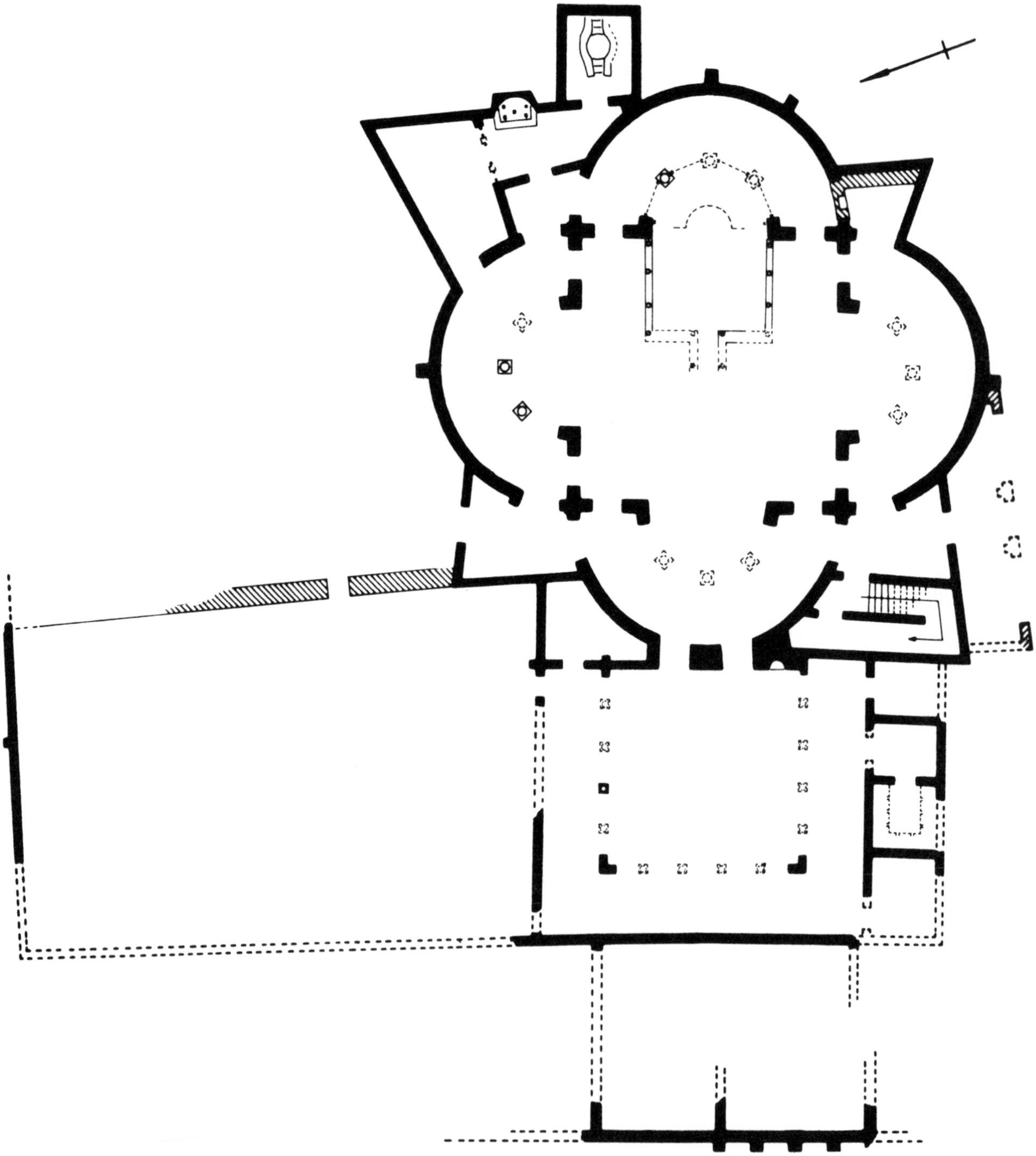

Plan of the East Church at Abū Mīnā. *Courtesy Peter Grossmann.*

to the Martyr Church, however, the fourfold form was also carried out in the external walls. Curiously enough, the rooms in the corners have an irregular angular shape with no recognizable symmetry. The church has a baptistery in the northeast corner and an atrium in the west, to which is connected a large, formerly paved courtyard to the north. This church may date from the middle of the sixth century. Prior to this date the church was a small basilica with a return aisle in the west and a narrow apse in the east but without adjacent apsidal rooms. These were added only later in the form of one single rectangular room surrounding the apse on three sides. In the neighborhood of the East Church are spread a great many little buildings that reveal the same simple two-room ground plan. Apparently they were hermitages. The East Church may thus be regarded as the center of an extensive settlement of hermits.

BIBLIOGRAPHY

Deichmann, F. W. "Zu den Bauten der Menasstadt." *Archäologischer Anzeiger* (1932):75–86.

Drescher, J. *Apa Mena. A Selection of Coptic Texts Relating to St. Menas.* Cairo, 1946.

Grossmann, P. "The Gruftkirche of Abū Mīna During the Fifth Century A.D." *Bulletin de la Société d'archéologie copte* 25 (1983):67–71.

______. *Abu Mina, a Guide to the Ancient Pilgrimage Center.* Cairo, 1986.

______. *Abū Mīna I. Die Gruftkirche und die Gruft.* Mainz, 1989.

Kaufmann, C. M. *Die Ausgrabung der Menas-Heiligtümer in der Mareotis-Wüste. I-III Vorbericht.* Cairo, 1906–1908.

______. *Die Menasstadt und das Nationalheiligtum der altchristlichen Ägypter in der westalexandrinischen Wüste,* Vol. 1. Leipzig, 1910.

______. *Die heilige Stadt der Wüste.* Kempten, 1921.

Khater, A. "La Translation des reliques de S. Ménas à son église au Caire." *Bulletin de la Société d'archéologie copte* 16 (1961–1962):161–81.

Krause, M. "Karm Abu Mena." In *Reallexikon zur byzantinischen Kunst,* Vol. 3, cols. 1116–58. Stuttgart, 1979.

Ward Perkins, J. B. "The Shrine of St. Menas in the Maryût." *Papers of the British School at Rome* 17 (1949):26–71.

PETER GROSSMANN

ABŪ MĪNĀ, SAINT. *See* Menas the Miracle Maker, Saint.

ABŪ AL-MUFAḌḌAL IBN AMĪN AL-MULK, fourteenth-century priest known from the colophons of three Arabic manuscripts of the prophets transcribed between 1582 and 1586 in the Church of the Virgin at Hārit Zuwaylah in Cairo. These manuscripts state that Abū al-Mufaḍḍal Amīn al-Mulk ibn Amīn al-Mulk Luṭfallāh was a priest in the Church of the Virgin in Damascus in 1355. He therefore came under the jurisdiction of Butrus II, bishop of Jerusalem (1341–1362).

At that time his son Jirjis lived in Cairo transcribing magnificent manuscripts with great care. Abū al-Mufaḍḍal's father occupied an important place in the Mamluk administration.

BIBLIOGRAPHY

Meinardus, O. F. A. *The Copts in Jerusalem.* Cairo, 1960.

KHALIL SAMIR, S.J.

ABŪ AL-MUNĀ, parish priest in Cairo in 1549. Information about Abū al-Munā comes from two manuscript colophons. In A.M. 1266/1549–1550, he acquired a manuscript now in the Bodleian Library, Oxford Huntington 240, one of the most precious manuscripts of this period for the number of unique or rare texts it presents, among them *Treatise on the Unity and the Trinity, the Incarnation and the Truth of Christianity* by BŪLUS AL-BŪSHĪ, *Treatise on the Priesthood* by AGATHON OF ḤOMṢ, and *Refutation of Proclus Concerning the Eternity of the World* by John Philopon. Revealing remarkable artistic talent, he added seven folios and ornamentation. He records on fol. 260r that he was a minister of the Church of the Virgin of Qaṣriyyat al-Rayḥān at Qasr al-Jamaʿ (*sic*) in Old Cairo. Beeston (pp. 199–200) misread this colophon and calls him Abū al-Munā Pallas Marcus.

The same year, A.M. 1266 (Simaykah read 1166), he transcribed a bilingual euchologion in Coptic and Arabic which contained the three eucharistic liturgies (Basil, Gregory, and Cyril), the office of incense, and the rite of the filling of the chalice. This manuscript is now lost, but it was at the Coptic Patriarchate of Cairo, in Ḥārit Zuwaylah, in 1578–1579, where the *qummuṣ* (see HEGUMENOS) Faḍlallāh found it and copied it. In January/February 1675 this copy was used as the model for the manuscript of the Coptic Patriarchate, Cairo (Liturgy 331; Simaykah, no. 790).

BIBLIOGRAPHY

Beeston, A. F. L. "An Important Christian Arabic Manuscript in Oxford." *Oxford Classical and Philosophical Monographs* 19 (1953):197–205.

Samir, K. *Traité de Paul de Būsh sur l'unité et la trinité, l'incarnation, et la vérité du Christianisme.* Patrimoine Arabe Chrétien 4, pp. 15, 74–75. Beirut, 1983.

KHALIL SAMIR, S.J.

ABŪ AL-MUNĀ, deacon (1663–1679). In 1663, while in Cairo, Johann Michael VANSLEB had copied for the Royal Library in Paris the large anthology of the Coptic canonical collection compiled by the priest Marcarius, monk of the monastery of Saint John Colobos (Graf, Vol. 1, pp. 560–63). This anthology was contained in two fine manuscripts that had been copied in A.D. 1372, which are now in the Vatican (Vatican Library, Arabic manuscripts 149 and 150). He entrusted the first (149) to a priest named Ghālī, who completed it on 12 Kiyahk A.M. 1380/9 December 1663, and the second (150) to the deacon Abū al-Munā, who completed it on 10 Bābah A.M. 1380/27 Rabīʿ A.H. 1075 (which should be corrected to read 1074/18 October 1663). The two manuscripts were then bound together in a large volume of 360 folios (National Library, Paris, Arabe 252). The section copied by Abū al-Munā (fols. 233–360) begins with the second book of the *Canons of the Kings.*

Sixteen years later, a priest in Cairo named Abū al-Munā copied the life and miracles of Anbā MARQUS AL-ANṬŪNĪ, which survive in a single manuscript (Coptic Patriarchate, Cairo, History 53; Graf, no. 492; Simaykah, no. 627; Graf, Vol. 1, p. 536, sec. 2 end). This manuscript was copied on commission from Father Buṭrus, a disciple of the 103rd Patriarch, JOHN (YU'ANNIS) XVI (1676–1718), and is dated 10 Abīb 1395/14 July 1679. Abū al-Munā may be the deacon employed sixteen years earlier by Vansleb, having in the meantime become a priest. A handwriting comparison has not yet been made.

KHALIL SAMIR, S.J.

ABŪ AL-MUNĀ IBN NASĪM AL-NAQQĀSH. Abū al-Munā is mentioned in a manuscript (Coptic Museum, Cairo, Liturgy 301; Graf, no. 167; Simaykah no. 164) that he restored. His name indicates that he or his father was a *naqqāsh* (wood inlayer). The small manuscript he restored is bilingual (Coptic and Arabic) and contains the office of prostration *(sajdah)* used on the day of Pentecost. M. Simaykah attributes it to the fifteenth century, whereas Graf, who is generally more reliable, attributes it to the seventeenth century.

BIBLIOGRAPHY

Graf, G. *Catalogue de manuscrits arabes chrétiens conservés au Caire,* p. 72. Vatican City, 1934.

KHALIL SAMIR, S.J.

ABUN, the highest spiritual leader of the Ethiopian Orthodox church. The term signifies "our father" and is applied to bishops, archbishops, and patriarchs, as well as to saints who were monks. The office of the *abun* was filled usually by a Coptic monk elected by his brethren in the monasteries of Egypt and was consecrated by the patriarch of Alexandria. Around 110 such metropolitans were sent to Ethiopia between the fourth and the twentieth centuries. Ethiopians could for the first time accede to the episcopate in 1948.

Only one metropolitan filled the office at a time, and in principle he could not be replaced except in the cases of decrepitude, infirmity, insanity, or doctrinal deviations. He was also expected never to leave his metropolitanate even temporarily. These norms have, nevertheless, not always been adhered to in practice. The dignitary often resided close to the imperial court, which was relatively mobile since the thirteenth century. But he was not always obliged to follow the royal camp. Axum, ʿAddi Abun, Gondur, Azazo, and Addis Ababa were the principal episcopal seats in various periods of Ethiopian history.

The *abun* derived his resources from the estates permanently endowed upon his office, from presents of the sovereign and the notables, and from the fees paid by the clerics he ordained. His major function consisted of ordaining priests and deacons, consecrating new or restored churches as well as articles pertaining to them, performing coronation ceremonies, saying Mass on special occasions, and attending church councils. He had practically little to do with church administration *per se,* which was under the auspices of his counterpart, the EČ̣ČAGĒ; but he was so highly respected and often trusted that he could participate even in the privy council. In the protocol of seats in council sessions, the *abun* sat to the right of the sovereign while the *eččagē* sat to the left.

BIBLIOGRAPHY

Dastā Takla Wald, ʿAddis Yāmāreñña Mazgaba Qālāt. *Bakāhnātennā Bahagara Sab Qwānqwā Taṣāfa.* Addis Ababa, 1962.

Guidi, I. *Vocabolario amarico-italiano,* p. 455. Rome, 1901; repr. 1953.

Heiler, F. *Die Ostkirchen,* 2nd ed., pp. 361–64. Munich and Basel, 1971.

Heyer, F. *Die Kirche Äthiopiens. Eine Bestandsaufnahme,* pp. 1–15. Berlin and New York, 1971.

Hyatt, H. *The Church of Abyssinia.* London, 1928.

Kidāna Wald Keflē, *Maṣḥfa Sawāsew Wagess Wamazgaba Qālāt Ḥaddis. Nebābu Bage'ez Feččew Bāmāreñā.* Addis Ababa, 1948.

Māhtama Śellāsē Walda Masqal. *Zekra Nagar,* pp. 651–53, 891–94. Addis Ababa, 1942; 2d ed., 1962.

BAIRU TAFLA

ABŪ NAṢR IBN HĀRŪN IBN ʿABD AL-MASĪḤ,

a thirteenth-century Coptic copyist whose handwriting was fine, clear, careful, and regular; the texts he copied are pleasantly spaced. Two manuscripts, now united in the Vatican Library (Arabic manuscript 103), provide information about him.

The first (fol. 1–234/7–240 of the original Coptic numbering) contains the first volume (chapters 1–21a) of the *Summa Theologica* by Mu'taman al-Dawlah ibn al-ʿAssāl, entitled *Majmūʿ Uṣūl al-Dīn wa-Masmūʿ Maḥṣūl al-Yaqīn* (Graf, 1947, pp. 409–412). A larger volume contains the rest of the work (chapters 21b–70). Indeed, on folio 234v, Abū Naṣr wrote, "Yatlū-hu al-juz' al-thānī. Awwaluhu 'min Dāwūd Ibn Yassā al-Nabī'" (part two follows, beginning "from David son of Jesse, the prophet"). This corresponds, in a manuscript in the National Library, Paris (Arabe 200; sixteenth century), to folio 155r, line 11. This second volume is now lost.

The second manuscript is small, being a quinternion (set or gathering of five sheets of paper) contained in folios 235–44 (1–10 of the original Coptic numbering). It contains the little treatise of Mu'taman al-Dawlah ibn al-ʿAssāl entitled *al-Tabṣirah al-Mukhtaṣarah* (Brief Instruction). A kind of catechism for children and simple people, it is divided into sixteen chapters in two sections: Unity and Trinity in God, and the Incarnation.

The *Brief Instruction* was composed in March or April 1260, and the *Summa Theologica* a few years later (cf. Samir, 1984). Abū Naṣr copied his manuscript while Ibn al-ʿAssāl was still alive, as can be seen from the invocation that God might prolong the author's life (cf. fol. 236r and 244v). He must have copied it around 1265–1270, probably for Ibn al-ʿAssāl himself.

BIBLIOGRAPHY

Samir, K. "Date de composition de la Somme Théologique d'al-Mu'taman b. al-ʿAssāl." *Orientalia Christiana Periodica* 50 (1984):94–106.

KHALIL SAMIR, S.J.

ABŪQĪR

(Canopus), a city located on the northern coast of the western Delta, 15 miles (24 km) northeast of Alexandria. The village's name is an abbreviated Arabic form of the name of the Coptic saint Apa Cyrus, who taught Christianity in this area in the third century and was buried there after his death.

Near Abūqīr is the ancient city known in Egyptian as Per-gwati and in Greek as Canopus, after the pilot of Menelaus, the Trojan War hero. Canopus is said to have died and been buried at this place in Egypt.

Canopus, one of the most famous centers of pagan religion in ancient Egypt, is mentioned frequently in classical authors, papyri, and inscriptions. From these sources we know a great deal about the religion, mythology, and history of the region.

The strength of the city's devotion to the Egyptian god Serapis made it difficult for Christianity to gain a foothold in the area. In 312 Athanasia and her daughters Theopiste, Theodora, and Theodoxia were imprisoned in Canopus because of their Christian faith. Cyrus and John, who journeyed to the city to strengthen the prisoners, suffered martyrdom together with them (Holweck, 1969, pp. 257–58). Holweck indicates that Canopus was more pagan than Christian in the early fourth century. RUFINUS (*Historia ecclesiastica* 2.26–27) relates that in his day (second half of the fourth century) Serapis still held sway in Canopus.

Eunapius says that Patriarch THEOPHILUS (385–412), acting under the aegis of the emperor Theodosius and with the support of the prefect Evagrius and strategus Romanus, went to Canopus and Alexandria, destroyed the Serapeum in each city, and established monks in its place (1922, pp. 418–24). Jerome relates that monks from the monasteries of PACHOMIUS settled in Canopus and followed the Pachomian rule. For the many Latin-speaking visitors and monks who were drawn to this monastery, Jerome translated the rules of Pachomius, THEODORUS OF ALEXANDRIA, and HORSIESIOS. In order to avoid the pagan associations evoked by the name Canopus, the monks changed the name of their dwelling to Monastery of the METANOIA. ARSENIUS OF SCETIS AND ṬURAH, the renowned father of monks, spent three years in this monastery (*Apophthegmata Patrum*, nos. 66, 80).

The Monastery of the Metanoia was one of the few monasteries to avoid destruction by the Persians around 618, but from the ninth century on no source mentions the monastery or any other Christian buildings in Abūqīr and no traces of their ruins have been found. In 1935 a new Coptic church of Cyrus and John in Abūqīr was dedicated (Muyser, 1979, pp. 6–7).

BIBLIOGRAPHY

Eunapius. *Lives of the Philosophers and Sophists*, ed. W. C. Wright. Loeb Classical Library. London and New York, 1922.

Holweck, F. G. *A Biographical Dictionary of the Saints*. Reprint edition. Detroit, 1969.

Muyser, J. *Les Pèlerinages coptes en Egypte*. Cairo, 1979.

Timm, S. *Das christlich-koptische Ägypten in arabischer Zeit*, pt. 1, pp. 438–46. Wiesbaden, 1984.

RANDALL STEWART

ABŪ SAʿĪD IBN SAYYID AL-DĀR IBN ABĪ AL-FAḌL AL-MASĪḤĪ, a "Coptic author who lived about 1322" and who might have been the author of the Canons of Ammonius and Eusebius (Sbath, 1938, 1939). But G. Graf did not treat him as an author and, apparently, by merely mentioning the manuscript without referring to the author's name, indicated that he had only been the copyist of the Canons.

Abū Saʿīd, in fact, did not recopy the Canons of Ammonius, which comprise only a few pages; rather, he composed a true diatessaron based on this work. He confirmed this himself in the colophon of his signed manuscript. "The gathering [*jamʿ*] of the Canons which bring together the four holy Gospels was achieved on Monday, 19th day of the month of Hatūr of the year 1039 of the pure Martyrs. This date corresponds to the 4th day of Dhū al-Qaʿdah of the year 722 of the Muslim Hijrah. The humble servant and sinner, Abū Saʿīd ibn Sayyid [or Sīd] al-Dār ibn Abū [*sic*] al-Faḍl al-Masīḥī, gathered them with his own hand for his personal use" (Sbath, 1946). This date corresponds to 15 November A.D. 1322.

Of this diatessaron we possess the signed manuscript (Sbath, no. 1038) and a copy that belonged to a Cairene Orthodox Coptic book dealer, Murqus Jirjis.

Abū Saʿīd did not translate the Gospels anew to compose his diatessaron. He used a translation, then widely accepted in the Coptic church, that is found in other manuscripts (e.g., Vatican Library, Sbath, no. 27 and Sbath, no. 1029, which differ from Sbath, no. 1035 [Sbath, 1928]). This version was the so-called Egyptian Vulgate, which was improved by al-Asʿad Abū al-Faraj ibn al-ʿAssāl about 1240. Abū Saʿīd, however, did not use the improved version.

Besides composing his diatessaron, Abū Saʿīd copied at least two manuscripts, one in 1312 and the other in 1330.

A manuscript of the Coptic Patriarchate in Cairo (Theology 152) forms a collection of spiritual and monastic writings containing extracts from John Sabas (named, in Arabic, *al-shaykh al-rūḥānī*, the spiritual old man; *Graf, 1944, pp. 434–36)* as well as the *Pinnacles of Knowledge* (*Ruʾūs al-Maʿrifah*) by Evagrius Ponticus. These constitute a supplement to *Kephalaia Gnostica* (Graf, 1944, p. 398, no. 2). This manuscript was transcribed by the priest Sulaymān ibn Saʿd ibn al-Rāhibah, minister of the Church of the Virgin of Ḥārit Zuwaylah. It was completed on 5 January 1739 (see fol. 118v) and was copied from a manuscript transcribed by Abū Saʿīd ibn Sayyid al-Dār ibn al-Faḍl al-Masīḥī and dated 1 Misrā A.M. 1028/13 July A.D. 1312. This notation in the text seems to apply only to the writings of John Sabas. This manuscript is described by Graf (1934) and by Simaykah (1942).

In October 1330, Abū Saʿīd copied the sermons for the Feast of the Lord, which were composed in 1240 by Būlus al-Būshī, a Coptic priest in Old Cairo. He copied them from a manuscript transcribed by Ibn Ṣadaqah, who himself had copied them from a manuscript written by CYRIL III Ibn Laqlaq (1235–1243), a contemporary of Būlus al-Būshī, of the Coptic Patriarchate, Cairo (Theology 339) described by Simaykah, 1942; this is not the manuscript described by Graf (Vol. 2).

BIBLIOGRAPHY

Graf, Georg. *Catalogue de manuscrits arabes chrétiens conservés au Caire,* p. 226, no. 622. Vatican City, 1934.

Sbath, P. *Bibliothèque de manuscrits Paul Sbath,* Vol. 1, p. 22; Vol. 2, pp. 141–43, 146–49, no. 1038. Cairo, 1928.

______. *Al Fihris (Catalogue de manuscrits arabes),* Vol. 1. p. 63, no. 515. Cairo, 1938.

______. "Manuscrits arabes d'auteurs coptes." *Bulletin de la Société d'Archéologie copte* (1939):159–73, especially p. 168, no. 63.

______. *Choix de livres qui se trouvaient dans les bibliothèques d'Alep,* p. 237, no. 1038. Cairo, 1946.

KHALIL SAMIR, S.J.

ABŪ ṢĀLIḤ THE ARMENIAN. Abū Ṣāliḥ is wrongly described as the author of the famous work entitled *The Churches and Monasteries of Egypt and Some Neighbouring Countries Attributed to Abū Ṣāliḥ the Armenian* (ed. B. T. A. Evetts, 1895). The real author of the work is a Copt named ABŪ AL-MAKĀRIM. The name of Abū Ṣāliḥ was inscribed on the only manuscript of the work as the proprietor of the codex, which had no author on the title page, thus misleading the reader as to its authorship.

AZIZ S. ATIYA

ABŪ SAYFAYN. *See* Mercurius of Caesarea, Saint.

ABŪ SHĀKIR IBN AL-RĀHIB. Abū al-Karam Buṭrus ibn al-Muhadhdhab was the son of al-Shaykh al-Mu'taman al-Saniy Anbā Buṭrus al-Rāhib, one of the leading Coptic personalities and eminent scribes of Egypt, who lived in the thirteenth century. After being widowed, he retired from public service, and on becoming a monk—which explains the use in his name of the epithet "al-Rāhib" (the monk), which appears in his son's name as well—he was appointed presbyter of the ancient Church of Abū Sarjah in Old Cairo (see BABYLON).

Abū Shākir the younger was a deacon in the famous Church of Our Lady known as al-Mu'allaqah in Old Cairo, and proved himself to be a writer of great distinction and one of the most eminent theologians of the Middle Ages. His precise date of birth is unknown, but he was probably born sometime before the investiture of Pope CYRIL III ibn Laqlaq, the seventy-fifth patriarch, who acceded to the throne of Saint Mark in A.D. 1235. Abū Shākir is known to have been a contemporary of Pope Cyril III, ATHANASIUS III, GABRIEL III, JOHN VII, and probably THEODOSIUS II, that is, the seventy-fifth to the seventy-ninth patriarchs, whose reigns extended from 1235 to 1300. He was made a deacon by Pope Athanasius III in 1260, although he had previously opposed the election of that same pope.

Abū Shākir distinguished himself as a theologian, a historian, and a linguist in perfect command of both Coptic and Arabic. His work on the dates of the patriarchs shows that he could have been equally proficient in mathematics and astronomy. Perhaps his most famous work was his theological study on the divinity and humanity of Jesus, entitled *Kitāb al-Shifā fī Kashf mā-Istatara min Lāhūt al-Masīḥ wā-ikhtafā* (The Book of healing of what was hidden of the divinity of Christ), of which an autographed copy dated A.M. 984/A.D. 1268 is preserved in the National Library in Paris; another copy dated A.M. 1398/A.D. 1611 is available in the Patriarchal Library in Cairo. This is mainly an exegetical work full of biblical commentaries with references drawn from the works of the fathers of the church.

Among his famous works is *Kitāb al-Burhān fī al-Qawānīn* (The Book of evidence in laws), a legal compendium in fifty-two chapters comprising a statement of Christian doctrines and traditions. A contemporary copy dated A.M. 987/A.D. 1270 exists in the Patriarchal Library. Other, later copies are available in the British Museum, the Vatican, and elsewhere.

As a historian, Abū Shākir composed a universal history under the title *Kitāb al-Tawārīkh* (The Book of histories) consisting of fifty-one chapters beginning with a section on astronomy and chronology followed by a chronicle of world events and the history of the patriarchs of Alexandria. His compilation of the dates of the Coptic popes is a significant contribution to Coptic chronology and historiography, in which he displayed his unusual skill in the use of astronomical and mathematical data. His treatise on the ecumenical councils *(al-Majāmi' al-maskūniyyah)* comprises the whole movement without excluding the later councils that were recognized by his own Coptic church.

In the field of Coptic linguistics, he stands as a towering figure in his philological works. These consisted of his *Sullam (scala),* a lexical compendium in which he assembled Coptic terms with their Arabic equivalents; it preceded his second major work, *Muqaddimah* (literally, preface), a superior grammatical treatise of the Coptic language.

Abū Shākir, like Ibn Kabar, was an encyclopedist of great stature in the golden age of Coptic literature in the Middle Ages. He probably died at an advanced age during the reign of the seventy-ninth Pope Theodosius II (1294–1300), toward the close of the thirteenth century.

BIBLIOGRAPHY

Ibn Kabar. *Miṣbāḥ al Ẓulmah fī Īḍāḥ al-Khidmah,* Vol. 1. Cairo, 1971.
Jirjis Phīluthāwus 'Awaḍ. *Ibn Kabar.* Cairo, 1930.
Nakhlah, Kāmil Ṣāliḥ. *Kitāb Tārīkh wa-Jadāwil Baṭārikat al-Iskandariyyah al-Qibṭ.* Cairo, 1943.

AZIZ S. ATIYA

ABŪṢĪR, a modern village a few miles south of Cairo and famous for the pyramids from the Old Kingdom of Sahurê (Fifth Dynasty), Neferikarê (Fifth Dynasty), and Ne-user-Rê (Fifth Dynasty). In the village itself are the remains of a temple from the New Kingdom, probably dedicated to Osiris. It is possible that the town Busiris, mentioned in Roman documents, lay in the same spot (cf. Calderini, 1988, p. 67). In the course of the German excavations in the courtyard of the pyramid of Sahurê, remains of a Christian chapel and a large multiaisled building were found. The chapel had a single aisle and a remarkably strong east wall acting as a support for the apse. Of the large building only the southwest corner with a door and a base of the southern row of columns have been preserved in situ. More building remains from the Christian period were discovered in 1978 in the mortuary temple of Hentj-Kazu; they were identified by the excavators as the living quarters of Coptic monks (Verner, 1980, pp. 158–69; 1978, pp. 155–59). These remains all belong to the late seventh or eighth centuries A.D. It has not been ascertained whether the hermits living there were connected with the monastery of DAYR APA JEREMIAH, whose main quarters were situated in the pyramid region of Saqqara.

BIBLIOGRAPHY

Borchardt, L. *Das Grabdenkmal des Königs Ne-User-Rê,* pp. 146f. Leipzig, 1907.
Calderini, A. *Dizionario dei nomi geografici e topografici dell'Egitto graeco-roman,* Vol. 2. Milan, 1988.
Timm, S. *Das christlich-koptische Ägypten in arabischer Zeit,* Vol. 1, pp. 50f. Wiesbaden, 1984.
Verner, M. "Excavations at Abusir, Season 1976, Preliminary Report." *Zeitschrift für ägyptische Sprache und Altertumskunde* 105 (1978):155–59; 107 (1980):158–69.

PETER GROSSMANN

ABŪṢĪR (Taposiris Magna), city on Lake Maryūt, near Alexandria, with access to the sea. Vital to ship traffic is a lighthouse there that originated in the Imperial period. The name of the town probably derives from the sanctuary of Osiris found in the same spot, to which belongs a temple originating in the Ptolemaic period. Today all that is left standing of this temple is the peribolos wall built with finely dressed ashlar blocks. The temple itself was almost certainly pulled down shortly after its desecration.

Presumably in the first half of the fifth century, the site within the area enclosed by the peribolos wall was used for a Roman military camp, mentioned by Zacharias Rhetor (*Historia ecclesiastica* 4.1). The well-planned single-story quarters for the soldiers lay adjacent to the wall, as was the rule in the time after Valentinian I (A.D. 364–378). In the southeast and southwest corners, respectively, remains of stairs have been preserved that secured access to the boundary wall. On the east side of the courtyard close behind the pylon stand the ruins of a small single-aisled camp church. Its discovery gave some grounds for erroneously regarding the above-mentioned structures in the temple as a monastery (Ward Perkins, 1943–1944, pp. 48–49). JUSTINIAN (528–565) richly endowed the town with buildings. Especially mentioned are the residences of the magistrates and baths. Further, the city figured prominently in the conquest of the country by the Persians in 619.

In the 1980s archaeological excavations were begun by an American mission in the course of which harbor buildings on Lake Maryūt and a palacelike villa were revealed. Remains of a large early Christian church complex were found outside the wall to the west of the city. It is a large basilica with an adjoined chapel to which two large courts were attached. Both courts are surrounded with single- and double-lined rooms.

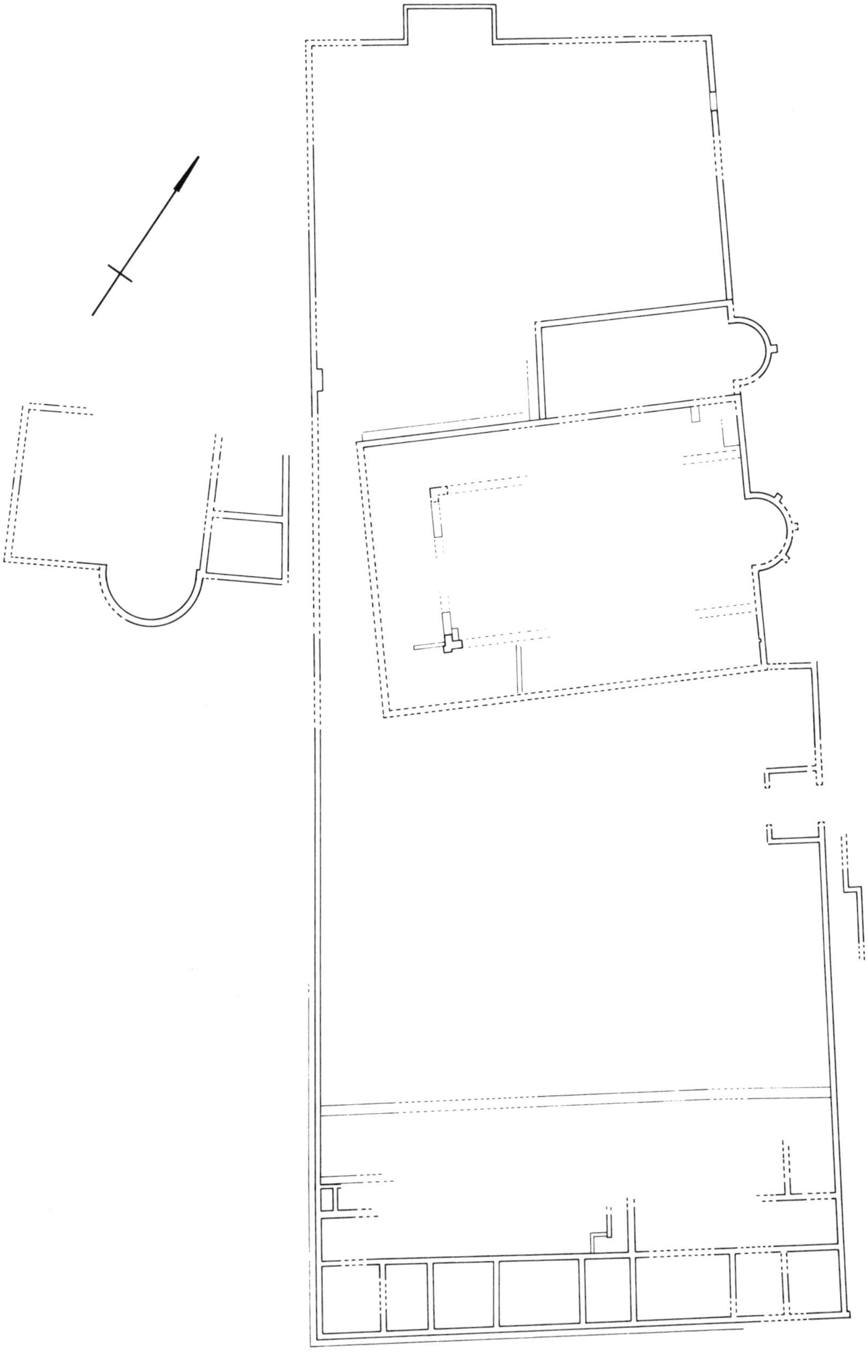

Plan of the early Christian church complex found to the west of Abūṣīr. *Courtesy Peter Grossmann.*

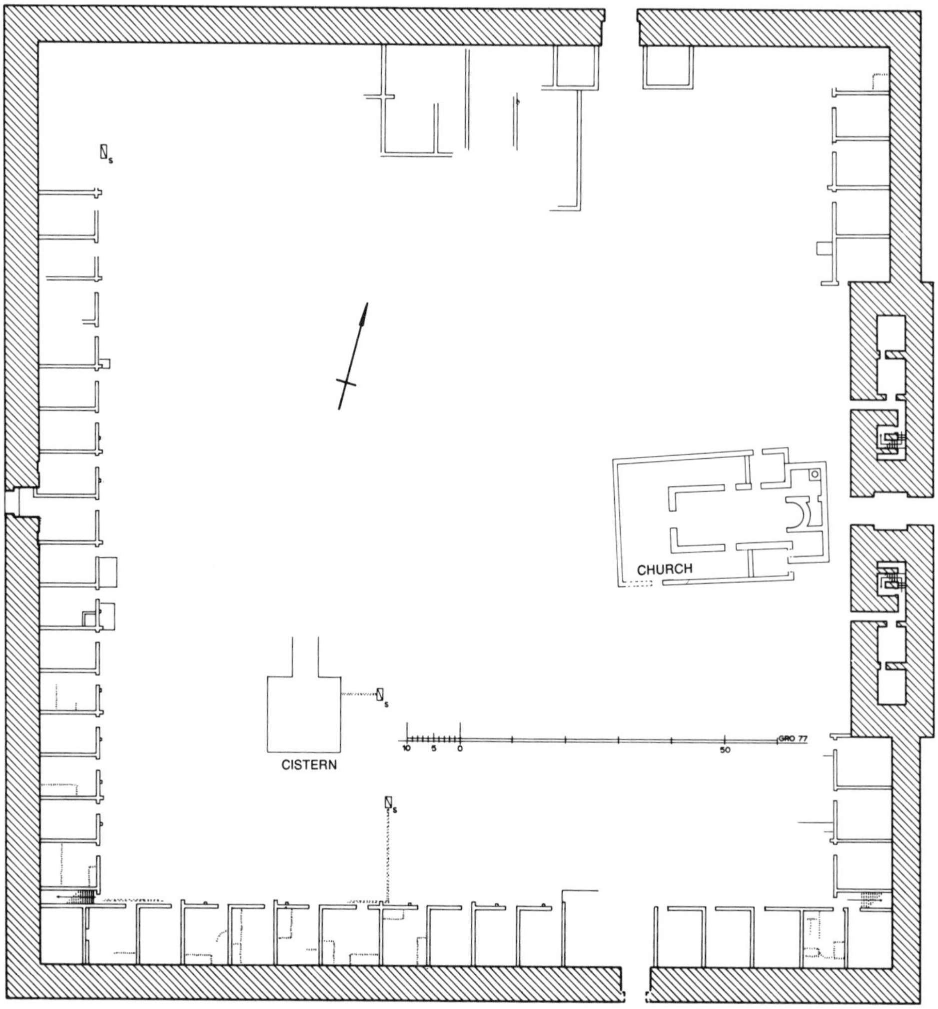

Plan of the area enclosed by the peribolos wall, Abūṣīr. *Courtesy Peter Grossmann.*

BIBLIOGRAPHY

Adriani, A. "Travaux des fouilles et de restaurations dans la région d'Abousir (Maréotis)." *Annales du Musée Gréco-Romain* 3 (1940–1950):129–39.

Amélineau, E. *La Géographie de L'Egypte à l'époque copte,* p. 122. Paris, 1893.

Dorman, P. "Diary of a Dig." *Science Digest* 79 (Sept. 1976):38–45.

Gauthier, H. *Dictionnaire des noms géographiques,* Vol. 4. Cairo, 1925–1931.

Grossmann, P. *Elephantine II.* Mainz, 1980.

______. "Die Kirche extra muros von Taposiris Magna." *Mitteilungen des deutschen archäologischen Instituts—Abteilung Kairo* 38 (1982):152–54.

John of Nikiou. *The Chronicle of John, bishop of Nikiou,* trans. from H. Zotenberg's Ethiopic text by R. H. Charles. London, 1916. German trans. in *Christentum am Roten Meer,* by F. Altheim and R. Stiehl. Berlin, 1971.

Ward Perkins, J. B. "The Monastery of Taposiris Magna." *Bulletin de la Société archéologique d'Alexandrie* 36 (1943–1944):48–53.

PETER GROSSMANN

ABŪṢĪR BANĀ, town located in the Egyptian Delta about three miles south of SAMANNŪD in the province of al-Gharbiyyah. Its Greek name was Busiris.

Although Abūṣīr Banā had a reputation as late as the Byzantine period for its devotion to Isis, Christianity also has a long tradition in the town. One of the bishops Melitius was able to win over to his side in 325 (see MELITIAN SCHISM) was Hermaion, bishop of Kynopolis and Abūṣīr Banā (Munier, 1943, p. 3). By the middle of the fifth century at the latest there was an orthodox bishop in Abūṣīr Banā as evidenced by the attendance of Bishop Athanasius at the Council of EPHESUS in 449 and the Council of CHALCEDON in 451 (Munier, 1943, pp. 19–20).

JOHN OF NIKIOU reports that at the time of the ARAB CONQUEST OF EGYPT Abūṣīr Banā was an important administrative center. The Byzantine regime maintained troops in the town under the leadership of a man named Zacharias. Nonetheless, the Arabs were able to capture the city with little difficulty (1883, p. 411).

The Coptic community in Abūṣīr Banā seems to have withstood the Arabic Conquest and to have remained intact. The HISTORY OF THE PATRIARCHS reports that in the time of Patriarch ALEXANDER II (705–730) Bishop John of Ṣa reunited the heretical Coptic congregation in Abūṣīr Banā with the orthodox church. By 744 a bishop was again situated in Abūṣīr Banā. We know that Bishop Jacob from the town was present at the synod that selected KHĀ'ĪL I (744–767) as the forty-sixth patriarch. Bishop Peter was in office in Abūṣīr Banā sometime shortly before 750. A student of Bishop Zacharias of ATRĪB, Peter was one of several church leaders who were imprisoned with Patriarch Khā'īl. Sometime during the patriarchate of PHILOTHEUS (979–1003), Bishop Severus from Abūṣīr Banā visited the patriarch in Alexandria. At the end of the eleventh century a man named Mark was bishop in Abūṣīr Banā. In 1078 Mark was present at DAYR ANBĀ MAQĀR in Wādī al-Naṭrūn for the selection of CYRIL II (1078–1092) as patriarch.

Given the long Coptic tradition of Abūṣīr Banā, it is not surprising that the town appears in the medieval Coptic-Arabic scales and in the lists of Egyptian bishoprics (Munier, 1943, pp. 48, 54, 63).

BIBLIOGRAPHY

Amélineau, E. *La Géographie de l'Egypte à l'époque copte,* pp. 9–10. Paris, 1893.

John of Nikiou. *Chronique de Jean, évêque de Nikiou,* ed. and trans. H. Zotenberg. Paris, 1883.

Munier, H. *Recueil des listes épiscopales de l'église copte.* Cairo, 1943.

Timm, S. *Das christlich-koptische Ägypten in arabischer Zeit,* pt. 1, pp. 459–63. Wiesbaden, 1984.

RANDALL STEWART

ABŪṢĪR AL-MALAQ, a town located between the Nile and the Fayyūm in the province of Banī Suef. It was known in Greek as Busiris and in earlier Arabic literature as Būṣīr Qūrīdis (M. Ramzī, 1960).

As evidenced by archaeological finds from the earliest period of Egyptian history, Abūṣīr al-Malaq has a very long history. It is likely that the story in the *Chronicle* of JOHN OF NIKIOU about the founding of a town called Busiris is about Abūṣīr al-Malaz. The tale states that a certain Mantunawis who was a devotee of Ayqasbera (Osiris?), the same who is known as Dionysus in Upper and Lower Egypt, established a city called Busiris (1883, pp. 224–45). Abūṣīr al-Malaq is mentioned in Greek papyri from as early as the third century B.C. to as late as the sixth century A.D.

In the Arabic period the name of Abūṣīr al-Malaq first arises in connection with the death of the last Umayyad caliph, Marwān ibn Muḥammad al-Ja'dī (744–751). Though the accounts of his demise differ, many of them relate that he died in a monastery and some say this monastery was near Abūṣīr al-Malaq. Even today a tombstone near the town is said to be that of Marwān. In one place ABŪ ṢĀLIḤ THE ARMENIAN says Marwān died in Abūṣīr near al-ASHMŪNAYN, but elsewhere he places Marwān's death in the area of Abūṣīr al-Malaq (Būsīr Qurīdis) and goes on to state that a church of the Virgin Mary and a monastery called Abirūn were located there. It was in this monastery that Marwān actually died. In no other sources do we find references to a church or a monastery near Abūṣīr al-Malaq, but it is possible that DAYR AL-ḤAMMĀN, located about 5 miles (8 km) north of al-Lāhūn, is the monastery mentioned in the sources that say Marwān died in a monastery in or near Abūṣīr al-Malaq.

There is today a Coptic church of uncertain age in Abūṣīr al-Malaq.

BIBLIOGRAPHY

Amélineau, E. *La Géographie de l'Egypte à l'époque copte,* p. 10. Paris, 1893.

John of Nikiou. *Chronique de Jean, évêque de Nikiou,* ed. and trans. H. Zotenberg. Paris, 1883.

Timm, S. *Das christlich-koptische Ägypten in arabischer Zeit,* pt. 1, pp. 465–67. Wiesbaden, 1984.

RANDALL STEWART

ABŪ TARBŪ. *See* Magic.

ABŪ TĪJ, a town on the west bank of the Nile just south of the city of Asyūṭ in the province of Asyūṭ. Abū Tīj served in antiquity as the depot for grain gathered for shipment to Rome. Accordingly it was known in Egyptian as Pa-Chna and in Greek as Apotheke, both of which mean "depot." The Copts transliterated the Greek name and used it as their own designation for the city. The Arabic Abū Tīj is based on this Greek-Coptic term.

The name of the town makes its first appearance in Christian sources in medieval Coptic-Arabic scales and the first attestation of a bishop in Abū Tīj is from the thirteenth century. The HISTORY OF THE PATRIARCHS states that there was a church of Abū Bīshah just south of Abū Tīj, in which the body of Abū Bīshah and that of the martyr Bīshyah or Bibsiyah were preserved in two chests. ABŪ ṢĀLIḤ THE ARMENIAN apparently meant the same church when he wrote that the bones of Pachomius and Shenute were preserved in two chests in a church south of Abū Tīj. A Coptic church of Macarius, the age of which is unknown, still stands in Abū Tīj.

[*See also:* Pilgrimages.]

BIBLIOGRAPHY

Amélineau, E. *La Géographie de l'Egypte à l'époque copte*, pp. 11–12. Paris, 1893.

Timm, S. *Das christlich-koptische Ägypten in arabischer Zeit*, pt. 1, pp. 57–59. Wiesbaden, 1984.

RANDALL STEWART

ABWĀB, AL- ("the gates"), a place or district in the medieval Nubian kingdom of ʿALWĀ. Several Arab authors agree in identifying it as the most northerly place within the territory ʿAlwā, although its exact location has not been established. L. P. Kirwan (1935, p. 61) places it somewhere in the vicinity of the old Kushite city of Meroë, while A. J. Arkell (1961, p. 194) favors a location much farther to the north, near the Fourth Cataract of the Nile.

Al-Abwāb is mentioned primarily in manuscripts dealing with the Mamluk military campaigns in Nubia in the thirteenth and fourteenth centuries. The Christian kings of MAKOURIA, when driven out of their kingdom by the Mamluks, apparently often fled to al-Abwāb for refuge. However, on two occasions the fugitive rulers were captured by the "kings of al-Abwāb" and were sent as prisoners to Cairo. It is possible that in these documents al-Abwāb is merely a synonym for the kingdom of ʿAlwā, so that the kings of al-Abwāb should be identified as the rulers of ʿAlwā. However, it is also possible that there was a petty principality of al-Abwāb with its own ruler.

There are no further references to al-Abwāb in any document after the fourteenth century, and no knowledge of its whereabouts survives today.

BIBLIOGRAPHY

Adams, W. Y. *Nubia, Corridor to Africa*, pp. 526–29; 536–37. Princeton, N.J., 1977.

Arkell, A. J. *A History of the Sudan, from the Earliest Times to 1821*, rev. ed., pp. 194–99. London, 1961.

Kirwan, L. P. "Notes on the Topography of the Christian Nubian Kingdoms." *Journal of Egyptian Archaeology* 21 (1935):57–62.

WILLIAM Y. ADAMS

ABYĀR, a city located in the Egyptian Delta about 9 miles (14.5 km) northwest of Ṭanṭā in the province of Gharbiyyah.

The earliest reference to Christians in the area of Abyār is the notice in the HISTORY OF THE PATRIARCHS that around 1117 a hermit named Mercurius lived near the city. The first attested bishop of Abyār was Mark, who was among the bishops who joined with Patriarch CYRIL III IBN LAQLAQ in 1240 to issue new canons (Munier, 1943, p. 31).

About one-half mile southwest of Abyār is Dayr al-Ḥabīs (Monastery of the Hermits) with its church of ABŪ MINĀ. The antiquity of this church is indicated by the fact that it is named in a medieval list of churches in Egypt (Amélineau, 1893, pp. 578, 580).

BIBLIOGRAPHY

Amélineau, E. *La Géographie de l'Egypte à l'époque copte*, p. 1. Paris, 1893.

Munier, H. *Recueil des listes épiscopales de l'église copte*. Cairo, 1943.

Timm, S. *Das christlich-koptische Ägypten in arabischer Zeit*, pt. 1, pp. 60–63. Wiesbaden, 1984.

RANDALL STEWART

ABYDOS, one of the most renowned sites in ancient Egypt. Situated on the left bank of the Nile about 7 miles (11 km) from the town of al-Balyanā, it was reputed to be the repository of the head of Osiris. For this reason, it was much frequented as a place of pilgrimage, as is shown by the inscriptions and graffiti in the temple of Seti I, called Osireion in the Egyptian period and the Memnonion in the Hellenistic period. In the Christian era the temple was very soon inhabited by Christian ascetics, of which we have both archaeological and literary testimony.

Archaeological and Literary Evidence

The pharaonic tombs are numerous, for in ancient Egypt it was desirable to have one's tomb, or at least a cenotaph, close to that of Osiris. We may distinguish first of all the tombs that were laid out behind the pharaonic temple. Evidence of their habitation by Christians has been noted by some authors (Peet, 1914, pp. 49–53; *Archaeological Report*, 1908–1909; 1911–1912, pp. 8–9).

Caves have been fitted up in the Darb al-Jir, a track leading to the Kharjah Oasis in the Libyan mountains [Daressy, 1898, pp. 282–84; Lady Petrie's contribution of "The Coptic Hermitage at Abydos" (1925); Badawy (1953) gives a synthesis of the preceding documents in his article "Les Premiers établissements," pp. 69–70].

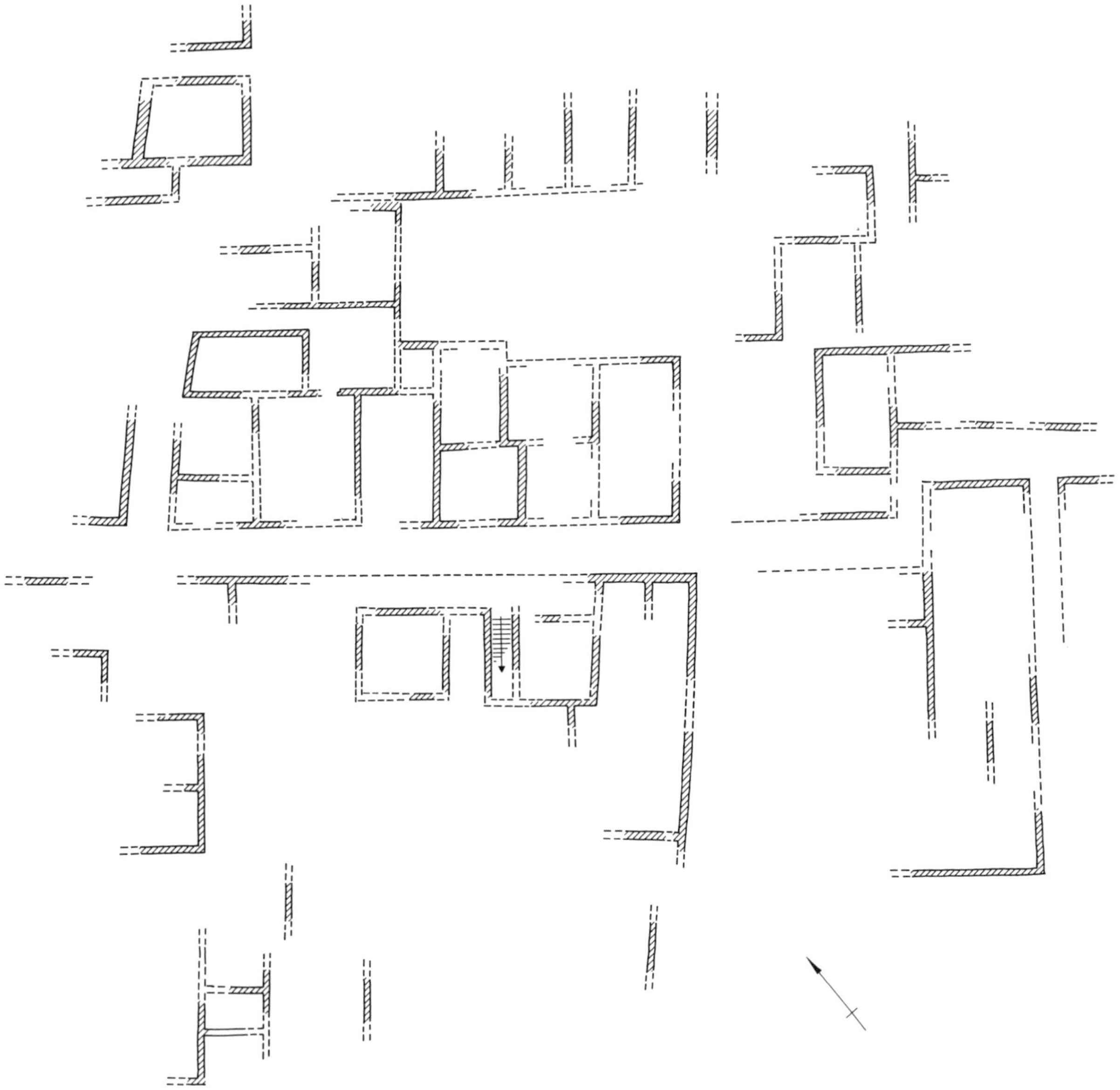

Plan of the remains of a settlement found at Abydos. *Courtesy Peter Grossmann.*

The temple of Seti I was occupied by a community of women, as is shown by the graffiti published by W. E. Crum (Murray, 1904, pp. 39–42). The whole was examined and completed by Piankoff (1958–1960, pp. 125–49). The most recent graffiti date from the tenth century.

The region of Abydos is named in the Life of the martyr monks PANINE AND PANEU (Orlandi, 1978, pp. 95–115). The Life attests that monasticism was present at Abydos at least from the fifth century. Thereafter we have no evidence until the sixth-century Life of Moses, who founded a monastery at Abydos. His Life is published only in part (Amélineau, 1886, 1888, pp. 680–706, 826–27; Till, 1936, pp. 46–81; Munier, 1916, pp. 53–54; see also Campagnano, 1970, pp. 223–46). This Life testifies that Moses founded two religious houses at Abydos, one for men to the south of the temple of Seti I, the other for women at a place unknown.

We have some testimonies about two monasteries situated at Abydos to the south of the temple of Seti I. The Jesuit C. Sicard (1982, p. 68) saw the ruins of a monastery that he calls "of Pachomius" (see DAYR ANBĀ BAKHŪM). That was perhaps the remains of the monastery founded by Saint Moses. Its ruins are called by Lefebvre "the monastery of the Greeks" (1911, pp. 239–40). In Arabic there is no great difference between Dayr Bakhūm and Dayr al-Rūm, but we do not know who of the two may have been mistaken.

To the northwest of the ancient temple of Osiris there is today a monastery sometimes called DAYR SITT DIMYANAH and sometimes that of Saint Moses (see DAYR ABŪ MŪSĀ).

BIBLIOGRAPHY

Amélineau, E. *Monuments pour servir à l'histoire de l'Egypte chrétienne aux IVe, Ve, VIe et VIIe siè-*

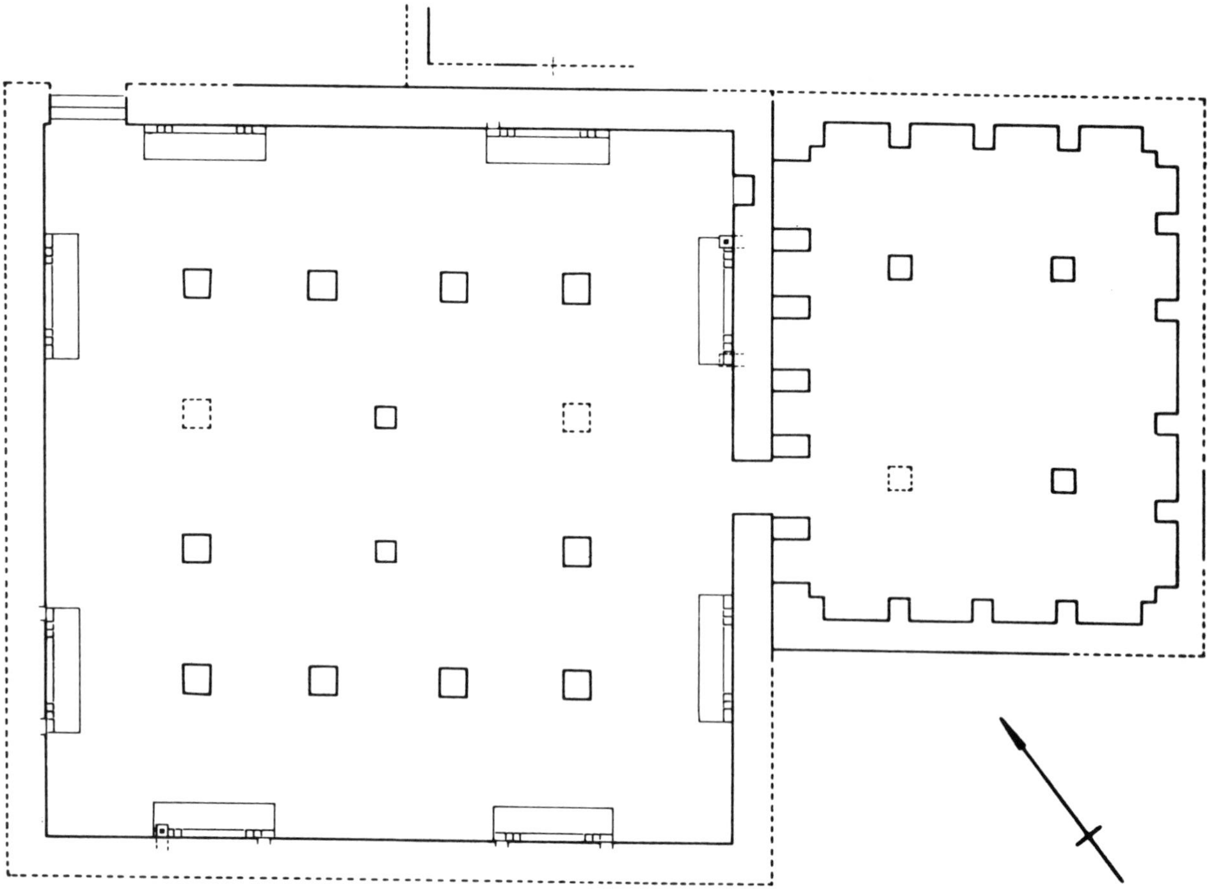

Weaving mill at Abydos. *Courtesy Peter Grossmann.*

cles. Mémoires publiés par les membres de la mission archéologique française au Caire 4. Paris, 1886, 1888.

Badawy, A. "Les Premiers établissements chrétiens dans les anciennes tombes d'Egypte." In *Tome commémoratif du millénaire de la Bibliothèque patriarcale d'Alexandrie,* Vol. 2. Alexandria, 1953.

Campagnano, A. "Monaci egiziani fra V e VI secolo." *Vetera Christianorum* 15 (1978):223–46.

Daressy, G. "Exploration archéologique de la montagne d'Abydos." *Bulletin de l'Institut d'Egypte* (1898):282–84.

Lefebvre, G. "Egypte chrétienne, IV." *Annales du Service des Antiquités de l'Egypte* 11 (1911):238–50.

Munier, H. "Les Manuscrits coptes." *Catalogue général des antiquités egyptiennes du Musée du Caire* 74. Cairo, 1916.

Murray, M. A. *The Osireion at Abydos.* London, 1904.

Orlandi, T. *Il dossier copto del martire Psote.* Testi e documenti per lo studio dell'antichita 61. Milan, 1978.

Peet, T. E. *The Cemeteries of Abydos,* pt. 2. London, 1914.

Petrie, H. E. "The Coptic Hermitage at Abydos." In *Tombs of the Courtiers and Oxyrhynchos,* ed. W. F. Petrie. London, 1925.

Petrie, W. F. *Tombs of the Courtiers and Oxyrhynchos,* ed. W. F. Petrie. London, 1925.

Piankoff, A. "The Osireion of Seti I at Abydos During the Graeco-Roman Period and the Christian Occupation." *Bulletin de la Société d'Archéologie copte* 15 (1958–1960):125–49.

Sicard, C. *Oeuvres,* Vol. 3, *Parallèles géographiques,* ed. S. Sauneron and M. Martin. Bibliothèque d'Etude 85. Cairo, 1982.

Till, W. *Koptische Heiligen- und Martyrerlegenden,* fasc. 2. Orientalia Christiana Analecta 108. Rome, 1936.

RENÉ-GEORGES COQUIN
MAURICE MARTIN, S.J.

Buildings

Abydos is one of the oldest and holiest places of pharaonic Egypt, for according to the old religion, here Osiris was buried and here he rose again from the dead. The area therefore served from earliest Egyptian times as a necropolis (Kaiser, 1979, pp. 162–63). In addition, several kings erected large cenotaphs for themselves there.

The real main temple of the place has not survived (on the few remains, see Kemp, 1968). On the other hand, the great temple of Seti I, with the cenotaph of this king (the so-called Osireion), is still standing. It is one of the best-preserved New Kingdom temples.

Until well into the Christian period, the temple was a bulwark of paganism (Piankoff, 1958–1960, pp. 128–31). It was only Moses of al-Balyanā who, at the beginning of the sixth century, brought about its end. To all appearance, however, the temple did not undergo any real Christianization. Nevertheless, there are Christian inscriptions and graffiti in several rooms. The larger service room on the west side of the so-called Butchers' Hall, in the south wing of the temple, is studded with Coptic inscriptions. This room appears to have taken on a new cultic significance in Christian times, but its purpose is not beyond dispute. At any rate, there are no indications of its conversion into a church. The content of the inscriptions implies that the room was particularly frequented by women and Christian nuns, which points to the existence of a convent in the neighborhood (Crum, in Murray, 1904, pp. 38–43). These inscriptions extend down to the tenth century A.D. In the area of the first temple court, behind the pylon, numerous late Roman architectural fragments were found. If there was a church in this temple, it can only have stood in this court.

Remains of a settlement in late antiquity have also been preserved on the top of the *kom* (mound) a few hundred yards northeast of the Seti temple, at the place where today stands the rest house of the Egyptian Antiquities Organization (EAO). We can recognize some traces of streets and a larger building that shows an extended inner court. The buildings as a whole are built of mud bricks. The thickness of the walls and the staircases that can be seen at several places indicate that the majority of the buildings were two-storied.

During the construction of the EAO rest house, the ruins of a church, probably a basilica, were found (unpublished). Isolated shafts of columns and several large capitals of limestone still lie in the surrounding fields. Some of them, for the adornment of the rest house terrace, were set up on the parapet of the wall.

A weaving mill from the early Christian period, perhaps of the seventh century A.D., with several pieces of Byzantine workmanship, was discovered to the south of the temple in the marketplace of the present-day village of ʿArābah al-Madfūnah.

There are also a few hermits' caves in the neighborhood of Abydos. These subterranean grave structures from the pharaonic period are approached by an outside staircase; with the addition of a few niches and benches, they were converted for living purposes. Some of these hermits' caves (e.g., Chapel D 68; Peet, 1914, fig. 14) have inscriptions and modest paintings.

BIBLIOGRAPHY

Abdallah Farag, R. "Excavation at Abydos in 1977: A Byzantine Loom Factory." *Mitteilungen des Deutschen Archäologischen Instituts, Abteilung Kairo* 39 (1983):51–57.

Bouriant, U. *Rapport au ministre de l'instruction publique sur une mission dans la Haute Egypte.* Mémoires publiés par les membres de la mission archéologique française au Caire 1. Paris, 1881–1884.

Calverley, A. M. *The Temple of King Sethos I at Abydos,* Vols. 1–4. London and Chicago, 1933–1958. (Ground plan is in Vol. 1, pl. 1A.)

Kaiser, W. "Umm el-Qaab." *Mitteilungen des Deutschen Archäologischen Instituts,* Abteilung Kairo, 35 (1979):162–63.

Kemp, B. J. "The Osiris Temple at Abydos." *Mitteilungen des Deutschen Archäologischen Instituts,* Abteilung Kairo 23 (1968):138–55.

Murray, M. A. *The Osireion at Abydos.* London, 1904.

Peet, T. E. "The Cemeteries of Abydos II, 1911–1912." *34th Memoir of the Egypt Exploration Fund* (1914):49–53.

Piankoff, A. "The Osireion of Seti I at Abydos During the Greco-Roman Period and the Christian Occupation." *Bulletin de la Société d'Archéologie copte* 15 (1958–1960):125–49.

PETER GROSSMANN

ACACIAN SCHISM, rupture of communion between Rome and Constantinople in the period 484–519. Behind the dispute between the two sees lay issues concerning the relations of both with Alexandria and diverging attitudes toward the Council of CHALCEDON.

The death of TIMOTHY II AELURUS ("the Cat"), the anti-Chalcedonian patriarch of Alexandria, failed to end the schism between supporters and opponents of Chalcedon in Alexandria. At Constantinople, Patriarch Acacius had acted in concert with Pope Simplicius (468–483) and maintained communion with Timothy II's rival, Timothy Salafaciolus ("Wobble-Cap"). The choice of the presbyter PETER III MONGUS as Timothy's successor had, if anything, strengthened Acacius' resolve not to support the anti-Chalcedonians in Alexandria. Peter, a deacon in Dioscorus' time, had little to commend him as an individual. Soon after Peter's consecration, Acacius wrote to Simplicius denouncing Peter as "a friend of darkness" and subverter of the canons of the church fathers, on the ground that he had "accepted consecration at dead of night while the body of his predecessor was still unburied" (*Acacii epistola ad Simplicium,* in *Collectio Veronensis,* pp. 4–5; *Epistolae romanorum pontificum,* ed. Thiel, *epistola* 8). This was a letter that Acacius would live to regret.

Between 478 and 482 events moved Constantinople increasingly away from Rome and toward Peter Mongus. First, popular opinion in Syria was becoming progressively more anti-Chalcedonian. In 479 Patriarch Stephen was murdered. Acacius maneuvered to secure a strong prelate loyal to Constantinople as his replacement. Although at first he worked in concert with Simplicius, against disturbers of the peace, he eventually consecrated Calendio as patriarch in Constantinople, assuring Simplicius that he had acted out of necessity and that the election would be confirmed by a provincial synod (i.e., he discounted the idea that Constantinople had established a precedent by consecrating a bishop of a see that many regarded as the mother see of the East). Simplicus seems to have accepted this explanation, though he protested against the precedent he saw being established. In the event, Acacius was unable to keep his undertaking to have Calendio's consecration ratified at Antioch, while the pope continued to be irked at what he regarded as Acacius' unwillingness to maintain communication with him. In this atmosphere of suspicion the doctrinal issue that had always been just under the surface since Chalcedon reemerged. The patriarch of Jerusalem, Martyrius (478–486), produced a compromise formula that seemed to offer the chance of reconciling the less rabid opponents of Chalcedon. His encyclical stated that the true faith was to be found in the decisions of NICAEA, CONSTANTINOPLE, and EPHESUS I, and that anyone who accepted different doctrines, whether pronounced at Serdica (Sofia), Ariminum (Rimini), or Chalcedon, was anathema. Chalcedon was not done away with but reduced to the status of a suspect and secondary assembly. To this, however, the papacy would never agree.

In the winter of 481/482 further moves took place that rendered Acacius' partnership with Simplicius more difficult. Timothy Salofaciolus felt himself aging and sent a delegation headed by his fellow Pachomian monk, John Talaia, to Constantinople to arrange for a successor. John, however, was suspected of intrigues against Emperor Zeno; and though Acacius agreed that Timothy should be succeeded by an Egyptian cleric, John was informed that he himself could not be appointed (though any other post was open to him) and renounced his claims on oath. When Timothy died in February 482, however, John found himself prevented from keeping his oath by his supporters. He gave further offense in Constantinople by not informing Acacius of his consecration and at the same time maintaining relations with the powerful Isaurian chieftain Illus, whom Zeno feared as a possible supplanter. When a rival delegation from Peter Mongus arrived in Constantinople, Acacius took the opportunity to state his terms for recognizing Peter as patriarch.

The result was the HENOTICON (Instrument of unity), dispatched on 28 July 482 to the "bishops, monks and laymen of Alexandria, Egypt and Cyrenaica." At this time there was no papal representative in Constantinople, and as a result Rome knew very little, or perhaps nothing, of these events. Simplicius had recognized John Talaia as the new patriarch of Alexandria, and therefore was horrified to learn of what he believed to be dire treachery on the part of Acacius. He had been urging the latter to initiate stronger action against Peter Mongus, to send him "far off," and in no way to accept him even as a deacon. The *Henoticon* itself seems to have played little part in the deteriorating relations between Rome and Constantinople. The quarrel remained disciplinary. On 15 July, a fortnight before the *Henoticon* was issued, Simplicius had sent two angry letters to Acacius, accusing him of perfidious conduct in recognizing Peter Mongus. In November the pope complained to Acacius about events in Alexandria but not about the *Henoticon*. The final straw appears to have been the rumor circulating in Rome that Acacius was asserting a claim to be "the head of the whole church."

The quarrel developed slowly. Simplicius, too ill to take action, died in March 483. His successor, Felix III (483–492), took time to assess the situation. He sent two bishops, Misenus and Vitalis, to Constantinople with letters to Zeno and Acacius demanding that the latter come to Rome and answer complaints brought by John Talaia against him. Acacius outwitted them, and the wretched legates found themselves communicating unwittingly with Acacius and representatives of Peter Mongus. On their return home they were excommunicated. In July 484, a synod of twenty-nine bishops assembled under Felix's presidency in Rome and excommunicated Acacius on the grounds not of heresy but of double-dealing and refusing to answer John Talaia's charges. At Constantinople the papacy had its supporters. The pro-Chalcedonian community of the Sleepless Monks had contributed toward stirring the papacy into action. One of its monks pinned the sentence on Acacius' pallium while the latter was celebrating the Eucharist. Acacius reluctantly replied in kind; Felix's name was removed from the diptychs, that is, he was not listed among the dignitaries for whom the patriarch would pray during the celebration of the Eucharist. When, on 1 August, Felix told Emperor Zeno that he must choose between the apostle Peter and Peter Mongus, the schism became a reality.

During the thirty-five years of schism, Constantinople stood on the defensive. Acacius died in 489, and his two successors, Fravitta (d. 490) and Euphemius (490–496), both sent letters to Rome announcing their election, only to be rebuffed by the reigning pope. In 496, Patriarch Macedonius wished to include Rome among the recipients of his synodal letter, but was forbidden to do so by Emperor Anastasius I (491–518). Except for the brief interlude of the reign of Pope Anastasius II (496–498), Rome made no effort to restore harmony. Felix III was succeeded by Gelasius I in 492. The latter, probably of African origin, left no doubt that he considered Acacius not only a hypocrite but also "an Eutychist" tainted with heresy by entering into communion with Peter Mongus. He was guilty by association with those who had been condemned at Chalcedon. He "had known the truth and yet had allied himself with enemies of the truth." During the four and a half years Gelasius occupied the papal throne, relations between the churches in the East and West worsened noticeably.

On the other hand, Acacius achieved his aim of restoring communion with the church of the majority of Christians in Alexandria. John Talaia was sent into exile and ended his days as a bishop of Nola in southern Italy. The Chalcedonian line of patriarchs was not renewed. The restoration of communion between Acacius and Peter Mongus caused rejoicing in Constantinople and the sending of a fulsome letter from Acacius to the Alexandrian patriarch. Peter, however, was not his own master. His position was threatened by anti-Chalcedonian extremist monks, the ACEPHALOI, who feared communion with the church in Constantinople would compromise their anti-Chalcedonian principles. Peter was forced to tack and turn. Before he died, he had had to denounce Chalcedon unreservedly and was close to another breach with Constantinople. His successor, Athanasius II, was of like mind, "openly and freely anathematizing the synod and Tome [of Leo]."

Communion, however, was not broken, and in the East no bishop denounced the *Henoticon*. Fravitta was succeeded by Euphemius (490–496), who, deposed as a result of an internal political crisis in 496, was followed by Macedonius (496–511). Macedonius reflected the outlook of his predecessors. The schism was regretted and Chalcedon would not be abandoned, but with that proviso, communion with the other Eastern patriarchates must be maintained. The *Henoticon*, however, was the touchstone of orthodoxy; and with the aim of securing universal assent to this symbol of the faith, an effort was made in 497 to restore the communion between Rome and Constantinople without rupturing the links between Constantinople and Alexandria. Though the mission of the Roman senator Festus to Constantinople was doomed to failure, it showed that, given goodwill, peace might have been restored on the basis of dropping Acacius from the diptychs, that is, making him a scapegoat guilty of disciplinary offenses, and the pope accepting the *Henoticon*. Surprisingly, the spirit of compromise affected Alexandria. Athanasius wrote to the pope, setting out in a confession of faith the terms on which communion between Rome and Alexandria could be restored: the *Henoticon*, Cyril's *Anathemas*, and the acceptance of Dioscorus, Timothy "the Cat," and Peter Mongus as orthodox. The last condition was, of course, impossible; but the fact that it was put forward at all suggests that the schism between Alexandria and Rome was not regarded as desirable or permanent.

Anastasius' death ended hope of a compromise. His successor, Symmachus (498–514), had to survive a schism launched by supporters of the archpresbyter Laurentius, but when he finally gained undisputed control in 506, he showed that his loyalties lay with the Italy of Theodoric the Ostrogoth. He was in no hurry to resolve the Acacian dispute except through surrender by Constantinople. Meanwhile, the relations between Alexandria and Constantinople continued on an even keel. Athanasius II's successor, John I Mula, signed the *Henoticon* without any additions, though he also denounced the *Tome* of Leo and Chalcedon.

The restoration of papal self-confidence coincided with a significant shift in imperial policy. Emperor Anastasius had always harbored anti-Chalcedonian opinions. He had the reputation of holding the Manichaean doctrine, but down to about 507 he had done nothing to upset the policies of his predecessor, Zeno. In this he was supported by his patriarch. From 507 on, however, a number of developments pushed him toward an increasingly anti-Chalcedonian stance. With the renewed hardening of the papal attitude, extreme anti-Chalcedonians began to find themselves welcome in Constantinople. First, in 507, came the visit of the metropolitan of Hierapolis in Mesopotamia, Philoxenus (Xenaias), and in the next year that of the monk SEVERUS OF ANTIOCH. The latter had been sent by his monastery near Gaza in Palestine to plead the cause of his and other anti-Chalcedonian monasteries in the Palestinian coastal plain, which were being harassed by the patriarch of Jerusalem, Elias (494–516), and his pro-Chalcedonian agents.

Severus had been strongly influenced in his vocation by Peter the Iberian. His theology was based on an unbounded reverence for the ideas of CYRIL I and those of the Cappadocian fathers. Gradually Severus gained influence over the emperor. The process was aided by a dispute between Flavian, patriarch of Antioch, and JOHN II of Nikiou, who had succeeded John Mula at Alexandria. Flavian refused to remain in communion with John when the latter followed his predecessor in denouncing Leo's *Tome* and Chalcedon.

The quarrel extended to include Philoxenus, who bore a grudge against Flavian, and in 510 they both appealed to Anastasius as arbitrator. Acting on Severus' advice, Anastasius issued *Typos tes plerophorias* (Formula of Satisfaction), which accepted the *Henoticon* but denounced the *Tome* of Leo and the Christological formula "in two natures," and passed over Chalcedon in silence. This brought about a rift between Severus and Patriarch Macedonius, and after a period of increasingly bitter conflict, Severus emerged victorious; Macedonius was deposed and exiled on the night of 6/7 August 511. His successor, Timothy (511–518), though remaining in communion with Elias of Jerusalem, took care to go as far as he could in repudiating Chalcedon in order to retain the goodwill of Severus and of John of Nikiou at Alexandria.

This incident, followed by riots in Constantinople

against the use of the Monophysite addition to the Trisagion ("who was crucified for us") in services, showed that the *Henoticon* was proving inadequate to maintain religious unity in the Byzantine empire. In 513 a new and ultimately decisive threat developed through the revolt of Vitalian. This was a military revolt, but it reflected the alienation of the European, and in particular the Latin-speaking, provinces of the empire against the emperor's religious policy. Pope Symmachus was now succeeded by Hormisdas (514–523). Pressure began to mount on the emperor.

In 512 the Illyrian bishops had written to Symmachus, stating their support for the Council of Chalcedon. Under Hormisdas the pro-Chalcedon movement gathered pace. In 515 forty bishops petitioned the pope to admit them to his communion after they had withdrawn communion from Dorotheus, bishop of Thessalonica. In the summer of that year Hormisdas was able to tell a Gallic synod that the churches in the provinces of Illyrianus, Dardanius, and Scythia had submitted to him.

Meanwhile, Vitalian had extended his hold over the European provinces of Scythia, Moesia, and Thrace, and Anastasius had been forced to restore the Trisagion without the "Monophysite" addition. In an increasingly difficult situation, the aging emperor turned to Hormisdas for mediation.

The pope's terms were severe. A delegation to Constantinople led by Ennodius, the aristocratic bishop of Ticinum (Pavia), told the emperor that the schism could be ended only by the unequivocal acceptance of Chalcedon and the denunciation of Dioscorus, Timothy "the Cat," and Peter Mongus and their abettor, Acacius. At this stage, Hormisdas seems to have been following in Pope Gelasius' footsteps and emphasizing Alexandrian doctrinal deviation and the fault of Acacius as an associate of the Alexandrians. The papal *libellus* (brief) did not mention Acacius' successors or even Severus, who in November 512 had become patriarch of Antioch. The conditions, however, were beyond anything the emperor would concede. In a letter to Hormisdas, he said that Chalcedon could be accepted as a disciplinary synod, not conflicting with Nicaea, and he would recall bishops who had recently been exiled. He also was prepared to reprimand the Egyptians for their continuous denunciation of Leo and Chalcedon, and NESTORIUS and EUTYCHES would remain under anathema. Acacius, however, he would not sacrifice, because of the result of such action on popular feeling. The living must not be made to suffer for the errors of the dead, and unity achieved under duress would be displeasing to God. Even in a moment of crisis, the unity of the Eastern patriarchates was seen to be more important than even the restoration of communion with "Old" Rome on Hormisdas' terms.

Negotiations dragged on through 516 and into 517. Vitalian's attempt to take Constantinople failed during 516 and provided the emperor with a much-needed respite. Finally, when yet another embassy from Rome was suspected of intriguing to consolidate pro-Chalcedonian opinion against the emperor, Anastasius lost patience. On 11 July 517 he wrote to Hormisdas, "From henceforth, we shall suppress in silence our requests, thinking it absurd to show the courtesy of prayers to those, who with arrogance in their mouths refuse even to be entreated." He ended with the words, which could be applied to relations between empire and papacy in later periods, "you may insult and thwart me, but you may not command me."

The emperor's time was running out. Even before he died on the night of 8/9 July 518, the situation had worsened. Pro-Chalcedonian feeling was rising in the eastern as well as the European provinces of the empire. In the vast patriarchate of Antioch, Severus' rule was becoming ever less popular. His passion for doctrinal "accuracy" in the anti-Chalcedonian sense was resented, and his active administration with its drive for efficiency and integrity was little understood. In particular, the clergy and monks of Syria Secunda, still predominantly Greek in language and sentiment, were becoming restive. It was, however, in Palestine that the storm broke. On 1 September 516 the emperor, probably at Severus' prompting, had deposed the patriarch Elias. Elias, however, had been supported by the majority of the monks led by Saint Saba in an increasingly strong pro-Chalcedonian attitude. His successor, John (516–524), was forcibly prevented from denouncing Chalcedon, and the monks raised the cry, "Four Councils even as Four Gospels." It was a cry that was heard often in the next few years.

The next year brought little joy to the anti-Chalcedon cause. In Alexandria, John of Nikiou, the patriarch, had died; his successor, DIOSCORUS II seems to have been a more open-minded individual. Completely secure in his own position, he saw little point in reiterating denunciations of Leo's *Tome* and the Council of Chalcedon. He seems to have been anxious to maintain good relations with Constantinople even at the expense of annoying Severus of Antioch. Severus's letters indicate a rift between them, and elsewhere Severus accuses

Dioscorus of dropping the anti-Chalcedonian addition to the Trisagion.

More serious was the outright revolt of a considerable number of the monks of Syria Secunda. Near the end of 517, 207 leading monks of the province, led by Alexander, presbyter and archimandrite of the great monastery of Maro, south of Damascus, sent a letter to Pope Hormisdas. In it they attacked Severus, accusing him of daily denouncing "the holy synod of Chalcedon" and "our blessed father Leo," and of using murderous violence to achieve his ends. Clearly, opinion in the Byzantine world was becoming polarized, with the advantage passing to the pro-Chalcedonians. Hormisdas' reply, sent on 10 February 518, was confident of victory. The accession of Vitalian's associate JUSTIN I to the imperial throne on 9 July ushered in a complete change of imperial policy toward Rome and the Council of Chalcedon. On the following Sunday and Monday, the solemn Eucharist was disturbed by popular outcries, which demanded the proclamation of the Council of Chalcedon; the restoration of the relics of the former patriarch, Macedonius, to the church; the deposition of Severus; and—most significant of all—reconciliation with Rome.

Justin was well qualified to heed the appeals. He had been born in Epirus, one of the remaining Latin-speaking areas of the empire, and by sentiment was pro-Chalcedonian, intent on restoring harmony and communion between the two Romes. Contemporaries described him as a "burning zealot." As early as 1 August 518, Justin sent the first of many messages to the pope, informing him of his election as emperor and begging "that by your saintly prayers you may supplicate the divine power that the beginning of our rule may be strengthened." Five weeks later, on 7 September, the first formal steps were taken to end the schism. Three letters to Pope Hormisdas were drawn up in Constantinople: one from Patriarch John, one from Justin, and one from his nephew, Count Justinian. The most significant of these was Justinian's. The patriarch declared his faith according to the four ecumenical councils and hoped that the true faith would be established by their joint efforts. He also stated his intention to add Pope Leo to the diptychs alongside Hormisdas, and asked the pope to send legates to Constantinople "in order that Christ, who through you has preserved this peace to the world, may be glorified." Justin supported the patriarch's plea for the restoration of unity, indicating that bishops had assembled in the capital to establish the union of the churches on the basis of the true and orthodox faith. Justinian, however, went further, revealing that restoration of union had been his uncle's first aim since his accession and asking the pope to come "without delay" to Constantinople, to bring about the final settlement of union.

Given the sentiment in Constantinople and the support he had in the empire, Hormisdas could set his terms high, and he did so. The imperial letters had made no mention of individuals to be anathematized and left the position of Acacius as a matter for negotiation. The papal letter, or *libellus*, carried by his legates to Constantinople in January 519 demanded, first, that the See of Constantinople should acknowledge the unblemished orthodoxy of Rome; accept anathema against Nestorius, Eutyches, Dioscorus, Timothy "the Cat," Acacius, "and his successors" (not further identified); and unequivocally accept the *Tome* of Leo.

What happened in the two months between the arrival of the legates on Byzantine soil and Patriarch John's signature of the *libellus* is not at all clear. Except at Thessalonica, the legates had a warm, at times tumultuous, welcome. Among their number, however, was the deacon Dioscorus, an exile from Alexandria and confidant of Hormisdas who harbored no friendly feelings toward Constantinople and its faith. This man, who coldly and unemotionally reported every move in the negotiations to Hormisdas, may have been instrumental for the far stiffer terms that were presented to the emperor and patriarchs when the legates arrived in the capital on 25 March. Papal instructions to the legates had allowed them a minimum of discretion regarding "the successors" of Acacius. If the emperor proved adamant, they would be permitted simply to pass over them in silence and erase them from the diptychs without formal anathema. In the event, Dioscorus convinced the emperor and a council held by Patriarch John on 27 March in the emperor's presence of Acacius' guilt. The next day, Maundy Thursday, John signed the papal *libellus* in the presence of Justin, the Senate, and the legates. Added to the name of Acacius were not only Fravitta, Euphemius, Macedonius, and Timothy (patriarch of Constantinople, 511–518) but also the emperors Zeno and Anastasius. A copy of the document of reunion, compiled in Latin and Greek, was sent to the papal archives for permanent safekeeping.

Had the agreement been maintained in its literal form, the triumph of the papacy would have been complete. Not only would the church of Constantinople and the whole of the Greek East have been humbled, but the papacy would have established a precedent for pronouncing anathemas on emperors, even dead emperors.

It is clear, however, that contemporaries did not regard the agreement of reunion as a humiliation for the see of Constantinople, let alone for the imperial majesty. A letter from Patriarch John to Hormisdas rejoiced at the unity of the churches of Old and New Rome. He then accepted the first four councils, naming them in turn. The significant point here is Constantinople's being referred to as "regarding the confirmation of the faith [i.e., of Nicaea] and the ordering of the Church," that is to say, confirming Constantinople's status as second see to that of Rome. Only Acacius was condemned by name, though his "successors" were also mentioned (the emperors were not). Moreover, as John pointed out in another letter, written to Hormisdas on 21 April, the initiative for reunion had lain with the emperor: "He most wisely prepared the union of the Churches." In addition, there had been no renunciation of canon 28 of Chalcedon. Only Acacius had been sacrificed—with the willing consent of emperor and patriarch.

The ending of the Acacian schism, however, meant that so long as Justin and Justinian ruled, the religion of the empire would be based on the four councils and the unity of the two Romes. Fundamentally there had been a power struggle between Rome and New Rome in which Rome had emerged as tactical victor. The experiment attempted by Zeno and Anastasius of uniting the four Eastern patriarchates, focused on Cyril's Christology as reflected in the *Henoticon,* failed; but on the other hand, that experiment had enabled a consolidation of anti-Chalcedonianism in Egypt and its firm establishment in the patriarchate of Antioch. Within a few years, however, the anti-Chalcedonians would be forced to establish their own Monophysite hierarchy as a result of Justin's repressive measures against anti-Chalcedonian clergy. The reunion of the two Romes in 519 inevitably led to the Monophysite schism. The majority churches of Alexandria, Antioch, and Constantinople would never again be united as one.

BIBLIOGRAPHY

Bardy, G. "Sous le régime de l'*Hénotique:* La politique religieuse d'Anastase." In *Histoire de l'église,* ed. A. Fliche and V. Martin, Vol. 4, *De la mort de Théodose à l'élection de Grégoire le Grand,* pp. 299–320. Paris, 1948. This work contains a good bibliography to 1945.

Bréhier, L. "Justin et le rétablissement de l'orthodoxie en orient." In *Histoire de l'église,* ed. A. Fliche and V. Martin, Vol. 4, *De la mort de Théodose à l'élection de Grégoire le Grand,* pp. 423–36. Paris, 1948.

Caspar, E. *Geschichte des Papsttums, von den Anfängen bis zur Höhe der Weltherrschaft,* Vol. 2. Tübingen, 1933.

Charanis, P. *Church and State in the Later Roman Empire: The Religious Policy of Anastasius the First, 491–518.* Madison, Wis., 1939.

Collectio Avellana, Epistulae imperatorum, pontificum aliorum, A.D. 367–553, 2 vols., ed. O. Guenther. Corpus Scriptorum Ecclesiasticorum Latinorum 35.1 and 35.2. Vienna 1895–1898. This is the most important primary source for the negotiations between the popes and emperors during the schism.

Collectio Veronensis. In *Publizistische Sammlungen zum acacianischen Schisma,* ed. E. Schwartz. Abhandlungen der Bayerischen Akademie der Wissenschaften, Philosophisch-historische Abteilung, new series 10.4. Munich, 1934. The documents and commentary in this work are indispensable for study of the schism.

Duchesne, L. *L'Eglise au Ve siècle,* chaps. 1 and 2. Paris, 1924.

Dvornik, F. "Pope Gelasius and the Emperor Anastasius I." *Byzantinische Zeitschrift* 44 (1951):111–16.

______. *Byzantium and the Roman Primacy,* chap. 4. New York, 1979.

Ensslin, W. *Theodoric der Grosse.* Munich, 1947.

Frend, W. H. C. *The Rise of the Monophysite Movement,* chaps. 4–6. 2nd ed. Cambridge, 1979.

______. "Eastern Attitudes to Rome During the Acacian Schism." In *Studies in Church History,* Vol. 13, *The Orthodox Churches and the West,* ed. D. Baker, pp. 69–81. Oxford, 1976. Reprinted in Frend, *Town and Country in the Early Christian Centuries,* chap. 11. London, 1980.

Gray, P. T. R. *The Defence of Chalcedon in the East.* Leiden, 1979.

Guenther, O. *Beiträge zur Chronologie der Briefe des Papstes Hormisdas.* Sitzungsberichte der Kaiserlichen Akademie der Wissenschaften, Vienna, Philosophisch-historische Klasse 126.11. Vienna, 1892.

______. *Avellana-Studien.* Sitzungsberichte der Kaiserlichen Akademie der Wissenschaften, Vienna, Philosophisch-historische Klasse 134.5. Vienna, 1896.

Haacke, R. "Die Glaubensformel des Papstes Hormisdas im acacianischen Schisma." *Analecta Gregoriana* 20 (1939):18–32.

———. "Die kaiserliche Politik in den Auseinandersetzungen um Chalkedon, 451–533." In *Das Konzil von Chalkedon,* ed. A. Grillmeier and H. Bacht, Vol. 2, pp. 95–177. Würzburg, 1953.

Hefele, C. J. *Conciliengeschichte,* 2nd ed., Vol. 2. Freiburg im Breisgau, 1875.

Hofmann, F. "Der Kampf der Päpste um Konzil und Dogma von Chalkedon von Leo bis Hormisdas." In *Das Konzil von Chalkedon,* ed. A. Grillmeier and H. Bacht, Vol. 2, pp. 13–94. Würzburg, 1953.

Jalland, T. G. *The Church and the Papacy,* pp. 314–41. London, 1944.

Jugie, M. *Le schisme byzantine: Aperçu historique et doctrinal.* Paris, 1941.

Michel, A. "Der Kampf um die politische oder petrinische Kirchenführung." In *Das Konzil von Chalkedon,* ed. A. Grillmeier and H. Bacht, Vol. 2, pp. 491–562. Würzburg, 1953.

Moeller, C. "Le *Type* de l'empereur Anastase." In *Studia Patristica,* pp. 240–47. Texte und Untersuchungen zur Geschichte der altchristlichen Literatur 78. Berlin, 1961.

Schwartz, E. *Codex Vaticanus graecus 1431: Eine antichalkidonische Sammlung aus der Zeit Kaiser Zenos.* Abhandlung der Bayerischen Akademie der Wissenschaften, Philosophisch-historische Abteilung 32.6. Munich, 1927.

Sellers, R. V. *The Council of Chalcedon.* London, 1951.

Stein, E. *Histoire du Bas-Empire,* Vol. 2, pp. 20–39, 157–74. Paris-Brussels-Amsterdam, 1949. A well-documented survey.

Ullmann, W. *The Growth of Papal Government in the Middle Ages.* London, 1955.

Vasiliev, A. A. *Justin the First.* Dumbarton Oaks Studies 1. Cambridge, Mass., 1950. A well-documented survey.

Wigram, W. A. *The Schism of the Monophysites.* London, 1923.

W. H. C. FREND

ACACIUS, BISHOP OF CAESAREA, to whom a Coptic *Encomium of the Martyr Mercurius (of Caesarea of Cappadocia)* is attributed. Some ambiguity exists concerning this attribution, for, whereas patrologists recognize only one Acacius, bishop of Caesarea in Palestine (340–366), Coptic literature makes mention of another Acacius in Dioscorus' *Encomium of Macarius of Tkow.* The first-named Acacius succeeded Eusebius as bishop, and was the predecessor to Gelasius (who continued the *Historia ecclesiastica* by Eusebius). An exponent of Arian theology, he wrote biblical commentaries, *Symmikta Zetemata* (Various questions), an essay *Against Marcellus,* and an *Encomium of Eusebius.* The second Acacius, according to pseudo-Dioscorus, was of Neocaesarea, and therefore of Cappadocia. He was deposed by the Council of EPHESUS (431) not as a heretic but rather as a "disobedient," and was then replaced by a certain Firmo, only to be reinstated later at Firmo's death.

It is not clear which of the two personalities was in the mind of the man who originated the attribution. He surely was active in the period known in Coptic homilectic literature as "The Period of the CYCLES" in the seventh and eighth centuries.

The above-mentioned *Encomium of the Martyr Mercurius,* bearing this equivocal attribution, has come down in two forms: one probably original, and a second derived from the first and elaborated therefrom. In its first form, the encomium has a title that makes vague mention of a "Saint Apa Acacius, Bishop of Caesarea." But the codices containing the encomium in its more extended form speak of a "Saint Apa Acacius, Bishop of Neo-Caesarea of Cappadocia," a reference that could indicate the latter of the two Acaciuses as its author.

The encomium in its original form has been transmitted only in the codex British Library Oriental 6802.25–43 (Sahidic, eleventh–twelfth centuries). It comprises a brief prologue followed by an exposition of the *Passio* in a somewhat lengthy form. As a matter of fact, this particular text is merely a modest reworking of the *Passio,* reduced to an encomium, so as to render it more fitting to the needs of the homiletic literature reserved for the feast of Mercurius.

The encomium in its derived and more elaborate form has been transmitted in two codices: New York Morgan Library 588.8–26 (Sahidic, ninth century), and New York Morgan Library 589 (Sahidic-Fayyumic, ninth century). It contains a prologue, a brief summary of the *Passio,* the miracle of the death of Julian the Apostate (in an expanded form when compared to the account in the *Historia ecclesiastica),* the cycle of the seven posthumous miracles (similar to the composition of the *Martyrium* of Mercurius), and lastly, a brief epilogue. This extended text was reconstructed by assembling works that had formerly appeared separately (this can be said at least for the *Passio* and the miracle relating to Julian). The fact that this longer and more detailed text is actually a compilation of many works would indicate that the so-called original form was probably the first. At any rate, this encomium is a typical work of the Period of the Cycles, and therefore can be dated to the seventh century.

BIBLIOGRAPHY

Budge, E. A. W. *Miscellaneous Coptic Texts,* pp. 231–55. London, 1915.

Orlandi, T., and S. di Giuseppe. *Passione e Miracoli di S. Mercurio.* Milan, 1976.

TITO ORLANDI

ACCOUNTS AND ACCOUNTING, HISTORY OF COPTIC.

Coptic accounts and accounting is not a familiar subject to students of Coptology. If the term "Coptic accounting" could seem excessive, its use here is quite justified, in spite of factors that may limit the period and the domain it covers.

It is true that Coptic was never the official language of Egypt. If accounting is a product of the administrative system, there was no nationwide official Coptic administration in Egypt, because Egypt was occupied during the Coptic period by the Byzantines and later by the Arabs. It could also be argued that Coptic as a written language extends from the third century until the present day, where it is fossilized as the liturgical language of the Coptic church, whereas Coptic accounting covers only some two centuries, the seventh and the eighth. But in that short period and after a long submission, Egypt knew a revival of the native identity opposite to the foreign domination. If this revival did not end in any military recovery or political independence, it resulted in a movement of rapid renewal of certain aspects of the civilization and a quick resurgence of quite a few traditions and practices of everyday life. The historian should investigate *all* these manifestations to assess their links with the past, to study their potentialities, and to evaluate their chances of survival in the rapid changes of events at that time. To work out the image of Coptic Egypt, research should not be limited to art, architecture, theology, monachism, habits, and popular beliefs, but enlarged to include all other manifestations as they contribute to that image. Accounting is a good example.

After the fifth century, to which the last demotic documents are dated, there is a period of absence of any account written in the native language of Egypt. In the seventh century and in different parts of the country, there appears a group of accounts written not in Greek, the official language of Egypt at that time, but in Coptic, the native tongue of the population. These accounts deal not only with private affairs but with relations of the central administration. The value of these documents is evident. Like accounts in general, they are connected with economic problems, which have a direct impact upon societies. They provide the historian with precious material that is needed and that is often absent from literary, epigraphic, and archaeological sources. This is needed even more for Coptic history, in spite of the inevitable limitation of this material and however unevenly spread the light it throws on Coptic Egypt might be. What is dealt with in Coptic accounts and in business documents does not only reflect the official policy of the foreign ruler and its impact on the country. It gives above all an image built up from sundry details of affairs of inhabitants of small towns, villages, and monasteries, composed of small property owners, merchants, clergymen, monks, fellahin, and fugitives, that is, the tissue of the population that was subdued by waves of foreign invaders and that ended up as a minority by the early Arab period, trying always to maintain its heritage. Moreover, this material could help to assess more objectively the policy of the evolution of the foreign rulers, and many of their edicts. In fact, since the economic framework of the population of Egypt was always based on agriculture, it helped them to resist imposed changes, and in particular the process of political unification applied by foreign rulers, whether Ptolemaic, Roman, or Byzantine, until the Arabs broke this resistance when they implanted their tribes within the native population in the country. What succeeded in Alexandria and in other cities had no chance in the country where the Ptolemization, the Romanization, and the Hellenization had no real chance to take root, since its inhabitants never wanted to part with their habits. The language of the ruler imposed as the official one was used in official acts and documents of the administration, but the population maintained its language, as it maintained its habits of millennia. As in other parts of the empire, the inevitable process of decay of the foreign domination gave way to a normal revival of what was left of the ancient structure. The heritage of the past centered on the national church and the native language. This heritage sprang up in a considerable renaissance, pushing aside the Greco-Roman culture and giving to the

Egyptian church an important role, and to the Coptic language quasi-official recognition.

In this context of political agitation, a historian would badly need this objective information, which seems more trustworthy than the florid official texts of Rome, Byzantium, or Damascus, whose aim was to fill their granaries. This is why certain studies that neglect this point or take into consideration only official sources cannot offer this true image but lead to biased conclusions like those of G. Rouillard in *L'Administration civile de l'Egypte byzantine*, largely drawn from official edicts in contrast with the more objective work of H. I. Bell and W. E. Crum based on papyrological material composed of business documents. On the other hand, this material could a priori also be more objective than some Coptic writers, who would have naturally preferred an Egyptian ruler, when they denounce the merciless attitude of foreign governors.

A good case to illustrate this is tax accounting, which seems to be much more eloquent than official texts in showing the aim of the ruler. A study of tax accounts can also settle important issues and controversies among scholars, including whether high taxation was imposed by the Arabs on clergymen and monks, and consequently the crucial question of the situation of the church, and finally the real conditions of conversion to Islam. In fact, documents from monasteries like DAYR AL-BALĀ'YZAH clearly show two points: how the number of accounts very sharply increased from the Arab period, a fact that should not be understood as accidental; and how monasteries had to pay the polltax, and that it was, together with other taxes, exorbitantly high upon monks whose resources were very limited (private money of some monks or of their superior, and what they could gain from some handicrafts). Monasteries and churches, exactly like individuals, had no alternative but to struggle hard and to borrow money, a fact that could explain the relatively high number of debt acknowledgments among these documents; the other alternative was to disappear. No wonder, then, that around the middle of the eighth century, many monasteries were abandoned. These tax accounts help to reveal a subtle Arab strategy of disarming the church, the backbone of the Coptic population, because in fact those taxes that were too high on the poor monks added next to nothing to the total taxes. It was an undeclared campaign diametrically opposite to their proclaimed political action and to their official policy. The peasantry was in no better condition; many Copts had no choice but to abandon their fields, houses, and villages, and to flee, another fact that explains the presence of lists of fugitives among tax accounts. This means that the same policy of the Romans and the Byzantines of taxing the population too highly, which was at first denounced by Arabs in order to attract Copts, was later applied by them in a more artful way.

This information drawn from the tax accounts would incite the historian to reconsider the problem of political stability and social order in Coptic Egypt by the early Arab period and to doubt the absence of revolts earlier than that of 725–726, stated by al-MAQRĪZĪ to have been the first Coptic revolt against Arabs, and to give more credit to papyrological sources when they indicate earlier revolts even before the end of the seventh century. At any rate, the harsh tone of the letters of Arab officials found in archives with accounts pushes the historian more and more to doubt the officially declared attitude—unquestioned by quite a few scholars—and urges him to retain the literal meaning of the famous command of Caliph Sulayman (715–717) to Usāmah ibn Za'id, when he was appointed governor of Egypt. This was to "milk the cow till milk is exhausted and draw the blood to the last drop." This attitude had an immense impact upon Egypt: rapid deterioration of the economic structure; degeneration of the social stability because of the growing poverty and of the resurgence of banditry due to the increasing number of "fugitives" escaping high taxes; the decline of the administrative framework and impoverishment of its agents; the increase of taxes to compensate declining totals; and finally the massive apostasy of Copts in 745–750, which neither stopped the process of decay of the social structure nor the harsh policy of the ruler, who taxed converted Copts, too.

Another direct contribution of accounts is that they help to draw a more objective image of everyday life in Coptic Egypt, the nature of commodities, their abundance or scarcity, their prices, and their consumption; wages and expenses; the volume of commerce or exchange; the mechanism of quite a few commercial activities; the kind of dealings among villagers or monks, what they could afford to borrow and the price they had to pay for it, and so forth. Such a matter-of-fact image is needed to soften the fervor and charity that sometimes emerge from quite a few Coptic documents.

Last, accounts contribute to lexical studies, as they contain many terms and names of commodities and instruments not found in other sources. The importance of this aspect is that it shows how the popular language moves faster than other layers of the language and tolerates loanwords more easily.

The absence of studies on accounts and accounting contrasts with their contribution. If some scholars include accounts in the publication of documents, others would briefly refer to them and concentrate on other subjects. Consequently, no study of Coptic accounting has ever been published. Such a study would help students to tackle unintelligible accounts. It could also throw light on two interesting points—the logical approach of Coptic accountants reflected in their accounts and the place one could assign for this practice in the long history of accounting in Egypt.

First, accounting is basically the practice of analyzing, classifying, synthesizing, and registering accountable data. It could thus be, like mathematical exercises, a possible means to evaluate the logical approach of the ancient accountant, which is a valuable element for the historian since scribes were more or less the "literate" layer of the population, and accounts were often written by members of the clergy.

Second, since Coptic accounting is the last stage of a very long accounting practice in Egypt, it has to be considered from the point of view of the long development of this practice that, already around the end of the fourth millennium, allowed the administrative organization to take an annual census of the population and its wealth, and to adjust taxes levied every year. Since that time it has continued to develop with an evident tendency to simplify its method. This could be seen in a flow of hieratic, and later on, demotic accounts until the Roman period. Even when the Ptolemies imposed Greek as the official language, demotic continued to be used in a parallel direction until the Roman period.

In the Byzantine period, Greek tightened its hold more and more, especially with the teaching of mathematics in that language in different parts of Egypt. This explains the predominance of Greek accounts as well as its predominance in administrative and legal documents. It was only the process of political decay described above that changed this situation in the late Byzantine period and gave to Coptic its quasi-official recognition in accounts as well as in other documents. The Arab invasion was not an immediate factor to upset this situation, since Arabs were not able to impose their language for a certain time. Consequently, Greek and Coptic accounts continued to be used at the same time.

This simultaneous use of accounts in both languages written sometimes by the same person underlines the necessity of analyzing Coptic accounts, not only from the point of view of links with ancient Egyptian bookkeeping but also from the point of view of reciprocity. Further studies of the Greek accounting system as reflected in papyri from Egypt and of its links with the accounting system applied in the Greek peninsula would pave the way for a study of the links between Greek and Coptic accounting in Egypt.

The meaning and the use of terms in modern bookkeeping systems do not necessarily accord with those of similar terms in ancient accounting. This does not only apply to technical or sophisticated modern expressions but also to terms expressing simple important notions as balance or even account, the meaning of which does not always coincide in the context of ancient accounting with their full modern acceptance. On the other hand, one could argue about what is to be considered an account in ancient documents and also about the exact significations of the Greek term *λόγος* (*logos*), usually translated by the word account and how its use in Coptic accounting—as well as in Greek documents—could convey the meaning of list, inventory, memorandum, notice, or even balance, remainder, and so forth. Besides, the structure of certain Coptic accounts greatly diverges from the normal form and falls within other categories of documents like those concerned with private law and letters. Since the terminology used by ancient accountants is, in fact, limited, lexicographical studies had better avoid too specific significations with modern connotations, unless it is illustrated beyond doubt.

For the most part Coptic accounts date from the seventh and eighth century. A few could, perhaps, be attributed to an earlier or a later date. Thus they generally belong to the period of native renaissance, parallel with the weakening of the Byzantine domination and later with the very slow subjugation of the administrative system in Egypt by Arabs. These accounts come from monastic communities—an important element for the historian concerning the active role of the clergy and monks—and they were also the work of local officials who could write in Coptic and in Greek, the latter being the language they used in their dealings with the central administration, while the former was used for their dealings with the native population. When the Arabs quickly got rid of the Byzantines they had to rely on local officials, who knew Greek and Coptic.

The period covered by Coptic accounting is relatively short, shorter than that covered by hieratic, demotic, or Greek accounts from Egypt. Their number is also smaller. Yet one of their interests is that they represent the last step of the long tradition of accounting that lasted for almost four thousand years, a step that was able to survive in spite of the official imposition of an accounting in another language. No wonder, then, that the influence of this last step is felt in Arabic accounting in Egypt from the moment the same Coptic scribes used the newly imposed language as the administrative one. The influence of the same Coptic accountants continued centuries after.

Important accounts, as for example tax accounts, were written on papyrus, the writing material invented by Egyptians. Big monasteries, like Dayr al-Balā'yzah, seem to have kept papyrus account books from the Arab period. These books, probably written by the prior of the monastery, were numbered (e.g., the first book of the income) to keep the records of income and income taxes. This is likely to have been one of the measures imposed by Arabs when they taxed monks and monasteries.

Only a few account books of big monasteries begin with a rather short protocol, used as a stamp giving the date and the name of the governor. These stamps, necessary for the acknowledgment of legal acts and documents, were destined to control the numbered books for the sake of taxation. Ordinary and unofficial accounts needed no such protocol. They begin directly with a title ⲡⲗⲟⲅⲟⲥ (*plogos,* account of) followed by details of what is accounted for. The term account or even the whole title could be omitted in less formal accounts.

The date is usually mentioned first, written partly in the margin to render it more obvious. Consecutive dates in long accounts and daybooks are written in the same way in the middle of the account. A full date does not bear any indication of a regnal year, but gives the month and the day of the indiction year, which was a cycle of fifteen years fixed as a fiscal arrangement. Shorter dates occur especially in the middle of accounts omitting the year. To quite a few documents, this absence makes it often difficult to ascertain a definite date and reflects the general lack of centralization of the administration, especially in the late Byzantine period. At that time Egypt was quite far from the solid administrative organization of the pharaonic period and its powerful centralization, reflected in the unified systematic form of datation even in provincial documents. Moreover, dates mentioning the *Lashane* (the headman of a village or small town) or other local administrative authorities in the Coptic period are mostly confined to the elaborate style of legal documents. One is also far from the full dates of the time of Justinian, giving his regnal year, the consul, and the indiction. The fiscal year based on months of the ancient Egyptian calendar continued to be used throughout Coptic and Greek accounts and later in Arabic ones too.

Official accounts, written by experienced scribes, are often tabulated. Each item is entered on a separate line, arranged in two or more columns with dates, names of persons, places or commodities, and the appropriate amounts. The indication of the unit used often appears at the top of the column. The whole is usually aligned in a more or less neat table without any grid, and dashes are sometimes used in broad columns to facilitate the alignment of amounts with their respective entries.

Less formal accounts, on the contrary, are written in continuous lines with no apparent unit of the text and seem to have been written by unprofessional scribes or even dictated by illiterate persons or peasants as the text of these accounts show. One also remarks here the absence of idiomatic expressions, or units of currency or measure. In accounts originating from monasteries or written by members of the clergy or local officials, crosses begin and end accounts. They could also begin paragraphs or important entries and mark the separation between different parts of the account or between independent entries written in the same line, and in these cases, crosses are overwritten. To this pious attitude are attributed monograms like ⲓ̅ⲥ̅ ⲭ̅ⲥ̅ (Jesus Christ) or ⲡϭ̅ⲥ̅ ⲓ̅ⲥ̅ (the Lord Jesus) that one often meets in accounts and other documents.

Generally, Coptic accounts do not use many stereotyped formulas repeated every now and then such as in certain other ancient accounts. The language is simple and in accord with the contemporary language. The sober style tends to abridge everything down to the limits of intelligibility: dates, proper names, titles, commodity names, units of measure and capacity, currency, bookkeeping or economic terminology. The reading of these elements, familiar to the scribe, is not always easy for the student, especially since the same word could be differently abridged from one scribe to another or from one region to another, perhaps as a result of the lack of centralization; and examples abound in accounts. This excessive abridgment is no doubt the result of a long habit of scribes condensing their work, and can be seen in hieratic, demotic, and Greek accounts. Many features in common of this habit occur in demotic and Greek documents. It is necessary to mention here that the shortening of proper names in accounts is not a difficulty, since the filiation of the persons in question is often given.

Ellipsis, contraction, and the use of symbols are other characteristics of this style of Coptic accounts. Ellipsis is used to reduce the number of words in the entry to the very strict minimum. This is usually the case in accounts with similar entries. By contraction, the scribe shortens the familiar words and especially proper names, sparing only the initials, a habit which recalls a similar characteristic of abnormal hieratic and demotic texts. Here the number of omitted letters varies greatly, and a stroke is added after the spared letters to denote the contraction. One or more of the omitted letters are usually overwritten to help to identify words. Overwritten letters form an intercalated line in these accounts. This contraction of frequently used words, which are rapidly written, results in the formation of symbols that, in Coptic as in Greek accounts, are not numerous but occur very often, especially for units of measure and currency as, for example, *νο* (usually written with the omicron reduced and placed over the nu) for *νομίσμα(τα)*, "coin(s)," that is, *nomisma* or *solidus*. Monograms could also be considered as symbols.

As in Greek accounts from Egypt, but also in ancient Egyptian ones, there is a personal style as if the accountant were writing for himself (e.g., "I have received the remainder of" or "I have the remainder of the account of"). Another characteristic is what could be called the epistolary form of many Coptic accounts as well as Greek and demotic ones. The same form characterizes many documents of private law and business texts, not only in Coptic. This is why it is sometimes difficult to distinguish between these categories of documents, especially in the case of fragmentary ones.

Coptic measures used in these accounts include the very old units like the *oipe* and its subdivisions for grain (the same units were used in the countryside of Egypt until very recently before the application of the new systematization of units). Foreign units, like the Persian *artaba* and its subdivisions, are also used in demotic, Coptic, Greek, as well as Arabic accounts.

The currency mentioned in these documents is that of the Byzantine period. Other units could be related to the ancient Egyptian system. The same habit used in Greek accounts of adding diacritical marks after the *nomisma* sign to fill the vacant place and show that no carats are to be mentioned, is also used here. As mentioned above, at a certain time Greek was the language of mathematics taught in schools. This explains the tendency to write numbers and the units of measure and currency, as well as fractions, in the tailed Greek form of letters.

The ancient Egyptian system of fractions as aliquot parts is followed; with few exceptions there is no numerator greater than one. Fractions are written in the Coptic way, by using the letters of the alphabet. The ancient Egyptian word *re* (part or fraction), which in hieratic and demotic accounts is reduced to a dot or a dash preceding the denominator, fully reappears in Coptic as ⲣⲉ- (re-).

Accounts bear different checking marks—dots and strokes added in the margin—and ink was erased with water. Some of these marks seem also to have been the work of young scribes, who used to go through the old accounts to learn accounting. They often copied old accounts either on the same documents or on separate ostraca, and one could tell from their paleographical characteristics that they are the work of beginners.

The handwriting of accounts is generally rapid. The writing is often ligatured; groups of letters or even of words familiar to the scribe are more or less attached. These paleographical features are common characteristics of business documents and are not always easily conclusive, for precise dating is different from that of the calligraphic uncial of liturgical or literary texts. This is also the case with similar documents from Egypt whether hieratic, demotic, or Greek. Analytical palaeography of Coptic accounts and business texts is in fact badly needed to date more precisely this important material for the historian.

Accounts were kept by local officials; the title "accountant" is found in documents. In villages where illiteracy was frequent, that role was played not only by the scribe of the village but also by the clergy, as for documents of Coptic law. The rich collection of documents from Djeme, a Coptic town that sprang up in the ruins of the funerary temple of Ramses III at MADĪNAT HĀBŪ in Thebes in Upper Egypt, shows that at a certain time it was more or less the property of the nearby monastery of DAYR APA PHOIBAMMON. This explains the presence in accounts of the repeated signs of the cross, monograms, and other pious expressions that reflect the impact of religion, the ever important factor in the Egyptian milieu, on clerics, ascetes, officials, and peasants. But since only a small percentage of these accounts is free from this pious character, it seems to be an indication of the repeated affirmation of the Coptic identity with regard to the Byzantines.

There is no trace in these documents of any double-entry bookkeeping, which was an unknown method before the Middle Ages. In Coptic and in Greek accounting, a transaction is entered only once, however elaborate the accounts were. On the other hand, Coptic accounts reflect the two major divisions of the double system of economy of Egypt at that time. They are drawn according to the nature of what is accounted for—money accounts and grain accounts. This practice was already followed in demotic and in Greek accounts from the Ptolemaic period.

Apart from this important distinction, accounts were kept according to the two main axes, receipts and expenses. One could also classify these documents in distinct general groups: itemized daybooks, inventories, lists, detailed different accounts for current commodities, and tax accounts, which form the bulk of Coptic accounts. These terms are used loosely, and one could identify other categories of texts of accounting. Moreover, the scribes who kept the accounts were generally the same persons responsible for drawing up the legal and administrative documents. It would be interesting to trace the interaction of these domains, as well as the interaction of demotic, Greek, and Coptic accounting systems, so as to be able to assess Coptic accounting and whether the features in common are the fruits of a normal independent evolution or the results of these interactions; especially considering that bilingual accounts—like bilingual civil law documents—are not a rarity.

The accounting practice called *ḥisāb-dobia* could be considered as one of the last steps in the history of accounting in Egypt. Although it was never done in Coptic, it became associated with Copts, because accounting used to be exclusively done by them, and even until the middle of the twentieth century it was one of their main occupations. The first element of this term is the Arabic word *ḥisāb* (account). It is here coupled with a foreign word that may be a deformed derivative of the Italian adjective *doppia,* in the technical term *partita doppia* (double-entry), used in accounting to define the method by which two entries are made of each transaction. *Ḥisāb-dobia* (var. *ḥisāb-ed-dobia* and rarely *ḥisāb-al-dobia*) is thus one of many hybrid terms that abound in spoken Arabic in Egypt. Its composition points to a fairly recent date.

The Italian origin of the loanword could be explained first by the long contact between the two countries and then by the genesis of the "double-entry" method in bookkeeping. Active relations between Egypt and the Italian cities have continued since the Roman domination of the Mediterranean. They were intensified by the polarization of commerce between Europe, Africa, and the East through Alexandria and the important Italian ports, in which the method of double-entry accounting among merchants engaged in these important transactions was first used.

BIBLIOGRAPHY

No study of Coptic accounting has yet been published. Coptic accounts are published among other documents in general publications. The most important are:

Bell, H. I., and W. E. Crum, ed. *Coptic and Greek Texts from the Excavations Undertaken by the Byzantine Research Account.* Copenhagen, 1922.

Crum, W. E. *Coptic Manuscripts Brought from the Fayum by W. M. Flinders Petrie.* London, 1893.

______. *Coptic Ostraca from the Collection of the Egypt Exploration Fund, the Cairo Museum and Others.* London, 1902.

______. *Catalogue of the Coptic Manuscripts in the British Museum.* London, 1905.

______. *Catalogue of the Coptic Manuscripts in the Collection of the John Rylands Library, Manchester.* Manchester, 1909.

______. *The Monastery of Epiphanis at Thebes.* New York, 1929.

______. *Short Texts from Coptic Ostraca and Papyri.* Oxford, 1931.

______. *Varia Coptica.* Aberdeen, 1939.

Hall, H. R. *Coptic and Greek Texts from the Christian Period from Ostraca, Stelae, etc. in the British Museum.* London, 1905.

Kahle, P. H. *Bala'izah. Coptic Texts from Deir El-Bala'izah in Upper Egypt.* London, 1954.

Rouillard, G. *L'Administration civile de l'Egypte byzantine,* 2nd ed. Paris, 1928.

Stefanski, E., and M. Lichtheim. *Coptic Ostraca from Medinet Habu.* Chicago, 1952.

Thompson, H. *Theban Ostraca.* London, 1913 (Coptic texts).

Till, W. *Die koptischen Ostraca der Papyrussammlung der Österreicheschen Nationalbibliothek.* Vienna, 1960.

For accounting methods, see:

Grier, E. *Accounting in the Zenon Papyri.* New York, 1934 (for the Greek collection of the Zenon Papyri from Egypt).

Megally, M. *Notions de comptabilité à propos du papyrus E. 3226 du Musée du Louvre.* Cairo, 1977 (for ancient Egyptian accounting).

MOUNIR MEGALLY

ACEPHALOI, extremist anti-Chalcedonians in Egypt who refused to recognize the Alexandrian patriarchs who accepted the HENOTICON. They first appear in history in 482 as Egyptian monks who opposed PETER III MONGUS's rapprochement with Constantinople (Zacharias Rhetor *Historia ecclesiastica* 6. 2). Their name denoted their community of purpose without the need of a personal leader, and least of all a Henoticist patriarch (see Leontius of Byzantium, *De sectis* 5, col. 1230). It is possible that these dissidents adopted the name of other irreconcilables who after the Formula of Reunion in April 433 rejected both CYRIL I and JOHN OF ANTIOCH (see Liberatus of Carthage *Breviarium* 9. 41).

At the end of the ACACIAN SCHISM, "Acephaloi" was used as a term of abuse by the Jerusalem Chalcedonians against SEVERUS OF ANTIOCH and his followers (*Sacrorum conciliorum collectio,* Vol. 8, col. 1085, recording popular outcries when John, patriarch of Jerusalem [516–524], visited the principal church at Tyre on 16 September 518). In 520, a petition to Emperor Justin from "the clerics and abbots and landowners of the province of Syria Secunda, and representatives from the patriarchates of Antioch and Jerusalem associated 'acephaloi' with 'Eutychians' and others whose excommunication they demanded" (*Collectio Avellana* 232a, p. 704).

The Acephaloi were condemned as a sect by the Home Synod of Constantinople in June 536 (*Sacrorum Conciliorum Collectio,* Vol. 8, col. 891). They continued to exist when THEODORUS was consecrated Monophysite patriarch of Alexandria in the summer of 575 (Severus, *History of the Patriarchs,* PO 5, p. 474). The clear separation between Chalcedonians and Monophysites in Egypt after the reestablishment of the Chalcedonians' patriarchate in 537 robbed the Acephaloi of most of their purpose, but they lingered on into Muslim times.

BIBLIOGRAPHY

Collectio Avellana, Epistulae imperatorum, pontificum aliorum, A. D. 367–553, 2 vols., ed. O. Guenther. CSEL 35.1 and 35.2. Vienna, 1895–1898.

Leontius of Byzantium. *De sectis.* In PG 86, cols. 1134–1268. Paris, 1865.

Liberatus of Carthage. *Breviarium,* ed. E. Schwartz. In *Acta conciliorum oecumenicorum* 2.5, pp. 98–141. Berlin, 1936.

Schaff, P. "Acephali." DCB 1. In Repr. New York, 1974.

Vasiliev, A. A. *Justin the First.* Dumbarton Oaks Papers No. 1. Cambridge, Mass., 1950. Contains references.

W. H. C. FREND

ACHILLAS, saint and eighteenth patriarch of the See of Saint Mark (311–312) (feast day: 19 Ba'ūnah). Achillas succeeded PETER I, who lost his life toward the end of the persecutions begun by DIOCLETIAN. He was a contemporary of emperors Galerius (305–310) and Licinius (308–324). During the term of Licinius, the church had a respite from persecutions after the abdication of Diocletian. Previously ordained a presbyter by THEONAS with Pierius, he was placed at the head of the CATECHETICAL SCHOOL after Pierius either went to Rome or was martyred in Alexandria. Apparently he distinguished himself so much in Greek philosophy and theological science that Athanasius later described him as "the Great" (*Historia ecclesiastica* 7.32).

Achillas inherited from Peter I the troubles of the church in the Melitian heresy and schism at Lycopolis in Upper Egypt, and the heresy of ARIUS in Alexandria. However, after his accession, a considerable number of supporters of Arius prevailed upon him to lift the sentence of EXCOMMUNICATION and ANATHEMA imposed by his predecessor on the future heresiarch. Thus, Arius was not only forgiven but also granted the priesthood of the Church at Bucalis, the oldest in Alexandria. This appears to be the only major event of Achillas' short episcopate, which according to the *History of the Patriarchs* (Vol. 1, Pt. 2, p. 401) lasted only six months. His early death was ascribed by the faithful to his breach of the command of his predecessor Peter in regard to Arius. He is commemorated in the Copto-Arabic SYNAXARION.

BIBLIOGRAPHY

Altaner, B. *Patrology,* Eng. trans. Hilda Graef. London, 1958.
Bardenhewer, O. *Geschichte der altkirchlichen Literatur,* 3 vols. Freiburg, 1902–1912.
Duchesne, L. *Early History of the Christian Church,* Vol. 1, pp. 341ff. London, 1909.
Quasten, J. *Patrology,* 3 vols. Utrecht and Antwerp, 1975.
Smith, W., and H. Wace. *Dictionary of Christian Biography,* 4 vols. New York, 1974.

AZIZ S. ATIYA

ACHILLAS, SAINT, a monk at Scetis in the golden age of monasticism (fourth–fifth centuries). Saint Achillas was outstanding among all the great ascetics. Abbot THEODORUS OF PHERME said of him, "He was like a lion at Scetis, considered formidable in his own day." The APOPHTHEGMATA PATRUM gives some examples not only of his austerity but also of his wisdom and the sensitivity of his charity. It was indeed in spite of himself that fame had come to him. He said, "Be like an animal so that you do not in any way let yourself become known." Later hagiography has liked to compare the ascetic achievements of this rough uncultured anchorite with the warlike exploits of his namesake, the hero of *The Iliad.*

BIBLIOGRAPHY

Arras, V., ed. *Collectio Monastica,* 13, 65, p. 100. CSCO 238. Louvain, 1963.
Cotelier, J. B., ed. *Apophthegmata Patrum.* In PG 65, pp. 124–25. Paris, 1864.
Leloir, L. *Paterica Armeniaca,* 11, 25, CSCO 371, p. 127. Louvain, 1976.
Rosweyde, H., ed. *Paschase,* 25. PL 72, p. 1049B. Paris, 1849.

LUCIEN REGNAULT

ACTA ALEXANDRINORUM, the propaganda literature of Greek Alexandrian groups, preserved on papyri. Since the form of a judicial record was often used, they are of significance for comparison with the Christian Acts of the Martyrs.

BIBLIOGRAPHY

Musurillo, H. *The Acts of the Pagan Martyrs.* Oxford, 1954.
______. *Acta Alexandrinorum.* Leipzig, 1961.

MARTIN KRAUSE

ACTA SANCTORUM, monumental hagiographical work whose beginnings go back to the Counter-Reformation, which took its stamp from the Council of Trent (1545–1563). Reformed criticism of the cult of saints was answered on the Roman Catholic side by efforts at moderation and orderliness in the veneration of the saints, and by a critical sifting of the traditions with a view to separation of the false from the true. In 1603 a Belgian Jesuit, H. Rosweyde (1569–1629), developed his plan of replacing the many apocryphal lives of the saints by a new collection based on the manuscript treasures of the Belgian libraries. In 1615 he published the *Vitae patrum,* which is important for the history of early Egyptian monasticism. When Rosweyde died, J. van Bolland (1596–1665) was entrusted with continuing the work. With G. Henschenius (1601–1681) he developed the principles of source criticism used in producing the two volumes of the *Acta sanctorum* that covered January.

For the first time in the history of hagiography, the effort was made to sift the sources by age and trustworthiness, and to give an account of this in the prolegomena to the printed texts. The group of researchers that established itself in Antwerp, and was joined in 1659 by D. Papebroch (1628–1714), came to be called the Society of the BOLLANDISTS, after Bolland. Thereafter the volumes for the rest of the months were published in the order of the Calendar of Saints. By 1773, when the Jesuit order was dissolved, the third volume for October had been reached. After a period of confusion, with many attempts to provide a new basis for the *Acta sanctorum,* the Society of the Bollandists was inaugurated at the Collège Saint Michel in Brussels, following the reestablishment of the Belgian province of the Jesuits.

Adoption of the methods of historical scholarship, which began to blossom in the nineteenth century, led to a considerable expansion in activities. Since 1882 the *Analecta Bollandiana* have been appearing, and alongside them the Subsidia Hagiographica series. In both, manuscript catalogs were published. Important aids for hagiographical work are *Biblio-*

theca hagiographica latina (2 vols., 1898–1901, with supplement of 1911); *Bibliotheca hagiographica graeca* (3rd impression, edited by F. Halkin, 3 vols. with *auctaria*, 1957 and 1969); *Bibliotheca hagiographica orientalis* (1910). Leaders in the field were H. Delehaye (on him and his writings, see P. Peeters, *Analecta Bollandiana* 60 [1942], I–LII) and, in the area of Oriental studies, P. Peeters (see P. Devos, *Analecta Bollandiana* 69 [1951], I–LIX, with bibliography), who also created the *Bibliotheca hagiographica orientalis.* These two scholars dealt with Egyptian hagiography in outstanding studies. In the *Acta sanctorum* Egyptian saints are also taken into account. In addition, scholarly handling of the Egyptian saints, whether in the Greek, the Coptic, or the Arabic texts, is dependent on the relevant studies and aids produced by the Bollandists.

BIBLIOGRAPHY

Aigrain, R. *L'Hagiographie. Les sources, ses méthodes, son histoire,* pp. 329–50. Paris, 1953.

Delehaye, H. *L'oeuvre des Bollandistes à travers trois siècles 1615–1915,* 2nd ed. Brussels, 1959. The work contains a bibliographical guide.

Peeters, P. *L'oeuvre des Bollandistes,* 2nd ed. Brussels, 1961.

THEOFRIED BAUMEISTER

ACT OF PETER, the fourth and last Coptic tractate in the Berlin Codex (BG 8502, 4). The *Act of Peter* is written on the final eleven pages (128.1–141.7), with one papyrus leaf missing from the middle of the text (133–34). The most important person in the story, of course, is the chief apostle, Peter. Unlike other early Christian pieces in which he is chiefly a teacher and almost never a worker of miracles (e.g., the Pseudo-Clementina), here one of Peter's greatest gifts is his ability to heal the blind, deaf, and lame (128.10–17), which he customarily does on Sundays. On one occasion, he is criticized by one of his acquaintances for not healing his own daughter, who lies partially paralyzed. In response, he heals his daughter in the presence of many, only to reverse the miracle after bolstering their faith, leaving the girl an invalid again. When the crowd pleads on her behalf, he relates to his visitors that her physical deformity had preserved her virginity when a certain Ptolemy abducted the girl so that he could marry her, heedless of the objections of Peter's wife. Apparently, Peter relates the unusual circumstances of Ptolemy's attention toward his daughter—then a beautiful, whole maiden—in the missing segment, including her becoming a cripple, an event that allowed her to retain her chastity. In the dramatic sequel, a repentant Ptolemy seeks out Peter, is himself healed of blindness, and becomes converted to the Christian faith. Before his death, which follows soon after, he wills a parcel of land to Peter and his daughter. Thereupon, in an act reminiscent of the requirement that the property of all proselytes be sold and the proceeds be entrusted to the church's leadership (Acts 4:32–5:11), Peter sells the land and gives "the entire sum of money to the poor" (139.16–27). After he has drawn from this story the lesson that God watches over his own people, Peter distributes bread to the crowd and then retires to his home.

It is generally agreed that the setting for the narrative is Jerusalem, where Peter lives with his wife and daughter. Further, Ptolemy's rash abduction and his evident intent to force the girl to become his wife seem to presuppose Jewish law. Moreover, on the question of the relation of this text with the collection known as the *Acts of Peter,* preserved in large measure in the Latin manuscript *Actus Vercellenses,* Schmidt (1924) has demonstrated convincingly that the *Act of Peter* was a part of the lost opening of the *Acts of Peter.* Krause (1972) has even suggested a connection with the ACTS OF PETER AND THE TWELVE APOSTLES in Nag Hammadi Codex VI. In addition, Schmidt has argued for an Encratite influence. But any such influence will have been slight, since the real point of the account is to show that God sought to preserve a Christian maiden's virginity, not to demonstrate that marriage and its attendant sexual relations are to be avoided at all costs. After all, in the story Peter is married and his wife has given birth to a daughter. In addition, Brashler and Parrott (1979) are doubtless correct in suggesting that the obvious Gnostic interests, which brought together the first three treatises in the Berlin Codex, also added the *Act of Peter* because of the allegorizing possibilities in the narrative. The document itself was likely composed in the late second or early third century.

BIBLIOGRAPHY

Brashler, J., and D. M. Parrott, eds. "The Act of Peter." In *Nag Hammadi Codices V, 2–5 and VI with Papyrus Berolinensis 8502, 1 and 4,* ed. D. M. Parrott, pp. 473–93. Leiden, 1979.

Krause, M. "Die Petrusakten in Codex VI von Nag Hammadi." In *Essays on the Nag Hammadi Texts in Honor of Alexander Bohlig,* ed. M. Krause, pp. 36–58. Leiden, 1972.

Schmidt, C. "Studien zu den alten Petrusakten I." *Zeitschrift für Kirchengeschichte* 43 (1924):321–48.

Till, W. C. *Die gnostischen Schriften des koptischen Papyrus Berolinensis 8502,* ed. H.-M. Schenke, pp. 296–321, 333. Texte und Untersuchungen 60. Berlin, 1972.

S. KENT BROWN

ACTS, MICHIGAN PAPYRUS OF, originally a papyrus about 27 × 14 cm in size (15 × 10 cm extant) with thirty-six lines to the page, of which twenty-one remain. It contains Acts 18:27–19:6, and 19:12–16. According to Sanders, it is from 200–250; Aland says about 300, and Roberts and Skeat place it in the third/fourth century. Probably deriving from the Fayyūm, the text essentially agrees with that of Codex Bezae (D); hence the attestation of this text type in Egypt is important.

In editions of the Greek New Testament this papyrus is designated P 38. Its inventory number in the Michigan collection is 1571, and it has been edited by H. A. Sanders as text 138 in *Miscellaneous Papyri* (Ann Arbor, 1936 [P. Mich. 3]).

[*See also:* Bible Manuscripts, Greek.]

BIBLIOGRAPHY

Aland, K. "Studien zur Überlieferung des Neuen Testaments und seines Textes." *Arbeiten zur Neutestamentlichen Textforschung* 2 (1967):120.

Haelst, J. van. *Catalogue des papyrus littéraires juifs et chrétiens,* p. 175. Paris, 1976.

Kenyon, F. *The Text of the Greek Bible,* 3rd ed. London, 1975.

Sanders, H. A. "A Papyrus Fragment of Acts in the Michigan Collection." *Harvard Theological Review* 20 (1927):1–19 (*editio princeps*).

MARTIN KRAUSE

ACTS OF THE APOSTLES. Coptic literature is particularly rich in so-called apocryphal texts. This is especially noticeable in the documents dealing with the apostles. The source of this phenomenon may be ascribed to the spirit of patriotism prevailing among the Copts or to the tradition of legendary and fictitious forms so commonly used in the monastic milieus for edification or entertainment. The importance of such texts in the Christian literature of the first few centuries was signaled by I. Guidi (1888, pp. 1–7) as a means for a better knowledge of the numerous apostolic acts to be found in Coptic manuscripts. In his estimation, they were the basis of the collections of acts known in Arabic and in Ethiopian.

In 1904, E. REVILLOUT undertook the publication of a number of fragments derived mainly from the National Library of Paris, as well as the Vatican Library and the libraries of Oxford and Strasbourg. These he presented under the inclusive and erroneous title of "The Gospel of the Twelve Apostles" (PO 2). That same year, P. Lacau also brought out a number of those fragments, but he classified them very carefully, distinguishing the *Acts of Pilate* from an *Apocalypse of Bartholomew* and some other pieces to which, for want of better title, he gave the name "Apocryphal Gospel."

Since then, the labors of different critics and in particular the effort to assemble pages of manuscripts spread throughout the various libraries of the West, put into action by T. Orlandi at the center of the *Corpus dei manoscritti copti letterari* in Rome, have allowed us to form a clearer idea of that group of apocryphal acts, preserved, translated, and recopied, at times revised and even rewritten by the Coptic church throughout the first six centuries.

If the Arabic (ed. Smith-Lewis) and Ethiopian (ed. Malan and Budge) collections inform us about the content of the legends inherited from Coptic sources, they tell nothing about the composition of the collections that preserved these legends. The work of reassembling the codices has brought to light the fact that, with the exception of acts about the great figures such as Peter, Paul, and John, the narratives concerning an apostle were practically never circulated in an isolated state. They were always inserted in a collection that was carefully arranged in a specific order. It is therefore possible to find collections that contain only the acts, namely, the teaching of the apostles, without the accompanying martyrdom narratives. Other collections contain only an account of a martyrdom, as does the manuscript of the Pierpont Morgan Library M 635—which alone is still in its original arrangement. In some collections the teaching and the martyrdom narrative alternate, and finally, some collections combine different acts of the apostles. Andrew is an example of such, for he is always associated with a companion. The apostle Simon, son of Cleophas, also called the Zealot or the Canaanite, and a virgin named Theonoe, are the subjects of a story apparently belonging to the local Egyptian patrimony, since it is not found in the Arabic and Ethiopian collections. It should in all probability fill a complete codex of its own.

The principal apostles, Peter, Paul, and John, have obviously received special treatment, since their acts and passion stories occupy a complete codex, or else the copyist has summarized the story —something that occurs from time to time with other apostles—or he has simply given an extract in a collection concerning the acts of the other apostles.

In this way, the *Acts of Paul* in the Coptic language are known primarily by the Heidelberg Papyrus No. 1 (ed. Schmidt), which gives, again in a fragmentary state, a witness of the Greek Acts of Paul, that is, not only the journey, the acts of Paul and of Thecla, but also the correspondence with the Corinthians and the martyrdom (cf. for that account, F. Bovon et al., 1981, pp. 295–98). C. Schmidt dates the papyrus as the sixth century being the latest possible date. Its language is Sahidic very strongly colored by Akhmimism. There are two other unedited fragments, one minute on a fourth-century parchment (John Rylands Library Suppl. 44, English translation by W. E. Crum in the *Bulletin of the Ryland's Library* 5, 1920, pp. 498ff.), and the other in a very bad state, on a fifth-century papyrus in the Bodmer Collection, translated provisionally by R. Kasser (*Revue d'histoire et de philosophie religieuses* 40 (1960): 45–57, and Hennecke and Schneemelcher, Vol. 2, pp. 268–70). The first of these gives again a passage from the beginning of Saint Paul's journey; the other, the Ephesus episode. The collections of reconstructed acts have, up to now, given only fragments of martyrdom, possible proof that the entire story of Paul's predication should have been the object of separate codices.

Perhaps it was the same with the *Acts of Peter*, though some fragments of manuscripts bring to light some passages that are difficult to insert in the existing collections (cf. Poirier and Lucchesi, 1984, p. 8, notes 2 and 4; p. 12, note 1).

As is the case with Paul, Peter's martyrdom is better testified (ed. Guidi, 1887–1888, Vol. II, pp. 25–29 and 31–34). The *Act of Peter*, preserved in the Gnostic Berlin Codex 8502, is of particular interest because it was cut out of the authorized version of *Acta Petri* known through the Vercelli manuscript (cf. Schmidt, 1903, 24, 1, pp. 3–7; Parrott, 1979, 11, pp. 478–93; Tardieu, 1984, pp. 217–22) but inserted in a Gnostic collection. Till and Schenke (1960, p. 333) and Tardieu (1984, pp. 67–72) have tried to explain why Gnostic people preserved this particular story. In the light of that text, it is striking to observe the role that popular and fictitious narrative could play in ethic and dogmatic paraenesis, like the narratives that are to be found in the collection of stories preserved in Coptic apostolic collections. These stories were surely linked with a solid reality, namely, that of the society of those times as well as its thoughts and its customs.

The *Acts of John* preserved in Coptic are those of Prochorus (fifth century). At least one manuscript keeps them in their entirety (M 576, Pierpont Morgan Library), and several others are in a fragmentary state (cf. Junod and Kaestli, 1983, pp. 377–97). The account of the apostle's death, or metastasis of the Greek acts, is covered widely enough, and particularly so in the British Museum manuscript Or 6782 (tenth century) edited by E. A. Wallis Budge (1913, pp. 51–58).

In the *Acts of Andrew*, the Coptic papyrus of Utrecht No. 1, now edited by R. van den Broeck in J. M. Prieur, 1989, pp. 653–671, with French translation (translated into German in Hennecke and Scheemelcher, Vol. 2, pp. 281–85 by Quispel and Zandee, and in Italian in Erbetta, Vol. 2, pp. 404–406; Moraldi, Vol. 2, pp. 1424–27) proves that the text of the Greek acts had itself circulated in Coptic, because the fragment, damaged at the beginning and in the center, is inserted very neatly in chapter 18 of the story of Gregory of Tours. On the other hand, the reconstituted codices and the Arabic and Ethiopian collections have preserved different acts about Andrew where the apostle always appears accompanied, either by Matthias or Philemon, or by Bartholomew, or by Peter or Paul. As to the martyrdom, the thin fragment that remains is very close to the Arabic version (Smith-Lewis, 1904, p. 28).

Finally, the Coptic text of the *Acts of Thomas*, the contents of which had been known until now from the Arabic and Ethiopian versions that derive from Coptic, was published in its fragmentary state by P. H. Poirier in 1984. E. Lucchesi in an appended codicogical study, determines the place of the fragments in the Coptic collections of the apocryphal acts. The story about Thomas's working of miracles and his conversions, as well as of his carrying on his shoulders the skin that had been torn from him, are not to be found in the Greek acts, nor in the Syriac or Latin traditions, but a Persian legend attributes the same torture to Bartholomew. As to the martyrdom, it seems to be a simplified version of that contained in the primitive Greek acts.

As to the other apostles, the fragments that remain allow us to establish the fact that, with some occasional differences, the narratives agree more or less with those of the Arabic and Ethiopian collections; the exceptions are the acts of Simon, son of Cleophas, and of the Virgin Theonoe. This story is preserved in Coptic by at least two manuscripts, of which one, very fragmentary (Zoega, 1810, no. 137) allows us to complete the other; this text was edited by I. Guidi (1887–1888, 3, 2, pp. 76–80). It is not to be found in the Arabic and Ethiopian collections. It is true that the Copts, judging from the pieces that have survived, should have possessed a considerable number of codices, distributed in various ways —either in the list of the apostles, which is never absolutely the same as that of the synoptic gospels or as that of the Arabic and Ethiopian collections, or in the orderly arrangement of the texts (sufferings, teachings, or an alternation of the two).

A link should be noted in the transmission of these apostolic Coptic legends: between the Sahidic collections (originating mainly from the White Monastery—see DAYR ANBĀ SHINŪDAH) or Sahidico-Akhmimic (*Acts of Paul,* for example) and the Arabic or Ethiopian collections existed the Bohairic collection of the Monastery of Saint Macarius in Wādī al-Naṭrūn. Unfortunately very few fragments remain from the acts of John of Prochorus, the metastasis, the teaching and martyrdom of Philip, the teaching of Bartholomew, and the martyrdoms of Matthias, Mark, and Luke. The content has a close resemblance to the Arabic and Ethiopian versions and remains in the category of a precious witness of the transition that the editor H. Evelyn-White (1926) dates to the thirteenth century or thereabouts.

The Coptic church was therefore rich in numerous collections of apostolic legends, which had been taken from the Greek tradition and translated or reshuffled, or which had been fashioned by the church itself. If one reflects on the numerous codices that were recopied, at the White Monastery for example, the church must have made great use of them in the liturgy as much as in the instruction and building of a Christian and monastic people.

BIBLIOGRAPHY

Acta Apocrypha in general

Bovon, F., et al. *Les Actes apocryphes des apôtres.* Publications de la Faculté de l'Université de Genève; Geneva, 1981.

Erbetta, M. *Gli Apocrifi del Nuovo Testamento,* Vol. 2, Atti e Legende. Turin, 1966.

Hennecke, E., and W. Schneemelcher. *Neutestamentliche Apokryphen,* Vol. 2. Tübingen, 1959–1964.

Lipsius, R. A. *Die Apokryphen Apostelgeschichten und Apostellegenden,* 2 vols. Brunswick, West Germany, 1883–1890; repr., Amsterdam, 1976.

Moraldi, L. *Apocrifi del Nuovo Testamento,* Vol. 2. Turin, 1971.

Acta Apocrypha Coptica

Budge, E. A. W. *Coptic Apocrypha in the Dialect of Upper Egypt,* pp. 51–58, 233–40. London, 1913.

Guidi, I. "Frammenti copti." *R. Accademia nazionale dei Rendiconti,* ser. 4, 31, 1887, 47–63; 3.2, 1887, 19–35; 65–81, 177–190; 251–270; 368–384; 4.1, 1888, 60–70. Rome, 1887–1888.

______. "Gli Atti Apocrifi degli Apostoli nei testi copti, arabi ed etiopici." *Giornale della Società asiatica italiana* 2 (1888):1–66.

Junod, E., and J.-D. Kaestli. *Acta Johannis (Corpus Christianorum, Series Apocryphorum* 1), Vol. 1, pp. 377–97. Turnhout, Belgium, 1983.

Lacau, P. *Fragments d'apocryphes coptes.* Mémoires de l'Institut d'archéologie orientale du Caire 9. Cairo, 1904.

Lemm, O. von. "Koptische apokryphe Apostelacten" 1–2. *Mélanges asiatiques* 10 (1890–1894):99–171, 293–386.

______. *Kleine Koptische Studien 1–58,* ed. P. Nagel. Leipzig, 1972.

______. *Koptische Miscellen 1–148,* ed. P. Nagel. Leipzig, 1972.

Lucchesi, E. "Deux nouveaux fragments coptes des Actes d'André et de Barthélemy." *Analecta Bollandiana* 98 (1980):75–82.

Lucchesi, E., and J. M. Prieur. "Fragments coptes des Actes d'André et de Barthélemy." *Analecta Bollandiana* 96 (1978):339–50.

Morard, F. "Notes sur le recueil copte des Actes Apocryphes des Apôtres." *Revue de théologie et de philosophie* 113 (1981):403–413.

______. "Les Recueils coptes d'actes apocryphes des apôtres. Un exemple: le codex R." *Augustinianum.* XI Incontro di studiosi dell' antichità cristiana 23 (1983):73–82.

Orlandi, T. "Gli Apocrifi copti." *Augustinianum.* XI Incontro di studiosi dell' antichità cristiana 23 (1983):57–71.

Parrott, D. M. *Nag Hammadi Codices V, 2–5, and VI with Papyrus Berolinensis 8502 1 and 4.* Nag Hammadi Studies 11, pp. 478–93. Leiden, 1979.

Poirier, P.-H. *Acts of Thomas.* Louvain-la-neuve, 1981.

———. *La Version copte de la prédication et du martyre de Thomas, avec une contribution codicologique au corpus copte des Acta Apostolorum Apocrypha par E. Lucchesi.* Subsidia Hagiographica 67. Brussels, 1984.

Revillout, E. *Les Apocryphes coptes.* PO 2, pt. 2.

Schmidt, C. "Die alten Petrusakten." *Texte und Untersuchungen zur Geschichte der alterchristlichen Literatur* 24, 1, pp. 3–7. Leipzig, 1903.

———. *Acta Pauli, aus der Heidelberger koptischen Papyrushandschrift Nr. 1.* Leipzig, 1904; 2nd ed., 1905; repr., Hildesheim, 1965.

Tardieu, M. *Codex de Berlin,* pp. 67–72, 217–22; 403–410. Paris, 1984.

Till, W., and H. M. Schenke. *Papyrus Berolinensis 8502.* Texte und Untersuchungen zur Geschichte der alterchristlichen Literatur 60, 2. Berlin, 1960.

Zoega, Georg. *Catalogus codicum copticorum manuscriptorum qui in Museo Borgiano Velitris adservantur.* Opus posthumum. Rome, 1810. Re-edited J. M. Sauget. Hildesheim, 1973.

Acta Bohairica

Evelyn-White, H. G. *The Monasteries of the Wadi n'Naṭrun,* Vol. 1, pp. 27–50. New York, 1926.

Acta Arabica

Smith-Lewis, A. *The Mythological Acts of the Apostles.* Horae semiticae 4. London, 1904.

Acta Ethiopica

Budge, E. A. W. *The Contendings of the Apostles,* 2 vols. London, 1899–1901.

Malan, S. C. *The Conflicts of the Holy Apostles.* London, 1871.

FRANÇOISE MORARD

ACTS OF THE MARTYRS. *See* Acta Alexandrinorum.

ACTS OF PETER AND THE TWELVE APOSTLES, first tractate in Codex VI of the NAG HAMMADI LIBRARY. While fragmentary in a number of crucial places within the first eight pages, this tractate clearly describes a journey taken by Peter and the other disciples at the beginning of their ministry and after the end of Jesus' earthly life. Since no missionary acts by the disciples are noted, it is not a missionary journey, but rather a journey of preparation for later missionary efforts. The disciples first travel to an island city called "Habitation" (the Coptic term is probably a translation of the Greek word meaning "inhabited world"). There Peter—but not the other disciples—witnesses the activities of a pearl merchant who subsequently identifies himself as Lithargoel, meaning, according to the text, "a lightweight, glistening stone," and still later he reveals himself as Christ. His actions involve hawking pearls, without actually displaying any. The rich turn away, but the poor respond favorably. However, when they want to see a pearl, he does not show one to them but instead invites them to his city, telling them that there they may not only see one but receive one as a gift.

At that point the poor turn to Peter (the reason is unclear) and ask about the difficulties of the way to the city. Peter tells what he has heard, but then asks the pearl merchant first who he is and then about the difficulties, implying in the latter case that the pearl merchant truly knows the difficulties, whereas Peter has only hearsay.

The merchant identifies himself again as Lithargoel and says that the journey requires both the renunciation of possessions and fasting. The reason is that the journey necessitates going through a wilderness filled with beasts of prey who will attack those with possessions, food, and drink. Peter sighs over the difficulties and suggests that Jesus could give them the power to make the journey. Lithargoel says that all that is necessary is to know the name of Jesus and believe in him. He then affirms that he believes in the Father who sent Jesus. (Note that he does not say that he believes in Jesus.) With regard to the name of his city, he says it is called "Nine Gates."

Peter is about to go and call his friends, but first he observes that the island city is surrounded by walls and endures in the face of the storms of the sea. In a discussion with an old man, he makes a comparison between it and the person who "endures the burden of the yoke of faith." He goes on to say that such persons will be included in the Kingdom of Heaven.

Peter then calls together his friends and they successfully make the journey to Lithargoel's city. It should be noted that the poor are no longer involved. The disciples remain outside the gate, and Lithargoel comes to them in the guise of a physician. He promises to show them Lithargoel's house but first performs a healing. He then reveals himself as Christ.

The remainder of the tractate follows the pattern of a revelation discourse. The eleven disciples prostrate themselves before Christ and indicate their willingness to do his will. He instructs them to return to Habitation. They are to teach, care for the needs of the poor, and heal the physical ills of the believers with medicine that he provides. The disciples and the poor will receive the promised pearl at some future time. The physical healing by spiritual means is to convince those who are healed that the disciples can heal spiritual ills also. They are not to deal with the rich, who ignored him. Those in the churches who show partiality to the rich are condemned, but the disciples are to judge the rich uprightly. The disciples accept the instructions, prostrate themselves, and worship Christ. He raises them up and departs.

Signs of editorial activity abound. Some are evident from the description above. Two others should be mentioned: (1) The inconsistency of the story time. At its start, the story appears to be the account of the first journey of the disciples following the Resurrection, but at its conclusion, at a time before any missionary activity, reference is made to the existence of established churches. (2) The physician's disguise of Lithargoel serves only to confuse the relationship between Lithargoel and Christ. Although we are told by the narrator (who is to be thought of as a disciple) that Lithargoel is Christ, there is in fact no way for the disciples to have learned that fact, until Christ begins to refer to things that Lithargoel had said earlier.

If one takes the indications of editorial activity into consideration, it is possible to identify a basic account and several editorial additions. The basic account is the allegory of the pearl merchant (referred to in the text as a parable that concerns both how the rich and poor respond to the preaching of salvation and how one can attain it). The allegory is contained in the section from 2:1 to 6:27. It is similar in theme and approach to the similitudes of *The Shepherd of Hermas* (see Hermas) from the second century A.D. (see particularly Similitudes 1:2 and 9:2, 12, 20). It is possible, as M. Krause has suggested (1972), that this account was originally non-Christian and had to do with a god named Lithargoel. However, there is no current evidence of a Lithargoel cult in late antiquity. In fact, the name Lithargoel is formed like the names of Jewish angels, for example, Gabriel and Michael (Schenke, 1973). Since there is only very late attestation for an angel with such a name, its original purpose would seem to have been to portray Christ as an angel in disguise.

Added to the allegory (and somewhat compromising its character) is the material about Peter and the other disciples preparing themselves for their ministry, which is to be in the city of Habitation. It may be that the proletarian stance of the allegory attracted the editor to it. This material exhibits an ambivalence about the character of the disciples; at times they are historical figures, and elsewhere, representative personalities.

At a later stage, the material having to do with Lithargoel's disguise as a physician and the instructions about physical healing were probably added, perhaps in reaction to the popular cult of Asclepius, the god of healing.

Finally, at some point Peter's vision of the city and his subsequent discussion with the old man were inserted. The connection with the rest of the account is too tenuous for these elements not to have been originally independent. There are significant parallels between it and *The Shepherd of Hermas.*

Nothing within the tractate compels one to identify it as Gnostic. Nor does its presence in Codex VI lead to that conclusion, since the codex contains several other tractates that are neither Gnostic (i.e., the selection from Plato's *Republic* and the two Hermetic tractates) nor possible to classify as such with any assurance. The renunciation required of those who would go to Lithargoel's city does not point at any particular direction, since renunciation is a theme common to a variety of Christian groups (Haas, 1981).

Judeo-Christian origins for the allegory may be inferred from the name Lithargoel, from the portrayal of Jesus as an angel—and even as a guardian angel—from the fact that only the poor respond to the pearl merchants, and from the parallels with *The Shepherd of Hermas.* Peter's vision could have had the same origin in view of its parallels with *Hermas.* However, the material about the disciples, with its assumption of a ministry within a church that includes both rich and poor, was probably the work of an orthodox writer, who may well have been responsible for the tractate in its penultimate form (i.e., without the addition of the physician–physical healing material). He appears to have been opposed to the increasing worldliness of the church and its leaders.

The title, which is found only at the end of the tractate, is probably secondary since the tractate speaks of eleven disciples, not twelve, and the term "acts," in the technical sense of missionary activity, is not accurate here.

As to the date, the allegory and Peter's vision are probably no later than the middle of the second century A.D., in view of their affinities with *The Shepherd of Hermas* (dated mid-second century or before). The final form of the tractate then would be dated late in the second century or early in the third.

It has been proposed that this tractate is somehow connected with the lost first third of the *Acts of Peter* (Krause, 1972), but no convincing arguments supporting that have yet been presented.

BIBLIOGRAPHY

Haas, Y. "L'Exigence du renoncement au monde dans *les Actes de Pierre et des Douze Apôtres, les Apophtègmes des Pères du Désert* et *la Pistis Sophia*," pp. 296–303. In *Colloque international sur les textes de Nag Hammadi*, ed. B. Barc. Louvain, 1981.

Krause, M. "Die Petrusakten in Codex VI von Nag Hammadi," pp. 36–58. In *Essays on the Nag Hammadi Texts in Honour of Alexander Böhlig*, ed. M. Krause. Leiden, 1972.

Krause, M., and P. Labib. *Gnostische und hermetische Schriften aus Codex II und Codex VI*, pp. 107–121. Gluckstadt, 1971.

Parrott, D. M., ed. *Nag Hammadi Codices V, 2–5, and VI with Papyrus Berolinensis 8502, 1 and 4*, pp. 197–229. Leiden, 1979.

Robinson, J. M., ed. *The Nag Hammadi Library in English*, pp. 287–94. San Francisco, 1988.

Schenke, H.-M. "Die Taten des Petrus und der zwölf Apostel." *Theologische Literaturzeitung* 98 (1973): 13–19.

DOUGLAS M. PARROTT

ADĀM, a Coptic chanting term and one of the two leading melody types in the music of the Coptic Church. The other type is called WĀṬUS. Coptic names have passed into the choir books of the Ethiopic church as well. The *Adām* melody (LAḤN) receives its name from the first word of the first verse of the Theotokia for Monday, "Adām *again* being sad."

If the day is one of the first three of the week, that is, Sunday to Tuesday, the Theotokia of the day and its *psali* (and similarly the *psali* of the feast), the LŌBSH, the DIFNĀR, and the *Ṭarḥ* are sung to the melody of *Adām*.

The second HŌS (ode) and its *Lōbsh* are, however, sung daily to the *Laḥn Adām*. Similarly the *Adām* doxology is sung after the office of the morning prayer in all the days of the week. The *Adām* ASPASMOS is also sung in the Anaphora each day.

[*See also:* Music: Description of the Corpus and Present Musical Practice.]

EMILE MAHER ISHAQ

ADAM AND EVE. *See* Biblical Subjects in Coptic Art.

ADAYMA. *See* Isnā.

ADORATION OF THE MAGI. *See* Christian Subjects in Coptic Art.

ADVENT, the ecclesiastical season immediately preceding the Nativity of Christ. In the Coptic church this period lasts six weeks starting on 16 Hātūr and ending on 29 Kiyahk. It is a period of fasting in preparation for the celebration of Christ's coming.

Throughout the month of Kiyahk, the Kiyahkian *psalmodia* is chanted in a manner popularly known as the "seven-and-four" *psalmodia (sab'ah wa-arba'ah),* so called because it includes seven Theotokia and four *hos* and is characterized by joyful singing in expectation of the coming of Christ (see MUSIC, Sec. 1).

Thus, the church not only commemorates the anniversary of the Nativity, that is, the first coming of the Savior, but also looks forward to His Second Coming, the day when the Lord comes in power and majesty (Mt. 24:42; Jn. 14:2). Although Christ has warned that the day and hour of His coming no one knows (Mt. 24:36), it is nevertheless assumed that the Second Coming would take place at a time similar to the first, that is, after the completion of a full circle of time.

BIBLIOGRAPHY

Botte, B. *Les Origines de la Noël et de l'Épiphanie,* pp. 263–84. Louvain, 1932.

Martimort, A. G. *L'Eglise en prière,* pp. 734–38. Paris, 1961.

ARCHBISHOP BASILIOS

AFLAH AL-ZAYTUN. *See* Monasteries of the Fayyūm.

AFLĀQAH, a town located in the Egyptian Delta in the Damanhur district of the Beheira Province. The HISTORY OF THE PATRIARCHS (Vol. 2, pt. 3, p. 323) relates that Patriarch CHRISTODOULUS (1047–1077) prophesied that his successor, the man who later became Patriarch CYRIL II (1078–1092), would be a monk named George who lived as a thresher in Aflāqah.

BIBLIOGRAPHY

Timm, S. *Das christlich-koptische Ägypten in arabischer Zeit,* pt. 3, pp. 1160–61. Wiesbaden, 1988.

RANDALL STEWART

AFRĀJŪN, AL- (Phragonis), the transmitted name of an Egyptian city, the exact location of which is unknown. The Greek, Latin, and Coptic lists of the bishops who participated in the Council of NICAEA in A.D. 325 mention a Harpocration from Alphocranon. SAWĪRUS IBN AL-MUKAFFA', in his Arabic version of this list, gives the name of Harpocration's diocese as al-Afrājūn (see Munier, 1943, p. 4). But the location of the place is unknown, which has led some to believe that the name Alphocranon results from a double writing of the personal name Harpocration (Αρποκρατιων-Αλ/ρποκρανων, Arpokratiōn-Al/rpokranōn). This theory is weakened, but not nullified, by the appearance of the place-name in a medieval list of Egyptian dioceses (National Library, Paris, manuscript copte 53, and John Rylands Library, Manchester, Coptic manuscript 53). Though the list is independent of the earlier catalogs of the bishops at Nicaea, it is notoriously corrupt in the very section that records the name Alphocranon. The name appears again in a late Arabic legend about a Christian from al-Afrājūn, but the source of the story is unknown and it is possible that the name is simply a fabrication in this tale (Crum, 1932, p. 139).

The fact that the name al-Afrājūn, as recorded in Sāwīrus, is much more similar to the Greek Phragonis (al-Farrājīn in Arabic) than to the Greek or Coptic form of Alphocranon makes possible the theory that the source(s) used by Sāwīrus had the name Phragonis and that al-Afrājūn and Phragonis are two names for the same place.

Phragonis/al-Farrājīn is well attested in ancient and medieval sources. Its exact location is unknown, but it appears to have been situated near Tīdah in the Gharbiyyah Province.

BIBLIOGRAPHY

Amélineau, E. *La Géographie de l'Egypte à l'époque copte,* pp. 46–47, 179–80. Paris, 1893.

Crum, W. E. "A Nubian Prince in an Egyptian Monastery." In *Studies Presented to G. L. Griffith,* pp. 137–48. London, 1932.

Munier, H. *Recueil des listes épiscopales de l'église copte.* Cairo, 1943.

Timm, S. *Das christlich-koptische Ägypten in arabischer Zeit,* pt. 1, pp. 73–75; pt. 2, pp. 940–44. Wiesbaden, 1984.

RANDALL STEWART

AFTHĪMĪ AL-MIṢRĪ. Afthīmī was a monk at the monastery of Saint Catherine on Mount Sinai, who on 10 January 1242 completed his copy of a Byzantine horologion in Arabic (Sinai Arabic 180, 137 fols.). He was a Melchite from Cairo, as is indicated by his *nisbah* (place of origin).

BIBLIOGRAPHY

Atiya, A. S., and J. N. Youssef. *Catalogue Raisonné of the Mount Sinai Arabic Manuscripts* (in Arabic), pp. 290–95, 358. Alexandria, 1970.

KHALIL SAMIR, S.J.

AGATHON, SAINT, fourth–fifth century anchorite. The different collections of the APOPHTHEGMATA PATRUM include about fifty items in which an Abba Agathon appears, but it is justifiable to doubt whether they all concern the same person, for in a collection preserved in Ethiopic he is designated "Agathon the Great" (*Collectio Monastica* 13, 98; 14, 45) and "the one from early times" (*Collectio Monastica* 13, 93). It is not certain if he is the one, relatively young at the time of POEMEN (Cotelier, 1864, Poemen 61), who was not considered worthy of being compared with the great men of olden times (Cotelier, 1864, Elias 2). The Alexandrian Synaxarion mentions, without details, Agathon the Hermit for the 8 Bābah. But his early maturity had soon won him the title *abba* and many disciples, among others Alexander and Zoïlus, who later lived with ARSENIUS OF SCETIS AND ṬURAH. Out of the thirty apothegms in the chapter devoted to Agathon in the alphabetical collection, at least ten come from the *Ascetikon* of Isaiah, who had received them orally from Abraham, Agathon's disciple. The whole forms a fine sketch of the spiritual aspect of the old man, with a sober and moving account of his last moments.

Agathon, hostile to offhandedness and flippancy, had a most sensitive conscience; he gave proof of constant vigilance and faithfulness in the smallest things. Diligent in his manual work, he abandoned it as soon as it was the hour for prayer, declaring that this was the monk's greatest work. Detached from earthly things, he was always ready to give away what he had. Such was his charity that he would willingly have exchanged his body for that of a leper. As death drew near, he recognized that he had always done his utmost to keep God's commandments, but added humbly that he did not rely on himself and his works. The narrator concludes, "So it was that he ended his life in joy, departing as a man who bids his friends farewell." Dorotheus of Gaza twice quotes the final words of Abba Agathon in his exhortations to his monks.

BIBLIOGRAPHY

Arras, V., ed. *Collectio Monastica,* 13, 93–94, 98–99; 14, 45; pp. 107–108, 121. CSCO 238. Louvain, 1963.

Cotelier, J. B., ed. *Apophthegmata Patrum.* PG 65, pp. 108–118. Paris, 1864.

Dorotheus of Gaza, Saint. *Oeuvres spirituelles,* ed. L. Regnault and J. de Préville. Sources chrétiennes 92. Paris, 1963.

Draguet, R. *Les Cinq recensions de l'Asceticon syriaque d'abba Isaïe, Logos VI 5.* CSCO 289, pp. 40–49; 293, pp. 47–73. Louvain, 1968.

LUCIEN REGNAULT

AGATHON OF ALEXANDRIA, thirty-ninth patriarch of the See of Saint Mark (661–677). Before his preferment to the Coptic patriarchate, Agathon was the assistant to BENJAMIN I from 644. During his predecessor's last illness, he assumed de facto patriarchal authority until his succession to the throne of Saint Mark in 661. He was a fierce fighter against Chalcedon, but never attempted to flee from the face of Cyrus, the Byzantine patriarch and prefect of Egypt. He remained in Alexandria disguised by day as a carpenter carrying the basket of his tools as he went around. By night, he officiated for his flock and comforted the faithful anti-Chalcedonians in the ensuing wave of persecution.

In his earlier years, Agathon had lived in the district of Mareotis. We must therefore assume that he was born somewhere in the neighborhood of Alexandria and that he took the monastic vow in one of the small monasteries of that area. He probably came from a Hellenized Egyptian family and spoke both Coptic and Greek. It is possible that he spoke some Arabic as well. As a monk and a priest, he lived through the period of the ARAB CONQUEST OF EGYPT; and, on Benjamin's return to Alexandria, the patriarch retained him by his side in the administration of the church, thus paving the way for his accession to Saint Mark's throne without any complications.

Agathon was truly a spiritual and compassionate person. During his reign, the Muslim armies are known to have raided the island of Sicily and to have returned to Alexandria with Sicilian Christian prisoners for sale in the slave market. In spite of the fact that they were technically heretical from the orthodox Coptic viewpoint, Agathon hastened to buy these captives and free them. The patriarch tried to establish communication not only with the Sicilians but also with the local heretical sects known as the Gaianites and BARSANUPHIANS. He continued the policy of Benjamin I of ordaining more bishops to attend to the spiritual needs of the faithful and to win back those who had strayed into disunion with their mother church. He also attended to the requirements of the Coptic monastic brotherhood, more especially in the region of Wādī al-Naṭrūn. The number of the monks was increasing, and their need for cells was growing. Agathon authorized the construction of multitudes of cells strewn all over the Naṭrūn marshland, for until the bedouin pillage of 869, the monasteries remained unprotected and unfortified by outer walls. Benjamin I had consecrated the sanctuary of Saint Macarius, and we must assume that Agathon continued the good work of his predecessor. He even dedicated a sanctuary to Benjamin and embellished it with adornments.

But Agathon's reign was not free from local troubles. The Chalcedonians were still much too numerous to be stifled or slighted. Their leader was a certain Theodosius (or Theodore) who happened to be in the good graces of Yazīd ibn Muʿāwiyah (A.H. 60–64/A.D. 680–683), the Umayyad caliph at Damascus. The HISTORY OF THE PATRIARCHS contains a statement that Theodosius supplied the caliph with funds in return for a diploma giving him authority over the population of Alexandria, Mareotis, and the surrounding districts. This included the collection of taxes from these areas. Theodosius was answerable to the caliph rather than to the governor of Egypt; the caliph even gave him police powers to facilitate his task. However, Theodosius proved to be unacceptable even to the Chalcedonians, and his aspirations to become rival patriarch were dampened.

Theodosius remained merely a tax collector for the Muslim state and a troublemaker for Agathon. With police power in his hands, he issued an order requesting the Alexandrian populace to stone the patriarch if he was ever seen in the open. He probably aimed at uniting secular and religious powers in his own hands, in keeping with the old system started by Justinian. The situation for Agathon was alleviated by the existence in Egypt of a rival caliph in the person of ʿAbdallah ibn al-Zubayr. Though confined to his cell by Theodosius, Agathon was nevertheless able to collect enough funds to pay the extra money Theodosius wanted and attend to the needs of the church.

An incident showing the state of confusion between Chalcedonians and anti-Chalcedonians occurred in the city of Sakhā, which was predominantly under the influence of a Chalcedonian majority. Apparently that city was the seat of a Coptic bishop from the year 431. Its Coptic name was Xeos in the old Byzantine province of Aegyptus II or the Delta east of Alexandria (Williams, 1977, pp. 492–505 and map, p. 512). It had a magistrate, an archon by the name of Isaac, who, in conjunction with its Muslim governor, was able to prevail over the Chalcedonian majority. The viceroy of Egypt at the time was Maslamah ibn Makhlad ibn Ṣāmit al-Anṣarī (667–689). He sent seven bishops to Sakhā to make an inquiry into the accusation that some officials had been branded. Together with Isaac, who was obviously a follower of Agathon, the situation was clarified, and the accused were absolved. Ultimately, Isaac became intendant for the whole district owing to the harm Theodosius had done to the patriarch. On the whole, the picture was a confused medley where the followers of Chalcedon tried to stir Muslim troubles against the Orthodox (Monophysite) Copts, but failed.

From the above accounts, it is evident that Agathon's life in Alexandria was marked by immense hardships. Nevertheless, he was able to go to the monastery of Saint Macarius (DAYR ANBĀ MAQĀR) in Wādī al-Naṭrūn, but he probably never went to Upper Egypt. From his residence and through the hierarchy, he continued to ordain priests for the country, in order to strengthen the orthodoxy of the Copts. In spite of his difficulties, he was very active and in good health until his last illness and death in 677. His body was carried to the monastery of Saint Macarius, where it was laid to rest next to the remains of his predecessor, Benjamin.

Agathon must have been an able preacher, but his homilies remain to be uncovered. A Coptic fragment ascribed to Agathon could possibly be part of his homiletic account of a vision of Benjamin at the consecretion of his sanctuary in the monastery of Saint Macarius.

BIBLIOGRAPHY

Brakmann, H. "Zum Pariser Fragment angeblich des koptischen Patriarchen Agathon. Ein neues Blatt der Vita Benjamins I." *Le Muséon* 93 309.

Williams, R. J. "Agypten II." In *Theologische Realenzyklopädie*, ed. G. Krause and G. Müller. Berlin and New York, 1977.

C. DETLEF G. MÜLLER

AGATHON AND HIS BROTHERS, saints and fourth-century martyrs (feast day: 7 Tūt). They are Agathon or Agathūn, Peter, John, Amūn, Ammūnah, and their mother, Rifqah or Rebecca.

The editors of the Copto-Arabic SYNAXARION, R. Basset (1907–1929) and I. Forget (1905–1926), tell us that they were from the district of Mamūnyah in the province of Qūṣ; in fact, this name should read Samnūṭiyyah, or, following E. Amélineau (1893, p. 399, n. 4, and p. 418, n. 1) Samnūtah. These are the forms attested for Sunbāṭ or Tacempoti, a well-known town in the district of Ziftah and the province of the Gharbiyyah.

As for Qūṣ, this cannot be the famous town in Upper Egypt, but is probably the capital of the Jazīrah Qūṣāniyyah, which was, according to B.T.A. Evetts ("The Churches . . ." 1895, p. 32, n. 1), the name of this district in the thirteenth century. Thus the family came from Sunbāṭ, which reconciles with the events recounted by the Synaxarion.

Agathon, the eldest son, was the town mayor and greatly loved by the people, who were not all Christians. Christ appeared to his family, telling them they would gain the crown of martyrdom at Shubrā of Alexandria and that their bodies would be taken to Niqrihā in the province of Beheira (read by Amélineau as "in the Jazīrah," p. 482, n. 4). This place-name was "corrected" by Amélineau and Basset to read "Taqrahā," whereas Forget changes it to "thaghrihā," which he translates as "ad huius fines." The identification of Niqrihā presents no problems; it is a suburb of Damanhūr (cf. Maspero and Wiet, 1919, p. 194, n. 1).

They thereupon distributed all their goods to the poor and made an early start for town. The military leader had them tortured, starting with Rebecca, their mother. However, he soon tired of torturing them and sent them off to Alexandria, since their constancy had already converted many people because they were loved by their fellow citizens.

In about 300, when they arrived in Alexandria at a place called Shubra, the *dux* Armenius subjected them to terrible tortures, cutting their flesh, roasting them in cauldrons, employing meat-hooks, crucifying them head downward, and so forth. They remained immovable. He finally had them beheaded, and their bodies were put into a boat to be thrown into the sea or the lake, according to other manuscripts.

An archon of Niqrihā, who had been informed of the martyrdoms by an angel, collected the bodies by bribing the guards. He buried them in the church of Niqrihā until the persecution passed. After the persecution he built a beautiful church for them, and their bones are said to have worked miracles.

At the beginning of the thirteenth century, the date of the redaction of the first and anonymous half of the Synaxarion, their bodies were carried to the town of Sunbāṭ, or Samnūṭiyyah, where their cult began to develop.

A long account of their martyrdom is found in three Arabic manuscripts originating from Sunbāṭ itself (National Library, Paris, Arabe 277; Egypt, 1524, fols. 41r–74r; Coptic Patriarchate, Cairo, History 40; Egypt, 1558, fols. 93r–112v, Graf, no. 478, Simaykah, no. 608; National Library, Paris, Arabe 4777; Egypt, nineteenth century, fols. 122r–40r, which seems to be a direct copy of the Cairo manuscript).

A translation of the incipit follows: At the time of the impious kings Diocletian and Maximian . . . there was a God-loving man, an archon, from a village in the district of the town of Qūṣ in the province of the Ṣaʿīd . . . called Aghātū, who was compassionate, in accordance with the very meaning of his name in Coptic." This shows that the account took Qūṣ as being the famous town in Upper Egypt.

BIBLIOGRAPHY

Amélineau, E. *La Géographie de l'Egypte à l'époque copte,* pp. 399–400 (Qous), 417–418 (Sanmouteh), 482–483 (Taqrahā). Paris, 1893.

Caraffa, F. "Agatone." *Bibliotheca Sanctorum,* Vol. 1, col. 343. Rome, 1962.

Graf, G. *Catalogue de manuscrits arabes chrétiens conservés au Caire,* pp. 183–84, no. 478. Vatican City, 1934.

Maspero, J. and G. Wiet. *Matériaux pour servir à la géographie de l'Egypte.* Cairo, 1919.

Troupeau, G. *Catalogue des manuscrits arabes [de la Bibliothèque Nationale de Paris].* Part 1: *Manuscrits chrétiens,* Vol. 1, pp. 244–45, no. 277, Paris 1972; Vol. 2, pp. 27–29, no. 4777. Paris, 1972–1974.

KHALIL SAMIR, S.J.

AGATHON OF ḤOMṢ, twelfth-century author and a bishop of Ḥomṣ, and mentioned by the encyclopedist Abū al-Barakāt IBN KABAR (d. 1324) in Chapter 7 of the *Miṣbāḥ al-Ẓulmah* ("Lamp of Darkness"). He classes him among the Coptic medieval authors after SĀWĪRUS IBN AL-MUQAFFAʿ, Michael of Damietta, and Butrus of Malīj, and before CYRIL III ibn Laqlaq (Samir, 1971, p. 315, no. 4). Concerning him, Ibn Kabar says, "He is the author of the book of the 'Account of the Faith and the Sacrament of the Priesthood.' He composed this work in order to justify his request to be freed of the bishopric of Ḥomṣ without being deposed from his rank."

G. Graf first mentioned Agathon among the Melchites (Graf, 1947, p. 71, no. 3), but then classed him more certainly among the Jacobites (Graf, 1947, p. 270, no. 4). Nevertheless, Agathon was probably a Melchite; it is unlikely that he was a West Syrian or Jacobite, and he was not a Copt. Haji-Athanasiou (pp. 120–21) has supported the Melchite thesis, because of the lack of importance given the title of metropolitan, the use of a biblical version close to the Septuagint, and the mention of the canons of the Council in Trullo of 692. Another evidence is Agathon's reference to Anastasius I, Greek patriarch of Antioch (593–599).

Agathon began life in Antioch as a layman called Iliyyā and nicknamed Ibn al-Ashall. He probably lived at the end of the eleventh century or at the beginning of the twelfth century, but at least before 1178, the date of the earliest known manuscript (the information given by Paul Sbath in *Fihris*, no. 2537, according to which Nīqūlāwus Naḥḥās of Aleppo possessed a manuscript dated A.D. 1128, is not trustworthy). A delegation of prominent citizens of Ḥomṣ came to visit him and proposed that he should become their bishop. He complied with their request, was ordained a priest, and then consecrated metropolitan of Ḥomṣ in Syria.

With reference to his works and manuscripts, according to the manuscript of Naḥḥās, Agathon composed a "Priests' Invitation." This information cannot be checked, as the manuscript of Naḥḥās is no longer accessible.

Agathon's only certain work, mentioned by Ibn Kabar, is known today from a single complete manuscript (Bodleian Library, Oxford, Huntington 240, (fols. 131r–60v). Copied by a Copt of Cairo in 1549, it was purchased the same year by ABŪ AL-MUNĀ, parish priest of the Coptic church of Qaṣriyyat al-Rayḥān in Old Cairo, who ornamented it and added seven folios.

A second manuscript, much more ancient, is found at the Byzantine monastery of Saint Catherine at Mount Sinai (Sinai Arabic 483, fols. 357r–80v). It was copied by the priest Yūsuf ibn Barakāt of the unidentified village of Qalḥāt, on the commission of the priest Yūḥannā ibn Abī al-Ḥasan, in June 1178. Unfortunately, between fols. 361 and 362 there is a lacuna of an estimated twelve folios, which eliminates one-third of the text, corresponding to fol. 135r, line 21, to fol. 135v, line 2, in the Huntington manuscript.

In this work, Agathon, after exercising his ministry for a certain time, expresses his discouragement in light of the scandal caused by certain priests and bishops, and feels unworthy of his heavy charge. He offers his resignation. Criticized by his people, he defends his right not to be stripped of his priesthood. He supports his point of view by mentioning three famous examples (cf. fol. 132r): Saint Gregory the Theologian, who resigned in 381; Narcisius, patriarch of Jerusalem (d. 212); and Anastasius I, patriarch of Antioch (593–599). This is the introduction (fols. 131r–33v).

He then explains the essence of the priesthood: "The priesthood is to become similar to God as far as is possible." It is like true philosophy, which also consists of "becoming similar to God as far as is possible," since God is the Wise One par excellence (fols. 133v–34r). This is required of every Christian, but especially of a priest (fols. 134r–34v). The bishop is at the same time "god," "father," "mediator," "illuminator," and "guardian of the Law" (fols. 134v–36v).

Man is created in the image of God. Just as God is threefold, so also man is threefold, being composed of intellect, word, and soul, corresponding to the Father, the Son, and the Spirit (fols. 137r–39v). To become the image of God, priesthood is necessary. God has instituted it in order to remit sins and in this way to preserve or restore the image of God in man. Thus the priest is the mediator, and for this task he must resemble God by his purity, illumination, and mercy, and men by his humility.

As for the conditions for the priesthood, they are also three, according to the image of the Trinity: (1) a specific, visible criterion: to be at least thirty years old; (2) tangible, visible criteria: equilibrium, dignity, and a pleasant, radiant countenance; and (3) spiritual criteria: purity, kindness, mercy, intelligence, etcetera, and all the virtues mentioned by Paul to Timothy and Titus.

This text is one of the few reflections we possess in Arabic on the role and nature of the priesthood. It was relatively well known to the Copts of the thirteenth to the sixteenth centuries. It is as yet unpublished, although M. Haji-Athanasiou (1978, p. 118, n. 1) has prepared an edition and a translation of it.

BIBLIOGRAPHY

Haji-Athanasiou, M. "Agathon d'Emèse et son traité sur le sacerdoce." *Parole de l'Orient* (1978):117–40.

Samir, K., ed. *Miṣbāḥ al-Ẓulmah/fī Īḍāḥ al-Khidmah, li-Shams al-Riyāsah Abī al-Barakāt al-maʿrūf bi-Ibn Kabar.* Cairo, 1971.

Sbath, P. *Al-Fihris* (*Catalogue de manuscrits arabes*), Vol. 1. Cairo, 1938.

KHALIL SAMIR, S.J.

AGATHON THE STYLITE, SAINT. Our only source of information about Agathon is the

SYNAXARION, which gives a summary of his life at 14 Tūt, the probable day of his death.

He was born at Tinnis, as E. Amélineau correctly saw (1893, pp. 507–508), and not at Tanis, as the name is translated by R. Basset (PO 1, pt. 3, p. 265) and J. Forget (CSCO 78, p. 15); at this period Tanis, the ancient pharaonic town, was no more than a village called Ṣā al-Ḥajar (Ramzī, 1954–1968, Vol. 1, pt. 2, p. 116, and Amélineau, 1893, pp. 413–14).

Agathon's parents were Christians, and he remained with them to the age of forty. He then left for Mareotis, and from there went to Scetis, where he was led by an angel in the form of a monk to the monastery of Saint Macarius. He became the disciple of ABRAHAM AND GEORGE OF SCETIS and remained with them for three years. Abraham and George spent three days in prayer over the *skhema* (monastic garment) that Agathon received from the hands of the *hegumenos* Anbā Yu'annis.

Agathon led a life of great austerity, engaged in prayer and in reading the Life of Saint Symeon the Stylite. Greatly influenced by this Life, he resolved after ten years at Scetis to imitate it. He asked the permission of the elders, who approved, then left Scetis and established himself near Sakha in the Delta, where the faithful raised a column for him. It is said that he accomplished many miracles there.

He died at the age of one hundred, having lived forty years in the world, ten in the desert, and fifty as a stylite (Evelyn-White, 1932, p. 281).

According to the *Life of John Kame* (ed. Davis, 1920, pp. 24–25), Agathon introduced into Scetis the use of the canonical hours. The ancient custom was to recite together only Vespers and the night office.

BIBLIOGRAPHY

Amélineau, E. *La Géographie de l'Egypte à l'époque copte.* Paris, 1893.

Davis, M. H. *The Life of Abba John Khamé.* PO 14, pt. 2. Paris, 1920.

Evelyn-White, H. G. *The History of the Monasteries of Nitria and of Scetis.* The Monasteries of the Wādī 'N Natrun, pt. 2. New York, 1932.

Muḥammad Ramzī. *Al-Qāmūs al-Jughrāfī.* Cairo, 1954–1968.

RENÉ-GEORGES COQUIN

AGATHONICUS OF TARSUS, probably a fictitious figure, supposed to have been bishop of Tarsus in Cilicia, about the middle of the fourth century. To him are ascribed a few works that have come down in various collections found in diverse editions. The most important collection is found in a papyrus codex now in the Bodmer Library, Geneva (ed. Crum, 1915). We follow its order in listing the works attributed to Agathonicus:

1. *De fide,* transmitted also by one codex from the White Monastery (see DAYR ANBĀ SHINŪDAH), where the doctrine is transformed in order to fit with anthropomorphism. It is a catechetical treatise, composed of (a) a prologue, in which the author describes the doubts that he must overcome before discussing the subject since his inspiration might come from a demon rather than from God; (b) a central discussion concerning anthropomorphism, where the primitive redaction was against anthropomorphism; and (c) an exhortatory conclusion regarding, above all, the correct way to pray.

2. *Dispute with Justin the Samaritan about the Resurrections,* transmitted also in three manuscripts, two from the White Monastery and one (Fayyumic) now in Copenhagen (ed. Erichsen, 1932). The Samaritan is persuaded to believe in the resurrection of the body with arguments based on passages from the Old Testament. At the end, he asks to be baptized.

3. *Dispute with the Cilicians,* transmitted also in one codex from the White Monastery. It is composed of (a) a historic prologue about some Council of Ancyra (Ankara) and the origin of the subsequent dispute; and (b) the dispute between Agathonicus and a group of Cilicians guided by Stratonicus, which deals first of all with the idea of providence, then proceeds to many other subjects, both ecclesiastic and monastic. This seems to be the work that "created" Agathonicus, after which his reputation spread so far that it caused other works to be attributed to him.

4. *Apologia de incredulitate,* transmitted also by the Fayyumic manuscript in Copenhagen (cf. above). A treatise in homiletic form, it is composed of (a) a prologue, in which the author describes his difficult spiritual condition and his decision to write in order to help any brothers in similar circumstances; (b) a central portion, in which phrases from the scripture are contraposed to phrases of the unbelievers, as a means of setting forth various moral arguments; and (c) a conclusion, which blames the defection of some Christians on their reading of such pagan texts as the works of Homer and Socrates. Some of the manuscripts also integrate into these texts (1) an apothegm on the Resurrection; (2) an apothegm on the passions of Christ as God and as man; and (3) an anti-Chalcedonian homily (evidently taken from a redaction later than that of the other texts).

The doctrines expounded seem to indicate that the group that produced them was that of some Evagrian monks. In fact, Evagrius is expressly quoted in the *Apologia on Incredulity,* and the theories expounded in the catechism *De fide* are in accord with the Evagrian Origenism of the monks at Kellia and Nitria during the end of the fourth and beginning of the fifth centuries. The original redactions were probably in Greek, but the different constituents of the corpora indicate the Pachomian milieu as the seat for their translation into Coptic. Interestingly, Shenute's White Monastery seems to be the place where theological elaborations of some texts were made, and where the works of Agathonicus became interpolated into the official canonical collections of the Coptic church.

BIBLIOGRAPHY

Crum, W. E. *Der Papyruscodex Saec. 6–7 der Phillips-Bibliothek in Cheltenham. Koptische Theologische Schriften.* Schriften der wissenschaftlichen Gesellschaft in Strassburg 18. Strasbourg, 1915.

Erichsen, W. "Faijumische Fragmente der Reden des Agathonicus Bischofs von Tarsus." *Danske videnskabernes selskab meddelelser* 19, no. 1. Copenhagen, 1932.

Orlandi, T. "Il dossier copto di Agatonico di Tarso: Studio letterario e storico." In *Studies Presented to H. J. Polotsky,* ed. D. W. Young. East Gloucester, Mass., 1981.

TITO ORLANDI

AGĀTHŪN IBN FAṢĪḤ AL-ṬŪRSĪNĪ, a monk of the monastery of Saint Catherine on Mount Sinai, if the *nisbah* (place of origin) refers to him. It is possible that he was the son of a monk of Sinai, if the *nisbah* refers to his father. He belonged to the Melchite community of Egypt.

In 1242 he copied in Cairo a Psalter, which he called *zabūr,* which also contains the apocryphal Psalm 151 (Sinai Arabic 55, fols. 1–172). Folios 173–233 were added and bound with Agāthūn's manuscript in the sixteenth century, as is confirmed by the note by Yuwākīm al-Karakī on the death of the Melchite patriarch of Alexandria, GREGORY V, on 6 April 1503 (cf. fol. 173r).

Agāthūn ibn Faṣīḥ al-Ṭūrsīnī may be the same Agāthūn who added observations to folios 1v and 176v of a thirteenth-century liturgical manuscript at Sinai (Arabic 226). On this occasion he signed himself as Ghāthūn, monk at the Monastery of Sinai. Since these two manuscripts have not been microfilmed, it is not possible to compare the handwriting.

BIBLIOGRAPHY

Atiya, A. S., and J. N. Youssef. *Catalogue Raisonné of the Mount Sinai Arabic Manuscripts* (in Arabic), pp. 111–12; 417–18. Alexandria, 1970.

KHĀLIL SAMIR, S.J.

AGENCY. *See* Law, Coptic: Private Law.

AGHARWAH, a town of uncertain location mentioned several times in the HISTORY OF THE PATRIARCHS. During the patriarchate of JOHN III, Agharwah and Sakhītus, both of which had been Chalcedonian (that is, Greek Orthodox) communities, entered into the Coptic national church. The patriarch MARK II (799–819) stopped at Agharwah while journeying from Cairo to Alexandria and healed a man who was possessed. Though the location of Agharwah (Aghrāwah) is uncertain, the *History of the Patriarchs* states that it was accessible from Alexandria, suggesting that it was somewhere in the Delta in the vicinity of Alexandria.

BIBLIOGRAPHY

Timm, S. *Das christlich-koptische Ägypten in arabischer Zeit,* pt. 1, pp. 75–76. Wiesbaden, 1984.

RANDALL STEWART

AGNOETAE, name given to those who attributed either ignorance (*agnoia*) to Christ relating to subjects such as the timing of the Day of Judgment (cf. Mk. 13:32) or, alternatively, a gradual ascension to knowledge and wisdom (cf. Lk. 2:52).

In Alexandria the issue grew out of the controversy between SEVERUS OF ANTIOCH and JULIAN OF HALICARNASSUS on the corruptibility or incorruptibility of Christ's flesh. About 534 an Alexandrian deacon, Themistius, pushed the argument for corruptibility a further step by pointing to Christ's ignorance concerning the moment of the Day of Judgment and in his dealing with Lazarus (Jn. 11:34; Liberatus *Breviarium* 19.137; John of Damascus *De haeresibus* 85). He also attributed to Christ the human tendency to fear (John of Damascus *De haeresibus* 85). Among many of Severus' supporters, however, the views of Themistius were rejected, in particular by the patriarch of Antioch, Timothy IV (d. 535) (Liberatus *Breviarium* 19.137).

The debate continued, however, Themistius' ideas being advanced by a certain Theodosius (not, probably, the Monophysite patriarch; see John of Damascus), but opposed within the Monophysite movement by John Philoponus, representing the tritheists. Later in the sixth century the controversy spread to the monks of Palestine. There exist two letters to the Chalcedonian patriarch of Alexandria, Eulogius, from Pope Gregory I (*epistolae* 10.35 and 10.39 of A.D. 599), drawing his attention to the issue and asking his advice. Gregory criticized the agnoetan standpoint, indicating that while total knowledge could not have arisen from Christ's human nature, it was clearly indicated from the union of the two natures, human and divine (*epistola* 10.39, in PL 77, col. 1097). Gregory's views were underlined by Patriarch Sophronius of Jerusalem (634–638), and agnoetism was formally condemned at the Sixth General Council in 680, at which Themistius was equated with Severus and Apollinaris of Laodicea as a heretic (*Sacrorum conciliorum collectio*, Vol. 11, col. 636).

BIBLIOGRAPHY

Gregory the Great. *Epistolae*, 2 vols., ed. P. Ewald and L. M. Hartmann. Monumenta Germaniae Historica, Epistolae 1–2. Berlin, 1887–1893.

John of Damascus. *De haeresibus*. In PG 94, cols. 677–780. Paris, 1864.

Stokes, G. T. "Themistius." In DCB 4, p. 898. Repr. New York, 1974.

Vacant, A. "Agnoètes." In *Dictionnaire de théologie catholique*, Vol. 1, cols. 586–96. Paris, 1923.

W. H. C. FREND

AGNUS DEI

AGNUS DEI, Lamb of God, a designation of Jesus Christ based on Isaiah 53:7 and used by John the Baptist who, upon seeing Jesus Christ, said, "Behold the Lamb of God, who takes away the sin of the world" (Jn. 1:29).

The formula sounds the theme of divine sacrifice, calling to mind the sacrifice of Christ on the cross and sacrifice of the lamb in the Old Testament. It appears in various forms of worship in the Coptic church.

In the Anaphora of Saint BASIL, during the prayers of oblation, the priest says, "Thou hast foreordained to make thyself the lamb without blemish, for the life of the world."

In the Anaphora of Saint Gregory, the priest says, "Thou camest as a lamb to the slaughter, even unto the cross." At the descent of the Holy Spirit, the deacon asks the congregation to "bow down to the Lamb, the Word of God." In the fraction prayers at the feasts of angels, the heavenly host, and the Blessed Virgin Mary, the prayer starts with these words, "Here He is present with us at this sacred table, this day, Emmanuel, our God, the Lamb of God who carries away the sin of the whole world." Prayers said on Holy Saturday, include, ". . . Thou of Whom the Prophet Isaiah hath prophesied saying, 'He is brought as a lamb to the slaughter, and as a sheep before her shearers is dumb, so he openeth not his mouth.'" And the fraction prayers according to Saint CYRIL OF ALEXANDRIA begin, "O Lamb of God who, by Thy suffering hast carried away the sins of the world . . ."

In the Gloria of the morning prayer is the invocation, "O Lord God, the Lamb of God, Son of God, Who raisest away the sins of the world, have mercy upon us. . . ." In the collect of None (the prayer of the ninth hour) following the reading of the Gospel is the phrase, ". . . when the Mother saw the Lamb and Shepherd, Savior of the world, on the cross. . . ."

Some church historians believe that the Agnus Dei was introduced into the Roman Catholic liturgy of the mass by Pope Symmachus (498–514), but others ascribe it to Pope Sergius I (687–701), who ordered it to be sung in the mass in protest against the decision of the Council in Trullo (692), which banned representation of Christ in the form of a lamb. The term is also given by the Roman Catholic church to a sacramental wax medallion carrying the figure of a lamb, which is blessed by the pope in the first year of his reign and every seventh year thereafter.

BIBLIOGRAPHY

ʿAbd al-Masīḥ al-Masʿūdī. *Kitāb al-Khūlājī al-Muqaddas*. Cairo, 1902.

Daniel, H. A. *Codex Liturgicus*, 2 vols. Leipzig, 1847–1848.

Duchesne, L. *Le Liber Pontificalis,* 2 vols. Paris 1886, 1892.
Froger, J. *Les Chants de la messe aux viii*[e] *et ix*[e] *siècles.* Tournai, 1950.
Henry, W. "Agnus Dei." In *Dictionnaire d'archéologie chrétienne et de liturgie,* Vol. 1. Paris, 1907.
Jungmann, J. A. *The Mass of the Roman Rite,* 2 vols., trans. F. A. Brunner. New York, 1951–1955.
Mangenat, E. "Agnus Dei." In *Dictionnaire de théologie catholique,* Vol. 1. Paris, 1923.

ARCHBISHOP BASILIOS

AGRIPPINUS, tenth patriarch (167–180) in the line of succession to Saint MARK. He held the office during the reign of Emperor Marcus Aurelius. He was laid to rest on 5 Amshīr near the remains of Saint Mark in the Church of Bucalis at Alexandria.

BIBLIOGRAPHY

Atiya, A. S. *History of Eastern Christianity.* Millwood, N.Y., 1980.

AZIZ S. ATIYA

AHD AL-ʿUMAR. *See* Covenant of ʿUmar.

AHL AL-DHIMMAH. The idea of this category of the population of the rising Arab empire originated in the lifetime of the prophet Muḥammad. This was at the time when he invaded the oasis inhabited by the Jewish tribe of Khybar, who automatically became distinguished as *Ahl al-Dhimmah,* or protected "people of the covenant," with rights and duties toward the Muslim states. During the period of the great conquests, mainly in the first Hegira century under the Orthodox caliphate, the world was evenly divided according to Muslim canon law into what was known as *Dār al-Islām,* the Muslim territory, and *Dār al-ḥarb,* the territories conquered by the Muslim hosts but inhabited by religions other than Islam. Christians or Jews were described as *Ahl al-Kitāb,* that is, people of the Scripture. Those willing to submit to Muslim rule became distinguished as *Ahl al-Dhimmah,* or Dhimmis, with the right of protection from foreign inroads by the Muslim military power, with security of personal property, and with a limited freedom to practice their religion.

First, *Dhimmis* were required to disarm completely and to submit to Muslim rule. Any person found to be armed was either killed or enslaved. Second, Dhimmis were allowed to practice their own faith within churches or synagogues established prior to the advent of Islam, but building of new religious houses was prohibited. It was understood that liturgies would be performed quietly, without ostentation or the organization of open processions or any other function that might prove offensive to Muslims. Each community was under the hegemony of a religious leader answerable to the Muslim governor. Throughout the Middle Ages, Coptic partriarchs bore the burdens of the community vis-à-vis the Muslim caliph, sultan, or governor. Third, the Dhimmis were liable to pay a tribute known as JIZYAH (poll tax) fixed by the Muslim authority on all able-bodied men, thus excluding women and children. Initially, the *jizyah* established by Caliph ʿUmar ibn al-Khaṭṭāb (634–644) was fixed at forty-eight dirhams for the rich, twenty-four for the middle class, and twelve for the poor (Bar Ye'or, 1985, p. 185). The *imām* was permitted to levy the enormous sum of one thousand dinars on those whose wealth was acquired by treachery from Muslims, thereby dispossessing the culprit of most of his fortune. Dhimmis were also subject to the imposition of the KHARĀJ, an annual tax on land used for agriculture. According to Muslim canon law, the conquered land belonged to the the Muslim state, but it was considered expedient to allow those who occupied it to use it because, in utilizing it, they could render a percentage of its crops to the state in kind to be commuted later into currency. If a Copt apostatized to Islam, he remained liable to render the *kharāj* but not the *jizyah.* The *kharāj* taxation disappeared as other levies, such as the *ʿushr* (tithing) and the *zakāt* (charitable gifts) emerged. At certain times, a third, irregular tax was imposed when need arose for the support of a military at a time of extremely expensive campaigning; but this was left to the whim or discretion of the ruler, with no fixed dimension.

On the social front, the Coptic Dhimmis were required to wear a vestment distinctive from that of the Muslims. They were also required to ride only donkeys and to desist from the use of horses. They were supposed to rise in the presence of Muslims. They were subjected to certain legal disabilities, though they were protected by criminal law. Though technically they were deprived of occupying administrative positions in the Muslim government, the Islamic rulers continued to employ them because they were the able accountants and knowledgeable administrators without whom the economy of the country would collapse. At times, they were dismissed from office by a bigoted ruler, but they were gradually reinstated as it became evident that they were necessary for the conduct of affairs. Numerous Copts reached the highest positions in the administration of Egypt. (See PROFESSIONAL ACTIVITIES OF COPTS IN LATE MEDIEVAL EGYPT.)

BIBLIOGRAPHY

Bar Ye'or. *The Dhimmi Jews and Christians under Islam.* Rutherford, Calif., and London, 1985.

Berchem, M. van. *La propriété territoriale et l'impôt foncier.* Leipzig, 1886.

Gottheil, R. J. H. "Dhimmis and Moslems in Egypt." In *Old Testament and Semitic Studies in Memory of William Rainers Harper,* 2 vols., ed. R. F. Harper, F. Brown, and G. F. Moore. Chicago, 1908.

Juynboll, T. W. "Kharādj." In *Encyclopedia of Islam,* Vol. 2, pp. 902–903, ed. M. Th. Houtsma, A. J. Wensinck, T. W. Arnold, W. Heffening, and E. Levi-Provencal. Leiden and London, 1927.

Kramer, A. von. *Kulturgeschichte des Orients unten den Califen,* 2 vols. Vienna, 1875.

Lane-Poole, S. *A History of Egypt in the Middle Ages.* New York, (1901) 1969.

Lokkegaard, F. "Fay'." In *Encyclopedia of Islam,* Vol. 2, new edition, p. 869, ed. B. Lewis, C. Pellat, and J. Schacht. Leiden and London, 1965.

Māwardī. *Al-Aḥkām al-Sulṭāniyyah.* Cairo, A.H. 1298.

MacDonald, D. B. "Dhimma." In *Encyclopedia of Islam,* Vol. 1, pp. 958–59, ed. M. Th. Houtsma, T. W. Arnold, R. Basset, and R. Hartmann. Leiden and London, 1913.

AZIZ S. ATIYA

AHNĀS (Ihnās al Madīnah, Ihnāsyah al-Madīnah, Byzantine Herakleopolis), settlement on the site of pharaonic *Nn-nswt,* Ptolemaic, Roman, and Byzantine *Herakleopolis.* The Coptic and Arabic names go back to Egyptian *Ḥwt-nn-nswt, Hnn-nswt,* the Greek name comes from the identification of *Hrj-š.f* (Herishef, Greek Harsaphes), the town's ram-headed local deity, with Heracles (Herishef was also identified with Dionysus). Ahnās lies in Middle Egypt 75 miles (120 km) south of Cairo and about 10 miles (16 km) west of Banī Suef, close to the entrance to the Fayyūm, between the canals al-Sulṭanī and al-Manāfrah.

History

From the Sixth Dynasty until the Late Period, Ahnās served as the capital of the twentieth and twenty-first Upper Egyptian nomes *n'rt ḫntt* and *n'rtpḫt* (Helck, 1974, pp. 121ff). The royal center of the First Intermediate Period of the Ninth and Tenth Dynasties and the seat of the family of local kings of Libyan origin, it also housed the shipmasters of Herakleopolis between 940 and 630 B.C. (Kitchen, 1973). During the Ptolemaic and Roman periods it became the capital of the Herakleopolitan nome; after the reorganization of the Egyptian administration early in the fourth century A.D., it was a metropolis; after 539, it came under the Comes of the province Arcadia; and after the Arab conquest, it became the center of a district.

The settlement was built around the temple of Herishef, part of which has been excavated, with a sacred lake of the deity attested since the First Dynasty. Other temples are mentioned as well: late sources name the Temple of Nehebkau; Roman papyri mention temples of Anubis and Kronas, as well as the cults of Apollo and of Rome. A Roman city wall of the second or third century B.C. appears in some records, and names of city quarters and of streets further the existence of an agora of the Greeks (246 B.C.) and an agora of the Egyptians (165 B.C.) as recorded in Ptolemaic documents. A gymnasium of the first or second century A.D., baths (A.D. 188), a hippodrome of about 193, and a palaestra with colonnade (176–180) are enumerated in the Roman papyri.

The necropolis of the pharaonic, Ptolemaic, and Roman settlement was situated at Sadamant al-Jabal, west of the Baḥr Yūsuf. A First Intermediate Period (2160–2000 B.C.) necropolis was, however, discovered within the territory of the ancient city. The fourth and fifth century A.D. pagan and Christian sepulchral buildings, from which some limestone sculptures originated, were situated near the Herishef temple. A mosque built under the Umayyads is mentioned in Aḥmad Kamāl's *Le livres des perles enfouies et du mystère précieux.*

Apparently its administration between the first and fourth centuries was similar to that of capitals of other nomes. And although a *pagarch* (administrator of a nome) is still attested in 647 and a *dioketes* (finance minister) between 643 and 647, the recorded activities of the senate after the reforms of Diocletian are sporadic. The first governor of the district of Herakleopolis appears in 653.

Tradition knows of several third-century Christian

martyrs of Herakleopolis. According to the *Patrum Nicaenorum nomina*, Peter, bishop of Herakleopolis, participated in the Council of NICAEA in 325. According to a more reliable source, in 431 Heraklios, bishop of Herakleopolis, appeared at the Council of EPHESUS. Monophysite bishops of Herakleopolis are recorded at Ahnās between the sixth and the fourteenth centuries by Severus, Dioscorus Stephanus, Georgius, and others.

A papyrus dating from 405 first mentions a church building—perhaps identical to the bishop's church of 534 and that recorded in later documents. Churches are also chronicled in 590–596 and in 604. A carving from an obviously expensive tomb building erected toward the middle of the fourth century shows the importance of the Christian community. Marble capitals discovered by E. Naville (Strzygowski, 1904, no. 7350) that belonged to a late fourth-century Christian structure—perhaps a funerary chapel—proclaim the influence of the Christian community. ABŪ ṢALIḤ THE ARMENIAN and AL-MAQRĪZĪ mention a monastery dedicated to the archangel Gabriel and the monastery of Saint George at Sadamant.

Before 1164 al-Idrīsī speaks of Ahnās as a prosperous city, but Yāqūt al-Ḥamawī (Y. ibn 'Abdallah al-Rūmī) describes it as almost totally ruined by the early thirteenth century (Maspero and Wiet, 1914, p. 28).

Archaeology

The mounds and the debris of ancient Herakleopolis cover a ⅔ square mile (1 sq. km) surface, extending from Baḥr Yūsuf to the al-Sultānī canal. The area of the ancient city is encircled, and to a great extent covered, by Ihnāsyah al-Madīnah and by small villages and *'izbas*, or farms.

Excavations at the Herishef temple were started in 1891 by Naville, who also made diggings to the east of the temple at a site called Kanīsah and perhaps at a further mound. In 1904, W. M. F. Petrie worked at the Herishef temple and cleared Roman houses. In 1961, Aḥmad al-Ṭāhir of the Antiquities Department discovered a Roman temple that may have been converted into a church north of the Kom al-Aqrab.

A Spanish mission in 1966–1969 and 1976–1977 excavated a necropolis of the First Intermediate Period within the territory of the ancient city. The pharaonic necropolis had been excavated by Naville in 1891 and by Petrie in 1920–1921, and in 1904 Petrie had also signaled a Roman cemetery at the village of Sadamant. The late antique architectural fragments and Ahnās sculptures came from clandestine diggings in one or two presently unidentifiable sites investigated by Naville. The carvings were found, however, in secondary position, as filling materials.

The Ahnās Sculptures

The excavations of Naville in 1891 and of Petrie in 1904, and clandestine diggings after 1904 have yielded a number of limestone architectural fragments with ornamental and figural decoration. These can be dated from late antique to early Coptic. Art historians still regard them as chronologically and stylistically within Egyptian late antique–early Coptic plastic art. Connections with sculptures from Oxyrhynchus had been stressed by E. Kitzinger, but relationships and sequences between Ahnās carvings and other sculptures from al-ASHMŪNAYN, BĀWĪṬ, SAQQARA, and elsewhere in fourth- to sixth-century Egyptian art are not understood.

The majority of the Ahnās finds are conserved in the Coptic Museum at Old Cairo; others are in the Greco-Roman Museum at Alexandria and in the State Museum in East Berlin. There are others in some museums in Egypt as well as in museums and private collections in Europe and the United States. The finds from Naville's excavations went first to the Egyptian Museum where they were cataloged by J. Strzygowski, two pieces going to Alexandria. Earlier pieces were later transferred to the Coptic Museum in Cairo where they were exhibited together with fragments of sculptures acquired from art dealers.

In 1923, U. Monneret de Villard published a list of the Ahnās carvings known at that time. He also identified the Ahnās finds in Trieste and East Berlin.

Due to Naville's misleading report, art historians generally maintain that the Ahnās carvings were made for Christian cult buildings. This belief resulted in an erroneous interpretation of early Coptic iconography. The Christian context of the mythological motifs was first doubted by Monneret de Villard and then by Kitzinger. In 1969, H. Torp proved that Ahnās carvings with non-Christian representations belonged to pagan tomb buildings and suggested that the building where Naville unearthed the majority of the sculptures was a funerary chapel built over the walls of a pagan sepulchral building. Torp's interpretation of the small quadrangular building with a small apselike niche to the north was confirmed by H. G. Severin, who identified analogous and related buildings at Oxyrhynchus, Bāwīṭ, and Saqqara. It is thus highly probable that the majority of the Ahnās carvings belonged to the architecture of medium-sized tomb buildings of late antique character, provided with one or more niches, doors, and corner pilasters, and cornices in their interior.

The material of the Ahnās sculpture consists of niche heads, column and pilaster capitals, fragments of cornices, and a small number of other architectural members (figural pilaster base, large tondo, etc.). The majority belonged to buildings of rather small dimensions. Some friezes come from the interior architecture of larger, perhaps public, edifices. The capitals made of imported marble are Egyptian works. The niche pediments are partly semicircular, partly variants of a broken pediment type known from the architecture of the eastern Roman provinces, the prototype of which seems to have been developed within late Hellenistic "miniature" architecture in Alexandria. It is also probable that the semicircular niche heads similarly followed late Hellenistic Alexandrian models. Most niche heads show figure work representing Greek mythological subjects that had a specific sepulchral significance in Roman and late antique art and were further personifications of Hellenistic and Roman characters. An exceptional broken pediment is decorated with two genies holding a cross. The friezes are also decorated with figural representations of Greek mythological subjects or with foliate ornaments including peopled scrolls. From the preserved fragments no canonical order(s) can be reconstructed but the use of traditional elements in niche heads (bead and reel, egg and dart, bracketed cornice, shell) and in cornices (egg and dart, leaves, frieze) does not differ to a considerable extent from the average reduced orders of late antique architecture.

Some of the themes on Ahnās sculptures are: personification of the Earth, the Earth and the Nile, the Nile alone, Tyche, the birth of Aphrodite, Dionysus, Leda and the swan, Daphne, Orpheus, and Herakles and scenes from his legend.

According to Monneret de Villard, the Ahnās carvings date from the period between the late second and late fifth centuries. Kitzinger distinguished a soft-style and hard-style group and demonstrated close connections between the soft style and the developed phase of Oxyrhynchus carvings. He proposed a date between the late fourth and the mid-fifth centuries for the first group. The hard style postdates in his view the soft group and predates the early phase of Saqqara and Bāwīṭ, that is, the sixth century. A later study classified the broken pediments according to a typological-chronological scheme, the starting point of which is the example in the Coptic Museum (No. 7050). The figural decoration displays stylistic connections with late tetrarchic–early Constantinian porphyry sculptures. The late phase of the development is marked, for example, by the sculpture in the Coptic Museum (No. 7065) and dated in the fifth century. This chronological scheme was accepted by H. G. Severin, who demonstrated that the so-called south church at Bāwīṭ was built originally in the fourth century as a pagan sepulchral chapel and was rebuilt in the sixth century with the use of fourth-century architectural elements left in their original place, of fourth- and fifth-century *spolia*, and of members (capitals, pilaster, bases, friezes) carved for the rebuilding.

In a later study Severin maintained (in contrast to Kitzinger's low, mid-fifth-century dating) the high dating of the Ahnās pilaster capitals, but also allowed other datings before the middle of the fifth century, thus disregarding the considerable stylistic differences between these and the firmly datable carvings in Suhāj from the middle of the fifth century.

A recent investigation tried to show that (1) Kitzinger's soft and hard styles were largely contemporaneous; (2) the Ahnās sequence is contemporary with the Oxyrhynchus sequence; (3) stylistic trends observed in the Ahnās and Oxyrhynchus material occur also in the fourth- and fifth-century architecture at al-Ashmūnayn, Bāwīṭ, and Saqqara; and (4) the early phase of the figural sculpture at Ahnās is related to Constantinian porphyry sculpture, and its further development received inspirations from Constantinople; however, the form of mediation is unknown.

The Ahnās material and related carvings from other sites can be divided into three chronological phases, each consisting of pieces demonstrating the survival of different stylistic traditions and trends. As a key monument of stylistic plurality, an example is a frieze showing side by side all soft and hard types of acanthus scrolls occurring in the course of the fourth century. The date of Phase I is indicated by two pieces in the Coptic Museum (Nos. 7051 and 7348), and further by Oxyrhynchus capitals: first third of the fourth century. The Coptic Museum's exhibits 7276, 7050, 7052, the Alexandria Greco-Roman Museum's No. 14145, and a series of mythological reliefs of unknown provenance also belong in Phase I. Phase II embraces carvings made around the middle of the fourth century: foliage friezes from Ahnās and Oxyrhynchus, hard-style niche pediments with figural decoration and interlaced acanthus foliage (the latter also appears independently on larger friezes). A niche head decorated with two genies holding a cross (Coptic Museum, No. 7285) belongs to this phase, and the characteristic acanthus foliage forms, as well as the angular style of the Ahnās pieces made in the third quarter of the century, also appear in al-Ashmūnayn, Bāwīṭ, and Saqqara. Phase III is stylistically and typologically connected to marble capitals found at Ahnās and al-Ashmūnayn and to limestone capitals from Ahnās, Oxyrhynchus, Bāwīṭ, and Saqqara. They are characterized by leaves with touching tips, degenerate or entirely omitted caulicdes, and unorthodox proportions; the uppermost tips of each acanthus lobe are curved up to the lowest tips of the next lobe in such a way that there appear small elliptical eyes between the lobes. These capitals slightly predate the propylaeum capitals of the Hagia Sophia and the capitals from the Golden Gate and other pieces in Jerusalem from the last quarter of the fourth century.

The type survived in Ahnās and Saqqara in a still more angular and dry style in the first half of the fifth century. Acanthus forms of capitals such as those mentioned above occur on friezes and niche heads with figures, in a rather clumsy execution attempting a graphic, linear effect as to the foliage. Monuments of Phase III range from the last quarter of the fourth century to the middle of the fifth. Its end is represented, for example, by the capitals in the Coptic Museum (Nos. 7074, 7068, 7035, 7062), and by some Oxyrhynchus fragments. The mid-fifth-century date of some pagan sepulchral buildings at Ahnās and Oxyrhynchus is indicated by the occurrence of the specific "Golden-Gate-type" acanthi. In Oxyrhynchus also appears an acanthus scroll type that goes back to the decoration of the entablature on the Hagia Sophia propylaeum.

BIBLIOGRAPHY

Aḥmad Kamāl, ed. *Le livres des perles enfouies et du mystère précieux.* Cairo, 1907.

Almagro, M., and F. J. Presedo. "Les fouilles à Hérakleopolis Magna 1976." *Acts of the 1st International Conference of Egyptology,* pp. 67–71. Berlin, 1979.

Badawy, A. *Coptic Art and Archaeology.* Cambridge, Mass., 1978.

Beckwith, J. *Coptic Sculpture, 300–1300.* London, 1963.

Bell, H. I. *Egypt from Alexander the Great to the Arab Conquest.* Oxford, 1948.

Bonnet, H. *Reallexikon der ägyptischen Religionsgeschichte.* Berlin, 1952.

Breccia, E. *Le Musée Gréco-Romain, 1931–1932.* Bergamo, 1933.

Brilliant, R. *Age of Spirituality,* ed. K. Weitzmann. Catalogue of the Metropolitan Museum Exhibition. New York, 1979.

Bouriant, U. *Actes du concile d'Ephèse. Texte copte,* pp. 71, 130. Cairo, 1892.

Calderini, A. *Dizionario dei nomi geografici e topografici dell' Egitto Greco-romano,* Vols. 2, 3. Milan, 1975.

Chassinat, E. "Fouilles à Bawit." *Mémoires publiés par les membres de l'Institut français d'Archeology orientale* 13 (1911):pls. 42/43.

Crum, W. E. *Catalogue of the Coptic MSS in the British Museum,* no. 532. London, 1905.

Diechman, F. W. *Die Spolien in der spätantiken Architektur,* pp. 60ff. Munich, 1975.

Del Francia, L. *Un tessuto copto con nascita di Afrodite. Alessandria e il mondo ellenistico-romano, Fs A. Adriani,* Vol. 2, fig. 6. Museum of Kom Washim, Rome, 1984.

Effenberger, A. "Scultura e arte minore copta." *Cahiers coptes d'archéologie biblique* 28 (1981):65–102.

Farouk Gomaa. "Herakleopolis Magna." In *Lexikon der Ägyptologie,* Vol. 2, p. 1125. Wiesbaden, 1977.

Gayet, A. *L'art copte,* pp. 106ff. Paris, 1902.

Grenfell, B. P. *Revenue Laws of Ptolemy Philadelphus.* Oxford, 1896.

Griffith, F. L. *Catalogue of the Demotic Papyri in the Rylands Library,* Vol. 1, p. 220, nos. 14, 347. Manchester, 1909.

Grossmann, P., and H. G. Severin. "Reinigungsarbeiten im Jeremiaskloster bei Saqqara. Vierter vorläufiger Bericht." *Mitteilungen des deutschen archäologischen Instituts—Abteilung Kairo* 38 (1982):155–93.

Helck, W. *Die altägyptischen Gaue.* Wiesbaden, 1974.

Ibn Ḥawqal. *Kitāb Ṣūrat al-arḍ,* ed. M. J. de Goeje. Leiden, 1873.

Ibn Khurdādhbah. *Kitāb al-Masālik wa-al-Mamālik,* ed. M. J. de Goeje. Leiden, 1889; repr. 1967.

Kautzsch, R. *Kapitelstudien,* nos. 1ff. Berlin and Leipzig, 1936.

Kitchen, K. A. *The Third Intermediate Period in Egypt (1100–650 B.C.).* Warminster, 1973.

Kitzinger, E. "Notes on Early Coptic Sculpture." *Archaeologia* 87 (1938):181–215.

Krautheimer, R. *Early Christian and Byzantine Architecture,* fig. 54. Harmondsworth, 1979.

Lauzière, J. "Le mythe de Léda dans l'art copte." *Bulletin de l'Association des amis de l'art copte* 2 (1936):38–46.

Maspero, J., and G. Wiet. *Matériaux pour servir à la géographie de l'Egypte,* Vol. 1. Cairo, 1914.

Monneret de Villard, U. *La scultura ad Ahnas. Note sull'origine dell'arte copta.* Milan, 1923.

Munier, H. *Recueil des listes époscopales de l'église copte.* Cairo, 1945.

Naville, E.; P. E. Newberry; and G. W. Fraser. *The Season's Work at Ahnas and Beni Hasan. Special Extra Report of the EEF 1890–1891*, pp. 7–8. London, 1891.

Naville, E., and T. Hayter Lewis. *Ahnas el Medineh (Heracleopolis Magna). Eleventh Memoir of the EEF*, pp. 32–34. London, 1894.

Pensebene, I. *I capitelli. Scavi di Ostia VII*, nos. 355–68. Rome, 1973.

Petrie, W. M. F. *Ehnasya 1904. Twenty-sixth Memoir of the EEF*. London, 1905.

______. *Sedment*. London, 1924.

Quibell, J. E. *Excavations at Saqqara 1908–1909, 1909–1910*. Cairo, 1912.

Raouf Habib. *The Coptic Museum. A General Guide*. Cairo, 1967.

Severin, H. G. "Zur Süd-Kirche von Bawit." *Mitteilungen des deutschen archäeologischen Instituts—Abteilung Kairo* 33 (1977a): 113–24.

______. "Frühchristliche Skulptur und Malerei in Ägypten." In *Spätantike und frühes Christentum*, ed. B. Brenk. Propyläen Kunstgeschichte Suppl. 1. Berlin, 1977b.

______. "Problemi di scultura tardoantica in Egitto." *Corsi Ravenna* 28 (1981a):315–36.

______. "Gli scavi eseguiti ad Ahnas, Bahnasa, Bawit e Saqqara: storia delle interpretazioni e nuovi risultati." *Corsi Ravenna* 28 (1981b):299–314.

______. "Egitto 3. Scultura." In *Dizionario patristico e di antichita cristiana*, Vol. 1. Casale Monferrato, 1983.

Strzygowski, J. *Koptische Kunst*. Wien, 1904.

Török, L. "On the Chronology of the Ahnas Sculpture." *Acta antiqua academiae scientiarum Hungaricae* 22 (1970):163–82.

______. "Notes on Pre-Coptic and Coptic Art." *Acta Archaeologica Hungarica* 29 (1977):125–53.

______. "Notes on the Chronology of Late Antique Stone Sculpture in Egypt." *Acts of the 3rd International Congress of Coptic Studies*. Warsaw, 1984.

Torp, H. "Leda Christiana. The Problem of the Interpretation of Coptic Sculpture with Mythological Motifs." *Acta IRN* 4 (1969):101–12.

Wace, A. J. B.; A. H. S. Megaw; and T. C. Skeat. *Hermopolis Magna: Ashmunein. The Ptolemaic Sanctuary and the Basilica*. Alexandria, 1959.

Wulff, O. *Altchristliche und mittelalterliche byzantinische und italienische Bildwerke*, Vol. 1. Berlin, 1909.

Zoega, G. *Catalogus codicum sopticorum manuscriptorum*, pp. 135ff. Rome, 1810.

LÁSZLÓ TÖRÖK

AHRŪN IBN A'YAN AL-QASS, a priest and physician of Alexandria who, with PAUL OF AIGINA, was one of the last great physicians of the School of Alexandria. Contrary to the opinion of F. Sezgin, who thinks that Ahrūn lived in the sixth century, he lived in the seventh century and at the beginning of the eighth century as can be deduced from a verse dated 720–721, composed by the poet al-Ḥakam ibn 'Abdal.

Ahrūn composed a thirty-volume medical anthology entitled *Pandektēs* or *Syntagma*, which was translated into Syriac by Gōsiōs in the thirteenth century, as stated by Bar Hebraeus (d. 1686). According to the ninth-century historian of medicine, Ibn Juljul, it would have been translated from Syriac into Arabic with the title *al-Kunnāsh* (Anthology) by the Jew Māsarjawayh al-Baṣrī at the beginning of the seventh century, but this is doubtful. The Greek text and the Syriac translation have been lost. Approximately one hundred extracts survive in the medical encyclopedia of Muḥhammad ibn Zakariyyā al-Rāzī (865–925), entitled *al-Ḥāwī* (*Continens* in Latin). These extracts have been listed by Sezgin (1970) and Ullmann (1970). Al-Qifṭī (p. 324, ll. 17–18) states concerning the Ahrūn anthology that it is "the best of the ancient medical anthologies."

This work was well known to the medieval Arabic physicians. It is quoted by Yuḥanna ibn Māsawayh (777–857), 'Alī ibn Ibrāhīm ibn Bakhtīshū' in the second half of the eleventh century, al-Ghāfiqī in the twelfth century, al-Qalānisī in 1194, Maimonides (1139–1204), Ibn al-Bayṭār (d. 1248), Najm al-Dīn Maḥmūd al-Shīrāzī (d. 1330), the vizier Lisān al-Dīn Ibn al-Khaṭīb (d. 1374), and others.

Apart from this magnum opus, al-Rāzī five times quotes a *Kitāb al-Fā'iq*, which is probably an extract of the foregoing. Another extract survives in Arabic with the title *Kitāb al-Adwiyah al-Qātilah* (Book of Lethal Medicines) in the manuscript library of the Museum of Baghdād.

BIBLIOGRAPHY

Dietrich, A. "Ahrun." In *Encyclopédie de l'Islam*, 2nd ed., suppl. 1–2, pp. 52–53. Leiden, 1980 (French edition).

Jamāl al-Dīn . . . Ibn al-Qīfti. *Tārīkh al-Ḥukamā'*, ed. Julius Lippert. Leipzig, 1903.

Sezgin, F. *Geschichte des arabischen Schrifttums*, Vol. 3, pp. 168–70 (with bibliography). Leiden, 1970. Still in progress.

Ullmann, M. *Die Medizin im Islam*, pp. 87–89 (with bibliography). Leiden, 1970.

KHALIL SAMIR, S.J.

AISLE. *See* Architectural Elements of Churches.

AJBIYAH. *See* Canonical Hours, Book of.

AKHBARIYYAH, AL-. *See* Karm al-Akhbariyyah.

AKHMĪM, city on the right bank of the Nile, about 250 miles (467 km) south of Cairo. In Byzantine times Akhmīm was known as Panopolis. It remains today the chief town of the province of Suhāj. Akhmīm is a name of pharaonic times (Chemmis) clothed in Arabic.

Monasteries

Pachomian Establishments

The Greek and Coptic lives relate that PACHOMIUS established three monasteries in the neighborhood of the town of Akhmīm. In chronological order, the first of the three was that of Tse or Tasi "in the land of Akhmīm," which was the sixth Pachomian establishment; the second came a little later at the request of Arius, bishop of Akhmīm, but the name of the place is not mentioned; the third was that of Tesmine, which in the Coptic (Sahidic) recension is ninth in the list of Pachomius' religious houses.

No doubt because L. T. Lefort did not know the Coptic leaves published by Coquin (1979, pp. 212–23), he did not mention the second monastery near Akhmīm in his article on the early Pachomian monasteries (1939, pp. 403–404) and thus counts only two at Akhmīm. Efforts to determine the precise locations of these three monasteries, reported by M. Jullien (1901) and H. Gautier (1904, 1912), have proved fruitless.

Other Monasteries

In discussing Akhmīm, al-Maqrīzī, the fifteenth-century Muslim historian of the Copts, mentions a number of monasteries in existence in his own day. These are the Monastery of the Seven Mountains (DAYR AL-SAB'AT JIBĀL); the Monastery of the Weeping Willow (Dayr al-Ṣufṣāfah); Dayr Ṣabrah; and the Monastery of Apa Bisādah the Bishop (Dayr Abī Bisādah al-Usquf).

Several monasteries still exist in the area. East of Akhmīm are DAYR AL-MALĀK MĪKHĀ'ĪL (called Dayr Ṣabrah by al-Maqrīzī); DAYR AL-SHUHADĀ'; DAYR AL-'ADHRĀ'; DAYR AL-MADWID (called Dayr al-Sab'at Jibāl by al-Maqrīzī; also named Dayr al-Ṣufṣāfah); and DAYR AL-QURQĀS (under the patronage of Dīsqūrūs and Sklābiyūs). North of Akhmīm are DAYR ANBĀ BĀKHŪM at Ṣawam'āt al-Sharq and DAYR MĀR TŪMĀS founded at Shinshif at Naj' al-Dayr. South of Akhmīm are DAYR MĀR JIRJIS AL-ḤADĪDĪ (also named of Awlūjiyūs and Arsāniyūs), and DAYR ANBĀ BISĀDAH al-Usquf, opposite al-Manshiyyah.

BIBLIOGRAPHY

Amélineau, E. *Géographie de l'Egypte à l'époque copte*, pp. 18–22, 485, 496–97. Paris, 1893.
Coquin, R.-G. "Un complément aux vies sahidiques de Pachôme: Le Manuscrit IFAO Copte 3." *Bulletin de l'Institut français d'Archéologie orientale* 79 (1979):209–247.
Gauthier, H. "Notes géographiques sur le nome panopolite." *Bulletin de l'Institut français d'archéologie orientale* 4 (1905) 39–101. On Akhmim, 93–4, 103.
______. "Nouvelles notes géographiques sur le nome panopolite." *Bulletin de l'Institut français d'archéologie orientale* 10 (1912): 93–94, 103.
Jullien, M. "A la recherche de Tabenne et des autres monastères fondés par saint Pachôme." *Etudes* 89 (1901): 238–58. On Akhmim, 254–56.
Lefort, L. T. "Les Premiers Monastères pachômiens: Explorations topographiques." *Le Muséon* 52 (1939):379–407.
Meinardus, O. F. A. *Christian Egypt, Ancient and Modern*, pp. 295–96. Cairo, 1977.
Salim, N. *Story of the Martyrs Anba Bākhūm and His Sister Datosham and the Martyrs of Akhmīm* (Arabic). Cairo, 1967.
Viaud, G. from the notes of J. Muyser. *Les Pèlerinages coptes en Egypte*, pp. 57–58. [Cairo], 1979.

RENÉ-GEORGES COQUIN

Churches in Akhmīm

Of the numerous churches in Akhmīm two are of some historical interest.

The Church of Abū Sayfayn is situated in the southeastern part of the city. A walled enclosure is partitioned into two unequal parts by a wall. The larger area contains a cemetery of the Ottoman period and some dependent structures. The smaller area leads to two adjoining churches. One, which was added in the twentieth century, is a three-aisled BASILICA with rectangular sanctuaries. The other, earlier church represents a local variant of a type that evolved in the Mamluk period, the domed hall church (*Hallenkirche*) with columns (for the type, see Grossmann, 1982, p. 196). As originally constructed, Abū Sayfayn was five units (i.e., rooms or bays) wide and three deep. The east end consisted of three sanctuaries flanked by rectangular rooms, with two bays in front of each sanctuary and room. The northern row of two bays and a corner room were destroyed when the adjoining church was built. Domes on squinches pierced by windows surmount the bays in front of the central sanctuary, and domes on pendentives cover the side bays. The three sanctuaries have a shape favored in other local churches: straight sides ending in semicircular apses (see DAYR AL-'ADHRĀ' near Akhmīm), each decorated with rounded niches. The sanctuaries are closed off by wooden screens, each with a door in the middle and two side windows. Geometrical designs are inlaid in the left screen and painted on the other two. The columns, arches, and domes are of fired brick painted black and red in cross patterns, not always following the mortar joints (see Dayr al-'Adhrā' [Akhmīm] for local parallels). The rest of the church is built of mud brick, plastered and whitewashed. To the right of the entrance stands a marble LAQQĀN (epiphany tank). Behind the central altar is the bishop's throne.

The second structure of interest is the complex of DAYR SITT DIMYĀNAH, which is situated on the northern edge of the city. From an outer court a corridor leads to Sitt Dimyānah. The Church of the Virgin is on the right of the corridor. Sitt Dimyānah is the older and sits 20 inches (50 cm) lower than the Church of the Virgin. It represents a modified form of the domed hall church with columns. It has three deep sanctuaries with straight walls culminating in curves, as in several other churches of the area, such as Dayr al-'Adhrā' near Akhmīm, but at Sitt Dimyānah each sanctuary is shaped and articulated slightly differently. At the back of the central sanctuary is a bishop's throne. Behind the northern sanctuary there is a corridor, probably originally sion.

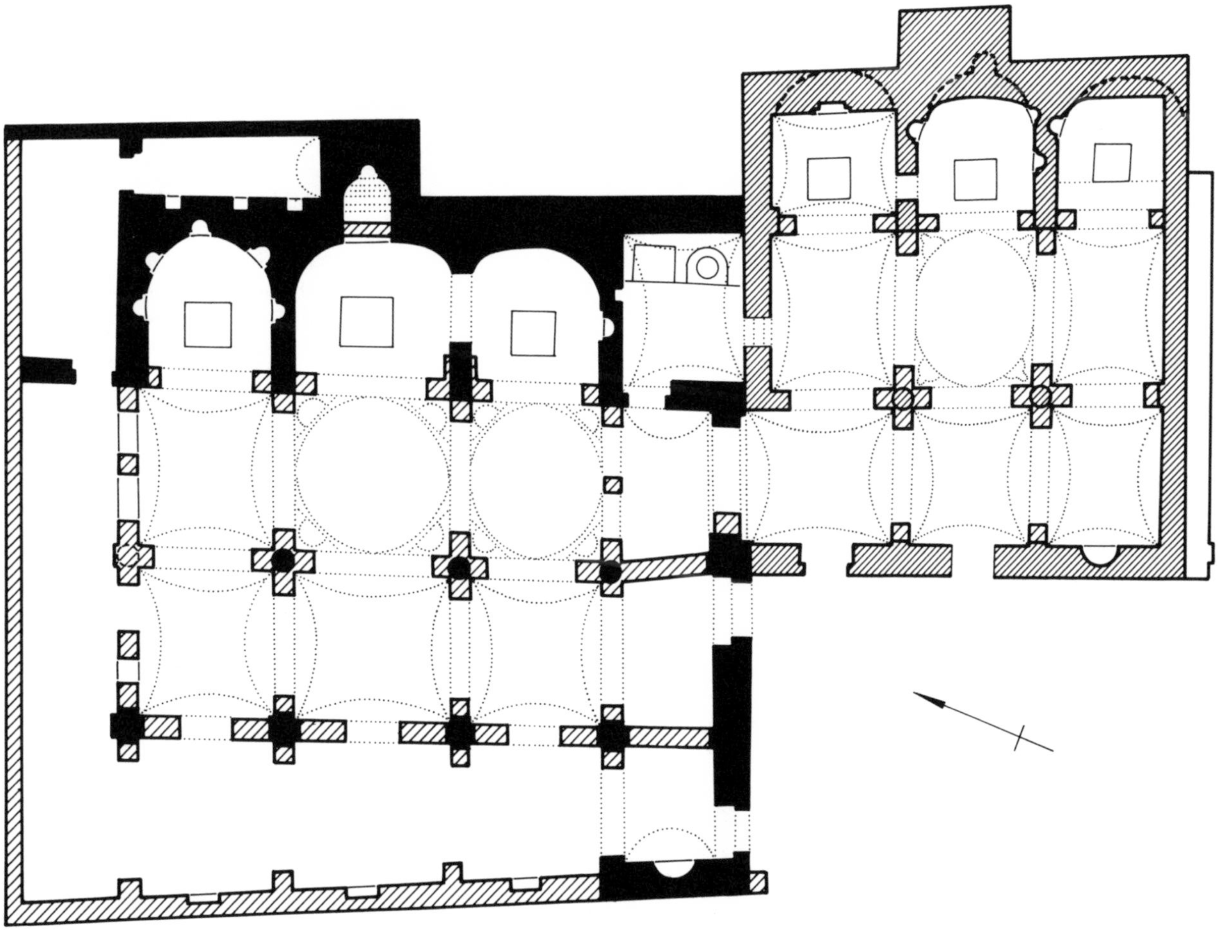

Plan of Dayr Sitt Dimyānah, Akhmīm. *Courtesy Peter Grossmann.*

balanced by one on the south, as in Dayr Mār Jirjis al-Ḥadīdī (for such corridors generally, see Dayr al-ʿAdhrāʾ). The two bays in front of the central and south sanctuaries are covered by domes on squinches; the southern three bays, by a barrel vault; and the remaining bays, by domes on pendentives. For better support, the originally free-standing columns between the bays have subsequently been built into walls, thereby forming irregularly shaped corridors. In the early 1980s the whole interior was plastered and painted. It is said to have been previously painted in red-and-black patterns with white divisions. A sixteenth-century date still visible on the extensively restored *hijāb* (iconostasis) provides a terminus ante quem for Sitt Dimiyānah and probably for the other local churches with similar sanctuaries and corridors. The later Church of the Virgin is in poor repair. It has a roughly square plan. As in Sitt Dimyānah, each sanctuary is shaped differently, and the supporting columns are embedded in the walls. The dome in front of the central sanctuary is on squinches, and the others, on pendentives.

BIBLIOGRAPHY

Grossmann, P. *Mittelalterliche Langhauskuppelkirchen und verwandte Typen in Oberägypten.* Glückstadt, 1982.

SHELA MCNALLY

AKHMĪM FRAGMENTS

AKHMĪM FRAGMENTS (P. Cair. 10759, in *Catalogue général des antiquités égyptiennes du Musée du Caire,* ed. B. P. Grenfell and A. S. Hunt [Oxford, 1903]), a parchment codex of thirty-three leaves (15 × 12 cm) with several apocryphal writings in Greek: parts of the Gospel of Peter (van Haelst no. 598), the Apocalypse of Peter (van Haelst no. 617), and two fragments of the book of Enoch (van Haelst no. 575). In the binding was found a parchment page with parts of the martyrdom of Julianus (van Haelst no. 707). The fragments, discovered in 1886/1887 in Akhmīm, date from between the eighth and the twelfth centuries, according to Bouriant and to Lods. Earlier datings are in van Haelst (nos. 575, 598, 617).

BIBLIOGRAPHY

Bouriant, U. "Fragments du texte du livre d'Enoch et de quelques écrits attribués à saint Pierre." *Mémoires de la Mission archéologique française au Caire* 9, 1 (1892):91–147.

Haelst, J. van. *Catalogue des papyrus littéraires juifs et chrétiens.* Paris, 1976.

MARTIN KRAUSE

AKHMIMIC DIALECT.

AKHMIMIC DIALECT. *See* Appendix.

ʿALAM ṢALĪB AL-IBNĀSĪ, AL-.

ʿALAM ṢALĪB AL-IBNĀSĪ, AL-. *Shaykh* al-ʿAlam is known from two colophons of Coptic Arabic manuscripts that are kept at the Vatican and London. They describe him as a deacon and archon (prominent citizen) who was very generous and devout, practicing hospitality to strangers, and educating orphans. He was the son of the deacon and archon al-MAKĪN JIRJIS. As the titles al-ʿAlam and al-Makīn show, this was a family of prominent citizens, who were high-ranking state officials from Ibnās but settled in Cairo. Al-ʿAlam lived there from 1585 to 1587.

This information is found in the long colophon of the Vatican manuscript (fol. 351b), published and translated by A. Hebbelynck and A. van Lantschoot (Vol. 1, pp. 22–23). Several corrections to their translation have to be made, of which three are essential: (1) al-ʿAlam is a title *(laqab)* given to certain prominent citizens. This was not grasped by Hebbelynek and Lantschoot, who read *al-shaykh al-muʿallim,* which they translated as "magister doctus"; (2) the word *najl* (son), which appears twice, was read as *JL* and translated "gloria"; and (3) the title *al-makīn* was also interpreted as an adjective and translated "gloria . . . magistri *constantis" (najl . . . al-shaykh al-Makīn).*

The London manuscript (British Library, Or. 1326) was written between 12 Baramhāt A.M. 1301/8 March 1585 and 13 Tūt A.M. 1303/10 September 1586. It comprises 326 folios, containing the second volume of the Arabic Bible from Ezekiel to Revelation, copied by the priest Faḍlallāh in his house in Ḥārit Zuwaylah, on commission from al-ʿAlam. This manuscript was used as the basis for the edition of the Arabic text of the Polyglot Bible of London.

The Vatican manuscript (Vatican Library, Coptic 8), dated 28 Bashans 1303/2 June 1587, comprises 353 folios (33 × 24 cm), containing the four Gospels in Bohairic Coptic and Arabic; the version is the Egyptian Vulgate, copied by Arghādiyūs or Arcadius ibn Yūḥannā, on commission from al-ʿAlam.

BIBLIOGRAPHY

Hebbelynck, A., and A. van Lantschoot. *Codices Coptici Vaticani Barberiniani Borgiani Rossiani,* Vol. 1. Codices Coptici Vaticani, pp. 19–23. Vatican City, 1937.

Rieu, C. *Supplement to the Catalogue of the Arabic Manuscripts in the British Museum,* pp. 1–4. London, 1894.

KHALIL SAMIR, S. J.

'ALAM SHALTŪT (Maryūt, about 18 miles [30 km] south of 'Amriyyah), site of the discovery of a building of several rooms with abundant painting from the early Christian period. Unfortunately, it is only incompletely excavated, so that the purpose of the building remains unclear.

BIBLIOGRAPHY

Adriani, A. *Annuaire du Musée Gréco-Romain,* pp. 151–58. Alexandria, 1940.

PETER GROSSMANN

ALEF. *See* Ethiopian Church Saints.

ALEXANDER I, nineteenth patriarch of the See of Saint Mark (312–326).

Life

Alexander succeeded ACHILLAS, who died in the year 312, after one of the shortest episcopates in Coptic history. His death was ascribed by the pious Copts to supernatural chastisement for breaking the command of PETER I, "Seal of the Martyrs," by accepting ARIUS into communion. On the eve of the succession of Alexander, the imperial throne was contested by six claimants after the abdication of Diocletian. They were Galerius, Maximinus, Maximianus, Maxentius, Licinius, and Constantine. One by one, these claimants disappeared either by natural death or by falling in the field of battle in civil wars.

The high point in this strife was the Battle of Milvian Bridge in 312, where Maxentius perished at the hands of Constantine, who reportedly saw a flaming cross in the sky with the Greek dictum *en toutoi nika,* "in this sign, conquer." Subsequently Constantine and Licinius converged on Milan in 313 as sole augustal survivors. There Constantine issued his famous Edict of Milan, confirming the religious toleration previously proclaimed by Galerius before his death, and recognizing Christianity as the official religion of the state. This was shortly after Alexander's accession to the throne of Saint Mark and the formal termination of Christian persecutions. In the following year, however, Licinius, in a struggle with Constantine for supreme and undivided authority, resumed some persecutions in the East as a punishment to the Christian supporters of his adversary. But in 324 Constantine inflicted final defeat on Licinius at Chrysopolis (modern Üsküdar) and had him executed in the following year, establishing himself as sole emperor, with the freedom to secure the unity of all Christians in a church in Alexandria where Alexander was facing schism.

Alexander had to deal with three problems throughout his episcopate. He was first troubled over the timing of Easter observance by a schismatic faction led by a certain Erescentius. Alexander was constrained to write a special treatise on this paschal controversy, referring to previous patristic declarations by DIONYSIUS THE GREAT. This subject remained a sore point until it was settled by the bishops at the Council of Nicaea in 325.

The second problem that faced the patriarch occurred at Lycopolis in Upper Egypt, where Bishop MELITIUS had been calumniating Achillas, as he later continued to do against Alexander, even lodging a formal complaint against him to the imperial court under Constantine. The court paid no great attention to it. Still more seriously, Melitius seems to have established a kind of alliance with the most dangerous of the patriarch's adversaries, Arius. Further, he consecrated his own schismatic bishops over his ecclesiastical superior's head. The Melitian schism remained in full force until it was temporarily settled at Nicaea in 325, through the wisdom of the patriarch, who compromised in order to win the bishop back to the fold, thus ending his union with Arius.

The third problem faced by Alexander concerned the most dangerous of all heretical movements, that of Arius, who was excommunicated by Peter I, only to be readmitted by Achillas and placed as presbyter of the most ancient of Alexandrian churches, at Bucalis. The church was located in the most populous district of the metropolis, where Arius could exercise a great influence on the Christian population. Arius had previously posed as a rival to Alexander at the time of his elevation to the episcopate. Open hostilities between the two occurred when Alexander declared the unity of the Trinity in one of his sermons. Arius at once branded his declaration as mere SABELLIANISM. Since the Son of God was created by the Father, he argued, the Son could not be coeternal with his Father. This was the beginning of a long argument, which the future heresiarch developed into horrifying dimensions as he acquired the support of expanding numbers of followers. He was supported in his views by a number of deacons, including Euzonius, Macarius, Julius, Menas, and Helladius, as well as a presbyter by the name of Colluthius, who separated himself from his bishop and started to ordain presbyters of his own. Arius was thus encouraged to preach his heretical views to a wider public, and his followers increased to a point where the bishop found it necessary to summon two assemblies of priests and deacons to discuss these views. This did not, however, restrain the heresy.

Thus, Alexander called a synod of Alexandria and the neighboring province of Mareotis in 320, this time for the trial and condemnation of those doctrines and their author. Thirty-six presbyters and forty-four deacons, including young ATHANASIUS, subscribed to a sentence of condemnation and signed a document to that effect. Nevertheless, the movement kept spreading, notably in Mareotis and Libya, where Arius prevailed upon Secundus, bishop of Ptolemais, and Thomas of Marmarica to unite with the MELITIANS in Lycopolis. The whole church was thus threatened with schism. In 321 Alexander decided to convoke a general council of the whole diocese to settle the problem on a national basis. Attendance at this council reached about one hundred members, and here again Arius asserted that the Son could not have existed before the time of his creation. He further proclaimed that the Son was not similar to the Father in substance, a proclamation that horrified the bishop and the whole council, whereupon Arius was placed under ANATHEMA until he recanted his errors.

The cornered Arius fled to Palestine, where he secured the support of numerous bishops, who wrote in his favor to Alexander. His greatest support came from Eusebius, bishop of Nicomedia, who was closely connected with the imperial court at the Byzantine capital. Thus, the Arian heresy began to assume international dimensions, and the emperor himself found it necessary to issue a written appeal for the unity of the church and the repudiation of what he had regarded as petty discussions on unintelligible minutiae. But neither the imperial brief nor the episcopal epistles could resolve these matters of serious dogma. The Arians in Alexandria took to violence in defense of their creed, and Alexander wrote an encyclical to all his brother bishops of Christendom, stating the history of the Arian doctrine and describing the errors of Arius. He was forced to expose Eusebius, bishop of Nicomedia, whose support for the heretical views of the religious outcast was demonstrated by the fact that he had assembled a provincial council of Bithynia, which scorned Arius' excommunication and anathematization by the councils and bishop of Alexandria by formally admitting him to the communion of the Syrian church. Arius also received a sympathetic hearing from Paulinus of Tyrus, Eusebius of Caesarea, and Patrophilus of Scythopolis, who seem to have allowed him to assemble his followers for the Divine Office in their churches as he used to do at Bucalis in Alexandria.

It was probably at this time that Arius composed his work entitled *Thalia,* which contains elegant poetry and hymns representing his views. So popular were these hymns that they could be heard everywhere in open places and at the shipyards. In the meantime, the multiple epistles issued by Arius and Alexander solved no problems; on the contrary, they seem to have fed the fire of theological uproar in the metropolis. In the face of what seemed like a universal rebellion against orthodoxy, Alexander issued his tome, a confession of the faith, on the advice of his brilliant deacon Athanasius. This he dispatched to all bishops, requesting them to endorse it by their signature. He succeeded in obtaining approximately 250 signatures on his tome, including about one hundred from his own diocese, fifteen from Cappadocia, thirty-two from Lycia, thirty-seven from Pamphylia, forty-two from Asia, and others that are untraceable. It is interesting to note that Alexander wrote to his namesake, the bishop of Byzantium, complaining about the violence of the Arians and their promulgation of Arius' views on female influence. While promoting his tome in Byzantium, Alexander also communicated with Sylvester of Rome, Macarius of Jerusalem, Asclepius of Gaza, Longinus of Ascalon, Macrinus of Yannina, and Zeno of Tyrus, as well as with many other bishops on the same subject.

The Arian heresy had become a universal problem threatening the peace and unity of the church and of the empire. Hence, Constantine, now sole emperor after the execution of Licinius, his remaining rival, needed to act to stop this disunity on what seemed to him simply theological jargon. He wrote his missive addressed "to Alexander and Arius." Since the letter was written from Nicomedia, we must assume that the Arian-oriented Bishop Eusebius participated in its composition. This royal brief was confided to Hosius, the old and reputed bishop of Cordova, who was to transmit it to the contestants in Alexandria. It ended, "Restore to me quiet days and nights void of care, that henceforward I may have the joy of Pure Light and the gladness of a quiet life. . . .Open to me your reconciliation, the way to the East, which ye have closed by your contentions; and allow me speedily to behold yourselves and all other people at union, so that I may be enabled, with the unanimous accordance of every mouth, to return thanks to God for the common concord and liberty of all" (Neale, 1947, p. 134).

On Hosius' arrival at Alexandria with this royal message, Alexander summoned another general council that seems to have confirmed his tome together with the term "consubstantial." The council sanctioned the excommunication of Arius and the condemnation of the Melitians, which further infuriated the Arians in the metropolis. Arius submitted a formal complaint to the emperor for the injustice imposed on him, and the emperor's response, carried by his imperial couriers, Syncletius and Gandentius, called for the defendant to plead his case before an ecumenical council at the city of Nicaea in Bithynia on 14 June 325. In this way the ecumenical movement was inaugurated. The movement lasted several centuries, and had an immense impact on the progress of the church and the definition of its dogma and doctrines.

At Nicaea, however, 318 divines came from Italy, Spain, Africa, Palestine, Cappadocia, Isauria, Mesopotamia, and Egypt. Even the Goths were represented. This impressive scene included such notable Christian leaders as Macarius of Jerusalem, Eustathius of Antioch, James of Nisibis, Leontius of Caesarea, Hypatius of Gangra, Paul of Neocaesarea, Alexander of Constantinople, Nicasius of Die from Gaul, Protogenes of Sardica, Melitius of Sebastopolis in Armenia, Spiridion of Tremithus in Cyprus, Achilleus of Larissa, Athanasius of Thessaly, Gelasius of Salamis, and many other prelates from the four corners of the old world. Sylvester of Rome was represented by two priests, Vitus and Vincentius. Bishop Alexander of Alexandria was accompanied by twenty prelates, who included Potamon of Heraclea, Paphnutius from the Thebaid, and the formidable young deacon Athanasius, acting as the eloquent mouthpiece of his bishop. The Arian team consisted mainly of Secundus, Zephyrius, Theonas, and Dathes, all from Libya and the Pentapolis. The Arians had their strong sympathizers; first and foremost in the person of Eusebius, bishop of Nicomedia, with his palace association and influence. Others included Eusebius of Caesarea, the ecclesiastical historian; Paulinus of Tyrus; Actius of Lydda; Menophantus of Ephesus; and Theognius of Nicaea.

The proceedings of the council, which opened on 20 May and lasted until 25 July, are monumental and varied. In their totality, they belong elsewhere; our focus here is the Arian controvery. From a special throne prepared for him, Constantine, speaking to the assembly in Latin with a Greek interpreter, pleaded for unity and unanimity. Alexander, who was supposed to preside over the council, replaced himself by Hosius of Cordova, since he could not be both judge and chief accuser. In the ensuing discussions, young Athanasius revealed himself to be the most powerful exponent of orthodoxy against Eusebius of Nicomedia, a fact that made him a target of Arian assaults to the end of his life.

One of the most famous results of the council is the NICENE CREED. Eusebius of Caesarea submitted the text of a creed that was rejected outright by the council, because it did not include specific mention of the consubstantiality of the Son with the Father. Consubstantiality implies that the Son is not only similar but inseparable from the Father, that He is not only like the Father, but of the same substance. This was the orthodox consensus to which the Arians would not subscribe at all.

Hence the orthodox party proceeded to develop their own creed, probably in a closer committee under the leadership of the highly respected Hosius. Contributors may have been Leontius, bishop of Caesarea in Cappadocia, and Hermogenes who later succeeded him in that see. However, the chief framer of the new text of the creed appears to have been Athanasius, who must have been inspired by Alexander. The final and rather short and pointed version presented to the council read as follows:

> We believe in one God, the Father Almighty, Maker of all Things, visible and invisible:
>
> And in one Lord Jesus Christ, the only Begotten Son of God, begotten of the Father, that is, of the Substance of the Father, God of God, Light of Light, very God of very God, begotten not made, consubstantial with the Father: by whom all things were made, both in heaven and on earth:

Who for us men and for our salvation came down, and was incarnate, and was made Man: He suffered, and rose again the third day, and ascended into heaven: and shall come again to judge the quick and the dead.

And we believe in the Holy Ghost.

And for them that say, concerning the Son of God, there was a time when He was not, and He was not before He was produced, and He was produced from things that are not, and, He is of another substance or essence, or created, or subject to conversion or mutation, the Catholic and Apostolic Church faith, let them be anathema

[text in Neale, 1947, p. 145].

The majority of the fathers accepted this text. Only seventeen opposed it—mainly because of the term "consubstantial." In the end and after some discussion, only five remained adamant in their opposition, and the rest were swayed to join the majority. The five dissenters were Eusebius of Nicomedia, Theognius of Nicaea, Maris of Chalcedon, and Secundus and Theonas from Libya. Eusebius attempted to use his influence at the imperial palace without avail, and he knew that his defeat might spell his deposition. Cornered between acceptance of the creed or exile, Maris reluctantly signed the document. Eusebius and Theognius are said to have subscribed to the creed with the addition of the Greek letter "iota" to the HOMOOUSION to turn the term into HOMOIOUSION, thus rendering the Son of God "of like substance" instead of "of the same substance," but this allegation is based on Arian sources (Neale, 1947, pp. 145–46). Eusebius, however, refused to accept the sentence of anathema against Arius. Secundus and Theonas remained firm in their total opposition and, with Arius, they were banished by imperial decree to the province of Illyria.

This ended Alexander's battle with Arianism, but the Arian troubles survived Nicaea and Patriarch Alexander into the age of Athanasius, who continued to combat the heresy and the heresiarch.

The council also dealt with the schism of Melitius, and here Alexander exercised leniency in order to try to keep the Melitians from aligning with the Arians. Melitius was allowed to remain in the communion of the church and even retain the title of bishop, but he was not permitted to exercise episcopal powers. His appointees could retain the title to which they were elevated by him, but their occupancy of an episcopal see would be contingent on the existence of a free seat vacated by death from those previously consecrated by Alexandria.

On the paschal controversy, the bishop of Alexandria was empowered to make his own decision and communicate it to Rome and the rest of Christendom. Another canon allowed the Egyptians to observe their ancient customs in regard to clerical celibacy. On the advice of Paphnutius, an anchorite, no priest could be allowed to marry after taking holy orders.

Five months after his return from Nicaea, Alexander died, according to one source on 22 Baramūdah/17 April 326. He is commemorated in the Copto-Arabic SYNAXARION on that date.

AZIZ S. ATIYA

Literature and Works

In Coptic literature, Alexander I is represented most fully in Eusebius' *Historia ecclesiastica;* he is also mentioned in the lives and encomiums of his successor, Athanasius the Apostolic. These accounts tend to present Alexander in the shadow of his great successor, who as his secretary (*notarius*) would have led the struggle against Arius and his disciples in his own name, both at Alexandria and at the Council of Nicaea if Alexander had not taken the initiative. According to CONSTANTINE OF ASYŪṬ, it is even said that Alexander was president of the Council of Nicaea (historically, it was Hosius of Cordova). As he was dying, Alexander is supposed to have named Athanasius as his successor.

Of his works, only one collection of letters relative to the Arian controversy was known in antiquity, and of these, only two have survived. Also, a homily *De anima et corpore* (On the soul and the body) is ascribed to him in a Syriac version, but the Coptic version attributes this work to Athanasius.

Coptic literature does attribute to Alexander an *Encomium of Peter the Alexandrian*, known in five codices: VC62.10 (Bohairic, ninth century), VC62.8 (Bohairic, two fragments, ninth century), and three fragmentary codices from the WHITE MONASTERY (ed. Orlandi, 1970). There is also an elaborated Arabic translation to be found in the chapter concerning Alexander in the HISTORY OF THE PATRIARCHS by SĀWĪRUS IBN AL-MUQAFFA'. It is possible to reconstruct the original redaction of this encomium by comparing the various versions in existence. It must have been composed of three segments, which can be characterized as follows: a literary prologue; the main body, which recounts his birth, life, and martyrdom, with vivid descriptions of the many miracles wrought at his birth, during his life, and after his death; and a literary epilogue. Except for a few minor variations, the Sahidic and Bohairic redactions are similar, save that the Bohairic version has excluded the martyrdom and posthumous miracles.

The text appears to be a typical, late construction, filled with biblical allusions, vague traditions, and the portrayal of Peter's Passion. The complexity of the literary structure, the theological competence, and the style make it one of the best examples of this literary period, and probably one of the first whose date can be proposed as being at the first half of the seventh century.

TITO ORLANDI

BIBLIOGRAPHY

Altaner, B. *Patrology,* trans. H. C. Graef, pp. 309ff. Freiburg, 1960.

Bardenhewer, O. *Geschichte der altkirchlichen Literatur,* Vol. 3, pp. 34ff. Freiburg im Breisgau and St. Louis, 1913–1932.

Cowell, E. B. "Alexander (St.)." DCB 1, cols. 79–82.

Duchesne, L. M. O., ed. *Le Liber Pontificalis,* Vol. 2, pp. 98ff. Bibliothèque des Ecoles françaises d'Athènes et de Rome, ser. 2. Paris 1886–1892.

Hyvernat, H. *Les Actes des martyrs de l'Egypte,* pp. 247–83. Paris, 1886–1887.

Neale, J. M. *The Patriarchate of Alexandria,* pp. 113ff. London, 1947.

Orlandi, T. "La versione copta (saidica) dell'Encomio di Pietro alessandrino." *Rivista degli Studi Orientali* 45 (1970):151–75.

Quasten, J. *Patrology,* Vol. 3, pp. 13–19. Utrecht and Antwerp, 1975.

ALEXANDER II, forty-third patriarch of the See of Saint Mark (705–730). Little is known about his early life as a layman before he took the monastic vow at ENATON in the region of Mareotis west of Alexandria. There he became well known for his chastity, sanctity, and religious scholarship.

After the death of his predecessor, SIMON I, in 701, the See of Saint Mark remained vacant for approximately four years, during which the faithful continued their search for a worthy successor. In the end, the secretary of the state (*mutawallī al-diwān*) in Alexandria, a Copt by the name of Athanasius, appealed to the governor to permit Anbā Gregorius, bishop of al-Qays, to take charge of the finances of the patriarchate until a new pope was elected. Governor 'Abd al-Azīz ibn Marwān approved, and the necessary steps were taken for the selection of a patriarch. Thus, Athanasius, together with the Coptic scribes, the clergy, and the bishops, unanimously chose Alexander, the monk of Enaton, whose virtues had become known to them. He was taken to Alexandria, where he was consecrated on Saint Mark's commemoration day in A.M. 420/A. D. 704, according to a passage in HISTORY OF THE PATRIARCHS (Vol. 1, pt. 3, p. 304 [text]; p. 50 [trans.]), though this year precedes the 705–730 given on the title page of the same work (p. 302 [text]; p. 48 [trans.]). Of course we have to allow a certain margin in the conversion of this early chronology.

Pope Alexander was a contemporary of several Umayyad caliphs with different attitudes toward the Copts: 'Abd al-Malik ibn Marwān (685–705), Al-Walīd ibn 'Abd al-Malik (705–715), Sulaymān (715–717), 'Umar ibn 'Abd al-'Azīz (717–720), Yazīd II (720–724), and Hishām (724–743). Thus, this patriarch must have lived through some of the most precarious years of Islamic history, including the years of the Umayyad siege of Constantinople (716–718), with its repercussions on the economic situation in Egypt. In fact, the Umayyad failure in the conquest of Byzantium was a signal for its decline and final downfall, which was precipitated by financial pressures aggravated by internal conflict with al-Zubayr's rebellion. In these dire circumstances, the Umayyad caliphs looked at Egypt as the closest resource on which they could prey without mercy to save themselves economically.

This situation started when the governor of Egypt, 'Abd al-Azīz ibn Marwān, decided to relegate his position to his own son al-Aṣbagh. The new governor proved to be one of the worst Egypt had had. His thirst for levying taxes was insatiable, and, curiously, he was aided by a Copt named Benjamin, who showed him all the hiding places of Coptic wealth that could be confiscated. Al-Aṣbagh imposed extraordinary taxation, beyond the normal capitation of the JIZYAH (poll tax), and for the first time in history imposed it on the monks in the desert. Furthermore, he imposed a levy of 2,000 dinars above the normal tax of the KHARAJ (communal tax) on every bishop. So squeezed were the Copts by both legal and illegal imposts that many of them were constrained to convert to Islam as a means of escape from these financial burdens. Such Coptic notables as Buṭrus, the viceroy of Upper Egypt, his brother Theodorus, and his son Theophanes, governor of Mareotis, feigned conversion.

Harboring so much hatred for the Christians, al-Aṣbagh was not satisfied with his financial loot from the Copts. He reviled Christ and spat in the face of the image of Our Lady during a Coptic procession at a monastery in Ḥilwān. The *History of the Patriarchs* states that he was chastized by sudden death, and that his father met his end forty days after his son. The Coptic archon Athanasius, accompanied by his sons, decided to go to Damascus to complain to the caliph, ʿAbd al-Malik. Instead of responding to their appeal by the application of justice, the caliph ordered the arrest of Athanasius and his companion, as well as the confiscation of the whole of their fortunes. In 705 he sent to Egypt a new governor, ʿAbd Allah ibn ʿAbd al-Malik, who proved to be worse than his predecessor. On his arrival in the capital, the patriarch went to greet him. Instead of receiving him, the governor ordered the patriarch's arrest and demanded the immediate payment of 3,000 dinars as a price for his freedom. A deacon by the name of Jirjā al-Tamrāwī, from Damrū, an influential Coptic archon, came forth to appeal for the release of the patriarch under his own guarantee for a few months, during which he would tour Upper Egypt to collect the amount requested from the faithful. Only after the payment of the illegal impost could the patriarch regain the full freedom to return to his capital.

The same story recurred throughout the patriarchate of Alexander II, the only differences being that the financial imposts were multiplied and were accompanied by ferocious treatment of the innocent and helpless subjects. It had been customary for every new caliph to appoint a new governor, who naturally renewed his claim for more taxation beyond the limitations of the *jizyah* and the *kharaj*. People began to flee their domiciles to escape this harsh treatment. The governors resorted to means of forcing the return of escapees and invented all means of realizing their aims, by tattooing, cauterizing, and even chaining their victims with lead and iron bracelets or pendants. Confiscation of property and cattle was not unusual in farmlands. Even death was treated irreverently, by confiscating the property of a deceased person, instead of passing the inheritance to the heirs. Unheard-of humiliations, contrary to the Covenant of ʿUmar with Patriarch BENJAMIN, together with brutal imposts, became the order of the day at the installation of all new governors, who descended on the people like vultures or ferocious animals, without the slightest regard for human dignity. Even the religious personalities, previously exempt from the merciless financial imposts, began to be subjected to the same treatment as the rest of the population. Incarceration, flogging, amputation of limbs, and even outright murder of a delinquent subject were customary punishments. No one could escape the clutches of a new viceroy (*wālī*).

The accession of al-Walīd ibn ʿAbd al-Malik brought about changes in provincial governors, as existing authorities were replaced by friends of al-Walīd. Qurrah Shurayk thus became governor of Egypt in 709. He turned out to be even worse in dealing with his subjects. During his reign, the condition of the country was worsened by a plague outbreak, which killed many Copts and Muslims, including Governor Qurrah in the year 714. His successor, ʿAbd al-Malik ibn Rifāʿah al-Fahmī (714–717), was inaugurated in the midst of an outbreak of famine that killed more people than the previous plague. It was also during the caliphate of al-Walīd that a royal decree was issued to the governor of Egypt to impose the use of Arabic instead of Coptic in the manipulation of the tax registers. In the period of the siege of Constantinople that began in 716, people were forbidden from hosting sailors from Byzantium—which halted the progress of international trade and impoverished the country even more than before, while the caliph's thirst for funding his Byzantine expeditions freed the governor's men to pillage whatever they could find in Egypt. All the gold and silver utensils used in sacramental services were looted, and even pillars of precious colored marble and beautiful carved wooden structures were taken from churches for other, profane uses. Occasionally, monasteries were invaded; some were completely ruined, and their monks carried away for slave work in the Islamic fleet. A Chalcedonian named Anastasius bribed the governor to place a Chalcedonian physician by the name of Onopus on the throne of Saint Mark instead of Alexander II. This movement was foiled by the Alexandrian people, and Onopus rescinded his claim and asked forgiveness.

With the accession of ʿUmar ibn Abd al-ʿAzīz (717–720) to the Umayyad caliphate, a period of respite dawned on the Copts, for the new caliph issued a number of edicts for the relief of churches and episcopates from past, illegal financial imposts. He also directed his men to concentrate on the restoration of ruined towns and villages. So people lived in relative peace and security until a new governor, Ayyūb ibn Sharḥabīl, was appointed for Egypt in 717. A reversal of the policy of understanding followed. The caliph wrote the governor that only Muslims should be in his employ, and Copts who wanted to remain in office would have to apostatize to Islam. In this way, according to the *History of the Patriarchs,* "he was like Antichrist" (p. 326 [text]; p. 72 [trans]).

The accession of Yazīd II (720–724) to the caliphate after ʿUmar brought a renewal of the rule of financial terror and miseries, since he restored the imposts suppressed by his predecessor and further ordered the destruction of crosses and all the sacred images from churches. The situation was somewhat mended only by his death and the succession of his brother Hishām (724–743), who, according to the *History of the Patriarchs,* "was a God-fearing man. . . .and he became the deliverer of the Orthodox" (p. 327 [text]; p. 73 [trans.]). Nevertheless, the appointment of a new viceroy for Egypt, ʿUbayd-Allāh ibn al-Ḥabḥāb, with full powers to raise the *kharaj* tax, did not leave either the patriarch, Alexander II, or the people, Copts and Muslims, in peace. Ibn al-Ḥabḥāb devised accurate registers of all landed property, vineyards, and even the cattle in all villages and towns, a kind of Domesday Book, to ensure the payment of all dues to the state. To ensure the execution of his financial policy, he ordered all subjects, young and old, aged twenty to one hundred, to wear a distinguishing leaden badge around their necks. Further, the Copts were to be branded with the mark of a lion on their hands as their passport to practice trading, and anyone found without that mark would have his hand cut off. Also, groups of townsfolk were mustered for slave labor in the building of palaces for the governor at Giza and Memphis, and the *kharaj* taxes were doubled.

The miseries and financial imposts resulted in a rebellious mood, and blood was spilled in the successive local revolts, especially in the cities of Banā, Ṣā, and Samannūd in Lower Egypt. These hard times weighed heavily on the conscience of the patriarch, who met them with fortitude. But when it was decided to brand the patriarch, he categorically refused to submit to this humiliation and asked to be allowed to go to al-Fusṭāṭ (Cairo) to present his case personally to the viceroy, ʿUbayd-Allāh. Thus, he was dispatched to the capital with a special military bodyguard. While his request to see the viceroy was denied, he remained at al-Fusṭāṭ under a kind of house arrest. There he became sick and, in the company of Anbā Shamūl, bishop of Awsīm, decided to flee from incarceration on a ship heading for Alexandria. Reaching Tarnūṭ, the sick patriarch died while the governor's soldiers pursued him, and when they found him dead, they seized Anbā Shamūl and returned with him to al-Fusṭāṭ, where he was accused of complicity in the patriarchal flight and fined 1,000 dinars. In the end, the faithful were able to raise 300 dinars for his captors and the impecunious bishop was consequently allowed to go.

After one of the hardest reigns in patriarchal annals, Alexander went to his rest. After twenty-five years of continuous suffering, his body was taken to Alexandria for burial amid the immense grief of his congregation.

BIBLIOGRAPHY

Atiya, A. S. *History of Eastern Christianity.* London, 1968.

Cambridge History of Islam, ed. P. M. Holt, A. K. S. Lambton, and B. Lewis. 2 vols. Cambridge, 1970.

Lane-Poole, S. *The Mohammadan Dynasties.* London, 1894.

______. *History of Egypt in the Middle Ages.* London, 1901.

SUBHI Y. LABIB

ALEXANDER OF LYCOPOLIS, Neoplatonist philosopher (c. A.D. 300). Photius of Constantinople indicates (*Contra Manichaeos* 1. 11) that he converted to Christianity and became archbishop of Lycopolis. He is known through his *De placitis Manichaeorum,* which shows him as a coolheaded critic of the teaching being spread in Egypt by Manichaean missionaries in the first generation after Mani's death in 277. Alexander states that he gained his knowledge of Mani's teaching from those "who had known the man." He opens the *De placitis* by contrasting the "simplicity" of Christian teaching with the complicated mythology purveyed by the Manichaeans. He follows with a well-informed, point-by-point refutation of Manichaean dualism, cosmology, moral teaching, and its purely docetic concept of Christ. He concludes with brief but trenchant attacks on the sectaries' refusal to eat living things and their abstinence from marriage. He shows how MANICHAEISM was gaining ground among people who were prepared to accept propositions without examination, and even some "who have studied philosophy with us" (*De placitis* 5).

Throughout, Alexander writes as a Platonist philosopher. The author of creation is the Demiurge (craftsman). He refers to "fellow students of philosophy," dispassionately discusses aspects of Greek religion relevant to his criticism of the Manichaeans, and singles out the founder of Stoicism, Zeno of Citium, for praise. At the same time, he praises Jesus for showing that goodness was the common heritage of all classes of mankind and for his simple teaching and discourses that raised the senses toward God (*De placitis* 25).

Alexander's attack on Manichaean asceticism may be compared with that of Patriarch THEONAS of Alexandria (282–300) at about the same time (Papyrus Rylands 469). It seems clear that abstinences and rejection of marriage were among the Manichaean tenets that found most support among the Copts at this time, and lends significance to the careers of Saint ANTONY and PACHOMIUS OF TABENNĒSĒ. Alexander himself is interesting as one who, though an educated Greek, could appreciate the value of Jesus' teaching uniting all men of whatever background in a common aspiration toward goodness. His work shows that among pagans as well as Christians, there was some understanding of the religious ideas that were increasingly penetrating among the Copts on the eve of the Great Persecution of Diocletian.

BIBLIOGRAPHY

Alexander of Lycopolis. *De placitis Manichaeorum.* In PG 18, cols. 411–48. Paris, 1857.

Alexandri Lycopolitani contra Manichaei opiniones disputatio, ed. G. Brinkman. Leipzig, 1895.

Catalogue of the Greek Papyri in the John Rylands Library, Manchester, Vol. 3, *Theological and Literary Texts,* ed. C. H. Roberts. Manchester, 1938.

Cowell, E. B. "Alexander of Lycopolis." In DCB 1, p. 86. Repr. New York, 1974.

Photius. *Contra Manichaeos.* In PG 102, cols. 15–264. Paris, 1900.

Schmid, W. *Geschichte der griechischen Literatur,* 6th ed., Vol. 2, pp. 861ff. Handbuch der klassischen Altertumswissenschaft, Vol. 7, pt. 2. Munich, 1924.

W. H. C. FREND

ALEXANDRA, SAINT

ALEXANDRA, SAINT, a fourth-century recluse (feast day: 7 Amshīr). The account of Saint Alexandra is given by the recension of the Copto-Arabic SYNAXARION of Upper Egypt (Basset, 1916, pp. 801ff.; Forget, 1954, p. 453 [text]; 1953, p. 480 [trans.]), but this passage is only a translation of Chapter 5 of the *Historia lausiaca* by PALLADIUS (Butler, 1904, p. 21; Lucot, 1912, p. 50).

Alexandra was a young woman of Alexandria who, pursued by the importunities of a young man, preferred to shut herself up in a tomb not far from Alexandria, where she remained for ten years and where she died. Melania the Elder succeeded in getting her to tell her story and how she employed her time. From morning to the ninth hour, she prayed every hour and spun flax. According to Melania's narrative, we can date the life of Alexandra to the second half of the fourth century.

The story in Palladius and the Synaxarion is interesting, for it shows reclusion as a form of the monastic life at Alexandria.

BIBLIOGRAPHY

Lucot, A. *Palladius: Histoire lausiaque.* Textes et documents 15. Paris, 1912.

RENÉ-GEORGES COQUIN

ALEXANDRIA, CHRISTIAN AND MEDIEVAL

ALEXANDRIA, CHRISTIAN AND MEDIEVAL. The capital of the Ptolemies and the seat of the Roman prefect and of innumerable patriarchs, heresiarchs, and other products of Christian sectarianism, Alexandria rapidly lost its importance after the establishment of AL-FUSṬĀṬ (Cairo) as the new Muslim capital in 973. As the former capital, Alexandria, according to some, particularly P. Kahle (1921), received special treatment from its new rulers and was permitted to retain something of the status that it enjoyed in the last days of Byzantine rule. Alexandria in the late sixth and early seventh centuries was a city where, in spite of revolts and tumultuous incidents caused by supporters of the Circus colors and others (John of Nikiou, 1883, chap. 109, sec. 15, pp. 118–19.), the imperial writ still ran; but it was a city where power lay effectively in the hands of the Augustal and a host of minor officials, and in the hands of the Melchite patriarch and his ecclesiastical officials.

Unlike in provincial towns, the mass of the Greek population had long since lost all significant organs of local self-government. That the Melchite church had in the course of time, since the Council of CHALCEDON, largely superseded the state as the instrument of effective government in the capital can be seen from the civil and legal powers assumed, clearly with the approval of Heraclius, by both John "the Almoner" informally and, in more special circumstances, by Cyrus the *Muqawqas.* In such a body politic the traditional organs of local government, as they had hitherto developed, counted for little. City councillors, like legionary commanders, belonged to the limbo of pre-Justinian Egypt, and it was only in the provinces that the village headmen and their village councillors (*protokometai*), and the pagarchs (administrative officials) of the *pagoi* (districts), together with the owners of large "autopract" estates, supported the structure of bureaucratic government. Nevertheless, Alexandria did possess from the conquest onward certain privileges, notably the continued appointment of a Greek Christian civil governor, who, like his Byzantine predecessor, was called *augoustalios*, and in Arabic by various paraphrases, including ARCHON. The use of the Greek title in a letter of Qurrah, dated A.H. 92/A.D. 710 (*P. Lond.*, no. 1392) signifies that the usage continued into the Umayyad period. In terms of the Arab administration, it may even have started then. However, this appointment probably reflects more a concession to the Arab government in dealing with the still partly Greek-speaking, former capital, where the sole presence of a purely military governor from al-Fusṭāṭ might lead to trouble, than a deliberate attempt to buttress the status of the city.

The real status of Alexandria differed fundamentally from that of al-Fusṭāṭ, in its role in the overall control of the country and of the Arab settlements in Egypt. First and foremost, there were no true personal, tribal, or military settlements; with one exception, the formation of *khiṭṭas* (districts) was forbidden at Alexandria (Ibn 'Abd al-Ḥakam, *Futūḥ Miṣr*, cf. *Arab Conquest of Egypt*, 1978, p. 130). In place of the semicivic form of life based on the *khiṭṭahs* that grew apace at al-Fusṭāṭ—and which Ibn 'Abd al-Ḥakam described in detail from his own direct, firsthand knowledge, without reliance on traditions—Alexandria was a *thaghr* (frontier post), with billeting in available property (*akhā'idh*), but no *khiṭṭahs* were allowed (*al-Ḥakam*, 1922, pp. 130–31). The billeting system introduced by 'Amr was based on the principle of a semestrial rotation of posting, by which troops from al-Fusṭāṭ occupied their quarters for half the year, to be replaced by others at the end of that time (*al-Ḥakam*, 1922, p. 130). This military role in itself led to a form of dependence on al-Fusṭāṭ, though in the Umayyad period the city was still ruled by a civic governor. In A.H. 45/A.D. 665 'Alqamah ibn Yazīd was sent by 'Utbah ibn Abī Sufyān, governor of Egypt, with 12,000 men to stay there permanently (*al-Ḥakam*, 1922, p. 192). Again in the governorship of 'Abd al-'Azīz ibn Marwān, brother of Caliph 'Abd al-Malik, sometime between 684 and 704, a new system was introduced by which the garrisons of both Alexandria and Khirbitā, in the eastern Delta, were placed on a permanent basis, and a garrison-population of Arab tribesmen sprang up. Nevertheless, the status of Alexandria as a frontier post remained unaltered at a much later date when its commercial role had increased, and it is so called, for example, by the Arab geographers and travelers. Furthermore, even before the change from temporary to permanent garrisoning, immigrants had been brought in from Arabia under 'Uthmān (*al-Ḥakam*, 1922, pp. 123, 128; al-Balādhurī, 1932, p. 226). Thus we may say that under the Orthodox caliphs and the Umayyads the city had been both largely militarized and arabized.

As the need for an Arab Mediterranean fleet grew, Alexandria resumed its role as a shipyard, and became one of the major shipbuilding centers of the eastern Mediterranean, after Babylon and Clysma. Moreover, since the Arabs had both a dislike and an incapacity for naval operations, their navy was partly manned by Copts, who received booty and payment for their annual campaigns. The papyri yield considerable evidence of this shipbuilding and of the use of native Egyptian crews alongside of the Arabs (cf. *P. Lond*, Vol. IV, pp. xxxiiff.) In the reign of Mu'āwiyah, the expeditions to Cyprus (649) and to Rhodes (672; al-Balādhurī, 1932, p. 375H), and that to Sicily (651 and 669) were launched from Alexandria. These maritime operations, unpopular as they were with the Orthodox caliphs, nevertheless laid the foundations of Muslim conquests overseas. Mu'āwiyah employed the same principle of rotating garrisons in Rhodes, in the seven years that the Muslims maintained their hold on the island, as obtained in Alexandria before the permanent garrison was installed (al-Balādhurī, 1932, p. 236). Its defensive role, on those occasions when the Byzantine fleet descended on the Delta coast and waterways, was equally vital, but the Arabs were not successful in holding off the Byzantine depredations at, for example, DUMYĀṬ in 720 and at Tarūjah, on the western edge of the Delta, in about 738. Most of these coastal and interior cities lying on the branches and canals of the Nile had to be refortified at a later date (cf. Fahmy, 1966, pp. 139ff). In general, the presence of the permanent garrisons, as no doubt also of the maritime elements in the population, formed an inevitable source of danger to the Umayyad government, whose viceroy sat in al-Fusṭāṭ, and there were not infrequent outbreaks of mutiny over pay and other issues at Alexandria in the Umayyad period.

Although the role of the city was to remain modest for several centuries until the Fatimid period and later, the development of overseas trade on a large scale gave it a new function as an entrepôt and commercial center. The impressions formed by the Arab conquerors, particularly ʿAmr himself as given in the letter to ʿUmar (*al-Ḥakam*, 1922, p. 82) describing his entry into the city, were totally devoid of reality, save in recognizing its foundation by Alexander, Dhū al-Qarnayn (or perhaps by Shaddād ibn ʿĀd). Oral and written impressions of the first settlers as chronicled were unrealistic as well. They had little else to record but Egyptian traditions. To them the city was built of blindingly white marble, so bright that a needle, as the Traditionists love to repeat (*al-Ḥakam*, 1922, p. 42), could be threaded at night without the aid of moonlight. The Pharos Lighthouse, still functioning for many centuries under the Muslims, was turned into a miraculous weapon against invaders, and descriptions of such were fantasized. The city that had been built in 300 years and had stood for 300 years and had taken 300 years to destroy, had been so embellished by Cleopatra that she might be termed the second founder of the Muslim al-Iskandariyyah, a view not confined to the Muslim world. She had built the Pharos and built the canals that brought it water. The Arabs had indeed captured from the Greco-Roman capital only the figures of Alexander himself, about whose identity they had the gravest doubts, but by whose bier Olympias and sages, named and unnamed, appropriate and inappropriate, were later to lament the passing of the conqueror of the world. They also knew of Cleopatra, Heraclius, and Cyrus the *Muqawqas*, but between these figures lay centuries that were blank. Thus in many ways the al-Iskandariyyah of the literature based on the traditions, as opposed to the later travelers' records of it, was a city of the imagination only, symbolic of greatness felt, though not understood. The Arab chroniclers created this elaborate mesh of fantasy in the absence of any true historical tradition. The reader of the Egyptian traditions must be struck by the contrast between the first-hand knowledge of al-Fusṭāṭ shown by Ibn ʿAbd al-Ḥakam, and emphasized by the absence of *isnāds* (traditional sources) in the description of the *khiṭṭahs* and the fantasies elaborated round the frontier post al-Iskandariyyah, based often on a vague and fabulous tradition.

The reality was different. Alexandria had undergone a profound transformation in the centuries of Roman and Byzantine rule. The city that had once been contained between Maryūṭ and the sea, to the south and the north, and between Shaṭbī and the western harbor on the east and west, had now spread far beyond its original circuit, particularly to the east, where the city almost joined up with Nikopolis, which, when founded by Augustus, had been five miles from the center of the city. As a result, the fortifications had come to have significance only in times of crisis, as Christian refugees had found sanctuary behind them during the Persian invasions of Palestine and Syria. These walls, according to the Arabs, were demolished by ʿAmr after the second capture of the city, but we read of them as standing or having been rebuilt later in the eighth century. It is likely that, although demolished, they were not wholly dismantled. Nor can there be doubt that the northern face of the city, the old Palaces or Brucheion area, had been so severely damaged in the first three centuries of the empire that Epiphanius could speak of that section of the city as a desert.

On the other hand, the main ridge of the city, running along the approximate line of the medial road of today, in front of the Kom al-Dikkah area, had maintained or increased its role in civic life, at a date when the Ptolemaic remains already lay meters below the late Roman street level. No very precise date can be assigned to the late Roman and Byzantine buildings, public and private, brought to light by the Polish excavations of Kom al-Dikkah. Nevertheless, the theater-like building that seems to have formed the central point of that area was still standing at the time of the earliest Arab occupation, as revealed both by dwellings and by burial pits. There is no sign of a regular destruction level, and it looks as if the first Arab settlers camped among the buildings and in the houses they found standing in the city. To this extent the excavations confirm the picture given by Ibn ʿAbd al-Ḥakam that the first Arab garrison troops occupied residential quarters, which the remaining Greeks tried to take back from them (al-Ḥakam, 1922, pp. 130–31; al-Balādhurī, 1932, p. 222). Thus the early Arab al-Iskandariyyah probably did not differ greatly in appearance from late Byzantine Alexandria.

Nevertheless, the change of faith, and the departure of the Melchite population changed the use of religious buildings. We learn from the *Futūḥ Miṣr* of the names of the five early mosques of the city, including a Mosque of ʿAmr, but the location of none of these is given in such a way as to help us locate them, save that the Mosque of Dhū al-Qarnayn lay near the market and the Caesareum. More historically plausible is the information provided by Severus and Eutychius that the Melchite churches were turned into mosques. There was no Melchite patriarch between 642 and 727, it may be noted. Of course the Monophysite churches continued, in normal circumstances, to fulfil their proper role. It is noteworthy that in his list of the mosques Ibn ʿAbd al-Ḥakam does not include the "Mosque of Mercy" that he tells us ʿAmr dedicated at the point where the Arab forces sheathed their swords during the second conquest of the city.

An unverifiable piece of information transmitted by *Futūḥ Miṣr* (pp. 42–44) is that the city of Alexandria consisted of three separate sections, side by side. They were each surrounded by a wall and called respectively Mannā, the area of the Pharos; al-Iskandariyyah, "the area where the citadel now is"; and Naqīṭah, which has been seen as an Arab reminiscence of the name of the general who won Egypt for Heraclius at the beginning of the seventh century. Some such attempt at regional division is not impossible; certainly the names are sufficiently unusual to give them an air of historicity. In any event, the toponymy of the city in early Muslim times is largely unknown.

We may say that the city was deliberately isolated from the main stream of events by ʿUmar's wish to ensure the provision of vital supplies from Egypt to the Arabian peninsula. He was not concerned with the expansion, or even continuation, of Mediterranean trade. ʿAmr was forbidden by ʿUthmān to establish his headquarters at Alexandria, and was allowed to reside there only a short time. As already emphasized, the city had no *khiṭṭas*, having instead garrisons dependent for the first generation on the organization of al-Fusṭāṭ. At the same time, the large-scale departure of the Melchite Greek merchant class meant the loss of the one element in the population able to provide commercial stability and communication with the outside world. An inevitable consequence of the geographical position of the city was that this state of affairs could not be permanent, and that new groups would fill the gaps left by the departed Greeks. The Jews came in time to fill the role of the Greeks. In later centuries, during the Fatimid period, Jewish commercial activities are richly documented in the commercial papers found in the old Cairo *Geniza* studied exhaustively by S. D. Goitein in his *A Mediterranean Society* (Univ. of California, in press, 1987–), which have revealed a trade with the West, by land and sea, no less than with the East, based on transit via Alexandria. But in the years following the conquest, and in the Umayyad period, there is no sign of such life, and the city remained a frontier post, though at the same time its links with the Delta and the interior were maintained by the continuing care given by caliphs and governors to the canals linking the city with the Nile.

When ʿAbd al-ʿAzīz ibn Marwān, the governor of Egypt, arrived in the city in 685, an elderly Greek was able to give Marwān an eyewitness account of the capture of the city (al-Ḥakam, 1922, pp. 74.19–75.22). The reference serves, by its very unexpectedness, to remind us of the scanty evidence of Greeks in the population of the early Muslim city. The story presents a lively picture of the old man as a youth in his capacity as servant of a Greek patrician named Markos. He and his master, the latter richly robed and caparisoned, together rode out of the fortifications to watch the activity in the Arab camp. A single Arab horseman left a tent, saddled his horse, gave chase to them, and killed the master, while the young Greek managed to reach the safety of the walls. Other Greeks, we know, were quick to occupy untenanted parts of houses in Alexandria allotted to the Arab garrison.

A cultural vacuum set in. Even before the conquest, secular Greek culture had been at a low ebb since the time of Justinian. Few Greek authors of this late date are known, though we may note a continuing tradition in the *Lives of the Saints* and other works concerned with supernatural healing, such as the *Miracula* of Sophronius. But the Melchite church of Alexandria had no theological literature to compare with the wealth of Coptic literature known from Upper Egypt, and with the departure of most of the Melchite population, the Alexandria Library no doubt closed its doors, even though ʿAmr did not burn it down. The next phase in the culture was found in the role played by Greek and Arabic doctors resident in Egypt, and particularly in Alexandria, who contributed to the transmission of Greek medical knowledge to Muslim lands; but the activity in this respect as compared with that in Nestorian lands is small indeed. Though Greek culture declined rapidly after the conquest, the same is not true of the Greek language itself, for it continued to be an essential language of the new bureaucracy until the eighth century. The new Islamic culture gained a slow footing in the city, which had little to attract Arab men of letters, because the whole of Arab tradition and tribal continuity and of Islam itself was placed, so far as Egypt was concerned, in the new capital at al-Fusṭāṭ. The contrast in this respect is apparent in the comparative importance of the mosques of

ʿAmr at al-Fusṭāṭ and at al-Iskandariyyah. The former remained the focal point of an early Muslim cult, enlarged first by Maslamah ibn Mukhallad in 674, and then rebuilt by Qurrah in 711, on the orders of the caliph Walīd I; it thus became the most splendid mosque in the city. The very location of the Mosque of ʿAmr at al-Iskandariyyah seems, on the other hand, to have been almost forgotten (but cf. *al-Ḥakam,* 1922, pp. 130, 5–6). When ʿAmr himself returned to Egypt as the military governor of Muʿāwiyah a few years later it was to al-Fusṭāṭ that he returned, the city he had founded in the shadow of Babylon.

BIBLIOGRAPHY

Bagnall, R. S. "The Arab Conquest of Egypt and the Last Thirty Years of the Roman Dominion," *Classical Journal* 75 (1979–1980):347–48.

Balādhurī, Aḥmad ibn Yahyā ibn Jābir, al-. *Kitab Futūh al-Buldān,* 3 vols., ed. Ṣalāḥ-al-Din al-Munajjid. Cairo, 1956.

———. *Liber expungnationis regionum,* 3 pts., ed. M. J. de Goeje. From author Imama Ahmed ibn Iahja ibn Djabir al-Baladsori. Leiden, 1863–1866. Reproductions of same made in Cairo, 1901, and again in 1932, without index, diacritical marks, or *apparatus criticus.*

Butler, A. J. *The Arab Conquest of Egypt.* Oxford, 1902. Second ed., P. M. Fraser. Oxford, London, and Glasgow, 1978. Includes Butler's later works, entitled *The Treaty of Miṣr by Ṭabari* (1913) and *Babylon of Egypt* (1914). Three-vol. edition, Cairo, 1956.

Caetani, L. C. *Annali dell'Islam,* Vols. 1–7. Milan, 1905–1914. Repr. Hildesheim, 1972.

Dennett, C., Jr. *Conversion and the Poll Tax in Early Islam.* Harvard Historical Monographs 22. Cambridge, Mass., 1950.

Fahmy, A. H. *Muslim Sea Power.* Cairo, 1966.

Ibn ʿAbd al-Ḥakam, Abu al-Zāsim ʿAbd al-Raḥmān ibn Abdullah. *Futūh Miṣr wa-Akhbaruha,* ed. C. C. Torrey from manuscripts in London and Paris—under the title *The History of the Conquest of Egypt, North Africa and Spain,* known as *Futūḥ Miṣr.* Yale Oriental Series, Researches 3. New Haven, Conn., 1922.

Kahle, P. "Zur Geschichte des mittelalterlichen Alexandria." *Islam* 12 (1921):29–84.

Kubiak, W. *Al-Fusṭat: Its Foundation and Early Urban Development.* Dissertation, University of Warsaw, 1982.

Lokkegarde, F. L. *Islamic Taxation in the Classic Period.* Copenhagen, 1950.

Makowiecka, E. "Polish Excavations at Kom el-Dikka in 1965 and 1966. Preliminary Report." *Africana Bulletin* 22 (1975):7–40.

Nikiou, J. de. *Chronique,* ed. H. Zotenberg. Notices et Extraits des MSS de la Biblioteque Nationale. Paris, 1883. English trans. R. H. Charles, *The Chronicle of Jean, Bishop of Nikiu.* Text and Translation Society. London, 1916.

P. M. Fraser

ALEXANDRIA, HISTORIC CHURCHES IN.

ALEXANDRIA, HISTORIC CHURCHES IN. As capital of Egypt prior to the ARAB CONQUEST OF EGYPT, Alexandria deserves special attention in regard to its religious institutions. This need is further accentuated by the fact that it was also the seat of the Coptic patriarchate throughout the Byzantine period and during the early centuries of Arab rule. Pope Christodoulus (1047–1077), the sixty-sixth patriarch, decided to move the seat of the patriarchate closer to the new central government, from Alexandria to the southern city of al-Fusṭāṭ (Cairo) where he resided in the area of the ancient Church of Our Lady known as al-Muʿallaqah within the precincts of the Fort of BABYLON in Old Cairo.

The most extensive record of the ancient churches established in Alexandria appears in the twelfth-century work of Abū al-Makārim on the history of Coptic churches and monasteries; and an analytical survey of its contents in the chapters devoted to Alexandria (1984, vol. 1, pp. 135–75) gives the right perspective on this important subject. It is interesting to note, however, that the religious foundations in that city must have suffered greatly when the Persians descended on Egypt in their conquest of the late sixth century, even before the Arabs appeared on the scene. Nevertheless, the churches of Alexandria survived that temporary havoc, and it is impossible to find a more detailed account of those ancient churches than we have in the work of Abū al-Makārim. A summary follows.

1. Saint Mark's church on the seashore, known as Bucalis, the spot where Saint Mark was martyred and buried.
2. Church of Mār Sābā (see no. 35, below).
3. Church of Saint John the Evangelist, consecrated by Pope Christodoulus.
4. Church of Saint Mercurius, consecrated by Pope Christodoulus.
5. Church of the Archangel Michael, consecrated by Pope Christodoulus.
6. Church of Saint Menas, situated outside the city fortress, consecrated by Pope Christodoulus.
7. Church of Saint George (Mār Jirjis), consecrated by Pope Christodoulus.

8. Church of the Virgin Mary, founded by Saint THEONAS (282–300), the sixteenth patriarch of the Coptic church, during the age of persecutions. Here, during the patriarchate of KHĀ'ĪL I (744–767), the forty-sixth pope, a story is told of a man who looked at the icon of the crucifixion and jeered at the idea of the stabbing in the side of the crucified Jesus. Then he took a cane and mounted to where the icon hung with the intent of stabbing the other side of Jesus while ten thousand spectators watched. As soon as he reached the icon, he felt that he was himself stabbed and hanging in mid air; he suffered mortal pains and decided to offer penitence and to become converted if he were relieved. The legend continues that he was relieved, became converted, and went to the monastery of Saint Macarius where he was baptized and became a monk and died.
9. Church of John the Baptist and the Prophet Elijah, which apparently suffered some damage in the age of persecutions, and was restored by Pope THEOPHILUS (385–412), the twenty-third patriarch. The body of John was laid there, but the head was later discovered in Emesa (Ḥomṣ) during the reign of Pope DIOSCORUS I (444–458), the twenty-fifth patriarch.
10. The Smaller Church in the Febrius (the island of Pharos), where the bodies of the martyrs Apa Cyr (Abūqīr) the monk and John the soldier were transferred from Saint Mark's Church during the patriarchate of CYRIL I the Great (412–444).
11. The Church on the Island (of Pharos), restored by Theophilus (385–412).
12. Church of the Angelion, a large cathedral with 140 priests in the west of Alexandria, restored by the Orthodox people in the papacy of THEODOSIUS I (535–567), the thirty-third patriarch; temporarily appropriated by the Chalcedonians; then returned to the See of Saint Mark. SIMON I (689–701) was consecrated forty-second patriarch in it.
13. Church of COSMAS AND DAMIAN, situated in the stadium west of the colonnade, founded in the year 284 during the reign of Emperor DIOCLETIAN.
14. Church of Our Lady, probably founded by the fifteenth patriarch MAXIMUS (264–282) during the reign of Emperor Aurelianus (270–275). Abū al-Makārim mentions the founder as the patriarch Taron (corruption of Theonas who succeeded Maximus), and states that it was in the reign of Aurelianus, who was a contemporary of Maximus.
15. Church of Archangel Michael, founded in a temple where Cleopatra installed a brass statue named Michael that the Alexandrians cherished with tremendous offerings. The nineteenth patriarch, ALEXANDER I (312–326), convinced them of the falsehood of that statue and replaced it with the archangel Michael. This ancient church suffered much damage by fire during the invasion of Alexandria by the North African tribe of Ḥabāsah in 912.
16. Legend describes an anonymous church that the unfaithful wanted to drown by a spring pouring from the mountain. It was saved by an angel who deflected the course of the stream by striking a rock asunder so that the water flowed away from the church.
17. Church of Thaddaeus, restored by Theophilus, the twenty-third patriarch.
18. Church of Our Lady (Martmaryam), restored by Theophilus.
19. Church of Saint John, also restored by Theophilus.
20. Church of Emperor Arcadius (395–408), son of Theodosius the Great (379–395), completed by Theophilus (385–412). A rich Jew by the name of Orbeit was converted to Christianity and was very charitable to the needy. One Easter he died there while distributing charities to 300 persons.
21. The Cathedral Church of the Jacobites, the finest and largest in Egypt, is situated in the section of Alexandria known as al-Masárij where the Copts firmly espoused the Orthodox Creed confirmed by the 318 church fathers at the Council of NICAEA and rejected the Arian heresy described here as the Melchite sect. The Melchite patriarch, supported by Emperor Constantine the Lesser (the second), ascended the pulpit and declared his heretical creed. Consequently, the Jacobites rebelled and stoned and killed the patriarch, and his body was transported outside the city and burned. Constantine was furious and appointed another patriarch in succession, who planned a conspiracy to chastise the Jacobites. The Melchites, armed with swords in the form of staves and crutches, invited the Copts to congregate in that cathedral. Once inside, the gates of the cathedral were locked and the swords were mercilessly used to kill the Orthodox congregation to avenge the murder of the Melchite patriarch. Much blood was spilled, and destruction of the edifice itself followed to the extent that only a staircase and a couple of doors survived

the havoc. This apparently happened during the reign of Pope ATHANASIUS I, the Apostolic (326–373), the immortal twentieth patriarch who combated and defeated the Arian heresy.

22. Church of Saint Peter the Apostle, restored by Severus of Antioch and appropriated by the Melchites.
23. Church of Mark the Evangelist, known as al-Qamḥah, outside Alexandria, restored by JOHN III (677–686) of Samannūd, the fortieth patriarch, who purchased property for it in Cairo, Alexandria, and Mareotis and with the help of the Christian population constructed for it a mill and a wine press.
24. Church of Saint George, originally the house of ANIANUS the Cobbler, the second patriarch after Saint Mark, and situated on the seashore.
25. Church of Saint Menas, situated outside the fort of Alexandria.
26. Church of Joseph (the Prophet), situated about nine miles outside Alexandria and used as the residence of PETER IV (567–569), the thirty-fourth patriarch, who used it as a shelter from the powerful Chalcedonian sect in Alexandria.
27. An anonymous church restored by the archons of Alexandria in the reign of CYRIL II (1078–1092), the sixty-seventh patriarch.
28. Church of Saints Sergius and Wachas, inside Alexandria, destroyed during the reign of the Fatimid caliph al-ḤĀKIM (996–1021) and restored by Pope ZACHARIAS (1004–1032), the sixty-fourth patriarch. It was enriched by the archon Abū al-Faḍl Ibrahim ibn Abū al-Makārim, who constructed a carved wooden ICONOSTASIS to the central altar in the year A.M. 893/A.D. 1175.
29. Church of Our Lady, known as al-Muʻallaqah, appropriated by the Venetians in Alexandria and restored by Zacharias.
30. Church of the Savior, built in the name of Jesus Christ in a vast area comprising several chapels built by Pope Mark II (799–819), the forty-ninth patriarch. It was destroyed by Andalusian arsonists within sight of that patriarch, who restored it nevertheless. It has many upper and lower chapels, as well as an extensive cemetery (Ṭafūs) nearby.
31. Church of Saint John (Abū Yuḥannis) located in the district of al-Ḥabbālīn in Alexandria. It was a fine structure containing the tomb of CYRUS the *Muqawqas*, who was viceroy of Egypt at the Arab conquest and who concluded the surrender on the basis of the Covenant of ʻUmar during the patriarchate of BENJAMIN I (622–661).
32. Church of Saint Sanutius (Abū Shinūdah), situated on an ancient gulf in the Mediterranean just outside Alexandria. It had a Greek inscription that describes Maximus and Basilius as the universal sovereigns.
33. Church of the Tomb of the Prophet Jeremiah located in an area of Alexandria known as Qubbat al-Warshān amidst a Muslim cemetery, now functioning as a mosque.
34. Church of Saint Nicholas (Mār Niqūlah) located in the district of Ḥammām al-Akhāwayn, which belonged to the Melchites.
35. Church of Mār Sābā in the district of Al-Qamrah, once belonging to the Melchites but returned to the Jacobites in the reign of COSMOS I (730–731) by Caliph Hishām ibn ʻAbd-al-Malik (724–743).
36. Church of John the Baptist, originally a fine and vast structure belonging to the Melchites, but later reduced by the Muslims, who constructed many shops within its area and left only a small section for the church.
37. Church of the Qayṣāriyyah (square) belonging to the Melchites.
38. Church of Creniua, where Proterius the Melchite patriarch was assassinated by the Jacobite populace. His body was transported on camelback to the Ptolemaic stadium where it was burned.
39. Church of Saint Menas (Abū Mīnā) in Mareotis, where the body of the saint is interred. It was constructed in the time of Theophilus (385–412), the twenty-third patriarch, and the emperors Arcadius (395–408) and Theodosius II (408–450). It was completed in the time of TIMOTHY II AELURUS (458–480) who enriched it with columns of colored marble, the like of which was seen nowhere else. With the help of a Chalcedonian, the Abbasid caliph transported these columns to Baghdad during the papacy of YŪSĀB I (830–849), the fifty-second patriarch, who tried to restore the structure and beautify it again.
40. Church of THEODOSIUS II, son of Arcadius (395–408), founded by Theophilus (385–412), the twenty-third patriarch.
41. An unknown church at Būkhīshā, a village in the district of Mareotis, built by a heretical sect that denied the passion of Jesus and professed that his physical tortures were unreal and only like a dream. This took place during the reign of Pope SHENUTE I (858–880), the fifty-fifth patri-

arch. Ultimately they came back to orthodoxy and were welcomed by the patriarch, who consecrated a priest for them from their group. That sect is reminiscent of the Qur'anic theory of the crucifixion of Jesus in Islam, which is unreal and only a semblance (*Qur'ān*, Sūrat al-Nisā', 4:157).

According to Sa'īd ibn AL-BIṬRĪQ (quoted by Abū al-Makārim, Vol. 1, pp. 151, 164) many other churches were founded in Alexandria and its environs but were later destroyed and could not be traced after the Persian invasion, which razed many religious monuments.

It is to be remembered that churches were not the only religious institutions in Alexandria. Several monasteries appeared in the city and became known as great landmarks. Perhaps the most conspicuous among them was the ENATON, known as Dayr al-Zujāj, which was started by one of the Coptic fathers toward the end of the age of persecutions and Coptic martyrdoms. PETER IV (567–569), the thirty-fourth patriarch, graduated from that monastery, which contained the relics of Peter the Confessor, bishop of Ghaza, as well as those of Abū Baṭra and Severus of Antioch. This monastery grew to considerable dimensions. Its fourteen wells and numerous water-wheels irrigated its arable terrains and the palm groves within its precincts. It had a solidly built KEEP with numerous monks. Another subsidiary monastery also arose on the seashore. It was inhabited by forty-four monks in the year A.M. 804/A.D. 1088, and it is even said that similar institutions were situated in that area for other monks and for nuns as well. The Nikious monastery, located in the northeast section of the city, was favored by Benjamin I (622–661), the thirty-eighth patriarch, contemporary of the Arab Conquest. The Dayr Baṭrah monastery was an episcopal seat. After destruction by fire, it was restored by Isaac (686–689), the forty-first patriarch. Other houses for monks as well as nuns were started by the presbyter ANASTASIUS before he became the thirty-sixth patriarch (605–616). A monastery known as that of the lower terrain (DAYR ASFAL AL-ARḌ) and bearing the name of Saint Mark existed in the east section of Alexandria amidst orchards and agricultural land. It was here that the evangelist celebrated mass. Bodies of martyrs were preserved in its caves, including the remains of Saint Sophia and her three daughters. It is said that this latter monastery was given to the Melchites in the partition of religious property with the Jacobites. Just outside Alexandria, in Mareotis, was another monastery that housed aged fathers and younger monks who tortured themselves by the use of iron fetters.

Alexandria, where Christianity took root in Egypt and where the ancient foundation of the Coptic Orthodox Church was laid by Saint Mark, continued to be a significant home of time-honored religious institutions, too numerous to be fully treated by scholars and historians.

BIBLIOGRAPHY

Abū al-Makārim. *Tārīkh al-Kanā'is wa-al-Adyirah,* 4 vols., ed. Ṣāmū'īl al-Suryānī. Cairo, 1984.

Meinardus, O. F. A. *Christian Egypt: Ancient and Modern.* Cairo, 1977.

AZIZ S. ATIYA

ALEXANDRIA, ISLAMIC PERIOD. *See* Alexandria, Christian and Medieval.

ALEXANDRIA IN LATE ANTIQUITY. Founded at the western end of the Nile Delta in 331 B.C. by Alexander the Great, Alexandria soon replaced Memphis as capital of Egypt and the Ptolemaic empire, thus focusing Egypt more resolutely than ever on the eastern Mediterranean and the Greek world. Alexandria became a center of Hellenistic civilization as the court of the Ptolemies attracted outstanding poets and scholars. It also played a leading role in economy and commerce, draining goods from the Egyptian chora (hinterland), the Red Sea, and the Indian Ocean, and forwarding them to the Mediterranean world. Alexandria must have been the most populous city of that area (one million inhabitants in the first century, by an optimistic estimate), until it had to cede this place to imperial Rome. With the victory of Octavian (later Augustus) and the death of Cleopatra VII in 30 B.C., Egypt became a Roman province with Alexandria as its capital. But even then the predominantly Greek city maintained an identity of its own compared with the Egyptian chora, a status acknowledged by a distinct citizenship and reflected in the official designation of *Alexandrea ad Aegyptum.*

We have a good description of the city by the Greek geographer and historian Strabo (*Geography* XVII.1.6–19), who visited Egypt in 25–24 B.C. in the

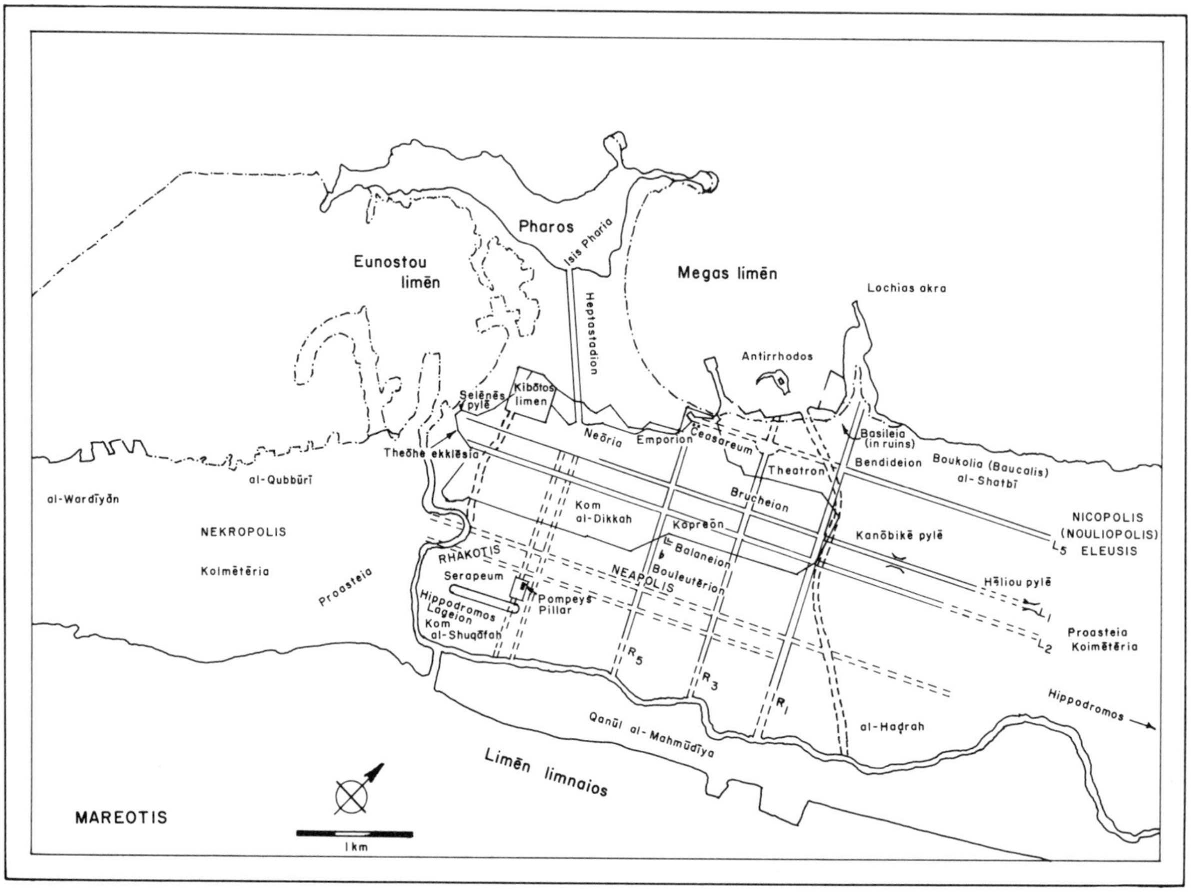

Alexandria in late antiquity.

company of Aelius Gallus, prefect of Egypt. Many of the features that were characteristic of Strabo's Alexandria had disappeared by the time of DIOCLETIAN (284–305) as a consequence of old age and new building activity, but also in the course of destruction due to natural disasters and warfare, particularly in the third century. There is thus a certain discontinuity between Hellenistic and early Roman Alexandria, on the one hand, and the Byzantine town, on the other; several important features remain, however, largely unaltered. As before, the two maritime harbors, the Great Harbor and the Harbor of Eunostus (of Fortunate Return), were in existence, separated by the Heptastadium, which linked the mainland and the island of Pharos, so called after the famous lighthouse of the third century B.C. Whereas these harbors assured the exchange of goods between the Mediterranean and Egypt, the port facilities on the southern side of Alexandria and the northern shore of Lake Mareotis brought the capital in contact, via canals, with the Canopic branch of the Nile, with the Nile Delta, and with Upper Egypt.

Beyond the city walls, to the east and west, lay necropoles (later to become Christian *coemeteria*) and suburbs, such as Eleusis on the east side and, still farther east, the Roman legionary camp of Nikopolis. West of the city wall, the burial grounds seem to have molded the whole area, Strabo therefore calling it simply Necropolis. The map joined to this article can give only a very approximate idea of the streets and sites of buildings in late Roman Alexandria. The slow decay following the ARAB CONQUEST OF EGYPT, the transfer of the capital of Egypt to Fusṭāṭ-Cairo, and, above all, the hectic building activity since the nineteenth century have partly destroyed and partly covered the older strata of the town. In the Serapeum area, Pompey's Pillar (a victory monument erected after the recapture of Alexandria by Diocletian c. 299) is one of the few monuments still erect in situ.

Despite excavations (mostly on very limited sites) and careful observations, many localizations and attributions of public buildings and churches remain hypothetical. The many cemeteries on the fringe of the town in particular yielded interesting results.

More recently, the Polish archaeologists digging in Kom al-Dikka, in the very center of Alexandria, discovered important sections of the Roman and Byzantine town: a small, very dense residential quarter of the late Roman period, baths (probably dating back to the third century A.D.), a public building (interpreted as an odeum), and another building with rows of marble seats that the excavators took to be a theater but that Balty has identified as the *bouleuterion*, the hall of the town council of Roman Alexandria (terminus post quem, 200). The same place yielded dozens of graffiti and drawings related to the games of the hippodrome and to other motifs.

As capital of the Roman *provincia Aegyptus*, Alexandria was the seat of the *praefectus Aegypti*, the representative of the emperor, who headed the provincial administration. Alexandria and its immediate surroundings were heavily garrisoned by the *classis Alexandrina* in the harbor and especially by the troops in the camp of Nikopolis. During the Roman period and until the reforms of Diocletian, Alexandria had its own mint and issued coins with representations of gods, emperors, and city buildings. Alexandria had been equipped by its founder with the institutional set of a Greek polis: assembly of the people (*ecclesia*), town council (*boule*), magistrates, and other officials. When Ptolemy I moved with his court from Memphis to Alexandria and monarchical rule made its impact felt during the reigns of the following Ptolemies, the development of polis autonomy was decisively restricted. Perhaps Alexandria lost its *boule* under one of the later Ptolemies (Bowman, 1971, pp. 12–14); another theory makes Augustus responsible for its abolition (Fraser, 1972, Vol. 1, pp. 94ff.; Geraci, pp. 176–82). Later Roman emperors, unimpressed by Alexandrian delegations, did nothing to restore their town council until Septimius Severus granted it in 200. But about the same time, the nome capitals of Egypt were also given town councils, so that the restoration of the Alexandrian *boule* was not much of a privilege.

But Roman Alexandria nevertheless had its own laws and its own citizenship, which set the Greek or Hellenized citizens apart not only from the Egyptians of the town and the chora but also from the numerous Jewish inhabitants. Dissensions between Alexandrian citizens and Jews about the latter's constitutional position and civic rights were a source of serious conflict and even civil war in the first and second centuries (especially the Jewish revolt of 115–117). As the capital of Ptolemaic, Roman, and Byzantine Egypt, and as a crossroads of men and products, Alexandria had acquired a quite varied population. Besides the immigrants from the Greek and Near Eastern areas, among them many Jews who had settled in Alexandria since the Hellenistic period, there was a nucleus of native Egyptians centered in the old village of Rhakotis, which had become an important quarter of the town around the Serapeum. Moreover, there was a constant supply of autochthonous Egyptians from the chora, threatening, as the city authorities felt, the Greek character of Alexandria and thus occasionally expelled by order of the Roman government.

Alexandria also played host to many foreigners attracted by a wide range of commercial, industrial, and other activities. Various languages were thus spoken in that Levantine metropolis, but Greek was dominant in official business, as in everyday life, from the time of Alexander the Great to the Arab conquest and even beyond (see GREEK LANGUAGE IN EGYPT). The often volatile mixture of Greeks and Egyptians, of Jews and Arabs, of people from black Africa, Central Asia, India, China, and the West gave the city a reputation of being frivolous and rebellious, deriding kings and emperors, intolerant of both Jews and Egyptians, finding in theater and hippodrome an outlet for their anger and their passions. In the second half of the first century, the speech of Dio Chrysostomus "To the People of Alexandria" (*oratio* 32; see Jones, pp. 36–44) bears eloquent testimony to the Alexandrian addiction to exciting music and circus. These tensions exploded often enough. The massacre of the Alexandrian population and the expulsion of native Egyptians by the emperor Caracalla provide a particularly dramatic example (Kolb, 1972). Alexandria kept its antagonistic structures and unruly character in Byzantine times, violent clashes occurring now between Christians and pagans (destruction of the Serapeum in 391, murder of the pagan philosopher Hypatia in 415) or between rival Christian factions (Orthodox *vs.* Arians and Melitians, Monophysites vs. Dyophysites).

Alexandria suffered terrible losses in human lives, as well as in public and private buildings, during the riots and wars of the second and third centuries. The quarter of the Brucheion, for example, had been ravaged in the course of the Jewish revolt of 115–117. That section of the town was obviously resettled afterward, and Alexandria in a more general way must have thoroughly recovered since the reign of Hadrian (117–138). If we may believe the figures given in a very short but precise survey of

Roman Alexandria in the Syriac *Chronicle* of Michael bar Elias, Jacobite patriarch of Antioch from 1166 to 1199, there were in Alexandria 2,478 temples (obviously shrines included), 47,790 (or 24,296?) houses, and 1,561 baths (not taking account of the important peripheral quarters of the town). Michael concludes, "Alexandria is the greatest of the cities of the inhabited world." If these figures are exact, his conclusion might well be correct, as a comparison with similar surveys of Rome and Constantinople shows.

Michael gives no precise information concerning the period to which his notice refers, but the text itself hints at a date after the accession of Hadrian in 117 and before the Palmyrene occupation of Alexandria in 270–272 (for English translation of Michael's text and commentary, see Fraser, 1951). The conquest of the town by the Palmyrene troops of Zenobia and its recapture by the emperor Aurelian in 272 caused lasting havoc, resulting in the abandonment of the coastal area in the northeast, once the core of the Ptolemaic city with the palace and other public buildings. The quarter of the Brucheion, again in ruins, was now given up.

The city walls were rebuilt under the Byzantine emperors, but they now included a smaller surface. This reduction is clearly indicated by both literary sources and archaeological investigations, illustrating the abandonment of the eastern quarters beyond the street R 1 of the map in Adriani's *Repertorio* (p. 269; cf. Rodziewicz, 1984, p. 335). The successive contractions of the city area resulted in the perimeter of the Arab wall of the eleventh century, leaving out substantial sections of the eastern and southern quarters of the town. In the absence of reliable data, it is, of course, very hazardous to give an estimate of the population of Alexandria in late antiquity, but 500,000 inhabitants is perhaps not too far off the mark. In Byzantine times, Alexandria with its reduced area, reshaped quarters, and rising churches must have looked very different from what it was in the Ptolemaic and early Roman periods. It must, however, have been a splendid metropolis in late antiquity, even if we allow for some exaggeration in the panegyrical descriptions of Alexandria by Ammianus Marcellinus (XXII.15–16) and other late authors (for *encomia* of Alexandria, cf. Jones; J. H. M. Hendriks et al.; and *Expositio totius mundi* 35–37).

As Alexandria had had to serve Rome by contributing largely to the food supply of the imperial capital during the first three centuries of the Christian era, so it had to bow to Constantinople when this city became the seat of the emperors of the Eastern Roman Empire. Products and taxes were now drained to the new imperial capital. Political directives issued by Constantinople, soon followed by ecclesiastical patronizing, often led to opposition and violent clashes between representatives of Byzantine and Egyptian interests. Notwithstanding several incisive changes in Byzantine times, Alexandria kept some of its former political structures. One of these was the *boule*, composed of a smaller number of notables, including essentially big landowners, rich merchants, and higher administrative personnel. The members of the *boule* were responsible for the application of the imperial edicts and the payment of taxes from their own funds.

Even in the Byzantine period, Alexandria probably remained the most important economic center of the not yet divided Mediterranean world. In this respect, the capital of Egypt was well served by an abundant and highly professional working force. The transportation services, of paramount importance in a commercial city, were operated through associations of shippers. Specialized workers were active in linen weaving, processing of papyrus, and glassblowing. The manufacture of perfumes, jewelry, and drugs, a traditional domain of Alexandria, was still widely practiced in Byzantine times. Well equipped with harbors both on the sea and on the northern shore of Lake Mareotis, Alexandria availed itself of the opportunities of its site at the conjunction of the Mediterranean and the Nile. Commerce continued to flourish not only with its Western and Near Eastern neighbors but also with the Middle and the Far East (cf. Rougé). From the Egyptian ports on the Red Sea, especially from Leukos Limen al-Quṣayr, goods were transported through the Eastern Desert to the Nile Valley. There the town of Coptos was the most important trading center from which products were shipped down the Nile to Alexandria and the Mediterranean. In the third century, Coptos had attracted many foreigners who not only were active in commerce but also propagated new beliefs (MANICHAEISM; cf. Koenen, 1983) and alien interests (sympathizers of Palmyra; Schwartz, 1976).

The important role of Egypt in sustaining Constantinople and the Byzantine armies not only mirrors the auxiliary function of Alexandria in regard to the Byzantine capital but also shows how essential it was for the emperor and the central administration to secure the loyalty of Egypt and especially of Alexandria. This helps to explain the often far-reaching compromises between imperial and Egyptian interests, and the liberties conceded to the Alexandrian patriarch and his church in ecclesiastical and overall policy. The interference of the Alexandrian clergy in worldly matters can be understood first in the light of the strong connection between religious policy and political allegiance. But there is another aspect not to be neglected—the influence exerted by the church and its agencies on the professional groups of Alexandria. Not only was the church the single most important organization providing social welfare but, as Christianity conquered the majority of the Alexandrian population during the second half of the fourth century, it could and did use its new muscle in the struggle against heterodox rivals (Arians and Melitians), pagans, and Jews. In the course of the next centuries, the church, besides being the most influential political and social unit, became a potent economic organization, accumulating property, attracting legacies, and running its own enterprises.

Besides the reasons for Alexandrian unruliness already mentioned, there was further potential for social conflict in the late Roman period. Many Egyptians of the chora, being unable to pay their taxes, fled to Alexandria, where unemployment, notwithstanding the economic opportunities of the place, could be a problem. This was especially true during the winter months, when navigation on the Mediterranean had to be interrupted and many sailors and dockers were idle. There was an antagonism between these poorer classes and the richer members of the Alexandrian town council, who ran the local administration. When these economic and social tensions were fueled by religious conflicts, as occurred in the fourth century, when pagans were still numerous, this could result in bloody outbursts of anger and frustration.

It comes as no surprise that a church leader like ATHANASIUS presents conflicts in terms of religious affiliation, accusing the Arians of allying themselves with pagans and Jews in their hostility to orthodoxy. But that even a writer like Ammianus Marcellinus does so is perhaps a better proof of the pervading influence of religion on political and social matters. Describing the situation in Egypt in 362, after the death of Constantius II, who had favored Arianism, and the accession of Julian, Ammianus (XXII.11) gives a vivid account of the gruesome excesses of Alexandrian pagans against leading Christians. Georgius, the Arian bishop of the town, was lynched because he had denounced fellow citizens to Constantius. He was also thought to have given damaging advice on the taxing of public buildings and had infuriated pagan Alexandrians by insulting remarks on the sanctuary of the *Genius* (the temple of the Agathodaimon or, perhaps, the Serapeum; cf. Thélamon, 1981, pp. 248–50). The wrath of the pagan *plebs* turned also on Dracontius, the *praepositus monetae,* for having destroyed an altar in the Alexandrian mint and against the *comes* Diodorus, who, while overseer of the building of a church, had offended pagan feelings by cutting off the curls of boys, "thinking that this also had to do with the worship of gods" (Ammianus XXII.11.9). Ammianus stresses that even the Christians did not come to the rescue of the victims, because of the general hatred for Georgius. (One might, of course, suspect the antagonism between Arians and Orthodox Christians as the real reason for this failure to help.) After having insulted and murdered Georgius, Dracontius, and Diodorus, the pagan rioters cremated the corpses and threw the ashes into the sea in order to avoid, as Ammianus specifies, the collecting of the remains and the construction of memorial buildings such as had been erected to the martyrs of the past. Learning of these events, the emperor Julian, while utterly unsympathetic to Georgius, expressed his strong displeasure with the popular lynch law but refrained from punishing the culprits (Julian, *epistula* 60, ed. Bidez).

From roughly the same period as Ammianus is the *Expositio totius mundi* by an anonymous author of the Greek East (probable date, 359–360). He gives an interesting account of the state of affairs in Egypt and Alexandria (chs. 34–37), not only describing the geographical features of the country and its products, but also stressing the cultural activity of Alexandria and the fervor of pagan worship. Popular unrest in Alexandria is tersely recorded, with a surprising explanation (37.1): *Iudices enim in illa civitate cum timore et tremore intrant, populi iustitiam timentes* (for the governors enter this city with dread and tremble, fearing the people's justice). The anonymous writer goes on to specify the violence against culpable governors (*peccantes iudices*). Obviously, the author of this passage combines an extraordinary admiration for the presumed sense of justice of the Alexandrian population with a deep distrust of representatives of the central government.

In the following centuries of Byzantine rule, urban unrest is a recurrent theme in Alexandrian history. Conflicts between Monophysites and Dyophysites, patriarch and emperor (or his representatives), were frequent. As in many Roman and Byzantine towns, there had been and still was in Alexandria a strong interest in spectacles and mass entertainment. The hippodrome and its chariot races enjoyed special popularity, and the charioteers were public celebrities.

In that context, a series of graffiti and drawings mentioning and depicting charioteers, discovered by Polish archaeologists in the central quarter of Kom al-Dikkah, in a building that may have been the *bouleuterion* of late Roman Alexandria (and not the theater; cf. Balty), could make an interesting contribution to our knowledge of Alexandrian circus factions. Borkowski, who first edited this material, connected it with the uprising of Heraclius and his partisans against the emperor Phocas in 608. This connection, however, has been seriously challenged by Cameron and Bagnall (discussing chronological problems and the general interpretation of circus inscriptions).

We cannot deal here with the details of the last phase of Byzantine Alexandria and Egypt, but a short concluding note on the Arab conquest of Alexandria is indispensable. While Byzantium and Sassanid Persia exhausted themselves by waging war against each other, the forces of Islam gathered strength for their onslaught on both the Persian Middle East and the oriental provinces of Byzantium. After the fall of Egypt's eastern stronghold, Pelusium, in 639, the Arab troops of ʿAmr forced their way through the Delta. Babylon fell on 6 April 641, and Alexandria followed on 12 September 642. Dynastic strife in Constantinople following the death of the emperor Heraclius in 642 and the resulting confusion had greatly helped the Arab cause. When, on the other hand, dissensions in the Islamic camp led to the demise of ʿAmr, the Byzantine general Manuel seized the opportunity and recaptured Alexandria in 645. This in turn provoked the reinstallment of ʿAmr and the final conquest of Alexandria in 646. It sealed the close of an epoch that had begun nearly a millennium before with the coming of Alexander the Great in 332–331 B.C. But the end of Greco-Roman rule did not generate total disruption. However, notwithstanding the numerous links with the past, Egypt was now set on a new course, which finally led to the decline of Alexandria and the ascension of Cairo.

In later Roman times, Alexandria still had the reputation of being intellectually active and a town of learning. In his description of fourth-century Alexandria (XXII.16.7–22), Ammianus emphasizes the importance of arts, mathematics, music, and medicine. In the second half of that century, the Museon was still in existence. The famous library had already suffered several serious losses in the course of the successive devastations of the town. It seems never to have regained its former significance. Nevertheless, teaching, research, and literary activity were still flourishing in late Roman times, paganism and Christianity following their own, often uncompromising ways. Open and brutal hostility often prevailed: the persecution of Christians, the destruction of pagan sanctuaries (e.g., the Serapeum in 391), the savage killing of the pagan philosopher Hypatia in 415. But the brightest of Christian intellectuals never completely shed the heritage of Hellenic philosophy and of a classical tradition deeply imbued with paganism. Even after his conversion to Christianity, Hypatia's pupil Synesius, bishop of Ptolemais and later bishop of Cyrene, maintained his veneration for his pagan teacher. In late antiquity, Alexandria still had its adepts of Platonist and Aristotelian philosophy, while Justinian had already closed the Academy at Athens in 529. But the philosophers of that age progressively lost their pagan affiliation, being or becoming Christians, for example, the Monophysite John Philoponus (born c. 490), author of philosophical and theological works.

Poetry in Byzantine Alexandria largely followed the patterns of classical Greek tradition. Its practitioners were mostly scholars and teachers, often active as rhetors and attached to political figures. One outstanding example is Claudian, a pagan Alexandrian writing Latin verse at the end of the fourth and the beginning of the fifth centuries, who was part of the entourage of Stilicho, his patron and *magister militum* of the Western Roman Empire. In late Roman Egypt, Alexandria was not the only center of literary activity. Notwithstanding the rise of Coptic in the Egyptian hinterland, Greek language and culture were still firmly entrenched in several towns of the chora—for instance, in Panopolis, hometown of Nonnos, who in the fifth century wrote an epic poem in forty-eight books on the god Dionysus (*Dionysiaca*) as well as a metrical paraphrase of the Gospel of John (*Metabole*).

The classical tradition, until its final absorption by Christianity, was only one branch of the intellectual life of late Roman Alexandria. There was another, more genuine contribution of Christianity to Alexandrian teaching and philosophy—the so-called CATECHETICAL SCHOOL. At first offering no more than a basic program for catechumens, it became in the second century something of a philosophical school, particularly under the direction of CLEMENT and, from 203/204 to 231, of ORIGEN, one of the greatest and most controversial teachers of the church. Origenist influence was still perceptible in the fourth century, when DIDYMUS THE BLIND (c. 313–398), author of theological treatises and of commentaries on the Old Testament, was head of the Catechetical School. There is a marked contrast between the widespread influence of this school on Christian intellectuals in the Mediterranean world and the absence of Coptic translations of the writings of, for example, Clement and Origen (Krause, 1983), whereas the festal Letters of the Alexandrian patriarchs were translated into Coptic. Various explanations for this situation may be possible, the most obvious being perhaps, besides a lack of intellectual interest in this kind of theoretical work, the presumed unorthodoxy of Origen and his tradition. The fact that the Coptic language played virtually no role in Alexandria, but prevailed in the chora, is a clear indication of the cultural barrier between that town and native Egypt.

That barrier, however, was not totally impermeable. Whereas the influence of Greek Christian spirituality and theorization on native Egyptian Christianity seems to have been limited, the impact of the Coptic church on Alexandria and, via Alexandria, on Christianity at large was considerable (Krause, 1981). Coptic influence on the formulation of trinitarian theology, on monophysitism, and on the worship of Mary, Mother of God (THEOTOKOS) is obvious. Native Egypt also contributed a large share to monasticism in the late Roman Empire, by direct contact (visitors staying with Egyptian hermits or in Egyptian monasteries) and by the appeal of writings such as the *Life of Antony* by Athanasius. This work, in its combination of Greek and Egyptian spiritual traditions, impressively illustrates the role of Alexandria as a mediator between Coptic and Mediterranean monasticism. (Athanasius was one of the very few patriarchs familiar with the Coptic language.) In the course of time, monks came to dominate the church organization in the chora almost completely. By the sixth century, nearly all bishops in Egypt originated from Egyptian monasteries, which bears testimony to the influence of autochthonous Christianity in a number of once Hellenized nome capitals.

Our knowledge of the beginnings of Christianity in first-century Alexandria is very insufficient, but the heritage of these early stages was still visible in Byzantine Alexandria. In the second century, GNOSTICISM played a significant role there through teachers like Basilides and his son Isidorus. This tradition survived into fourth-century Alexandria but finally succumbed to orthodoxy.

Because of the nearly total absence of reliable archaeological data, our knowledge of the churches of Byzantine Alexandria rests almost completely on literary sources (Calderini, 1935; Krause, 1966; Martin, 1984). As for monasteries, there were none or very few within the walls of late Roman Alexandria, but they were extraordinarily numerous in the immediate surroundings of the town (Krause, 1981, p. 57). Among the most important was the monastic complex of ENATON at the ninth milestone west of Alexandria. Many churches were built on the ruins or within the existing structures of pagan sanctuaries. Alexandria counted seven or more churches before the victory of Constantine in 324. Constantine himself does not stand out as a builder or benefactor of Alexandrian churches, since the capital of Egypt was neither an imperial residence like Constantinople nor a holy place like Jerusalem. His successor, Constantius II (337–361), authorized the construction of a church in the former Caesareum as a favor to the Arian bishop Georgius. The chief promotor of Alexandrian church building was the patriarch THEOPHILUS (385–412). On the ruins of the Serapeum, devastated in 391, he erected a martyrium and a church of Saint John the Baptist, which is probably identical with the church named after the emperor Arcadius. Another church, bearing the name of the emperor Theodosius, was perhaps built on the site of the Serapeum as well. On the island of Pharos, Theophilus had a church consecrated to Saint RAPHAEL, the archangel then replacing Isis Pharia as a protector of navigation.

Only a few of the Alexandrian churches can be localized exactly or approximately. The Baucalis Church (where Arius had been presbyter) derived its name from the eastern suburb of Boukolia or Boukolon. In the vicinity stood the martyrium and the Church of Saint Mark. More to the west, in the quarter of the former temple of the god Bendis, probably near the Great Harbor, Athanasius had built in 268–270 the Church of Bendideion or Mendideion, which later took his name. Another church, called by the name of the predecessor of Athanasius, ALEXANDER I (312–326), was perhaps a former temple of the god Kronos Saturnus transformed by Alexander into a church of Saint Michael. When, about 325, Constantine ordered the transfer of the Nile cubit from the Serapeum to an unnamed church, this church may well have been the Church of Saint Michael (following Martin, p. 219), since elsewhere this saint replaced the god Hermes Thoth as the patron of inundation (see also Thélamon, pp. 276ff.). The main church of early

Christian Alexandria stood in the western part of the town and bore the name of Bishop Theonas (282–300). It was the cathedral of the Alexandrian patriarchs until this function was transferred to the Church of Saint Dionysius and later to the church built in the former Caesareum (Augusteum or Sebasteum), which Constantius II put at the disposal of the Arian bishop Georgius. Later it was taken over by Athanasius and was designated the Great Church. A church in the western necropole had received the name of the martyr-bishop Peter (300–311); it was later consecrated to Saint Mary Theotokos.

After the Council of CHALCEDON in 451 and the ensuing schism between Monophysites and Dyophysites, Alexandria was torn by rival communities. The Dyophysites, siding with the Orthodox emperor and thus called Melchites (from *melech,* which means king or emperor), competed with the Monophysites for the patriarchate and the possession of the Alexandrian churches. In the Egyptian chora, the Monophysites held a near monopoly, and they certainly represented the majority in Alexandria. This conflict finally led to the simultaneous existence of two rival patriarchs in Egypt, the Melchite one (most of them of non-Alexandrian and non-Egyptian origin) being recognized by the emperor, whereas the Monophysite patriarch was virtually excluded from Alexandria, finding shelter in the numerous monasteries surrounding Alexandria, especially in the Enaton. When the Arabs conquered Alexandria, the Melchite patriarch Cyrus al-Muqawqas left the town with the Byzantine troops, whereas the Monophysite patriarch BENJAMIN I seized the opportunity and returned to Alexandria. His successors maintained their see there until the eleventh century. Only then did the patriarch CHRISTODOULUS (1047–1077) transfer his see to the political capital, Cairo.

BIBLIOGRAPHY

Adriani, A. *Repertorio d'arte dell'Egitto greco-romano,* Ser. C, Vols. 1–2, pls. 1–113, nos. 1–146. Palermo, 1966.

Balty, J.-C. 'Le 'bouleuterion' de l'Alexandrie sévérienne." In *Etudes et travaux* 13. Travaux du Centre d'Archéologie Méditerranéenne de l'Académie Polonaise des Sciences 26. Warsaw, 1983.

Bernhard, M. L., ed. *Starozytna Aleksandria w badaniach polskich.* Warsaw, 1977.

Bernand, A. *Alexandrie la grande.* Paris, 1966.

Bidez, J. *Julian der Abtrünnige.* Munich, 1947.

Bonacasa, N., and A. di Vita, eds. *Alessandria e il mondo ellenistico-romano. Studi in onore di Achille Adriani,* 3 vols. Studi e Materiali, Istituto di Archeologia, Università di Palermo 4–6. Rome, 1983–1984.

Borkowski, Z. *Inscriptions des factions à Alexandrie.* Warsaw, 1981.

Bowman, A. K. *The Town Councils of Roman Egypt.* American Studies in Papyrology 11. Toronto, 1971.

———. *Egypt After the Pharaohs 332 B.C.–A.D. 642: From Alexander to the Arab Conquest,* pp. 203–233. London, 1986.

Breccia, E. *Alexandrea ad Aegyptum. A Guide to the Ancient and Modern Town, and to Its Graeco-Roman Museum.* Bergamo, 1922.

Butler, A. J. *The Arab Conquest of Egypt and the Last Thirty Years of the Roman Dominion,* 2nd ed., ed. P. M. Fraser. Oxford, 1978.

Calderini, A. *Dizionario dei nomi geografici e topografici dell'Egitto greco-romano,* Vol. 1, pt. 1, pp. 55–205. Cairo, 1935.

Cameron, A., and R. S. Bagnall. *Bulletin of the American Society of Papyrologists* 20 (1983):75–84 (review of Z. Borkowski, *Inscriptions des factions à Alexandrie*).

Fraser, P. M. "A Syriac *Notitia urbis Alexandrinae.*" *Journal of Egyptian Archaeology* 37 (1951):103–108.

———. *Ptolemaic Alexandria,* 3 vols. Oxford, 1972.

Geraci, G. *Genesi della provincia romana d'Egitto.* Studi di Storia Antica 9. Bologna, 1983.

Grimm, G. *et al.,* eds. *Alexandrien. Kulturbegegnungen dreier Jahrtausende im Schmelztiegel einer mediterranen Grossstadt.* Aegyptiaca Treverensia 1. Mainz, 1981.

Hendriks, I. H. M.; P. J. Parsons; and K. A. Worp. "Papyri from the Groningen Collection I: *Encomium Alexandreae.*" *Zeitschrift für Papyrologie und Epigraphik* 41 (1981):71–83.

Jones, C. P. *The Roman World of Dio Chrysostom,* pp. 36–44. Cambridge, Mass., and London, 1978.

Koenen, L. "Manichäische Mission und Klöster in Ägypten." In *Das römisch-byzantinische Ägypten. Akten des internationalen Symposions 26.–30. September 1978 in Trier,* ed. G. Grimm et al. Aegyptiaca Treverensia 2. Mainz, 1983.

Kolb, F. "Das Strafgericht Caracallas über die Alexandriner." In *Literarische Beziehungen zwischen Cassius Dio, Herodian und der Historia Augusta,* pp. 97–111. Antiquitas, Ser. 4, Vol. 9. Bonn, 1972.

Krause, M. "Alexandria." In *Reallexikon zur byzantinischen Kunst,* Vol. 1, cols. 99–111. Stuttgart, 1966.

———. "Das christliche Alexandrien und seine Beziehungen zum koptischen Ägypten." In *Alexandrien. Kulturbegegnungen dreier Jahrtausende im*

Schmelztiegel einer mediterranen Grossstadt, ed. G. Grimm et al. Aegyptiaca Treverensia 1. Mainz, 1981.

———. "Das Weiterleben ägyptischer Vorstellungen und Bräuche im koptischen Totenwesen." In *Das römisch-byzantinische Ägypten. Akten des internationalen Symposions 26.–30. September 1978 in Trier,* ed. G. Grimm et al. Aegyptiaca Treverensia 2. Mainz, 1983.

Leclercq, H., and F. Cabrol. "Alexandrie." In *Dictionnaire d'archéologie chrétienne et de liturgie,* Vol. 1, cols. 1098–1210. Paris, 1924.

Martin, A. "Les premiers siècles du christianisme à Alexandrie. Essai de topographie religieuse (IIIe–IVe siècles)." *Revue des études augustiniennes* 30 (1984):211–25.

Müller, C. D. G. "Alexandrien. I. Historisch." *Theologische Realenzyklopädie* 2 (1978):248–61.

Rodziewicz, M. "Nouvelles données sur le quartier de Kopron à Alexandrie." In *Etudes et travaux* 11. Travaux du Centre d'Archéologie Méditerranéenne de l'Académie Polonaise des Sciences 22. Warsaw, 1979.

———. *Les habitations romaines tardives d'Alexandrie à la lumière des fouilles polonaises à Kom el-Dikka.* Alexandrie III. Warsaw, 1984.

———. "Excavations at Kom el-Dikka in Alexandria 1980–1981 (Preliminary Report)." *Annales du Service des antiquités de l'Egypte* 70 (1984–1985):233–42.

Rougé, J. *Recherches sur l'organisation du commerce maritime en Méditerranée sous l'empire romain.* Paris, 1966.

Schubart, W. "Alexandria." In *Reallexikon für Antike und Christentum,* Vol. 1, cols. 271–83. Stuttgart, 1950.

Schwartz, J. "Palmyre et l'opposition à Rome en Egypte." In *Palmyre. Bilan et perspectives. Colloque de Strasbourg (18–20 Octobre 1973).* Travaux du Centre de Recherche sur le Proche-Orient et la Grèce antique 3. Strasbourg, 1976.

Thélamon, F. *Païens et chrétiens au IVe siècle. L'apport de l'"Histoire ecclésiastique" de Rufin d'Aquilée.* Paris, 1981.

HEINZ HEINEN

ALEXANDRIAN THEOLOGY. When Saint Mark introduced Christianity into Egypt, the city of Alexandria was already a great center of learning where Hellenistic thought thrived side by side with Hebrew teachings. The most eloquent exponent of philosophy of the time was PHILO OF ALEXANDRIA (20 B.C.–A.D. 50), who sought to fuse and harmonize Greek thought and Hebrew religion. When Christianity found a fertile ground in Alexandria, a school that was originally established to teach CATECHUMENS soon developed into a flourishing center for the dissemination of all types of knowledge and was able to stand against the influence of other centers of learning in the metropolis, such as the schools founded by Ptolemy I and Ammonius Saccas (in 323 and 193 B.C., respectively). The new Christian school soon attracted many of the luminaries of law, philosophy, logic, and rhetoric, and eventually evolved a new system of thought in harmony with Christian teaching.

Among the outstanding figures of this school were Athenagoras, PANTAENUS, CLEMENT OF ALEXANDRIA, and ORIGEN. Athenagoras advocated the idea that the subtle, mysterious references uttered by the ancient high priests concerning the breaking forth of the light had at last been fully realized. Pantaenus was busy culling material from a variety of sources to strengthen the spirits of believers. Clement of Alexandria, described by Saint Jerome as the most learned scholar of his time, spared no effort in establishing the Christian church on sure foundations. Origen, the philosopher par excellence, was the supreme teacher during the postapostolic period (Rufinus *Apologiae in Sanctum Hieronymum* 2.20). He was the finest elucidator of the Christian mysteries and paved the way for those who desired to comprehend the majesty of the Creator (Daniélou, 1948).

These great thinkers codified the Alexandrian theology, which had the following distinctive features:

1. The use of philosophical studies not merely as an introduction to the understanding of religious science but, more important, as an effective means toward the proper assimilation of Christian doctrine. Clement of Alexandria was able to harness philosophy in the service of faith and to use the weapons of philosophical arguments to refute the claims of his opponents. He argued that real gnosticism brooks no contradiction between faith and knowledge—on the contrary, it generates a certain harmony, which leads to the attainment of perfect Christianity and perfect gnosticism. To him, faith is the beginning and end of philosophy.

2. The supremacy of Logology in the attempt to narrow the gap between God and the world. To Clement, the Logos is a member of the Trinity: the Creator, the Divine Mind, the Teacher, and Savior of humanity who, through faith, knowledge, contemplation, and love, will lead human beings to eternal life. Christ, the Incarnate Word of God, is at the same time God who became man. It was Origen who enriched ecclesiastical vocabulary with the Christological terminology that is still in current use, though perhaps differently applied at times: Hypostasis, Physis, Theanthropos, Homoousios, and Ousia.

3. The use of allegory in the interpretation of the Scriptures for non-Christians. In this respect Origen may have been influenced by Philo of Alexandria, who differed from the school of Antioch, which kept to the literal and historical approach in the interpretation of biblical texts.

4. The contrastive textual method in the translation of both Old and New Testaments into Coptic, said to have been carried out by Pantaenus and Clement—an achievement that undoubtedly encouraged the spread of Christianity among Egyptians. The first attempt at verifying the text of the Old Testament was undertaken by Origen, who compiled the following works:

a. a *Tetrapla* comprising four parallel columns, including the translations of the Septuagint, Aquila, Symmachos, and Theodotion, with Origen's own commentary on the Septuagint.

b. a *Hexapla* comprising the previous four translations in four columns, to which are added a Hebrew text in Hebrew characters, and the same text in Greek characters.

c. an *Octapla,* comprising the previous six columns, to which are added the two translations found in Jericho and Nikopolis.

Origen's works amounted to about fifty volumes, representing a unique and unparalleled attempt in the study of the Scriptures by one man, who can rightly be called the founder of the science of exegesis.

BIBLIOGRAPHY

Asad Rustum. *Abā' al-kanīsah fī al-qurūn al-thalāthah al-ulā.* Beirut, 1963.

Daniélou, Jean. *Origène.* Paris, 1948.

Grillmeier, A. *Christ in Christian Theology,* trans. S. Bowden. London, 1965.

Ighnāṭyus Aphram. *Al-durar al-nafīsah fī mukhtaṣar al-kanīsah.* Ḥoms, 1940.

Kelly, J. N. D. *Early Christian Doctrines,* 5th ed. London, 1968.

Nautin, P. *Origène: Sa vie et son oeuvre.* Paris, 1979.

Osborne, E. F. "Teaching and Writing in the First Chapter of the *Stromateis* of Clement of Alexandria." *Journal of Theological Studies* n.s. 10 (1959): 335–343.

Oulton, J. E. L., and H. Chadwick. *Alexandrian Christianity.* London, 1968.

Rufinus. *Apologia in Sanctum Hieronymum.* In PL 21, cols. 541–624. Paris, 1849.

Trigg, J. W. *Origen: The Bible and Philosophy in the Third Century Church.* Atlanta, 1983.

ARCHBISHOP BASILIOS

ALLBERRY, CHARLES ROBERT CECIL AUSTIN (1913–1943), English Coptologist. He was educated at Christ College, Cambridge, and became the first Lady Wallis Budge scholar. He edited and published the Chester Beatty Manichaean Psalm Book and other Coptic texts. He also published articles in *Journal of Egyptian Archaeology,* of which he became the editor in 1939. He joined the Royal Air Force in 1940 and was killed in action over Germany in April 1943. A list of his specific contributions to Coptic studies can be found in *A Coptic Bibliography* (Kammerer, 1950, 1969).

BIBLIOGRAPHY

Dawson, R. and E. P. Uphill. *Who Was Who in Egyptology.* London, 1972.

Kammerer, W. comp. *A Coptic Bibliography.* Ann Arbor, 1950; repr. New York, 1969.

AZIZ S. ATIYA

ALLELUIA, an expression of praise to God, occurring in a number of Psalms and in the book of Revelation. It is used extensively in the church rites and ceremonies, usually preceding the Gospel.

Like the term "Amen" (meaning "verily") Alleluia (also spelled Halleluiah and Hallelujah) was adopted into Christian worship in both Eastern and Western churches. Sozomen, the fifth-century historian, states that in A.D. 389 the Christian population of Alexandria sang Alleluia while pulling down a temple of the cult of Serapis.

BIBLIOGRAPHY

Cabral, F. "Alleluia, acclamation liturgique." In *Dictionnaire d'archéologie chrétienne et de liturgie,* Vol. 1, cols, 1229–46. Paris, 1907.

Mattā al-Miskīn. *Al-Ifkhāristiyyā.* Cairo, 1977.

ARCHBISHOP BASILIOS

ALLOGENES, the third tractate from Codex XI (45.1–69.20) of the NAG HAMMADI LIBRARY, is a "book" (68.21; cf. 69.17–18, where the plural is used) said to be written by a certain Allogenes ("stranger," "one of another race") for Messos ("middle one," i.e., the one between the divine and the lower realms). The recipient of revelation, Allogenes is told to transcribe the book and preserve it on a mountain for the sake of posterity (68.16–25); he passes this revelatory work on to his disciple Messos, whom he describes as his "son," so that he in turn may proclaim these truths to those who would hear (cf. the instructions of the heavenly being addressing Allogenes at 68.19–20: "those who will be worthy after you"). Allogenes is given its title as a subscript (69.20), and certainly must be related to the revelations of Allogenes and Messos mentioned by Porphyry in his *Life of Plotinus* 16 (cf. also Epiphanius, *Panarion* 39.5.1, 40.2.2, on "the books called Allogeneis").

The tractate records the nature of the divine as revealed to Allogenes. Although a few lines are missing at the tops of many pages, the tractate apparently opens at 45.1 with the first of several speeches delivered to Allogenes by Youel, "she who is of all the glories" (50.19–20 ff.). In these revelatory speeches Youel explicates the character of the Triple Power and the aeon of Barbelo: the Triple Power truly exists, and is manifested in existence, life, and mind (49.26–38; cf. the Neoplatonic triad *to on, zoe, nous*), while the aeon of Barbelo is the divine First Thought, "possessing the patterns and the forms of those who truly exist" (51.14–16) and also correcting the defects of nature (51.28–32). As in *The Three Steles of Seth* (Nag Hammadi Codex VII,. 5.126, 4–16 ff.), praises are offered (here, it seems, by Youel) to the heavenly glories (53.37–54.37ff.). Meanwhile, Allogenes is filled with goodness and light, and can even exclaim, "I became divine" (52.12–13). When Youel finally departs (57.24–27), Allogenes spends a full century preparing for further visions of the godhead, and he is not disappointed in his hopes. He is taken up in ecstasy to a marvelous holy place where heavenly powers explain how he may receive "a primary revelation of the Unknown One, the One whom, if you would know him, be ignorant of him" (59.28–32). With a profound silence and calm Allogenes ascends up through the Triple Power, from the blessedness of self-knowledge (cf. mind) to the eternal motion of vitality and the stillness of existence itself. In such a manner Allogenes attains to the Unknown One, who subsequently is described in utterly transcendent and paradoxical terms (61.25–67.20).

Allogenes thus is a non-Christian Gnostic text with a strongly philosophical orientation. Using terms and perspectives characteristic of Neoplatonism, the tractate probably was composed, in Greek, during the late second or early third century.

BIBLIOGRAPHY

Robinson, J. M. "The Three Steles of Seth and the Gnostics of Plotinus," pp. 132–42. In *Proceedings of the International Colloquium on Gnosticism,* ed. G. Widengren. Stockholm, 1977.

Turner, J. D. "XI, 3: Allogenes." In *Nag Hammadi Codices XI, XII and XIII,* ed. C. W. Hedrick. Nag Hammadi Studies. Leiden, forthcoming.

Wire, A. C.; J. D. Turner; and O. S. Wintermute. "Allogenes (XI,3)." In *The Nag Hammadi Library in English,* ed. J. M. Robinson. San Francisco, 1977.

MARVIN W. MEYER

ALODIA. *See* ʿAlwā.

ALPHA AND OMEGA. *See* Symbols in Coptic Art.

ALPHABET IN COPTIC, GREEK. *See Appendix.*

ALPHABETS, COPTIC. *See Appendix.*

ALPHABETS, OLD COPTIC. *See Appendix.*

ALTAR, a place, structure, or table on which sacrifices are offered to a divinity. The word comes from the Latin *altare* related to the verb *adolēre,* to "burn up."

Pagan Altars

Since prehistoric times, offerings to subterranean gods were made in pits, and offerings to heavenly gods were presented on altars raised above the ground. The latter usage was influenced not only by awe of the deity but also by considerations of expedience, whether the object sacrificed was a burnt offering of meat or a simple offering of fruit or grain. At first a pile of wood and branches or a large, freestanding stone may have sufficed.

When such sacrificial acts were regularly repeated at the same spot, it was natural to create a permanent artificial support for them. In Judaism, altars built of earth or unhewn stones (Ex. 20:24–25) were required. The Greeks and Romans, as well as the Egyptians, at first used brick altars. Later they built altars of hewn stones or even monoliths. In Egypt a brick altar belonging to the Fourth Dynasty was identified in the area of the Satet temple at Elephantine (Dreyer, 1977, pp. 73–81), but Egyptian altars usually consisted of movable wooden offering tables, sometimes overlaid with metal, which were kept in storehouses when not in use. The few stone altars fixed in position are cubical and suggest the wooden altars that were their prototype. The upper surface is enclosed by a frame and, in some cases, contains bowl-shaped depressions.

For a long time in the Greco-Roman world most altars were built in a simple block form. From the beginning of the classical period, however, the form of the altar became artistically richer, modeled on the bases of statues and elements of temple architecture. The altars of some important temples were even adorned with reliefs, for example, the altar at Pergamum and the Ara Pacis in Rome. At the same time, their size was increased. While most altars were small and humble, there were some of enormous dimensions and of an unusual height, so that the officiating priest could ascend to them only by a staircase. The enhancement of their size had the purely practical purpose of affording the largest possible number of people a view of the sacrificial rites.

Christian Altars

In Christianity also, the altar is the place of sacrifice, for it is only at the altar, considered as holy, that the transformation of the bread and wine into the Body and Blood of Christ is accomplished in the EUCHARIST, through which worshipers are in communion with God. In some texts of the Coptic tradition, the concept of sacrifice is given very clear expression. In the early period of Christianity the altar also served as the table (Greek *trapeza*) on which the gifts of bread and wine to be used for the Eucharist were laid by the congregation. The altar thus became the place of sacrifice only after the development of the liturgy in which the priest officiated. When congregations had grown to large numbers in the Constantinian period separate tables for gifts were set up alongside the actual eucharistic sacrificial altar (Klauser, Vol. 43, 1935, pp. 179–86).

When in the course of the fourth and fifth centuries the practice of the congregation making such offerings again fell out of use and the elements to be used for the Eucharist had increasingly to be supplied by the church, these gift tables also fell into disuse. Nevertheless, there are still traces of such subsidiary tables. One is in a side niche in the central church of Makhūrah al-Qiblī (Grossmann, 1980, pp. 225–27). In the church in front of the pylon of the Luxor temple such a table stood at the side wall of the apse. Both could properly be interpreted only as gift tables in the sense mentioned. Otherwise in the Eastern churches the gifts intended for the Eucharist were deposited in a room called the *scevophilacion,* situated near the entrance or even outside the church; they were ceremonially brought to the altar only in the "great entrance," which has its origin in this rite (Descoeudres, 1983, pp. 49–61).

Form. Probably because of its original subsidiary function as a table for the gifts brought by the congregation, the altar in the early Christian period frequently took the form of an ordinary table. It consisted of a top (*mensa*) carried on one or more legs, which were themselves fixed in a base or simply into the floor. The Coptic church also used movable wooden altars. Altars with six legs are less common but occur in both main churches of the Kellia. The altar of the later East Church of Qaṣr Waḥaydah was round. Several built-in altar bases of the early Christian period have a further depression in the middle as in the East Church of the pilgrim center of ABŪ MĪNĀ, (Grossmann, 1977, pp. 35–38), which was probably the place for a reliquary.

Besides these simple table-altars, massive monolithic altars and altars built of stone or bricks were in use at an early date. The former often consisted of blocks that originally came from another structure and were reworked for their new use. Thus, the altar of the East Church of Abū Mīnā consisted of a simple column drum flattened on the back (Grossmann, 1977, p. 37). In the church in the Isis temple at PHILAE dedicated to Saint Stephen, a former pagan altar was taken over for church use.

The form of altar in use today in Egypt appears to have developed in the Fatimid period. It consists of a cube built up of quarried stone or, more rarely, of bricks, as at DAYR SITT DIMIYANAH, which in only a few cases is furnished with an upper cornice. Notable exceptions are in Cairo. The latter probably has its origin in the monolithic marble slab used earlier. A shallow rectangular depression was let into the upper surface of the block, which originally held a relic. Today, in the same place, there is a consecrated wooden board (*maqṭa'*). In the back of the altar, facing the east, a small but relatively deep cavity like a niche is left open close to the floor; this must be regarded as the last vestige of the original table-shaped form of the altar. Today the consecrated oil is frequently kept in it.

Location. As a rule, in the early Christian period, the altar in a church stood not within but in front of the apse, in an area surrounded by low screens (cancelli), the presbytery (see ARCHITECTURAL ELEMENTS OF CHURCHES). In the Great Basilica of Abū Mīnā it stood in the center of the intersection of the nave and the presbytery, and in the North Basilica of the same place, it stood in the area of the second eastern intercolumnium. Only in very simple churches—such as those of the anchorite settlements of Kellia, which instead of a semicircular apse had only a rectangular cult chamber furnished in the east wall with a simple prayer niche—is the altar accommodated within this cult chamber. The latter accordingly represents the presbytery. In very small oratories, the altar consists of no more than a *mensa* let into an eastern niche, usually semicircular. In some cases, the space under the *mensa* is not even left open but is imitated by dark painting. In these oratories the niche serves as both altar room and apse. Even after the introduction of the *khūrus* (room at the eastern end of the nave) in the late seventh century, the altar remained located in front of the apse and of necessity came to be in the area of the *khūrus*. An exception, however, is the al-'Adhrā' church of DAYR AL-SURYĀN in Wādī al-Naṭrūn, deriving from the early eighth century, where the altar, despite the original presence of a *khūrus*, was evidently accommodated from the beginning in the central cult chamber at the eastern end of the church (Grossmann, 1982, pp. 115–19).

An alteration to this pattern resulted from the introduction of churches with several altars in the late twelfth and early thirteenth centuries. In all probability the typical simple anchorite church served as the model for this new development. The altar is now occasionally accommodated in a room designated as the *haykal* (Hebrew, *hēkal*, the room in front of the Holy of Holies in the Temple) or *sharqiyyaḥ* (Arabic for "the eastern"). This room, the sanctuary, is closed off toward the nave by a screen called the *hijāb*, or ICONOSTASIS, built of wood, stone, or brick.

BIBLIOGRAPHY

Apophthegmata Patrum, ed. J. B. Cotelíer. PG 65, cols. 71–440. Paris, 1864.

Braun, J. *Der christliche Altar in seiner geschichtlichen Entwicklung*, Vols. 1–2. Munich, 1924.

Burmester, O. H. E. *The Egyptian or Coptic Church*. Cairo, 1967.

Butler, A. J. *The Ancient Coptic Churches of Egypt*, Vol. 2. Oxford, 1884; repr., 1970.

Daumas, F. "Rapport sur l'activité de l' Institut français d'Archéologie orientale du Caire an cours des années 1968–1969. *Comptes rendus de l'Académie des Inscriptions et Belles-Lettres*, pp. 496–507. Paris, 1969.

Descoeudres, G. *Die Pastophorien im syro-byzantischen Osten*. Wiesbaden, 1983.

Galling, K.; J. P. Kirsch; T. Klauser; and L. Ziehen. "Altar I–III." *Reallexikon für Antike und Christentum* 1 (1950):310–54.

Grossmann, P. "Abū Mīnā, Die Ostkirche." *Mitteilungen des deutschen archäologischen Instituts—Abteilung Kairo* 33 (1977):35–38.

______. "Abū Mīnā, Die Ostkirche." *Mitteilungen des deutschen archäologischen Instituts—Abteilung Kairo* 36 (1980):222–224.

______. *Mittelalterliche Langhauskuppelkirchen und verwandte Typen in Oberägypten*. Gluckstadt, 1982.

______. "Funde im Presbyterium der Gruftkirche." *Mitteilungen des deutschen archäologischen Instituts—Abteilung Kairo* 40 (1984):126–31.

Kaiser, W. "Stadt und Tempel von Elephantine." *Mitteilungen des deutschen archäologischen Instituts—Abteilung Kairo* 33 (1977):73–81.

Kasser, R. *Kellia Topographie*. Geneva, 1972.

Klauser, T. "Die konstantinischen Altäre der Lateransbasilika." *Römische Quartalschrift für christliche Altertumskunde und für Kirchengeschichte* 43 (1935):179–86.

Munier, H. *La Scala copte 44 de la Bibliothèque nationale de Paris*, Vol. 1. Cairo, 1930.

Muyser, J. "Des Vases eucharistiques en verre." *Bulletin de la Société d'archéologie copte* 3 (1937):9–28.

Nussbaum, O. *Der Standort des Liturgen am christlichen Altar vor dem Jahre 1000*. Bonn, 1965.

Onasch, K. *Kunst und Liturgie der Ostkirche*. Vienna, 1981.

Rassart-Debergh, M. "La Decoration peinte." In *Le site monastique des Kellia*. Louvain, 1984.

Stadelmann, R. "Altar." *Lexion der Agyptologie* 1 (1975):145–49.

PETER GROSSMANN

ALTAR, CONSECRATION OF. Anointing a new altar is the culmination of the ceremonial consecration of a new church. The elaborate service, rich in prayers and petitions, is a reflection of the reverence felt toward the holy table, the place where, at every celebration of the Divine Liturgy, the actual transformation of the bread and wine into the Body and Blood of our Lord Jesus Christ takes place. The following is a brief account of this service.

Standing at the altar with the rest of the clergy, the bishop first offers incense and says the prayer of incense, followed by Psalms 22 and 23. Again he offers incense, and makes the sign of the cross over the altar, without using the chrism oil. Then Psalms 25, 26, 83, and 92 are read, followed by the Pauline Epistle (Heb. 13:10–16). The deacons sing the *Trisagion* and a priest recites the intercession of the Gospel. The Gospel reading is taken from Matthew 16:13–19, the last two verses of which are, "And I tell you, you are Peter, and on this rock I will build my church, and the powers of death shall not prevail against it. I will give you the keys of the kingdom of heaven, and whatever you bind on earth shall be bound in heaven, and whatever you loose on earth shall be loosed in heaven."

This is followed by the seven greater intercessions: for the sick, for travelers, for waters (or crops or vegetation according to the season of the year), for the ruler, for the dormant, for oblations, and for catechumens.

Then the bishop reads a number of petitions, each of which is concluded with the words, "We beseech Thee, God our Savior, hearken to us and have mercy upon us," to which the congregation respond "Kyrie eleison." In these prayers reference is made to the following points: (1) the creation of man in the image of God, his fall, and his reinstatement; (2) the incarnation of Jesus Christ; (3) the birth of the Only-begotten Son of God in the fullness of time; (4) the establishment of the holy church upon the immovable rock; (5) the blessing of the Patriarch Abraham by Melchizedek, with bread and wine according to the grace of the new covenant given to the church; (6) the manifestation of the promise of salvation to Isaac; (7) Jacob's vision of the ladder reaching up to heaven, with the angels descending upon it and his setting up of a stone as a pillar and pouring of oil on its corner, calling the place the house of God; (8) the granting of the law to Moses upon Mount Sinai and his building of the tabernacle; (9) the command of God to Moses to place an ark in the tabernacle, and a golden pot with manna, representing the bread of life descending from heaven; (10) the adorning of the tabernacle by Belzaleel according to the pattern seen by Moses; (11) the making of a covenant with David for the building of the house that was later completed by his son Solomon; (12) the sanctification of the house by God, in answer to Solomon's prayers; (13) the granting to the apostles the pattern of heavenly things and the hieratic orders and rituals; (14) the prayer to Jesus Christ, the lover of man, to have mercy upon the congregation; (15) the prayer to God to send down the Holy Spirit, the Paraclete, as He had done to the apostles, to bless this new place and transform it into a holy church, a house of salvation, a place of forgiveness of sin, an assembling place of the angels, a haven of safety, a holy tabernacle, a heavenly altar, and a cleansing place of stained souls; (16) the prayer for the well-being of the patriarch and the bishops; and (17) the prayer for the clergy and the congregation, by the intercessions of the THEOTOKOS, the archangels, John the Baptist, Saint Mark, and all the saints.

The three greater intercessions follow—for peace, for the church fathers, and for the congregation—and then all recite the Creed. The bishop offers incense for the third time, makes the sign of the cross over the altar, also without using oil, and prays to the Almighty God to send His Holy Spirit upon this altar that He may purify it for a place on which to offer the bloodless sacrifice of the Holy Body and Precious Blood of Jesus Christ.

After some petitions said by the deacon, the bishop continues, saying, "Almighty God, receive this fervent supplication of Thy servants . . . Lord, God, receive this fervent supplication of Thy servants . . . Lord, God of our salvation, who has substituted ecclesiastical ritual for symbolical types, who has released us from the vanity of material things . . . grant us the blessing of Christ who raised up the church and set up the altars, who gave us the baptism of regeneration. . . . Give help to those who offer sacrifices on our behalf. Complete the consecration of this altar with the oil of grace, the mystery of the Holy Spirit, to offer the bloodless sacrifice through the mystic unction, to partake of the Holy Body and the Precious Blood."

The bishop concludes his prayers with these short petitions: "A pure altar; a harbor for troubled souls; a refuge from sin, both voluntary an involuntary; deliverance from unjudicious intentions; provision of heavenly graces; fulfillment of all righteousness," after each of which the congregation responds "Amen."

Finally the bishop takes the pot of myron oil, pours the oil upon the altar three times in the form of the cross, saying each time "Alleluia." With his thumb he makes three crosses with the myron oil, saying, "With this holy myron, we consecrate this altar which has already been placed, for the name of [Saint] in the name of the Father, and of the Son, and of the Holy Spirit."

He proceeds to anoint the entire altar, while reciting Psalms 84:1–3, 4, 6–7, 8–10 and 26:6–8, and says a prayer of thanksgiving. New coverings are laid on the altar, and the gospel book, the cross, and the altar vessels are placed on top. The *Trisagion* and the prayer of inclination follow. The bishop offers incense, says the prayer of incense, and goes around the altar three times, joined by the clergy. Then all go around the church carrying lighted candles and singing appropriate hymns. Then he says the prayer of thanksgiving, standing at the altar, and reads Psalm 26:8, 7: "O Lord, I love the habitation of thy house, and the place where thy glory dwells. Singing aloud a song of thanksgiving, and telling all thy wondrous deeds." The Gospel reading is taken from Luke 19:1–10.

A priest says the three intercessions (for church peace, the fathers, and the congregation), and finally the bishop says the absolution. Then they proceed to consecrate the baptismal font.

BIBLIOGRAPHY

Abū al-Barakat ibn Kabar. *Miṣbaḥ al-Ẓulmah,* Vol. 1, pp. 1–43. Cairo, 1971.

Horner, G. W. *The Service for the Consecration of a Church and Altar According to the Coptic Rite.* London, 1902.

ARCHBISHOP BASILIOS

ALTAR-BOARD (*maqṭa'* or *al-lawḥ al-khashab*), consecrated rectangular wooden panel set into a special slot on the surface of the altar to be used as a substitute reliquary. Usually it is decorated with a cross and bears the signs ⲓⲏ ⲭⲣ ⲩⲥ ⲑⲥ (Jesus Christ Son of God) in the four squares between the arms of the cross.

[*See also:* Antimension.]

BIBLIOGRAPHY

Burmester, O. H. E. *The Egyptian or Coptic Church,* pp. 21–22. Cairo, 1967.

Butler, A. J. *The Ancient Coptic Churches of Egypt,* Vol. 2, pp. 3–7. Oxford, 1884; repr., 1970.

PETER GROSSMANN

ALTAR LIGHTS, lights to illumine the church, its sanctuary, and the altar, which must be lit during the liturgy and other prayers, even if services are held in broad daylight.

In the Old Testament the Lord commanded Moses to make a lampstand of pure gold according to a particular symbolical design (Ex. 25:31–40; 37:17–24, etc.) and place it at the south side of the tabernacle opposite the table (Ex. 26:35). When Solomon built the temple, he made ten lampstands of gold in the minor shrine (1 Kgs. 7:49; 2 Chr. 4:7). These, together with the other contents of the temple, were removed to Babylon in 587 B.C. (Jer. 52:18).

In the Christian church, the kindling of light is associated with the coming of Christ, "the light of the world" (Jn. 12:46). The book of Revelation describes seven lampstands of gold encircling the Son of Man; the author saw the Lord as One who holds the seven stars in His right hand and walks among the seven lamps of gold (Rev. 1:12; 2:1). Saint Jerome (c. 342–420) was particularly impressed by the use of light in Eastern churches: "Through all the churches of the east, when the Gospel is to be read, lights are kindled, though the sun is already shining; not, indeed, to dispel darkness, but to exhibit a token of joy; . . . and that under the figure of bodily light, that light may be set forth of which we read in the psaltar, 'Thy word is a lantern unto my feet, and a light unto my paths.'"

Inside the sanctuary of a Coptic church two candle lamps must remain constantly lit: one in the eastern niche, and the other hanging down from the dome above the altar. For the liturgy two large candles, placed in candlesticks, one to the north and the other to the south of the altar, are lit by a deacon, who extinguishes them at the end of the service.

Candles (made of beeswax) and olive oil—in accordance with God's commandment to Moses to use pure oil of pounded olives (Ex. 27:20)—are the only things allowed to be brought to the altar in addition to the bread and wine around the incense.

Candle lamps used in Coptic churches throughout the ages, many of which are scattered over the museums of the Western world, exhibit a considerable degree of craftsmanship. To this, many travelers and church historians have testified, among them A. J. Butler, who writes, "First of all—to be mentioned only with sorrow and regret—come the ancient lamps of glass enamelled with splendid designs and bands of Arabic writing in the most lovely colours. These, the work of thirteenth century artists, were once hung before the haikal in many Coptic churches, but have now entirely disappeared: one or two specimens however may be seen at the British Museum and at South Kensington [the Victoria and Albert Museum] . . . ." (1884, Vol. 2, pp. 69, 70).

BIBLIOGRAPHY

Butler, A. J. *The Ancient Coptic Churches of Egypt,* Vol. 1, pp. 321, 324. Oxford, 1884.
Ibn al-'Assāl, al-Safī. *Kitāb al-Qawānīn.* Cairo, 1927.

ARCHBISHOP BASILIOS

ALTAR VEIL. *See* Eucharistic Veils.

'ALWĀ, or Alodia, the most southerly of the Christian kingdoms of medieval Nubia. Its territorial extent is unknown but was apparently considerable. According to IBN SALĪM AL-ASWĀNĪ, it was larger than the neighboring kingdom of MAKOURIA. The frontier between Makouria and 'Alwā was at AL-ABWĀB (the gates), which was evidently somewhere between the Fourth and Fifth Cataracts of the Nile. The capital, and presumably the largest city, was at SOBA, close to the confluence of the Blue and White Niles. How much farther the kingdom extended to the east, south, and west is not recorded.

Nothing is known of the history of 'Alwā prior to the time of its conversion to Christianity in the sixth century. Presumably its principal inhabitants were the Noba, a Nubian-speaking people who overran much of the old territory of the empire of KŪSH in the fourth century. According to John of Ephesus, the conversion of 'Alwā to Coptic Christianity was effected by the missionary LONGINUS in the year 580.

'Alwā is mentioned by a number of medieval Arab historians, but only IBN ḤAWQAL was a firsthand observer. However, his description of 'Alwā is very brief. Ibn Salīm al-Aswānī recorded a good deal that he had heard about 'Alwā while visiting in the neighboring kingdom of Makouria, but he does not seem to have traveled to the southern kingdom in person. His account contains some fairly accurate geographical information but says almost nothing about the history or administration of the kingdom. He was led to believe that "the Chief of 'Alwā is a greater person than the Chief of Makouria, he has a stronger army, and his country is more extensive and more fertile," but modern scholars question the reliability of this statement. ABŪ ṢĀLIḤ THE ARMENIAN also wrote about 'Alwā at second hand in his *Churches and Monasteries of Egypt and Some Neighbouring Countries.* Much of his information is evidently copied from Ibn Salīm, but he goes on to speak of 400 churches and numerous fine monasteries, apparently drawing mainly on the resources of his imagination.

There is no reliable information about the organization of the church in 'Alwā, although a late medieval source indicates that there were six episcopal sees within the country. All authors agree that the inhabitants were Jacobite Christians. According to Ibn Salīm, "their [holy] books are in the Greek tongue, which they translate into their own language." Only a few very fragmentary texts in the Old Nubian language have been recovered from the territory of 'Alwā. On the basis of some peculiarities of writing, F. L. GRIFFITH concluded that the language spoken here may have been different from the Old Nubian of the kingdom of Makouria.

'Alwā is mentioned incidentally in a number of late medieval Arabic documents, dealing mostly with the various Mamluk campaigns into Nubia. On a number of occasions when the Mamluks attempted to depose the ruler of Makouria, the latter fled for safety to the district of al-Abwāb, within the territory of 'Alwā. This strategy was not always successful, for on at least two occasions the fugitive ruler was captured by the "king of al-Abwāb" and was sent as a prisoner to Cairo. It is not clear from these accounts whether the king of al-Abwāb was in fact the king of 'Alwā or whether the southern kingdom at this time was divided into petty principalities, each with its own ruler. A thirteenth-century Mamluk emissary, 'Alam al-Dīn Sanjar, reported that he had to deal with nine individual chiefs while on a diplomatic mission to 'Alwā.

From the thirteenth century onward 'Alwā, like the neighboring kingdom of Makouria, was increasingly overrun by Arab nomads. A familiar Sudanese folk tradition, the so-called Funj Chronicle, attributes the final downfall of 'Alwā and its capital city of Soba to a combined attack of bedouin Arabs and the black Funj Sultans of Sennar in 1504. Modern scholarship has suggested that the attack probably took place at an earlier date, and was the work of the 'Abdallab Arabs alone. When the 'Abdallab in their turn were subjugated by the Funj, the latter appropriated to their own history the story of the capture of Soba. At all events, the place was in ruins when it was visited by David Reubeni in 1523, although a few surviving inhabitants were living in temporary shelters. The missionary John the Syrian, who had visited the country at about the same time, reported that the people "are neither Christians, Moors, nor Jews, but they live in the desire of becoming Christians."

As a political entity the kingdom of ʿAlwā perished along with the Christian faith. It was incorporated first within the tribal territory of the ʿAbdallab, and later in the Funj kingdom of Sennar.

BIBLIOGRAPHY

Adams, W. Y. *Nubia, Corridor to Africa,* pp. 438–538. Princeton, N.J.; 1977.

Kirwan, L. P. "Notes on the Topography of the Christian Nubian Kingdoms." *Journal of Egyptian Archaeology* 21 (1935):57–62.

Monneret de Villard, U. *Storia della Nubia cristiana,* pp. 68–221. Orientalia Christiana Analecta 118. Rome, 1938.

Vantini, G. *Christianity in the Sudan,* pp. 44–207. Bologna, 1981.

WILLIAM Y. ADAMS

AMA. *See* Apa.

AMAZONS. *See* Mythological Subjects in Coptic Art.

AMBO. Derived from the Greek word ἄμβων, ămbōn, the ambo (Arabic, *anbīl*) is a raised pulpit that stands at the northeast side of the nave. It is built of white or colored marble, stone, or wood, supported on pillars, and is reached by a staircase. It is sometimes carved with crosses and flowers, finely sculptured and filled with rich designs. It can also be decorated with the images of the four evangelists or inscriptions of certain verses from the Bible. On the ambo of the Church of Saint Mercurius (DAYR ABŪ SAYFAYN) in Old Cairo are inscribed the words from Psalm 107:32, "Let them extol him in the congregation of the people, and praise him in the assembly of the elders."

From the ambo the Gospel is sometimes read to the people, and also certain addresses such as papal

Ambo in the Church of al-Muʿallaqah (Old Cairo). *Courtesy Arab Republic of Egypt.*

or episcopal encyclicals and messages. Particular use is made of it during Holy Week, as on Maundy Thursday and Good Friday, when the priest and deacons ascend the ambo, bearing with them crosses, candles, and icons of the Crucifixion.

Many old Coptic churches still have their original ambos, despite the ravages of time. A. J. Butler supplies detailed descriptions of the ambos of some churches in Old Cairo. In the CHURCH OF AL-MUʿALLAQAH "the body of the ambo has a coping of white marble carved with most exquisitely minute and graceful pendentives" (Butler, 1884, p. 218). At the Church of Saint Mercurius in Dayr Abū Sayfayn, "the pillars and wedges are covered with a minute mosaic of coloured marble and shell-pearl," whereas the ambo of Mār Mīnā Church is "inlaid with various devices in red, black and white marble mosaic, while the side of the balcony is formed by a slab of white marble carved with five beautiful designs in low relief . . . three are large conventional roses, the other two in panels dividing them represent graceful vases overflowing with chrysanthemums and other flowers" (Butler, p. 50). An outstanding pulpit made of wood that dates from the eighteenth century can be seen in the Church of Saint Mercurius in Ḥārit Zuwaylah.

BIBLIOGRAPHY

Butler, A. J. *The Ancient Coptic Churches of Egypt.* Oxford, 1884.

Malaṭī, T. Y. *Al-Kanīisah Bayt Allāh.* Alexandria, 1982.

Simaykah, M. *Dalīl al-Mathaf al-Qibṭī wa-Ahamm al-Kanā'is wa-al-Adyurah al-Athariyyah*, pt. 1. Cairo, 1932.

ARCHBISHOP BASILIOS

AMBULATORY. *See* Architectural Elements of Churches.

AMELINEAU, EMILE CLEMENT (1850–1915), French Egyptologist and Coptologist, born at La Chaize-Giraud, Vendée. He was initially trained for the church and was ordained in the Catholic diocese of Rennes. He became attracted to Egyptology by Felix Robiou, whose lectures he attended. Later he studied Egyptian and Coptic in Paris under Gaston MASPERO and Sylvain Grébaut.

In 1882 he joined the French Archaeological Mission in Cairo for four years. He left the Catholic church in 1887. He excavated at Abydos from 1894 to 1898. The antiquities he collected were sold in Paris on 8–9 February 1904, not having been adequately catalogued.

He was professor of the history of religions in the Ecole des Hautes Etudes. His best work was in the field of Coptic studies, in which he published widely; he also wrote a number of Egyptological works not cited here. He died at Châteaudun.

His major contributions to Coptic studies include *De historia lausiaca quaenam sit hujus ad monachorum aegypticorum historiam scribendam utilitas . . .* (Paris, 1887); *Monuments pour servir à l'histoire de l'Egypte chrétienne aux IVe, Ve, VIe et VIIe siècles*, Coptic texts with French translations (2 vols., Paris, 1888–1895); *Monuments pour servir à l'histoire de l'Egypte chrétienne, Histoire des monastères de la Basse-Egypte, Vie de Saints Paul, Antoine, Macaire, Maxime et Domèce, Jean le Nain etc.*, Coptic texts with French translations (Musée Guimet Annales 25, Paris, 1894); *Oeuvres de Schenouti*, Coptic text with French translation (2 vols., Paris, 1907–1914); *Monuments pour servir à l'histoire de l'Egypte chrétienne au IVe siècle, histoire de Saint Pachôme et de ses communautés*, unedited Coptic and Arabic documents (Musée Guimet Annales 17, Paris, 1889); *Essai sur le gnosticisme égyptien, ses développements et son origine égyptienne* (Musée Guimet Annales, 14, Paris, 1887); *Pistis Sophia, ouvrage gnostique de Valentin*, French translation with introduction (Paris, 1895); *Contes et romans de l'Egypte chrétienne* (2 vols., Paris, 1888); and *La géographie de l'Egypte à l'époque copte* (Paris, 1893). Other titles are listed in *A Coptic Bibliography* (Kammerer, 1950, 1969).

BIBLIOGRAPHY

Balteau, J., et al. *Dictionnaire de biographies françaises*. Paris, 1933–.
Dawson, W. R., and E. P. Uphill. *Who Was Who in Egyptology*. London, 1972.
Kammerer, W., comp. *A Coptic Bibliography*. Ann Arbor, 1950; repr. New York, 1969.

AZIZ S. ATIYA

AMĪN AL-DĪN ʿABD-ALLĀH IBN TĀJ AL-RIYĀSAH AL QIBṬĪ. A nephew of the vizier al-Sadīd al-Shāʿir on his mother's side, Amīn al-Dīn obtained his professional training through working with his uncle who occupied the post of *mustawfī* (superintendent of finances). As a result, he later succeeded his uncle in that position. He accepted Islam at the hands of his patron, the amir Baybars al-Jashankīr, and consequently was appointed to the office of *istīfā'* (finance officer). Though he thrice became a vizier, he constantly regretted having had to give up the office of *istīfā'*, which gave him satisfaction and enabled him to live free from danger. He distinguished himself by his courtesy and tolerance toward everyone. The sources lay special emphasis on his good calligraphy even when utmost speed in writing was necessary. He transcribed part of the Qur'ān in exquisite script and composed many eulogistic poems on the Prophet of Islam. He went to Tripoli in Syria as *nāẓir* (intendant). On the termination of his service in Syria, he went to Jerusalem, where in 1322 he heard of his appointment for the third time as vizier—upon the arrest of Karīm al-Dīn al-Kabīr. Two years later he was relieved from office, but without confiscation of his property. In 1328 the sultan al-Nāṣir Muḥammad ibn Qalāwūn gave him the office of *naẓir al-dawlah* (secretary of state).

At this point, Amīn al-Dīn advised the sultan to nominate a Turk in the office of vizier in anticipation of enhancing the falling revenues of the state. He even promoted the name of Mughlaṭāy al-Jamālī for the office. In 1332 Amīn al-Dīn occupied the post of *naẓir al-dawāwīn* (prime minister) in Damascus. In 1339, after the arrest of al-Nashw, the Copt, Amīn al-Dīn was suspended or perhaps dismissed. Fearing for his life, he retired to his residence. In the end he was arrested with his son Tāj al-Dīn, who at the time was *nāẓir al-dawlah*, and another by the name of Karīm al-Dīn, who was *Mustawfī*. They fell into disgrace and were tortured in prison, where Amīn al-Dīn was strangled in the end, in October or November 1340.

BIBLIOGRAPHY

Ibn Ḥajar al-Asqalāni. *al-Durar al-Kāminah fī A'yān al-Mā'ah al-Thāminah*, 2nd ed. Cairo, 1966–1967.
Ibn Taghrī-Birdī. *Al-Nujūm al-Zāhirah fī Mulūk Miṣr wa-al-Qāhirah*. Cairo, 1963.

SUBHI Y. LABIB

AMMON, LETTER OF. *See* Letter of Ammon.

AMMONAS, SAINT, Anchorite and Bishop. The APOPHTHEGMATA PATRUM includes about fifteen items relating to a fourth-century Abba Ammonas who spent at least fourteen years at SCETIS and was in touch with Saint ANTONY (Cotelier, 1864, pp. 120–24, Ammonas 7–8, Antony 26) before becoming a bishop. It is not too bold to identify this person with the Ammonas who is mentioned in Chapter 15 of the HISTORIA MONACHORUM IN AEGYPTO and who is supposedly Antony's immediate successor as leader of the monks of Pispir. This Ammonas is also thought to be the author of spiritual exhortations in the form of letters, preserved in different languages. Along with the letters of Antony, with which they have been intermingled in the Coptic and Arabic tradition, these letters of Ammonas are among the few documents that tell us something about the mysticism of the desert fathers. Their central theme is the acquisition of the Spirit, coming to perfect the purification and illumination of the monk's soul. According to his own experience, the author describes the wonderful effects of this divine gift, what one must do to make oneself worthy of it, the trials to be borne and the temptations to be overcome. This original teaching is, it appears, completely independent of EVAGRIUS PONTICUS. It is of basically biblical origin.

The most complete collection of the letters of Ammonas is preserved in Syriac (Kmosko, 1913). Seven letters preserved in Greek have been published by F. Nau (1914). A Latin translation from Arabic has been published in J. P. Migne in Patrologia Graeca. An unpublished Georgian series is almost as complete as the Syriac collection (Garitte, 1952, pp. 103–107).

BIBLIOGRAPHY

Chitty, Derwas J. *The Desert a City*, pp. 38–39. Oxford, 1966.
Cotelier, J. B., ed. *Apophthegmata Patrum*. PG 65, pp. 120–24. Paris, 1864.
Festugière, A. J., ed. *Historia monachorum in Aegypto*, p. 111. Brussels, 1971.
Kmosko, M. *Ammonii Eremitae Epistolae*. PO 10, pp. 567–616. Paris, 1913.
Nau, F. *Lettres d'Ammonas*. PO 11, pp. 432–64. Paris, 1914.

LUCIEN REGNAULT

AMMONIUS OF KELLIA, a disciple, with his three brothers, of PAMBO, the celebrated monk of NITRIA (Palladius, 1904, chap. 11, pp. 32–33). Because he and his brothers were of great stature, they were nicknamed "the tall brothers" (Socrates, 1964, 6.7, 684 D). They were distinguished not only by their stature but also by their learning. The eldest, Dioscorus, was at first a priest in Nitria and then was consecrated bishop of Hermopolis by the twenty-third patriarch, THEOPHILUS, who took the two youngest, Eusebius and Euthymius, into his household in Alexandria (Socrates, 1964, 685 A). Ammonius himself was entreated to become a bishop by Theophilus' predecessor, TIMOTHY. He had stolen away and, to avoid being consecrated, cut off his ear, whence the sobriquet Parotes (ear lobe) was given him (Palladius, 1904, pp. 32–33; Socrates, 1964, 4.23, 521 A; Sozomen, 1964, 6.30, 1384 AB). Palladius and Rufinus (1849, 445 B–447 B) give equal praise to his learning and his asceticism. He lived as a monk at KELLIA, where he became the friend of EVAGRIUS PONTICUS, who was also very well educated and a great reader of ORIGEN. The two became the masters of a community of monks that their adversaries dubbed "Origenists." When Theophilus set himself to persecute the Origenists and organized an expedition against them to Nitria and Kellia in 400, Ammonius, along with the majority of the Origenist monks, had to go into exile; he found refuge with JOHN CHRYSOSTOM at Constantinople, where he died in the first years of the fifth century (Palladius, 1904, p. 34). None of his writing has been preserved, but it is not known whether any ever existed.

ANTOINE GUILLAUMONT

AMMONIUS OF TŪNAH, fourth-century hermit. The name of Ammonius of Tūnah (Thone in Coptic) is mentioned in the Coptic inscriptions of al-Jabrāwī (see DAYR AL-JABRĀWĪ), on the right bank south of ASYŪṬ, in tombs used by the hermits, along with the names of Apollo, Anoup, Phib, and Pshoi of Jeremiah (Crum, 1902, pp. 45–46 and pl. 29, no. 3). He is represented on a fresco from Bāwīṭ (Clédat, 1904–1916, p. 91) and also at FARAS (Kubinska, 1974, no. 90 and fig. 80). A summary of his life is given by the Copto-Arabic SYNAXARION (PO 16, pp. 399–401; CSCO 67, pp. 130–31 [text]; 90, pp. 129–31 [trans.]). A papyrus leaf preserves part of the Coptic life (Crum, 1913, pp. 162–64). Mount Tūnah is situated on the left bank of the Nile, to the west of al-ASHMŪNAYN (Shmūn or Hermopolis Magna) in central Egypt, about 12 miles (20 km) north of BĀWĪṬ.

After experiencing a vision in which Saint ANTONY invited him to become a monk, Ammonius went to Saint Isidorus (perhaps ISIDORUS OF SCETIS) (Evelyn-White, 1932, pp. 101–02), who clothed him in the monastic habit. After his initiation, he withdrew to Mount Tūnah. One day, the devil tempted him by persuading a woman to seduce him, but Ammonius converted her and she remained near him as an ascetic. The devil then took the semblance of a monk and made a circuit of the monasteries, crying out, "Anba Ammonius, the hermit, has married a wife who lives in his cave, and thus he dishonours the monks and does shame to the holy habit." Apollo, "the fellow of the angels," no doubt APOLLO OF BĀWĪṬ, accompanied by Ānbā Yūsāb (Joseph) and Anbā Papohe (perhaps author of the life of Phib), went to Mount Tūnah to investigate. There they found the woman, called al-Sādij by the Synaxarion. An angel revealed to Apollo that they had been brought to Ammonius to be present at the death of al-Sādij, which then took place; she had spent eighteen years with Ammonius without ever looking upon him and living only on bread and salt. Ammonius himself died soon after.

Perhaps we have here a distant witness to the *agapetae* (beloved) who lived with ascetics (Guillaumont, 1969). If it is indeed Apollo of Bāwīṭ, this Ammonius lived toward the end of the fourth century. H. Torp (1965, pp. 167–68) thinks that this Ammonius of Tūnah is the Amoun mentioned in Chapter 9 of the HISTORIA MONACHORUM IN AEGYPTO (Festugière, 1971, pp. 71–75).

BIBLIOGRAPHY

Clédat, J. *Le Monastère et la nécropole de Bawit.* Mémoires publiés par les membres de l'Institut français d'Archéologie orientale 12. Cairo, 1904–1916.

Crum, W. E. *The Rock Tombs of Deir el-Gebrawi,* Vol. 2, ed. N. de G. Davies. London, 1902.

______. *Theological Texts from Coptic Papyri.* Oxford, 1913.

Evelyn-White, H. G. *The Monasteries of the Wadi'n Natrūn,* Pt. 2, *The History of the Monasteries of Nitria and Scetis.* New York, 1932.

Festugière, A. J., ed. *Historia monachorum in Aegypto.* Subsidia Hagiographica 53. Brussels, 1971. Two parts in 1 vol., Greek text and Latin trans.

Guillaumont, A. "Le Nom des 'Agapètes.'" *Vigiliae Christianae* 63 (1969):30–37.

Kubinska, J. *Inscriptions grecques chrétiennes* (Faras IV). Warsaw, 1974.

Torp, A. "La date de la fondation du monasterè d'Apa Apollo de Baouît et son abandon." *Mélanges d'archéologie et d'histoire* 77 (1965):153–177.

RENÉ-GEORGES COQUIN

AMPHILOCHIUS OF ICONIUM. Some scholars have thought that Amphilochius of Iconium deserves to rank alongside BASIL THE GREAT of Caesarea, GREGORY OF NYSSA, and GREGORY OF NAZIANZUS as the fourth great Cappadocian of the end of the fourth century. Educated at the school of Libanius at Antioch, then an advocate in Constantinople, Amphilochius was invited to accept the episcopate of the town of Iconium by Basil of Caesarea in 373, in order to stand in the way of the Arians who were endeavoring to gain possession of all the sees. He died after 394; Basil had died in 379. More than one letter exchanged between them testifies to their preoccupation with countering APOLLINARIANISM and the doctrines of the Arian Eunomius.

The extant writings of Amphilochius are less numerous and in general less theological than those of the other Cappadocian fathers. He left a treatise against the heretics in which the moral deviations of the ascetic sects—the Apotactites, the Messalians, and the Gemellites—are the principal target.

Eleven homilies are considered to be authentic (Geerard, 1974, pp. 230–23). They already witness to a liturgical cycle in the preaching at Iconium. Some of them give evidence of a desire to oppose ARIANISM and Eunomianism in a more developed form than that encountered by Basil and Gregory in the years up to 380. Amphilochius answers Eunomius' doctrine of the innate names by an orthodox interpretation of the Gnostic speculations on the names of Christ. One of the homilies has been handed down only in Bohairic Coptic. It is preserved in a tenth-century codex of Saint MACARIUS (Vatican Coptic 61, fols. 194r–209v). The text of this homily on Abraham has been edited by L. van Rompay (Datema, 1978, pp. 269–307).

It contains some theological traits parallel to the other homilies, of which one of the most remarkable formulas, no doubt retouched by an ardent Monophysite, is "One who came forth from Mary will suffer in (his) body, but outside of his Godhead." A parallel development on the sacrifice of Isaac in the Greek homily VII runs: "While the flesh suffered, the divinity did not suffer" (Datema, 1978, p. 302). Amphilochius also left some canonical writings: the *Iambi ad Seleucum* (Geerard, 1974, no. 3230), a synodical letter and a creed (nos. 3243–3244). Nearly twenty-five fragments have also been collected.

Georg Graf (1944–1953, Vol. 1, p. 329; Vol. 3; p. 139, n. 20) points out that in the eighteenth century Ilīyā ibn al-Fakhr included the *Iambi ad Seleucum* in his canonical collection preserved in the manuscripts of Beirut 517 (autograph) and Jerusalem, Holy Sepulcher 1 (1886, pp. 397–99). But the works of Amphilochius that were especially widespread in Arabic were two writings generally considered apocryphal: a panegyric on Basil of Caesarea (Geerard, no. 3252) and a series of miracles of the same Basil (no. 3253).

The panegyric on Saint Basil is contained, unfortunately mutilated, in the very old Arabic codex Sinaiticus 457, the writing of which dates from the end of the ninth century. The manuscript was amply described by J.-M. Sauget in 1972. The title on folio 70 is "Of the sermon which Amphilochius bishop of Iconium pronounced on Basil and . . ." (p. 154). The complete panegyric is chiefly known in Syriac. The oldest copy is Vatican Syriac 369, of the eighth century, fol. 5–15, also described by Sauget in 1961. It has been published several times in Syriac.

P. J. Alexander (1953, p. 61, no. 22) has found a Greek fragment in the *testimonia* of the acts of the Iconoclastic Council of Saint Sophia in 815. Arguments against authenticity were advanced by A. Vööbus in 1960. They are not really convincing unless we accept that in the patristic period the idea of a panegyric included a need to recall the elements of a biography. This is not the case. Gregory of Nyssa left the life of Melitius in complete obscurity at the point when he wrote his panegyric. Vööbus has shown the parallelism between the anonymous life of Rabbula of Edessa, preserved in Syriac and dating from the sixth century, and that of Basil by Amphilochius. There is nothing to prevent our believing that the anonymous author drew his inspiration from the panegyric on Basil, which he already knew.

The problem of the Life, or rather the Miracles, of Saint Basil is entirely different. In the Greek tradition they are attributed either to Amphilochius of Iconium or to Basil's successor Helladius of Caesarea. The series of the miracles consists of anecdotes badly stitched together. Since Helladius speaks in the first miracle, one can understand the attribution being gradually transferred to him. It is less obvious to think of the attribution to Amphilochius as added to that of Helladius. F. Combefis, the first editor in 1644, published the Miracles under the name of Amphilochius. The majority of patrologists rejected this association, quoting in particular the story in which Ephraem is present at Basil's ordination. One of them even suggested that we should recognize here the hand of Amphilochius of Cyzicus, a contemporary of Photius in the ninth century. The enormous diffusion of the collection makes this untenable, and the Eastern translations are generally ancient.

In Arabic, the Miracles are attributed to *'ladyus* in Manuscript Sinai 457, as well as in the Strasbourg codex Orientalis 4226, the colophon of which, today in Leningrad, is dated to 885 and is due to Antony of Baghdad, who wrote at Saint Sabas. The story of Peter of Sebaste, pointed out among the Leningrad fragments by G. L. Fleischer in 1854, is in reality part of the same codex as that of Strasbourg, and is one of the Miracles of Basil. The later Arabic tradition transformed the name Helladius into Hilarion, and under this name Graf lists seven manuscript witnesses. Several other collections have transcribed the same miracles anonymously, as Graf again points out. Whatever the objections against authenticity, it should not be forgotten that the literary genre of the miracles is quite different from that of the panegyric. Gregory of Nyssa did not scorn the popular miracles transmitted with regard to Gregory Thaumaturgus. And the Life of Saint Antony contains anachronisms that have not prevented the majority of patrologists from acknowledging the attribution to ATHANASIUS I of Alexandria.

One of the Lives of Amphilochius (*Bibliotheca hagiographa Graeca* 72–75) also passed into Arabic, but it has not been established which one. See Manuscript British Museum Add. 9965 (Arabic Christian 28, collection of Macarius Ibn al-Za'īm), fols. 200r–204v; Sinai Arabic 397 (A.D. 1333) 6 and 475 (thirteenth century); Graf, 1944–1953, Vol. 1, p. 515.

BIBLIOGRAPHY

Alexander, P. J. "The Iconoclast Council at St. Sophia (815) and Its Definition (*Horos*)." *Dumbarton Oaks Papers* 7 (1953):35–66.

Datema, C., ed. *Amphilochii Iconiensis Opera*. Corpus Christianorum, Series Graeca 3. Turnhout-Louvain, 1978. Includes bibliography.

Esbroeck, M. van. "Un Feuillet oublié du codex arabe Or. 4226 à Strasbourg." *Analecta Bollandiana* 96 (1978):383–84.

———. "Amphiloque d'Iconium et Eunome: l'homélie CPG 3238." *Augustinianum* 21 (1981):517–39.

Garitte, G. "Homélie d'Ephrem sur la mort et le diable." *Le Museon* 82 (1969):125–26.

Geerard, M. *Clavis Patrum Graecorum*, Vol. 2, Corpus Christianorum, pp. 230–42. Turnhout-Louvain, 1974.

Sauget, J. M. "Deux homéliaires syriaques de la Bibliothèque Vaticane." *Orientalia Christiana Periodica* 27 (1961):414.

———. "La Collection homilético-hagiographique du manuscrit Sinai arabe 457." *Proche-Orient chrétien* 22 (1972):129–67, 147–52.

Schiwietz, S. *Das morgenländische Mönchtum*, pp. 129–32. Mödling, 1938.

Vööbus, A. "Das literarische Verhältnis zwischen der Biographie des Rabbula und dem Pseudo-Amphilochianischen Panegyrikus über Basilius." *Oriens Christianus* 44 (1960):40–45.

MICHEL VAN ESBROECK

AMPULLA. An ampulla is a small container about 3–4 inches (9 cm) high of pale yellow or orange clay, produced in the neighborhood of the sanctuary of Saint Menas, near Alexandria. Ampullae, filled with water from a spring near the saint's tomb, were widespread in Egypt and throughout many regions of the Christian world. Their dating

Ampulla shaped like the head of Abū Mīnā. Alexandria. Polish excavations of Kom al-Dikka. *Courtesy Zsolt Kiss.*

Ampulla showing full figure of Abū Mīnā. Warsaw, National Museum. *Courtesy Zsolt Kiss.*

Ampulla of Abū Mīnā with "classical" medallion. Alexandria. Polish excavations of Kom al-Dikka. *Courtesy Zsolt Kiss.*

corresponds to the period when the Sanctuary of Saint Menas flourished, from the beginning of the fifth century to the end of the first half of the seventh century. Coptic ampullae appear in two main forms:

1. Containers in the shape of the pilgrim's flat gourd, with a narrow neck edged with two handles, the belly being decorated on both surfaces with round medallions in relief. The illustrations within this form evolved as follows:

a. The essential schema was a representation of Saint Menas in military dress, with both hands raised as a sign of prayer; at his feet, he is venerated on each side by a camel. The representation of the model, still classical or very swollen, was placed in a circular border of chevrons, laurel, and smooth taeniae. Other motifs—rosette, boat, basket with bread—as well as the identifying inscription *eulogia tou agiou mena* (blessing of the Holy Menas) also appeared. From this period there are large-sized ampullae, about 6 inches (15 cm) high, with the figure of Saint Menas praying or a representation of Saint Thecla venerated by dogs, following the same schema.

b. About the year 600, the output of ampullae increased and the schema of representations on the medallions was restricted. The same medallion with the worshiping figure of Saint Menas venerated by the camels within a circular milled border ordinarily appeared on both sides of the belly. The representation had become more schematic and linear. Another type of decoration of the ampulla consisted on one side of a medallion with the above schema and on the other of the eulogistic legend encircled by a border of laurel. In the final phase of production of Coptic ampullae, another medallion was elaborated with a schematic head in profile, negroid features, and frizzled hair, within a double border of milling.

2. Small molded vases in the shape of a man's head with frizzled hair on a round base surmounted

Ampulla of Abū Mīnā with text of the Eulogy. Alexandria. Polish excavations of Kom al-Dikka. *Courtesy Zsolt Kiss.*

Ampulla in praise of Abū Mīnā (St. Menas). Terra cotta. Seventh-eighth century. *Courtesy Louvre Museum, Paris.*

by a slim neck. The mouth and nose were modeled in clay, the eyes painted, and the whole touched up with color. Their production paralleled that of the gourd-shaped ampullae, as well as statuettes of women and horsemen from the same workshops.

BIBLIOGRAPHY

Kaufmann, K. M. *Die Menasstadt I.* Leipzig, 1910.

______. *Zur Ikonographie der Menas-Ampullen.* Cairo, 1910.

Kiss, Z. *Les Ampoules de St. Ménas des fouilles polonaises à Kôm el-Dikka.* Warsaw, forthcoming.

Metzger, C. *Les Ampoules à l'eulogie au Musée du Louvre.* Paris, 1981.

ZSOLT KISS

ʻAMRIYYAH (Maryūt), a towering site close to the Mediterranean coast west of Alexandria now occupied only by bedouins. In Kom Abū Driʻah (formerly called al-Kurūm al-Ṭuwāl) situated about 8 miles (12 km) south of ʻAmriyyah, numerous ancient capitals and pillars lie about on the ground even to this day.

During excavations carried out in 1929, remains of a small, three-aisled, pillared church were found with a narthex, baptistery, and access to the roof. It had no return aisle. The sanctuary was destroyed. The excavators dated the building from the sixth to the seventh century A.D. Another interesting complex in the area of Kom Abū Driʻah is an underground early Christian tomb standing below what was probably a three-aisled, above-ground structure.

A second group of ruins to the north of ʻAmriyyah is called al-Dayr by the inhabitants and, according to O. Meinardus (1965, p. 136), is to be identified with the OKTOKAIDEKATON monastery mentioned in early Christian sources.

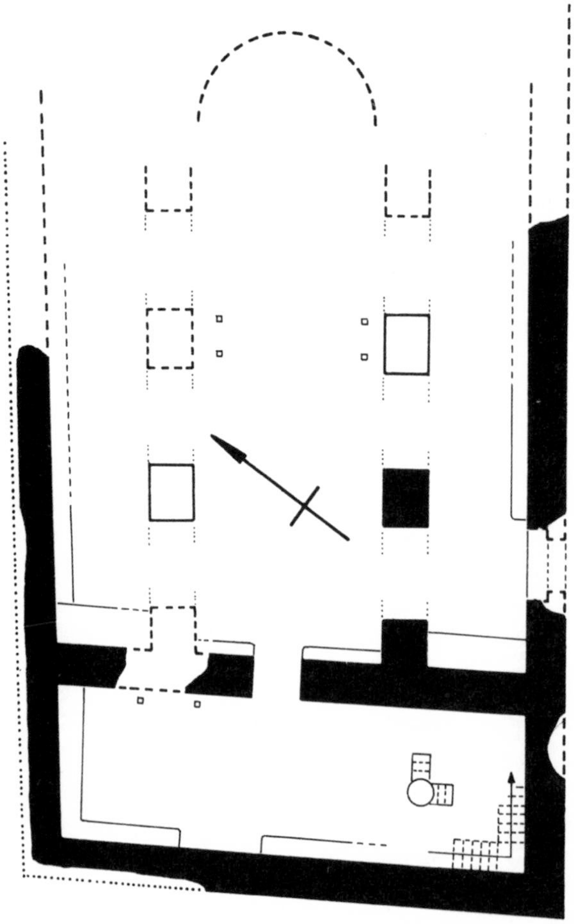

Plan of the three-aisled church at ʻAmriyyah. *Courtesy Peter Grossmann.*

BIBLIOGRAPHY

Eilmann, R.; A. Langsdorf; and H. E. Stier. "Bericht über die Voruntersuchungen auf den Kurûm el-ṭuwâl bei Amrîje." *Mitteilungen des deutschen archäologischen Instituts—Abteilung Kairo* 1 (1930): 106–129.

Meinardus, O. *Christian Egypt: Ancient and Modern,* p. 136. Cairo, 1977.

PETER GROSSMANN

AMULET. *See* Magical Objects.

AMUN, SAINT, fourth-century anchorite. Around the year 320, Amun became the first monk to settle in the desert of NITRIA. Orphaned early, he had been obliged to marry by an uncle, but lived with his wife in total continence for eighteen years. After becoming a monk, he was in touch with Saint ANTONY, who advised him about the establishment of a new monastic center in the desert of KELLIA (PG 65, col. 85). Amun died some time before Antony, who, from a distance, saw his soul carried up to heaven. The collections of apothegms that come especially from the communities of SCETIS have only a few items relating to Amun.

BIBLIOGRAPHY

Athanasius. *Vita S. Antonii* 60. PG 26, col. 929. Paris, 1857.

Chitty, D. J. *The Desert a City,* pp. 11, 29, 32. Oxford, 1966.

Cotelier, J. B., ed. *Apophthegmata Patrum.* PG 65, p. 128. Paris, 1864.

Evelyn-White, H. G. *The Monasteries of the Wadi'n Natrūn,* Pt. 2, *The History of the Monasteries of Nitria and Scetis.* New York, 1932.

Festugière, A.-J., ed. *Historia monachorum in Aegypto,* pp. 128–30. Brussels, 1971.

LUCIEN REGNAULT

ANACHORESIS, the step by which an ascetic, following the example of Saint ANTONY, leaves his village "to withdraw" (Greek, *anachorein*) to the desert and thus becomes an ANCHORITE (*anachoretes*). But the oldest attestations of the word in Egypt relate to a phenomenon of a social character. Crushed by excessive fiscal burdens, peasants fled from their villages to the desert or some other place. This phenomenon, already noted in pharaonic Egypt (Posener, 1975) and again under Arab domination, is particularly well known, thanks to papyri from the Greco-Roman period (Martin, 1934; Henne, 1956; Braunert, 1964).

Several historians, such as A. Piganiol (1947, p. 376), have thought that there is a close relationship between this *anachoresis* of the peasants and the monastic *anachoresis.* In 373 and 377 the emperor Valens adopted measures against those among the monks who sought to escape their civil and military obligations (Piganiol, 1947, pp. 380–81). The monasteries sometimes served as refuges for crowds of people who fled before the exactions of the civil officials, as is apparent in the fifth century from the testimony of Isidorus of Pelusium (letter 191 PG 78, cols. 305A and B). The Pachomian Rules (see PACHOMIUS OF TABENNĒSĒ), in prescribing the conduct to be adopted with regard to candidates for the monastic life, call attention to the case—which must therefore have occurred—of those who presented themselves in order to escape judicial proceedings. Such candidates were naturally to be rejected.

The monastic *anachoresis,* in fact, must be made, as it is said in the *Life of Saint Antony* (Athanasius, 1857, col. 853A), "out of virtue." It is thus of a quite different nature from the *anachoresis* of peasants fleeing from their fiscal obligations. In accomplishing it, the monk separates himself from "the world," that is, from all the objects (people and things) and occupations that excite the passions and distract the spirit, thus preventing him from being mindful of God alone. In this the monastic *anachoresis* is rather in the tradition of the philosophers and sages of Hellenism who withdrew from public life to devote themselves solely to philosophy (Festugière, 1960). Like them, the monk, by his *anachoresis,* sought what was called *hesychia,* the solitude and the leisure that allow one to devote oneself exclusively, without distraction, to what is considered the supreme good. But, more than that of the sages and philosophers, the *anachoresis* of the monks is a step of an essentially religious character and, as such, belongs to a phenomenon widely represented in the history of religions, particularly in Judaism and early Christianity. Before the appearance of monasticism, there had been faithful souls who, following the example of Jesus (cf. M. 1:35; Lk. 5:16), withdrew to the desert or into solitude to pray.

The anchoritic life took diverse forms, from the absolute anchoritism of a Saint Antony or a PAUL OF THEBES, who spent the greater part of their lives in complete solitude, to more moderate forms like the semi-anchoritism of the monks of NITRIA and SCETIS, where a judicious balance had been established between the solitary and the communal life. Complete and lasting solitude was not without its own dangers. If the monk in the desert was far removed from the passions and the occupations of the world, he still had to face up to his own thoughts and the assaults of demons; the desert was in fact considered the home of the demons (Guillaumont, 1975). The demons warred against the monk either directly, according to the hagiographers, or indirectly, as is shown by the profound analyses of EVAGRIUS PONTICUS, by suggesting to him evil thoughts, which maintained the passions in him in an even more lively manner than the actual objects in the world. Thus, complete *anachoresis* was not advised for beginners and was recommended only for those who already had a long experience of cenobitic, or community, life (cf. Cassian, 1959, 18.4). Reserved for the perfect, it appeared as the highest form of monastic life, as an ideal practically inaccessible to the majority of monks. The hagiographic literature has embellished with marvelous features the life of the anchorites in the desert. It shows them dwelling in the company of wild animals, without any clothing, and subsisting on the desert plants. They are also said to have been miraculously fed by the angels, receiving from them, or sometimes from Christ himself, the Eucharist, of which the anchorites found themselves deprived by reason of their isolation. Completely ignored by humans, the anchorite is only discovered at the moment of his death, in order that a decent burial may be assured him and, above all, that his extraordinary life may be known and serve for the edification of all. A fine specimen of this marvelous literature concerning the anchorites is the story of the journey of the monk PAPHNUTIUS into the desert (Amélineau, 1885).

BIBLIOGRAPHY

Amélineau, E. "Voyage d'un moine égyptien dans le désert." *Recueil de travaux relatifs à la philologie et à l'archéologie égyptiennes et assyriennes* 6 (1885):166–94.

Athanasius. *Vita et Conversatio S.P.N. Antonii.* PG 26, cols. 837–976. Paris, 1857.

Braunert, H. *Die Binnenwanderung; Studien zur Sozialgeschichte Ägyptens in der Ptolemäer- und Kaiserzeit.* Bonner historische Forschungen 26. Bonn, 1964.

Festugière, A.-J. *Personal Religion Among the Greeks,* pp. 53–67. Berkeley, Calif., 1954; 2nd ed., 1960.

Guillaumont, A. "La conception du désert chez les moines d'Egypte." *Revue de l'histoire des religions* 188 (1975):3–21.

Henne, H. "Documents et travaux sur l'anachôresis." *Mitteilungen aus der Papyrussammlung der österreichischen Nationalbibliothek (Papyrus Erzherzog Rainer) redigiert von H. Gerstingen,* pp. 59–66. Vienna, 1956.

Isidorus of Pelusium. *Epistolarum,* Liber I, 191. In PG 78, cols. 119–454. Paris, 1864.

Martin, V. "Les papyrus et l'histoire administrative de l'Egypte." *Münchner Beiträge zur Papyrusforschung und antiken Rechtsgeschichte* 19, pp. 144ff. Munich, 1934.

Piganiol, A. *L'Empire chrétien, 325–95,* p. 376. Paris, 1947.

Posener, G. "L'ἀναχώρησις dans l'Egypte pharaonique." In *Hommages à Claire Préaux: Le monde grec. Pensée, littérature, histoire et documents,* pp. 663–69. Brussels, 1975.

ANTOINE GUILLAUMONT

ANAMNESIS, a word of Greek origin meaning remembrance, memorial, or commemoration, and as such part of the liturgy for the Eucharist. Greek versions of the scriptures use the word to translate various forms of the Hebrew root *zkr,* which in Arabic is pronounced *dhikr.*

The text of the anamnesis reminds the faithful of the Lord's salvific work through His sufferings, crucifixion, resurrection, and ascension to heaven. The Eucharist is not only the mystery of the crucifixion but is also the fulfillment of the Lord's instruction to His apostles, "Do this in remembrance of me" (I Cor. 11:24). It is also related to the Passover that was ordered to be celebrated by the Israelites every year as a commemoration of God's salvation, insofar as the Lord made Himself the true Passover of the new covenant replacing the symbol or figure of the old covenant (I Cor. 5:7-8).

In the three eucharistic Divine Liturgies used by the Coptic Orthodox Church (Saint Mark's, or the so-called Cyrillian; Saint Basil's; and Saint Gregory's), the anamnesis comes before the words of consecration, and in most of them is also summed up after the consecration and immediately before the EPICLESIS. Hence, in a Coptic context, the anamnesis does not only have the sense of the remembering, but also the representing of all the main events and of making them present in the minds of the faithful. This is why the anamnesis is preceded by the remembrance of the Lord's incarnation, birth, and teachings.

The whole process of remembrance, whether in the preanamnesis or anamnesis, requires the preparation of the minds of the faithful in order that they may share effectively in worship. The officiating priest and the deacons are dressed in their white and gold vestments, the priest as figure of the Lord, and the deacons as figures of the angels. They together have to prepare the altar for the holy sacrifice. In this aspect three elements should be distinguished: the altar, the deacons, and the preparation, which are all figures of heavenly realities. Therefore, the officiating priest expresses these meanings inaudibly in the prayers of preparation. Even the entombment of the Lord is presented on the altar when, after the prayer of thanksgiving, the priest covers the paten with a mat and likewise the chalice with another mat, and he covers both with the veil then places another mat on the veil, which represents the large stone that closed the Lord's tomb. The triangularly folded mat on the veil is a figure of the seal on the stone.

When after the prayer of reconciliation the priest and deacon raise the veil, an action symbolic of the removal of the stone from the Lord's sepulcher, the deacon draws the attention of all worshipers to the presence of the Lord on the altar, asking them to enter effectively into the everlasting sacrifice of the risen Lord.

After the people's chanting of the cherubim's hymn of "Holy," the priest continues the anamnesis, expressing in humility to God the Lord how man, who was created by Him and placed in the paradise of grace, disobeyed His commandments and consequently was exiled from this paradise.

> Thou hast never abandoned us unto the end but didst ever visit us by Thy Saintly Prophets. In the fullness of time Thou didst appear to us, we who are living in darkness and the shadows of death; through Thine Only-Begotten Son, Our Lord, God and Savior Jesus Christ; Who is of the Holy Spirit and of Saint Mary the Virgin; He took flesh and became man and taught us the way to salvation; He blessed us with the grace of the high birth through water and spirit; and made of us a congregation that is sanctified by His Holy Spirit; He is the One Who offered Himself for our redemption from death that has swayed upon us; that to which we are all bound in abeyance because of our sins; He descended into Hades as accorded to the Cross.
>
> He rose from the dead on the third day, ascended to the heavens and sat at the right hand of the Father; and appointed a day for retribution, whence He shall appear to judge the world in equity and give each according to his deeds.

It is noteworthy that the center of this anamnesis is the priestly action of Christ in His incarnation, His passion, His resurrection, His ascension, and His second coming for the resurrection of the dead. His sacramental presence in this anamnesis abstracted from time and place, granting us communion with Himself, constitutes the heart of this heavenly liturgy. Saint JOHN CHRYSOSTOM explains this action in his commentary, "We offer even now what was done then, for we perform the anamnesis of His death."

BIBLIOGRAPHY

Agpeya, The. New York, 1981.

Atiya, A. S. *History of Eastern Christianity*. London, 1967.

Dalmais, I. H. *Introduction to the Liturgies*. London, 1961.

Danielou, S. J. J. *The Bible and the Liturgy*. Ann Arbor, Mich., 1956.

Ishak, F. M., trans. *The Coptic Orthodox Mass and the Liturgy of Saint Basil*. Toronto, 1977.

Khulājī al-Muqaddas, al-. Cairo, 1959.

Kropp, M., O. P. "Die Koptische Anaphora des Heiligen Evangelisten Mattäus." *Oriens Christianus*, ser. 3, 7 (1932):111–25.

Lee, R. D. "Epiclesis and Ecumenical Dialogue." *Diakonia* 9 (1974).

Yuḥannā Salāmah. *Al-La'ālī' al-Nafīsah fī Sharḥ Ṭuqūs wa Mu'taqadāt al-Kanīsah*, 2 vols. Cairo, 1909.

GABRIEL ABDELSAYYED

ANAPHORA OF SAINT BASIL, anaphora normally used in the Coptic church, and one of the three retained in Coptic service books when others were abandoned in the Middle Ages. The expression "Anaphora of Saint Basil" is used to designate either (1) that anaphora within its strict limits (from the dialogue introducing the eucharistic prayer to the concluding doxology before the preface to the

Fraction), or (2) that anaphora together with other prayers, or (3) the entire eucharistic liturgy of the Coptic church from beginning to end, with the Anaphora of Saint Basil and the prayers used with it inserted in their proper places within the common order, which also supplies the prayers not proper to the other Coptic anaphoras, of Saint Gregory and of Saint Cyril.

The anaphora in the strict sense, like that of Saint Gregory, but unlike that of Saint Mark/Saint Cyril, is not of Egyptian but of Syrian origin, with Syria taken broadly enough liturgically to include Cappadocia if need be. It has the structural components of Antiochene anaphoras like that of Saint James, and differs structurally from Byzantine and Armenian anaphoras—themselves strongly influenced by Syrian usage—in only a few details. With the Antiochene Syrian anaphoras, but not those of the Byzantine and Armenian rites, it shares the distribution of roles between priest, deacon, and people in the intercessory prayers after the epiclesis, and the acclamation of the people, "We show forth Thy death, O Lord . . ." after the institution narrative. Its eucharistic prayer, especially, is similar to the longer one in the anaphoric part of the Byzantine Liturgy of Saint Basil.

In assessing the textual relationship of the two, scholars differ in their opinions. Of those accepting a direct relationship between the two, some hold the older view that the Egyptian anaphora is an abridgment of the Byzantine one, reworked in conformity to traditional Egyptian usage, while many accept the view of H. Engberding (1931, pp. lxxiii–lxxix) that the Egyptian text is closer to the original, while the Byzantine text is an expansion of the original one, with additions showing a taste for theological speculation based on biblical passages. Engberding has even suggested Basil the Great as the author of the theological expansions, and a more thorough demonstration of the same thesis has been attempted by B. Capelle in his appendix to J. Doresse and E. Lanne (1960). One can be impressed with the arguments for Basilian composition of the longer Byzantine anaphora while remaining skeptical about its being an expansion of a shorter and older anaphora whose primitive text is more faithfully retained in the Egyptian Saint Basil; the verbal similarities between the two have not been explained to everyone's satisfaction.

While the Egyptian Anaphora of Saint Basil in the strict sense is fundamentally Syrian in both composition and structure, with some Egyptian retouching, the Basilian formulary (Anaphora of Saint Basil in the second sense given above), outside of the properly anaphoric section, includes a few Syrian prayers borrowed outright for use in a structural order, which is Egyptian. A prayer of the veil that can easily be isolated as the first prayer of the formulary is taken from the Syrian Liturgy of Saint James. In the Syriac manuscript tradition a prayer of the veil is the first element found in an anaphoric grouping, but while in the structure of a Syrian liturgy it is actually said immediately before the historical beginning of the anaphora in the strict sense, in the Egyptian order it finds its place immediately after the prayer following the Gospel. Between it and the beginning of the anaphora proper, several other prayers intervene in the Egyptian order, and the placement of a prayer of the veil at the beginning of the Egyptian anaphoric formulary is probably due to imitation of Syrian formularies, without such imitations leading to alteration of the Egyptian order of service.

The structure of the Coptic common order of service now joined to the anaphoric formulary to form the Anaphora of Saint Basil in the widest sense (the third sense above) is peculiar to Egypt. Although most of its components can be found elsewhere in another structural order, some are specifically Egyptian, for example, the reading of four passages from the New Testament (from Saint Paul, the Catholic Epistles, the Acts of the Apostles, and the Gospels), the absolutions before the prayer of incense preparing the readings and after the prayer of inclination following the Lord's Prayer, and the homologia (a confession of faith in the presence of Christ's body on the altar and in the mystery of His saving actions). The fraction of the consecrated bread takes place before the Lord's Prayer, as in the West and East Syrian rites, but actions that would naturally follow (a consignation and commiction) are postponed until after the elevation following the Lord's Prayer with its embolism and prayer of inclination. The lack of ancient textual witnesses to the common order makes it impossible to trace its history, but its prayers can be presumed generally to be Egyptian compositions. Its regular integration with the Egyptianized Syrian Anaphora of Saint Basil in order to constitute the full text of an ordinary Coptic liturgy was a practical step, as that anaphora became the one normally used in the Coptic church.

Greek texts both of the anaphora with its properly associated prayers and of the Coptic common order have survived. There is some reason to think that a recension of the Greek text, at least from the prayer of the veil, was also used in the Melchite church of Alexandria until its local usages gave way to the integral observance of the Byzantine rite. In the Coptic church, the Greek text, which may have been used only in particular circumstances, has not been used for centuries, with Coptic and, increasingly Arabic, being the only liturgical languages retained. Some short Greek elements have been retained in the Coptic text, especially in parts reserved to the deacon and the people.

BIBLIOGRAPHY

The Greek text is in E. Renaudot, *Liturgiarum orientalium collectio* (2nd ed., Frankfurt and London, 1847; repr. Franborough, 1970); also in Anton Hänggi and Irmgard Pahl, eds., *Prex eucharistica* (Spicilegium friburgense 12, Fribourg, 1968), pp. 347–57, only the anaphora in the strict sense); and in William F. Macomber, *Orientalia christiana periodica* 43 (1977):308–334 (with the common order).

For a list of service books containing the Bohairic and Arabic texts printed before 1961, see H. Malak in *Mélanges Eugène Tisserant,* Vol. 3, pp. 6–8, 27 (Studi e testi 233, Vatican City, 1964). A fourteenth-century Arabic text has been published by Khalil Samir in *Orientalia Christiana Periodica* 44 (1978):342–90. An important Sahidic witness has been published by J. Doresse and E. Lanne, *Un témoin archaique de la liturgie copte de S. Basile* (Bibliothèque de Muséon 47, Louvain, 1960), which can be supplemented by fragments published by P. E. Kahle, *Bala-izah* (Vol. 1, p. 404, London, 1954) and by H. Quecke in *Orientalia* 48 (1979):68–81.

Translations in English are found in John, Marquis of Bute, *The Coptic Morning Service for the Lord's Day* (3rd ed., pp. 46–134, London, 1908); *The Coptic Liturgy,* authorized by H. H. Abba Kyrillos (Vol. 6, pp. 57–117, Cairo, 1963); Fayek M. Ishak, *A Complete Translation of the Coptic Orthodox Mass and the Liturgy of St. Basil* (Hong Kong, 1974). French translations are found in *Notre messe selon la liturgie copte dite de saint Basile le Grand* (Cairo, 1963), Italian in *Guida facile per seguire la Messa di rito alessandrino copto* (Vatican City, 1956), and Latin in E. Renaudot, *Guida facile, etc.* (Vol. 1, pp. 1–25 [of the Coptic recension] and Vol. 1, pp. 57–86 [of the Greek text], the anaphoric part of the latter being reprinted in Hänggi-Pahl, *Guida facile, etc.,* pp. 348–58).

Studies on the subject are O. H. E. Burmester, "Rites and Ceremonies of the Coptic Church, Part II" (*The Eastern Churches Quarterly* 8 [1949–1950]:1–39) re-edited in Burmester, *The Egyptian or Coptic Church,* pp. 46–90 (Publications de la Société d'Archéologie Copte, Textes et documents 10, Cairo, 1967).

Others are H. Engberding, *Das eucharistische Hochgebet der Basileiosliturgie* (Theologie des christlichen Ostens 1, Münster, 1931) and Habīb Iskandar Masīhā, *Sharḥ wa-Tafsīr al-Quddās al-Ilāhī* (2 vols., Cairo, 1965–1966 and 1977).

AELRED CODY, O.S.B.

ANAPHORA OF SAINT CYRIL, the most typically Egyptian of the three anaphoras retained in the euchologion of the Coptic church. It is basically the same as the anaphoric part of the Greek Liturgy of Saint Mark that was formerly used in the Melchite church of Alexandria. Although it is regularly called the Anaphora of Saint Cyril, it is introduced in Coptic euchologia as "the Anaphora of our holy father Mark the Apostle, which the thrice-blessed Saint Cyril the Archbishop established."

Although both the Coptic Saint Cyril and the Greek Saint Mark contain textual variants peculiar to the one or to the other, both seem to be derived from the same recension of the old Egyptian anaphora, whose earliest textual witnesses are fragments in Greek. A few Coptic fragments in the Sahidic dialect have also been found. The extant witnesses to the text of the present Coptic Saint Cyril, none of them earlier than the twelfth century, are in the Bohairic dialect, but a Greek text apparently meant for occasional use in the Coptic church survives in a few manuscripts, one of which has been published. It is still impossible to say whether the Bohairic version was made from a Greek text or from a Sahidic intermediary. In general, the readings of the early fragments, both Greek and Sahidic, are closer to those of Coptic Saint Cyril than to surviving manuscripts of the Melchite Saint Mark.

Superficial influence of the Syrian Liturgy of Saint James is less evident in Saint Cyril than in Saint Mark, and the Byzantinizing tendencies that appear in extant manuscripts of the Liturgy of Saint Mark are absent from the Anaphora of Saint Cyril. On the other hand, Coptic Saint Cyril has textual additions of its own that are not found in the anaphoric part of Melchite Saint Mark. In the Coptic euchologia the Anaphora of Saint Cyril in the strict sense, prefaced by proper prayers of the veil and of the kiss of peace and followed by proper prayers of the fraction (with its preface), of embolism and of inclination after the Lord's Prayer, and of thanksgiving and of inclination after communion, is designed for insertion into the common order of the eucharistic liturgy which is given in connection with the Anaphora of Saint Basil. The three great prayers of intercession after the prayer of the veil are either to be omitted or to be substituted with shorter prayers when the Anaphora of Saint Cyril is used.

In modern times the Anaphora of Saint Cyril is rarely used, and most of the music proper to it has grown dim in the memory of the singers, if it has not been forgotten altogether. Some celebrants use prayers drawn from it in place of the corresponding prayers in the Anaphora of Saint Basil, and some efforts are made to restore its integral use. Traditionally it was seen as especially apt for use in Lent and in the Coptic month of Kiyahk before Christmas.

BIBLIOGRAPHY

A Greek text once used in the Coptic Church has been published by W. F. Macomber, "The Anaphora of St. Mark according to the Kacmarcik Codex." *Orientalia christiana periodica* 45 (1979):75–98.

For a list of printed liturgical editions of the Bohairic and Arabic texts, see H. Malak in *Mélanges Eugène Tisserant,* Vol. 3. Studi e Testi 233, pp. 6–8, 27. Rome, 1964.

An English translation is in F. E. Brightman, ed., *Liturgies Eastern and Western,* Vol. 1, pp. 144–88; Oxford, 1896; the Anaphora of Saint Cyril is combined with the Coptic common order of the liturgy. A Latin version can be found in E. Renaudot, *Liturgiarum orientalium collectio,* 2nd ed., Vol. 1, pp. 38–51, Frankfurt and London, 1847; reproduced without the intercessions, with editing by A. Raes, in A. Hänggi and I. Pahl, eds., *Prex eucharistica,* Spicilegium friburgense 12, pp. 135–39, Freiburg, 1968.

AELRED CODY, O.S.B.

ANAPHORA OF SAINT GREGORY, one of the three anaphoras retained by the Coptic church in its service books. In the manuscript tradition, followed by modern printed editions, the anaphora in the strict sense (from the beginning of the eucharistic prayer to the doxology before the fraction and Lord's Prayer) is supplemented by certain prayers preceding and following it and meant for use with it, which are to replace the corresponding prayers used with the Coptic ANAPHORA OF SAINT BASIL. For other elements of the service, rubrics direct the celebrant to the common order of Coptic service now attached to the Anaphora of Saint Basil.

The anaphora in the strict sense, like the Anaphora of Saint Basil, shows the structure of an Antiochene or Syrian anaphora, without the more strikingly Egyptian features of the anaphora part of the Liturgy of Saint Mark and the ANAPHORA OF SAINT CYRIL, and it is presumably of Syrian origin. Its adaptation to Egyptian use has led to some structural duplication not found in the Basilian anaphora. In the dialogue at the beginning of the anaphora there is a mixture of Syrian elements with the Egyptian, and there are two introductions to the triple Holy, the first characteristically Egyptian in stressing the "Holy" sung by those present, the second typically Syrian in its emphasis on the "Holy" sung by the angelic choirs. A peculiarity of the anaphora lies in its being addressed not to God the Father but to God the Son, to whom divine acts in the history of salvation before and after the Incarnation are attributed, both in the eucharistic prayer after the triple Holy and in the first of the two prayers of the kiss of peace preceding the anaphora proper. In the EPICLESIS, Christ is asked to change the gifts "with His own voice" as well as to send His Holy Spirit to hallow and change them.

Although one of the two alternative prayers of the kiss of peace preceding the anaphora proper may be a secondary addition, both are addressed to Christ and thus fit that peculiarity of the anaphora. These prayers are preceded by a prayer of the veil that is clearly secondary, for it is addressed not to the Son but to the Father. In the Greek recension, probably Melchite, there is also an alternative prayer of the veil which is identical with the Byzantine prayer of the *cherubikon,* and this is itself preceded by three other prayers absent in the Coptic recension. Of these three, the second, for the end of the prothesis, is addressed to Christ and is not known in another context; the first, for the beginning of the prothesis, is borrowed from the Antiochene Liturgy of Saint James and the third, to precede the Gospel, is identical with the prayer of the Gospel in the Coptic common order. One concludes that, just as in the case of the Anaphora of Saint Basil, the original Anaphora of Saint Gregory as an independent formulary began with a prayer of the kiss of peace, with a prayer of the veil added afterward in imitation of the beginning of anaphoras in Syrian collections, while the additional prayers in the Melchite formulary were further accretions felt to be opportune in Melchite Egyptian practice.

Traditionally, the Anaphora of Saint Gregory is used on major feasts such as Christmas, Epiphany, and Easter, and on PALM SUNDAY, because it is addressed to Christ. In modern times, some celebrants do not use it at all, and some use parts of it in place of the corresponding parts of the Anaphora of Saint Basil, on appropriate feasts.

BIBLIOGRAPHY

A slightly Byzantinized Greek text is found, with Latin translation, in E. Renaudot, *Liturgiarum orientalium collectio,* Vol. 1, pp. 85–115 (2nd ed.; Frankfurt and London, 1847). The anaphoric part of the same text and translation, edited by A. Raes, is given in A. Hänggi and I. Pahl, eds., *Prex eucharistica,* pp. 358–73 (Spicilegium friburgense 12; Fribourg, 1968). For a list of printed liturgical editions of the Bohairic and Arabic texts, cf. H. Malak in *Mélanges Eugène Tisserant,* Vol. 3, pp. 6–8, 27. (Studi e testi 233; Vatican City, 1964). The Bohairic text of a modern Coptic euchologion is given with some emendations and selected variants by E. Hammerschmidt, *Die Koptische Gregoriosanaphora,* pp. 10–78 (Berliner byzantinistische Arbeiten 8; Berlin, 1957).

Translations (of the Coptic version) are given in German in Hammerschmidt, pp. 11–79; in English in J. Medows Rodwell, *The Liturgies of S. Basil, S. Gregory, and S. Cyril from a Coptic Manuscript of the Thirteenth Century,* pp. 1–10 (Eastern Church Association: Occasional Paper 12; London, 1870); Latin in Renaudot, Vol. 1, pp. 25–37.

AELRED CODY, O.S.B.

ANASTASIA, SAINT (feast day, 26 Ṭūbah), sixth-century founder of a monastery. The story of Saint Anastasia is transmitted by the Lower Egyptian recension of the Copto-Arabic SYNAXARION (Basset, 1916, p. 703; Forget, 1954, p. 234 [text]; 1953, p. 414 [trans.]) and by the tale of DANIEL HEGUMENOS of SCETIS (Wādī al-Natrūn), in which it occupies the second place (Guidi, 1900, pp. 535–64; 1901, pp. 51–53).

Anastasia was the wife of a consul and a patrician. She was pursued by the emperor JUSTINIAN and thus aroused the jealousy of the empress THEODORA. To avoid the worst, she went off to Alexandria, and at a place called the PEMPTON she founded the monastery called by her name (also known as the Monastery of the Patrician). After Theodora died in 548, Justinian tried to get Anastasia to return to Constantinople, but she left her monastery and went in search of Apa Daniel, who was then HEGUMENOS of Scetis. Daniel installed her in a cell 18 miles (27 km) from Scetis. He secretly paid her a visit once a week and supplied her with water through one of his disciples. In 576, twenty-eight years after her arrival in Scetis, Daniel's disciple found an ostracon with the words "Bring the spades and come here." When Daniel received this message, he knew that Anastasia's death was near. He went with his disciple to give her communion and receive her last words. Daniel revealed her story to his disciple after burying her.

BIBLIOGRAPHY

Cauwenberg, P. van. *Etude sur les moines d'Egypte.* Paris and Louvain, 1914.

Delehaye, H. *Synaxarium Ecclesiae Constantinopolitanae.* Brussels, 1902.

Evelyn-White, H. G. *The Monasteries of the Wadi'n Natrūn,* Pt. 2, *The History of the Monasteries of Nitria and Scetis.* New York, 1932.

Guidi, I., ed. "Vie et récits de l'abbé Daniel de Scété." *Revue de l'Orient chrétien* 5 (1900):535–64; 6 (1901):51–53.

RENÉ-GEORGES COQUIN

ANASTASIUS, thirty-sixth patriarch of the See of Saint Mark (605–616). Anastasius was a priest in Alexandria, a man of profound learning in the Scriptures and the doctrines of the Coptic faith, when he was unanimously selected by the bishops and the clergy of the Coptic church to succeed DAMIAN to the archiepiscopal throne of Alexandria. Although his biography has been compiled in detail by SĀWĪRUS IBN AL-MUQAFFA' in the HISTORY OF THE PATRIARCHS, it seems strange that his name does not appear in the standard biographical dictionaries of the Christian church. As we may be able to learn from the accounts of Sāwīrus, however, his election would have taken place at a time when the Chalcedonian influence must have been strong, not only in the capital city of Alexandria but also at the Byzantine court in Constantinople.

Actually, Coptic orthodox bishops of the Monophysite profession were forbidden entrance into Alexandria. Apparently, the Monophysite Coptic congregation in the capital city was subjected to great troubles, first by the Byzantine emperor, Tiberius II (578–582), and an adjutant of his by the name of Belisarius. The policy of persecution was maintained by Tiberius' son and successor, Maurice (582–602). When Maurice was murdered by a rebel named Phocas, who laid his hand on the Byzantine throne and became emperor in 602, circumstances surrounding Anastasius became even worse. In Alexandria at this time, there was a Chalcedonian by the name of Eulogius who wrote a defamatory letter to Phocas about Anastasius. Consequently, the infuriated emperor issued an order to the prefect of Alexandria that the Coptic patriarch should be dispossessed of the important church of Cosmas and Damian and all its dependencies and all that belonged to it; it should be given to Eulogius, the misguided Chalcedonian. The saddened Anastasius apparently fled to a neighboring monastery where he could bury his grief.

Due to his increasing difficulties on the internal front, the Coptic patriarch turned his attention to the unity of the church beyond his frontier where he was rewarded by the renewal of close contacts with Antioch. Athanasius had succeeded Peter, a supporter of Chalcedonian doctrine, on the archiepiscopal throne of Antioch, which had been led into disunion with Egypt by Peter. With Peter's death, anti-Chalcedonian doctrines received more favor.

When Anastasius heard of this change in the church of Antioch, he wrote a synodal letter to Athanasius commending him for his wisdom and good faith in the rectification of errors and aberrations of Peter and urging him to work for the unity of the churches of Egypt and of Antioch. Consequently, on receiving this synodal missive, Athanasius summoned an ecclesiastical council of his bishops whom he addressed in that vein, and it was decided to pursue the new trend by sending a delegation from Antioch to Alexandria in an attempt at cementing the unity. Together with five bishops from Antioch, Athanasius sailed to Alexandria. On their arrival, however, they understood that Anastasius was still in a neighboring monastery. Although it is not known where the delegation met Anastasius, the possibility remains that they must have headed directly to the monastery where he resided, because the Coptic Orthodox bishops were not allowed to enter a city preponderantly held by the Chalcedonians. On the arrival of the Antiochene delegation, Anastasius at once summoned his bishops and the Coptic clergy for a show of unity between Egypt and Antioch. Athanasius, quoting the Psalms, said in a warm discourse: "At this hour, O my friends, we must take the harp of David and sing the voice of the psalm, saying: Mercy and truth have met together . . . " (*History of the Patriarchs*, Vol. 1, pt. 2, p. 482 [218]). The two patriarchs then embraced one another with a kiss of peace. Egypt and Syria were declared to become one in doctrine. Afterward, the two leaders remained in the Coptic monastery "for a whole month meditating together upon the holy scriptures and profitable doctrine, speaking of these matters and discussing them." Then Athanasius returned to his province in peace and great honor after the conclusion of an act of unity between Antioch and Alexandria, which remains in effect today.

Anastasius spent his remaining years assiduously attending to the affairs of the church. Evidently, he was a prolific writer on theological matters, though most of his work has been lost. From the day he sat on the archiepiscopal throne of Alexandria, he wrote an epistle, festal letter, or homily each beginning with a different letter from the Coptic alphabet. According to the *History of the Patriarchs*, he wrote a book every year of his reign, whether mystagogic or synodal. In all, he presumably completed twelve books in his reign of twelve years.

AZIZ S. ATIYA

ANASTASIUS, abbot. Anastasius is said to have been the abbot of a Pachomian monastery, probably that of PBOW. His period is not indicated, but he is the author of several stories, one of which, relating to the adventures of a Nubian prince, Qafrī, has been retained in the recension of the Copto-Arabic SYNAXARION of the Copts from Upper Egypt. The name Qafrī may be a play on words, as Crum points out, for this word is related to the Arabic *qafr* (desert) and describes an anchorite. Using a Nubian invasion for cover, the prince reached the village of Abnūd, which is near Qifṭ (Ramzī, 1953–1963, Vol. 2, pt. 4, p. 174)—and became a monk in a monastery of Pachomius. This story will be found in the European editions of the Synaxarion, either that of Basset (1907, pp. 514–16) or that of Forget (1905–1922, Vols. 47–49, pp. 353–55). Two other stories of Athanasius have been published by Crum (1932).

Such episodes recall for us a historical event, the Nubian invasion, which would otherwise pass unnoticed. At the same time, they allow us to date Athanasius before the Islamic conquest.

BIBLIOGRAPHY

Crum, W. E. "A Nubian Prince in an Egyptian Monastery." In *Studies Presented to F. Ll. Griffith*, pp. 137–48. London, 1932.

Muḥammad Ramzī. *Al-Qāmūs al-Jughrāfī lil-Bilād al Miṣrīyyah*, 3 vols. in 8 pts. Cairo, 1953–1966.

RENÉ-GEORGES COQUIN

ANASTASIUS OF EUCAITA, a fictitious character invented in the Period of the CYCLES (eighth century), in relation to the legends concerning the martyr THEODORUS STRATELATES, who was from Eucaita. Anastasius is said to have been bishop of Eucaita, the successor of a certain Sukianus, and it is stated that he composed an encomium in honor of Theodore, the complete text of which exists in Sahidic (Morgan Library M591, unpublished). Portions of the text survive in Bohairic (National Library, Turin; now lost; ed. Rossi, 1893–1894).

This text gives a lengthy account of the life of Theodorus, starting with his family. His father, John, is said to have been a bold Egyptian soldier from the village of Apot (or Apor) near Shotep. After fighting under the emperor Numerian, he married the daughter of a prefect and went to live in Anatolia, where his son Theodore was born. Theodore was educated by his pagan mother and became a bold warrior. There follows the account of his battle with the dragon near the town of Eucaita, his conversion, and his martyrdom for refusing to offer sacrifice.

This text seems to have been created in order to "Egyptianize" the famous military martyr. It is based on the Passion of Theodorus before he was associated with the other Theodorus, known as Anatolius—who, in the Coptic tradition, forms part of the cycle of BASILIDES the General. They are, of course, independent of each other. The encomium attributed to Theodorus of Antioch substantiates that they are different persons.

Although in the Greek tradition the two Theodores develop from a single figure, for hagiographical reasons, the Coptic tradition seems at first to be acquainted with the two Theodores as separate figures, and then to place them in some sort of relation to each other, albeit in a very casual manner.

BIBLIOGRAPHY

Delehaye, H. *Légendes grecques des saints militaires*, pp. 11–43. Paris, 1909.

Rossi, F. "Di alcuni manoscritti copti che si conservano nella Biblioteca Nazionale di Torino." *Memorie Accademie di Torino*, 2nd ser., 43 (1893):223–340; 44 (1894):21–70.

TITO ORLANDI

ANATHEMA, either a votive offering set up in a temple (2 Macc. 2:13; Philo, *De vita Mosis* 1.253) or, in general terms, that which is devoted to a divinity either consecrated or accursed. In New Testament times, the meaning was moving in the direction of the latter, the best example being in Paul's First Letter to the Corinthians (1 Cor. 12:3): No one who speaks by the Spirit of God says "Jesus is accursed." Added to this was the sense of swearing an oath that would involve a curse if it was not fulfilled. Thus, in Acts 23:14 it is recorded that the conspirators against Paul "bound themselves to the plot by oath" (*anathemati*).

Paul also used the term to denote separation from the church of an offender guilty of sins such as preaching a gospel other than his (Gal. 1:8) or not loving the Lord (1 Cor. 16:22). The term most usually retains this sense in the history of the early church. It is noticeable that the bishops who judged the opinions of Paul of Samosata at Antioch in 265 merely stated that he who did not acknowledge the preexistence of Christ was "alien from the Catholic Church" (the text of the council's letter is in Mansi (1901), Vol. 1, cols. 1033–40). In the West, the Council of Elvira (in southeast Spain c. 309) used the term "anathema" to castigate offenders (see canon 52). At Nicaea in 325 the term was applied to what the council deemed to be the opinions of Arius: "And those who say, 'Once he was not' and 'Before His generation he was not' and 'He came to be from nothing' . . . the Catholic Church anathematizes" (Socrates *Historia ecclesiastica* 1.8).

With the example of the Council of Nicaea in front of them, the fourth-century church councils regularly anathematized their opponents. The only exception was the statement of the Third Council of Sirmium in 357, that while there "was no question that the Father is greater than the Son" and that the terms HOMOOUSION and HOMOIOUSION were objectionable, dissidents were not subject to anathema (Hilary of Poitiers *Liber de synodis* 11).

In Egypt the ferocity of ecclesiastical debate, first between ATHANASIUS I and his opponents and then between CYRIL I and NESTORIUS, made anathema and counteranathema part and parcel of the armory of vituperation. The most important example of doctrinal statements, opposition to which would involve the culprit in anathema and deposition from clerical office, was Cyril's Twelve Anathemas, drawn up in November 430 (Cyril, *Epistula* 17), which Cyril required Nestorius to accept on pain of excommunication. Nestorius' Counter Anathemas to Cyril precipitated the summons of the First Council of EPHESUS in June 431 by Emperor Theodosius II.

Anathemas continued to be appended to doctrinal statements agreed by the councils in the Eastern and Western churches through the Middle Ages. Anathema was regarded as the most serious disciplinary measure, involving complete separation from the faithful (Gratian, *Decretum* 11, canon 106). It survives to the present day in the Coptic church as a means of imposing severe ecclesiastical discipline on refractory clergy and laymen.

BIBLIOGRAPHY

Bindley, T. H., and F. W. Green. *Oecumenical Documents of the Faith*, 4th ed., pp. 124–37. London, 1950.

Cyril. *Epistolae*. In PG 77, cols. 9–390. Paris, 1864.

Hilary of Poitiers. *Liber de synodis*. In PL 10, cols. 479–546. Paris, 1845. Translated as *On the Councils* by L. Pullam in *A Select Library of Nicene and Post-Nicene Fathers of the Christian Church*, ed. P. Schaff and H. Wace, ser. 2, Vol. 9, pp. 4–29. Repr. Grand Rapids, Mich., 1955.

Vacant, A. "Anathème." In *Dictionnaire de théologie catholique*, Vol. 1, cols. 1168–71. Paris, 1923.

W. H. C. FREND

ANATOLIUS, SAINT, fourth-century martyr (feast day: 9 Ṭūbah). He is one of the personages of the Basilidian cycle referred to in different texts in relationship with the more famous Theodore Anatolius. The most important part of his martyrdom is recorded in one incomplete codex (Balestri and Hyvernat, 1908); two fragments from Leipzig consist of the beginning and some other passages (Leipoldt, 1906, p. 388). The complete text may be reconstructed from the abstract of the Copto-Arabic SYNAXARION, probably derived through a different redaction.

According to the Synaxarion, Anatolius was a general of Persian origin under DIOCLETIAN. When the persecutions began he confessed his faith. Diocletian tried in vain to have him persuaded away from his faith by the general Romanus.

From here the Coptic text continues. The scene is set in Antioch. Anatolius, having been tortured because of his opposition to the apostasy of Diocletian, is praying. Jesus appears to him, cures, and comforts him. As Anatolius leaves to go to the emperor, he stumbles over the corpse of a dead man in the square and raises him. The crowd acclaims him, and the emperor is informed. He charges Anatolius with magic and tortures him by fire. Because the martyr endures the tormenting without visible suffering, 800 people are converted to Christianity.

Anatolius' head is peeled and bathed in vinegar, but the martyr does not suffer; he prays, and the archangel MICHAEL cures him. He is placed in a hole and burned, but God preserves his body from fire. The emperor gives orders to have him beaten, but the soldiers in charge of this task become blind. Invoking the Christian God, he saves the soldiers, causing their conversion and their martyrdom.

Anatolius is taken before wild beasts to be martyred, but a lion speaks, praising Anatolius and assailing the emperor. Other spectators in the crowd adopt the Christian faith. Anatolius cures the emperor, who once again is found in the devil's hands.

The text is interrupted when Romanus the general (another famous character of the Cycle) advises the emperor to jail Anatolius indefinitely. This is one of the latest texts of the Basilidian Cycle, at least in the preserved version. For this reason the typical features of the epic Passions (see HAGIOGRAPHY) are particularly unpolished and exaggerated.

BIBLIOGRAPHY

Balestri, I., and H. Hyvernat, eds. *Acta Martyrum*, 2 vols. CSCO 43, 44. Paris, 1908.

Leipoldt, J. "Verzeichnis der koptischen Handschriften." *Katalog der Handschriften der Universitätsbibliothek zu Leipzig*, Vol. 2, ed. C. Vollers. Leipzig, 1906.

TITO ORLANDI

ANBĀ. *See* Apa.

ANBĀ FARIJ. *See* Anbā Ruways.

ANBĀ RUWAYS (c. 1334–1404), saint and monk known for his holiness (feast day: 21 Bābah). He was born at Minyat Yamīn in the Gharbiyyah province. His original name was Isḥāq Furayj, but he is known in Coptic as Ruways, a diminutive Arabic pseudonym referring to the young camel that was his constant companion.

After a short time as a farm laborer, Isḥāq Furayj devoted himself entirely to a life of prayer, asceticism, and self-abnegation. He used to fast for long periods, as testified by Patriarch MATTHEW. He was also blessed with the power of clairvoyance that earned for him the epithet of Theophanius (the beholder of God).

Anbā Ruways was buried with four patriarchs in the crypt of the small church now named after him, but previously known as the Church of Saint Mercurius (Abū Sayfayn) in the ground of Anbā Ruways Monastery, at one time known as DAYR-AL-KHANDAQ, in the Abbassiyyah district of Cairo.

In recent history a cemetery arose around the Church of Anbā Ruways. But this cemetery was later transferred to the Red Mountain (al-Jabal al-Aḥmar) region north of Cairo, and all that was left behind was the small Church of Anbā Ruways. However, on that vast terrain that automatically reverted to the patriarchate, a number of stately buildings arose, including the Anbā Ruways building that accommodates the INSTITUTE OF COPTIC STUDIES and its library, as well as some episcopal and patriarchal offices. The same grounds also contain the CLERICAL COLLEGE, the patriarchal residence, and the new majestic Cathedral of Saint Mark.

BISHOP GREGORIOS

ANCHORITE. [*This entry consists of two parts:* History *and* Folklore. *The first treats the development of the movement and names some famous anchorites. The second alludes to folklore associated with the philosophy.*]

History

Anchorites are those ascetic hermits who embraced the highest degree of monastic life by retreating into the Egyptian desert and living in complete seclusion and self-mortification.

The annals of the Coptic church abound in names of anchorites who lived between the third and seventh centuries. An anchorite could spend many decades in caves or cells cut off from all human contact until some saintly men's footsteps were directed to the spot where he dwelt, this encounter usually taking place when the anchorite's death was imminent. Thereupon, he would acquaint his visitors with his life story. When death came, the anchorite would be buried in the sand.

The SYNAXARION lists the dates for the commemoration of saints, many of whom were anchorites, notably Anbā Būlā (Paul; 2 Amshīr), Apa Nofar (Onophrius; 16 Ba'ūnah), Anbā Pidjimi (11 Kiyahk), Anbā Hadrā (12 Kiyahk), Anbā Miṣā'īl (13 Kiyahk), Anbā Timotheus (23 Kiyahk), Anbā Karās (Cyrus; 8 Abīb), and the penitent MARY THE EGYPTIAN (6 Baramūdah). But however numerous the names of anchorites included in the Synaxarion, the *Paradise of the Fathers* (Budge, 1907), and the various manuscripts kept at Coptic monasteries, there must have been many more anchorites who lived and died unknown to history.

The man credited with instituting the anchoritic life is Anbā Būlā, the anchorite or hermit par excellence who spent eighty years as a recluse in the Eastern Desert before he was visited by Saint ANTONY, who later buried him and wrote his life story. Antony is also credited with instituting anchoritic life, although he had supplies brought to him every six months, and after twenty years, received many visitors who were directed by him to the ascetic way of life. Similarly, Anbā Kārās was discovered by a holy man named Anbā Pambo after fifty-seven years of solitary life. Anbā Samuel the Confessor recorded the history of Anbā Moses; Saint Babnūdah wrote the life stories of Apa Nofar and Anbā Timotheus; Anbā Isaac, abbot of al-Qalamūn monastery, wrote those of Anbā Miṣā'īl and Anbā Ghalyūn; and Anbā Buqṭur, the abbot of DAYR AL-ZUJĀJ, wrote the life stories of many more anchorites. Coptic monasteries include the names of other anchorites, such as Anbā Harmīnā, Anbā Iliyyā, Anbā Sīlās, Anbā Ḥizīqyāl, Anbā Murqus al-Tarmaqī, and Anbā Ulāgh.

For the most part, anchorites were initially cenobites who belonged to certain monasteries. Anbā Pidjimi spent twenty-four years in the company of elderly monks, and when they had all died, he went

Anchorite's cave, Wādī al-Natrūn.

out in search of solitude. Apa Nofar, we are told, was so moved by the stories he heard about anchorites that he decided to become one; and Anbā Ghalyūn lived to an advanced age at DAYR ANBĀ SAMŪ'ĪL OF QALAMŪN before he finally became an anchorite.

On the other hand, some anchorites never belonged to a monastery. As in the case of Anbā Būlā, this was because monasticism had not yet been established. Mary the Egyptian embarked on a life of solitude in the desert without having previously belonged to a convent, and was later met by Anbā Zosima (Zosimus), who wrote her story.

The extent of physical subjugation and self-mortification that many anchorites endured can be inferred from the fact that Anbā Būlā lived on a daily ration of half a loaf of bread, said to have been brought to him by a raven. This is reminiscent of the story of the prophet Elijah, who was similarly supported by God near the brook Cherith (1 Kgs. 17:2–6).

Apa Nofar dwelt close to a palm tree and a spring of water. Anbā Pidjimi and Anbā Mūsā each fed on herbage and drank dewdrops off leaves of trees. It should not, however, be assumed that anchorites were ethereal figures or phantasmal beings, as some believed. Some anchorites, we are told, suffered mortal diseases in their seclusion: Anbā Timotheus was afflicted by a liver disease, and Apa Nofar died of fever.

Certain of them were also subject to the weaknesses of the flesh, as in the case of Anbā Mūsā, who eventually repented with the help of Anbā Samuel the Confessor and partook of Holy Communion before he departed this life.

As to clothing, we are told that Anbā Būlā wove palm leaves and fibers into a garment. A few anchorites, however, went naked as a token of mortification of the flesh: Apa Nofar grew his hair long to cover his body. Anbā Pidjimi preferred, after a period of nakedness, to cover his body, since God gave raiment to Adam and Eve, and since the cherubim cover their bodies with their wings. We also note that Mary the Egyptian hid behind a tree on seeing Anbā Zosima, and asked him to give her his cloak to cover herself.

Anchorites spent their lives in constant communion with God. We read of certain anchorites who were directed to alter the course of their lives for the benefit of others. Anbā Pidjimi left the desert for a mountain cave in the vicinity of his native town, where through his influence and teachings people were led to better lives and to embrace Christianity. Anbā Hadrā became a cenobite who exercised the gift of healing and was eventually consecrated bishop of Aswan.

Anchorites, on the whole, led angelic lives while completely unknown to the outside world and immersed themselves in prayer and meditation.

BIBLIOGRAPHY

Budge, E. A. Wallis. *The Paradise or Garden of the Fathers*, 2 vols. London, 1907.

POPE SHENOUDA III

Folklore

The word *sā'iḥ* (pl., *suwwāḥ*), meaning "wanderer," is the Arabic term for an anchorite. To be among the *suwwāḥ* is to have reached the highest spiritual rank for a monk. The popular belief is that a *sā'iḥ* feels no bodily pain, hunger, thirst, or lust. He is also believed to be invisible except to those to whom he reveals himself. But some humans may hear him or see the incense he or a group of *suwwāḥ* have burned during a mass. There is much controversy as to their number, which is believed in some instances to be four hundred, and in others twelve only, while some hold that it is unlimited. Those who believe their number is limited emphasize the fact that it never varies. It is also held that if one of the *suwwāḥ* dies, the other *suwwāḥ* choose someone to replace the deceased among the monks and summon him to join them. At the *suwwāḥ* level, there is no distinction made between men and women, and *suwwāḥ* are held to be nearer in their bodily and spiritual qualities to heavenly beings than are other human beings.

MALEK WASSEF

ANDREW OF CRETE (660–740), a hymn writer and theologian who became archbishop of Gortyna in Crete. The Arabic Christian tradition has preserved for us at least six homilies of Andrew of Crete:

On the Nativity of Mary (PG 97, cols. 805–820; Clavis Patrum Graecorum 8170); On the Presentation of Mary in the Temple (PG 97, cols. 861–81; Clavis Patrum Graecorum 8173); the First Homily on the Dormition of the Virgin (Bibliotheca Hagiographica Orientalis 1121), which is very rare and therefore not published by J. P. Migne in the Patrologia Graeca, nor mentioned by M. Geerard in his

Clavis Patrum Graecorum, nor identified by G. Graf (1944); the Third Homily on the Dormition of the Virgin (PG 97, 1089–1109; Clavis Patrum Graecorum 8183); on Saint Nicholas (PG 97, cols. 1192–1205; Clavis Patrum Graecorum 8187); and the Canons on Penance (Clavis Patrum Graecorum 8219), which are not yet properly identified.

Only On the Presentation of Mary in the Temple is found in the Arabic tradition of the Copts. It is still unpublished, but it is found in at least three manuscripts of Coptic origin (Coptic Patriarchate, Cairo, History 36, Graf, no. 564, Simaykah, no. 643, Egypt, 1717, fol. 38b–54b; National Library, Paris, Arabe 150, Egypt, 1606, fols. 193a–201a; and Vatican Library, Arabic 698, Egypt, 1371, fols. 139b–55b).

The homily was read at the liturgy on 3 Kiyahk. The incipit, following the Paris catalog, reads: "That the width of the earth could be surveyed by hand span or that the width of the ocean could encompass the surface . . . ."

This Arabic homily is also found in manuscripts that are not of Coptic origin, such as Melchite and West Syrian origin eighteenth century (Oriental Library, Beirut, 510, Syria, pp. 520–25; Oriental Library, Beirut, 511, Syria, 1867, pp. 29–40; and National Library, Paris, Syriac 209, Western garshūnī, 1645, fols. 504a–17b, with an identical incipit).

No homilies of Andrew of Crete are found in Coptic.

KHALIL SAMIR, S.J.

ANDRONICUS, thirty-seventh patriarch of the See of Saint Mark (616–622). Andronicus was unanimously elected by the clergy and the bishops of the Coptic church. His election was universally acclaimed by the people of Alexandria to whom he was well known not only for his piety but also for his charitable character, since he gave generously to the poor of his community. Even the Chalcedonian dissidents among the inhabitants did not contest his nomination.

Andronicus was a man of immense wealth, and his family had a high social and political standing. His cousin became Alexandria's chief administrator, "the head of the council of Alexandria," according to the HISTORY OF THE PATRIARCHS (p. 484 [220]). By vocation, Andronicus was an accomplished scribe, and although there is no record to prove that he was a theological scholar, he was undoubtedly a man of profound faith and a religious leader in his church. He was one of the very few laymen to attain the patriarchal dignity in Coptic history, for he was only a simple deacon in the Church of the Angelion at the time of his election. Though he was not a monk or a full-fledged presbyter, he remained a bachelor all his life and confined himself to a cell adjacent to the Church of the Angelion.

The reign of Andronicus came to pass during one of the most critical periods in Egyptian history, since it coincided with the last Persian invasion of the country at the beginning of the seventh century and before the Arab conquest of 642. Egypt was still under Byzantine rule during the reign of Emperor Heraclius (610–641). The Persians had no regard for Christianity and Christians. According to the *History of the Patriarchs,* their armies, under the leadership of the Persian emperor Chosroes II Parviz, descended upon Egypt and the Egyptians like locusts and "trod them down as the oxen tread the thrashing floor, and collected their wealth and all that they had into his [Chosroes'] treasuries" (p. 484 [220]). After the conquest of the country, the Persian emperor dispatched a section of his armed forces, under the command of a certain Salar (probably a corruption of Shahr Baraz), to seize Alexandria and the adjacent district of Mareotis in the northern Nile Delta. On his way toward the capital, the Persian commander surrounded the rich area of the ENATON monastery and seized all its establishments by storm. The Persians slaughtered all its monks save a few who succeeded in concealing themselves in hiding spots. The troops pillaged everywhere and denuded what was probably the richest of Coptic monasteries of all its wealth and vast possessions. They left the Enaton completely in ruins. Once a flourishing monastic institution, it disappeared from the map, never to rise again.

When the news of this terrible catastrophe reached Alexandria, its authorities decided to negotiate a peaceful surrender in the hope of saving the city from being sacked and ruined. Thus they opened the city gates to the invaders who entered it without lifting a finger. Apparently the Persians feigned a peaceful entry. After establishing themselves in headquarters later known as the Castle of the Persians, they invited the young men of Alexandria from the age of eighteen to fifty years to go out of the walls to receive a gift of twenty gold denarii each in a show of magnanimity. The unsuspecting citizens, eighty thousand in number, responded, and as soon as they were assembled unarmed, Salar issued an immediate order to his troops to surround them and slay them all. After this sacrilege, the Persians left with their loads of loot and returned to Upper Egypt. When they reached the city of NIKIOU, a native traitor who may have been a Chalcedonian showed them the way to some adjacent monasteries, which were destroyed in the same way as all other places seized by the Persian battalions.

It was not until the Byzantine emperor Heraclius was able later in his reign to recapture his lost territories that Egypt could shake off the Persian yoke. Throughout that period, Andronicus remained hidden in his cell at the Angelion church. Although safe himself, he must have suffered at the loss of his people and the ruined monasteries. Within six years of his accession, he died on 20 Ṭūbah, the day of his annual commemoration in Coptic churches.

BIBLIOGRAPHY

Milne, J. *A History of Egypt Under Roman Rule.* New York, 1898.

AZIZ S. ATIYA

ANGEL, one of the myriad of incorporeal creatures whose natural abode is heaven and who, on certain occasions, appear to man in the shape of human beings to reveal God's will and carry out His commands. The appellation "messenger" or "angel" used in the prophecy of Malachi was confirmed by Christ when He said of John the Baptist, "This is he of whom it is written, 'Behold, I send my messenger [or angel] before thy face, who shall prepare thy way before thee'" (Mt. 11:10 quoting Mal. 3:1). The same usage was applied to some bishops in charge of churches in Asia Minor (Rev. 1:20; 2:1, 8, 12, 18; 3:1, 7, 14).

The fathers of the church recorded their views of the celestial hierarchy. CLEMENT OF ALEXANDRIA (c. 150–215) holds that "the grades here in the church of bishops, presbyters, deacons, are imitations of the angelic glory . . ." (*Stromata* 13, in *Ante-Nicene Fathers,* Vol. 2, p. 505; Jurgens, 1970, Vol. 1, p. 184). According to CYRIL OF JERUSALEM (c. 315–386), "After this we make mention of heaven . . . of the Angels, Archangels, Virtues, Dominations, Principalities, Powers, Thrones, of the Cherubim with many faces: in effect repeating that call of David's, 'Magnify the Lord with me.' We make mention also of the Seraphim . . ." (*On the Mysteries* 5.6, in *A Select Library,* 1955, Vol. 7, p. 154; Jurgens, Vol. 1, p. 362).

BASIL THE GREAT (c. 330–379) states that "Accordingly the mode of creation of the heavenly powers is passed over in silence, for the historian of the cosmogony has revealed to us only the creation of things perceptible by sense . . . , glorify the Maker by whom all things were made, visible and invisible, principalities and powers, authorities, thrones, and dominions, and all other reasonable natures whom we cannot name . . ." (*On the Spirit* 16.38, in *A Select Library,* Vol. 8, p. 23; Jurgens, Vol. 2, p. 17).

For GREGORY OF NAZIANZUS (329–389), "The Angel, then, is called spirit and fire; Spirit as being a creature of the intellectual sphere; Fire, as being of a purifying nature. . . . But, relative to us, at least, we must reckon the Angelic Nature incorporeal, or at any rate as nearly so as possible. Do you see how we get dizzy over this subject, and cannot advance to any point, unless it be as far as this, that we know there are Angels and Archangels, Thrones, Dominions, Princedoms, Powers, Splendours, Ascents, Intelligent Powers or Intelligencies . . ." (*Oration* 28.31, in *A Select Library,* Vol. 7, p. 300; Jurgens, Vol. 2, p. 31).

JOHN CHRYSOSTOM (c. 347–407) states that "If visible things are sufficient to teach us the greatness of the power of the Creator, and if you then come to the invisible powers, and you strain your mind to the armies of Angels, Archangels, Virtues above, Thrones, Dominations, Principalities, Powers, Cherubim, Seraphim, what thought, what word can declare His indescribable magnificence?" (*Homilies on Genesis* 4.5, in Jurgens, Vol. 2, p. 102). And Augustine (354–430) writes "Certainly the Apostle says: 'Whether Thrones, whether Dominations, whether Principalities, whether Powers.' And therefore I do most firmly believe that in the heavenly splendors there are Thrones, Dominations, Principalities and Powers, and I believe with an unhesitating faith that they somehow differ among themselves. But . . . what they are and how they are different from each other I do not know." (*To Orosius against the Priscillianists and Origenists* 11:14, in Jurgens, Vol. 3, p. 115).

[*See also:* Archangels, Cherubim and Seraphim, Guardian Angel, Demons.]

BIBLIOGRAPHY

Jirjis Mīkhā'īl Ḥunayn. *Kitāb al-Khalīqah Ghayr al-Manzūrah ay al-Malā'ikah wa-al-Shayāṭīn,* pp. 15–78. Cairo, 1949.

Jurgens, W. A. *The Faith of the Early Fathers,* 3 vols. Collegeville, Minn., 1970–1979.

Leclercq, H. "Anges." In *Dictionnaire d'archéologie chrétienne et de liturgie,* Vol. 1, cols. 2080–2161. Paris, 1907.

Mīkā'īl Mīnā. *'Ilm al-Lāhūt,* Vol. 2, pp. 75–90. Cairo, 1936.

Roberts, A., and J. Donaldson, eds. *The Ante-Nicene Fathers,* Vol. 2. Grand Rapids, Mich., 1956.

Schaff, P., and H. Wace. *A Select Library of Nicene and Post-Nicene Fathers of the Christian Church,* 2nd ser., Vols. 7 and 8. Grand Rapids, Mich., 1955.

Turmel, J. "Histoire de l'angélologie des temps apostoliques à la fin du Ve siècle." In *Revue d'histoire et de littérature religieuses,* Vol. 3, pp. 531–52. Paris, 1898.

ARCHBISHOP BASILIOS

ANGLICAN CHURCH IN EGYPT. Since 1815, when the Church Missionary Society (CMS) in London commissioned William Jowett to lead a team of missionaries, whose initial mandate was not to make converts among Muslims but to seek to bring about the "enlightenment and elevation" of "those who are already outwardly members of Christian churches," the Anglican Church has been active in Egypt. Jowett was well received by the Coptic Orthodox patriarch, who granted him letters to principal priests and monasteries. From 1824 to 1862 CMS missionaries, mostly Lutherans from the Basel Missionary Society, journeyed throughout Egypt, distributing scriptures and tracts.

In a separate but parallel development, expatriate members of the Anglican communion in Egypt grouped together to hold services and build churches in Alexandria and Cairo. The first Anglican Church in Egypt was consecrated in 1855; this was the Church of Saint Mark in Alexandria. It was served by chaplains appointed by the bishop of London until the formation of the Diocese of Egypt and the Sudan in 1920.

In 1887 the CMS returned to Egypt with a mandate to develop schools and hospitals as part of an attempt to evangelize Muslims. They also formed church congregations and established perhaps the first social welfare center in Egypt. In 1925 forty Egyptian members of CMS-founded congregations were constituted as the (Arabic) Episcopal Church in Egypt. The first Egyptian was ordained to the Episcopal ministry later that year. Since then there have been ten further Egyptian ordinations. There were in 1984 five Egyptian congregations served by five national clergymen: the Church of Saint Michael and All Angels, Heliopolis; the Church of Jesus the Light of the World, Old Cairo; the Church of the Good Shepherd, Giza; the Egyptian congregation of All Saints' Cathedral, Zamalek; and a small congregation attached to the hospital in Minūf.

The Episcopal diocese of Egypt is geographically the largest of the four dioceses that comprise the province of Jerusalem and the Middle East. The Episcopal church is one of the smallest denominations in Egypt, and total church membership in the diocese is estimated at about one thousand. Only in Egypt itself is there an indigenous congregation; elsewhere members are exclusively expatriate.

BIBLIOGRAPHY

Burrell, A. *Cathedral on the Nile, A History of All Saints' Cathedral, Cairo.* Oxford, 1984.

Lasbrey, F. O. *These Fifty Years, The Story of the Old Cairo Medical Mission from 1889 to 1939,* 2nd ed. Cairo, 1946.

Parry, E. G. *"Unto Him Be the Glory in the Church," Being an Account of the Arabic Anglican Church in Egypt.* Cairo, 1937.

Vander Werff, L. L. *Christian Mission to Muslims: The Record, Anglican and Reformed Approaches in India and the Near East, 1800 to 1938.* South Pasadena, Calif., 1977.

HILARY WEIR

ANIANUS, the immediate successor as patriarch (68–85) to Saint MARK I the Evangelist and his first convert to the new religion in the region of Alexandria. When Mark I entered Rakotis, a suburb of Alexandria, following his journey from Cyrene in the Pentapolis, the strap of his sandal broke off. He found a cobbler named Anianus to repair it. While working on the sandal, an awl slipped and pierced Anianus' hand. He then cried "Heis ho Theos," the Alexandrian Greek for "God is one," an utterance that opened the way for Mark to preach monotheistic Christianity to him while miraculously healing his wound in the name of Jesus.

It is difficult to know whether Anianus was Jewish or a pagan native under the influence of the opulent Jewish community and its monotheistic teachings in Alexandria. Consequently, Mark was invited to Anianus' home, where he taught his family the Gospel and baptized them all. This proved to be the beginning of a rich harvest of other converts in this area, which provoked the pagan citizens to defend their local gods against the intruder.

Thus Mark decided to disappear for the time being from the scene of imminent strife. He ordained Anianus as bishop, together with three presbyters and seven deacons, to watch over the spiritual welfare of the flock during his absence. He was away for two years and is said to have gone to Rome, Aquileia, and the Pentapolis, performing miracles and baptizing an increasing number of converts. He returned to Alexandria to find that the new faithful had multiplied and were able to build their own church at Bucalis on the shore of the eastern harbor—the Portus Magnus of the Ptolemies. The HISTORY OF THE PATRIARCHS describes that place as "the Cattle-Pasture, near the sea, beside a rock from which stone is hewn" (Vol. 1, pt. 1, p. 145 [47]).

After Mark's martyrdom on the 30th of the Coptic month of Baramūdah, the second day after Easter, which happened to be the same day as the festival of the Alexandrian god Serapis, Anianus assumed the leadership of the nascent church as its second patriarch. He remained in this capacity for seventeen years, six months, and nine days, during which the believers in Christ increased in numbers and he ordained new priests and deacons for them. It is not known whether other churches were built in addition to Bucalis, but we must assume that most of the missionary work was limited to Alexandria and that it was conducted secretly to avoid the hostility of the pagan population. At any rate, the new patriarch survived the rule of the Roman emperors Nero, Galba, Otho, Vitellius, Vespasian, and Titus. During the reign of Domitian (81–96), he died in his bed, probably in 83 or 85, and was laid to rest next to Saint Mark in Bucalis.

The Western view that Anianus was the first patriarch of the Coptic church is denied by the Copts, who place him as the second, insisting that their first patriarch was Saint Mark, the founder of their church. The official church view is the one adopted throughout this work.

BIBLIOGRAPHY

Atiya, A. S. *History of Eastern Christianity.* Millwood, N.Y., 1980.

O'Leary, D. *The Saints of Egypt.* Amsterdam, 1974.

Roncaglia, M. *Histoire de l'église copte,* Vol. 1. Beirut, 1966 (6 vols., in progress).

Smith, W., and H. Wace. *Dictionary of Christian Biography,* 4 vols. New York, 1974.

Tillemont, L. S. N. *Mémoires pour servir à l'histoire ecclesiastique,* Vol. 2. Paris, 1711.

AZIZ S. ATIYA

ANKH, ancient Egyptian sign of life in hieroglyphics, transmitted to the Christian Egyptians as the cross or sign of eternal life. The ankh in the form of a cross with a rounded head was always carried by the gods of Egyptian mythology as well as by the pharaohs, who were also regarded as gods. The regular cross is also to be found in ancient Egyptian art. The child god Horus, wearing a chain with a cross round his neck, is sometimes seen sucking at the breast of the goddess Isis. The same is encountered with the god Nefer-Hotep and the god Bess. In the early Christian period, the ankh was automatically adopted as a cross, sometimes with a regular cross inside the rounded head of the ankh. According to the church historian Socrates (380–450), when Pope THEOPHILUS (385–412), the twenty-third patriarch, ordered the destruction of the Temple of Serapis in Alexandria, numerous cross signs were found engraved on its walls amid the hieroglyphic writings *(Historia ecclesiastica* 5.16). The Christians affirmed this feature exultingly as signals of the life to come in the new religion, which was consequently adopted by throngs of converts. The Temple of Serapis, full of ankh or cross signs, was eventually turned into a Christian church, accord-

Cross shaped like an *Ankh. Courtesy Coptic Museum, Cairo.*

ing to such writers of Christian antiquity as RUFINUS (345–410) and SOZOMEN (fifth century).

BIBLIOGRAPHY

Budge, E. A. *The Gods of the Egyptians,* 2 vols. London and Chicago, 1904; New York, 1969.
Cramer, M. *Das altägyptische Lebenzeichen im christlichen-koptischen Ägypten.* Wiesbaden, 1955.
Neale, J. M. *A History of the Holy Eastern Church—The Patriarchate of Alexandria.* London, 1847.

EMILE MAHER ISHAQ

ANNO MARTYRUM. *See* Calendar, Coptic.

ANNONA, term for Egypt's annual wheat crop during Roman times. A substantial part of the *annona* was destined to feed the people of Rome *(annona civica, annona urbis).* In economic terms, the contribution Egypt had to furnish after its conquest by the Romans in 30 B.C. was of paramount importance, as the shipments from the Nile to the Tiber provided the imperial capital every year with wheat for four out of twelve months. Augustus himself assumed in 22 B.C. the *cura annonae* (the responsibility for the grain supply), a fact that underlines the political importance of the *annona* as a means of feeding and controlling the *plebs urbana* (city population). After the foundation of Constantinople in 324–330, Egypt's civil *annona* was shipped to the new capital of the Roman East. The organization of the *annona,* its collection, its transport down the Nile, its storing in Alexandria, and finally its conveyance to Rome (or later to Constantinople) was carefully supervised by the *praefectus annonae Alexandriae* (superintendent) and was of great concern to the emperors, as is shown by the well-known Edict XIII (538–539) of Justinian. (For the general context of the *annona civica,* see TAXATION.)

During the first three centuries of Roman rule in Egypt, the *annona militaris* (supply for the army) was normally secured by the administration, which spent part of the annual tax revenue to buy food and other items for the troops at prices fixed by the state *(coemptio).* Other supplies may have been provided by the imperial estates in Egypt.

The term *annona* for provisions destined for Roman troops in Egypt appeared in the papyri only at the end of the second century A.D., sometimes in connection with the visits of the Severan emperors in that country (Thomas and Clarysse, 1977, pp. 199f.). As in other provinces of the empire, it was not unusual to levy taxes or to impose deliveries in kind for certain requirements of the army such as food, clothes, and fuel. Another obligation was to provide billets *(metatum)* and transport services for the army *(angariae),* especially in time of war or during movements of troops.

The extant papyrological documentation does not yet allow us to discern exactly how the military *annona* emerged and evolved. It may have started with irregular impositions for military supplies, demanded when the need arose—hence perhaps a frequent feature in the troubled years of the third century (see conflicting discussion of evidence in Van Berchem, 1937, and Carrié, 1977). The *annona militaris* was to become a regular part of the taxation system with the reforms of DIOCLETIAN. As for the organization of the military *annona,* the network and methods already in existence for the overall tax collection were applied to the military contributions, too. That is, the central state authorities, represented by the *praefectus,* communicated to the *strategi* (commanders) the nature and amount of taxes to be collected for the army. These regional authorities then charged the town councils (*curiae, boulai,* created about A.D. 200) of their respective districts with the actual collection of the *annona militaris.* In their turn, the town councils designated some of their members as curators *(epimeletai)* of the *annona.* These *epimeletai* performed their service as a liturgy (i.e., as an unpaid obligation), but to make absolutely sure that these obligations were fulfilled, the town councils were compelled to assume collective responsibility for the curators they had appointed (Bowman, 1971, pp. 77–82). This system, which had evolved in the third century, seems not to have changed basically in the fourth, as far as the military *annona* is concerned. One new feature, however, is the insertion of the *diadotai* (distributors of provisions) between the *epimeletai* and the soldiers. The *diadotai* appear in records until the end of Byzantine rule in Egypt.

During their period of service, the soldiers normally did not receive their pay in cash, but in kind. That meant that the population of Egypt provided nearly everything for the maintenance of the soldiers and their mounts. In the almost complete absence of general data, the sources provide abundant details on the nature of military supplies and the ways of their collection. The military *annona* consisted of a great variety of items: cereals (bread, wheat, barley), meat, wine, vinegar (or cheap wine), oil, vegetables, etcetera. Hay and chaff were delivered for the mounts (horses, camels, mules, asses). Other items were collected for equipment and fuel, for example, hides (leather) and iron. Another important part of the military *annona* in the wider sense were clothes for the soldiers. These military taxes were paid in kind, but they could be replaced by payments in cash, a method that was rarely applied in the fourth century, but that spread later in the course of the Byzantine period. The money collected in that way was spent entirely, in principle at least, for the maintenance of the troops.

There were still other taxes related to the military sector, one of the most important being an amount of gold that served to buy recruits *(aurum tironicum)*, in fact an *adaeratio* (funding) of recruits that the land had to furnish proportionally to its surface (cf. the list of taxes in Lallemand, 1964, pp. 191–205).

In addition to the current requirements of military *annona* in late antiquity, special levies were organized in times of crisis or when the emperor was on the move with his entourage and army. Two substantial papyri of the Chester Beatty collection have preserved the minutiae of such circumstances (cf. Skeat, 1964). The first of them is concerned with preparations for the forthcoming visit of Diocletian to Panopolis (AKHMĪM) in September 298, especially with arrangements for provisioning the troops accompanying the emperor. This text shows an evident lack of enthusiasm and cooperation on the side of the municipal authorities. The second papyrus consists entirely of official correspondence between the *strategos* of the Panopolites and the *procurator (epitropos)* of the Lower Thebaid, all dated from 300. It contains a long series of orders issued to the *strategos* to supply money or provisions to a wide variety of military units throughout the Thebaid. It is striking to see deliveries (oil, salt) being made from the nome of Panopolis to places as far away as Syene (ASWAN).

The military organization in Egypt was rearranged several times in the course of the Byzantine period (see ARMY, ROMAN). Justinian's Edict XIII gives some interesting information on such changes in the service of the military *annona*. Edict XIII, chapter 13, states that the military expenditures in Alexandria and in the two provinces of Aegyptus are now to be placed under the direct supervision of the *augustalis* (imperial superintendent) and his office. They had formerly been administered by a secretary *(scrinarius)* for military affairs *(stratiotika)*. Another reform of Justinian is concerned with the *annona* for the *dux* of the *Libycus limes* (Libyan boundary), for his office and his troops (Edict XIII, chap. 18). Because Libya was too poor to deliver the necessary provisions, the districts of Mareotes and Menelaites in Aegyptus prima (Egypt I—that is, the Delta) were joined to the administrative sphere of the Libyan *dux* in order to secure sufficient annonary supplies. These measures were part of a wider reorganization aiming at a more efficient policing of the troubled region to the west of Alexandria (Edict XIII, chaps. 17–22). There is ample papyrological evidence for the collection and distribution of military *annona* in Byzantine Egypt, for instance, in the papyri concerned with sixth-century Aphrodito in Upper Egypt. They show, among other things, payment of the *annona* in cash (gold) in three installments per annum and deliveries to troops stationed in Antaeopolis, Antinoopolis, and Hermopolis. What was the percentage of the overall tax revenue of Egypt destined to the military *annona*, and did the latter become ever more oppressive in the course of late antiquity? In the absence of really satisfying statistical data, these questions are difficult to answer and have led to very divergent evaluations (cf. Carrié, 1977, with debate on p. 392f.). The problem is basically complicated by our ignorance of the total number both of the inhabitants of Byzantine Egypt and of the army stationed there.

A Greek ostracon, probably found in Idfū, is among the latest mentions of the military *annona*, the delivery being made through horsemen (Gascou, 1978). As the technical term *annona* had not yet occurred in the Greek papyri of the Arab period, Gascou proposed for this ostracon a date toward the end of Byzantine rule in Egypt (but see the mention of *annona* in a Coptic document of the post-Conquest period, MacCoull, 1986, p. 33, no. 29, 1.5; cf. also el Abbadi, 1984, on military *annona* in early Arab Nessana).

BIBLIOGRAPHY

Abbadi, M. el. "'Annona militaris' and 'Rizḳ' of Nessana." In *Atti del XVII Congresso Internazionale di Papirologia* 3, pp. 1057–62. Naples, 1984.

Berchem, D. van. "L'Annone militaire dans l'Empire Romain au IIIe siècle." *Mémoires de la Société nationale des antiquaires de France*, 8th ser. 10 (1937):117–202.

Bowman, A. K. *The Town Councils of Roman Egypt*, pp. 77–82. American Studies in Papyrology 11. Toronto, 1971.

———. "The Military Occupation of Upper Egypt in the Reign of Diocletian." *The Bulletin of the American Society of Papyrologists* 15 (1978):25–38.

Carrié, J.-M. "Le Rôle économique de l'armée dans l'Egypte romaine." In *Armées et fiscalité dans le monde antique*, pp. 373–93. Colloques nationaux du Centre national de la recherche scientifique 936. Paris, 1977.

Gascou, J. "Ostrakon grec tardif de l'IFAO." *Bulletin de l'Institut français d'Archéologie orientale du Caire* 78 (1978):227–30, pl. 68.

Johnson, A. C., and L. C. West. *Byzantine Egypt: Economic Studies*, pp. 218–229. Princeton University Studies in Papyrology 6. Princeton, 1949.

Lallemand, J. *L'Administration civile de l'Egypte de l'avènement de Dioclétien à la création du diocèse (284–382). Contribution à l'étude des rapports entre l'Egypte et l'Empire à la fin du IIIe et au IVe siècle*, pp. 168–220. Académie Royale de Belgique. Classe des Lettres, Mémoires, 2nd ser., Vol. 57, fasc. 2. Brussels, 1964.

Maccoull, L. S. B. *Coptic Documentary Papyri from the Beinecke Library (Yale University)*. Publications de la Société d'Archéologie copte. Textes et Documents 17. Cairo, 1986.

Segre, A. "Essays on Byzantine Economic History, I. The *Annona Civica* and the *Annona Militaris*." *Byzantion* 16 (1942–1943):393–444.

Skeat, T. C. *Papyri from Panopolis in the Chester Beatty Library Dublin*. Chester Beatty Monographs 10. Dublin, 1964.

Thomas, J. D., and W. Clarysse. "A Projected Visit of Severus Alexander to Egypt." *Ancient Society* 8 (1977):195–207.

HEINZ HEINEN

ANNUNCIATION. *See* Christian Subjects in Coptic Art.

ANNUNCIATION, FEAST OF THE. *See* Feasts, Major.

ANOINTING, the application or pouring of oil on a person or an object as a sacred rite, practiced from time immemorial by various peoples and in several religions. It is known in Arabic as *mas*ḥ.

Judaism

Anointing was common for both religious and mundane purposes, to consecrate certain persons or set particular things apart as sacred. Jacob took the stone he had used for his pillow and set it up as a monument, pouring oil over the top of it (Gn. 28:18, 31:13). Mosaic law prescribed the anointing of persons, places, and vessels in consecrating the tabernacle of the congregation, the Ark of the Covenant, the table and its furnishings, the lampstand and its accessories, the altar of burnt offering, the altar of incense and their vessels, and the basin and its stand (Ex. 30:23–28). Priests, prophets, and kings were also anointed to consecrate their lives to the service of God.

Self-anointing with fragrant oil and unguents was a common practice as a sign of gladness of celebration and as an indication that a period of mourning was over (e.g., Ru. 3:3; Ps. 23:5). Anointing the head or feet of a special guest was a sign of particular esteem and hospitality (Lk. 7:38–46); thus Mary, sister of Martha and Lazarus, anointed the feet of Jesus with ointment of spikenard (Jn. 12:3).

Christianity

Anointing may be applied to persons and objects for religious purposes. With persons, two special kinds of consecration oil are used in the ritual of the catechumenate, which is part of the baptismal rite of the Coptic church. The first is the oil of catechesis, which is applied prior to the renunciation of Satan. The priest anoints the person to be baptized first on the forehead, saying, "I anoint you [name] in the Name of the Father and of the Son and of the Holy Spirit, One God; oil of catechesis for [name] in the Holy, One Only, Universal and Apostolic Church of God, Amen." Then he anoints him on the heart, the palm and wrist of the right hand, and the palm and wrist of his left hand, saying, "May this oil bring to nought all the opposition of the adversary, Amen."

The second is the oil of exorcism, called the *gallielaion* (from the Greek meaning "cultivated olive," thus pure olive oil). After the person to be baptized has renounced Satan, personally if he is a catechumen or through a parent or sponsor in the case of a child, and repeated the confession of faith, the priest anoints him on the heart, the two arms, the hands, and the back thirty-six times, saying, "I anoint you [name] with the oil of beatitude against all the deeds of the adversary, that you may be grafted into the sweet olive tree of the Holy Universal Apostolic Church of God, Amen."

It is worthy of note that this anointing, as part of the prebaptismal service, was originally practiced by all churches, Eastern and Western alike. According to the Constitutions of the Holy Apostles (1970), "Thou shalt first anoint him with holy oil and afterwards baptize him with water" (vii, 11: see also iii, 16). CYRIL OF JERUSALEM also stated, "Then, when ye were stripped, ye were anointed with exorcised oil, from the very hairs of your head to the soles of your feet. After that ye were led by the hand to the holy font of baptism" (1955, pp. xxii–xxiii; see also Chrysostom, *Homilies on the Epistle to the Colossians,* p. 4).

Confirmation

The anointing of confirmation is done immediately following baptism. The priest takes the chrism and prays over it, saying, "Lord, to Whom alone is power, Who works all miracles, and to Whom nought is impossible, but through Thy Will, O Lord, Thy might is active in all things. Graciously grant that through the Holy Spirit in the outpouring of the Holy Chrism, it may become a living seal and confirmation to Thy servants, through Thy Only Son Jesus Christ our Lord."

After this prayer, the priest anoints the baptized person with the unction, working the sign of the cross with his right thumb thirty-six times on various parts of his body, saying, "In the Name of the Father and of the Son and of the Holy Spirit. An unction of the grace of the Holy Spirit, Amen. An unction of a pledge of the Kingdom of the Heavens, Amen. An unction of the fellowship of life eternal and immortal, Amen. A holy unction of Christ our God and an indissoluble seal, Amen. The perfection of the Grace of the Holy Spirit and the breastplate of the Faith and the Truth, Amen. I anoint you [name] with the holy oil in the Name of the Father and of the Son and of the Holy Spirit, Amen." The priest then lays his hand upon the baptized one and says, "May you be blessed with the blessings of the Heavenly and of the Angels. The Lord Jesus Christ bless you, and in His Name." Here he breathes on the face of the baptized one, saying, "Receive the Holy Spirit, and be a purified vessel through Jesus Christ our Lord, to Whom is due Glory with His Righteous Father and the Holy Ghost."

The first reference to anointing with the chrism after baptism was made by Tertullian (160–220): "After coming from the place of washing we are thoroughly anointed with a blessed unction, from the ancient discipline by which they were accustomed to be anointed with a horn of oil" (1970; see Ex. 29:30). Likewise, Cyprian, bishop of Carthage: "It is also necessary that he should be anointed who is baptized, so that having received the chrism, that is, the anointing, he may be anointed of God, and have in him the Grace of Christ" (1951, p. 377; *Constitutions of the Holy Apostles,* Bk. VII, 27, 42, 44, 1951, pp. 470–77).

While other Orthodox churches, both Chalcedonian and non-Chalcedonian, prescribe unction with the chrism after baptism, they differ from the Coptic church in the way it is applied. According to the Greek church, the priest anoints the forehead, eyes, nostrils, ears, breast, hands, feet, and the back. In the Armenian church, the forehead, ears, eyes, nostrils, mouth, hands, breast, shoulders, feet, and shoulder blades are anointed. The Syrian churches prescribe the anointing of the entire body.

Anointing with the chrism was administered by bishops and by priests. Hilarion the Deacon (c. 291–371) stated that "among the Egyptians presbyters give the seal if a bishop be not present" (quoted in Scudamore, 1908, p. 2003). Later, Photius, patriarch of Constantinople (c. 810–895), asserted the right of priests to administer the unction of the chrism as they are entitled to administer the sacrament of baptism (p. 2002). In the sixteenth century, Gabriel Severus, metropolitan of Philadelphia in Asia Minor (1541–1616), stated, "The Eastern Church considerably permits it [the anointing with chrism] not to bishops only, but to presbyters also after the sacred rite of baptism" (p. 2002).

Anointing of Heretics

During the third century, a question that gave rise to much controversy was whether persons who were baptized by heretics and were later restored to the church had to be rebaptized. According to the Church of Rome, it was sufficient for such persons to be absolved, whereas in the churches of Egypt, Africa, Asia Minor, Syria, Cappadocia, Caclicia, and Galatia, they had to be rebaptized, as their other baptism was considered invalid. In 381 the Council of Constantinople (CONSTANTINOPLE, COUNCIL OF) affirmed the following procedure (Percival, 1956, p. 185):

> Those who from heresy turn to orthodoxy, and to the portion of those who are being saved, we receive according to the following method and custom: Arians and Macedonians, and Sabbatians, and Novatians, who call themselves Cathari or Aristeri, and Quarto-decimans or Tetradites, and Apollinarians, we receive, upon their giving a written renunciation [of their errors] and anathe-

matize every heresy which is not in accordance with the Holy, Catholic, and Apostolic Church of God. Thereupon, they are first sealed or anointed with the holy oil upon the forehead, eyes, nostrils, mouth, and ears; and when we seal them, we say, 'The Seal of the gift of the Holy Ghost.' But Eunomians, who are baptized with only one immersion, and Montanists, who are here called Phrygians, and Sabellians, who teach the identity of Father and Son, and do sundry other mischievous things, and [the partisans of] all other heresies—for there are many such here, particularly among those who come from the country of the Galatians:—all these, when they desire to turn to orthodoxy, we receive as heathen. On the first day we make them Christians; on the second, catechumens; on the third, we exorcise them by breathing thrice in their face and ears; and thus we instruct them and oblige them to spend some time in the Church, and to hear the Scriptures; and then we baptize them.

Unction of the Sick

Unction of the sick is one of the seven sacraments of the church, in keeping with the teaching of James the Apostle: "Is any among you sick? Let him call for the elders of the church, and let them pray over him, anointing him with oil in the name of the Lord; and the prayer of faith will save the sick man, and the Lord will raise him up; and if he has committed sins, he will be forgiven" (Jas. 5:14–15).

From Mark 6:13 ("they . . . anointed with oil many that were sick and healed them") one learns that the practice was carried out by the disciples and apostles in fulfillment of the commandments of Christ. Accordingly the early fathers of the church emphasized its significance, among whom were ORIGEN, Saint JOHN CHRYSOSTOM, Cyril of Jerusalem, and Victor, presbyter of Antioch.

In the Coptic church, this sacrament (known in Arabic as *masḥat al-marḍā* or *ṣalāt al-qandīl)* may be performed by any person at any time. It is preceded by confession and an avowal of true repentance. If the sick person's condition does not permit him to go to church for the service, the actual unction may be given to him on his sick bed by the priest. The service is also performed for all the congregation once a year on the last Friday before Passion Week, which begins the Sunday *before* Palm Sunday, when all those who are present are anointed by the bishop or the priest. The service comprises seven prayers; hence, ideally, seven priests should take part. Any number, however, will do, and often one priest alone performs it.

Holy Matrimony

During the service of matrimony, the priest prays over the oil of anointing, saying, "O Master, Lord God Almighty, Father of our Lord and our God and our Savior Jesus Christ, Who with the fruit of the sweet olive tree anointed priests, kings and prophets, we pray Thee, Good Lover of man, to bless this oil with Your blessing. May it be an oil of sanctification to Thy servants [names]." Then he anoints the bridegroom and the bride, while the deacons sing part of Psalm 23: "Thou anointest my head with oil; my cup overflows." The Coptic church is apparently unique in following this practice, which is immediately succeeded by placing crowns on their heads.

Anointing of Kings

This service (known in Arabic as *tartīb masḥat al-mulūk)* used to be performed immediately before the crowning of a king or emperor. The patriarch would pray over the oil of anointing, saying, "Send, O Lord, from Thy Sacred Heights . . . and the Throne of Thy Kingdom's Glory, the Holy Spirit, the Comforter, upon this oil with which we anoint [name]. Let it be a sacred anointing, a holy oil, an oil of joy, a royal anointing, a girdle of light, a vestment of salvation, a protection of life, a spiritual grace for the purification of soul and body, an eternal joy . . . , a breastplate of power to sanctify Your servant [name] whom thou hast called king [emperor] . . . in the Name of Jesus Christ our Lord." Then he anoints him on the forehead, eyes, nostrils, heart, and hands.

Consecration of Buildings and Objects

When a church is consecrated, it is anointed with the chrism after prayers of consecration. The priests carry vessels of water, crosses, candles, censers, and the ornamented Gospel in front of the bishop, chanting various appropriate hymns until he comes to the window in the eastern wall behind the altar. He sprinkles it with water, saying, "Unto a holy consecration of the House of God." Then he takes the pot of the chrism and consecrates the middle part of the window in front of the altar, making the sign of the cross with his thumb, saying, "We consecrate this place for a Catholic church of . . . , in the Name of the Father and of the Son and of the Holy Spirit." He consecrates all windows, columns, and corners of the church, saying, "Blessed be the Lord God, now and forever, Amen." He also consecrates the altar by pouring the holy oil upon the table three times in the form of the cross, saying, "Alleluia, How lovely is thy dwelling place, O Lord of Hosts . . . [Ps. 84:1-4]." Finally, he consecrates the baptismal font with chrism, anointing it five times, saying, "We consecrate this font for the name of Saint John the Baptist, in the Name of the Father and of the Son and of the Holy Spirit." (See also BAPTISTERY, CONSECRATION OF.)

Consecration of Vessels and Icons

New vessels, the paten, chalice, spoon, and the like have to be anointed with the chrism before use. Similarly, all icons are consecrated after the reading of the appropriate prayers prescribed for the purpose. (See EUCHARISTIC VESSELS.)

In all the above-mentioned cases, anointing is performed by making the sign of the cross with the right thumb, a practice common to Eastern and Western churches.

BIBLIOGRAPHY

'Abd al-Masīḥ al-Mas'ūdī. *Al-Ma'mūdiyyah al-Muqaddasah.* Cairo, 1906.

Athanasius. *Kitāb Tartīb Qismat Rutab al-Kahanūt wa-Takrīs Jamī' Awānī al-Madhbah.* Cairo, 1959.

Bloch, M. *Les Rois thaumaturges.* Strasbourg, 1924.

Butler, A. J. *The Ancient Coptic Churches of Egypt,* Vol. 2, pp. 338-40, 343-45. Oxford, 1884.

Buṭrus 'Abd al-Malik. *Tartīb Mashạt al-Mulūk.* Cairo, 1930.

Cabrol, F. "Huile." In *Dictionnaire d'archéologie chrétienne et de liturgie.* Paris, 1907-1953.

"Constitutions of the Holy Apostles." In *The Ante-Nicene Fathers,* Vol. 7, ed. A. Roberts and J. Donaldson. Grand Rapids, Mich., 1951.

Cyprian, bishop of Carthage. "Epistle 70." In *The Ante-Nicene Fathers,* Vol. 5, ed. A. Roberts and J. Donaldson. Grand Rapids, Mich., 1951.

Cyril of Jerusalem. "Ceremonies of Baptism and Chrism." In Introduction to *The Catechetical Lectures of S. Cyril.* In *A Select Library of Nicene and Post-Nicene Fathers of the Christian Church,* 2nd ser., Vol. 7, ed. P. Schaff and H. Wace, Grand Rapids, Mich., 1955.

Dūmadyūs al-Baramūsī. *Al-Kanz al-Anfas fī al-Riḥlah al-Baṭriyarkiyyah wa-'Amal al-Mayrūn al-Muqaddas.* Cairo, 1930.

Gaudemet, J. "Anointing." In *New Catholic Encyclopedia,* Vol. 1, pp. 566-68. New York, 1967.

Ibrahīm Philūthā'us. *Kitāb Rutbat al-Iklīl al-Mubārak.* Cairo, 1888.

McClintock, J., and J. Strong. "Anoint." In *Cyclopedia of Biblical, Theological, and Ecclesiastical Literature,* Vol. 1, pp. 239-41. New York, 1894.

Murqus Bisādāh and Iqlādiyūs Labīb. *Kitāb al-Mashạh al-Muqaddasah.* Cairo, 1909.

Pange, J. de. *Le Roi très chrétien.* Paris, 1949.

Percival, H. R., ed. and trans. "The Seven Ecumenical Councils." In *A Select Library of the Nicene and Post-Nicene Fathers of the Christian Church,* ed. P. Schaff and H. Wace, ser. 2, Vol. 14. Grand Rapids, Mich., 1955.

Scudamore, W. E. "Unction." In *A Dictionary of Christian Antiquities,* Vol. 2, pp. 2000-2006. London, 1908.

Ṭaqs Takrīs al-Kanā'is al-Jadīdah. Gīza and Cairo, 1974.

Tertullian. "Baptism." In *The Faith of the Early Fathers,* Vol. 1, ed. W. A. Jurgens. Collegeville, Minn., 1970.

ARCHBISHOP BASILIOS

ANOINTING OF THE ETHIOPIAN EMPEROR. The most powerful prince succeeded to the Ethiopian throne immediately upon the death or removal of a sovereign, but his enthronement had to be legitimized sooner or later by the solemn anointment at the hands of the metropolitan. The time, the place, and to some extent the manner of the coronation varied throughout Ethiopian history. The question whether the empress should be crowned at the same time was also left to the discretion of the new sovereign. Traditionally, the cathedral of Zion in Axum was the venue, although several other churches have increasingly played a role in the coronation practice since around 1500. The investiture was conducted in three phases—the prelude, the anointment, and the sequel. The site and the occasion were announced at least a month earlier to the public, who were encouraged to attend. An immense banquet was prepared, and the royal articles were brought to the altar to be prayed upon for about fourteen days. Throughout the night preceding the anointment, prayers were held in the church in which the emperor also took part. He left in the morning for a particular place where he then nominated officials to key posts, decorated the grandees of the empire, and led them all in a procession that had to pass a few hurdles before entering the church. He was intercepted by a group of "virgins of Zion" who stretched a silk thread across his path and posed questions pertaining to his person and intentions. His response that he was the

King of Kings of Ethiopia being twice rejected, the questions were reiterated for the third time, and he cut the thread with his sword and continued on his way, thereby symbolizing the obstacles he might encounter in his reign and his determination to surmount them. A group of clergymen then led him singing to the accompaniment of the drum, sistrum, and sticks. The procession again halted, as the church gate was shut and as the singing clergy from within posed questions. The singing clergy from outside replied, and the gate opened. The sovereign spread gold pieces, thereby symbolizing that the kingdom of heaven would not be gained by force but by the giving of alms. The convocation culminated with the process of anointment.

When the emperor sat on his throne, the metropolitan administered to him a solemn oath to remain loyal to the Orthodox faith, to rule with justice, and to defend the state and the religion. The metropolitan confirmed the oath by an anathema against all opponents to his rule and urged the people to rally behind their sovereign. A special mass was then celebrated with a great deal of readings from the Holy Scriptures and the works of the fathers, in the course of which the ABUN dipped his thumb in the ointment and anointed the emperor on the forehead, the chest, and the shoulders. Then he blessed the regal articles consisting of the crown, a robe, a golden sword, two golden spears, an orb, and a diamond ring, which were handed to the emperor one by one, pronouncing the idea each represented. An official announced to the huge crowd waiting outside that the elect of God was now anointed King of Kings of Ethiopia. The army responded with thundering rifle volleys and 101 gun salutes, the women with ululations, and the men with songs and dances. Finally, the emperor went to a specified place where he sat on his throne with the *abun* to his right and the EČČAGĒ to his left. He declared himself the shepherd of his people by reading aloud to his subjects from the Psalms and had the basic principles of his rule spelled out through a herald. The ceremony was concluded by a series of rich feasts that lasted for a minimum of seven days.

BIBLIOGRAPHY

Guèbrè Sellasié. *Chronique du règne de Ménélik II, roi des rois d'Ethiopie,* trans. Tèsfa Sellassié, pp. 264–78. Paris, 1930–1931.

Ludolphus, J. *A New History of Ethiopia. Being a Full and Accurate Description of the Kingdom of Abessinia, Vulgarly Though Erroneously Called the Empire of Prester John,* pp. 207–209. London, 1682.

Māhtamā Sellāsē Walda Masqal. *Zekra Nagar,* pp. 727–42. Addis Ababa, 1962; 2nd ed., 1969–1970.

Rossini, C., ed. *Historia Sarṣa Dengel (Malak Sagad).* In CSCO 20, *Scriptores Aetiopici* 3, pp. 78–80.

Tafla, B., ed. and trans. *A Chronicle of Emperor Yoḥannes IV.* Äthiopistische Forschungen 1. Wiesbaden, 1977.

Varenbergh, J. "Studien zur abessinischen Reichsordnung (Sĕrʿata Mangest)." *Zeitschrift für Assyriologie und verwandte Gebiete und vorderasiatische Archäologie* 30 (1915–1916):1–45.

BAYRU TAFLA

ANOMOEANS, the name given to the radical group of Arians who emerged about 356 under the leadership of Eunomius, bishop of Cyzicus (360–364), and the "godless" deacon Aetius. It is based on the Greek word *anomoios* (unlike), referring to the relationship between the Father and Son within the Godhead. The Son was stated to be "unlike" the Father, in contrast with those who believed He was "like" (homoeans) or of "like substance" (homoiousians), as well as the adherents of the Nicene Creed, the homoousians ("of the same substance").

Eunomius and Aetius exemplified the relatively socially mobile population that seems to have been associated with the growing triumph of Christianity during the reign of Constantius II (337–361) and that tended to be attracted to non-Nicene interpretations of Christianity. The grandfather of Eunomius had been a slave, but by hard effort the family had risen in the social scale to the point that Eunomius felt able to leave his father's small holding and emigrate from his native Cappadocia to the schools of rhetoric in Constantinople. (See Basil *In Eunomium* 1.2; Gregory of Nyssa *In Eunomium* 1.6.)

Aetius, son of a minor government official who had died bankrupt, had tried his hand at many trades, including that of goldsmith, before settling for teaching that had a strong theological bias. His targets were the Gnostics and Manichaeans, and he made his name through a celebrated debating victory over the Manichaean leader Aphthonius at Alexandria about 345 (Philostorgius *Historia ecclesiastica* 3.15). After a spell at Antioch coinciding with Athanasius' return to Alexandria from his second exile in 346, he was ordained deacon, and took advantage of Athanasius' third exile to return to Alexandria in 356. There he established himself as a teacher and was accepted by Athanasius' rival, Bishop George of Cappadocia, as deacon (Epiphanius *Panarion* 76.1.). He was joined in Alexandria by Eunomius, who became first his secretary and then the champion of the Anomoean cause (Gregory of Nyssa *In Eunomium* 1.6, cols. 260, 264; Socrates Scholasticus *Historia ecclesiastica* 3.22; Philostorgius *Historia ecclesiastica* 3.20).

Anomoean views, however, were too much for Constantius and his theological advisers, and especially for the homoiousians grouped around Basil, bishop of Ancyra. Aetius's case was made worse by his association with the luckless Caesar Gallus (Philostorgius *Historia ecclesiastica* 3.27; Gregory of Nyssa *In Eunomium* 1.6, col. 257), executed at Constantius's orders in November 354. At a council held at Ancyra in 358, the Anomoeans were anathematized and Aetius was sent into exile. Anomoean doctrines, however, continued to spread (see letter of George, bishop of Laodicea, cited in Sozomen *Historia ecclesiastica* 6.13, concerning their success in Antioch), and under Emperor Julian (361–363), Aetius was recalled from exile and invited to the emperor's court (Julian, letter 31; Sozomen *Historia eccesiastica* 5.5). The high-water mark in the success of the Anomoeans was reached in 362, when a council held at Antioch by Bishop Euzoius declared that "the Son was unlike the Father in all respects [*kata panta anomoios*], in respect of will as well as substance."

In the reign of Valens (364–378) the Anomoeans, now led by Eunomius, continued to flourish, attracting the polemics of BASIL THE GREAT and his brother, GREGORY OF NYSSA. Eunomius, however, gained the hostility of Eudoxius, the semi-Arian bishop of Constantinople, and was exiled. An Anomoean creed was presented to Emperor Theodosius along with other statements of Arian belief in 383, but after that time the Anomoeans found themselves singled out for special repressive attention (*Codex Theodosianus* 16, 5.31, 32, 34, 49, 58) by Theodosius and his successors. By the middle of the fifth century the party was practically extinct.

Anomoeanism was a logical system of belief that pushed the Arian premise of the consequences of the transcendence of God for the relations of the persons of the Trinity to their ultimate conclusion. It was a creed that might win debates but could not inspire multitudes. In Alexandria it was one of the alternatives to Nicaea that Athanasius rejected. It does not seem to have had much support outside Alexandria among Egyptian Christians as a whole, though curiously, the Anomoeans are cursed as an "evil heresy" in the "Concept of the Great Power," a Gnostic writing preserved in the Nag Hammadi Library.

BIBLIOGRAPHY

Basil. *In Eunomium*. In PG 29, cols. 497–774. Paris, 1886.

Gregory of Nyssa. *In Eunomium*. In PG 45, cols. 243–1122. Paris, 1863.

Julian. *The Works of the Emperor Julian*, 3 vols., ed. and English trans. W. C. Wright. Loeb Classical Library. London and New York, 1913–1923.

Le Bachelet, X. "Anoméens." In *Dictionnaire de théologie catholique*, Vol. 1, cols. 1322–26. Paris, 1923.

Philostorgius. *Historia ecclesiastica*, ed. J. Bidez. Die griechischen christlichen Schriftsteller der ersten drei Jahrhunderte 21. Berlin, 1913.

Venables, E. "Aetius." In DCB 1, pp. 51–53. Repr. New York, 1974.

______. "Eunomius." In DCB 2, pp. 286–90. Repr. New York, 1974.

Wickham, L. R. "Aetius and the Doctrine of Divine Ingeneracy." *Studia Patristica* 11 (1972): 259-63.

W. H. C. FREND

ANṢINĀ, the Arabic name of the city known in Greek as Antinoë or ANTINOOPOLIS. Located on the east side of the Nile about 6 miles (9.5 km) north of Mallawī in the province of Asyūṭ, the city was founded in 130 by the emperor Hadrian in honor of his friend Antinous, who had drowned in the Nile. The ruins of Antinoë/Anṣinā are located just east of Shayk ʿAbādah.

The earliest attestation of Christianity in Antinoë/Anṣinā is a notice in the writings of EUSEBIUS OF CAESAREA that Bishop Alexander of Jerusalem wrote a letter to the Christians in Antinoë, which indicates that Christianity had been established in the city by the middle of the third century (*Historia ecclesiastica* 6.11.2). Coptic-Arabic hagiographic literature indicates that Antinoë/Anṣinā was a bishopric by the beginning of the fourth century when a man named Timotheus administered as bishop in the city. In 325, Antinoë was represented at the Council of NICAEA by its bishop, Tyrannos (Munier, 1943, p. 5).

Antinoë/Anṣinā was the birthplace or place of martyrdom of many Christians in the early years of the fourth century (for a list with bibliography, see Timm, 1984, pp. 113–16). Monasticism also made an early entry into the city. Among the most important monks was Apa Pammon, a contemporary of Patriarch ATHANASIUS I (Halkin, 1932, p. 119). At the beginning of the fifth century there were twelve nunneries in Antinoë and its environs; the monasteries in the same area were beyond counting (Palladius, *Lausiac History* 59).

[*See also:* Antinoopolis; Dayr al-Dīk; Dayr al-Naṣārā (Antinoopolis); Dayr Sunbāṭ; and Shaykh Ṣaʿīd.]

BIBLIOGRAPHY

Amélineau, E. *La Géographie de l'Egypte à l'époque copte,* pp. 48–51. Paris, 1893.

Halkin, F. *S. Pachomii Vitae Graecae.* Subsidia Hagiographica 19. Brussels, 1932.

Munier, H. *Recueil des listes épiscopales de l'église copte.* Cairo, 1943.

Timm, S. *Das christlich-koptische Ägypten in arabischer Zeit,* pt. 1, pp. 111–28. Wiesbaden, 1984.

RANDALL STEWART

ANTHROPOMORPHISM, the belief that God possesses a bodily form like that of human beings. The belief derives from a literal reading of the many Old Testament references to the eyes, face, and hands of God.

This belief seems to have been widely held by the monks of Egypt in the late fourth and early fifth centuries. THEOPHILUS, patriarch of Alexandria (385–412), refuted this belief in his festal letter of 399 and aroused a great deal of resentment among the monks. It is not clear how widespread the anthropomorphite beliefs were. John Cassian's account (*Collationes* 10.2ff.) indicates that the majority of the monks in SCETIS (Wādī al-Naṭrūn) were anthropomorphites. Sozomen (*Historia ecclesiastica* 8.11) states that a delegation of angry, threatening monks visited Theophilus, who did not retract his criticism of anthropomorphism but accommodated the monks by condemning Origenism and attacking suspected Origenist monks.

The Audians, a fourth-century anthropomorphite sect, were condemned and exiled to Scythia by Constantine. It is not clear whether there is any connection between the Audians of Syria and the anthropomorphite monks of Egypt. The Egyptian monks suffered no persecution for their beliefs, perhaps because of their numerical strength.

BIBLIOGRAPHY

Augustine. *De haeresibus.* In PL 42, cols. 21–50. Paris, 1841. See sec. 50.76.

Drioton, E. "La discussion d'un moine anthropomorphite audien avec le patriarche Théophile d'Alexandrie en année 399." *Revue de l'Orient chrétien* 20 (1915/1917):92–100, 113–32.

Gennadius. *Liber de scriptoribus ecclesiasticis.* In PL 58, cols. 1059–1120. Paris, 1847. See sec. 34.

Orlandi, T. "Il dossiere copto di Agatonico di Tarso: Studio letterario e storico." In *Studies Presented to Hans Jacob Polotsky,* ed. D. W. Young, pp. 269–99. East Gloucester, Mass., 1981.

JANET TIMBIE

ANTICHRIST, term occurring first in Christian literature but as conception of a powerful being opposed to God at the end of the world found in earlier Jewish apocalyptic literature (e.g., D. 7:7ff.; 11:40). This probably originated in Iranian eschatology (the battle of Ahura Mazda with Angra Mainyu), and from there influenced Jewish apocalyptic writings. There were many variations within Judaism reflecting dualist ideas current at the time. The powerful being is sometimes called Satan or Belial (e.g., *Testament of Levi* 18.12 in Charlesworth, 1983, p. 795), and is described as "the prince of this world." The Qumrān sect believed that Belial would be at the head of the army of the Sons of Darkness against whom the Sons of Light wage war. In one of the Qumrān hymns (16.15) there occurs the prayer: "Suffer not Belial to arise and immerse himself in Thy servant's spirit" (trans. Gaster, 1976, p. 202). Sometimes this powerful being was identified with historical persons (e.g., Caligula, who had threatened to desecrate the Jewish Temple in A.D. 39/40). A cycle of traditions also arose around the belief that Nero would return with a Parthian army to take vengeance on Rome.

Christian as well as Jewish apocalyptic literature took up this belief and identified Nero with Antichrist (Rev. 13, 17; *Sibylline Oracles* 5; *Ascension of Isaiah* 3.13–4.18). In Christianity the opponent of Christ (the Messiah) in the last days, whether human or demonic, was identified as Antichrist (Mk. 13:14; 2 Thes. 2:3–12; 1 Jn. 2:22, 4:3; 2 Jn. 7). Later Christian thought sometimes identified Antichrist with a Jewish figure (so Hippolytus and Irenaeus). Various enemies such as ARIUS and Muḥammad were also equated with this figure, and Emperor Constantius II was denounced by Bishop Lucifer of Cagliari as "the forerunner of Antichrist."

In Coptic eschatological thought, which is strongly influenced by Judaism, earlier ideas of a powerful being opposed to God and Christ predominate, and the identification of heresy, especially Nestorianism, with Antichrist came easily to the Copts.

BIBLIOGRAPHY

Bousset, W. *Antichrist.* London, 1896.
Charlesworth, J. H., ed. *The Old Testament Pseudepigrapha,* Vol. 1. Garden City, N.Y., 1983.
Cohn, N. *The Pursuit of the Millennium.* London, 1957.
Gaster, T. H., trans. *The Dead Sea Scriptures.* New York, 1976.
Hanson, P. D., ed. *Visionaries and Their Apocalypses.* London, 1983.
Rigaux, B. *L'Antéchrist.* Paris, 1932.
Rowley, H. H. *The Relevance of Apocalyptic.* London, 1944.
Russell, D. S. *The Method and Message of Jewish Apocalyptic.* London, 1964.

LESLIE W. BARNARD

ANTIMENSION, a consecrated linen or silk cloth used on an altar during the celebration of the Eucharist; it is decorated with biblical texts and artistic representations of the Passion of Jesus Christ.

In the Coptic church, however, instead of the antimension, a portable ALTAR-BOARD or altar-slab is used, called ⲡⲓⲛⲁⲝ in Coptic, usually of copper, brass, or wood, but sometimes made of stone or marble. A large cross is engraved in its middle and four smaller crosses in the corners, with Coptic inscriptions of the name of Jesus Christ and some verses from the Psalms (e.g., Ps. 86:1–3).

Special prayers are used in consecrating it, and then it is anointed with the holy chrism. It is placed on top of the ALTAR in a special area that fits its size, which is not standard, but large enough to fit the chalice and the paten (see EUCHARISTIC VESSELS). In thickness it measures usually between about ¾ and 2 inches (2 and 5 cm). It is used for the celebration of the liturgy where there are no proper altars, or where the altar has not been consecrated.

A. J. Butler relates an incident of relevant interest: "When Zacharias, king of Nubia, about 850 A.D. sent his son and heir George to Egypt . . . he was granted as a very great privilege by the Patriarch [YŪSĀB I] a portable altar of wood to carry to his father. Tradition says that such a thing was never known before . . ."

BIBLIOGRAPHY

Butler, A. J. *The Ancient Coptic Churches of Egypt,* 2 vols. Oxford, 1884.
Manqariyūs ʿAwaḍallah. *Manārat al-Aqdās fī Sharḥ Ṭuqūs al-Kanīsah al-Qibṭiyyah wa-al-Quddās.* Cairo, 1947.

ARCHBISHOP BASILIOS

ANTINOË. *See* Antinoopolis.

ANTINOOPOLIS (Arabic, Ansinā). [*The entry on this ancient town in Upper Egypt consists of two articles:* Literary and Archaeological Sources *and* Architecture.]

Literary and Archaeological Sources

In the fourth and fifth centuries the town of Antinoopolis flourished, for it was the capital of the province of the Thebaid as far as Aswan. The nuns were numerous, and the hermits and monks lived in the vicinity. This we learn from contemporary documents: the texts relating to Saint PACHOMIUS repeatedly speak of it; the LETTER OF AMMON quotes one of the monks living at Antinoopolis (ed. Halkin and Festugière, 1982, pp. 115, 164); Palladius' *Historia Lausiaca* speaks of the twelve convents of women in the town of Antinoopolis and of the 1,200 hermits living around the town. It speaks of the monasteries and of the caves where they lived (1898, Vol. 1, pp. 151–54). In the sixth century, John Moschus still knows this monastic community (Chaps. 143 and 161, PG 87). The Coptic texts also mention two places where veneration was paid in particular to the relics of the saints Claudius and Colluthus (Drescher, 1942, p. 77; Muyser, 1937, p. 21; Till, 1935–1936, Vol. 1, pp. 168, 181; Godron, 1970, p. 566).

In the Middle Ages the only author who gives a general view is ABŪ ṢĀLIḤ THE ARMENIAN (beginning of thirteenth century). He wrote after the destruction of Anṣinā by Ṣalāḥ al-Dīn (Saladin, 1169–1193), according to A. Grohmann (1959, p. 44b). Abū Ṣāliḥ (*The Churches,* 1895, pp. 228–29, 244–45) places the monastery at Antinoopolis, no doubt through confusion between the place-names Anṣinā and Isnā, then the monastery of the great saint Shinūdah, which he puts at the mountain Andariba. We may wonder if the author has not confused Andariba and Atrīb, and must also remember that the province at this period was called Ṭaḥā wa-Shinūdah (*cf.* Grohmann, 1959, p. 43a). We may raise the question of the existence of another celebrated monastery dedicated to Saint Shinūdah, whose name was added to that of the province. Abū Ṣāliḥ also names the monastery of Saint Colluthus with his relics, that of Abū Ṭabyah with his relics, and finally the DAYR AL-KHĀDĪM, which al-MAQRĪZĪ and the *State of the Provinces* place in the province of al-Bahnasā. Abū Ṣāliḥ thus seems rather confused about the region of Antinoopolis. Al-Maqrīzī (1853, Vol. 2, p. 502) names only the monastery of Yuḥannis al-Qaṣīr near Antinoopolis. We must also note the testimony of the travelers, for they saw the town before its remains were used for the building of a sugar works at Rūḍah. We may note in particular:

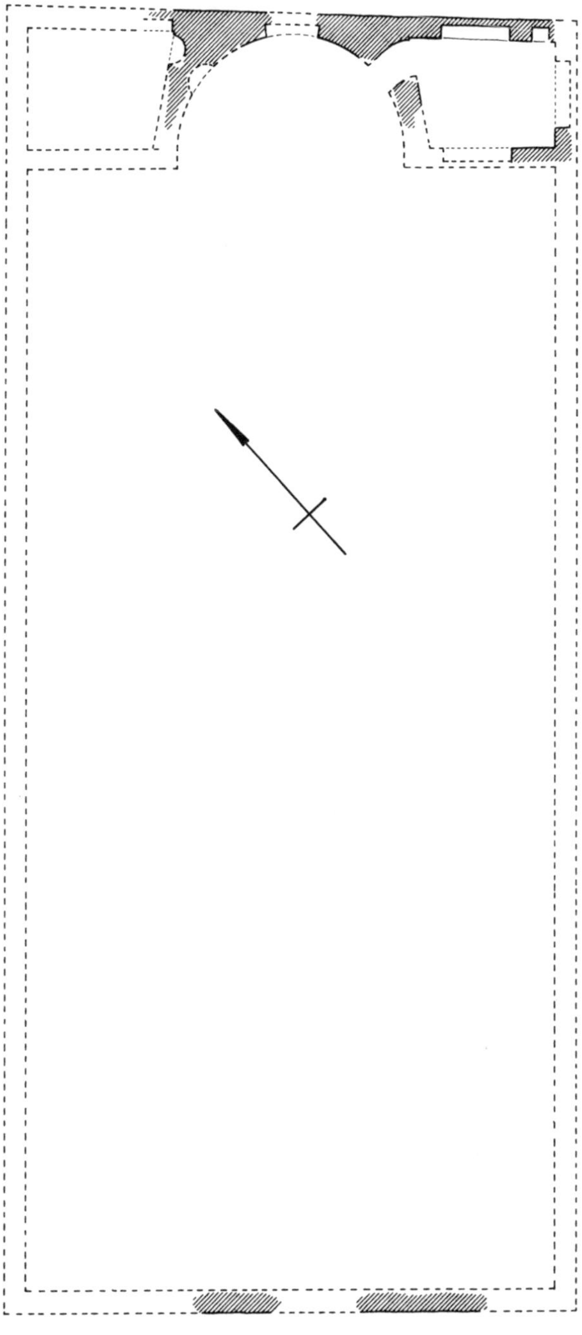

Part of the ruins of the medieval cenobite monastery at Antinoopolis. *Courtesy Peter Grossmann.*

1. The anonymous Venetian of 1589 who describes ancient Antinoopolis in detail (*Voyages en Egypte*, 1971, pp. 57–63).
2. J. VANSLEB, who in 1673 spent several days at Abū Ḥinnis (1677, pp. 141–52; Eng. ed., 1678, pp. 232–40). He also saw the tomb of Ammonius, martyr bishop of Isnā, transformed into a mosque, and thought that Shaykh ʿAbādah (the present name of the village close to the ruins of Antinoopolis) comes from a confusion between the appellation *ʿābid* (devout), given to Ammonius and misunderstood by the Arabs, and ʿAbādah, the name of the village.
3. C. SICARD, who in 1714 described at some length what he saw at Antinoopolis, and in particular the inscription mentioning Saint Colluthus (1982, Vol. 2, pp. 82–110; Vol. 3, pp. 60–63).
4. Father Jullien, who toward 1890 still saw the church of Saint Ammonius "on the river's edge" (Munier, 1940, pp. 158ff.).

Two series of excavations have been carried out in the town and the necropolises that surround it.

1. Between 1898 and 1910 Gayet excavated especially the necropolises. A critical account of these excavations is given by H. Leclercq in *Dictionnaire d'archéologie chrétienne et de liturgie* (Vol. 1, pt. 2 cols. 2326–60) and by A. Mallon in the same dictionary (Vol. 3, cols. 2819–86). Their information was completed by G. Lefebvre (1910, 1915). A general view with a bibliography on the subject can be found in H. Munier (1949).

2. Since 1936 the Italian missions from the universities of Rome and Florence have excavated chiefly the town (Breccia and Donadoni, 1938; Donadoni, 1974, 1975).

BIBLIOGRAPHY

Breccia, E., and S. Donadoni. "Le prime ricerche italiane ad Antinoe." *Aegyptus* 18 (1938):285–310.

Donadoni, S. "Antinoë 1965–1968." *Missione archeologica in Egitto dell'Università di Roma*, pp. 14ff. Istituto di Studi del vicino oriente, serie archeologica 21. Rome, 1974.

______. "Antinoopolis." *Lexicon der Ägyptologie*, Vol. 1. Wiesbaden, 1975.

Drescher, J. "Apa Claudius and the Thieves." *Bulle-*

tin de la Société d'Archéologie copte (1942):63–87.

Godron, G. *Textes coptes relatifs à Saint Claude d'Antioche.* Patrologia Syriaca 35 (1970).

Grohmann, A. *Studien zur historischen Geographie und Verwaltung des frühmittelalterlichen Ägypten.* Österreichische Akademie der Wissenschaften, Phil.-Hist. Klasse, 77, Vol. 2, Vienna, 1959.

Halkin, F., and A.-J. Festugière. *Le Corpus athénien de Saint Pachôme.* Cahiers d'orientalisme 2. Geneva, 1982.

Lefebvre, G. *Egypte chrétienne,* pts. 2 and 5. Annales du Service des Antiquités de l'Egypte 10, 1910, pp. 50–65; 15, 1915, pp. 113–39.

Mallon, A. "Copte (Epigraphie)." In *Dictionnaire d'Archéologie chrétienne et de Liturgie,* Vol. 3, pt. 2, ed. F. Cabrol and H. Leclercq. Paris, 1914.

Moschus, J. *Pratum Spirituale.* PG 87, pt. 3. Paris, 1860.

Munier, H. "Les monuments coptes d'après les explorations du père M. Jullien." *Bulletin de la Société d'Archéologie copte* 6 (1940):141–68.

———. "Stèles chrétiennes d'Antinoë." *Aegyptus* 29 (1949):126–36.

Muyser, J. "Des vases eucharistiques en verre." *Bulletin de la Société d'Archéologie copte* 3 (1937):9–28.

Sicard, C. *Oeuvres,* Vols. 2 and 3. Bibliothèque d'étude 84–85. Cairo, 1982.

Till, W. *Koptische Heiligen- und Martyrerlegenden.* Orientalia Christiana Analecta 102, 108. Rome, 1935–1936.

Vansleb, J. *Nouvelle relation en forme de journal d'un voyage fait en Egypte en 1672 et 1673.* Paris, 1677. Trans. as *The Present State of Egypt.* London, 1678.

Voyages en Egypte des années 1589, 1590 et 1591. Le Vénitien anonyme; le Seigneur de Villamont; le Hollandais Jan Sommer. Cairo, 1971.

RENÉ-GEORGES COQUIN
MAURICE MARTIN, S.J.

Architecture

In the second and third centuries A.D. the town, which enjoyed great favor from several Roman emperors, must have been one of the most beautiful and most splendidly equipped towns in Upper Egypt. Parts of this splendor, such as the theater, a triumphal arch and several columned streets, and a large bath building, were still standing at the time of the Napoleonic expedition (Jomard, 1822, pls. 53–61). In the interval, however, almost all has been carried away, reused as building material, burned into lime, or sifted by diggers for *sabākh* (fertilizer).

Church Buildings in the Old Town

The many church buildings mentioned in several sources are no longer in existence. The Italian archaeological missions, which have been present on the site since 1965, came across a few small church buildings but only in marginal areas of the former town. There is the severely plundered ruin of an early Christian basilica in the southeast quarter of the town. We can see the course of part of the outer wall and the stylobate, which also give the position of the return aisle, as well as a crypt accessible by stairs on both sides (Uggeri, 1974, pp. 37–67).

A second small church was discovered in the area of the north necropolis of Antinoopolis. It consists of a small basilica with a three-part sanctuary but without a return aisle. In the south there is an adjoining court, bounded on the east side by several rectangular chambers. One of these has several small soldier's sketches on one wall. The building was dated to the fourth century by the excavators (Manfredi, 1966, p. 191; sketch-plan in Pericoli, 1978, pp. 307–309, fig. 9).

A third church probably of the same date was discovered in the so-called south necropolis. It is a particularly large building of basilican shape with an unusually modeled tripartite sanctuary. The apse is adorned with an inner ring of applied columns and in addition to the central main opening has two smaller and half-rounded entrances to form the sides.

The other church buildings traceable in the center of the town (Mitchell, 1982, pp. 177–79, d,1–d,4), and until now not excavated, are of a later date, belonging probably to the sixth century.

Beside these, many hermit dwellings have been identified in the former quarries in the surrounding desert plateau. Among the most important are the foundations of DAYR AL-DĪK and DAYR AL-NASĀRĀ, which both lie to the north of Antinoopolis.

Buildings in the Southern Suburb

A somewhat larger number of church buildings has been preserved in the later southern suburb of Antinoopolis called Upper Anṣinā, the ruins of which are called al-Madīnah by the population living in the area (Clarke, 1912, pp. 187f.). They were evidently inhabited down to the Fatimid period. Among the ruins there are some very large building complexes. A number of churches and chapels were also identified in this area (some ground plans in Grossmann, 1969, pp. 150–68), some of them belonging to monastic foundations. Chronologically

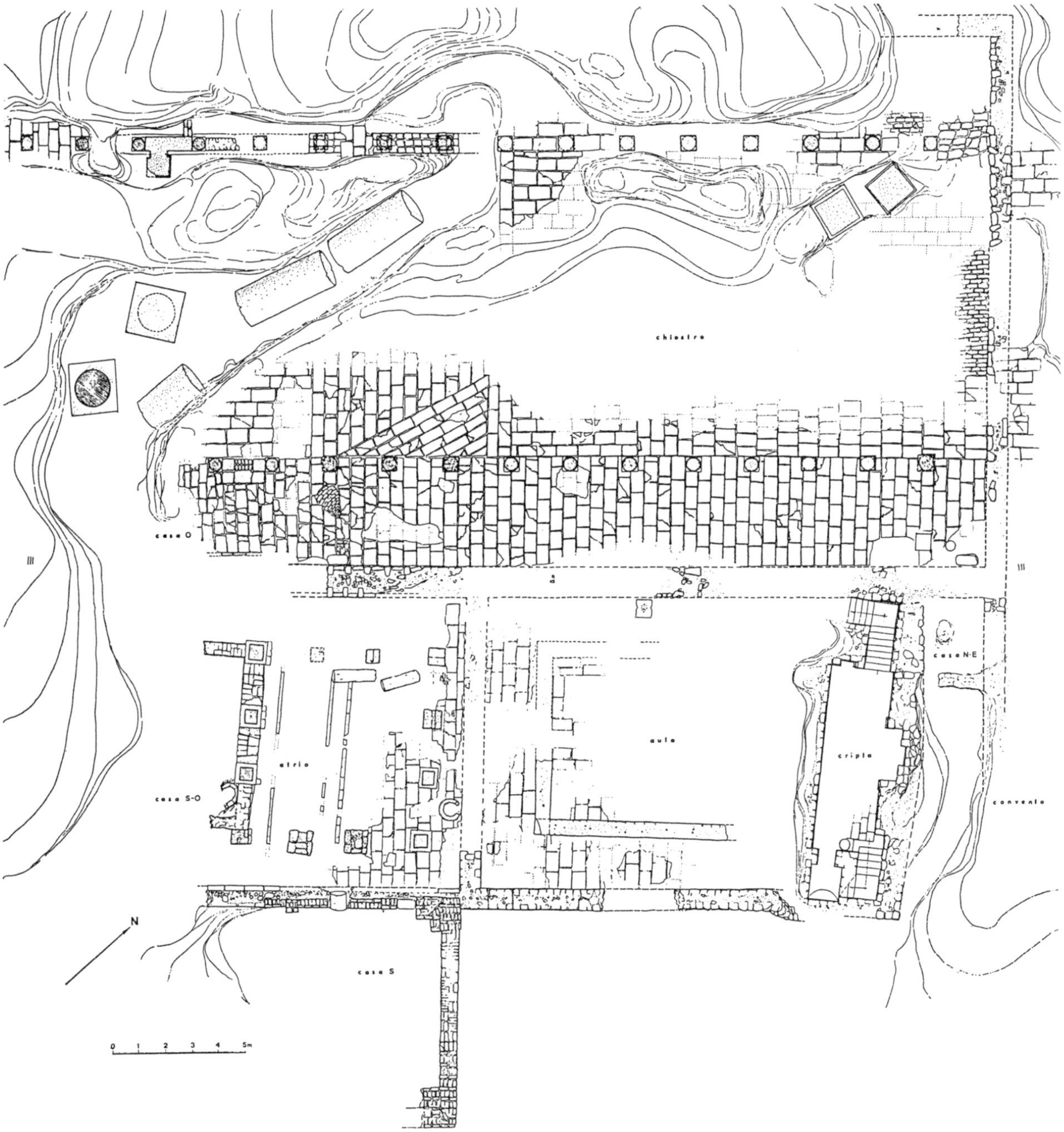

Plan of the church in the southeast quarter of Antinoopolis. *Courtesy Peter Grossmann.*

they derive from the end of the late antique period. One of these churches has a sanctuary developed as a triconch. It lies on the south edge of a large walled precinct that also contains many two- or three-storied single buildings. At another place there is an accommodation block of several rooms, each room containing several bedsteads. Unfortunately, all these buildings are still largely buried, so that important elements are so far not available for examination.

Only a small complex of ruins lying near the river was actually excavated by the Egyptian Antiquities Organization, and this was evidently a small medieval cenobite monastery. Within an area surrounded by a meager wall lie a church, several accommodation buildings, and a tower. The church has a single aisle and in the west a narthex separated from the nave by a row of columns. The sanctuary as usual consists of three chambers, in front of which is placed a *khūrus* (room between the sanctuary and naos) occupying the entire width of the church. Of the accommodation blocks, the larger one in the northeast calls for particular attention. The layout included two or three evidently communal dormitories on each side of a wide corridor. From the number of wall niches it appears that these were intended for seven or eight occupants each. On the left beside the entrance were presumably the stairs to the upper story. The whole west side of the building was occupied by a two-aisle refectory. The tower is square, but only the inner partition walls have survived. The outer walls were presumably built of stone and have been lost, but three rooms are apparent, in addition to the stairwell. Entrance may have been from the east by a drawbridge at the level of the first upper story. From a chronological point of view, the whole complex, because of the developed form of the church as well as of the accommodation block, is dated to the late eighth century, perhaps even into the ninth.

BIBLIOGRAPHY

Clarke, S. *Christian Antiquities in the Nile Valley.* Oxford, 1912.

Donadoni, S. "Scavi dell'Università di Roma in Egitto e in Sudan (1964–1975)." *La ricerca scientifica* 100 (1978):278–83.

Grossmann, P. "Die von Somers Clarke in Ober-Anṣinā entdeckten Kirchenbauten." *Mitteilungen des Deutschen Archäologischen Instituts* 24 (1969):144–68.

Jomard, E. F., ed. *Description de l'Egypte,* Vol. 4, *Antiquités.* Paris, 1821.

Leclercq, H. "Antinoë." In *Dictionnaire d'Archéologie chrétienne et de Liturgie,* Vol. 1, pt. 2., ed. F. Cabrol and H. Leclercq. Paris, 1907.

Manfredi, M. "Scavi in Egitto II." *Atène e Roma* n.s. 11 (1966):188–92; 14 (1969):39–41.

Mitchell, E. "Osservazioni topografiche preliminari sull'impianto urbanistico di Antinoe." *Vic. Oriente* 5 (1982):171–79.

Pericoli, A. "Antinoe—Projetto di carta alla scale 1:2000." *La ricerca scientifica* 100 (1978): Vol. 1, 307–10.

Uggeri, G. "La chiesa paleo-cristiana presso la porta orientale." *Antinoe (1965–1968),* pp. 37–67. Rome, 1974.

SERGIO DONADONI
PETER GROSSMANN

ANTIPHON, a form of liturgical chant performed by two cantors or two groups of cantors, referred to as the northern and southern chorus with regard to their position next to the iconostasis where they stand in the church. Each sings four verses alternately. This form is commonly used in the annual and Kiyahkian psalmody.

Antiphonal chanting has its origin in the Old Testament, where it was used in the tabernacle and later in the temple. In 1 Chronicles 25 we learn how David divided the Levites into groups to perform before the tent, until Solomon built the temple in Jerusalem, and in Ezra 3 we read about the sons of Asaph praising the Lord with their cymbals in the manner prescribed by David. In the days of Nehemiah at the dedication of the wall of Jerusalem the Levites were brought to celebrate this event in two choirs singing to the accompaniment of cymbals, lutes, and harps (Neh. 12:27–42). It was also in antiphonal singing that Isaiah heard the seraphim praising the Lord, calling ceaselessly to one another: "Holy, holy, holy is the Lord of hosts; the whole earth is full of his glory" (Is. 6:3).

Ecclesiastical historians differ as to the time and the process by which antiphonal chanting was introduced into the Christian church. Some attribute it to a vision seen by Saint Peter, and others to the initiative of Saint Ignatius of Antioch (c. 70–c. 107) who followed Saint Peter as bishop of that city (Rustum, 1958, Vol. 1, p. 52). According to Socrates, "Ignatius, third bishop of Antioch in Syria from the apostle Peter, who also had held intercourse with the apostles themselves, saw a vision of angels hymning in alternate chants the Holy Trinity. Accordingly he introduced the mode of singing he had observed in the vision into the Antiochian church; whence it was transmitted by tradition to all the other churches" (*Ecclesiastical History* 6.8).

In Theodoret's view, "That excellent pair, Flavianus [bishop of Antioch] and Diodorus [bishop of Tarsus] though not yet admitted to the priesthood and still ranked with the laity, worked night and day to stimulate men's zeal for truth. They were the first to divide choirs into two parts, and to teach them to sing the psalms of David antiphonally. Introduced first at Antioch, the practice spread in all directions, and penetrated to the ends of the earth" (1953, p. 85).

It is also possible to trace the ancestry of the antiphon to the Therapeutae, the Jewish community of ascetic converts to Christianity, and, through them, to the musical renderings performed in the ancient Egyptian temples. These Therapeutae, who lived in the vicinity of Lake Mareotis near Alexandria, at the time of Philo, may have played a significant part in introducing this manner of religious chanting. At Pentecost "they spent the whole night until sunrise in offering up praises and in songs of Thanksgiving sung in chorus by men and women. . . . The singing itself was rendered according to the laws of musical art, which seems to have been borrowed from Egyptian temples, and was then transmitted to the Christian Church" (Kohler, p. 139).

[*See also:* Music: Description of the Corpus and Present Musical Practice.]

BIBLIOGRAPHY

Kohler, K. "Therapeutae." In *The Jewish Encyclopedia,* Vol. 12, ed. Isidore Singer. New York, n.d.

Lightfoot, J. B. *The Apostolic Fathers,* pt. 2, p. 31. London, 1889.

Rustum, A. *Kanīsat Madīnat Allāh Anṭakiyah al-'Uẓmā.* Beirut, 1958.

ARCHBISHOP BASILIOS

ANTIPHONARY.

See Difnār.

ANTONY OF EGYPT, SAINT

(feast day, 22 Ṭūbah), third–fourth-century hermit. The principal source of our knowledge of the life of the man whom an ancient tradition calls "the Father of the Monks" is the biography written shortly after Antony's death (356) by Saint ATHANASIUS, patriarch of Alexandria. Its authenticity as a work of Athanasius was contested first by Weingarten (1877) and again by Draguet (1980), the editor of the Syriac version, but it seems firmly established. It was attested in ancient times, in the first Greek life of Saint PACHOMIUS (Halkin, 1932, p. 66) and in Latin by Rufinus (*Historia ecclesiastica* I, 8) and by Saint Jerome (*De viris illustribus* 87). In addition to the Greek text, there are two ancient Latin versions, the second being the work of Evagrius of Antioch, and versions in various Oriental languages. There is also a Coptic version, in the Sahidic dialect, which was published by G. Garitte (1949).

Several modern critics have called the work's historical value into question, in consequence of the writings of R. Reitzenstein (1914), who showed that Athanasius took as his literary models the lives of the pagan philosophers, in contrast to which he wished to portray the Christian sage. The influence of these models is beyond dispute, but it does not impair the value of the testimony of Athanasius, who knew Antony personally and affirms in his Prologue that he used not only his own memories but also the information given him by someone who was for some time a disciple of Antony. (On this point, the published Greek text must be corrected in accordance with the Coptic and Syriac versions.) This was probably SERAPION OF TMUIS, who was at the same time a disciple of Antony and a friend of Athanasius.

In addition to the biography written by Athanasius, there are some other sources that reveal certain aspects of Antony's life and personality. The alphabetical collection of the APOPHTHEGMATA PATRUM has collected under his name thirty-eight apothegms, which Dörries (1966) thought give a better knowledge of Antony's true personality than the book by Athanasius. PALLADIUS (1904, pp. 63–74) reported the recollections of a priest of NITRIA, Cronius, who in his youth lived near Antony and his disciples. The Arabic-Jacobite SYNAXARION adds some new information to that given in the sources cited above.

Antony was born of Christian parents in the village of Qimān (modern-day Qimān al-'Arūs, in the region of al-Wasṭah) about 251. After experiencing the death of his parents when he was some twenty years old and being mindful of the words of Jesus on renunciation (Mt. 19:21) read in the church, he gave away his goods, entrusted his young sister to a community of virgins, and lived as a hermit outside the village, following the example of other ascetics at this time. Then he moved away, reaching the mountainous region where the tombs were, and shut himself up in one of them, where he lived as a recluse for about ten years, heroically enduring, according to his biographer, the most violent assaults of the demons. Harassed by visitors, he went off to the other bank of the Nile and installed himself in the ruins of a Roman fort. Disciples then came to live around him, thus forming the first community of the monastery of Pispir, situated in proximity to the river. Some twenty years later, he desired to live in greater solitude, and so, under the guidance of bedouins, he penetrated into the Eastern Desert and established himself in a hermitage situated about 20 miles (30 km) from the Red Sea at the foot of Mount Qulzum, near the place where today stands the monastery of Saint Antony (DAYR ANBĀ ANṬŪNIYŪS). It was there that he lived for about forty years, until his death, maintaining himself with the work of his hands and the produce of his garden or with what his disciples brought him. Quite frequently, according to the account of Cronius reported by Palladius, he went to visit the disciples in the monastery on the banks of the Nile. His great renown drew people from all over Egypt to visit this place, where they could meet him in person. On two occasions he went to Alexandria to support Athanasius in his struggle against the Arians; it was in the course of one of these journeys, in 338, that he stopped at Nitria and counseled AMUN to undertake the founding of the monastic settlement of KELLIA.

Writings

In his lifetime, Antony won an immense reputation, which spread beyond Egypt. Athanasius (chap. 81, col. 956) asserts that he kept up a correspondence with the emperors Constantine, Constantius, and Constans. If this correspondence really existed, nothing of it remains. There has come down to us, in an Arabic version, a corpus of twenty letters bearing his name (Latin translation by Abraham Ecchellensis in PG 40, cols. 963–1066; the Arabic text published in Cairo, 1899). Only the first seven should be retained under the name of Antony. The others, as F. Klejna (1938) has shown, correspond for the most part to the letters otherwise known in Greek and in Syriac under the name of AMMONAS, a disciple of Antony. These seven letters were already known, under Antony's name, by Saint JEROME (*De viris illustribus* 88, PL 23, col. 731). A Latin translation was made in the fifteenth century from a Greek text now lost (PG 40, cols. 977–1000). A Georgian version, made directly from a Greek text, was published by G. Garitte (1955). There is a fragment in Coptic, edited by E. O. Winstedt and republished by Garitte (1955), giving one complete letter, the end of another, and the beginning of a third. Quotations in Coptic (also published by Garitte) are found in the fifth century in the works of SHENUTE and his disciple BESA.

The authenticity of the letters is questionable. There are several testimonies to the epistolary activity of Antony. In addition to the correspondence exchanged with the emperors of which Athanasius speaks, there is mention in the first Greek Life of Saint Pachomius (Halkin, 1932, p. 78) of a letter that Antony addressed to Athanasius through the medium of two Pachomian monks who had come to see him on their way to Alexandria. Another document, the *Letter of Ammon* (Halkin, 1932, pp. 116–17), gives the text of a letter written by Antony to Theodore, the successor of Pachomius, a letter written in Egyptian (i.e., in Coptic). Antony, in fact, was ignorant of Greek (Palladius, 1904, pp. 68–69), and this is probably what Athanasius means when he says that he was unlettered (*Life*, chap. 1, col. 841). The style and composition of these letters are devoid of any art and bear witness to a real lack of culture. But more surprising in such an author are some opinions suggestive of Origenism and, hence, of the highest intellectualism. Thus, we read, for example, that all prelapsarian beings formed a single essence and that they became diversified, taking various names, according to the degree of their fall. Antony was perhaps in contact with the Origenist circles of Alexandria. Palladius (chap. 4) affirms that Antony, on the occasion of his journeys to the city, went several times to visit DIDYMUS THE BLIND in his cell. But the text of the letters is still very poorly established, and there are great divergences between the various versions. It is not certain that the Coptic fragments themselves represent the original text. Arguments in favor of authenticity are, in addition to the ancient testimonies, the polemic against Arianism, of which we know Antony was an adversary, and the fact that one of these letters is addressed to monks in the region of Arsinoë, where we know from the *Life* (chap. 15, col. 865) that Antony had disciples whom he sometimes visited.

Other texts, certainly pseudepigraphic, have been handed down under Antony's name. At the head of the famous *Philocalia* (1957, pp. 3–27) there is under his name a paraenesis (exhortation) that is in reality a work of Stoic origin, strongly influenced by Epictetus (cf. Hausherr, 1933, pp. 212–16). In addition to the corpus of the twenty letters, the Arabic tradition has handed down a collection of diverse writings under this same name, the origin of which remains obscure. (A Latin translation is given in PG 40, cols. 963–78, 1065–1102.) In one of them, entitled *Spiritualia documenta*, a long passage has been identified by W. P. Funk (1976, pp. 8–21), which recurs literally in *The Teachings of Silvanus* (Codex VII 97, 9–98, 22), one of the treatises discovered at Nag Hammadi (see NAG HAMMADI LIBRARY). It could be a case of direct borrowing or, as Funk thinks, the common use of an older document.

The influence of Antony on the history of monasticism was considerable—in Egypt itself at first, since it was exerted either directly or through MACARIUS THE EGYPTIAN and Amun at the very origins of the great monastic movement of Lower Egypt, but also throughout the Christian world, by reason of the very wide diffusion, through translations, of the *Life* written by Athanasius. It is enough to recall, by way of example, the story told by Saint Augustine of the sudden conversion to the monastic life of two imperial officers of Trier on reading the *Life of*

Saint Antony found in a hermit's cabin and the role that this story, as well as Antony's example, played in the conversion of Augustine himself (*Confessions*, VIII, 6, 14–15 and 12, 29).

BIBLIOGRAPHY

Amélineau, E. *Histoire des Monastères de la Basse-Egypte*, pp. 15–45. Annales du Musée Guimet 25. Paris, 1894.
Antony (Letters of), Latin trans. A. Ecchellensis. In PG 40, cols. 999–1066, 1075–1080. Paris, 1863.
Athanasius. *Vita S. Antonii*, ed. B. de Montfaucon. In PG 26, cols. 835–976. Paris, 1887.
______. *The Life of Saint Antony*, trans. R. T. Meyer. Ancient Christian Writers 10. Westminster, Md., 1950.
Bartelink, G. J. M. *Vita di Antonio*. Milan, 1974.
Chitty, D. J., ed. *The Letters of St. Antonius translated*. Oxford, 1975.
Cotelier, J. B., ed. *Apophthegmata Patrum*. In PG 65, cols. 75–88. Paris, 1887.
Dörries, H. *Wort und Stunde*, Vol. 1, pp. 145–224. Göttingen, 1966.
Draguet, R., ed. *La Vie primitive de S. Antoine conservée en syriaque*. In CSCO 417–418. Louvain, 1980.
Funk, W.-P. "Ein doppelt überliefertes Stück spätägyptischer Weisheit." *Zeitschrift für ägyptische Sprache und Altertumskunde* 103 (1977): 8–21.
Garitte, G., ed. *S. Antonii Vitae versio sahidica*. In CSCO 117–18. Louvain, 1949.
______. *Lettres de S. Antoine. Version géorgienne et fragments coptes*. In CSCO 148–49. Louvain, 1955.
Halkin, F. *Sancti Pachomii Vitae graecae*. Subsidia Hagiographica 19. *Vita Prima*, pp. 1–96; *Epistula Ammonis episcopi*, pp. 97–121. Brussels, 1932.
Hausherr, I. "De doctrina spirituali christianorum orientalium." *Orientalia Christiana* 30 (1933): pt. 3, pp. 212[70]–216[74].
Jerome. *De viris illustribus*. In PL 23, cols. 631–760. Paris, 1883.
Klejna, F. "Antonius und Ammonas. Untersuchung über Herkunft und Eigenart der ältesten Mönchsbriefe." *Zeitschrift für katholische Theologie* 61 (1938):309–348.
Reitzenstein, R. *Das Athanasius Werk über das Leben des Antonius. Ein philologischer Beitrag zur Geschichte des Mönchtums*. Heidelberg, 1914.
Steidle, B., ed. *Antonius Magnus Eremita 356–1956*. Studia Anselmiana 38. Rome, 1956.
Weingarten, H. *Der Ursprung des Mönchtums im nachconstantinischen Zeitalter*, pp. 10–22. Gotha, 1877.

ANTOINE GUILLAUMONT

ANTONY THE GREAT. *See* Antony of Egypt, Saint.

ANṬŪNIYŪS MULŪKHIYYAH, eighteenth-century Coptic Catholic priest. Information about him comes from five Arabic manuscripts, three of which are at the Coptic Patriarchate of Cairo, and from a report made in Cairo on 4 October 1747 by the Franciscan priest Jacques de Kremsier, apostolic prefect of Egypt.

According to a manuscript from Faytrūn, his father's name was Mu'nis. Anṭūniyūs was born in Cairo in 1703. He was one of a generation of Coptic Catholics who came to Rome to live as regular monks with the Ethiopian monks installed at San Stefano dei Mori from 1732. He was professed there according to the rule of Saint ANTONY of the desert, as he was always to emphasize in later years. At Rome he continued his studies in philosophy, and in 1735 he copied a manual of logic, which he probably used for his studies. After his theology studies at Rome, he was ordained a priest.

On 26 February 1743 he arrived in Cairo, where he began his work as a missionary secular priest. His mission consisted of "preaching in the people's homes, visiting the Catholics, and not failing in his duty." Thus in October 1747 he was in Cairo; how many years he continued to exercise this apostolate is unclear.

Much later, in 1760, we have evidence that Anṭūniyūs was in Rome, copying manuscripts until 1763. He was still working in liaison with the missionaries of Egypt; thus the *Ḥawādith al-I'tirāf* (Tales of Confessions) were copied "at the request and for the use of the Coptic Catholic monks and the missionaries" (Graf, no. B 3). He must have died shortly after 1775, the date of the last manuscript bearing his name.

In 1735, Anṭūniyūs copied an anonymous manual of logic. On this occasion he signed himself Anṭūniyūs ibn Mu'nis Mulūkhiyyah.

In 1760, Anṭūniyūs copied eighty-two sermons, probably translated from the Italian, dealing principally with death, the Last Judgment, heaven, purgatory, hell, etcetera. (Coptic Patriarchate, Cairo, Theology 277; Graf, no. 513; Simaykah, no. 378).

In 1761 he copied the *Casos raros de la confesión* by the Spanish Jesuit Christoval de Vega (1595–1672), translated from Italian to Arabic with the *Riflessioni* of Antonio Heraudo di Levenzo, under the title *Ḥawādith al-I'tirāf.* The translation is by the Maronite Ibrāhīm Jalwān al-Simrānī (Graf, 1949, p. 471, no. e; Coptic Patriarchate, Cairo, Theology 281; Graf, no. 514; Simaykah, no. 379).

In 1763 he copied a large folio manuscript of 686 pages containing the commentary on the Gospel of John by the Dutch Jesuit Cornelius a Lapide (d. 1637) for the use of the small Coptic Catholic community of San Stefano. The text was probably translated by the Copt RŪFĀ'ĪL AL-ṬŪKHĪ, who was living with him at San Stefano dei Mori (d. 1787). This is the only known manuscript of this commentary (Graf, 1951, p. 163, no. 8e; Coptic Patriarchate, Cairo, Theology 52; Graf, no. 508; Simaykah, no. 382).

Finally, in 1775, when he was probably too old to copy the manuscript himself, at his own expense he had copied in Cairo a large folio manuscript of 922 pages containing a lectionary of Holy Week, in Bohairic Coptic and Arabic, including the entire book of Revelation. The copy was made by the deacon (*shammās*) Dāwūd Mīnā al-Jizāwī, nicknamed al-Muwaqqi', who professed to be "Coptic by race and Catholic by belief," in the house of the Muallim Yūḥannā Abū Ghubriyāl. It was completed on 11 September 1775. Anṭūniyūs donated this manuscript to Rūfā'il al-Ṭūkhī, as can be seen from fol. 1r: "MSS Copti di Monsig. Tuki Num. XIII." It is now in the Vatican Library (Borgia Coptic 52; cf. Graf, Vol. 2, pt. 1, pp. 199–204, with the colophon reproduced in full).

BIBLIOGRAPHY

Graf, G. *Catalogue de manuscrits arabes chrétiens conservés au Caire,* pp. 192–93. Studi e testi 63. Vatican City, 1934.

Trossen, J.-P. *Les Relations du patriarche copte Jean XVI avec Rome* (1676–1718); pp. 201–18: Answer by Fra Giacomo da Cremsirio. Luxembourg, 1948.

KHALIL SAMIR, S.J.

ANUB, SAINT, martyr under Diocletian (feast day: 24 Abib). His Passion has come down in only one Bohairic manuscript (Rome, Vatican Library, Copto 66, fols. 233–68; Balestri and Hyvernat, 1908, Vol. I, pp. 200–241).

The text opens with the usual situation, in which Diocletian sends out an edict to the whole empire ordering sacrifices to the Roman gods. The edict reaches the dux Armenius in Alexandria, who sends it to Cyprianus, prefect of Atrīb. An account of various episodes of martyrdom follows. After hearing a sermon in church, Anub, who lives at Naesi, near Atrīb, distributes his possessions among the poor and goes to the prefect Lysia in Cemnuti, who has also begun the persecution. In a vision, the Archangel MICHAEL exhorts Anub to martyrdom, after which occurs the first exchange of words with Lysia, who takes Anub to Atrīb. At this point another argument with Cyprianus takes place, followed by torture, which is without effect. Other forms of torture are described, and also a vision.

In the end Anub is sent to Armenius in Alexandria, where a further exchange of words and further torture take place. Julius of Aqfahṣ visits Anub in prison, after which Anub is martyred. This is followed by the "signature" of Julius of Aqfahṣ.

The text is a typical production of the late Coptic hagiographical school and is included in particular in the Cycle of Julius of Aqfahṣ. (see HAGIOGRAPHY; CYCLES). It can be dated to the seventh/eighth centuries.

BIBLIOGRAPHY

Balestri, I., and H. Hyvernat, eds. *Acta Martyrum,* 2 vols. CSCO 43, 44.

Baumeister, T. *Martyr Invictus. Der Märtyrer als Sinnbild der Erlösung in der Legende und im Kult der frühen koptischen Kirche.* Münster, 1972.

TITO ORLANDI

APA. The Coptic term *apa* is interchangeable with the Arabic *abbā*, which occurs in Semitic languages, including Syriac, Aramaic, and even Hebrew, all meaning "father." This is a title of reverence usually preceding names of persons in the church hierarchy. Historically the title is extended to the names of secular martyrs as well. It is also inspired by the opening of the Lord's Prayer, and its Latin equivalent of *pater* appears in the Latin Vulgate, originally in the Coptic ⲁⲡⲁⲧⲏⲣ (*apatēr*) or ⲁⲡⲁ ⲡⲁⲧⲏⲣ (*apa patēr*). Sometimes it is also cited in Coptic as ⲁⲛⲃⲁ (*anba*) or ⲁⲙⲡⲁ (*ampa*), which is generally used in modern Arabic with the names of bishops, archbishops, and patriarchs, such as Anbā Shinūdah. Derived from it is the word *abūnā* meaning "our father" which is used in addressing a priest or a monk. The word *apa* is widely quoted in the SYNAXARION sometimes as ⲁⲡⲟⲩ (*apou*; Arabic, *abū*), and the APOPHTHEGMATA PATRUM where it also occurs as ⲁⲃⲃⲁ (*abba*) or ⲁⲃⲃⲁⲥ (*abbas*). The term became firmly established in the Coptic lives of Saint Pachomius in the fourth century and was transmitted to medieval Europe in the Latinized form of *abbas,* from which are derived the terms abbot in English and *abbé* in French. Its Greek equivalent appears in the New Testament in three places: Mark 14:36, Romans 8:15, and Galatians 4:6. The Orthodox Ethiopians still call the head of their church ABUNA (our father).

The feminine occurs as ⲁⲙⲁ (*ama*) or ⲁⲙⲙⲁ (*amma;* mother) as the title for nuns. The term ⲡⲁⲡⲁ (*papa*) or with the definite article ⲡⲡⲁⲡⲁ (*ppapa*) is the equivalent of the Greek πάπας (papas), signifying priest.

BIBLIOGRAPHY

Crum, W. E. *A Coptic Dictionary.* Oxford, 1939.

Dupont, J. *Le Nom de l'abbé chez les solitaires d'Egypte.* La Vie spirituelle 77. Paris, 1947.

Lefort, L. T. *Les Vies coptes de S. Pacôme.* Lausanne, 1943.

Pelleccia, G., and G. Rocca. *Dizionario degli Istituti de Perfezione.* Rome, 1947.

AZIZ S. ATIYA

APAIULE AND TOLEMAEUS, SAINTS, a monk and a soldier martyred under DIOCLETIAN (feast day: 21 Ṭūbah). The text of their Passion exists in only one codex in Sahidic dialect (Pierpont Morgan Library, New York, M 583), edited by E. A. E. Reymond and J. W. B. Barnes (1973, pp. 131–37). As usual, it begins with the edict of Diocletian being sent to the provinces of the empire. After receiving it, the dux Sebastianus sets out on the Nile and reaches the village of Psutumet near Hnes. He orders sacrifice here, but the soldier Tolemaeus refuses to carry out the order. This is followed by the traditional scenes of discussion with the dux, imprisonment, and the vision of Jesus. At this point the monk Apaiule is introduced; he goes to visit Tolemaeus in prison, is recognized as a Christian, and is in turn tortured by Sebastianus. Finally both are martyred.

The text is part of the Cycle of the Diocletian martyrs and seems to date to the period of true Coptic production (see HAGIOGRAPHY) and is thus late (seventh century). However, its shortness, its disappearance in later tradition, and its remaining in the Sahidic dialect would lead one to conclude that it dates to the beginning of that period and remained isolated in local tradition.

BIBLIOGRAPHY

Baumeister, T. *Martyr Invictus. Der Märtyrer als Sinnbild der Erlösung in der Legende und im Kult der frühen koptischen Kirche.* Münster, 1972.

Reymond, E. A. E., and J. W. B. Barnes. *Four Martyrdoms from the Pierpont Morgan Coptic Codices.* Oxford, 1973.

TITO ORLANDI

APA JEREMIAH MONASTERY. *See* Dayr Apa Jeremiah.

APHRODITE. *See* Mythological Subjects in Coptic Art.

APHRODITO, a large town on the left bank of the Nile to the south of Asyūṭ, 31 miles (50 km) away, and to the southwest of Ṭimā. In the middle of the Roman empire and even in the Byzantine period and at the beginning of the Arab era, it was the capital of a nome (the tenth in Upper Egypt) and, judging from the mass of papyri discovered there, a very important city. In the sixth century A.D. this nome was swallowed up into the nome of the right bank, which had as its capital Antaeopolis (the present Qāw al-Kabīr).

Information about the arrival and expansion of Christianity in this city is still lacking, but it is known that in the town and its environs were many churches and monasteries. It is impossible sometimes to distinguish one from another, because each is called simply *topos* (place). Like L. Antonini and P. Barison, A. Calderini, in his *Dizionario* (1935–1987), enumerated more than thirty churches, and an even larger number of monasteries, without counting the vague references to a *topos.*

One must take care not to confuse this Aphrodito with the (five or six) other cities in Egypt that bear the same name. The interested reader will find in the studies of Calderini (1972, Vol. 1, pt. 2, pp. 325–40), Antonini (1940, pp. 191–98), and Barison (1938, pp. 98–122) the details of the churches and monasteries of this city and its immediate neighborhood. Since each site is simply designated *topos,* it is not known whether a church or a monastery is meant, although the appellation seems to relate to a church in the majority of cases. However that may be, the large number of religious buildings proves that Christianity was important in this town.

It was the discovery of a quantity of papyri relating to the town that allowed scholars to form some idea of the implanting of Christianity in this region, a discovery that took place at the end of the nineteenth century and was further investigated at the beginning of the twentieth century. This discovery has provided a better knowledge of the economic and social role that the Christians and their clergy were able to play before the ARAB CONQUEST OF EGYPT (cf. Wipszicka, 1972). As for the dialectal peculiarities, P. E. Kahle (1954, Vol. 1, pp. 51ff.) examines them, grouping them with those of the texts of Dayr al-Balayzah and Wādī Sarjah.

BIBLIOGRAPHY

Antonini, L. "Le chiese cristiane dell'Egitto dal IV al IX secolo secondo i documenti dei papiri greci." *Aegyptus* 20 (1940):129–208, esp. 191–98.

Barison, P. "Ricerche sui monasteri dell'Egitto bizantino ed arabo secondo i documenti dei papiri greci." *Aegyptus* 18 (1938):29–148, esp. 98–122.

Calderini, A. *Dizionario dei nomi geografici e topografici dell'Egitto greco-romano*, 5 vols. Milan and Cairo, 1935–1987. Vol. 1, repr., 1972.

Kahle, P. E., ed. *Balā'izah*, 2 vols. London, 1954.

Timm, S. *Das christlich-koptische Ägypten in arabischer Zeit*, 3 vols. to date. Wiesbaden, 1984–.

Wipszicka, E. *Les Ressources et les activités économiques des églises en Egypte du IVe au VIIIe siècle.* Papyrologica Bruxellensia 10. Brussels, 1972.

RENÉ-GEORGES COQUIN

APHRODITOPOLIS. *See* Itfīh.

APHU, monk and bishop of Oxyrhynchus during the second half of the fourth century and the beginning of the fifth. He is best known through Coptic sources and, later, from Arabic sources as well. A complete account of his life is handed down in a manuscript from Turin (Cat. 63000, ed. Rossi, 1887–1892). He is also mentioned in the life of PAUL OF TAMMAH. The Apophthegmata (Greek collection) ascribed to him only one apothegm, the content of which seems to be in agreement with the Coptic sources.

According to the Life, he was a disciple of the first hermits, and he chose a very unusual kind of ascesis. He mixed himself with a herd of buffalo in the desert and lived as they did. Once a year only he would be visited by a brother who reminded him about Easter, at which time he returned to town and participated in the ceremonies. During one of these visits he heard someone reading Theophilus' Festal Letter against the anthropomorphite doctrine. Presumably this was the letter dated 399.

Inspired by God, he went to the archbishop of Alexandria to dispute the orthodoxy of such a point of view. After a long disputation, essentially based on the literal or typological interpretation of scriptural passages, Theophilus was convinced and changed his mind completely. The impression of Aphu's personality so affected Theophilus that at the death of the archbishop of Oxyrhynchus, he obligated the inhabitants to elect that unknown monk as their bishop. Aphu accepted unwillingly, but refused to spend days other than Saturdays and Sundays in town and continued to reside in a monastery during the rest of the week until his death.

His last words expressed regret for the solitude of the desert, which alone allowed growth toward spiritual perfection. The apothegm mentioned above is also inspired by such sentiments.

The disputation with Theophilus aroused a certain interest among the scholars, who are not inclined to give it any importance as a strictly historic event. Nevertheless, we cannot exclude that beyond the literary disguise there could be an allusion to real events. The literal or allegorical interpretation of the famous verse of Genesis 1:26, "Let us make man in our image, after our likeness," which was one of the questions linked with the Origenist controversy, blossomed under Theophilus and was emphasized by the monastic milieu. The monks related it to the motivation of the ascesis, in order to keep the body in its original purity.

The exegesis and theology of the Egyptian monks in Upper and Central Egypt (apart from the Pachomian community) are substantially unknown to us, but there are elements that lead us to believe that the silence of the sources conceals literalistic ways of thinking, perhaps of Asian influence.

It is then possible that Aphu's life is the product of that environment and situation, and it shows how a part of the Nile Valley monasticism interpreted the events of 399–400, choosing a person particularly venerated as a spokesman of its own point of view. On the other hand, it is quite possible that Aphu might have taken part in all those events.

BIBLIOGRAPHY

Drioton, E. "La Discussion d'un moine anthropomorphite audien avec le patriarche Théophile d'Alexandrie en l'année 399." *Revue de l'Orient chrétien,* series 2, 10 (1915):92–100, 113–28.

Florovsky, G. "Theophilus of Alexandria and Apa Aphou of Pemdje." In *Harry Austryn Wolfson Jubilee Volume on the Occasion of his Seventy-fifth Birthday,* Vol. 1. Jerusalem, 1965.

Revillout, E. "La Vie du bienheureux Aphou évêque de Pemdje (Oxyrinque)." *Revue d'Égyptologie* 3 (1885):27–33.

Rossi, F. *I Papiri copti del Museo Egizio di Torino,* 2 vols., 10 issues. Turin, 1887–1892.

TITO ORLANDI

APION, FAMILY OF, wealthy landowners prominent in Egyptian imperial and public life in the first half of the sixth century. The earliest known member of the family, Apion I, held land around Herakleopolis Magna (see AHNAS AL-MADĪNAH) in 497 (*Oxyrhynchus Papyri* 1982; *Studien zur Palaeographie und Papyruskunde* 20.129). He was already prominent, having held an honorary consulship between 492 and 497. The date of his death is not known.

Better known is a member of the next generation, Flavius Strategius Apion. He was *patricius* in 503 and vice-prefect of the East in 503–504. Emperor Anastasius (491–518) appointed him to reorganize the commissariat of the Roman armies on the Persian frontier, and he supplied the town and garrison of Edessa with enough wheat to provision the garrisons of Dara and Amida. Flavius was regarded as very efficient (Theodorus Lector *Epitome* 482). He moved to Alexandria in May 504 with similar duties—"to make the soldiers bread there and send a supply" (Joshua Stylites, *History of the Calamities Which Befell Edessa, Amida, and All Mesopotamia*) —but was later recalled to Constantinople, allegedly for conspiring to obstruct the Persian campaign (Theophanes, *Chronographia* A.M. 5998).

While in Constantinople (508–510) Flavius made the acquaintance of SEVERUS OF ANTIOCH, who dedicated his work *Against Eutyches* to him and a certain Paul. (He thus at this time must have been an anti-Chalcedonian.) In 510, however, Flavius was condemned by the emperor Anastasius on political grounds and ordained presbyter at Nicaea by force (Lydus, *De magistratibus* 3.17; Theodorus Lector, *Epitome* 482; Theophanes *Chronographia* A.M. 611). He was recalled by Emperor Justin I in 518 and promoted to the rank of praetorian prefect of the East in 519 (*Chronicon Paschale* sub anno 519). He became a convinced supporter of the new dynasty's Chalcedonian Creed, a conviction shared by his son. He died about 530.

His son Flavius Strategius was even more distinguished than his father. In 518 he was honorary consul and honorary *magister militum,* and was sent to Egypt as *praefectus Augustalis* (518–523). He was *patricius* by December 530 (*Oxyrhynchus Papyri* 2779). His government, in a time of increasing tension between pro- and anti-Chalcedonians following the arrival of Severus of Antioch at Alexandria in the autumn of 518, was successful—peace was kept. In 532, bearing the rank of *agens vicem magistri officiorum,* Flavius was sent by Emperor Justinian to negotiate with the Persians. In this capacity he attended the meeting arranged by the emperor to attempt to solve the differences between orthodox and Monophysites. The meeting took place late in 532 at Constantinople, in the palace of Hormisdas. Flavius took part in the discussion but did not influence either side decisively. From 535 to 538 he held various senior offices in the financial administration of the empire. His last known position was in 538, when he was sent by Justinian to arbitrate in a dispute between Arab *shaykhs,* which the Persians had hoped to use to renew war against the empire (Procopius of Caesarea, *The Persian War* 2.1.9). He was a landowner at Oxyrhynchus (*Oxyrhynchus Papyri* 1984, 2779) and died about 545.

His son, Flavius Strategius Apion, was consul in 539 and held the title of *protopatricius* (probably, "leader of the Senate") (*Papyri Oxyrhynchus* 136, 137). He lived until May 577, but is not known to have filled any senior positions after his consulate, though he remained closely connected with the dynasty of Justinian. His grandson, Apion III, had as his mother Praejecta (*Papyri Oxyrhynchus* 1989), the daughter of the elder Praejecta who had been the wife of the grandson of Hypatius, Justinian's kinsman, who had momentarily seized power at the time of the Nika riot in 532.

The Apions were great landowners whose estates were minutely organized through a hierarchy of bailiffs, overseers, and local leaders ruling over an army of servile labor. They served the empire well. They seem to have been as liberal in religious conviction as the age allowed, but placed greater emphasis on ability to serve the state than on the "accuracy of doctrine" demanded by Severus and his supporters. They made their mark in the service of JUSTIN I and JUSTINIAN.

BIBLIOGRAPHY

Chronicon Paschale, 2 vols., ed. B. G. Niebuhr. Bonn, 1832.

Hardy, E. R. *The Large Estates of Byzantine Egypt.* New York, 1968.

Jones, A. H. M. *The Later Roman Empire,* 2 vols. Norman, Okla., 1964.

Joshua Stylites. *History of the Calamities Which Befell Edessa, Amida, and All Mesopotamia,* ed. W. Wright. Cambridge, 1882.

Lydus, John. *De magistratibus populi Romani,* ed. R. Warensch. Leipzig, 1903.

Martindale, J. R. *The Prosopography of the Later Roman Empire,* Vol. 2, pp. 110–12 and 1034–36. Cambridge, 1980.

The Oxyrhynchus Papyri. 51 vols. Published by the Egypt Exploration Society in *Graeco-Roman Memoirs.* London, 1898.

Procopius of Caesarea. *The Persian War,* ed. and trans. H. B. Dewing. Loeb Classical Library. London and New York, 1914.

Studien zur Palaeographie und Papyruskunde, Vol. 20, *Catalogus Papyrorum Raineri. Series Graeca. Pars I. Textus Graeci papyrorum, qui in libro "Papyrus Erzherzog Rainer—Führer durch die Austellung Wien 1894" descripti sunt,* ed. C. Wessely. Leipzig, 1921.

Theodorus Lector. *Epitome,* ed. G. C. Hansen. Die griechischen christlichen Schriftsteller der ersten drei Jahrhunderte. Berlin, 1971.

Theophanes. *Chronographia,* 2 vols., ed. J. Classen. Bonn, 1839–1841.

W. H. C. FREND

APOCALYPSE OF ADAM, the fifth tractate in Codex V of the NAG HAMMADI LIBRARY. It purports to be a revelation given by Adam to his son Seth, "in the 700th year," that is, just prior to Adam's death (Gn. 5:3–5). This feature gives the document the character of a "last testament" and associates it with other testamentary literature in antiquity. Adam describes his fall in the Garden of Eden as a lapse into ignorance. Three heavenly figures then appear to Adam, and their revelation to him becomes the subject of Adam's last testament to Seth. He describes to Seth the origin of a special race of men and their struggle against the creator god (called Sacla, the Almighty). Three attempts are made by the creator to destroy this race of men who possess the knowledge of the eternal God. Two of these threats are drawn from well-known Jewish traditions, but here they are given a new interpretation. For example, the biblical flood narrative is interpreted as the attempt of a wicked creator god to destroy the pure race of men that possess the special knowledge of the eternal god (67.22–76.7).

Adam describes the descent of a heavenly figure, the illuminator of knowledge. His appearance shakes the cosmos of the creator god and his evil host. They persecute him, yet he succeeds in revealing his knowledge to the special race of men. The narrative ends with an apocalyptic scene reminiscent of Matthew 25, in which those who oppose the illuminator fall under the condemnation of death but those who receive his knowledge "will live forever."

The narrative breaks down into two sections that appear to be two sources harmonized by an ancient editor with appropriate redactional comments at the point of literary seams. One source (64.1–65.23; 66.12–67.12; 67.22–76.7; 83.7–84.3; 85.19–22) can be described as standing near the border between Jewish apocalypticism and gnosticism. The general character of its gnosticism and the strong influence of Jewish traditions suggests that the author stood within a system that may be described as emerging gnosticism. In form, this narrative source is actually a midrashic commentary on the Genesis account of creation (Gn. 6:10) and the biblical account of the great flood (67.22–76.7). The Midrash of the flood paraphrases the biblical text (67.22–69.10; 70.3–71.4; 72.15–17; 73.25–27) and follows each paraphrase with an "exegesis" (69.18–70.2; 71.8–72.15; 72.18–73.24; 73.27–76.7) that embellishes and expands the biblical account with the narrative of the special race of men as the "real story of the flood."

The second source (65.24–66.12; 67.12–67.21; 76.8–83.7), on the other hand, contains few references to Jewish traditions and reflects a developed Gnostic mythology. The most interesting feature of this material is its close parallel with Christian traditions about Jesus. The illuminator comes to leave "fruit bearing trees" whose "souls" he will "redeem from the day of death." He "performs signs and wonders" and is punished "in his flesh" by the creator god. Thirteen erroneous explanations are given by the powers in a highly stylized form to explain the illuminator's origin. One of these attributes his origin to a virgin birth (78.27–79.19). The correct explanation given by the "kingless generation" describes him as being "chosen" from all the aeons. These parallels to the Christian traditions are not necessarily evidence of Christian influence, and many have argued that the document is evidence of the existence of a type of non-Christian gnosticism possessing a redeemer mythology.

These two sources were edited probably sometime prior to the beginning of the second century A.D., during an early stage in the development of the Sethian-Archontic tradition by a group that argued for a spiritualized understanding of baptism and an ascetic lifestyle. The redactor's views are most clearly expressed in his concluding statement (84.4–85.18, 22b–31).

The document was composed originally in Greek and was later translated into Coptic (Sahidic).

BIBLIOGRAPHY

Hedrick, C. W. *The Apocalypse of Adam: A Literary and Source Analysis.* SBL Dissertation Series. Missoula, Mont., 1980.

MacRae, G. W. "The Apocalypse of Adam." In *Nag Hammadi Codices V,* 2–5, and VI with Papyrus Berolinensis 8502, 1 and 4, ed. Douglas M. Parrott. Nag Hammadi Studies 11. Leiden, 1979.

Scholar, D. M. *Nag Hammadi Bibliography 1948–1969.* Nag Hammadi Studies 1. Leiden, 1971. Updated annually in *Novum Testamentum.*

CHARLES W. HEDRICK

APOCALYPSE OF JAMES, FIRST. This *Apocalypse of James* is the first of two such apocalypses in the NAG HAMMADI LIBRARY, constituting the third tractate of Codex V. It is a revelation containing a dialogue between the Lord Jesus and James, the Lord's brother. Here, however, James is not the Lord's brother "materially" (24.15–16).

The first part of the writing (24.10–30.11) is dominated by the fearfulness of James in the face of impending disaster. To encourage him, the Lord discusses various doctrines with him concerning Him-Who-Is, the seventy-two heavens existing under the authority of the twelve archons, the affinity of James with Him-Who-Is, and so forth, and then promises to reveal the way of redemption to him. Then "the Lord said farewell to him and fulfilled what was fitting" (30:12–13)—that is, Jesus is crucified.

After several days, the Lord comes to James and his disciples as they walk on Mount Gaugelan (possibly Golgotha; although there is a Mount Gaugela in Syria). The Lord first explains that he was not really harmed by those who put him to death. The heart of the following exchange is the revelation to James of various formulas that will enable him to escape the hostile powers, including three heavenly "toll collectors" who stand between him and the Preexistent One.

The text becomes increasingly fragmentary as it draws to a conclusion. But the following matters may be identified. First, the secret tradition is entrusted to James to hand on to Addai who is later to write it down (36:13ff.). Further particulars, now obscure, about the line of tradition are also given, involving, it seems, a certain Levi and his two sons.

Second, James is puzzled by the many women who are the Lord's disciples (38.15ff.). The problem of womanhood occupies the background throughout. The question is abruptly raised near the beginning (24.26–27); the formulas handed on to James by the resurrected Lord include references to Sophia and Achamoth and the problem involved in the fact that the latter is "female from a female" (35.10–13); finally we learn that the female followers of the Lord are to be encouraged by James since "the perishable has [gone up] to the imperishable and the female element has attained to this male element" (41.15–18).

Third, James is the leader of the early Christian community. At one point he is presented as rebuking "the twelve" (42.21–22).

The last two pages (43–44) contain a much mutilated version of James's martyrdom. This event is probably regarded as the prelude to the fall of Jerusalem previously announced (36.16–19). The fate of Jerusalem and its inhabitants is apparently linked with the defeat of the cosmic powers that threaten James. For Jerusalem "is a dwelling place of a great number of archons" (25.18–19).

The *Apocalypse of James* is connected with Valentinian gnosticism, especially through the formulas revealed to James by the Lord after the resurrection. They are placed by Irenaeus (Schmidt, 1907, 1.21.5; cf. Epiphanius, *Panarion* 36.3) in the setting of the apolytrosis—a Valentinian rite of extreme unction. One of the formulas is also echoed in the *Corpus hermeticum* 13.3: "I am an alien, a son of the Father's race." The prominence of James and of other matters may owe something to Jewish Christianity (Böhlig, 1968). But reflections on James's martyrdom and the fall of Jerusalem were also important in Catholic Christianity (cf. Hegesippus, Origen, Eusebius), and nothing else in the apocalypse is unequivocably Jewish-Christian (Brown, 1972). The references to Addai and, possibly, Mount Gaugelan point to a Syrian milieu of a Semitic character (cf. Eusebius, *Historia ecclesiastica* 1.13) and perhaps thereby also to Jewish Christianity. The teaching about the seventy-two heavens is probably a fragment of esoteric Jewish doctrine (Schoedel, 1970; Séd, 1979).

BIBLIOGRAPHY

Böhlig, A. "Mysterion und Wahrheit: Gesammelte Beiträge zur spätantiken Religionsgeschichte." *Arbeiten zur Geschichte des späteren Judentums und des Urchristentums* 6 (1968):102–118.

Böhlig, A., and P. Labib. *Koptisch-gnostische Apokalypsen aus Codex V von Nag Hammadi im Koptischen Museum zu Alt-Kairo.* Special issue; *Wissenschaftliche Zeitschrift der Martin-Luther-Universität.* Halle-Wittenberg, 1963.

Brown, S. K. "James: A Religio-Historical Study of the *Relations* between Jewish, Gnostic and Catholic Christianity in the Early Period Through an Investigation of the Traditions about James the Lord's Brother." Ph.D. dissertation, Brown University, 1972.

Grese, W. C. "Corpus Hermeticum 13 and Early Christian Literature." *Studia ad Corpus Hellenisticum Novi Testamenti* 1979):85–86.

Kasser, R. "Textes gnostiques: Nouvelles remarques à propos des Apocalypses de Paul, Jacques et Adam." *Le Muséon* 78 (1965):299–306.

______. "Textes gnostiques: Remarques à propos des éditions récentes du livre secret de Jean et des Apocalypses de Paul, Jacques et Adam." *Le Muséon* 78 (1965):71–98.

Schenke, H.-M. "Koptisch-gnostische Apokalypsen." *Orientalische Literaturzeitung* 61 (1966):23–34.

Schmidt, Carl. "Irenäus und seine Quelle in Adv. Haer. I, 29." In *Philatesia. Paul Kleinert zum* LXX. *Geburtstag,* ed. Hermann Diels, Karl Holl, Paul Gennrich, and Emil Kautzsch. Berlin, 1907.

Schoedel, W. R. "The First Apocalypse of James." In *The Nag Hammadi Library,* ed. James M. Robinson. San Francisco, 1977.

______. "The (First) Apocalypse of James." In *Nag Hammadi Codices V, 2–5 and VI with Papyrus Berolinensis 8502, 1 and 4,* ed. D. M. Parrott. Nag Hammadi Studies 11. Leiden, 1979.

______. "Scripture and the Seventy-two Heavens of the First Apocalypse of James." *Novum Testamentum* 12 (1970):118–29.

Séd, N. "Les Douze hebdomades, le char de Sabaoth et les soixante-douze langues." *Novum Testamentum* 21 (1979):156–84.

Tröger, K.-W., ed. *Gnosis und Neues Testament,* pp. 44–45. Berlin, 1973.

WILLIAM R. SCHOEDEL

APOCALYPSE OF JAMES, SECOND. This apocalypse constitutes the fourth tractate in Codex V of the NAG HAMMADI LIBRARY. It is called the Second Apocalypse of James in order to distinguish it from its immediate predecessor in Codex V; both texts have the same ancient title, *The Apocalypse of James.*

The presence and order of the two apocalypses in Codex V may be attributed to deliberate scribal organization. Although the two documents stress different aspects of the James tradition, the recipient of the revelation is the same in both tractates: James, the brother of Jesus (24.12–13; 50.1–23). In the First Apocalypse, James is warned about his future sufferings (25.12–14; 30.13–15) at the hands of an angry mob (33.2–5), which James will stir to anger against himself (32.9–11). In its fragmentary conclusion, however, this document contains only scant reference to James's suffering in accordance with these predictions. The Second Apocalypse, on the other hand, gives a detailed report of the suffering and death of James at the hands of a mob angered by his discourses. In short, the Second Apocalypse of James fulfills the predictions of the First Apocalypse of James.

Although it is titled an "apocalypse," the second James text takes the form of a two-part report to Theuda, the father of James, by a priest who was apparently present at the ritual stoning of James. The first part of the report narrates the discourses of James that immediately preceded and apparently caused his stoning (46.1(?)–60.29(?). Interestingly, James's reports include two revelation discourses of the resurrected Jesus, which exhibit Gnostic tendencies (48.1(?)–49.30(?); 51.1(?)–57.11). The second part of the priest's report (61.15–62.12) describes the ritualistic stoning of James, which accorded exactly with the Jewish execution prescribed for "deceivers" (*Mishnah, Sanhedrin* 6.6). The document closes with the final prayer of the martyred James (62.12–63.29).

At least four major sections were written in a sufficiently stylized form that they have been described by Böhlig and Labib (1963) as consisting of "harmonic prose." Three of these segments are aretalogies (49.5–15; 58.2–20; 55.15–56.13) and the fourth forms the final prayer of James.

The document clearly falls within the Christian-Gnostic tradition. Yet the author shows remarkable restraint in treating the usual Gnostic themes and draws extensively from Jewish-Christian tradition, particularly in his description of James's martyrdom (Eusebius, *Historia ecclesiastica* 2.23).

Little is known about the date and provenance of the document. Like other texts from the Nag Hammadi Library, it was probably written originally in Greek and then translated into Coptic (Sahidic) sometime before the middle of the fourth century A.D. The lack of allusions to the developed Gnostic systems of the second century A.D. and the New Testament suggest an early date for the tractate, possibly sometime before A.D. 150.

BIBLIOGRAPHY

Böhlig, A., and P. Labib. *Koptisch-gnostische Apokalypsen aus Codex V von Nag Hammadi im Koptischen Museum zu Alt-Kairo.* Special issue, *Wissenschaftliche Zeitschrift der Martin-Luther Universität.* Halle-Wittenberg, 1963.

Brown, S. K. "Jewish and Gnostic Elements in the Second Apocalypse of James (CG V, 4)." *Novum Testamentum* 17 (1975):225–37.

Funk, W. P., ed. *Die Zweite Apokalypse des Jakobus aus Nag-Hammadi-Codex V.* Texte und Untersuchungen 119. Berlin, 1976.

Hedrick, C. W. "The (Second) Apocalypse of James." In *Nag Hammadi Codices V, 2–5, and VI with Papyrus Berolinensis 8502, 1 and 4,* ed. D. M. Parrott. Nag Hammadi Studies 11. Leiden, 1979.

Little, D. H. *The Death of James the Brother of Jesus.* Ph.D. dissertation, Rice University, 1971.

CHARLES W. HEDRICK

APOCALYPSE OF PAUL, part of Codex V of the NAG HAMMADI LIBRARY. This is the account of a heavenly journey made by the apostle, from the third sphere to the pleromatic circles of the Ogdoad, the Ennead, and the Decad. Paul begins his journey on the mountain of Jericho with the aim of reaching Jerusalem, that is, the heavenly Jerusalem, where the twelve apostles are gathered. On his way, Paul is accompanied by a small child, the Holy Spirit, who shows him the direction and suggests how he should conduct himself when confronted by the obstacles of the spheres. The aim of the journey is the acquisition of knowledge: "Let your mind awaken, Paul, and see that this mountain upon which you are standing is the mountain of Jericho so that you may know the hidden things in those that are visible."

In the course of this journey to heaven, which at times takes on the appearance of a descent to hell, Paul glimpses the organization of the heavenly hosts, angelic and demonic, the interlocking of the spheres with their doors and their keepers, and the punishment of a wicked soul. Arriving at the seventh heaven, Paul faces a demiurgic power who questions him before allowing him to pass on to the Ogdoad. When Paul reaches the eighth heaven, he joins the twelve apostles, his spiritual companions, and with them goes to the tenth and last heaven.

The framework of the heavenly journey, as it is briefly sketched by the author of the *Apocalypse of Paul,* is of a literary genre common to many Jewish writings (patriarchs' and prophets' journeys to heaven, including the *Ascension of Isaiah; 2, 3 Enoch, Apocalypse of Baruch, 4 Esdras, Apocalypse of Abraham, Testament of Abraham;* cf. Widengren, 1955; Schwartz, 1977). The Gnostics frequently took up this schema to illustrate a theme that was dear to them: the mounting of the soul to God by a dangerous ascent through the heavenly spheres (cf. the *Apocryphon of James,* the *Dialogue of the Savior,* the *First Apocalypse of James,* the *Paraphrase of Shem, Zostrianos, Marsanes, Allogenes,* the *Gospel of Mary,* all in the Nag Hammadi Library).

The elements supporting Paul's ascent in this *apocalypse* are common to all heavenly journeys: the passage from sphere to sphere, questionings by the appointed toll-collectors at the gates, passwords and signa that the soul must give in order to advance, and finally the presence of an escorting angel who helps the soul in her wanderings (for a discussion of this imagery, cf. Scholem, 1960).

The *Apocalypse of Paul* does not seem to be closely related to the apocryphal literature about Paul that flourished in the first centuries of the Christian era: the *Acts of Paul* (Hennecke and Schneemelcher, 1975) and *Visio Pauli.* There is only one fairly close parallel between the Nag Hammadi text and the *Visio Pauli:* the scene of the punishment of the hypocritical soul. This scene is worth a comment. The men acting as witnesses in the *Visio Pauli* become the demons who have urged the soul to sin in the *Apocalypse of Paul.* This psychologized interpretation by the author of the *Apocalypse of Paul* reflects the influence of the Jewish apocryphal speculations on the evil tendency dwelling in man's soul (cf. *Testament of Reuben* 11;2–3: the seven spirits are the cause of human sins). Here one can as well think of the case of demonic possession of the soul; the sentence "I saw you and desired you" is very expressive in this connection (cf. the case of the possession of Sarah by the demon Asmodeus in the *Book of Tobit*). We should note, too, that the punishment adjudged to the soul in the *Apocalypse of Paul* consists of casting her into a body prepared for her. Here we have the idea of metempsychosis, expressed also in the phrase: "the whole race of demons, the one that reveals bodies to a soul—seed." It is the demons, then, who are responsible for the new incarnation of the wicked soul. Furthermore, Tartarus, the infernal place of punishment, is situated not under the earth nor in the sublunar part of the heavens but on earth—an earth which the author does not hesitate to define as "land of the dead" or "world of the dead."

Another scene takes place in the seventh heaven, with Paul as protagonist, and is also worth noting. He meets an old man there, a demiurge, who asks Paul three questions before allowing him to proceed: "Where are you going, Paul? . . . Where are you from? . . . How will you be able to get away from me?" To these questions Paul gives the answers: "I am going to the place from which I came"; "I am going down to the world of the dead in order to lead captive the captivity that was led captive in the captivity of Babylon." Paul is presented here as the savior going down into the world of the dead to deliver them from the captivity of sin (Kroll, 1963; for *aichmalosia* [captivity], cf. Testament of Daniel 5, 8, 11, 13, where a Levitic Messiah will come and deliver from the captivity of Beliar the souls of the saints and will take them to rest in Eden and New Jerusalem; see also *Midrash of Melchizedek*, ed. Woude, 1965; *Apocryphon of Jeremiah*, ed. Kuhn, 1970). Paul does not answer the third question but he gives the old man a sign such that the keeper of the seventh heaven opens up to him the way to the Ogdoad. This question-and-answer section resembles closely the *First Apocalypse of James* from the Nag Hammadi Library. Through his answers, James, like Paul, escapes the vengeance of the toll-gatherers. So, to the toll-gatherer's question, "Where are you going?" one and the same answer is given by Paul and James, "I am going to the place from which I came." The kernel of all *gnosis* is condensed in this brief formula, which is not without echoes of that classic example in *Extract 78 from Theodotos* (and also Irenaeus 21.5).

BIBLIOGRAPHY

Cumont, F. *Lux Perpetua*, pp. 196ff. Paris, 1949.

Festugière, A. J. *La Révélation d'Hermès Trismégiste*, Vol. 1, p. 257, n. 2. Paris, 1944.

Hennecke, Edgar. *New Testament Apocrypha*, Vol. 2, ed. W. Schneemelcher. London, 1963. English trans. R. McL. Wilson, pp. 322–89. Great Britain, 1975.

Kroll, J. *Gott und Hölle, Der Mythos von Descensuskämpfe*, repr. Darmstadt, 1963.

Kuhn, K. H. "A Coptic Jeremiah Apocryphon." *Le Muséon* 83 (1970):291–350.

Murdock, W. R., and G. W. MacRae. "The Apocalypse of Paul," pp. 47–63. In *Nag Hammadi Codices V, 2–5 and VI*, ed. D. M. Parrott. Nag Hammadi Studies 1. Leiden, 1979.

Scholem, G. *Les Grands courants de la mystique juive*, chap. 2. Paris, 1968.

Schwartz, J. "Le Voyage au ciel dans la littérature apocalyptique." In *L'Apocalyptique, Etudes d'histoire des religions*, ed. M. Philonenko-M. Simon. Paris, 1977.

Widengren, G. *Muhammad, the Apostle of God and His Ascension.* Uppsala, 1955.

Woude, A. S. van der. "Melchisedek als himmlische Erlösergestalt in den neugefundenen eschatologischen Midraschim aus Q-Höhle 11." *Oudtestamentische Studiën* 14 (1965):354–73.

MADELINE SCOPELLO

APOCALYPSE OF PETER, the third text of Codex VII and consisting of a report of three visions seen by the apostle Peter, along with instructions from Jesus, during the night prior to the Crucifixion. In a passage that recalls Matthew 26:34, Jesus tells Peter, "He [You?] will accuse you [him] three times during the night" (72.2–4). On the whole, the text seems to represent an attempt to accentuate the interchange between Peter and Jesus on this memorable evening, a feature known from the canonical Gospels (Mt. 26:33–35, 37–38, 40–41, and parallels; Jn. 13:6–9, 36–38; 18:10–11).

Briefly, the setting is the temple at Jerusalem (70.15), although the description is unfamiliar, tempting one to postulate a scene in an otherworldly temple (70.14–20). But nothing else in the text points to such an idea. The instruction to Peter opens with the Savior's Gnostic discourse both on those "who come from life" and on the heavenly Son of Man (70.20–71.15). Next, Jesus addresses the nature of Peter's leadership of the elect that will oppose "the imitation of righteousness" (71.15–25), with Peter coming to know the Son of Man through a ritual act (71.25–72.4). The third section, which concerns spiritual blindness, opens with a vision of the approaching persecutors, who are obviously blind to the true nature of Jesus; Peter, by contrast, sees the "new light" descend on Jesus, illustrating the difference between the Gnostic disciple and all others with inferior spiritual capabilities (72.4–73.14). The fourth segment is made up of the Savior's instructions about the coming apostasy from "our word" and the variety of ways in which deceptive leadership will appear in coming generations (73.14–79.31). In the fifth portion, Jesus responds to Peter's worry about the "little ones" being deceived, assuring him that the apostasy is to be brought to an end by a renewal of "the agelessness of immortal thought" and the deception being uprooted (79.31–80.23). The key sixth section is made up principally of the vision of the Savior's escape from crucifixion, introduced by promises to Peter of protection by the "Invisible One." Peter then sees the grand vision in which the heavenly "Living Savior" not only escapes those who would nail him to the cross but also laughs at such an attempt, while a substitute is crucified in his place (80.23–83.15). The text ends with Jesus instructing Peter to teach others the "mystery" that he has witnessed (83.15–84.13).

While this text exhibits nothing of the myth of the fall of Sophia, its Gnostic character is undeniable. First, the esoteric teaching of the Savior is passed on only to one disciple, Peter, a trait shared by the Nag Hammadi tractates. Further, Peter is charged with a strict guardianship of this knowledge (73.14–18), transmitting it solely to "those of another race," the worthy initiates (83.15–19). In addition, those who are linked to the feared "deception" are of an unchanging nature, so that they cannot receive salvation (80.21–23). Moreover, when those from above mingle with those of the world, the former are made captive, a situation from which they can escape only by possessing the saving *gnosis* (73.21–74.3). In fact, the "immortal ones" from above alone are receptacles of glory (83.19–26).

Without doubt, the docetic view of Jesus' escape from suffering is clearer here than in any text in the library. It is the narration of Peter's final vision that clinches the case: "And I said: 'Who is it that I am seeing, O Lord, since you yourself are taken and it is [also] you restraining me? Or who is this happy one above the tree [cross] who is laughing while another is being struck on his feet and on his hands?' The Savior said to me: 'The one whom you see above the tree, who is glad and is laughing, is the living Jesus. But that one, into whose hands and feet they are driving the nails, in his fleshly counterpart, the substitute . . . But look at him and Me'" (81.6–24). One further feature is worth mentioning. The garment that Peter wears throughout serves as a vehicle for revelation (72.13–28), perhaps recalling the revelatory character of the ephod worn by the Israelite high priest.

The date and place of composition of the Apocalypse of Peter are impossible to fix, since it makes no clear historical allusions to contemporary events. P. Perkins (1975) and A. Werner (1974) have demonstrated that there are allusions to Matthew's Gospel and other New Testament traditions about Peter. One is left to conclude that the earlier Greek version of this text reached its current shape by the beginning of the second century.

BIBLIOGRAPHY

Brashler, J. A. "The Apocalypse of Peter." Ph.D. diss. Claremont (Calif.) School of Theology, 1977.

Brown, S. K., and C. W. Griggs. "The Apocalypse of Peter: Introduction and Translation." *Brigham Young University Studies* 15 (1974–1975):131–45.

Krause, M., and V. Girgis. "Die Petrusapokalypse." In *Christentum am Roten Meer,* ed. F. Altheim and R. Stiehl, pp. 152–79. Berlin and New York, 1971.

Perkins, P. "Peter in Gnostic Revelation." *Society of Biblical Literature 1974 Seminar Papers,* Vol. 2, ed. G. W. MacRae, pp. 1–13. Los Angeles, 1975.

Schenke, H.-M. "Bemerkungen zur Apokalypse des Petrus." *Essays on the Nag Hammadi Texts: Nag Hammadi Studies VI,* ed. M. Krause, pp. 277–85. Leiden, 1975.

Werner, A. "Die Apokalypse des Petrus: Die dritte Schrift aus Nag-Hammadi-Codex VIII." *Theologische Literaturzeitung* 99 (1974):575–84.

S. Kent Brown
C. Wilfred Griggs

APOCRYPHAL LITERATURE. Properly speaking, this consists of the so-called Old Testament pseudepigrapha. The Old Testament books called "apocryphal" by Protestants and "deuterocanonical" by Roman Catholics were until recently included in the biblical canon of the Coptic church. Only at the beginning of the twentieth century and by order of CYRIL V (1874–1927) were the following books removed from the canon: Tobit, Judith, the complement of Esther, the Wisdom of Solomon, Ecclesiasticus, the Epistle of Jeremiah, Baruch, the complement of Daniel (Susanna and the Three Youths in the Fire) and 1, 2, and 3 Maccabees. These books are normally included in the Coptic versions of the Bible.

The term *apokriphon* or the more usual *apografon* had already acquired a pejorative meaning in the 39th *Festal Letter* of Saint ATHANASIUS, in which the Old Testament apocrypha of Enoch, Isaiah, and Moses are condemned as heretical. Originally, the Greek word meant simply hidden or secret (cf. 4 Esd. 16:45–48). The condemnation of the apocrypha, caused no doubt by the extensive use made of them, put a stop to their diffusion in orthodox circles, particularly in the Coptic church. In spite of this, a surprising number of Coptic apocryphal manuscripts have come down to us. They share the following general characteristics: their dates of composition are late as compared to Greek and Aramaic texts, for the most part being translations from Greek; to a greater or lesser degree they show the effects of Christian reworking; they are normally works originating in, or strongly influenced by, Egyptian Judaism; and they frequently take up motifs and expressions from the ancient Egyptian religion.

In several ways the Coptic tradition adds significantly to our knowledge of the Old Testament apocrypha in general. At times it is the only, or the oldest, witness to apocryphal works quoted in early times; or because it is independent of the known Greek or other traditions, it helps to explain the history of the tradition of certain books. In general, it adds elements from particular traditions that enrich those already known from other literatures. In order to emphasize these aspects, the Coptic Old Testament apocrypha are here considered together with the other Old Testament apocrypha, grouped according to their genre.

Literature of Enoch

Enoch, father of Methuselah, "walked with God, and he was not, for God took him" (Gn. 5:24). He was taken up into heaven and there received the revelation of the divine mysteries concerning the people of Israel and the end of the world, thus becoming the most important representative of the apocalyptical revelations. His age, 365 years, gave rise to astronomical and chronological speculations. Thus, from the third century B.C. there appear apocalyptic and astronomical traditions and writings attributed to this patriarch. The book called 1 Enoch or the Ethiopic Enoch gathers these traditions, some of which were composed originally in Aramaic, as is shown by the fragments of eleven Aramaic manuscripts identified among the Dead Sea Scrolls (Milik, 1976). The collection was translated into Greek and from Greek into Ethiopic toward the year 500, in which version alone the entire collection is preserved (Charles, 1906). It can be divided into five sections, which differ in contents and proceed from different periods:

1. The Book of Watchers (1–36) relates the fall of the angels and the corruption of mankind (Gn. 6:5–6) and describes the journeys of Enoch to hell and to paradise. It is a product of the period before 175 B.C.
2. The Parables of Enoch (37–71) that announce the coming of the great judgment are in three parts called parables or similitudes. This section is not found in the Qumran fragments, and there is some discussion as to whether the date of composition is pre-Christian.
3. The Astronomical Book (72–82) promulgates the ancient priestly calendar of 364 days and is prior to 175 B.C.
4. The Book of Dreams (83–90) contains a vision of the flood and another vision of the history of the world until the Maccabean period, during which this section was composed.
5. The Epistle of Enoch (91–108) contains an exhortation to faith, steadfastness, and joy and the Apocalypse of the Weeks, in which the history of the world is described in ten periods, from the creation to the end of the world.

The Greek version of 1 Enoch was known in Egypt, as is shown by the fragments cited by M. Black (1970). But there was also a Sahidic Coptic version of at least the last section of the book, as can be seen from a fragment found in 1937 in ANTINOOPOLIS (Istituto Papirologico "G. Vitelli," Florence, Coptica Antinoë, 9), dating from the sixth or seventh century, and containing 1 Enoch 93:3–8 (Donadoni, 1960). A comparison of this Coptic text with the Aramaic texts on the subject shows that it is a very faithful version, the readings of which are to be preferred to those of the Ethiopic version, with which it differs in places. The Coptic version is of help in reconstructing the Greek version (cf. Milik, 1976, pp. 81–82). The few surviving Coptic manuscripts suggest that although 1 Enoch was known in the Coptic church, it was not widely available. No Coptic manuscript has been discovered of 2 Enoch, or Slavonic Enoch, or Book of the Secrets of Enoch, seemingly composed in Greek in the ninth or tenth century, but transmitted only in sixteenth- or seventeenth-century Slav manuscripts. Nor are there Coptic manuscripts of 3 Enoch, or Hebrew Enoch, a mystical apocalypse from the medieval period in the opinion of G. G. Scholem. However, H. Odeberg (1973) considers it to date from the second or third century A.D. and suggests that the traditions concerning Enoch-Metraton circulated in Egypt, and were taken over by some Gnostic groups there. This would parallel with the books of Jehu (c. Schmidt, 1892).

In Christian circles in Egypt the figure of Enoch was important, and they gathered many Jewish traditions (see *the Pierpont Morgan Fragments of a Coptic Enoch Apocryphon,* Coptic Theological Texts 3, fols. 1–9, found in Hou, ed. W. E. Crum, 1913; A. Pierson in Nickelsburg, ed., 1976; Latin trans. Garitte in Milik, 1976, pp. 100–103). These fragments are extremely deteriorated and consist of very poor quality papyrus in a codex of several quires. The order of the folios is a matter of debate. In Pearson's arrangement, the text relates in the first place how the Lord received Enoch into heaven where he saw "the mysteries that are hidden in the aeons of the Light." We next find Enoch in a mountain, where an angel of God (possibly Michael) appears to him and instructs him in the mysteries of the Holy Trinity and the task that he, Enoch, will have in the judgment. Then Enoch's sister, a prophetess (perhaps Sibylla), appears and informs him that he will be taken up into heaven in the same way as Elijah and Tabitha. Finally the judgment is described. The special character of this Enoch apocryphon is based upon the older Jewish apocryphal literature. The ascension and exaltation of Enoch is similar to that shown in the Parables of Enoch and 3 Enoch. His task in the judgment is to act as scribe of the sins and good deeds of the just, which are then weighed in the balance, and this connects with the Testament of Abraham and other apocryphal works. It might well have been composed in Egypt in the fifth century A.D. There are also the Sahidic fragments found at Aswan in 1909 containing meager remnants of an apocryphon apparently devoted to Enoch (Cairo Museum, n. 48085, ed. Munier, 1923, pp. 212–15, n. 3.; Latin trans. Garitte in Milik, 1976, pp. 103–104). In these fragments the role of Enoch as scribe of righteousness is emphasized in a way that is parallel to, though independent of, the Pierpont Morgan fragments. These characteristics of the figure of Enoch appear in other Coptic works, including those of a liturgical nature (cf. C. D. G. Müller, 1962, p. 73; E. A. W. Budge, pp. 345–46, 909; I. Ballestri and H. Hyvernat, Vol. 43, p. 236).

Testaments of the Patriarchs

In Judaism the "testament" is a well-known literary genre: in a speech uttered before his death a famous person transfers his spiritual or material legacy to his children or his followers. Examples of this genre can be found in the Old Testament (Dt. 33; Gn. 49) and in the New Testament (Jn. 13–17). The apocryphal literature developed this genre, producing many works that received the name of testaments. The most representative of these is the Testament of the Twelve Patriarchs, relating the testament of each of the twelve sons of Jacob. Each testament contains a prediction about the future of the tribe or of Israel and illustrates a particular virtue or vice, exhorting emulation of the virtuous conduct of the patriarch. The present form of the collection of Testament 12 has been transmitted in Greek, and is clearly Christian. There is still debate about whether it is a second-century B.C. work written in Hebrew and translated into Greek and interpolated by Christian authors, or whether it is a second-century A.D. work written in Greek by a Christian using existing Jewish material. Among the scrolls of Qumran have been found fragments of various testaments in Aramaic—Levi, Kohat, Amran—and of one in Hebrew—Naphtali, the text of which differs from that of Testament 12 (cf. Milik, 1959).

There is also a work called the Testament of Moses (sometimes called the Assumption of Moses) preserved only in a Latin manuscript. Following Deuteronomy 31–34, it describes the predictions made by Moses concerning the history of Israel; it is considered to date from the time of Antiochus Epiphanes, but to have been reworked in the first decades of the Christian era. Everything seems to show that in primitive or even medieval Judaism, there were many individual testaments that were joined together in Christian or perhaps Jewish circles to form collections used for homiletic purposes.

There are no known Coptic versions of the above-mentioned testaments. However, other testaments of the patriarchs do exist in Coptic. A manuscript of the Monastery of Saint Macarius (DAYR ANBĀ MAQĀR) dating from 962 in the Vatican Library contains the Testament of Abraham, Isaac, and Jacob in Bohairic, as well as writings attributed to Athanasius (manuscript no. 61, fols. 163v–98v; ed. Guidi, 1900, pp. 157–80 and 223–64; German trans. Andersson, in *Sphinx* 6, 1903, pp. 220–36, and 7, 1903, pp. 77–94 and 129–42; French trans. M. Chaine, in M. Delcor, 1973, pp. 186–213; English trans. of Testament of Isaac and Testament of Jacob, S. Gaselle, in Box, 1927, pp. 55–89; trans. of Testament of Abraham, G. Macrae, 1972, pp. 327–40). The Vatican manuscript is a fine example of how a collection of testaments attributed to the three patriarchs was formed in Christian circles; this collection is referred to in *Constitutiones Apostolicae* and Priscilianus. The three testaments narrate the death of each of the patriarchs, mixing discourses, narratives, and visions. They begin with the sending of the archangel Michael to announce their deaths. But before the divine plan is fulfilled there is a series of episodes that give a dramatic air to the narratives. They are a mixture of Haggadic legend, moral exhortation, and apocalypse.

Two of the testaments are based on the *Testament of Abraham*, substantial fragments of which have also been preserved from the fifth century in the Sahidic dialect (Institut für Altertumskunde, Cologne University, Inv. N. 3221) and in more than twenty Greek manuscripts, the oldest of which dates from the thirteenth century and contains two different recensions of the work: a long recension (A) and a short one (B). Which of the two Greek recensions is the earlier has not been determined. The Coptic version, together with the Arabic and Ethiopic versions, represents an intermediate recension closer to B. In the Coptic text, Abraham asks Michael to be allowed to visit heaven before he dies. There he observes the judgment of a soul after death. This soul is accused of his own sinful deeds, which are written in a book read by Enoch, the scribe of righteousness. Later comes Abraham's dialogue with death prior to his leaving this world. The hospitality and mercy of Abraham are emphasized, and in contrast to the Greek recensions, the judge is God and not Abel. In the opinion of M. Delcor, the Testament of Abraham was composed in Egypt by a Hellenist Jew in the first century before or after Christ. Yet, F. Schmidt (1986) considers it to be a document produced in Palestine in the first century A.D. in popular Essene circles (recension B) and later (first half of the second century) revised in Jewish circles in Egypt. Both are mere hypotheses.

The Testament of Isaac has also been preserved in Sahidic in a manuscript dated 894 (Pierpont Morgan Library, M577, fols. 12v–15v, ed. Kuhn, 1957, pp. 225–39, trans. Kuhn, 1967, pp. 325–36). It coincides with the Bohairic text, although they appear to be independent translations from the Greek. The Arabic and Ethiopic versions are known, but not the Greek text. The Testament of Isaac is more clearly paraenetic (exhortatory) in character than the Testament of Abraham, on which it depends. Isaac instructs the multitude gathered around him on the fulfillment of the law and on their duties as regards prayer. He is then taken up into heaven, where he observes how the condemned are punished and the just rewarded. A dialogue with Abraham serves to bring to mind the divine favors afforded to those who honor the memory of Isaac. The Testament of Isaac, with its allusions to the Trinity and its Christological expressions, would appear to be a Christian document. But Essene influences can be observed in references to fasting, ritual baths, the holiness of priests, and the river of fire. Thus it is difficult to be exact in details of the history of its redaction.

The Testament of Jacob is known only in Bohairic and in later Arabic and Ethiopic versions. It follows closely the biblical narrative of the patriarch but also includes a visit to heaven and to hell. In the description there is a clear reference to I Corinthians 2:9.

The Testament of Job appears in Coptic in a fifth-century Sahidic manuscript, the fragments of which also include the Testament of Abraham (Cologne University, Inv. N. 3221; transcription and translation of some fragments by Philonenko, 1968). The Greek text shows no direct dependence on any of the three known Greek manuscripts of this apocryphal work. The oldest of these versions is from the eleventh century (ed. S. P. Brox, in Picard, ed., 1967). Characteristic of this testament is the abundance of hymns and poetic material. The patience and mercy of the patriarch are emphasized. The work has a clearly Jewish character, although it may be the work of a Jewish Christian. The Coptic text is of great help in the understanding of the rhythm of the hymns, which is somewhat confused in the Greek version.

Reference to a Testament of Joshua can be found in a Coptic work on biblical characters, contained in a fragmentary manuscript (ed. Winstedt, 1907–1908, pp. 372–87, and 1908–1909, pp. 389–412). This testament is an important authority for the story of the destruction of his father's gods by Abraham. However, the testament could be referring to Joshua 24, and not to any other particular source. The fragments edited by Winstedt contain abundant elements from the apocryphal tradition concerning characters of the Old and New Testaments.

Apocalypses

Although the apocalyptic genre is present in many apocryphal works, some of them are expressly given the title apocalypse. They contain the revelation of the mystery of God's plans concerning the end of the world. The most widely known work is the book of Daniel. But there is an abundance of contemporary and later works, such as the Book of Jubilees, also known as Apocalypse of Moses and Leptogenesis, which narrate God's revelation to Moses on Mount Sinai in a manner similar to Genesis and Exodus 1–16; the story is presented in periods of forty-nine years, or jubilees. Written in Hebrew toward the end of the second century B.C., as shown by fragments found in Qumran, the only complete version is the Ethiopic (ed. Dillmann, 1859; trans. Charles, 1902). The name Apocalypse of Moses is also given to a work transmitted in Greek. This deals with the Life of Adam and Eve and is a midrashic work narrating Genesis 1–4, dated to the first century A.D. (ed. Tischendorf, 1866, pp. 1–23). There are some small fragments in Coptic Bohairic on the same subject from the Monastery of Saint Macarius (ed. Evelyn-White, 1926, p. 31).

The book of 4 Ezra or Apocalypse of Ezra gathers various materials, among which are the visions of Ezra in Babylon concerning the fate of the people of Israel abandoned in the hands of the gentiles and of the judgment and resurrection of the dead. This work was compiled toward the end of the first century A.D. and has been transmitted in Latin, Syriac, Ethiopic, Arabic, and Coptic versions. The Latin version is the most important, and it is included, together with other texts attributed to Ezra, as an appendix to the Latin Vulgate under the name of 3 Ezra. Chapters 3–14 belong to 4 Ezra. A small fragment of the Coptic version containing 4 Ezra 13:29–46 has been preserved (ed. and trans. Leipoldt and Violet, 1904, pp. 138–40). This fragment is a noteworthy aid in the reconstruction of the lost Greek text, which is the basis for all the versions. The Syriac Apocalypse of Baruch and the Greek Apocalypse of Ezra, the Coptic versions of which are unknown, show a literary dependence on 4 Ezra.

The Apocalypse of Elijah is extant only in Coptic, and although it deals with similar subjects, is distinct from the Book of Elijah (Sefer Eliyyahu) and other medieval Hebrew works. The apocryphal book of Elias quoted by Origen and others as the source of 1 Corinthians 2:9 does not correspond to any of the pseudepigraphic books of Elias known to us. The Coptic Apocalypse of Elijah has been preserved in four manuscripts dating from the fourth and fifth centuries. One of these is an Akhmimic text, which has been almost completely reconstructed from fragments at present in Paris and Berlin (ed. Steindorff, 1899, pp. 19–44); three texts are in Sahidic, one of them represented by six folios (ed. Steindorff, 1899, pp. Sahidic 3–14), another by a fragment in the British Library (Or. 7594, ed. Budge, 1912), and the third contains the complete text (Chester-Beatty Papyrus no. 1493; ed. Pietersma, Comstock, and Attridge, 1981). A small Greek fragment has also been discovered (ed. Pistelli, 1912, p. 16, n. 7; translations: German, Steindorff, 1899; Riessler, 1928, pp. 114–25; W. Schrage, 1980, pp. 192–288; English: Hougton 1959, pp. 43–67 and 176–210, with a transcription of the Coptic text; Pietersma, Comstock, and Attridge, 1980; French: Rosenstiehl, 1972). The Coptic Apocalypse of Elijah begins with a section dedicated above all to fasting and prayer, continues with the narration of wars and calamities in Egypt, and ends with the appearance of the Antichrist, who is opposed by the virgin Tabitha, Elias, Enoch, and the sixty just men. In a final battle Elias and Enoch slay the Antichrist and Christ appears. Because of the references to the Egyptian wars, it is considered to be a third century A.D. work written by a Jew, who drew on existing apocalyptic traditions and on Jewish messianic ideas from the first century B.C. to the first century A.D. The present version shows traces of Christian rewriting. The hypothesis put forward by Rosenstiehl concerning a prototype related to Essene circles has not been proved.

One sheet of the manuscript from which Steindorff (1899, pp. Sahidic 1–2) identified the Coptic Apocalypse of Elijah belongs to an Apocalypse of Zephaniah, and nine sheets of the Akhmimic manuscript containing the Coptic Apocalypse of Elijah belong to an Anonymous Apocalypse (Steindorff, 1899, pp. Akhmimic 1–18). Both apocalypses are so similar that they could well be two recensions, Sahidic and Akhmimic, of the same work. The fragment of the Apocalypse of Zephaniah can be completed from the reference to a work with the same name by Clement of Alexandria (*Stromata* V.IX.77.2) and from a Sahidic fragment of another manuscript (ed. Lefort, 1938, pp. 31–32). An interesting characteristic of the Apocalypse of Zephaniah is the description of the judgment in terms similar to those employed in the Testament of Abraham, the weighing of good and bad deeds on a scale. It is considered to be Egyptian-Jewish in origin together with the Apocalypse of Elias, with which it forms a collection.

The 14th Vision of Daniel or Apocryphal Apocalypse of Daniel is medieval in origin. It has been preserved in Coptic and other versions and contains references to the Fatimid Arabs and the Crusades (ed. Woide, 1799, trans. Macler, 1896, pp.

163–69). Very different in character are some Gnostic works from Nag Hammadi. Although contrary to the Jewish religion, they can be considered as Old Testament apocrypha. The APOCALYPSE OF ADAM, for example, supposes familiarity with Jewish apocalyptic testaments and judgment scenes, and history is presented in periods, as is true also of the PARAPHRASE OF SHEM, which is also independent of Christian traditions.

Lives of the Prophets

This is a genre that originated in Judaism and was developed among Christians. The most famous work is the Ascension of Isaiah. This includes a Jewish nucleus called the Martyrdom of Isaiah, in which the death of the prophet under King Manasses is related. A complete Ethiopic version and fragmentary Greek, Latin, and Slav versions of the Ascension of Isaiah have been preserved (ed. Charles, 1900). The substance of this material is a legend referred to in Hebrews 11:37 and is similar in character to the Teacher of Righteousness of the Qumran scrolls. As a consequence, it has been dated from the first century B.C. to the first century A.D. Parts of two manuscripts are known in Coptic. One is in Sahidic consisting of two fragments in the University of Louvain collection, which were lost in a fire in 1941 (ed. Lefort, 1938). These fragments contained the Ascension of Isaiah 3:3–6, 9–12, and 11:24–32, 35–40. The other is in Akhmimic and is made up of four fragments belonging to M. Scherling of Leiden (ed. Lefort, 1939) and others now lost (copied and ed. Lacau, 1946). In a fragmentary form they cover practically the whole of the text, which, curiously, was copied on a papyrus scroll. The Ascension of Isaiah was widely known among fourth-century Copts.

Clearly Jewish in character is the Paralipomena Jeremiou, also known as Rest of the Words of Baruch, written during the second Jewish revolt. It narrates the last deeds of Jeremiah who, according to the apocrypha, accompanies the captives to Babylon, and on their return restores the cult. It has been transmitted in Greek (ed. Harris, 1889; Kraft, 1972) and in Armenian and Ethiopic versions. Dependent on this work, at least so far as the traditions it draws on are concerned, is a Coptic work, the Coptic Apocrypha of Jeremiah in the Captivity of Babylon, also transmitted in an Arabic version. Evidence for the Coptic version is a codex in the Pierpont Morgan Library (M 578, fols. 97v–130v), fragments in Paris and Vienna that belong to the same manuscript dating from the ninth century, and an eighth-century Fayyumic fragment in the British Library (all ed. Kuhn, 1970). Although there are clear traces of Christian reworking, this apocryphon is basically Jewish and has important parallels in rabbinic literature.

Didactic and Poetic Literature

Only a few fragments of 4 Maccabees are in Coptic, and these are still being reconstructed (cf. Luchessi, 1981). It would appear to be a good version made from the Greek. This work, erroneously attributed to Josephus, is a philosophical discourse on the preeminence of religious reason over human passions and suffering. In the first century B.C., the Palestinian Jews continued to compose psalms. A collection in Greek of eighteen such psalms attributed to Solomon has come down to us. It is of particular interest, as it shows Jewish messianic ideas in that period. This is the collection known as the Psalms of Solomon (ed. Gebhart, 1895). No Coptic version of them is known. There is, however, a fine penitential psalm in fifteen verses, the Prayer of Manasses, transmitted in Greek in some manuscripts of the Septuagint. In many manuscripts it appears as an appendix to the psalms, together with other canticles taken from the Bible. It is considered to be the work of a first- or second-century A.D. Jew and is written in Greek. The Coptic Bohairic version is preserved in many codices of the psalms. The Sahidic version is preserved only in a manuscript in Vienna (K 8706; ed. Till and Sanz, 1939, pp. 90–97).

BIBLIOGRAPHY

General

Balestri, I., and H. Hyvernat. *Acta Martyrum,* 2 vols. CSCO 43, 44. Paris, 1908.

Budge, E. A. W. *Miscellaneous Coptic Texts in the Dialect of Upper Egypt.* London, 1915.

Charles, R. H. *The Apocrypha and Pseudepigrapha of the Old Testament,* 2 vols. Oxford, 1912.

Charlesworth, H., ed. *The Pseudepigrapha and Modern Research.* Missoula, Mont., 1976.

Denis, A.-M. *Introduction aux pseudépigraphes grecs d'Ancien Testament.* Studia in veteris testamenti pseudepigrapha 1. Leiden, 1970.

Diez Macho, A. *Apocrifos del Antiquo Testamento,* 5 vols. Madrid, 1982–1987.

Dillmann, A., ed., and R. Charles, trans. *The Book of Jubilees of the Little Genesis.* London, 1902.

Kraft, R. A., ed. *The Methodology of Textual Criticism in Jewish Greek Scriptures with Special Attention to the Problems in Samuel-Kings.* Society of Biblical Literature. Texts and Translations 1. Pseudipigrapha Series 1. Missoula, Mont., 1972.

Maser, M. *Bibliographie zur jüdisch-hellenistischen und intertestamentarischen Literatur: 1900–1970. Texte und Untersuchungen zur Geschichte der altchristlichen Literatur* 106/2. Berlin, 1975.

Milik, J. T. *Ten Years of Discovery in the Wilderness of Judea.* Studies in Biblical Theology 26. London, 1959.

Müller, C. D. G. *Die Bücher der Einsetzung der Erzengel Michael und Gabriel.* CSCO 225, *Scriptores Coptici* 31. Louvain, 1962.

Nickelsburg, G. W. E. *Jewish Literature Between the Bible and the Misnah.* London, 1981.

Scholem, G. *Jewish Gnosticism, Merkabah, Mysticism and Talmudic Tradition,* 2nd ed. New York, 1965.

Tischendorf, C., ed. *Apocalypses apocryphae.* Leipzig, 1866.

General Coptic

Grossouw, W. "De apocriefen van het Oude en Nieuwe Testament in de Koptische letterkunde." *Studia Catholica* 10 (1934):334–36; 11 (1934–1935):19–36.

Hallock, F. H. "Coptic Apocrypha." *Journal of Biblical Literature* 52 (1933):163–64.

Orlandi, T. "Gli Apocrifi copti." *Augustinianum* 23 (1983):57–71.

Schmidt, C. *Gnostische Schriften in Koptischer Sprache aus dem Codex Brucianus, herausgegben, übersetzt und bearbeitet.* Texte und Untersuchungen zur Geschichte der altchristlichen Literatur 8. Leipzig, 1892.

Winstedt, E. O. "Some Coptic Apocryphal Legends." *Journal of Theological Studies* 9 (1907–1908):372–87; 10 (1908–1909):389–412.

Books of Enoch

Black, M. *Apocalypsis Henochii Graece.* Pseudepigrapha veteris testamenti Graeca 3. Leiden, 1970.

Charles, R. H. *The Ethiopic Version of Enoch.* Oxford, 1906.

Crum, W. E. "Theological Texts from Coptic Papyri." *Anecdota Oxoniensia. Semitic Series* 12 (1913):3–11.

Donadoni, S. "Un frammento della versione copta del 'Libro de Enoch.'" *Acta Orientalia* 25 (1960):197–202.

Lawlor, H. J. "The Book of Enoch in the Egyptian Church." *Hermatema* 13 (1904–1905):178–83.

Milik, J. T. *The Books of Enoch, Aramaic Fragments of Qumran Cave 4.* Oxford, 1976.

Munier, H. "Mélanges de littérature copte III. Manuscrits coptes saʿidiques d'Assouan." *Annales du Service des Antiquités de l'Egypt* 23 (1923):210–88.

Odeberg, H., ed. *3 Enoch or the Hebrew Book of Enoch.* Cambridge, 1928. Repr. New York, 1973.

Pearson, B. A. "The Pierpont Morgan Fragments of a Coptic Enoch Apocryphon." In *Studies on the Testament of Abraham,* ed. George W. E. Nickelsburg, Jr. Missoula, Mont., 1976.

The Testaments

Andersson, E. "Abraham's Vermächtnis aus dem Koptischen übersetzt." *Sphinx* 6 (1903):220–36.

______. "Isak's Vermächtnis aus dem Koptischen übersetzt." *Sphinx* 7 (1903):77–94.

______. "Jakob's Vermächtnis aus dem Koptischen übersetzt." *Sphinx* 7 (1903):129–42.

Box, G. H. *The Testament of Abraham.* London, 1927. With an appendix containing a translation from the Coptic version of the *Testaments of Isaac* and *Jacob* by S. Gaselee.

Brox, S. P. "Testamentum Iabi," In *Apocrypha Baruchi Graeca,* ed. J. C. Picard. Leiden, 1967.

Delcor, M. *Le Testament d'Abraham.* Studia in veteris testamenti pseudepigrapha 2. Leiden, 1973.

Guidi, I. "Il Testo copto del Testamento di Abramo." *Rendiconti dell'Academia dei Lincei,* ser. 5, no. 9 (1900):157–80.

______. "Il Testamento de Isacco e il Testamento di Giacobbe." *Rendiconti dell'Accademia dei Lincei,* ser. 5, no. 9 (1900):223–64.

Hofius, O. "Das Zitat 1 Kor. 2.9 und das koptische Testament des Jakob." *Zeitschrift für die neutestamentliche Wissenschaft* 66 (1975):140–42.

Kuhn, K. H. "The Sahidic Version of the Testament of Isaac." *Journal of Theological Studies* 8 (1957):225–39.

______. "An English Translation of the Sahidic Version of the Testament of Isaac." *Journal of Theological Studies* 18 (1967):325–36.

MacRae, G. "The Coptic Testament of Abraham." In *Studies on the Testament of Abraham,* ed. G. W. E. Nickelsburg, Jr. Missoula, Mont., 1972.

Nagel, P. "Zur sahidischen version des Testament Isaaks." *Wissenschaftliche Zeitschrift der Martin Luther Universität Halle Wittenberg* 12, 3–14 (1963):259–63.

Nickelsburg, G. W. E., ed. *Studies on the Testament of Abraham.*

Nordheim, E. von. "Das Zitat von Paulus in 1 Kor. 2.9 und seine Beziehung zum koptischen Testament Jakobs." *Zeitschrift für die neutestamentliche Wissenschaft* 65 (1974):112–20.

Philonenko, M. "Le Testament de Job." *Semitica* 18 (1968):61–63.

Schmidt, F. *Le Testament grec d'Abraham*. Tübingen, 1986.

Woide, C. G. *Appendix ad editionem Novi Testamenti graeca*. Oxford, 1799.

Apocalypse of Elijah

Bouriant, U. "Les Papyrus d'Akhmim, fragments des manuscrits en dialecte achmourique et thébain." *Mémoires de la Mission archéologique française au Caire* 1 (1889):260–79.

Bousset, W. "Beiträge zur Geschichte der Eschatologie: Die Apokalypse des Elias." *Zeitschrift für Kirchengeschichte* 20 (1900):103–112; 275–78.

Budge, E. A. T. W. *Coptic Biblical Texts in the Dialect of Upper Egypt*, pp. 270–71. London, 1912.

Houghton, H. P. "The Coptic Apocalypse." *Aegyptus* 39 (1959):34–67; 176–210.

McNeil, B. "Coptic Evidence of Jewish Messianic Beliefs (Apocalypse of Elijah 2:5–6)." *Rivista degli Studi Orientali* 51 (1977):39–45.

Nützel, J. M. "Zum Schicksal des escatologischen Propheten." *Biblische Zeitschrift* 20 (1976):59–94.

Pietersma, A., S. T. Comstock, and H. A. Attridge. *The Apocalypse of Elijah Based on P. Chester Beatty 2018*. Texts and Translations 19. Chico, Calif., 1981.

Pistelli, E. *Papiri graeci et latini*, no. 7, p. 16. Florence, 1912.

Reissler, P. *Altjüdisches Schriftum ausserhalb der Bibel*, pp. 114–25. Augsburg, 1928.

Rosenstiehl, J.-M. "Un Sobriquet essénien dans l'apocalypse copte d'Elie." *Semitica* 15 (1959): 97–99.

———. *L'Apocalypse d'Elie, introduction, traduction et notes*. Textes et études pour servir à l'histoire du judaisme intertestamentaire 1. Paris, 1972.

Schmidt, C. *Der Kolophon des Ms. Orient 7594 des Britischen Museum, eine Untersuchung zur Elias-Apokalypse*. Sitzungsberichte der Preussischen Akademie der Wissenschaften, pp. 312–21. Berlin, 1925.

Schrage, W. *Die Elia-Apokalypse*. Jüdische Schriften aus hellenistisch-römischer Zeit 5, pt. 3. Gütersloh, 1980.

Steindorff, G. *Die Apokalypse des Elias, eine unbekannte Apokalypse und Bruchstücke der Sophonias Apokalypse, koptische Texte, Übersetzung, Glossar. Texte und Untersuchungen zur Geschichte der altchristlichen Literatur* 17/3a. Leipzig, 1899.

Stern, L. "Die koptische Apokalypse des Sophonias: Mit einem Anhang über den untersahidischen Dialect." *Zeitschrift für ägyptische Sprache und Altertumskunde* 24 (1886):115–29.

Stone, M. E., and J. Strugnell. *The Books of Elijah*, pts. 1 and 2. Texts and Translations 18. Missoula, Mont., 1979.

Apocalypse of Zephaniah

Diebner, B. J. "Literarkritische Probleme der Zephanja-Apokalypse." *Nag Hammadi and Gnosis*, ed. R. McL. Wilson. Leiden, 1978.

———. "Bemerkungen zum Text des sahidischen und des achmimischen Fragments der sog. Zephanja-Apokalypse." *Dielheimer Blätter zum Alten Testament* 14 (1979):54–60.

Lefort, L. T. "Coptica Lovaniensia." *Le Muséon* 51 (1938):31–32.

Apocalypse of Daniel

Macler, F. "Les Apocalypses apocryphes de Daniel." *Revue d'histoire des religions* 33 (1896):163–76.

Meinardus, O. F. A. "A Commentary on the XIV Vision of Daniel According to the Coptic Version." *Orientalia Christiana Periodica* 32 (1966):394–449.

———. "A Judaeo-Byzantine 14th version of Daniel in the Light of a Coptic Apocalypse." *Ekklesia Pharos* 60 (1978):645–66.

Apocalypse of Ezra

Leipoldt, J., and B. Violet. "Ein saïdisches Bruchstück des vierten Esrabuches." *Zeitschrift für ägyptische Sprache und Altertumskunde* 41 (1904):137–40.

Life of Adam

Evelyn-White, H. G. *The Monasteries of the Wadi'n Natrun*, Vol. 1, pp. 3–6. New York, 1926.

Gnostic Judaism

Perkins, P. "Apocalypse of Adam: The Genre and Function of a Gnostic Apocalypse." *Catholic Biblical Quarterly* 39 (1977):382–95.

Sevrin, J. M. "A propos de la Paraphrase de Sem." *Le Muséon* 88 (1975):69–96.

Life of Prophets

Amélineau, E. C. *Contes et romans de l'Egypte chrétienne*, Vol. 2. Paris, 1888.

Aranda, G. "Apocrifo de Jeremias sobre la cautividad de Babilonia." In *Apocrifos del Antiquo Testamento*, Vol. 2, ed. Alejandro Diez Macho. Madrid, 1982.

Ascension of Isaiah, ed. R. H. Charles. London, 1900.

Harris, J. R., ed. *The Rest of the Words of Baruch*. London, 1889.

Hyvernat, H. *Bibliothecae Pierpont Morgan codices coptici . . .* , Vol. 31, pp. 194–260. Rome, 1922.

Kuhn, K. H. "A Coptic Jeremiah Apocryphon." *Le*

Muséon 83 (1970):106–135, 291–326.

Lefort, L. T. "Coptica Lovaniensia." *Le Muséon* 51 (1938):24–32.

______. "Fragments d'apocryphes en copte-akhmimique." *Le Muséon* 52 (1939):1–10.

Lacau, P. "Fragments de l'Ascension d'Isaie en copte." *Le Muséon* 59 (1946):453–67.

Marmorstein, A. "Die Quellen des neuen Jeremia-Apocryphons." *Zeitschrift für die neuetestamentliche Wissenschaft* 27 (1928):327–37.

Sapiential Literature

Gebhardt, O. von. *Die Psalmen Solomons, zum ersten Male mit Benutzung der Athashand Schriften und des Codex Casanatensis herausgegeben.* Texte und Untersuchungen zur Geschichte der altchristlichen Literatur 13. Leipzig, 1895.

Lucchesi, E. "Découverte d'une traduction copte du quatrième livre des Maccabées." *Analecta Bollandiana* 99 (1981):302.

Ryle, E., and M. R. James. *Ψαλμοὶ Σολομῶντος,* Psalms of the Pharisees, Commonly Called The Psalms of Solomon. Cambridge, 1891.

Till, W., and P. Sanz. *Eine griechisch-koptische Odenhandschrift.* Rome, 1939.

Worrel, W. H. "The Odes of Solomon and the Pistis Sophia." *Journal of Theological Studies* 13 (1912):29–46.

GONZALO ARANDA PEREZ

APOCRYPHON OF JAMES, also known as the Apocryphal Epistle of James, the second tractate in Codex I of the NAG HAMMADI LIBRARY. It occupies sixteen pages, all well preserved except for the first three. The Coptic text apparently had no title. It is a translation into Subakhmimic Coptic of a Greek work that taught a rather conservative Christian gnosticism. Since it deals extensively with the subject of martyrdom, its unknown author must have produced it before the peace of the church in A.D. 314; how long before is uncertain. Equally uncertain is the place of writing, though this must have been in the eastern Mediterranean world, and Egypt is likely.

The main body of the work, which consists of a series of speeches put in the mouth of the risen Jesus, calls itself an "apocryphon." Jesus is represented as reappearing to the "twelve disciples" 550 days after the Resurrection and taking James the Lord's brother and Peter aside. To them he imparts —"openly" rather than "in parables"—a definitive revelation superior to the canonical one. The "apocryphon" closes on page 15 with an account of Jesus' real and final ascent into heaven. In a mystical vision, James and Peter follow him in stages that correspond to the ascents of the heart, the mind, and the spirit. The unexpected return of the other disciples during the vision, however, prevents their spirits from penetrating to the throne of God.

This "apocryphon" is preceded and followed by a "letter" from James "in the Hebrew alphabet," addressed to a recipient whose name is mutilated. Opening in typical Hellenistic letter form, the letter segment informs the recipient that James is sending this apocryphon at his request, and reminds him of "another apocryphon" sent "ten months ago." Attempts to identify the "other apocryphon" have failed. The letter, which resumes on page 16 following the "apocryphon" section, predicts the appearance of "sons who will be born"—presumably the Gnostic community for whom the work was written —and states that the revelation is for their sakes.

As important as the "letter" and "apocryphon" are, the exhortations to martyrdom that occupy pages 5 and 6 of the apocryphon are central. Stylistically this segment has much in common with other such exhortations in the second and third Christian centuries, but it goes beyond them in seeming to demand that the believer volunteer to be martyred. Thus he will be made "equal" with Jesus and gain the Kingdom of God.

It is notable that James's name regularly precedes Peter's and that the tractate emphatically makes James chief of the apostles (cf. Acts 15; Gal. 2:9). In this it joins various Gnostic and Jewish Christian works, in addition to the New Testament, in which James, rather than Peter, is the guarantor of true doctrine. It is difficult to identify this apocryphon with any form of gnosticism named and described by the church fathers.

The *Apocryphon of James* shows many points of agreement with doctrines in the New Testament. Recipients of its message will be filled with the Spirit, have the Kingdom of Heaven within them, and be assured of salvation. They are invited to believe, to gain knowledge, and then to enter the Kingdom by effort, zeal, and earnest prayer. They will thus follow the Savior where he has gone or, alternatively, "be received" into the Kingdom. The document's Gnostic terminology, its lack of doctrines of the atonement, Second Coming, and general resurrection, and its claim to be a later and superior revelation have led most interpreters to declare it Gnostic.

The exhortation to martyrdom as well as many similar admonitions toward faith, zeal, effort, and knowledge make up the main themes of the tractate. There is a question whether the work is composite or the product of one author, but its overall purpose was clearly to kindle courage and zeal in an afflicted community.

BIBLIOGRAPHY

Brown, S. K. *James.* Ph.D. Dissertation, Brown University, 1972.

Kipgen, Kaikhohen. *Gnosticism in Early Christianity: A Study of the Epistula Jacobi Apocrypha with Particular Reference to Salvation.* Ph.D. Dissertation, Oxford University, 1975.

Kirchner, D. *Epistula Jacobi Apocrypha, Die erste Schrift aus Nag-Hammadi-Codex I, neu herausgegeben und kommentiert,* 2 vols. Ph.D. Dissertation, Berlin-Humboldt University, 1977.

Malinine, M., et al. *Epistula Jacobi Apocrypha.* Zürich, 1968.

Schenke, H. M. "Der Jacobusbrief aus dem Codex Jung." *Orientalistische Literaturzeitung* 66 (1971):117–30.

Williams, F. E. "The Apocryphon of James." In *The Nag Hammadi Library in English,* ed. J. M. Robinson. New York, 1977.

FRANK E. WILLIAMS

APOCRYPHON OF JEREMIAH, part of the body of the pseudepigraphal literature about the Old Testament characters Jeremiah and Baruch. It exists in a Coptic (Sahidic) version as well as in Arabic and Garshuni versions. In the Coptic, it bears the title "Paralipomena Ieremiae," but it is not identical with the other work known by this name. In the latter versions, it sometimes appears under the title "History of the Captivity in Babylon." For its subject matter, the work drew largely on the Bible, but the author felt free to elaborate on the biblical framework and to enrich it from other sources. He was careless, however, and often disregarded details of history and geography. The author seems also to have known and used the "Paralipomena Ieremiae" and possibly other sources such as 2 Maccabees. But it is not always clear whether he relied on his imagination when embroidering the biblical narrative or drew from extrabiblical sources. The resulting apocryphon, with its heightened drama and strong miraculous element, shares characteristics with other apocryphal books.

In its present form, the piece is Christian. But A. Marmorstein (1928) suggests in his study of the Garshuni Jeremiah Apocryphon that the original form of the work was Jewish, and was only secondarily Christianized. It may also be tentatively suggested that the Coptic version of the work is a translation of a Greek original that no longer survives. The dating of the work also presents difficulties, although Marmorstein suggested that it may have originated in the third or fourth century.

The work may be summarized briefly. God sends Jeremiah to King Zedekiah of Judah with a message of rebuke to his people for their sinfulness and unfaithfulness. After a confrontation with the false prophet Hananiah, Jeremiah is cast into prison by Zedekiah. The Ethiopian Ebedmelech intervenes and obtains his release.

A second divine message of rebuke is written down by Jeremiah and read by Baruch to the king. The king orders the book to be burned, Baruch to be scourged, and Jeremiah to be imprisoned once more. Jeremiah predicts Israel's captivity in Babylon. Again Ebedmelech intervenes, and the prophet is moved from the pit of mire within the prison to the prison yard. The prophet promises that Ebedmelech, because of his kindness, will not see the destruction of Jerusalem and the captivity of the people of Israel.

The archangel MICHAEL commands Nebuchadnezzar to make war on Israel to punish the disobedient people. Nebuchadnezzar, after having tested God's will, invades Judah. Meanwhile it is arranged for Ebedmelech to sleep in the garden of Agrippa during the destruction of Jerusalem and during the period of the captivity of the Hebrews. Nebuchadnezzar meets Jeremiah, who intercedes with him for his people. Before himself going into captivity, Jeremiah deposits securely the high priest's garment, the temple vessels, and the keys of the temple. Then the Hebrews are marched off to Babylon, while Jeremiah rides in a chariot with Nebuchadnezzar and his generals.

The Hebrews suffer many hardships and indignities both on the journey and in Babylon. Zedekiah dies after forty years in captivity. Ezra, the future deliverer of his people, while still a schoolboy, is mocked by his Chaldean fellow pupils and performs astounding miracles, one being identical with a miracle attributed to Jesus in the Infancy Gospel of Thomas. At the end of seventy years, Jeremiah's prayer is answered, and King Cyrus of Persia is persuaded, through God's miraculous intervention, to let the people of Israel return.

Ebedmelech awakes from his long sleep and witnesses Jeremiah's entry into Jerusalem. After the recovery of the temple vessels, a service of thanksgiving is held in which the whole people of Israel join.

BIBLIOGRAPHY

Charlesworth, J. H. *The Pseudepigrapha and Modern Research,* pp. 88ff. Missoula, Mont., 1976.

Kuhn, K. H., ed. "A Coptic Jeremiah Apocryphon." *Le Muséon* 83 (1970):95–135, 291–350.

Marmorstein, A. "Die Quellen des neuen Jeremia-Apocryphons." *Zeitschrift für die neutestamentliche Wissenshaft* 27 (1928):327–37.

K. H. KUHN

APOCRYPHON OF JOHN, apocryphal work dealing with the risen Christ. A Coptic version of this "secret book" appeared in Berlin Papyrus 8502. It was then noted that Irenaeus may have used a Greek version in his treatise *Against All the Heresies* (1.29) written before A.D. 180. Notably, the NAG HAMMADI LIBRARY contains no fewer than three other versions, each placed at the beginning of a codex, thus demonstrating the importance of the work. Although the four texts present important variations, one may recognize a short version (the Berlin Papyrus and that of Nag Hammadi Codex III) and a long one (that of Codices II and IV of the Nag Hammadi Library), the latter unfortunately badly damaged. The question arises whether the longer version—in which the Christian elements are more numerous—constitutes a "Christianization" of a treatise that originally contained nothing of Christian character. According to other hypotheses (e.g., Giversen, 1963), it is the longer version of Codices II and IV that is the older.

The work purports to be a revelation from the risen Savior to John son of Zebedee. The Revealer pronounces terrible curses upon anyone who dares to divulge the mysteries to be revealed, a customary feature of "apocalypses" of a Gnostic type. The subject of the revelation is the creation both of the world and of man, as well as the origin of evil and the saving power of knowledge (*gnosis*). To summarize the contents, we note that from the Invisible Spirit there emanated twelve aeons of light of whom the last, Sophia, wished to produce by herself—without her heavenly consort—a copy of the Adam of light. She produced only an abortion, a demiurge named Ialdabaoth. Guarding jealously the power that he derived from his mother, he created the world of darkness, including archons, powers of evil, and so forth. Thinking to produce an image of the Father, the archons fashioned a human body. But being purely psychic, it was incapable of moving until Ialdabaoth was led by a ruse to breathe a particle of light into it. The man immediately showed himself superior to the frustrated demiurge, who with his archons then fashioned a purely material body, in which he imprisoned the man, as in a "tomb" and covered his senses with a veil to make him forget his divine nature. A long struggle then ensued between the Holy Spirit and the powers of evil, until the Savior was to come to convince men of their divine origin. We note also that the Revealer declared himself to be at once the Father, the Mother, and the Son, a typically Gnostic triad.

Although this document is an essentially Gnostic work, it is difficult to determine the sect to which it belonged. At its base we may find the mythological cosmogony described by Irenaeus (1.29), who designated the adherents of this doctrine by the general term "Gnostics." Because of the important place occupied by the first aeon, Barbelo, his followers have often been termed "Barbeloites," as if a separate sect actually existed under this name. Moreover, a certain kinship between the Apocryphon of John and some other texts from Nag Hammadi—particularly the Hypostasis of the Archons (II, 4), the Gospel of the Egyptians (III, 2, and IV, 2) and the Trimorphic Protennoia (XIII, 1)—has lead to the supposition that here is a connection with a Sethian text, even though the name Seth does not appear. However that may be, we possibly have here a witness to a very ancient *gnosis,* pre-Christian according to some hypotheses. Irenaeus presented it as an ancestor of the doctrines of the Valentinians. Some elements common to Valentinianism already appear in it: aeons, the fall of Sophia, the birth of an abortion, archons, the ignorance of the demiurge, the material and the psychic body, the spark of light, and so forth.

The "basic document," if one may so call it, is followed by a Gnostic commentary on the early chapters of Genesis. The biblical elements are almost always accompanied by the denial, "Not as Moses said. . . ."

Apart from the possible "Christianization" mentioned above, other influences may have come together in the text as we now have it. Some have noted occasional allusions to Iran (S. Giverson and R. Kasser). For instance, the demiurge Ialdabaoth, "darkness of ignorance," may be modeled on Ahriman, the principle of evil in Zoroastrianism, of whom Plutarch wrote that he was like "darkness and ignorance" (*Isis and Osiris* 46). Further, at the very beginning of the text, a Pharisee named Arimanios insidiously suggests to John that the "Nazorean" has deceived them. Notably, in Greek literature the name Arimanios appears only in connection with Zoroaster. Hence it might well be symbolic in our text. Additionally, there is even explicit reference to a "Book of Zoroaster," which is said to give precise information about the role of the angels.

Incidentally, at the very end of the long version in Codex II there appears a series of self-revelations in "I am" style that has led to comparisons with the Isis aretalogies. On the whole, the Apocryphon of John is a very important source both for the study of *gnosis* and very possibly for the primitive Gnostic mythology.

BIBLIOGRAPHY

Broek, R. van den. *Autogenes and Adamas: The Mythological Structure of the Apocryphon of John.* Nag Hammadi Studies 17. Leiden, 1981.

Giversen, S. *Apocryphon Johannis: The Coptic Text of the Apocryphon Johannis in the Nag Hammadi Codex II,* with translation, introduction, and commentary. Copenhagen, 1963.

Janssens, Y. "L'Apocryphon de Jean." *Le Muséon* 83 (1970):157–65; 84 (1971):43–64; 403–432.

Kasser, R. "Le Livre secret de Jean." *Revue de théologie et de philosophie* 14 (1964):140–50; 15 (1965):129–55; 16 (1966):163–81; 17 (1967):1–30.

Krause, M. and P. Labib. *Die Drei Versionen des Apokryphon des Johannes im Koptischen Museum zu Alt-Kairo.* Abhandlungen des Deutschen Archäologischen Instituts Kairo, Coptic series, Vol. 1. Wiesbaden, 1962.

Till, W. C. *Die gnostischen Schriften des koptischen Papyrus Berolinensis 8502,* 2nd ed., ed. H.-M. Schenke. Texte und Untersuchungen zur Geschichte der alterchristlichen Literatur. Berlin, 1972.

Wisse, F. "The Apocryphon of John." In *The Nag Hammadi Library in English,* ed. J. M. Robinson. San Francisco, 1977.

YVONNE JANSSENS

APOLI, SAINT, fourth-century martyr of Antiochian origin, who was put to death in Egypt (feast day: 1 Misrah). He appears only in the later hagiographic Coptic tradition. Of his Passion, ascribed to an eyewitness, the servant Sergius, two Bohairic fragmentary manuscripts are preserved. The first consists of four folios from Cairo (ed. Evelyn-White, 1926, pp. 88–93) and the continuation of the text in the Vatican Library (Copt 61ff, pp. 223–27, ed. Balestri and Hyvernat, Vol. I, pp. 242–48); of the second there are only two folios left in Leipzig (ed. H. G. Evelyn-White, 1926). The beginning of the text in the Coptic language is lost, but the reconstruction is possible through the abstract of the SYNAXARION and from the Ethiopic version, which is close in content even though different in form (ed. Pereira, 1907, pp. 73–98).

The Ethiopic text includes three passions—that of the general JUSTUS, his wife, Theoclia, and his son, Apoli, preceded by a narration of the previous history according to the typical late tradition of the Basilidian Cycle (see HAGIOGRAPHY). At the time of DIOCLETIAN, a war is waged by the great generals Justus and Theodore Anatolius. The events of the war are mainly centered on the capture of Nicomede, son of the king of Persia, and on the treason of the bishop of Antioch, who returns Nicomede to his father. Diocletian, according to the advice of Romanus, another great general and brother of Justus, refuses the Christian faith; both Diocletian and Romanus try to convince Apoli to retract in vain. After consideration of the situation, Justus, Theoclia, and Apoli voluntarily choose to be martyred. With this purpose they leave for Egypt, where they confess their faith first in the presence of Armenius and then before Tolomeus; both prefects are unwilling to put them to death. At last Tolomeus will pronounce the condemnation.

The Coptic text begins when Apoli is already before Tolomeus who tortures him in various ways. As is usual, next follows the apparition of Christ, who comforts and cures the martyr—along with Michael and Gabriel. Then there is a long discussion with Tolomeus, who tries to persuade Apoli to refuse the Christian faith and the martyrdom.

It is hard to state how much the first part of the Ethiopic text is a true representative of previous Coptic redaction. Taking into account that Justus' Passion preceded, in at least one code, Apoli's Passion, the Coptic material at our disposal seems rather to witness the previous existence of separate passions. These are related in content, since they belong to the same legendary Cycle built around Diocletian's abjuration and around the war with the Persians in the episode of the king of Persia and the traitor bishop (see ANATOLIUS). Later some writers may have also formally grouped the narrations together, obtaining the actual Ethiopic text, but this could have happened either in Coptic or in Arabic (it should be assumed between Coptic and Ethiopic), or directly in Ethiopic.

BIBLIOGRAPHY

Balestri, I., and H. Hyvernat. *Acta Martyrum*, 2 vols. CSCO 43, 44.

Baumeister, T. *Martyr Invictus. Der Märtyrer als Sinnbild der Erlösung in der Legende und im Kult der frühen koptischen Kirche.* Münster, 1972.

Evelyn-White, H. G. *New Coptic Texts from the Monastery of Saint Macarius.* New York, 1926.

O'Leary, D. E. *The Saints of Egypt*, pp. 80–1. New York, 1937.

Pereira, M. E. *Acta Martyrum*, 2 vols. CSCO 37, 38. Paris, 1907.

TITO ORLANDI

APOLLINARIANISM is the heresy of Apollinarius or Apollinaris (c. 310–c. 390), who in about 360 became bishop of Laodicea, a Hellenistic city in the Roman province of Syria.

Apollinarius adopted the Alexandrian-Nicene teaching concerning the Son of God. He maintained that the Second Person of the Blessed Trinity is coeternal and coequal with God the Father, but in order to defend the full and perfect divinity of Christ and the full and perfect union of godhead and manhood in Christ against ARIANISM, he fell into a heretical teaching by denying the existence of a human rational soul in Christ.

ARIUS taught that Christ was changeable and was liable to sin, although He Himself did not commit any sin. He was infallible. But His infallibility was not due to His divinity but to His conquest over sin and His fight against all temptations of sin to which He was exposed. And He was liable to sin because He, as human, was free to do good or bad. Nevertheless, He did good by His free will and did not do evil or bad.

Here Apollinarius, in the light of the Nicene Council (see NICAEA, COUNCIL OF) teaching said that Arius was wrong. The Son of God is not changeable, nor is he liable to commit sin. Christ was infallible, but His infallibility was not due only to His victory over sin to which He was liable, but rather to His very nature as a divine being. Apollinarius then said that Christ has no human rational soul. The human rational soul is created free and consequently is liable to change and hence, to sin. According to Apollinarius, who followed Platonist anthropology, man is composed of three elements: the body, an unrational soul *(psyche alogos)*, and the Logos.

The spirit, or the rational soul, is replaced in Christ by the Divine Logos. The Divine Logos is, in fact, the predominant principle, the most powerful and influential element of action in Christ and the overwhelming power that animates the body and the irrational soul with the divine supernatural and sublime life.

Apollinarius could not admit the possibility of a real union between the Logos and the rational human soul. He felt that in this case the rational human soul either maintains its free will—and consequently there would be no real union because the human free will would remain active—or loses its free will, being absorbed utterly into the Logos. In order to save the teaching that Christ is one Person and to demolish the Arian teaching of the duality in Christ, Apollinarius denied the existence of a rational soul in Christ and taught that the Logos replaced the rational soul.

The main and fundamental objection against the teaching of Apollinarius is that if Christ had no human rational soul then Christ's manhood was incomplete, and consequently Christ could not redeem the whole of human nature but only its spiritual elements. Christ must have had a complete human nature united to his divinity in order to redeem man's nature completely. The complete human nature is composed of a body and a rational soul, and thus, the human nature in man could not be redeemed if the Redeemer had not a rational soul. But Christ, who in fact is God the Logos Incarnate, came especially to the world for the salvation of men and to redeem the whole human nature.

Apollinarianism was refuted ably and competently by Saint ATHANASIUS the Great at the end of his life, in a huge work composed of three volumes. It was criticized strongly by BASIL THE GREAT and GREGORY OF NAZIANZUS (1955, Epistle 102). The essentials of the teaching of Apollinarius had already been condemned in a synod held in Alexandria under the chairmanship of Saint Athanasius the Apostolicos in 362.

It should be noted here that Saint Athanasius of Alexandria defended the full and perfect divinity of Jesus the Christ against Arius, and he was also the one who defended the full and perfect humanity of Jesus the Christ against Apollinarius. Christ, then, in the teaching of Alexandria as professed and confessed by Saint Athanasius and his successors, is the God-Man, the Incarnate Logos, who is not only divine and not only human; He is the Incarnate Logos, who is perfect in His divinity and perfect in His humanity. His divinity and humanity are united together in one person, in one nature that acquires the properties and qualities of the two natures united together in one, in a real and true union without separation. In other words, this unique union is inseparable.

The teaching of Apollinarius was repeatedly condemned in several other synods held in Rome under the chairmanship of Damasus of Rome between 374 and 380. Apollinarius himself was not condemned until 375.

Apollinarius and his teaching were finally and ecumenically condemned by the Second Ecumenical Council held in Constantinople in 381. Several imperial edicts were issued from 388 to 428, condemning Apollinarius and Apollinarianism, but despite this it remained influential in the religious thought of the people, and many of the leaders of Eastern Christianity, not least that of EUTYCHES. The real opposition to Apollinarius came from the revived Antiochene School of theologians represented by Diodore of Tarsus (330-c. 390) and THEODORE OF MOPSUESTIA. It formed the background to the clash of the Alexandrians and Antiochenes that dominated the history of the church in the time of NESTORIUS and CYRIL.

BIBLIOGRAPHY

Cross, F. L., ed. *Oxford Dictionary of the Christian Church.* Oxford, 1958.

Gregory of Nazianzus. "Against Apollinarius, the Second Letter to Cledonius." *In Nicene and Post Nicene Fathers of the Christian Church,* Vol. 7, series 2, pp. 443–445, ed. P. Schaff and H. Wace. Grand Rapids, Mich., 1955.

Lietzmann, H. *Apollinaris von Laodicea und seine Schule* (Texte und Untersuchungen 1). Tübingen, 1904.

Ludwich, A. *Apolinari Metaphrasis Psalmorum.* Leipzig, 1912.

Riedmatten, H. de, O. P. "Les Fragments d'Apollinaire à l"Eranistes'." In *Das Konzil von Chalkedon,* 3 vols., ed. A. Grillmeier and H. Bacht. Würzburg, 1951.

Voisin, G. *L'Apollinarisme, étude historique, littéraire et dogmatique sur le début des controverses christologiques au IVe siècle.* Louvain, 1901.

BISHOP GREGORIOS

APOLLO OF BĀWĪṬ, SAINT.

See Phib.

APOLLO AND DAPHNE.

See Mythological Subjects in Coptic Art.

APOLLONIUS AND PHILEMON, SAINTS

(feastday: 7 Baramhāt), fourth-century martyrs. Their story has come down to us in two versions: the original Coptic and a later Arabic tradition.

Coptic Tradition

The oldest account of the martyrdom of Apollonius and Philemon is found in chapter 19 of the HISTORIA MONACHORUM IN AEGYPTO, written around 400 (see the edition by Festugière). According to this text, Apollonius was a monk and a deacon whose love for his enemies so impressed Philemon, a flute player who had been reviling him in prison, that the latter confessed himself a Christian before the judge. When the two men were to be burned, a cloud of dew miraculously extinguished the fire.

They were then taken to the prefect in Alexandria. En route, Apollonius instructed the soldiers in the Christian faith. At the command of the prefect, all were drowned in the sea, their corpses being later found on the shore. The author of the *Historia* reports that the travelers had visited the martyrs' sanctuary on their pilgrimage to the Egyptian monks. Of Apollonius he says, "We too saw him, along with those who died with him as martyrs, while we were praying in the martyrium. And we fell down before God and venerated their bodies in the Thebaïs."

It can be taken as historical fact that before 400 there was a sanctuary consecrated to these martyrs. In it, following the Egyptian practice, the mummified corpses probably were placed on stands, where they could be venerated. The Greek Passion (*Bibliotheca hagiographica graeca* 1514; *Acta sanctorum martyrum,* Vol. 1 [Paris and Rome, 1865], 887–90) shows that the location of this sanctuary was ANTINOOPOLIS. Otherwise this second text differs considerably from the account in the *Historia monachorum.* It could be a fictitious elaboration of a later stage in the local tradition (perhaps fifth century), whereas the first account comes from the monastic milieu of the closing years of the fourth century. The second legend attaches to the martyrdom of Apollonius and Philemon an account of the change of heart and martyr's death of ARIANUS, the governor who was persecuting the Christians.

The Sahidic reworking of *Bibliotheca hagiographica graeca* 1514, probably undertaken in the sixth century, has been edited by F. Rossi (*Atti della R. accademia dei Lincei*, ser. 5, 1 [1893]:3–136, 307, with Italian translation). The text begins with a Martyrdom of Aclas, which is missing in the Greek version. There are relatively large changes in the part dealing with Arianus. In the tenth century Symeon Metaphrastes reworked the Greek legend and loosely attached it at 14 December to the martyrdom of saints Thyrsus, Leucius, and Callinicus (PG 116, 537–560). In the West the theme of the actor converted was taken up afresh by the baroque drama. The prototype for the *Philemon Martyr* of Jakob Bidermann (1578–1639) was the Latin translation of Metaphrastes' text by Laurentius Surius (*De probatis sanctorum historiis* . . . 6 [Cologne 1575], 911–15).

BIBLIOGRAPHY

Baumeister, T. *Martyr invictus*, pp. 105–108. Münster, 1972.

______. "Der Märtyrer Philemon." In *Pietas. Festschrift für Bernhard Kötting*, ed. E. Dassmann and K. S. Frank. Münster, 1980.

Delehaye, H. "Les martyrs d'Egypte." *Analecta Bollandiana* 40 (1922):5–154, 299–364.

THEOFRIED BAUMEISTER

Arabic Tradition

Neither the Arabic tradition in general nor the Coptic Arabic tradition in particular offers a Passion of Saints Apollonius and Philemon. Nevertheless, the Copto-Arabic SYNAXARION, in the part compiled by MĪKHĀ'ĪL, bishop of Atrīb and Malīj between about 1240 and 1250, commemorates these two martyrs on 7 Baramhāt. The following day, 8 Baramhāt, has a commemoration of their persecutor, ARIANUS, the prefect of ANTINOOPOLIS frequently mentioned in the Acts of the Martyrs, and historically well attested in the year 307. Because of them he was converted and was subsequently martyred himself.

The accounts of the Passions of Philemon and Apollonius and of Arianus are brief. They differ from the Greek and the Coptic accounts. In them Apollonius is the flute player, while Philemon is the musician and singer. They are both pierced by arrows and killed, but one of the arrows rebounds and pierces the eye of the prefect Arianus. A Christian suggests he put some of the martyrs' blood on his eye, and it is healed. Arianus is thereby converted to Christianity.

When Diocletian learns of the conversion, he summons Arianus to Alexandria to be tortured. He orders him thrown into a cistern, but an angel lifts Arianus out and places him at the foot of Diocletian's bed. Terrified, Diocletian instructs that Arianus be put into a sack and thrown into the sea, where he drowns. A dolphin brings the body to the shore of Alexandria, and his servants take it to Antinoopolis, as Arianus had requested prior to his death. They lay it to rest beside the bodies of Philemon and Apollonius.

Since the Synaxarion mentions Philemon before Apollonius, he appears to be the principal figure. Nothing concerning his conversion through the example of Apollonius is recorded.

KHALIL SAMIR, S.J.

APOLLO THE SHEPHERD, SAINT, monk at Scetis. Our knowledge of Saint Apollo is limited to the APOPHTHEGMATA PATRUM.

Apollo's place of origin is nowhere given. He was from a humble milieu, since, like his parents, he was a shepherd, whence his epithet. While keeping his flocks, he had a flight of fantasy, asking himself how a child looked in its mother's womb. Unfortunately Apollo passed from the fantasy to the act. He cut the womb of a pregnant woman in order to see how the fetus looked. After the death of the woman and the child, he was so stricken with remorse that he became a monk at Scetis and remained persuaded that his twofold crime could not be pardoned by God.

The Ethiopian Synaxarion gives this story as an example of repentance and focuses on the modality of his expiation. The text of the *Apophthegmata* says simply that he prayed without ceasing. The Ethiopian Synaxarion adds to this that in his youth he had committed all kinds of faults, and it embroiders somewhat on the manner of his penitence. He is said to have gone into the "interior" desert—that is, the most remote from the valley of the Nile, ten stades (about a mile and a half) from Scetis—without bread to eat or water to quench his thirst and there lived like the beasts. He is said to have lived in the desert like this for fourteen years, at the end of which time an angel caused him to meet a desert father who assured him that God had pardoned even the death of the child. After the desert father miraculously gave the Eucharist to him, Apollo died in the arms of the father, who wrote the story and made it known to the monks of Scetis. The moral lesson of this pious story is that whatever the magnitude of the crime one has committed, one must never despair of divine mercy.

Some doubt surrounds the festal date of Apollo, 5 Amshīr, for on the same day APOLLO OF BĀWĪṬ is commemorated. The memory of the latter may have attracted that of this Apollo.

BIBLIOGRAPHY

Budge, E. A. W., trans. *The Book of the Saints of the Ethiopian Church,* 4 vols. Cambridge, 1928.

Graf, G. *Catalogue des manuscrits arabes chrétiens conservés au Caire.* Studi e testi 63. Vatican City, 1934.

Troupeau, G. *Catalogue des manuscrits arabes,* Pt. 1, *Manuscrits chrétiens,* 2 vols. Paris, 1972–1974.

Waddell, H., trans. *The Desert Fathers.* London, 1981.

Ward, B., trans. *The Sayings of the Desert Fathers in the Alphabetical Collection.* Cistercian Studies. Kalamazoo and Oxford, 1981.

RENÉ-GEORGES COQUIN

APOLOGIST, one of a group of Christian writers who presented an apologia, or defense of the Christian faith, to the non-Christian world. In the New Testament, Luke through Acts provides such an apologia. However, in the second century, Christians were accused of various kinds of calumnies, and the Apologists attempted to vindicate Christians of false accusations and to show that the Christian way of life was the highest ethical ideal the world had yet seen. In this they were following the example of JOSEPHUS and PHILO OF ALEXANDRIA, who had already undertaken the same task in defense of Judaism. In addition to refuting calumnies and presenting Christianity as a rational faith, the Apologists were concerned with the questions of thoughtful men about the nature of the God in whom Christians believed. Using the prevailing Middle Platonist philosophy, some of the Apologists attempted to prove that Christianity was the true philosophy and the fulfillment not only of Judaism and the Old Testament but also of Greek thought. Moreover, their use of the Logos doctrine (i.e., that the Logos or Word was generated by God's will with a view to bringing about creation, and that the Word assuming flesh and being [cf. John 1:14] was incarnate as Jesus Christ) won that doctrine a permanent place in Christian theology.

The Apologists include Aristides, the writer of the *Epistle to Diognetus;* Justin Martyr; Tatian; Athenagoras; Theophilus of Antioch; Minucius Felix; and Tertullian. Of these, Justin Martyr (c. 100–c. 165) and Tertullian (c. 160–230) are the most important, representing the Greek and Latin worlds, respectively. Justin held that the Logos summed up the whole history of Christian and non-Christian thought in the coming of Christ. He was not conscious that he was grafting onto the biblical basis of Christianity a philosophical interpretation that was bound to modify it. However, although his writings reflect the eclectic Middle Platonism of his day, the heart of Christianity is for him God's care and love for men shown in the Bible and in Jesus Christ. Tertullian, on the other hand, sought in his *Apology* to develop a Christian philosophy on a classical basis, although it is doubtful that he intended to synthesize pagan and Christian thought. His skepticism about secular culture is, in fact, expressed in unyielding and sarcastic terms. The *Apology* is, however, a successful defense of the Christian faith, perhaps intended as an open letter to a wider public, as well as to the magistrates to whom it is addressed.

Later Christian writers are not usually included among the Apologists, although many use apologetic methods (they defend the faith by rational means). CLEMENT OF ALEXANDRIA (c. 150–c. 215) claims that all learning, whatever its source, is sacred, and he has much to say about the Logos as the divine enlightener of humanity. Although his vast biblical and classical learning was somewhat undisciplined, he set the tone of the Alexandrian school of Christian thought, which it retained throughout its history. His successor in the CATECHETICAL SCHOOL OF ALEXANDRIA, ORIGEN (c. 185–c. 254), was an outstanding systematic Christian thinker, the first to produce a full, logical interpretation of the faith (*On First Principles*) set within the widest intellectual framework. Origen had an enormous influence both as a writer and as a teacher. He wrote an important reply to a literary attack on Christianity made by the pagan philosopher CELSUS about 178. Origen's *Contra Celsum* enables us to discover the main points of Celsus's attack. While praising the Logos doctrine, Celsus objected to the exclusiveness of Christian claims and criticized the Bible, often with considerable acuteness. Celsus appealed to Christians to abandon their alleged religious and political intolerance. Origen, however, succeeded in countering Celsus's attack.

A further onslaught on Christianity was made by the apostate emperor Julian (332–363) in his *Against the Galileans,* written during the Persian campaign. No manuscript of this work survives, but almost the whole text can be recovered from CYRIL OF ALEXANDRIA'S refutation, *Contra Julianum.*

Later apologetic, such as is found in the works of Augustine (354–430), had to cope with the new philosophical challenge of Neoplatonism. Augustine's work reached a climax in his celebrated *City of God,* which N. H. Baynes called "the last and greatest of the Apologies for Christianity produced by the early Church" (1955, p. 288).

BIBLIOGRAPHY

Augustine. *City of God,* trans. M. Dods. New York, 1950.

Barnard, L. W. *Justin Martyr, His Life and Thought.* New York and Cambridge, 1967.

______. *Athenagoras: A Study in Second Century Christian Apologetic.* Paris, 1972.

Baynes, N. J. "The Political Ideas of St. Augustine's *De Civitate Dei.*" In *Byzantine Studies and Other Essays,* pp. 288–306. London, 1955.

Chadwick, H. *Early Christian Thought and the Classical Tradition.* Oxford, 1966.

Cyril of Alexandria. *Contra Julianum.* In PG 76, cols. 489–1058. Paris, 1863.

Daniélou, J. *The Gospel Message and Hellenistic Culture;* trans. J. A. Baker. London, 1973.

Grant, R. M., ed. "Studies in the Apologists." *Harvard Theological Review* 5 (1958):123–34.

______, ed. and trans. *Theophilus of Antioch, Ad Autolycum.* Oxford, 1970.

Malley, W. J. *Hellenism and Christianity.* Analecta Gregoriana 210. Rome, 1978. A discussion of Cyril of Alexandria's *Contra Julianum.*

Meecham, H. G., ed. *The Letter to Diognetus.* Manchester, 1949.

LESLIE W. BARNARD

APOPHTHEGMATA PATRUM, the collection of memorable words and anecdotes of the desert fathers. In the sixth century in Palestine, the monk Zosimus was already mentioning "the apophthegms of the holy old men" (Zosimus, 1864, col. 1679), but that does not seem to be the oldest or most common name. At the same period, also in Palestine, BARSANUPHIUS and John of Gaza, as well as their disciple Dorotheus, do not use it, whereas they frequently quote the *Lives and Words of the Fathers* or the *Gerontica.* Another title must have been in fairly common use, that of *Paradise* or *Garden* of the fathers, monks, or holy old men. We find it as the heading of the Syriac collection of Enanisho (seventh century). In the Coptic tradition, the life of JOHN COLOBOS written at the end of the seventh century by ZACHARIAS, BISHOP OF SAKHĀ, in Lower Egypt, mentions the "*Book of the Holy Old Men* . . . to which the title of *Paradise* has also been given" (1894, p. 322). The Arabic Manuscript 547 from Sinai contains "a part of the *Paterikon* known under the name of the *Garden* which consists of accounts of the Old Men and Fathers" (Sauget, 1973, p. 10). It is also under the title *Garden of the Monks* that the Arabic collection of the apothegms is published nowadays in Egypt.

The collections are very different from one another in both the material included and the arrangement of the items. But they have a common base, consisting of a majority of words and reports of the great monks of SCETIS of the fourth and fifth centuries. Handed down orally at first, probably in Coptic, principally by the disciples of the ancients, these apothegms were then put into writing and grouped into various small collections. At the end of the fifth or the beginning of the sixth century, no doubt in Palestine, these anthologies were brought together and integrated into huge collections containing several hundred items, presented in two main forms: one, alphabetical, in which each monk's words are gathered together in separate units classified according to the first letter of the name; the other, a systematic series in which the items are grouped in chapters according to subject matter. Most of the collections that we know in the manuscripts or publications belong to these two types, and the earlier collections have almost entirely disappeared. One of the few still in existence is in the Syriac Ascetikon of Abba Isaiah (Draguet, CSCO 289, pp. 30–51; 293, pp. 27–83).

To some extent, monastic life appeared everywhere in the Christian world in the third and fourth centuries, but from the outset, Egyptian monachism shone with such special splendor that it appeared everywhere as the pattern to be reproduced. The apothegms contributed much to the fame of the great anchorites of SCETIS. From the sixth century, the apothegms were translated from Greek into Latin and soon also into Syriac, Arabic, Georgian, and Armenian. It is impossible to evaluate the influence they may have had in the history of spirituality. Many traces of it are found even in the profane literature of all the European countries. This influence was exercised, especially in the Coptic church, either directly through the reading of the collections in Coptic and Arabic or indirectly through the place given to the holy monks of the apothegms in the liturgy. In the monasteries, the reading of the *Garden of the Monks* has always had an honored place during the common meals. It is still the daily practice in the Monastery of Saint Macarius (DAYR ANBĀ MAQĀR). The popular edition published in Cairo, which has reappeared many times, has been much appreciated also by the laity. Coptic Christians have never had a conception of spirituality peculiar to the laity, and it is in the school of the desert fathers that they are trained in the practice of the virtues, asceticism, and prayer.

BIBLIOGRAPHY

Bousset, W. *Apophthegmata: Studien zur Geschichte des ältesten Mönchtums.* Tübingen, 1923.

Chaine, M. *Le Manuscrit de la version copte en dialecte sahidique des "Apophthegmata Patrum."* Cairo, 1969.

Cotelier, J. B., ed. *Apophthegmata Patrum.* In PG 65, cols. 71–440. Paris, 1864.

Draguet, R. *Les Cinq recensions de l'ascéticon syriaque d'abba Isaïe.* CSCO 289, Scriptores Syri 120. Louvain, 1968.

Guy, J. C. *Recherches sur la tradition grecque des "Apophthegmata Patrum."* Subsidia Hagiographica 36. Brussels, 1962.

Hopfner, T. *Über die koptisch-sa'idischen Apophthegmata Patrum Aegyptiorum und verwandte griechische, lateinische, koptisch-bohairische und syrische Sammlungen.* Kaiserliche Akademie der Wissenschaften in Wien. Philosophisch-historische Klasse, Denkschriften 61.20. Vienna, 1918.

Regnault, L. *Les Sentences des pères du désert: Troisième Recueil et tables.* Solesmes, 1976.

———. "Les Apophtègmes des pères en Palestine au Ve-Ve siècles." *Irènikon* 54 (1981):320–30.

———. *Les Pères du désert à travers leurs apophtègmes.* Solesmes, 1987.

Rufinus. *Verba seniorum.* In PL 73, cols. 739–1066. Paris, 1849.

Sauget, J. M. "Un nouveau témoin de collection d'Apophthegmata Patrum: Le Paterikon du Sinai arabe 547." *Le Muséon* 86 (1973):10.

Zacharias. *Vie de Jean Colobos.* Annales du Musée Guimet 25. Paris, 1894.

Zosimus. *Alloquia.* In PG 78, cols. 1679–1702. Paris, 1864.

LUCIEN REGNAULT

APOSTATIZED COPTIC DIGNITARIES.

See Professional Activities of Copts in Medieval Egypt.

APOSTLES, 127 CANONS OF THE.

See Canons, Apostolic.

APOSTLES, FAST OF THE.

See Fasts.

APOSTLES' CREED,

a brief statement of faith, used only in the Western church, based upon belief in the Holy Trinity as expressed in the New Testament. There is no definite evidence to support the claim of RUFINUS, who wrote a commentary on it (Kelly, 1972, p. 1), that every apostle contributed a section to it, although statements of faith laid down by the apostles in their various epistles were incorporated into the formulation of the Apostles' Creed.

An eighth-century writer, Pirminius, was the first to cite it in its present form, but baptismal formularies in use at Rome and in other Western churches in the fourth century bear a strong resemblance to it. Marcellus, bishop of Ancyra (c. 340), transcribed it in Greek, which shows that it was in use before the middle of the third century, when Greek was still the language of the liturgy in Rome.

Since the beginning of Christianity, the apostles had laid down a formula to be repeated by catechumens at baptism (e.g., Rom. 1:3–5; 1 Cor. 15:3–5; 1 Pt. 3:18–22). When the Apostle Philip baptized the Ethiopian eunuch who had gone to Jerusalem, the latter said, "I believe that Jesus Christ is the Son of God" (Acts 8:37). Paul also reminds his disciple Timothy, "You made the good confession in the presence of many witnesses" (1 Tm. 6:12), which confession is believed to have been made at his baptism.

Such statements expressing belief in the Holy Trinity came to be known later as the Apostles' Creed and, originally including only nine clauses, was expanded at successive stages in the generations that followed. In his treatise on the APOSTOLIC TRADITION, HIPPOLYTUS mentions a terse expression of faith, in the form of three questions dealing with belief in the Holy Trinity that were asked by priests during baptism.

In Eastern churches other statements of faith were common, such as the formula still in use by the Coptic church for baptism: "I believe in One God, the Father Almighty, and His only-begotten Son Jesus Christ our Lord, and in the Holy Spirit, the Life-giver, and in the Resurrection of the body. I believe in the one, holy, catholic, apostolic church, Amen." Other formulas were used by the churches of Punt, Jerusalem, Caesarea (Palestine), and Antioch.

Before Nicaea (see NICAEA, COUNCIL OF), two statements of faith were in use, one Eastern and the other Western, that were similar in substance though different in wording. Of the two, the Eastern one was abandoned after the adoption of the Niceno-Constantinopolitan Creed in all services and liturgies.

In the *Book of Common Prayer* of the Anglican church, the Apostles' Creed is used daily in the services of matins and evensong, except on the thirteen days in the year in which the Athanasian Creed is used in its place at matins. Here is the text in its latest form:

"I believe in God the Father Almighty, Maker of Heaven and Earth, and in Jesus Christ, His only Son, our Lord, Who was conceived by the Holy Ghost, born of the Virgin Mary; suffered under Pontius Pilate, was crucified, dead, and buried; He descended into hell; the third day He rose from the dead; He ascended into Heaven, and sitteth on the right hand of God the Father Almighty, from thence He shall come to judge the quick and the dead. I believe in the Holy Ghost; the Holy Catholic Church, the communion of Saints; the forgiveness of sins; the resurrection of the body; and the life everlasting. Amen."

BIBLIOGRAPHY

ʿAbd al-Masīḥ al-Masʿūdī. *Kitāb al-Maʿmūdiyyah al-Muqaddasah.* Cairo, 1896.

Asad Rustum. *Kasnīsat Madīnat Allāh Anṭakiyah al-Uẓmā,* 3 vols. Beirut, 1958.

Burn, A. E. *An Introduction to the Creeds.* London, 1899.

______. *The Apostles' Creed.* Oxford Church Text Books, 1906.

Carpenter, H. J. *Creeds and Baptismal Rites in the First Four Centuries.* Journal of Theological Studies 44. Oxford, 1943.

Creha, J. H. *Early Christian Baptism and the Creed.* London, 1950.

Ghellinck, J. "Histoire du symbole des apôtres à propos d'un texte d'Eusèbe." *Recherches de science religieuse* 16 (1928):118–25.

Kelly, J. N. D. *Early Christian Creeds.* Oxford, 1950; 3rd ed., 1972.

Kīrullus Maqār. *Al-Waḍʿ al-Ilāhī fī Ta'sīs al-Kanīsah,* 3 vols. Cairo, 1925.

Lietzmann, H. *Symbole der alten Kirche.* Berlin, 1931.

ARCHBISHOP BASILIOS

APOSTLES AND EVANGELISTS. *See* Christian Subjects in Coptic Art.

APOSTLES PETER AND PAUL, FEASTS OF THE. *See* Festal Days, Monthly.

APOSTOLIC CONSTITUTIONS, a vast canonical and liturgical work circulated in Christian antiquity under this name from the end of the fourth century, but without the name of the author. It is a reworking from several sources, composed by a Syrian. Books 1–6 have as their base the DIDASCALIA, which is here adapted to contemporary institutions, with some of its prescriptions weakened. Book 7 contains three parts: Chapters 1–36 are a development of the DIDACHE; Chapters 33–38 contain five prayers, which were perhaps inspired by Jewish prayers; Chapters 39–45 give a baptismal ritual in which borrowings from the APOSTOLIC TRADITION can be recognized, here very much developed. The book ends with various appendices in Chapters 46–49. Book 8 is also composed of three elements: Chapters 1–2 constitute a treatise on the charismata, which must have as its basis the one that preceded the text of the *Apostolic Tradition;* Chapters 3–46 rework the *Apostolic Tradition,* except for the ritual of initiation, already given in Book 7; finally, Chapter 47 gives a series of eighty-five canons, in which the author appears to have relied on various sources.

The author seems to have been an Arian, and the work shows clear traces of this. The work must have been compiled after the Council of CONSTANTINOPLE in 381, for its eighty-five canons were inspired by it, but before the council in the same city in 394, for the latter recalls this work.

The eighty-five canons of Book 8 were circulated in Coptic under the title *Apostolic Canons,* and the text has come down to us. The canons were edited by a P. de Lagarde, which was the pseudonym for Paulus Böetticher (1883). They were freely translated into Arabic and form the *Canons of the Apostles* (canons 1–56 of Book 2, ed. and trans. J. Périer and A. Périer). Without doubt, a Coptic translation existed, for fragments are known (Leipoldt, 1904; Lefort, 1911).

An epitome (abridgment) of Book 8 of the *Apostolic Constitutions* had been compiled in Greek, edited as the *Apostolic Constitutions* by F. X. Funk (1905, Vol. 2, pp. 72–96). In the *Sources chréti-*

ennes edition (Metzger, 1985–1986), this epitome has not appeared. It is taken up in part in the Coptic *Ecclesiastical Canons* and hence indirectly into Book 2 of the *Canons of the Apostles.*

Some parts of the *Apostolic Constitutions* exist also in Arabic translation in the *Octateuch of Clement,* with an arrangement different from that of the Syriac recension.

Finally, Books 1–6 are translated into Arabic and are called *Didascalia of the Apostles* (Ḥāfiẓ Dāwud, 1924, 1940, and 1968).

BIBLIOGRAPHY

Funk, F. X. *Didascalia et Consititutiones Apostolorum.* 2 vols. Paderborn, 1905; repr. Turin, 1959.

Ḥāfiẓ Dāwud. *Al-Dasqūliyyah aw ta'līm al-rusul.* Cairo, 1924; repr. 1940, 1968, and 1975.

Lagarde, P. de. "Apostolic Canons." In *Aegyptiaca,* pp. 208–238. Göttingen, 1883; rep. Osnebrück, 1972. Coptic text without trans.

Lefort, L. T. "Note sur le texte copte des Constitutions apostoliques." *Le Muséon,* n.s. 12 (1911): 23–24.

Leipoldt, J. *Saïdische Auszüge aus dem 8. Buche der Apostolischen Konstitutionen.* Texte und Untersuchungen, N. F. 11. Leipzig, 1904.

Metzger, M. *Les Constitutions apostoliques.* vols. Sources chrétiennes 320, 329, and 336. Paris, 1985–1987. Greek text with French trans.

Périer, A., and J. Périer. *Les "cent-vingt-sept canons des apôtres."* PO8. pt 4, pp. 664–93. Paris, 1912.

Reidel, W. *Die Kirchenrechtsquellen des Patriarchats Alexandrien.* Leipzig, 1900; repr. Aalen, 1968.

RENÉ-GEORGES COQUIN

APOSTOLIC FATHERS. The designation "apostolic fathers" goes back to J. B. Cotelier, who in 1672 published a two-volume edition of the *Sanctorum patrum qui temporibus apostolicis floruerunt.* Since then it has been usual to group under the name of *Patres apostolici* certain early Christian writers who were regarded as disciples of the apostles, still belonging to the apostolic age. Cotelier included among them Barnabas, CLEMENT OF ROME, IGNATIUS OF ANTIOCH, POLYCARP OF SMYRNA, and HERMAS, and he edited their genuine or supposed writings together with *Acts of the Martyrs* relating to Clement, Ignatius, and Polycarp.

In the nineteenth century the circle was widened. Included now in editions of the apostolic fathers were the *Epistle of Diognetus,* the surviving fragments of Papias of Hierapolis and Quadratus, the fragments of the Presbyter in Irenaeus of Lyons, and the DIDACHE that was discovered in 1873.

During the twentieth century the number of critical voices increased. The notion that the writings of the apostolic fathers follow those of the New Testament chronologically cannot be sustained because the latest parts of the New Testament and the oldest elements of the apostolic fathers came into being at the same time. These writings must therefore be studied together (cf. Vielhauer, 1975). We must also keep in mind that the term "apostolic fathers" covers writings that vary greatly among themselves.

An edition of the remnants of Coptic translations was produced in 1952 by L.-T. Lefort. It contains portions from the *Shepherd of Hermas;* the *Didache;* the first pseudo-Clementine epistle *De virginitate;* the letters of Ignatius, with the inauthentic epistle to Hero; the fictitious, so-called Roman martyrdom of Ignatius and the Laus Heronis; and a later eulogistic and petitionary prayer directed to Saint Ignatius. Lefort did not include Clement's first epistle and the *Martyrdom of Polycarp* in his edition. For these he refers to the editions of C. Schmidt and of I. Balestri and H. Hyvernat (1924). In 1981, E. Lucchesi announced supplements to Lefort from Paris folios: for Ignatius, *To the Philadelphians,* for the *Shepherd of Hermas,* and for the first pseudo-Clementine epistle *De virginitate.*

BIBLIOGRAPHY

Acta martyrum II, ed. I. Balestri and H. Hyvernat. CSCO 86, *Scriptores Coptica* 6, pp. 62–89. Paris, 1924; Louvain, 1953. CSCO 125, *Scriptores Coptica* 15, trans. into Latin by H. Hyvernat, pp. 43–50. Louvain, 1950.

Altaner, B., and A. Stuiber. *Patrologie,* 8th ed., pp. 43–58. Freiburg, Basel, and Vienna, 1978.

Fischer, J. A. *Die apostolischen Väter,* 8th ed., pp. 9–15. Darmstadt, 1981.

Lefort, L.-T., trans. *Les Pères apostoliques en Copte.* CSCO 135–36, *Scriptores Coptica* 17–18. Louvain, 1952.

Lucchesi, E. "Compléments aux pères apostoliques en Copte." *Analecta Bollandiana* 99 (1981):395–408.

Quasten, J. *Patrology I,* pp. 29–105. Utrecht, Brussels, 1950.

Schmidt, C. *Der erste Clemensbrief in altkoptischer Übersetzung.* Texte und Untersuchungen 32, 1. Leipzig, 1908.

Vielhauer, P. *Geschichte der urchristlichen Litera-*

tur. Einleitung in das Neue Testament, die Apokryphen und die apostolischen Väter. Berlin and New York, 1975.

THEOFRIED BAUMEISTER

APOSTOLIC SEE. Since the apostolic age, all episcopal seats have been considered equal in honor and rank, as all bishops were "equal legates of Jesus Christ" (Ignatius of Antioch, A.D. 35–107). Saint Cyprian, who presided over the Council of Carthage in 256, stressed the parity of episcopal rank, contending that since all churches were equal members of one catholic (universal) church, so were all bishops equal members of one episcopacy, with Christ their Head, and to Whom they were all answerable.

Following the expansion of Christianity and the proliferation of the Christian population, episcopal seats multiplied in number. Some of them acquired more prominence than others, in view of their greater civic responsibilities.

One factor, however, is of particular importance in distinguishing one episcopal see from another: certain sees were founded by the apostles themselves and enjoyed an unbroken apostolic succession. Hence they are designated as apostolic sees, the most important of which are Jerusalem, Alexandria, and Antioch in the East, and Rome in the West.

BIBLIOGRAPHY

Isidhūrus. *Al-Kharīdah al-Nafīsah fī Tārīkh al-Kanīsah.* Cairo, 1923.
Jerassimus Masarrah. *Tārīkh al-Inshiqāq.* Beirut, 1931.
Kīrullus al-Anṭūni. *'Aṣr al-Majāmi'.* Cairo, 1952.
Kīrullus Maqār. *Al-Waḍ' al-Ilāhī fī Ta'sīs al-Kanīsah.* Cairo, 1925.
Leclercq, H. "Siège apostolique." In *Dictionnaire d'archéologie chrétienne et de liturgie,* Vol. 15. Paris, 1907–1953.
Sullivan, F. A. "Apostolic See." In *New Catholic Encyclopedia.* New York, 1967.

ARCHBISHOP BASILIOS

APOSTOLIC SUCCESSION, term referring to the unbroken chain of spiritual authority passed to the bishops from the apostles of Jesus Christ, to whom He said "As the Father has sent me, even so send I you" (Jn. 20:21). The apostles appointed bishops who in turn chose others to follow them, a practice that has continued until the present age. Accordingly, ever since the dawn of Christianity, these bishops have been considered the successors of the apostles, as they were entrusted with the privilege of ministry as given to the apostles, such as the consecration of bishops, presbyters, and deacons.

Apostolic succession is also a continuation of Old Testament teachings. Aaron was chosen by God to minister to Him and, on his death, was followed by his sons (Ex. 28, Nm. 18). The infringement of this sole right resulted in grave consequences, and so when Korah, Dathan, and Abiram and their accomplices rose against God and His chosen they met with utter perdition (Nm. 16:16–21); likewise, when Uzziah, king of Judah, transgressed against the Lord and entered the sanctuary to burn incense he was struck with leprosy (2 Chr. 26).

In the New Testament the twelve disciples were chosen by Christ (Mt. 10; Jn. 6, 15), and Matthias was later chosen to replace Judas (Acts 1:23–26). Paul and Barnabas were also chosen through the Holy Spirit (Acts 13:2–3). They consecrated bishops to succeed them, as well as various priests and deacons. Paul also consecrated Timothy and Titus and granted them authority to consecrate and ordain others, and according to the epistle to the Hebrews (5:4), "And one does not take the honor upon himself, but he is called by God, just as Aaron was."

Each APOSTOLIC SEE, Jerusalem, Alexandria, Antioch, and Rome, maintained the apostolic succession in an uninterrupted chain, imparting the title of apostolic successor upon the patriarch of each church. Thus in Jerusalem he is the successor to Saint James, in Alexandria to Saint Mark, and in Antioch to Saint Peter. Ancient church historians recorded the names of apostolic successors from the apostolic age down to their own times (see Eusebius, *Ecclesiastical History* 2, 3, 4, 5, 6, and 7). The lists of names of these heads of churches were evidence of the origin and ancestry of their churches, and were used in refuting the arguments of heretics and non-Orthodox dissidents.

Apostolic succession is adhered to by all Eastern and Western churches, with the exception of those Protestant churches that do not recognize the principle of priesthood.

BIBLIOGRAPHY

Aléos, A. *La Théologie de S. Cyprien.* Paris, 1922.
Clarke, W. K. L. *First Epistle of Clement to the Corinthians.* London, 1937.
Ehrhardt, A. *The Apostolic Succession in the First Two Centuries of the Church.* London, 1953.
Ḥabīb Jirjis. *Asrār al-Kanīsah al-Sab'ah,* 2nd ed. Cairo, 1950.
Isidhūrus, Bp. *Naẓm al-Yāqūt fī Sirr al-Kahanūt.* Cairo, 1894.
______. *Bayān al-Buhtān al-Mawjūd fī Kitāb Sharḥ Uṣūl al-Īmān li-al-Brutestān.* Cairo, n.d.
Jerasimus Masarrah. *Al-Anwār fī al-Asrār.* Beirut, 1888.
Kirk, K. E. *The Apostolic Ministry.* London, 1946.
Sullivan, F. A. "Apostolic Succession." In *New Catholic Encyclopedia,* Vol 1, pp. 695, 696. New York, 1967.

ARCHBISHOP BASILIOS

APOSTOLIC TRADITION, a liturgical treatise, previously known as the Egyptian Church Order, by the ecclesiastical writer and theologian of the Roman church, HIPPOLYTUS (170–236). The original Greek text was lost, but Arabic, Coptic, Ethiopian, and Latin versions have survived, the oldest being the Sahidic Coptic translation made about 500. The Arabic version was made from a Coptic text not earlier than the tenth century.

In his work Hippolytus described among other things the consecration ceremony of bishops, the ordination of priests and deacons, and the sacrament of baptism. He gives the three catechismal steps of expression of faith in baptism in the following questions: "Do you believe in God the Father Almighty? Do you believe in Jesus Christ, the Son of God, Who was born of the Holy Spirit and of the Virgin Mary, Who was crucified at the time of Pontius Pilate, dead, and buried, Who rose from the dead on the third day, ascended to Heaven, and sat at the right hand of His Father, whence He will come to judge the quick and the dead? Do you believe in the Holy Spirit, the Holy Catholic Church, and the resurrection of the body?" Thereupon the priest anoints the baptized with consecrated oil, in the name of Jesus Christ.

BIBLIOGRAPHY

Connolly, R. H. *The So-called Egyptian Church Order and Derived Documents.* Cambridge Texts and Studies 8, 4. Cambridge, 1916.
Dix, G. *Treatise on Apostolic Tradition of St. Hippolytus of Rome,* trans. with *apparatus criticus* and some crititical notes. London, 1934.
Hanssens J. M. *La Liturgie d'Hippolyte.* Rome, 1959.
Hauler, E. *Didascaliae Apostolorum Fragmenta Veronensìa Latina.* Leipzig, 1900.
Horner, G. *The Statutes of the Apostles (Ethiopic, Arabic and Bohairic).* London, 1904.
Wilmart, A. "Un Règlement ecclésiastique du début du IIIe siècle, 'La Tradition Apostolique' de Saint Hippolyte." In *Revue du clergé français* 96 (1918):85.

ARCHBISHOP BASILIOS

APSE. *See* Architectural Elements of Churches.

AQBĀṬ, AL- (Latin, Lacbat). The village of al-Aqbāṭ is mentioned in twelfth-century documents of Norman Sicily. The name means "the Copts." The village is located about 9 miles (15 km) south of Palermo, near the present town of Altofonte (Cusa, 1868, pp. 185, 229, 730). The Sicilian Orientalist Michele Amari believed the town to be the village of Caputo, which is just over half a mile (1 km) east of Monreale (Dufour, 1859, p. 39), but Bercher (1979, p. 545) has shown it to be in the vicinity of Altofonte.

Medieval documents give little information about al-Aqbāṭ and only mention its jurisdictional borders. The town seems to have been founded during the period of Muslim rule on the island, but it appears that there were Copts in Sicily earlier, when it was under Byzantine administration (Gregorius I, 1957, Vol. 2, p. 362). The extent of their presence on the island and the nature of their settlement there are still not precisely known. There is, however, one piece of tangible evidence that sheds some light on the nature of their stay, at least in part. A tomb with Latin inscriptions belonging to a Coptic merchant from Alexandria who died in 602 has been uncovered in Palermo (Guillou, 1980, p. 258).

The town of al-Aqbāṭ had a church and a Christian population during the twelfth century, while the surrounding settlements seem to have been predominantly Muslim. But other than its name, there is no information indicating the ethnic composition of its inhabitants. The town was located near the Oreto River in a well-watered area where sugar cane was cultivated. Close by was a silk-, linen-, and cotton-producing region with textile manufacturing (Bercher, 1979, p. 545). It is very possible that the

Copts were involved in the textile industry for which they were famous in medieval times. On the other hand, they may have been brought to Sicily to introduce cultivation of sugarcane on the island.

BIBLIOGRAPHY

Bercher, H., et al. "Une Abbaye latine dans la société musulmane: Monreale au XIIe siècle." *Annales* 34 (1979):528–48.

Cusa, S. *I Diplomi Greci ed Arabi di Sicilia.* Palermo, 1868.

Dufour, A., and M. Amari. *Carte comparée de la Sicile moderne avec la Sicile au XIIIe siècle.* Paris, 1859.

Gregorius I. *Registrum Epistolarum,* 3 vols., ed. L. Hartmann, 2nd ed. Berlin, 1957.

Guillou, A. *Longobardi e Bizantini.* Turin, 1980.

LEONARD CHIARELLI

AQFAHṢ, village to the southwest of the *markaz* (district) of al-Fashn on the left bank of the Nile about 25 miles (40 km) south of Banī Suef, celebrated as the birthplace of Julius of Aqfahṣ, biographer of the martyrs and himself a martyr (see MARTYRS, COPTIC). E. Amélineau (1893, pp. 56–58) fully established the exact location of Aqfahṣ, which his predecessors had wished to place in the Delta.

A monastery dedicated to Saint Philemon the Martyr, no doubt the one mentioned by the Copt-Arabic SYNAXARION for 7 Baramhāt, is mentioned by the work attributed to Abū Ṣāliḥ (fol. 91[a]; Abū Ṣāliḥ, 1895, p. 254), as being in the southern part of the district. Al-Maqrīzī refers very briefly to a monastery at Aqfahṣ, and indicates that it is in ruins. This is probably the same as the one of which Abū Ṣāliḥ speaks. The latter notes (fol. 80[a]; Abū Ṣāliḥ, p. 230) that Anbā Sanhūt, bishop of Miṣr, took refuge there when he was excommunicated by the patriarch MICHAEL IV in the month of Bashans in the year A.M. 818 (May 1102). The patriarch wished to make the Church of Saint Sergius in Old Cairo, which was Sanhūt's episcopal seat, into the patriarchal church. However, the HISTORY OF THE PATRIARCHS, which relates this episode (Vol. 2, pt. 3, 1959, pp. 248 [text], 396 [trans.]), indicates as Sanhūt's place of refuge the Monastery of Saint Severus on Mount Asyūṭ.

BIBLIOGRAPHY

Amélineau, E. *La Géographie de l'Égypte à l'époque copte,* pp. 56–58. Paris, 1893.

RENÉ-GEORGES COQUIN

ARAB CONQUEST OF EGYPT. The conquest, under ʿAmr ibn al-ʿĀṣ, was the last of the rapid series of victories in the years A.H. 13–19/A.D. 635–640 that had led the Arabs to overthrow the weakened Byzantine provinces of the Near East. The conquest of Egypt marked the virtual end of a rapid period of expansion, since after the swift conquest of the Pentapolis, the victorious Arab forces were compelled to mark time in the western parts of North Africa. During the period of the Orthodox caliphs and Umayyads, until the Fatimid conquest, Egypt remained on the margin of the Islamic world, and the story of its conquest is of relevance to the affairs of the rest of the Arab world.

The sources include Arabic chronicles of high quality. The brief but standard accounts in Balādhurī's *Futūḥ al-Buldān* and Ibn ʿAbd al-Ḥakam's *Futūḥ Miṣr* (which contains the earliest and most reliable accounts) form the basis of many of the later traditions. These are recorded by writers such as Ibn Duqmāq, al-Maqrīzī, and al-Suyūṭī, and comprise the largest body of collective evidence, but for our purpose provide little that is not already found in the two sources named. Furthermore, these later accounts are based on a long and largely unverifiable chain of traditions, and reveal the characteristic and familiar weaknesses of Arabic historiography. This is particularly obvious with reference to the termination of various phases of the hostilities between Muslim and non-Muslim, the confusion of dates and events, an uncritical reliance on oral or written *ḥadīth* (unconscious and conscious repetition), and the excessive details concerning unimportant individual episodes. Except for short sketches of narrative, the chronicles present no sense of the general course of events. These are strictures from which only Balādhurī is relatively free.

At the same time, the Chronicle of John, the Monophysite bishop of Nikiou (the important city of the western Delta), is of primary importance as a contemporary document independent of Arab traditions; it survives, however, only in an Ethiopic translation of an Arabic version of a Coptic or Greek original. Besides being naive and disjointed in style, it is mutilated and incomplete in its present form. Nevertheless, it provides the main thread on which our narrative must hang, both for the information that it uniquely provides and as a corrective to the untrustworthy, though beguiling, Arab sources.

Late Byzantine and early Arabic papyri also provide documentary evidence for administrative and fiscal history. In addition, eccesiastical histories (particularly that of SĀWĪRUS IBN AL-MUQAFFA') and the lives of the saints, which now survive largely in Arabic versions of Greek or Coptic originals, offer individual items of significance to the secular historian. They form the basis of the history of the national church itself as well.

At best, therefore, the historian may hope to extract only an outline of what occurred from all these inadequate sources. The brief account that follows omits detailed discussion of the insoluble problems raised by many episodes (for these the reader is referred above all to the works of Butler and Caetani) and attempts only to provide a framework against which more detailed studies can be consulted with a clearer understanding. A few words of introduction regarding the condition of Byzantine Egypt will provide a background for the narrative of the conquest itself.

In terms of its links with the rest of the empire, the political stability of the province, which had not been achieved by the measures of Justinian, had been severely shaken a generation before the arrival of 'Amr's forces. First, the revolt of the elder Heraclius in Africa against the vicious government of Emperor Phocas (602–610) that placed the young Heraclius (610–641) on the throne of Byzantium was largely fought out on Egyptian soil. Second, a decade later, Egypt, like the other Byzantine provinces of the Middle East, was invaded by the Sassanid forces of Chosroes II (A.D. 619–628). As a result of the Persian occupation, both Alexandria and the whole of the Nile Valley were subjected to severe material and religious oppression for a decade. Some aspects of this period are described in vivid colors in the encomiastic Life of the Melchite patriarch, John the Almoner *(Eleemon)* of Cyprus. He was sanctified because of his eleemosynary works in Alexandria on behalf of the refugees from the Persian advance. They crowded into the city from all over the Middle East, and especially from Jerusalem. The delayed but victorious "crusade" of Heraclius against the Persians in 628–629 resulted in the reconquest of all the eastern provinces, but the wounds inflicted by the Persians could have healed only partially all the time the Arab forces advanced on the Nile Valley.

We can now recover few of the events of that tumultuous generation. The Arabs certainly knew very little of the true history (Torrey, 1922, pp. 33–34). We can say with some certainty that the life of Alexandria was profoundly shattered by the Persian invasion. It could hardly have recovered its stability after its reoccupation by Byzantine forces, nor at the time of the arrival of the Arabs. Furthermore, Sassanid rule, as had the Achaemenid rule a millennium before, undoubtedly led to the establishment of garrisons and centers of Persian life and religion in the provinces and in the area around Alexandria. John of Nikiou's narrative of the Persian occupation falls within a lacuna, but we learn from al-Ḥakam, *Futūḥ Miṣr* (Torrey ed., 1922, p. 74, 1. 16) and later derivatives that there was (at the time of the Arab conquest) a locality, near the Alexandrian suburb called by the Arabs Ḥilwān, still called Qaṣr Fars (the Persian Fort). There is, however, little evidence to suggest wholesale religious persecution. The life of the province as a whole seems to have been relatively undisturbed. Indeed, the large estates that were so conspicuous a feature of the provincial life of Byzantine Egypt certainly continued to exist during the Persian interlude. The religious incompatibility of Monophysite and Melchite may have prompted the Persian authorities to leave them to mutual destruction.

After the Byzantine reconquest of the province and on the eve of the Arab invasion, intersectarian disharmony was considerably increased. Heraclius appointed Cyrus (then probably bishop of Phasis in the Caucasus, and known to the Arabs as al-MUQAWQAS) to the combined secular and religious leadership of the province, in the role of augustal and Melchite patriarch (Sāwīrus ibn al-Muḳaffa', ed. Evetts, 1907, pp. 225–26). This left to separate authority only the command of the armed forces garrisoned in and near the city and at Babylon, the great Roman fortress opposite Giza. This was not the first such dual appointment made by Heraclius, for it is explicit at several points in the *Life* of John the Almoner that he himself had authority bestowed on him by Heraclius to issue edicts in his own name and to sit in judgment in civil cases. Earlier evidence for such a dual part can perhaps be seen in the appointment of JOHN II as augustal and patriarch by JUSTIN II in about 570. It is, therefore, in no way surprising that Cyrus should have played the leading role both on the ecclesiastical (Melchite) and civil fronts at the time of the final collapse of Byzantine power in Egypt. But the reputation of Cyrus as the unyielding foe of the Monophysites had preceded him to Egypt, and thus from the outset threatened the relations of the two churches at a fateful moment in Egyptian history.

Arab testimony is unanimous but doubtless incorrect in recording that the Prophet had had contacts with Egypt before the Arab invasion. The tradition is not impossible that as far back as A.H. 6/A.D. 628

Muḥammad had communicated with the rulers of the world, demanding recognition, and that his messenger to Egypt, Ḥāṭib ibn Abī Balṭā', had been kindly received by al-Muqawqas (who, however, was not in office at that time). It was further written by the Egyptian traditionalists that the "ruler" sent back various gifts with the messenger. Two of these were Egyptian slave girls, one of whom, a native of ANTINOOPOLIS, became the mother by Muḥammad of a son named Ibrāhīm. This embroidery is of considerable age, for *Futūḥ Miṣr* quotes it (pp. 45ff.) from a tradition reaching back to Hishām ibn Isḥāq and it occurs, with only a brief reference to Egypt, in the *Sīrah* of Ibn Isḥāq.

There seems little reason to doubt the tradition, recorded at length by *Futūḥ Miṣr* (pp. 53ff.) of the previous visit of 'Amr to Egypt in the company of a Christian deacon whose life he had saved in Palestine. In so journeying, 'Amr was following the normal practice of the caravan traders from the eastern side of the Red Sea; even if the story has received much romantic accretion, there seems no reason to doubt its basic truth. Previous familiarity with the wealth of the Nile Valley provides the strongest motive for 'Amr's insistence that 'Umar should approve the invasion of Egypt.

The conquest of Egypt itself stands in our traditions, both Arab and non-Arab, as an episode in which 'Amr exerted pressure upon the more cautious judgment of 'Umar and caused the latter reluctantly to yield (*Futūḥ Miṣr*, pp. 55ff.). The story is widely recorded that, after 'Umar's discussion with 'Amr at al-Jābiyah near Damascus, giving permission to proceed, he wrote 'Amr a letter that was to recall him if it reached him before he had crossed the Palestinian border into Egypt, south of al-'Arīsh. If, on the other hand, the letter was received and read when he was already inside Egypt, he should proceed with his campaign. According to this account, 'Amr, on receiving the missive, left it unopened and unread until he was safely inside Egyptian territory. The variant version, that this moral equivocation had been agreed between them at the meeting at al-Jābiyah, seems a pointless elaboration.

Whether 'Amr had a clear political plan in his campaign may be doubted, but it cannot be doubted that his strategy was based on a just appreciation of the geographical and military factors involved, as well as on the need to preserve his very limited forces—largely contingents from the northern Ḥijāz and the Yemen. Inevitably, his route led him past al-Faramā, down the old desert caravan route through the Wādī Ṭūmaylāt to the eastern flank of the Delta. His goal was Babylon, which would give him the most strongly fortified point in Egypt and would enable him to isolate the Delta before launching his attack on Alexandria. He could thus gain mastery of the whole Nile Valley by holding the crossing of the Nile at Giza. The decision to head straight for the Nile Valley was thus a preconceived strategy, which had the tactical advantage of enabling the Arabs, familiar with the desert routes, to pass outside the various Roman defensive positions until they reached Tendunias, the Arabs' Umm Dunayn. In taking this route, 'Amr was probably following in the steps of the Persians twenty years before. They, too, no doubt, wished to avoid the dangerous entanglements of the many branches of the Nile and the complexities of the canal system that led to Alexandria.

The reduction of al-Faramā is said to have occupied 'Amr for approximately a month—a conventional rather than an exact figure. According to Arab traditions, the assistance rendered by the Coptic population to the Arabs began at this point (*Futūḥ Miṣr*, pp. 58–59). The truth of this statement and of its consequences is discussed below. 'Amr advanced from al-Faramā without serious opposition to Bilbeis, where the caravan route reaches the cultivation, and this fell after a brief resistance. Further southwest, a few miles north of Babylon, at Tendunias (Umm Dunayn; *Futūḥ Miṣr*, p. 59, 10; Nikiou, p. cxii, 7–10), somewhere in the Azbakiyyah region of modern Cairo and a strongly defended Roman encampment, 'Amr met stronger resistance and sent urgently for reinforcement to 'Umar. According to the most trustworthy traditions, 'Umar sent him 4,000 foot soldiers under Khārijah ibn Khudhāfah, bringing the approximate total of 'Amr's troops to 8,000 *(Futūḥ Miṣr)* but making no allowance for losses incurred en route. With these reinforcements, a further battle was fought at 'Ayn Shams (Heliopolis), north of Tendunias, perhaps after the siege of Babylon had already begun. Here the battle was won by a successful Arab cavalry maneuver that outflanked the strong Roman entrenchments (Nikiou, p. cxii, 8; *Futūḥ Miṣr*, p. 59, 14ff., links this maneuver with the battle of Umm Dunayn). As a result of these victories, whatever their exact sequence, 'Amr was able to concentrate his energies on the siege of Babylon, whose great circular walls surrounded by a moat dominated the area between the Nile (which then ran close beside it) and the Muqaṭṭam hills to the east and controlled the route southward. It appears, however, that in spite of the natural advantage of striking hard at Babylon, ʿAmr at this point sent at least some of his troops to overcome the Roman forces scattered rather loosely in the Fayyūm and farther south, although the conquest of Upper Egypt itself was left to a later phase of operations. The fact reminds us that the Arabs were not adept at siege warfare (Nikiou, pp. cxi, 5f.; cxv, 9–10; cf. Butler, 1902, p. 219, n. 1; not in *Futūḥ Miṣr,* which gives a later account of a conquest of the Fayyūm, pp. 169–70, cf. Butler, pp. 218f.).

The number of the Roman defenders of Babylon, and indeed of Egypt as a whole, is very uncertain. John of Nikiou mentions numerous generals who were active at various points in the operations, but their individual roles are vaguely described. Theodorus seems to have been commander in chief and certainly played the leading role, and another George (?) was the commander of Babylon. Nor do we learn anything of the size or composition of the forces themselves. There is no doubt that the strict military formations of the early Byzantine period had been replaced in the reign of Justinian by troops *(arithmoi)* and garrisons commanded by tribunes *(tribuni),* and by the levies of *bucellarii* (private soldiers) raised by the owners of large estates. It is likely that these loosely associated forces, whose normal duties were probably protective in the manner of a police force rather than military, were neither well equipped nor well trained to meet the mobile and powerful Arab thrusts in open warfare. The multiplicity of command may itself have been a factor in the piecemeal defeat of the Roman forces.

The siege of Babylon began at the end of the flooding of the Nile (August–September) of A.H. 19/A.D. 640, and continued for seven months before its final capitulation in April 641. In the interval two attempts at negotiations failed. The first, probably about the end of September, is recounted in the Arab traditions. Cyrus, after consultation with his colleagues in the fortress, had himself secretly ferried over to "the island" Rawḍah (Roḍah). There he conducted a lengthy but abortive parley with ʿAmr, first through his own emissaries to the Arab camp, and then with the Arab envoys sent to Rawḍah, led by the powerful figure of ʿUbādah ibn al-Ṣāmit. This episode has the ring of truth, but the different traditions recorded by *Futūḥ Miṣr* (pp. 64ff.) are sufficiently at variance with each other on fundamental points to prevent acceptance of any single version. In any case, the options offered by the Arab delegation through ʿUbādah—either submission and the payment of tribute or continuation of the war—are no doubt historically correct. After some debate among the Romans, they were refused, and the siege continued.

The second episode is undoubtedly historical though it has to be pieced together from *Futūḥ Miṣr* and other sources. According to *Futūḥ Miṣr* (71–72), very shortly after this (in or about November 640), pessimistic over the outcome of the siege, Cyrus had returned from Rawḍah to Babylon and offered submission to ʿAmr, who in return offered the same alternatives of submission and payment of tribute or continuation of the war. This time a provisional treaty was signed, to be approved by the emperor (*Futūḥ Miṣr,* p. 71). Cyrus returned to Alexandria and wrote to Heraclius, who was not enthusiastic about the letter. Apparently he forthwith summoned Cyrus to Constantinople, where he was soundly berated for his cowardice in dealing with the Arab invasion (Nikiou, pp. cxvi, 14; cxix, 19–20; cxx, 4).

Meanwhile, having left a detachment to continue the siege, ʿAmr had been able to turn his attention to the subjugation of the Delta. However, he made little progress, and soon returned to the siege. In February 641 Heraclius had died, and by March news of this reached the Arab camp outside the citadel. On learning of it, the Roman garrison lost hope, and the Arabs pressed the siege still harder. The dramatic but probably unhistorical tradition of the feat of al-Zubayr ibn al-ʿAwwām seems to belong to this phase of the siege (*Futūḥ Miṣr,* pp. 63–64; not in Nikiou).

Al-Zubayr devoted himself to Allāh, undertaking to scale the walls and capture the fortress. He, and others who followed him, reached the top of the wall. They were recalled from entering by ʿAmr, who feared for Zubayr and at the same time insisted, in answer to Zubayr's protestations, that the Roman capitulations should be by surrender and not by force. The Roman garrison, under its acting commander, surrendered after a further brief resistance, and ʿAmr had thus achieved his aim.

The terms of the agreed treaty are not recorded in full in any recognizable form, but they are given in a very succinct version by John of Nikiou (p. cxvii, init.). The conditions of surrender seem to be of a strictly military nature.

> And ʿAmr, the chief of the Muslim forces, encamped before the citadel of Babylon and besieged the troops that garrisoned it. Now the latter received his promise that they should not be

put to the sword, and they on their side undertook to deliver up all the munitions of war, which were considerable. Thereupon he ordered them to evacuate the citadel, and they took a small quantity of gold and set out. And it was in this way that the citadel of Babylon in Egypt was taken on the second day after the [festival of the] Resurrection.

The text of the "Treaty of Miṣr" given in Butler, (Vol. 2, pp. 32–33), whatever its origin, does not seem to be a relevant document in this context. The doubts cast on its authenticity by S. Lane-Poole and L. C. Caetani are not wholly dispelled by Butler's subsequent vigorous treatment of the text.

With Babylon fallen, the forces of ʿAmr again turned northward and proceeded up the western side of the Delta, capturing Terenuthis, Nikiou (the main link between Babylon and Alexandria, and later the seat of Bishop John), Kom Sharīk and Sulṭays, and reached the outskirts of Alexandria at Ḥulwā and Max (*Futūḥ Miṣr,* pp. 73–74). ʿAmr, as always at his least effective when facing a siege, failed to take the city (Nikiou, p. cxix, 3) and left a detachment to continue the siege. He once more returned south to his new garrison at Babylon in order to meet Cyrus, who had returned in September from Constantinople via Rhodes to Alexandria (together with the commander-in-chief Theodore).

Cyrus came armed with authority to negotiate a permanent peace from the successive short-lived successors of Heraclius. This was signed between the two protagonists at Babylon in A.H. 20/A.D. 641. This final treaty of Alexandria, recorded by John of Nikiou (p. cxx, 17ff.), unlike the previous submission at Babylon, covered the whole field of future relations in Egypt to Muslim rule and acceptance of subject status, with payment of tribute and a two-dinar poll tax (JIZYAH) by all unconverted adult males. It provided for an armistice of eleven months during which the Byzantine troops were to evacuate all Egypt, including Alexandria; ʿAmr used this period to complete the reduction of the rest of the country as far as the Thebaid (Nikiou, p. cxv, 9; cf. *Futūḥ Miṣr,* pp. 139–40; 169–70). Alexandria finally opened its gates at the end of the period of armistice in A.H. 21/A.D. 642.

The termination of the period of armistice was followed by the evacuation of the Byzantine forces accompanied by Greek civilians, who are reported to have sailed to Constantinople. Jews were allowed to remain, though according to one tradition 7,000 left (*Futūḥ Miṣr,* p. 82). The number of departing Greeks is uncertain. The evacuation population is said to have consisted of 100,000 troops and civilians (*Futūḥ Miṣr,* p. 82; cf. Butler, 1902, p. 366, n. 3), although the ships were assembled for the purpose of carrying 30,000 persons with their goods and chattels. Prisoners numbering 600,000 were said to have been held, women and children excepted. These figures are certainly exaggerated, and there is no doubt that numbers of free Greeks remained behind in the city for a considerable time. According to John of Nikiou, Cyrus himself had already died during the period of armistice in March 642, grief-stricken at the fall of his city. The news of the fall of the great city was conveyed to ʿUmar in Medina by ʿAmr's envoy, Muʿāwiyah ibn Hudayj (*Futūḥ Miṣr,* p. 81).

The whole reduction of the country had taken only three years from the arrival of the first troops at al-Faramā. During this period the Arab forces had been living on the sustenance provided by the country itself. The pressure this placed on the peasant population is attested by numerous surviving Greek and Arabic papyri, which contain *entagia,* demands for requisition of livestock, fodder, and supplies for troops. Such requisitions continued to be a feature of Muslin rule, and papyri of a later date (of the period A.D. 698–722) include the voluminous correspondence of the most notable of all the early governors of Egypt, the much-disliked Qurrah ibn Sharīk. Many of these letters deal with the same or similar topics. (See the analysis in Butler, 1977, pp. 76ff.; for the Qurrah papyri, see pp. 80ff.; cf. also Nikiou, p. cxiii, 4).

There is an epilogue to the conquest. Four years after the evacuation, the Byzantine government engineered a revolt in Alexandria, headed by one Manuel, who was sent from Constantinople. This attempt to oust the Muslim conquerors extended over the Delta but was put down without difficulty and marks the end of the conquest (*Futūḥ Miṣr,* p. 80, without reference to Manuel, but clearly referring to the later siege; also pp. 175.3–176.8, on the death of Manuel; Theophilus 338; cf. Butler, 1902, p. 481). It should be stressed that the double siege and double surrender, once by voluntary submission *(ṣulḥ)* and once by force *(ʿunwatan),* led to that profound confusion in the minds of the Egyptian traditionalists, who in a short time inextricably conflated the terms imposed after the second conquest with those imposed after the first. Unfortunately, no clear statement as to a second treaty, if one existed, survives, and we should probably accept the conclusion that the status assigned to Alexandria and the villages associated in the revolt was, on the instruction of ʿUthmān, left unchanged from that imposed after the original conquest. That is to say, the conquered remained protected persons on payment of the poll tax (the matter is recorded at length in *Futūḥ Miṣr,* pp. 82ff.). There is, in any case, no doubt that the second siege was conquest by force (*Futūḥ Miṣr,* pp. 175–81; Balāhurī, 1956, pp. 260–61, 347–84; Butler, 1902, pp. 465–83). This was also conducted by ʿAmr, who was recalled from a post to which he had been assigned outside Egypt to command the Muslim forces (*Futūḥ Miṣr,* pp. 173–74). He spent only a month in Alexandria after the original conquest. He is said to have handed the city over to destruction and to have razed its fortifications, although the walls were either soon rebuilt, or, as frequently in the past, had been only partially demolished (Balādhurī, pp. 347–48). At the point at which the Arabs sheathed their swords ʿAmr erected the "Mosque of Mercy" (Masjid al-Raḥmah).

The relative ease with which Egypt fell before the small Muslim forces was long explained as the result of the cooperation of the Monophysite population, which, under the leadership of their patriarch, BENJAMIN I, could no longer brook the long-standing Melchite persecutions, which reached a climax under Cyrus himself. This view was challenged in forceful terms by A. J. Butler, who regarded the Copts as having remained faithful to their imperial allegiance in spite of all their tribulation, until after the surrender of Babylon or the capture of the Fayyūm, when they saw that further resistance would be fruitless. They then collaborated with the invading forces. Others have not been convinced by this argument, and indeed the evidence, in spite of all the confusion in either direction, seems to point to the traditional view. In Ibn ʿAbd al-Ḥakam (*Futūḥ Miṣr,* p. 58.20ff.) there is a tradition going back to vague Egyptian sources that Benjamin himself, on hearing of the arrival of ʿAmr at al-Faramā, wrote to his flock that the power of Byzantium was broken and that the "Copts" should rally to ʿAmr. That, if true, was not unduly prescient of him, in view of the speed of the Arab conquests elsewhere, nor was he likely to be unaware that the Muslim treatment of religious minorities would be governed by more rational procedures than those of Melchite persecution.

On the other hand, John of Nikiou, our earliest and normally most reliable source, appears to imply that the collaboration of the Copts began only after the approximate time of the submission of Babylon (Nikiou, p. cxiii, 1). The issue is historically crucial, but the chaotic state of the surviving text of John at this point does not permit a decision in favor of prolonged Coptic allegiance to Byzantium; the subsequent persecutions of the Copts carried out by Cyrus after his return from Constantinople (Nikiou, p. cxvi, 14, misplaced) hardly affect the issue. Cyrus himself seems to have regretted his role in the final fall of Egypt but is not reported to have felt any particular remorse over his treatment of the Copts. Ironically, the Arab traditionalists frequently regard him as a Copt, that is, as Egyptian and not Roman. Perhaps no solution of this problem is possible with the evidence in its existing state. In any case, the causes of defeat were complex. The military failure of the Byzantine government, the personal character of Cyrus, in particular his persecution of the Copts, and the hostility of the overwhelmingly Monophysite population must all in different degrees have contributed to the defeat. The hostility of the Copts, amply justified in their own eyes, was probably the decisive factor in terms of local assistance provided to the Muslim troops, particularly in the Delta. This assistance is recorded beyond doubt in the later stages of the campaign by the Arab chroniclers, possibly in exaggerated terms (*Futūḥ Miṣr,* pp. 73, 3ff.; 74, 16–17).

ʿAmr had established a new era in Egyptian history when he first set up his standard just north of Babylon, on the site known henceforth as al-Fusṭāṭ (*fossatum,* the camp, perhaps from a previously existing Byzantine camp). From A.H. 22/A.D. 643 onward the area between the river and the Muqaṭṭam Hills was divided into tribal and military allotments. These familiar inalienable *khiṭṭahs* (districts) rapidly grew into a town that, in turn, spread farther north and east of the fortress. Their partially excavated ruins are a familiar sight today. Gradually, however, the center of urban gravity moved slightly farther north, and the area of al-Fusṭāṭ began to be abandoned when the Abbasid dynasty built al-ʿAskar as a residential area, in the neighborhood later occupied by the Mosque of Ibn Ṭūlūn. This transference was consummated in A.D. 969, by the foundation of al-Qāhirah by the Fatimid commander Jawhar al-Siqillī. The settlement was slightly farther north in the area between Babylon and the old Tendunias. References to al-Fusṭāṭ still occur in the twelfth century, and the excavations have yielded considerable material from this latest phase, before its destruction by fire in A.D. 1168.

The material consequences of the conquest weighed heavily on the native population. The protection of the *Dhimmis* (unconverted) was guaranteed in return for a payment of *jizyah* (poll tax) of supposedly fixed taxes, which were embodied in the terms of the capitulation, at two dinars per adult male, and an additional *kharaj* (land tax) payable by those (including churches) possessing land in the provinces. In addition, the protected population was required to provide a measure of clothing and hospitality to any itinerant Muslim. This description is vague enough to cover the innumerable variations of interpretation offered by Arab chroniclers, jurists, and writers on taxation, to say nothing of many of their modern successors concerning the imposition of these taxes. Much of this confused material reflects the theoretical variations of a later date. Nevertheless, contemporary papyri as well as some historical sources show clearly that the Dhimmis in early Muslim Egypt were, in fact, the victims not so much of a system fixed *ab origine* by the capitulation but of frequent and seemingly haphazard changes in status and in levels and incidence of taxation. Of these, the poll tax weighed heavily on lay people and eventually clerics alike, and at some periods even the converted were not exempt.

In most other respects the Arab authorities did little more than adapt the existing bureaucratic system to a more efficient standard of administration. This was focused on the person of the PAGARCH, whose role is amply documented for us in two sets of correspondence, that between Qurrah and Basilius of Aphrodito, and that between Papas, pagarch of Apollonos Ano, and the amīr of the Thebaid. The main effect of this was certainly to be seen in the provinces, where the large estates and autopract domains of Coptic landowners that had dominated the life of the country and country towns, were swiftly abolished and appropriated for allotment. The pagarchic system survived long after the Umayyad period, and, correspondingly, Greek remained the main vehicle of intercourse between governor and governed until the ninth century. On the other hand, the steady stream of Arab military settlers and garrison troops, who virtually repopulated the Delta and other areas in the early period, led to the rapid predominance of the Muslim faith, and, in time, to the almost complete predominance of the Arab tongue.

BIBLIOGRAPHY

Ibn Abd al-Ḥakam. *Futūḥ Miṣr wa-Akhbāruhā*, edited from manuscripts in Paris and London by Charles C. Torrey under the title *The History of the Conquest of Egypt, North Africa and Spain*, known as *Futūḥ Miṣr*. Yale Oriental Series, Researches 3. New Haven, 1922. First printing in Leiden, 1920. Another earlier edition under the title *Futūḥ Miṣr wa-al-Maghrib* was edited by Abd al-Mun'im Āmir; Cairo, 1911. References in this article are to the Torrey edition.

Balādhurī, al-, Aḥmad ibn Yaḥyā ibn Jābir. *Kitāb Futūḥ al-Buldān*, 3 vols., ed. Ṣalāḥ-al-Din al-Munajjid. Cairo, 1956. First edited by De Joeje, *Liber expugnationis regionum*, 3 pts., Auctore Imama Ahmed ibn Iahja ibn Djabir al-Baladsori. Leiden 1863–1866. Reproductions of the Leiden ed. made in Cairo 1901 and again in 1932 without index, diacritical marks, or critical apparatus.

Butler, A. J. *The Arab Conquest of Egypt*. Oxford, 1902. Second, amplified ed. P. M. Fraser, Oxford, 1977. My edition includes Butler's later pamphlets entitled *The Treaty of Miṣr by Ṭabarī* (1913) and *Babylon of Egypt* (1914). In the introductory section of the second edition, I have given in considerable detail an analysis of other relevant works both in general and by chapter. The reader should consult this edition, to which some further modern items might be added, but no additional ancient evidence has come to light directly relating to the conquest. As explained in Butler, 2nd ed., p. 50, the full text of Abd al-Ḥakam was not available to Butler, though Caetani was able to use one of the two Paris manuscripts of the *Futūḥ Miṣr* (see p. 51).

Caetani, L. C. *Annali dell'Islam;* vols. 1–7. Milan, 1905–1914. Repr., Hildesheim, 1972. Most important are sections analyzed in Butler, 2nd ed., pp. 163–69.

Kubiak, W. *Al-Fusṭāṭ: Its Foundation and Early Urban Development*. Dissertation, University of Warsaw, 1982. Contains a valuable discussion of Arab sources, including Ibn 'Abd al-Ḥakam, pp. 18ff.

Lane-Poole, S. *Egypt in the Middle Ages*, 8 vols. London, 1901.

———. *The Story of Cairo*. Mediaeval Towns Series. London, 1902.

Nikiou, John of. *Chronique*, in *Notices et Extraits des manuscrits de la Bibliothèque Nationale*, Vol. 24, ed. H. Zotenberg. Paris, 1883. English trans. R. H. Charles, *The Chronicle of John, Bishop of Nikiu*. London, 1916.

For further bibliographical material, including that relating to the Polish reports of their excavations at Kom al-Dik, which embrace both the Byzantine and the early Islamic periods, see ALEXANDRIA, CHRISTIAN AND MEDIEVAL.

P. M. FRASER

'ARAJ, AL-, small oasis on the road that joins the oasis of Siwa, west of Alexandria, to BĀWIṬ in the oasis of al-Baḥariyyah, about 65 miles (100 km) from Siwa. A. Fakhry thinks that the ancient tombs that he excavated there preserve traces of paintings of the Christian period, which would indicate that they must have been occupied by hermits (Fakhry, 1939, p. 614; 1973–1976, Vol. 1). However, A. de Cosson, who had written earlier, advanced an opposing opinion (1937, pp. 226–29).

BIBLIOGRAPHY

Cosson, A. de. "Notes on the Bahrên, Nuwêmisah and el-Areg Oases in the Libyan Desert." *Journal of Egyptian Archaeology* 23 (1937):226–29.

Fakhry, A. "The Tombs of el-ʿAreg Oasis in the Libyan Desert." *Annales du Service des Antiquités de l'Egypte* 39 (1939):609–19.

MAURICE MARTIN, S.J.
RENÉ-GEORGES COQUIN

ARCHANGEL

ARCHANGEL (Coptic, ⲁⲣⲭⲏⲁⲅⲅⲉⲗⲟⲥ, from the Greek ἀρχάγγελος, arkhággelos), superhuman being dwelling in heaven who reveals to man God's will and executes His commands. Archangels occupy the eighth of the nine ranks in the hierarchy of the heavenly host, which has a threefold structure (see ANGELS).

A Coptic doxology, forming part of the service of the evening and the morning offering of incense, includes the names of seven archangels who constantly glorify the Almighty: MICHAEL (Mīkhā'īl), GABRIEL (Ghubriyāl), RAPHAEL (Rūfā'īl), SURIEL (Suryāl), Sadakael, Saratael, and Ananael: they are the great, pure, and luminescent beings who intercede on behalf of humanity.

Commemoration dates of the first four archangels are Michael on 12 Hatūr, Gabriel on 22 Kiyahk, Raphael on 3 al-Nasī, and Suriel on 27 Ṭūbah.

BIBLIOGRAPHY

Marriott, W. B. "Angels and Archangels." In *Dictionary of Christian Antiquities*, Vol. 1, pp. 87–89. London, 1876.

Payne, D. F. "Michael the Archangel." In *The New International Dictionary of the Christian Church*, p. 657. Great Britain, 1974.

ARCHBISHOP BASILIOS

ARCHBISHOP

ARCHBISHOP. Following the apostolic age, all bishops of the church were considered equal in rank and dignity. According to Saint Cyprian (d. 258), "The episcopate is one, of which each bishop holds his part within the undivided structure. The church also is one however widely she has spread among the multitude" (*The Unity of the Catholic Church*, in Jurgens, 1970, Vol. 1, p. 221).

With time, however, certain bishops came to be distinguished over others through their longer tenure in office and their experience in organization and administration, thus deserving the title of archbishop. Again the church had to follow the civic division of the country into provinces, whereby the bishop of the capital city of each province took precedence over other bishops. In addition, some apostolic episcopates, such as Jerusalem, Alexandria, Antioch, Ephesus, and Rome had acquired seniority due to the honor of having been established by the apostles themselves.

In the fourth century, the rank of METROPOLITAN came into use, thereby giving the metropolitan bishop authority over other bishops in his province. *Apostolic Canon* 34 stipulates: "The bishops of every nation must acknowledge him who is first among them and account him as their head, and do nothing of consequence without his consent; but each may do those things only which concern his own parish and the country places which belong to it. But neither let him (who is the first) do anything without the consent of all; for so there will be unanimity, and God will be glorified through the Lord in the Holy Spirit" (*The Apostolical Canons*, 1956, p. 590).

Likewise Canon 9 of the Council of Antioch (341) lays down the following:

> It behooves the bishop in every province to acknowledge the bishop who presides in the metropolis, and who has to take thought for the whole province; because all men of business come together from every quarter to the metropolis. Wherefore it is decreed that he have precedence in rank, and that the other bishops do nothing extraordinary without him (according to the ancient canon which prevailed from the times of our Fathers) or such things only as pertain to their own particular parishes and the districts subject to them. For each bishop has authority over his own parish, both to manage it with the piety which is incumbent on everyone, and to make provision for the whole district which is dependent on his city; to ordain presbyters and deacons; and to settle everything with judgment. But let him undertake nothing further without the bishop of the metropolis; neither the latter without the consent of the others (*The Canons of the Blessed and Holy Fathers*, 1956, p. 112).

From the above and other canons, it is clear that the archbishop's prerogative was to preside over the synod, to head the ceremony of consecration of bishops in his diocese, and to look into grievances as well as decisions of other local episcopal councils.

Following the introduction of the rank of patriarch in the fifth century, the bishops of patriarchal sees, for example, Rome and Constantinople, were designated archbishops at the Council of CHALCEDON (451).

BIBLIOGRAPHY

Canons of the Blessed and Holy Fathers Assembled at Antioch in Syria. In *A Select Library of the Nicene and Post-Nicene Fathers of the Christian Church,* 2nd ser., Vol. 14, ed. P. Schaff and H. Wace. Grand Rapids, Mich., 1956.

Cyprian of Carthage. *The Unity of the Catholic Church.* In *The Faith of the Early Fathers,* Vol. 1, ed. W. A. Jurgens. Collegeville, Minn, 1970.

Kīrullus al-Anṭūnī. *'Aṣr al-Majāmi',* pp. 69, 70, 112. Cairo, 1952.

Salīm Sulaymān. *Mukhtaṣar Tārīkh al-Ummah al-Qibṭiyah fī 'Aṣray al-Wathaniyyah wa-al-Masīhiyyah),* p. 337. Cairo, 1914.

ARCHBISHOP BASILIOS

ARCHDEACON. The rank of archdeacon dates back to the apostolic age. Having appointed seven deacons, "men of good repute, full of the Holy Spirit and of wisdom," the apostles selected one of them, Stephen, to be their chief (Acts 6:1–6). However, no mention is made to this particular rank in the letter written by Cornelius, bishop of Rome (251–253), to Fabius, bishop of Antioch, although Cornelius refers to other ranks of the diaconate (Eusebius, *Historia ecclesiastica* 6.43).

The position of archdeacon became fully established in the Eastern and Western churches in the fourth century, as evidenced by the writings of Saint Augustine (*De Diversis Questionibus ad Simplicianum* III.9). Theodoret, bishop of Cyrrhus (393–466), in his history of the Council of NICAEA, describes the position of ATHANASIUS as the principal deacon (reported in *Eusebius* 1. 25). The archdiaconate equally figures in the proceedings of the Council of EPHESUS (431).

Seniority in the diaconate appears to have been the criterion for promotion to the archdeaconate. This rule, nevertheless, was not without its exceptions, as Athanasius became head of the deacons though still young, without being the most senior of deacons when the patriarch ALEXANDER I (312–326) appointed him archdeacon. Likewise Saint JOHN CHRYSOSTOM (347–407) ordained Serapion deacon and then archdeacon of the church of Constantinople (Socrates, *Historia ecclesiastica* 6.4; Sozomen, *Historia ecclesiastica* 8.9).

On the recommendation of the congregation and the clergy, a bishop ordains an archdeacon in accordance with the sacrament of holy orders. The ordination service follows immediately after the prayer of the aspasmos (Kiss of Peace) and before the congregation sings the hymn of the aspasmos. The bishop says: "Our Master, Lover of man . . . do send the grace of Thy Holy Spirit upon Thy servant [Name] who is called to be an archdeacon through the vote and judgment of those who have brought him into our midst and the request of those who have given account of him. Make him worthy to be archdeacon for Thy holy church . . . that he may hold the chalice of the precious Blood of the Lamb without blemish which is Thine only-begotten Son; that he may minister unto the orphans and help the widows, having care of the servers . . . nor is this grace given through the imposition of our hands, we being sinners, but by the visitation of Thy rich compassion, it is given to those who are worthy of it. . . . We pray and beseech Thee, the Good One and Lover of man, on behalf of Thy servant [Name], that Thou shouldst make him worthy of the grace of the calling of the archdiaconate through the descent upon him of Thy Holy Spirit."

The bishop then lays hands upon him, and he takes part in the celebration of Divine Liturgy.

The archdeacon is charged with making necessary arrangements for church services, assigning various tasks to deacons and subdeacons; safekeeping of church books, vessels, and vestments; ensuring that church charity is received by the needy; acting as a liaison on behalf of the bishop; and participating in recommending candidates for the diaconate and for promotion to higher ranks.

BIBLIOGRAPHY

Burmester, O. H. E. *The Egyptian or Coptic Church.* Cairo, 1967.

Cummings, D. *The Rudder.* Athens, 1908.

Iqlādyus Yuḥannā Labīb. *Kitāb al-Abṣalmudiyyah al-Sanawiyyah al-Muqadassah.* Cairo, 1911.

Mas'ūdī 'Abd al-Masīh Ṣalīb, al-. *Al-Khūlājī al-Muqaddas.* Cairo, 1902.

Stanley, A. P. *Lectures on the History of the Eastern Church.* London, 1906.

ARCHBISHOP BASILIOS

ARCHELAUS OF NEAPOLIS is an imaginary figure invented by the Coptic authors of the period of the CYCLES. Various homilies are attributed to him. Information on his fictional personality can be drawn only from the content of his homilies, and his mention in the Coptic-Arabic SYNAXARION on 22 Kiyahk also derives from one of these. He is said to have been bishop of Neapolis (it is not specified which, but probably Nablus of Palestine was intended), the successor of a certain Nikolaus; he traveled in the Holy Land and built a church in his town dedicated to the Archangel GABRIEL.

We possess a complete homily attributed to him and a fragment of another (not published; Paris, National Library, Copte 131.1.28) that is an exegesis of a moral character of certain passages of Isaiah (in particular Is. 5:22).

The complete homily, *In Honor of the Archangel Gabriel,* exists in Sahidic (New York, Pierpont Morgan Library M 583.1–16, unpublished; fragments of a codex of DAYR ANBĀ SHINŪDAH, or the White Monastery) and in Bohairic (Rome, Vatican Library, Coptic 59.30–49, ed. Vis, 1929, pp. 246–91, fragments of another codex of Saint Macarius). The redactions are in substantial agreement with each other.

In order to celebrate Gabriel, Archelaus gives an account of a pilgrimage he made to the Holy Land, especially to the monastery of Saint Romanus. In the library of this monastery he found an old book narrating Jesus' revelations to the apostles concerning Saint Gabriel. When, with the help of Bishop Nikolaus, he returned to Neapolis, Archelaus had a church built in honor of the archangel. The rest of the homily consists of an account of the miracles Gabriel worked to help in the building of the church and then to establish its authority.

The elements of this homily are traditional. The journey to the Holy Land and the discovery of an old book with revelations of Jesus are found in many Coptic texts of the same period. For miracles during the building of a church, see the text attributed to ACACIUS OF CAESAREA in honor of Saint MERCURIUS.

BIBLIOGRAPHY

Vis, H. de, ed. and trans. *Homélies coptes de la Vaticane.* Coptica 1, 5. Copenhagen, 1922, 1929.

TITO ORLANDI

ARCHELLIDES, SAINT, a Roman noble who became a monk in Palestine (feast day: 13 Ṭūbah). The account of his life has been preserved in Sahidic in a complete codex (New York, Pierpont Morgan Library M 579.1) and in various fragments from DAYR ANBĀ SHINŪDAH (ed. Drescher, 1947), and is attributed to one Eusebius, a historiographer of Rome who, in the mind of whoever composed it, was obviously the same person as EUSEBIUS OF CAESAREA, without apparent reason for such an attribution.

We are told that Archellides came from a noble and very pious family of the city of Rome. He is educated by "philosophers" and sent to complete his education in Athens and Beirut. Along the way he meets a corpse and is so struck by this that he takes a vow of virginity and goes to the Palestinian monastery of Saint Romanus. He is accepted by the monks, performs great acts of asceticism, and is also respected for his wisdom.

Without any news of him, his mother is very sad; she opens a hostel where she takes care of wayfarers. After twelve years some passing merchants discuss Archellides, and his mother learns where he is. She gives her belongings to the poor and sets out. When she reaches the monastery, she asks to see her son, who refuses her an audience [presumably because he has vowed not to look at the face of a woman]. The mother insists, and in his difficulty Archellides prays intensely for death. His mother thus manages to see him, although he is already dead; she prays that she too may die, and her prayer is granted.

The text is one of the fictitious stories not linked to a Cycle and seems to have been composed directly in Coptic in about the seventh century.

BIBLIOGRAPHY

Drescher, J. *Three Coptic Legends: Hilaria, Archellites, the Seven Sleepers.* Supplement to *Annales du Service des Antiquités de l'Egypte* 4. Cairo, 1947.

TITO ORLANDI

ARCHIMANDRITE, a term of Greek origin (*archein,* to rule, and *mandra,* fold, byre) denoting the superior of a monastery. Although its precise application is the subject of controversy, one thing is certain: it was a higher-ranking term than others such as father, PROESTOS, and HEGUMENOS. The title "archimandrite" emerged in the Syrian and Mesopotamian regions during the course of the fourth century and subsequently became part of the terminology employed by Eastern Christianity as a whole. Undoubtedly, its precise application changed from one country or period to another.

The oldest examples of the use of the title in texts referring to Egypt are to be found in the *Historia Lausiaca* of PALLADIUS and the letters of ISIDORUS OF PELUSIUM (c. 360–440).

The *Historia lausiaca,* written around 410, contains the recollections of the author's stay in Egypt at the end of the fourth century. PACHOMIUS (7.6) and an anonymous superior of a monastic community from which the young Cronius escaped (21.1) are described as archimandrites. The second example could prove that the word was universally used in reference to "ordinary" superiors, and not only to such personalities as Pachomius, if we could only be certain that Palladius really heard it from his collocutor. This cannot be ascertained.

Isidorus, the author of numerous letters, among which are some addressed to an archimandrite (Epistles I, 49, 117, 258, 283, 298, 318, 392), also uses the term *hegumenos;* this clearly proves that these words were differentiated.

In later literary texts, both Coptic and Greek, the title archimandrite is applied to Pachomius and later superiors of the whole Pachomian congregation, as also to SHENUTE and his successors. Famous monks known from hagiographic sources, such as MOSES OF ABYDOS and Apollo, the abbot of the Monastery of Isaac, are also described as archimandrites. The same title was held by Apa Jeremiah, the founder of the monastery at Saqqara (DAYR APA JEREMIAH) and by his successors. No evidence is presently available as to whether it was applied in reference to the superiors of NITRIA. Both in the Pachomian congregation and in the monastery at Saqqara, the term "archimandrite" denoted the superior of the entire community while the superiors of its components were described as *proestos.* Apart from the above-mentioned cases, the title of archimandrite was used by monastic superiors of less well-known and certainly smaller communities in various parts of Egypt.

It is not possible to determine exactly the criteria for using the title, since there are not enough texts to indicate the principles according to which one superior was known as archimandrite while another one was given a different title. The title was not exclusively reserved for superiors of congregations or groups of monasteries. The example of Shenute, whose great monastery was not divided into smaller units, proves that. Moses of Abydos also did not lead a congregation. The title was not even reserved for superiors of the cenobite monasteries, as W. E. Crum (1926) believed, since it appears in documents referring to lauras in al-Balayzah (Kahle, 1954, p. 33) and in Wādī Sarjah (Thompson, 1922), which leave no doubt as to the type of monastic community existing there. Moreover, Apa Paulos, the superior of a group of anchorites, was titled archimandrite (Crum and Steindorff, 1912, no. 106), while his successors held only the title of *proestos.* W. Hengstenberg tried to explain this, assuming that Apa Paulos not only directed his own group but also supervised the ascetics of the entire region. This hypothesis is worthy of careful consideration, since it presumes the existence of a sort of superstructure over various forms of ascetic communities in a given area, which could have been established by bishops and sometimes by the patriarch. The existence of certain forms of supervision is sometimes actually attested. As early as 330, Pachomius refused the offer of such a function from the bishop of Dandarah (Vita Prima 29, Halkin, 1932, p. 19). Another famous but much later example concerns JOHN OF NIKIOU, who was granted by the patriarch SIMON I "the management of the affairs of the monasteries because he was conversant with the life of monks and he knew their rules, and he gave him the authority over them" (Sāwīrus, 1910, pp. 32–33).

However, if we were to prove the universal existence of such superstructures—and this is a difficult task—it would by no means signify that the title of archimandrite was always applied to that person who supervised all the monks of a given region.

An explanation of the use of this title must come from elsewhere. It was probably an honorific term that was due to the superiors of famous and great monasteries because of their rank in the monastic world. It was also given to the superiors of smaller centers if they happened to be famous for their piety, literary activity, influence upon local brothers, or the like (Lampe, 1961–1968, under "archimandrites"). The honorific nature of the title is the reason it appears in some literary texts if someone addresses a superior, while in the story told in the third person other expressions are employed, as in A. Alcock's life of SAMŪ'ĪL OF QALAMŪN (1984, p. 41).

This use of the term corresponded to the mentality of a milieu that carefully observed the application of titles that reflected hierarchy but at the same time recognized informal authority which was the consequence of personal merits and a charismatic personality rather than an official post. It is difficult to say who had the right to grant this title—bishops in their dioceses, the patriarch, or public opinion as a result of use.

Papyri published by Crum (1909, no. 124) and by P. V. Jernstedt (1959, no. 3) show that the term "archimandrite" was sometimes replaced by the Coptic *noh nrome.*

BIBLIOGRAPHY

Alcock, A. *The Life of Samuel of Kalamoun.* London, 1984.

Crum, W. E. *Catalogue of the Coptic Manuscripts in the Collection of the John Rylands Library.* Manchester, 1909.

———. *The Monastery of Epiphanius at Thebes,* Vol. 1, p. 130; Vol. 2, commentary to text no. 133. New York, 1926.

Crum, W. E, and G. Steindorff, eds. *Koptische Rechtsurkunden des achten Jahrhunderts aus Djeime.* Leipzig, 1912.

Halkin, F. *Vitae Graecae.* Brussels, 1932.

Hengstenberg, W. "Review of *Ten Coptic Legal Texts* by A. A. Schiller." *Byzantinische Zeitschrift* 34 (1934):90.

Isidorus of Pelusium. *Epistulae.* PG 78. Turnhout, n.d.

Jernstedt, P. V. *Koptskie teksty Ermitazha.* Moscow, 1959.

Kahle, P. *Bala'izah: Coptic Texts from Deir el-Bala'izah.* London, 1954.

Lampe, G. W. H. *A Patristic Greek Lexicon.* Oxford, 1961–1968.

Pargoire, J. "Archimandrites." In *Dictionnaire d'archéologie chrétienne et de liturgie.* Paris, 1903.

Thompson, C. R. *Introduction to Wadi Sarga. Coptic and Greek Texts.* Copenhagen, 1922.

EWA WIPSZYCHA

ARCHITECTURAL ELEMENTS OF CHURCHES

[*This entry consists of forty-one articles. Most were written by Peter Grossmann. "Baptistery" is by W. Godlewski, "Column" by Hans-Georg Severin. They are as follows:*

Aisle
Ambulatory
Apse
Atrium
Baptistery
Cancelli
Ceiling
Choir
Ciborium
Coffer
Colonnade
Column
Crypt
Diaconicon
Dome
Gallery
Horseshoe arch
Iconostasis
Khūrus
Maqṣūrah
Naos
Narthex
Nave
Niche
Pastophorium
Pillar
Porch
Presbytery
Prothesis
Prothyron
Return aisle
Roof
Sacristy
Saddleback roof
Sanctuary
Synthronon
Tetraconch
Tribelon
Triconch
Triumphal arch
Vault

[*See also:* Altar; Baldachin; Basilica; Iconostasis.]

Aisle

An aisle is a passage on the side of the nave in a basilica-plan church. It is narrower than the nave and is usually separated from it by a row of columns connected by an architrave (beam) or arches. The purpose of aisles is to enlarge the interior of a church beyond the nave. Thus a church may have a nave or a nave and two or four aisles, depending on the size of the community it serves.

The aisle roof is lower than that of the nave. In Syria, North Africa, and Europe it formed a lean-to, but in Egypt it was usually flat. Egyptian basilicas, like those of other Eastern countries, show traces of windows in the aisles. Western basilicas have had aisle windows since the fifth century (Günter, 1968, pp. 39–42).

Characteristic of the Egyptian basilica, except on the north coast, are the niches (see below) let into the outer walls of the aisle, often in close sequence (Deichmann, 1937, p. 34). They are probably a relic of the older mud-brick building method, and they contribute to the often enormous strength of the walls.

BIBLIOGRAPHY

Deichmann, F. W. *Grundrisstypen des Kirchenbaus in frühchristlicher und byzantinischer Zeit im Morgenlande.* Halle, 1937.

Günter, R. *Wand, Fenster und Licht.* Herford, 1968.

Monneret de Villard, U. "La basilica cristiana in Egitto." In *Atti del IV congresso internazionale di archeologia cristiana,* Vol. 1. Rome, 1940.

Orlandos, A. K. Βασιλική, pp. 154–205. Athens, 1952.

PETER GROSSMANN

Ambulatory

An ambulatory is a covered walkway around the central part of a building, which is usually a covered hall but may be an open court. The Latin *ambulatio,* like the Greek *peridromos,* originally meant only the open space around a house. An ambulatory may be in the form of a peristyle, or colonnade (see below), such as those surrounding Greek temples or courtyards, but more often it is enclosed in walls, as in churches of the basilica plan. The inner walls may be connected with the central part of the building by one or more openings, and the outer walls may open into small chapels. An ambulatory may be carried around all four sides of the central area, or it may be U-shaped.

Ambulatories were used in temples and palaces in ancient Ur, Assur, Babylon, and Egypt. Examples in Egypt are in the grave temple of Peribsen, an early king of the Second Dynasty at Abydos (Um al-Qa'b), and the innermost sanctuary of temples of the New Kingdom to the Roman period in Karnak.

In early Christian architecture of the sixth century under Justinian, ambulatories were incorporated in large churches on the central plan. Famous examples are the churches of San Vitale in Ravenna and Saints Sergius and Bacchus in Constantinople (Krautheimer, 1965, pp. 161–70). The East Church of Abū Mīnā, near Alexandria, had an ambulatory. Ambulatories were also used in Egyptian churches of the basilica plan, notably a linking of the two side aisles with the return aisle (see below) across the western end of the church, as in the churches at Pbow. Ambulatories were used in a group of four-columned churches in the Nile Valley, some of which survived in Nubia until the completion of the Aswan High Dam in 1971 (Grossmann, 1980, pp. 85–111). Some buildings of the Fatimid period (tenth to twelfth century) with a central plan have ambulatories, for example, DAYR AL-KUBĀNIYYAH.

The roofing of the corner positions in the ambulatory presented a technical problem, since at these points supports were missing on one side. Therefore, to bridge the area in question, additional stone beams or auxiliary arches had to be introduced. From a spatial point of view, the corner areas were thereby always merged with one of the two sections of the ambulatory; from a constructional point of view, it did not matter which. In ancient Mesopotamian buildings, a symmetrical arrangement was preferred as in Ur and Assur (Hrouda, 1971, pp. 143–46, 155–58). In the tomb of King Peribsen at Abydos (Petrie, 1901, Vol. 2, p. 11) the merging circulates in a definite direction. The same solution appears in the fire temple of the great Parthian sun god at Hatra in Mesopotamia (Reuther, 1938, pp. 437–39). In other Iranian fire temples the corner area of the ambulatory was generally completely separated off and roofed with a small cupola of its own (Reuther, 1938, pp. 550–57). In the small four-columned churches of the Nile Valley a symmetrical solution was again chosen. Only in the vaulted buildings of the Fatimid period was a solution found that made it unnecessary to use auxiliary arches in the corner areas to carry the vaulting. In these examples, squinch arches constructed diagonally over a corner were used to serve as the support for larger arches over the remaining space. Examples of this construction have survived in the corridor vaulting of the accommodation building in DAYR ANBĀ HADRĀ, Aswan (Grossmann, 1982, pp. 245–46).

BIBLIOGRAPHY

Borchardt, L. *Ägyptische Tempel mit Umgang.* Cairo, 1938.

Delvoye, C. "Ambitus." In *Reallexikon zur byzantinischen Kunst,* Vol. 1, pp. 124–26. Stuttgart, 1966.

Grossmann, P. *Elephantine,* Vol. 2. Mainz, 1980.

______. *Mittelalterliche Langhauskuppelkirchen und verwandte Typen in Oberägypten.* Glückstadt, 1982.

Hrouda, B. *Vorderasien,* Vol. 1. Munich, 1971.

Krautheimer, R. *Early Christian and Byzantine Architecture.* New York, 1965.

Petrie, W. M. F. *The Royal Tombs of the First Dynasty,* Vol. 2. Memoirs of the Egyptian Exploration Fund 21. Oxford, 1901. Repr. 1975.

Reuther, O. "Parthian Architecture" and "Sasanian Architecture." In *A Survey of Persian Art,* Vol. 1, ed. A. U. Pope. Oxford, 1938.

PETER GROSSMANN

Apse

An apse is an extension of a rectangular hall, usually semicircular and roofed by a semicircular dome. Because of its strong visual effect, it draws every eye to itself and therefore was used in Roman temples to display the image of the god and in Roman basilicas for the emperor's throne. For similar reasons it was used at the sanctuary end of early Christian churches for the altar. In episcopal churches it also accommodated the synthronon (the bishop's throne and seats of priests on either side, see below) against the back wall. Later, after the seventh century, when the clergy moved forward nearer the nave, the altar was sometimes moved to the back of the apse.

Generally the apse is only slightly narrower than the nave. Churches in Egypt, more than in other Roman provinces, made great efforts to decorate the apse richly. The arch at the entrance received particular attention (see "triumphal arch" below). In several churches of the fifth and sixth centuries, columns were introduced as abutments to the arch and adorned with the finest capitals. From the ninth century, the arch was often decorated with an archivolt (ornamental molding). In a large number of churches the curved wall of the apse was provided with a ring of engaged columns, sometimes in two tiers, as in the churches of DAYR ANBĀ SHINŪDAH and DAYR ANBĀ BISHOI at Suhāj. Often the apses also contained a ring of niches. At Dayr Anbā Shinūdah rectangular and semicircular niches alternate in the horizontal and vertical planes. In the church of DAYR ABŪ FĀNAH at Mallawī, shallow niches alternate with deep ones. In the church in front of the pylon of the Luxor temple, at least one niche, flanked by columns, reaches from the apex of the apse to the floor.

As a rule, the greatest care was applied to the formation of the semidomed area above the apse. In several churches at Abū Mīnā, numerous discoveries of small mosaic tiles point to the existence at one time of an apse mosaic. In the Upper Egyptian churches the half-dome was usually adorned with paintings.

BIBLIOGRAPHY

Monneret de Villard, U. "La basilica cristiana in Egitto." *Atti del IV congresso internazionale di archeologia cristiana,* Vol. 1, pp. 308–315. Rome, 1940.

Orlandos, A. K. *Βασιλική,* pp. 206–224. Athens, 1952.

PETER GROSSMANN

Atrium

An atrium is an approximately square courtyard surrounded on four or at least three sides by porticoes. It was the chief interior court of a Roman house, as a peristyle was in a Greek house. An atrium served as an entrance court in many early Christian churches and continued in use in the West until about 1000, although it was seldom used in Egypt.

The atrium lies in front of the western end of the church and usually matches it in width. A well (*kantharos*) was often built in the center to be used for the ritual washings, particularly of the hands, that were customary there, at least in the early period. In addition, the porticoes offered protection from the rain and sun. Members of the congregation repenting of grievous sins were restricted to the atrium.

No rules governed the formation of the porticoes. Normally they were the same on all four sides, although Basilica A of Nea Anchialus has one curved portico (Soteriou, 1931, pp. 36–39). Sometimes the east portico, fronting on the church, has a more elaborate elevation or a different arrangement of columns because it forms part of the church facade. In such instances the church often has no proper narthex (see below) because its function as an entrance is served by the east portico. Conversely, sometimes if the church has a narthex, there is no east portico. Hagia Sophia in Constantinople has both a narthex and a distinctive east portico (Stube, 1973, pp. 33–39).

It is surprising that few Egyptian churches had atria, since similar courts were common in pharaonic temples, such as those in Luxor, MADĪNAT HĀBŪ, and IDFŪ, and there was no hesitation about adapting temple structure to church architecture. The only church atria so far known in Egypt are in the East Church and the North Basilica in ABŪ MĪNĀ, buildings that are to be ranked with imperial architecture rather than local building. These atria have porticoes on three or four sides. Synesius (1612, epistle 121, p. 258B) mentions some further examples. Otherwise only the great church of al-ASHMŪNAYN (Hermopolis Magna) presents an atrium, but it has a form very much of its own. Instead of conforming with the axis of the church, it is divided into four sections, like a garden, by two-sided open porticoes. Evidently Egyptians preferred courts of optional form and plan that were only generally coordinated with the church. Examples are several churches in ANṢINĀ and ANTINOOPOLIS (Mitchell, 1982, pp. 171–79). Presumably the great central court in the pilgrim center of ABŪ MĪNĀ had a similar significance.

BIBLIOGRAPHY

Binding, G. "Atrium." In *Lexikon des Mittelalters,* Vol. 1, pp. 1175–76. Munich and Zurich, 1980.

Brightman, F. E., ed. *Liturgies, Eastern and Western.* Oxford, 1896.

Delvoye, C. "Atrium." In *Reallexikon für Antike und Christentum,* Vol. 1, pp. 421–40. Stuttgart, 1966.
Mitchell, E. "Osservazioni: topografiche preliminari sull' impiarto urbanistico di Antinoe." *Vicino Oriente* 5 (1982):171–79.
Orlandos, A. K. *Βασιλική*, pp. 94–110. Athens, 1952.
Paulinus of Nola. *La Correspondance de Saint Paulin de Nole et de Sulpice Sévère.* Paris, 1906.
Strube, C. *Die westliche Eingangsseite der Kirchen von Konstantinopel in justinianischer Zeit.* Wiesbaden, 1973.

PETER GROSSMANN

Baptistery

A baptistery is a part of a church or a separate church building used for the sacrament of BAPTISM. It contains a basin, pool, or font for water. The basic problem in analyzing Egyptian baptisteries is to establish their date. The fact that many are in churches of an earlier date or underwent several stages of alteration does not mean that baptistery and church evolved simultaneously. This article will consider baptisteries unveiled during archaeological investigations; although medieval ones, reflecting changes in the baptismal ceremony, should also be studied. Some rooms thought to be baptisteries by some scholars—in churches at DANDARAH, KHIRBAT AL-FILŪSIYYAH, and OXYRHYNCHUS—are not discussed here because their function has not been confirmed by archaeology or furnishings.

Baptisteries dated from the fifth to the ninth century occur throughout Egypt. The largest group is in the Western Delta and the Abū Mīnā region, chiefly because of the archaeological research there. All known Egyptian baptisteries are connected with churches, either as an integral part or as an annex. None is freestanding. They are connected to large churches, such as the Martyr Church of Abū Mīnā, the basilica of al-Ashmūnayn, and the church of Dayr Anbā Shinūdah, and to smaller ones in places such as Ṭūd or Madīnat Hābū. These churches might be the seat of a bishop, as at al-Ashmūnayn and Qifṭ; pilgrim centers, as at Abū Mīnā; monastery churches, as in KELLIA and at Dayr Anbā Shinūdah; or parish churches.

The location of the baptistery within the church building was not strictly defined, but there can be seen a clear trend toward placing it in the eastern end of the building, usually adjoining the sanctuary (or altar area, see below). In Egypt generally the predominant trend seems to have been to locate the baptistery in the northeastern part of the church, irrespective of the size of the building or the baptistery. In some churches in Upper Egypt, however, at Ṭūd, Madīnat Hābū, and Suhāj, the baptistery was in the southeastern part of the complex. In Abū Mīnā the baptistery occupies the western part of the church complex. Though this location seems to have been quite alien to Egyptian practice, there are other examples of a western location in churches in Kurūm al-Ṭuwāl, by the pylon in Luxor, and in Medamud. In the enlarged church of Makhūrah, a baptistery has been confirmed in the extreme eastern part of the building, behind the sanctuary. A similar site is used in the North Church in Khirbat, if the small basin in the space behind the altar has been correctly interpreted.

Egyptian baptisteries are usually square or rectangular, with no special architectural treatment. This is because as an integral part of the church, they are completely subordinated to the shape of the building. In the larger church complexes, such as those at al-Ashmūnayn, Abū Mīnā, and Luxor (church by the colonnade of Ramses II), the baptistery is more extensive and consists of two or more rooms, functionally situated. The only baptistery that received a separate architectural shape was that of the Martyr Church of Saint Menas in Abū Mīnā; it was a central octagonal room with four corner niches and a dome and was connected by passages with all the surrounding rectangular rooms.

From the liturgical point of view, the most complete example is the baptistery of the North Basilica in Abū Mīnā, which consists of several rooms in a row, the central one having a large baptismal basin and the eastern one having three small apses with altars on its eastern wall. It seems also that the baptisteries of the East Church in Abū Mīnā and in Makhūrah were each connected with a room with an altar, although in different architectural arrangements.

The main furnishing of a baptistery is the baptismal pool, basin, or font. The early receptacles are usually large pools, built below floor level, for the total immersion of adults. They are usually in the center of the room, sometimes occupying almost the whole interior. They are generally made of brick or stone lined inside with waterproof plaster. Those at Abū Mīnā and Qifṭ were incrusted in decorative marble. Some pools had a ciborium (superstructure, see below) supported by four or six columns over them, as in Makhūrah, the North Basilica at Abū Mīnā, and the church in front of the

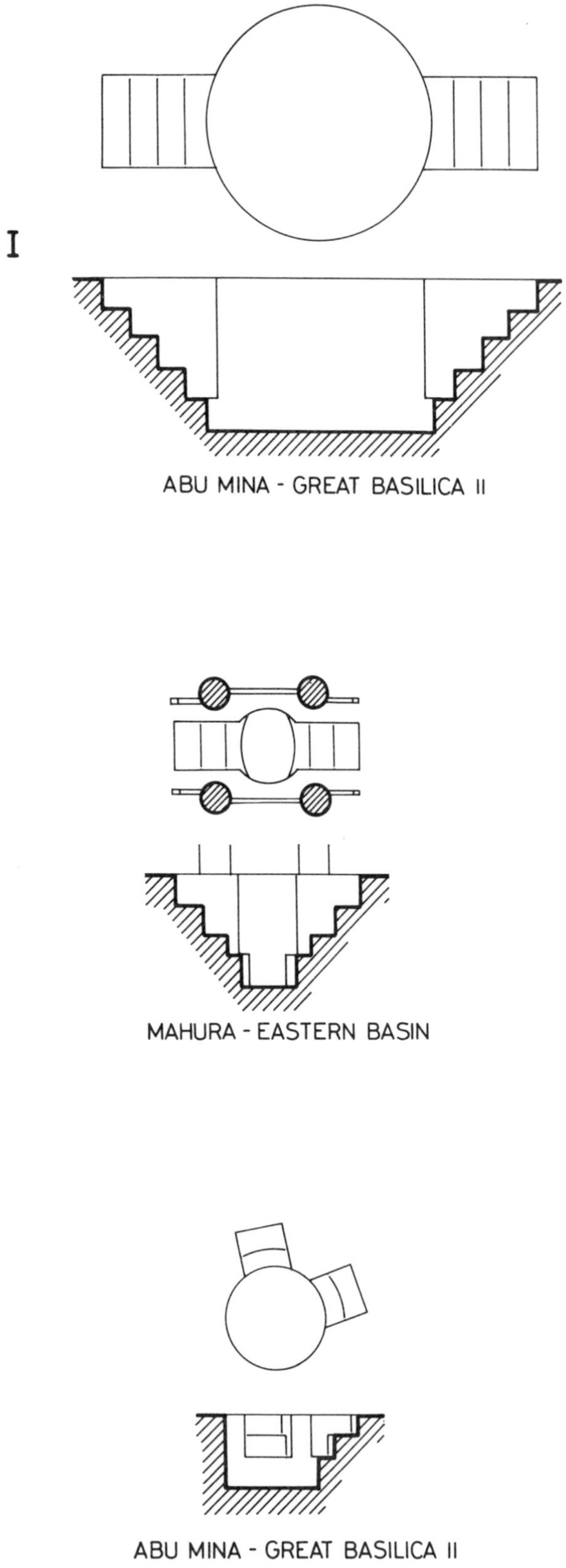

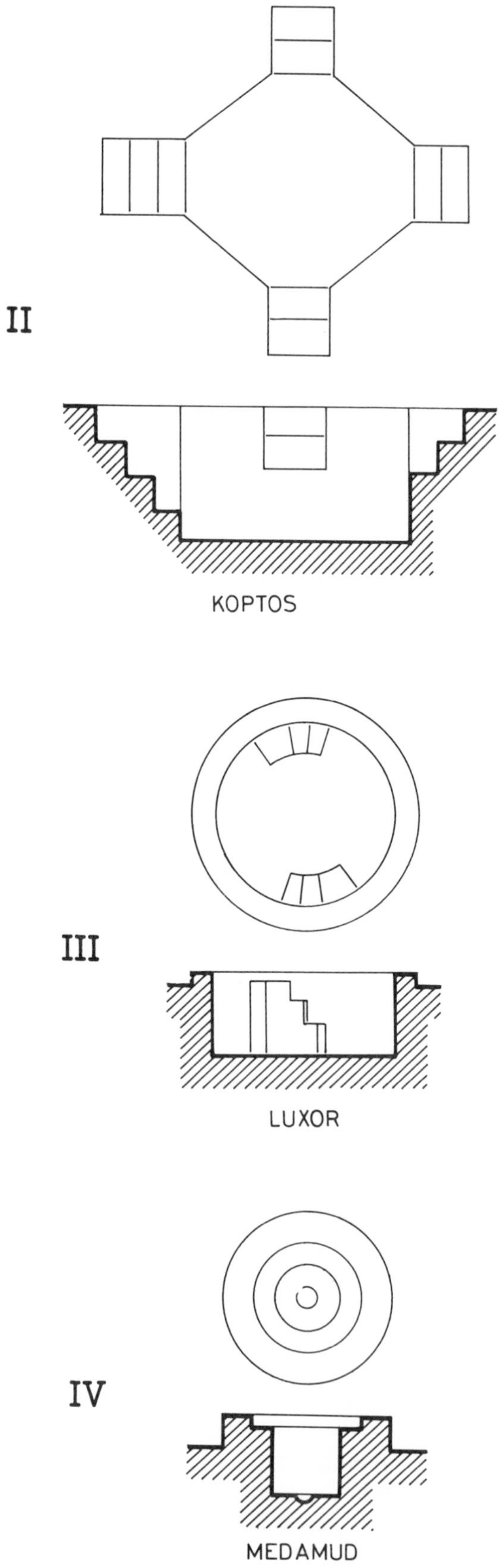

Samples of baptistery plans in large and small churches. *Courtesy Peter Grossmann.*

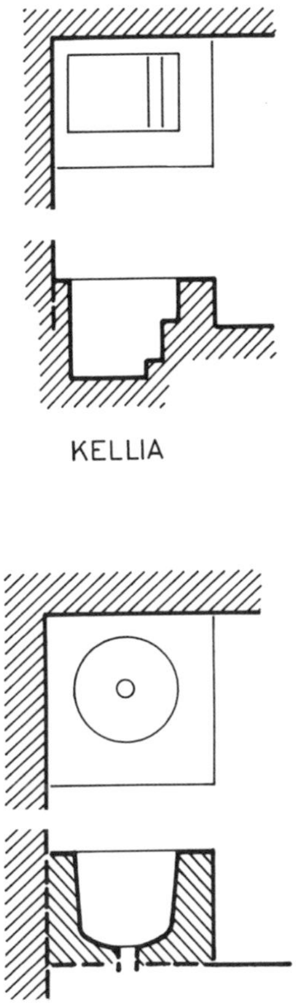

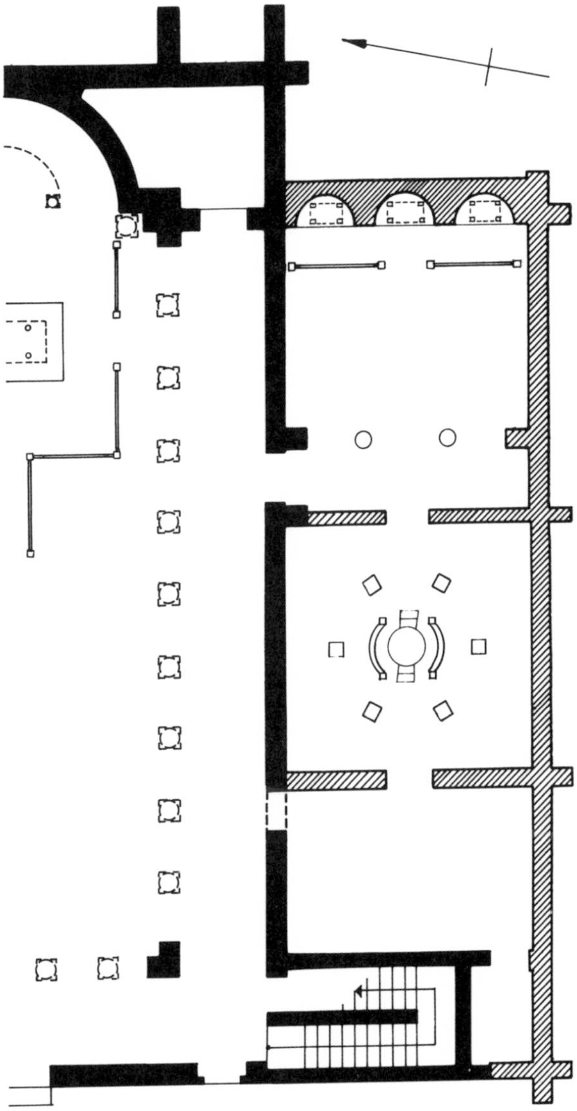

Baptistery of the North Basilica at Abū Mīnā. *Courtesy Peter Grossmann.*

pylon at Luxor. Others were surrounded with a low superstructure repeating their shape, as at Kellia and Medamud.

Later, especially during the Middle Ages, by which time infant baptism was general, the large pool was replaced by a smaller basin of terra-cotta or stone close to the eastern wall of the room or in a niche in the wall.

Taking into account three criteria—the shape of the pool or basin, the access to its interior, and the level on which it was placed—one can group Egyptian baptismal receptacles into the following types:

1. Large circular pools with vertical walls and two flights of stairs leading down into them, as at Abū Mīnā, al-Ashmūnayn, Qaṣr al-Waḥāydah at Kellia, Makhūrah, and Suhāj. One version of this type is the western pool of the sixth-century baptistery of Abū Mīnā: two flights of stairs, one above the other, lead into the round basin. Such an arrangement results from limited access to the pool, which is in a shallow niche in a relatively narrow room.
2. Large cruciform pools with steps in the western arm of the cross leading down into it, as at Qifṭ and Kurūm al-Ṭuwāl.
3. Large circular pools with internal stairs on either side, an evolution of type 1, as in Luxor's church by the colonnade of Ramses II.
4. Circular pools built below the floor level with a high shoring on the floor and without stairs, as at Medamud, Ṭūd, and Luxor's church in front of the pylon.
5. Rectangular pools built below floor level with a high shoring and internal stairs, as at Kellia and Quṣūr 'Isā, a type related to types 3 and 4.

6. Small circular basins built within a square or rectangular structure on the floor of the baptistery room, a type very popular in the Middle Ages.

BIBLIOGRAPHY

Adriani, A. "Travaux de fouilles et de restaurations dans la region d'Abousir (Maréotis)." In *Annuaire du Musée greco-romain,* Vol. 3, p. 12. Alexandria, 1940–1950.

Clédat, F. "Fouilles à Khirbet el-Flousiyeh (1914)." *Annales du Service des antiquités de l'Egypte* 16 (1916):29–32, fig. 21.

Daressy, G. "Notes sur Luxor de la période romaine et copte." *Annales du Service des antiquités de l'Egypte* 19 (1920):173, fig. 3.

Egloff, M. "Kellia: la poterie copte." *Recherches suisses d'Archéologie copte* 3 (1977):pl. 117.

Eilmann, R.; A. Langsdorf; and H. E. Stier. "Bericht über die Voruntersuchungen auf den Kurum el-Tuwal bei Amrije." *Mitteilungen des deutschen archäologischen Instituts—Abteilung Kairo* 1 (1930):113, fig. 3 and 5, pl. XXb.

Grossmann, P. "Abu Mena. Siebenter vorläufiger Bericht." *Mitteilungen des deutschen archäologischen Instituts—Abteilung Kairo* 26 (1970):55–82.

———. "Eine vergessene frühchristliche Kirche bei Luxor-Tempel." *Mitteilungen des deutschen archäologischen Instituts—Abteilung Kairo* 29, 2 (1973):16–69, ill. 1.

———. "Abu Mena. Achter vorläufiger Bericht. Kampagnen 1975 und 1976. *Mitteilungen des deutschen archäologischen Instituts—Abteilung Kairo* 33 (1977):35–45.

———. "Arbeiten in Mahura al-Qibli." *Mitteilungen des deutschen archäologischen Instituts—Abteilung Kairo* 36 (1980):225–27.

———. "Recenti risultati dagli scavi di Abu Mina." *Corsi Ravenna* 28 (1981):145–47.

———. "Abu Mina. Zehner vorläufiger Bericht, Kampagnen 1980 und 1981. *Mitteilungen des deutschen archäologischen Instituts—Abteilung Kairo* (1982):17–22.

———. *Mittelalterliche Langhauskuppelkirche und verwandte Typen in Oberägypten.* Glückstadt, 1982.

Hölscher, T. *The Excavation of Medinet Habu,* Vol. 5, pp. 55–6, fig. 59, pl. 46. Chicago, 1954.

Legrain, G. "Rapport sur les nouveaux travaux exécutés à Louqsor à l'ouest du Temple d'Amon." *Annales du Service des antiquités de l'Egypte* 17 (1918):49–75.

Leroy, J. "Deux baptistères paléochrétiens d'Orient réconnus." *Cahiers archéologiques* 25 (1976):4–6, fig. 3–4.

Muḥammad Abdul Qader. "Preliminary Report on the Excavations Carried Out in the Temple of Luxor. Seasons 1958–1959 & 1959–1960." *Annales du Service des antiquités de l'Egypte* 60 (1960):227–29.

Müller-Wiener, W. "Abu Mena. 3. Vorläufiger Bericht." *Mitteilungen des deutschen archäologischen Instituts—Abteilung Kairo* 20 (1965):126–37.

———. "Abu Mena. Fünfter vorläufiger Bericht." *Mitteilungen des deutschen archäologischen Instituts— Abteilung Kairo* 22. (1967):206–24.

Petrie, W. M. F. *Koptos,* pp. 25–26, pl. XXVIa. London, 1896.

Reinach, A. J. "Rapport sur les fouilles de Koptos (1910)." *Annales du Service des antiquités* 11 (1911):5, pl. V.

Vincent, H. "Un type de baptistère byzantin." *Revue biblique* 31 (1922):583–89.

Wace, A. J. B.; A. H. S. Megaw; and T. C. Skeat. *Hermopolis Magna, Ashmunein. The Ptolemaic Sanctuary and the Basilica,* p. 49, pl. 23, fig. 3. Alexandria, 1959.

Ward-Perkins, J. B. "The Monastery of Taposiris Magna." *Bulletin de la Société archéologique d'Alexandrie* 36 (1946):48–53.

W. GODLEWSKI

Cancelli

Cancelli (Greek, *kankelloi*) are screens used to enclose the presbytery (see below), the part of an early Christian church reserved for the clergy. The area enclosed, also called the *bema, hierateion, abaton, adyton,* or *hapsis* (apse, see above), contained the altar; it could be entered by the laity only for the reception of the EUCHARIST. In large cathedrals such as the one at al-Ashmūnayn, cancelli were also used to subdivide the presbytery. In the Martyr Church at Abū Mīnā, the open rooms on both sides of the eastern concha (semicircular room) are screened off from the altar by cancelli.

Cancelli, simple constructions of wood, stone, or metal, consist of a row of posts (*stipites*) permanently fixed to the floor and joined together by low screen panels (*transennae*), which may be either plain or pierced. Not uncommonly, such panels are also simply inserted between the columns along the sides of the nave. Doors are located generally in the center of the short side on the west, across the nave, as well as on the long sides, as was required. The middle entrance serves the clergy for its various entrances from the presbytery into the nave and is also used by the laity when receiving the

Eucharist at the altar. In large pilgrim churches, where a great onrush of believers was expected, a narrow entryway with similar cancelli on each side was set up in front of the altar. Examples are the Great Basilica at Abū Mīnā and Basilica B at Thebes.

In the early Christian church, these cancelli were never very high; thus, the proceedings at the altar could easily be observed from the nave. The posts of the cancelli in the basilica in front of the pylon of the Luxor temple, dating as late as 600, are only about 3 feet (1 m) high.

An ornate version of the cancelli called the templon apparently gained popularity from the sixth century onward, above all in Byzantine areas (Soteriou, 1931). Here the posts are made taller by having column shafts joined to, or set on top of, them and are joined together above the capitals by architraves or arches. The apertures that are thus produced above the *transennae* could be filled in by curtains if need be (first mentioned in the West in the seventh century; Duchesne, 1886, Vol. 1, p. 375). In Egypt this type of cancelli is rare, though attested several times in the region of Abū Mīnā. Instead, one finds a similar arrangement in some edifices, not older than the late seventh century, which already possess a *khūrus*, a room between the presbytery and the nave (see below). In these, the central opening of the *khūrus* is sometimes provided with a row of several columns of medium height, into which are sunk wooden frames reaching up to the capitals, as in the main church of Dayr Apa Jeremiah at Saqqara and the Church of Saint Mercurius at Dayr Abū Sayfayn in Cairo. The function of these frames was perhaps to carry a curtain that closed off the space between the columns. The Byzantine templon developed from the fourteenth century into the iconostasis (see below), a high screen that completely closed off the presbytery. In the Egyptian church, however, the curtain was replaced by the iconostasis some time during the Fatimid period.

BIBLIOGRAPHY

Chatzidakis, M. "Ikonostas." In *Reallexikon zur byzantinischen Kunst,* Vol. 3, pp. 326ff. Stuttgart, 1978.

Delvoye, C. "Cancelli." In *Reallexikon zur byzantinischen Kunst,* Vol. 1, pp. 900–931. Stuttgart, 1966.

Duchesne, L. ed. *Le liber pontificalis,* 3 vols. Paris, 1886–1957.

Klauser, T. "Cancelli." In *Reallexikon für Antike und Christentum* Vol. 2 cols. 837–838. Stuttgart, 1954.

Orlandos, A. K. Βασιλική, pp. 509–535. Athens, 1952.

Pauty, E. *Bois sculptés d'églises coptes (époque fatimide).* Cairo, 1930.

Schläger, H. "Abu Mena. Zweiter Vorläufiger Bericht." *Mitteilungen des deutschen archäologischen Instituts—Abteilung Kairo* 20 (1963):122–125.

PETER GROSSMANN
HANS GEORG SEVERIN

Ceiling

A ceiling (Arabic, *khasār'*) is the overhead surface of a room. In Egypt, except for vaulted structures, such as the mid-section of the *khūrus* of Dayr Anbā Anṭūniyūs, it is almost always flat. A flat ceiling is supported on wooden beams that rest on the walls of the room and, in large rooms, on interior rows of columns. The most commonly used building timber, since early pharaonic times, was cedar from Lebanon. Later, other kinds of wood were used, including less valuable, indigenous palm. In important buildings, beams were securely positioned in a regular series of recesses built into the structure of load-bearing walls, as in Dayr Anbā Shinūdah. In less carefully executed buildings, the beams were placed on top of the walls and the space between the beam ends was filled in as the ceiling was further constructed. Sometimes another layer of beams was laid at right angles to the first.

Over the beams was a compact layer of rushes, bundles of straw, or palm leaves. Above that was a thick layer of dry earth or even ashes to smooth the surface. Clay or plaster strips, or occasionally bricks, provided a top finish.

Only when the ceiling was complete was the building of the walls continued. In this building method, contact with the lower walls was often lost. A frequent consequence was that the walls of an upper story appear to have moved in relation to those of a lower story, which tended to weaken the walls.

Ceilings were rarely decorated. However, in rooms with plastered walls, the ceiling was plastered. The supporting framework of beams remained visible under the thin plaster as in the *khūrus* of the old church of Dayr Anbā Anṭūniyūs. In some churches, the surfaces of the beams were decorated with floral ornaments occasionally enriched with different kinds of animals. Other churches, beginning in the Ptolemaic period, had ceilings decorated with coffers (see below). A strictly flat ceiling occurred only in temple buildings, and then it consisted of stone. They were decorated with a starry sky, painted or in light relief, or with geometric and other patterns.

BIBLIOGRAPHY

Arnold, D. "Holxban" In *Lexikon der Ägyptologie,* Vol. 2, pp. 1269–70. Wiesbaden, 1977.

Balcz, H. "Die altägyptische Wandgliederung." *Mitteilungen des deutschen archäologischen Instituts —Abteilung Kairo* 1 (1930):73ff.

Boak, A. E. R., and E. E. Peterson. *Karanis. Seasons 1924–28,* pp. 26f. Ann Arbor, Mich., 1931.

Deichmann, F. W. "Kassettendecken." *Jahrbuch der österreichischen Byzantinistik* 21 (1972):83–107.

Haeny, G. *Lexicon der Ägyptologie,* Vol. 1, p. 999. Wiesbaden, 1975.

Lucas, A. *Ancient Egyptian Materials and Industries,* pp. 429ff. London, 1964.

Nowicka, M. *La Maison privée dans l'Egypte ptolémaique,* pp. 27f. Warsaw, 1969.

Schütz, A. R. *Der Typus des hellenistisch-ägyptischen Hauses,* pp. 58ff. Würzburg, 1936.

PETER GROSSMANN

Choir

The choir, or forechoir, is the small area, usually rectangular, between the apse and the naos (see below), or area for the laity. It is the place where the clergy or choir sings the divine service; hence its name. The choir is common in Western church architecture, where it is roughly equivalent to the presbytery or chancel, the area shut off from the naos by cancelli.

In middle and late Byzantine churches, which usually have a very small apse, the choir is often provided with side conchas. The side walls may also contain passages to the pastophoria (two rooms flanking the choir). In other Eastern churches the choir is very rare. Among early Christian churches of Syria and Asia Minor it is found only in the basilica of Qalblūzy and in some centrally planned buildings such as those in Apamea and Amida (Diyarbakr). In Egypt the oldest examples derive from the eighth century—the subsidiary church of the Church of Saint Menas in Cairo, dedicated to Mār Bahnām (Grossmann, 1982, pp. 13ff.), and a building from Ḥilwān (Grossmann, p. 83, ill. 28). An example from Nubia is the basilica in TAMĪT (Grossmann, pp. 16ff.).

BIBLIOGRAPHY

Butler, H. C. *Early Churches in Syria,* 2nd ed. pp. 187ff. Amsterdam, 1969.

Grossmann, P. *Mittelalterliche Langhauskuppelkirchen und verwandte Typen in Oberägypten.* Glückstadt, 1982.

PETER GROSSMANN

Ciborium

A ciborium is a freestanding, columned structure, surmounted by a cupola or, less commonly, a pyramid, that protects and architecturally emphasizes an altar, tomb, or throne. It may be put up in the open or inside a building. The terms "ciborium" and "baldachin" are often used synonymously in English, but a baldachin was originally a fabric canopy hung over an altar or door and only later became an architectural term. Similarly *tabernacle* originally meant a tent covering the Hebrew ark of the covenant but later came to mean a small cubical structure housing the host in Roman Catholic churches.

Since the New Kingdom, the throne of Egyptian rulers stood under a ciborium, as can be seen from many pictorial representations (Erman and Ranke, 1923, 1981, p. 67). Similarly, the imperial throne of Rome was covered by a ciborium. Also many pagan Roman altars had ciboria over them (Klauser, 1957, Vol. 3, pp. 77f.).

In the Christian era the use of ciboria was widespread. They appear over the thrones of Western rulers (Corippus, 1836, pp. 191ff.) and bishops (Klauser, 1953, p. 18), altars, tombs, wells, and baptismal basins. In Egypt, remains of such ciboria in stone and wood have been found in several early Christian churches such as those in Abū Mīnā and Makhūrah. All the older Cairo churches are furnished with altar ciboria of this kind, which confirms their use down to the present time. In those examples the cupola is usually of wood, and it has the form of a sail vault (see below), the underside of which is often richly painted.

BIBLIOGRAPHY

Alföldi, A. "Insignien und Tracht der römischen Kaiser." *Mitteilungen des deutschen archäologischen Instituts—Römische Abteilung* 50 (1935):127–32.

Butler, A. J. *The Ancient Coptic Church of Egypt,* Vol. 1, 2nd ed., p. 114; Vol. 2, pp. 28–35. London, 1970.

Erman, A., and H. Ranke. *Ägypten und ägyptisches Leben im Altertum.* Tübingen, 1923; repr. 1981.

Klauser, T. *Der Ursprung der bischöflichen Insignien und Ehrenrechte,* 2nd ed. Bonner Akademische Reden 1. Krefeld, 1953.

______. "Ciborium." In *Reallexikon fur Antike und Christentum,* Vol. 3, cols. 68–86. Stuttgart, 1957.

Lantschoot, A. van. "Allocution de Timothée d'Alexandrie." *Le Muséon* 47 (1934):13–56.

Orlandos, A. K. Βασιλική. pp. 471–80. Athens, 1952.

Wessel, K. "Ciborium." In *Reallexikon zur byzantinischen Kunst,* Vol. 1, cols. 1055–65. Stuttgart, 1966.

PETER GROSSMANN

Coffer

A coffer is a recessed panel. Ceilings covered with coffers were known in ancient Greek architecture. They had considerable importance in Roman houses (Vitruvius 7.2) and temples and were occasionally used in Egyptian buildings in the Roman, Byzantine, and early medieval periods. Coffers were made in flat wooden ceilings by subdividing the space between the large ceiling beams with short transverse beams. The areas thus formed, usually rectangular, were closed off on top by boards, which served as the substructure for the floor above. The beams could either be adorned with carved work or covered with wood, metal, or terracotta. In Roman vaulting, which usually consisted of a concrete shell made of small chips of stone or broken bricks and mortar, coffers were used as decorative forms on the undersurface of the vault, since the recesses could be very easily accommodated by the requisite thickness of the vault. Such coffers could take on triangular or polygonal forms. Famous examples are the vaults of the Pantheon and the Temple of Venus and Roma in Rome.

How far coffers were employed in Christian basilicas has not yet been determined with any certainty. Despite some basilicas in the city of Rome that certainly had a ceiling, several indications suggest that most basilicas probably had an open-frame roof (Deichmann, 1957, pp. 249ff.). Nevertheless there is evidence that individual parts of churches had a ceiling.

That there were coffered ceilings in Egypt in the Roman and early Byzantine periods is shown by a number of wooden boards preserved in the Coptic Museum, Cairo. Some have a richly bordered painted surface but at the edges generally show no painting at all (Deichmann, 1972, pp. 83ff.). There is hardly any doubt that these are panels from ceilings. Terra-cotta slabs with pictorial motifs to cover coffers were found in Alexandria (Wace, 1948, pp. 50f., pl. 3). In several tombs in Alexandria, coffers were simply painted on the ceiling (Adriani, 1940–1950, pp. 36–40, ills. 43 and 53, pl. A and B). In the same way, the former presence of a coffered ceiling may be deduced in some structures from an unusually close positioning of the beams. One example is the annexed southeast corner room of the church built into the front of the Temple of Isis at Philae under Bishop Theodorus in the eighth century. Another is the later baptistery in the newly discovered central church of Makhūrah al-Qiblī on the Mediterranean coast (Grossmann, 1980, pp. 225ff., pl. 50b). Both instances, moreover, involve false ceilings closing off an area above. Finally, over the central area of the *khūrus* in the old church of Dayr Anbā Antūniyūs, there is an interesting coffered ceiling curved as a barrel vault in an imitation of gypsum, where wide boards with a series of octagonal openings sawn in them have been inserted into the spaces between the beams (Grossmann, 1982, p. 50, pl. 59a).

BIBLIOGRAPHY

Adriani, A. "Nécropolis de l'île de Pharos." In *Annuaire du Musée gréco-romain,* Vol. 3, pp. 47–128. Alexandria, 1940–1950.

Deichmann, F. W. "Untersuchungen zu Dach und Decke der Basilika." In *Charites: Studien zur Altertumwissenschaft,* ed. K. Schauenberg. Bonn, 1957.

______. "Kassettendecken." *Jahrbuch der österreichischen Byzantinistik* 21 (1972):83–107.

Durm, J. *Baukunst der Etrusker und Römer,* pp. 244ff. Stuttgart, 1905.

Gross, W. H. "Lacunar." *Der kleine Paulys* 3 (1975):441f.

Grossmann, P. "Arbeiten in Mahūra al-Qibli." *Mitteilungen des Deutschen Archäologischen Instituts—Abteilung Kairo* 36 (1980):225ff, pl. 50b.

______. *Mittelalterliche Langhauskuppelkirchen und verwandte Typen in Oberägypten.* Glückstadt, 1982.

Wace, A. J. B. "Later Roman Pottery and Plate." *Bulletin de la Société d'archéologie d'Alexandrie* 37 (1948):50f., pl. 3.

PETER GROSSMANN

Colonnade

A colonnade is a row of columns relatively closely spaced, usually in a straight line connected by an architrave or arches. It is a characteristic element of basilica construction. A colonnade is the same as a portico. Sequences of round columns alternating with square-sided pillars in a distinct rhythm do not count as colonnades. If a colonnade forms a connection between two parallel walls, the columns closest to the walls are generally treated as engaged columns or pillars, that is, attached to the respective walls. In the architecture of Egypt, however, classical arrangement was generally abandoned in the pharaonic period, and instead imposts were positioned high on the wall to carry the architrave or arches.

In classical architecture down to the fourth century A.D., only uniform columns were normally used within a colonnade. A rare exception is formed by the courtyard porticoes of the Temple of Isis at Philae, belonging to the second century A.D., which in part contain different types of columns. From the fifth century A.D., probably as a result of the frequent use of elements stolen from earlier buildings, people began to accept columns of very different types into one colonnade. Down to the sixth century, however, care was taken in church building to place columns of different kinds together in matching pairs, a practice later abandoned (Deichmann, 1940, pp. 114–30). The introduction of the vault and especially of the dome (see below) divided the space beneath into individual bays, supported by widely separated columns. Thus as the character of a closed sequence was lost, the colonnade fell out of use.

BIBLIOGRAPHY

Deichmann, F. W. "Säule und Ordnung in der frühchristlichen Architektur." *Mitteilungen des deutschen archäologischen Instituts—Römische Abteilung* 55 (1940):114–30.

Orlandos, A. K. *Βασιλική*, pp. 351–56. Athens, 1952.

PETER GROSSMANN

Column

A column is a vertical architectural support that is circular in plan and slender in contrast to a pillar (see below), which is often rectangular and usually heavier. A column consists of two elements—a shaft and a capital—and usually a base; often it has entasis, a slight convexity. In the Ptolemaic and early Byzantine periods, Egyptian architects abandoned their traditional baseless columns and adopted two of the five classical orders developed in Greece and Rome, the Ionic and the Corinthian.

Elements

Base and Pedestal. The base consisted of circles of moldings superimposed on a plinth (a square floor slab), fashioned out of a single block of stone. As a rule, the plinth remained without ornament. The circular element was normally developed as an Attic base, that is, with the following sequence of shapes: the upper torus (a convex molding), the scotia or trochilus (a concave molding or channel), and the lower torus. Various adaptations of this traditional form were carried through in the late classical and early Byzantine periods with a view to simplification and refinement, as in the reduction of the upper torus to one or two fillets (narrow, flat bands) or the reduction of the lower torus to a half-torus leading into the vertical surface of the plinth. In the course of development, bases made of marble generally remained more closely tied to the traditional forms; early on, bases worked in local stone showed simplified forms such as simple beveling.

In special cases a square pedestal (also called a postament) was placed under the base; in late antiquity the two components were fashioned as a single, monolithic piece. The traditional decoration of the pedestal consisted of a relatively complicated sequence, or profile, consisting of supporting fillets above, making a cover slab, a contracted central field, and foot fillets below. These conventional forms were eventually simplified in various ways: the combining of the base and the cover slab of the pedestal into a single element, the discontinuation of individual moldings of the profile, the combination of supporting fillets and foot fillets, and their replacement by simple beveling.

The use of pedestals in late classical and early Byzantine buildings in Egypt appears to have been less restricted than Roman imperial architecture by any architectural canon, but presumably the aim was basically the elevation of column shafts with standard measurements, especially in basilicas such as the Great Basilica at Abū Mīnā and the main church at Dayr Apa Jeremiah. A special form of the late fifth and sixth centuries was the octagonal pedestal fashioned together with its base from a single

Square pedestal. Dayr Abū Mīnā. Late Antiquity. *Courtesy Hans-Georg Severin.*

block. Such pedestals were set up, for example, in exedras (semicircular rooms formed by a recess), as in the Great Basilica and the Martyr's Church at Abū Mīnā and at Dayr Apa Jeremiah.

Shaft. In the late classical period, the column shaft was fashioned as a monolith instead of being built up out of drums. It had no entasis but tapered upward in a slightly conical shape. The frugal decoration consisted of a foot ring and slight molding at the neck. Marble shafts with crosses in low relief were special cases. Occasionally workshops using local stone provided shafts with additional decoration—for example, a protruding tondo (medallion) with relief decoration—but these were small shafts, used for niches, and not full-size architectural supports. Shafts from local workshops completely covered with decoration for example, at Dayr Apa Apollo, Bāwīṭ, and Dayr Apa Jeremiah, were probably only half-columns.

Capital. The crowning member of the column was the capital, which provided support for the architrave or archivolt. The capital was the most richly and diversely decorated component of the column and therefore more subject to changing styles than the base or even the shaft. It can thus be dated within a narrower span of time.

It is not possible to describe here all the types of capitals known in late-classical and Byzantine Egypt. The most important and most widely distributed are the Corinthian, the Ionic, the composite, the capital with acanthus and flutes, the capital with olive branches on flat leaves, various types of two-zone capital, the impost capital (and its special refinement, the impost capital of fold type), and finally the basket-shaped capital (cf. Severin, 1977, nos. 274–77).

In the fully developed *Corinthian capital,* an upper crown and a lower crown, of eight acanthus leaves each, surround the calathus (cup-shaped body of the capital). On each of the four sides, cup-shaped sheath leaves spring from two stems visible between the leaves of the upper crown. The sheath leaves conceal the origin of spiral forms—helices, which curl inward, and volutes, which curl outward. The volutes run from the calathus to the corners of the abacus (coping stone or top slab), which is concave and may carry in the center an ornamental blossom or knob. In the course of time, some of these motifs were discarded, such as the helices, and the sheath leaves and volutes were merged into one form. But one cannot say that the simpler a Corinthian capital is, the later its date. As early as Roman times, small capitals show fewer motifs. Also regional peculiarities must be taken into account; for example in the fifth-century tomb church of Dayr Apa Jeremiah, greatly simplified Corinthian capitals were normal, whereas at the same time, large capitals at Oxyrhynchus had a relatively complete stock of motifs.

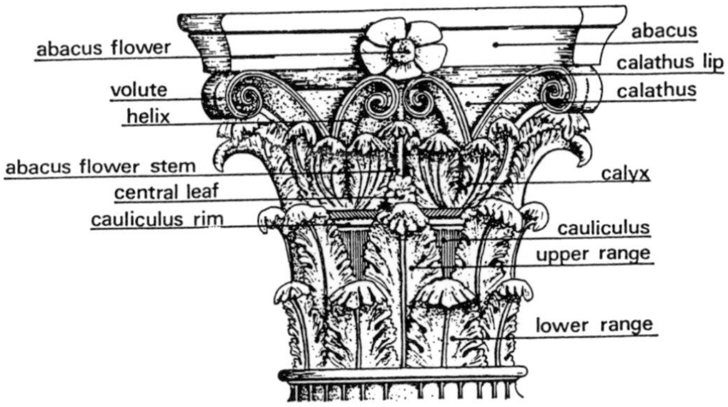

Schematic drawing of Corinthian capital. Components and nomenclature. *Drawing by R. Shevin and M. Fischer.*

Fully developed Corinthian capital. Late Antiquity. Cairo, Coptic Museum. *Courtesy Hans-Georg Severin.*

The Corinthian capital of marble, whether imported or carved in Egypt, reached a spectacular zenith and widespread diffusion in the fourth and fifth centuries. It appears in hundreds of examples reused in churches and Islamic buildings, especially in and around Cairo. The Corinthian capital was the primary form of capital made of local stone until the Arab conquest.

In the *Ionic capital,* a broad cap, or coussinet, curls down at the sides into sturdy volutes. It overhangs an echinus molding decorated with the egg-and-dart motif, which runs between the volutes. An astragal (narrow molding) leads from the echinus to the shaft. A slender abacus finishes off the capital above the cap.

The conventional Ionic capital was seldom used in Egypt. A special local type in marble shows four tongue-shaped leaves arranged diagonally below the volutes; it is squat and short and was perhaps used as a capital in a gallery. More common were composite capitals combining Ionic and other elements. The Ionic impost capital (a capital with a pyramid-shaped impost block superimposed on it) made as a monolith, which was characteristic of the Eastern Roman Empire, was known in late fifth- and early sixth-century Alexandria but not in Middle or Upper Egypt and was not copied in local stone.

The *composite capital* combined the two acanthus leaf crowns of the Corinthian capital with the superimposed abacus, volutes, and echinus of the Ionic capital. It was more rarely used than the Corinthian capital but is well attested in Egypt. An artificial form with fine-toothed acanthus, made in many subtypes, was popular in the Eastern Empire in the late fifth century but reached Egypt only as an import and was not copied.

In the *capital with acanthus and flutes,* the lower zone is covered with acanthus leaves or has only four acanthus leaves arranged diagonally. Above them (or between the four leaves) is a crown of flutes; the abacus has straight or concave sides. This capital was much in use in marble throughout the fourth and fifth centuries. It was the model for works in local stone, which as a rule replaced the flutes with reed leaves or the like as in Dayr Apa Jeremiah.

The *capital with olive branches on flat leaves* was a short-lived creation of the Constantinople workshops in the early sixth century. It has only a single range of large undivided leaves, on which an olive branch is superimposed. It is either carved with the volutes of the Corinthian capital and an echinus in the upper section or follows the regular Ionic pattern. Found only in marble, this capital, through ready-made imports and probably local copies, is well represented by twelve examples in Egypt, a surprising number for so rare a type.

In the *double-zone capital,* a leaf crown, a branch, or some basketwork is surmounted by one or more animals. In addition to various ready-made imports in marble, copies in local stone have survived (Deichmann, 1982, pp. 255–68, ills. 1–4).

The *impost capital* makes the transition from the circular cross-section of the column shaft to the square or rectangular shape of the abacus in its own body, which is a block that splays out at the top. The oldest firmly dated examples of this type of capital, which marked a decided departure from ancient tradition, are works in Constantinople of the early sixth century. The appearance of this form in Egypt can therefore be set in the second quarter of the sixth century at the earliest. Most of the various types of marble impost capitals in Egypt are ready-made imports. Regular impost capitals, in which the capital block is carried right to the corners of the abacus, seem rarely to have been manufactured in local stone. (For local works influenced by the imported marble impost capitals, see below.)

The *impost capital of the fold type* is a special form of the impost capital, formed by coussinets running diagonally from the corners of the abacus to the neck and in the middle from the abacus knob to the neck. This type of capital, of which ready-made marble imports are attested in Egypt, was imitated in local stone with small but significant variations that betray a lack of understanding of the imported form. In especially fine examples at Dayr Apa Jeremiah, the diagonal coussinets are not drawn right up to the corners of the abacus, and over the central coussinets an angular block appears in place of the abacus knob of the original design.

The *basket-shaped capital* has a convex, basket-shaped body under a thick abacus, which is usually modeled on the concave abacus of the Corinthian capital, especially at Dayr Apa Jeremiah and Dayr Apa Apollo, but also at al-Ashmūnayn and Tebtunis. The ornamentation of these local works (e.g., the vertical twisted bands) demonstrates that they were conceived under the influence of imported marble impost capitals, especially the capital of the fold type. Some highly imaginative local pieces are relatively remote from the original design. These basket-shaped capitals are not to be considered impost capitals, because the corners of the abacus project freely and are not engaged with the capital block. Since they were influenced by impost capitals, they are later in date.

The *impost block* could be inserted between a capital and an archivolt around an arch. Unlike the classical and late-classical capital with its square abacus, which did not allow any extension in one dimension only, the impost block could be lengthened on its upper surface to form a rectangle, so that the column could be adapted to the varying thicknesses of the archivolts.

The impost block seems to have been used in Egypt only in the area of Alexandria and very rarely there; at any rate, it did not become widespread in the interior. There are a few examples from Abū Mīnā in Nummulite limestone and probably also in marble. These pieces presumably served to equalize the heights of uneven columns, inasmuch as the upper surfaces have the same dimensions. In this connection, it appears noteworthy that the Ionic impost capital also may have been used only sporadically, as marble work in Alexandria; that the imitations of the imported impost capitals did not take over the ideal and formal consistency of their models; and that local workshops did not shy away from extending the abacus of a traditional capital in one direction in individual situations (i.e., giving the impost clearly rectangular proportions) in order to shape the piece suitably for a particular position (e.g., in the Corinthian capitals in Dayr Apa Jeremiah). Egyptians did not seem to have felt it necessary to analyze and clarify such problems of architectural decoration in terms of theory, plan, and design.

Impost capital. Marble. Sixth century. Cairo, Mosque of Sultan al-Nāṣir Muḥammad (Citadel). *Courtesy Hans-Georg Severin.*

Evidently the impost block was scarcely understood as an achievement, and with the exception of Alexandria, it was deleted as superfluous from the list of Eastern Roman imports.

Half-Column. The half-column is treated separately, in order to emphasize characteristic phenomena of Egyptian architectural decoration in the late-classical and early-Byzantine epochs. A half-column, consisting of base, shaft, and capital, is engaged (attached) to a pillar or wall. It is generally used in pairs to flank an apse or other opening in a wall.

Half-columns were used at full length, as attested by projecting half-column capitals worked in a stucco composite in DAYR AL-BARAMŪS in Wādī al-Naṭrūn and a pair of limestone impost capitals of the fold type reused in the main church of Dayr Apa Jeremiah. Half-columns were also frequently employed in smaller sizes. In an alternating arrangement of semicircular and rectangular niches, they flanked the concave niches while pilasters (engaged rectangular pillars) flanked the rectangular niches. From these smaller half-columns come the characteristic examples with shafts decorated in several zones, a continuance of Roman imperial decoration. The best-known examples from Dayr Apa Apollo and Dayr Apa Jeremiah were, however, found in unskillful secondary constructions, and the original system in the church of Dayr Anbā Shinūdah cannot easily be recognized under disfiguring repairs and patchings.

BIBLIOGRAPHY

Deichmann, F. W. "Zu einigen spätantiken Figuralkapitellen." In *Rom, Ravenna, Konstantinopel und Naher Osten.* Gesammelte Studien zur spätantiken Architektur Kunst und Geschichte. Wiesbaden, 1982.

Fischer, M. "The Corinthian Capitals of the Capernaum Synagogue: A Revision." *Levant* 18 (1896):133, fig. 1.

Kautzsch, R. *Kapitellstudien.* Studien zur spätantiken Kunstgeschichte 9. Berlin and Leipzig, 1936; 2nd ed., 1970.

Kramer, J.; and U. Peschlow. *Corpus der Kapitelle der Kirche von San Marco zu Venedig,* ed. F. W. Deichmann. Forschungen zur Kunstgeschichte und christlichen Archäologie 12. Wiesbaden, 1981.

Severin, H.-G. *Spätantike und frühes Christentum,* ed. B. Brenk, nos. 274–77. Propyläen Kunstgeschichte, Suppl. Vol. 1. Frankfurt am Main, Berlin, and Vienna, 1977.

Strube, C. *Polyeuktoskirche und Hagia Sophia,* pp. 78ff. Munich, 1984.

HANS-GEORG SEVERIN

Crypt

A crypt is a partly or entirely underground room, usually under a church. In ancient times a crypt was simply an underground vaulted room or passage (*cryptoporticus*), and in early Christian times it was a subterranean burial chamber. In the Greek-speaking Eastern Roman Empire, such a chamber was called a *taphos* (Arabic, *ṭafūs*).

Since cemeteries in the pagan world were considered a sacred area, whose occupants were free of persecution, Christians took advantage of this privilege to meet there for worship. After the Edict of Milan in 313, ending persecution, this custom led to the erection of numerous cemetery churches. Since, in addition, some martyrs had already been buried in almost all cemeteries, it was natural that their graves should be associated with the churches there. This development was encouraged in particular by the pagan custom of organizing a regular commemoration festival on the birthday of the deceased, which the Christians turned into a celebration of the death of the martyr.

At first, spatial proximity between the grave and the church was not important for this association. The intensifying of the cult of the saints toward the end of the fourth century, however, led to a need for linking the sanctuaries of the cemetery churches more closely with the martyrs' graves and facilitating access to them. A desire also arose for supplying churches in towns with martyrs' graves, which formerly had not been possible because of the Roman prohibition against burials within a town. A series of changes followed. New churches were erected so that their apse lay directly over the grave of a saint or martyr, and the grave itself was made accessible by a staircase from the interior of the church. Usually two staircases were built, one for descending and the other for ascending, to expedite the traffic of visitors. In addition, there was need for a crypt or confession, a room directly adjoining the grave or linked with it, in which brief devotions might be held in the neighborhood of the tomb. In later days these rooms were furnished with altars and so made suitable for celebration of a complete liturgy.

There was also a wish among many believers to be buried in the neighborhood of a martyr's grave. At first, people were content to obtain a grave in the same cemetery. Once there were large churches at the martyr's graves, people sought to have a place in the interior of these churches, a privilege accorded to only a few of the faithful and, as a rule, only to members of the higher clergy. If a memorial church was founded by private citizens, they could naturally ensure for themselves a place of the first rank in the crypt itself, close to the martyr's grave. From this developed in the late Middle Ages the great subterranean crypts under many collegiate churches, which had a small chapel but essentially served to receive the graves of the founding family.

Crypts that were burial places and were under church floors, or at least entered from the interior of a church, are known in Egypt but do not appear to be widespread. They are not commonly called by a term equivalent to "crypt" but only *ṭafus* and are not linguistically distinguished from an ordinary subterranean grave such as might be in any hypogeum (underground room). The only early Christian example of a crypt that stood in close association with a grave, the remains of which can still be identified, is under the Martyr Church at Abū Mīnā (Grossmann, 1980). It shows clearly regulation of visitor traffic by entrance and exit. Some medieval examples of crypts with graves are known from the literature. The crypt at the north wall of the Church of Saint Mercurius at Dayr Abū Sayfayn is the room in which Abū Barsūm, one of the last saints of the Coptic church, spent part of his life. An altar was later placed there. A genuine modern crypt is the grave of Patriarch Cyril VI (who died in 1971), under the church of the modern monastery of Saint Menas in Maryūt.

In all the other crypt chambers so far identified in Egypt, there is no indication of a directly adjoining grave, although there are frequently two staircases, sometimes symmetrically arranged, which implies the proximity of a grave. They thus have only the significance of a memorial room (Onasch, 1981, pp. 261–62). Characteristic examples are the crypts of the church on the east wall of Antinoopolis (Uggeri, 1974, pp. 42–46), the Church of Saint Sergius in Cairo (Middleton, 1885, pp. 405–407), and a new church in al-Faramā (ancient Pelusium). The crypt of Saint Sergius took on a cruciform shape because of two semicircular niches at the sides, which likewise suggest an ecclesiastial function. Presumably the chamber was originally provided with four central supports, and it is conceivable that it served at least for a time as a burial place. The crypt in al-Faramā exhibits all the details of a chapel intended for liturgical use. It seems to have been an important foundation, for side walls of the staircase are encrusted with marble slabs. Two crypt chambers only recently discovered, under two large buildings in Manqabād, are without any fittings. One of them is remarkable for its rich figurative painting. The other, belonging to a second building phase, has traces of a central dome. Finally, a domed crypt without superstructure, only half sunk into the ground, was found in Abū Mīnā. A bench running along the walls suggests that it could have served as the commemoration room for a grave in the neighborhood.

BIBLIOGRAPHY

Claussen, H. "Krypta." In *Lexikon für Theologie und Kirche*, cols. 651–53. Freiburg, 1961.

Grossmann, P. "Aufnahmearbeiten in der Gruft." *Mitteilungen des deutschen archäologischen Instituts— Abteilung Kairo* 36 (1980):206–212.

______. "Weitere Beobachtungen zur baulichen Gestalt der Märtyrergruft." *Mitteilungen des deutschen archäologischen Instituts—Abteilung Kairo* 38 (1982):137–39.

Middleton, J. H. "On the Coptic Churches of Old Cairo." *Archaeologia* 48 (1885):397–420.

Onasch, K. *Kunst und Liturgie der Ostkirche*. Leipzig, 1981.

Uggeri, G. "La chiesa paleo-cristiana presso la porta orientale." In *Antinoe (1965–1968): Missione archeologica in Egitto*. Rome, 1974.

PETER GROSSMANN

Diaconicon

A diaconicon is a room in a church for the use of the deacons in carrying out their duties. Etymologically the word "diaconicon" means "belonging to the deacon." In antiquity the exact location of the diaconicon in the church does not seem to have been specified. From what is known so far, the designation "diaconicon" was used in Syria for the two side rooms off the apse (pastophoria). Early Christian texts from Egypt attest the diaconicon as a side room in the church accessible from the church proper.

In conformity with the manifold duties of the deacons, the diaconicon accommodated a variety of functions. According to early Christian texts from Egypt, it served, among other things, for the setting up of the incense altar. According to other texts, the sacred vessels were kept there. Thus it is the same as a sacristy (see below). According to G. Graf, the room was called *qunūmiyyah*, which was another word for "sacristy" (Munier, 1930, fol. 60r, 1.12).

A related term is the Arabic *diqūniyyah*, used for a room in which, according to old witnesses, Coptic monks kept their bread (Graf, 1954, p. 46). This is, however, a room in a monastery, not in the church. The designation is rather derived from the *diaconia*, the institution for poor relief, which was among the oldest duties of the diaconate and later was a particular concern of the monasteries. In the monastery of Saint Matthew the Poor, the *diaconia* was a building of several stories, from which one could look far into the distance (Till, 1936, p. 12).

BIBLIOGRAPHY

Amélineau, E. *Étude sur le Christianisme en Egypt au septième siècle*. Paris, 1887.

Descoeudres, G. *Die Pastophorien im syro-byzantinischen Osten*. Wiesbaden, 1983.

Graf, G. *Verzeichnis arabischer kirchlicher Termini*. CSCO 147, Supp. 8. Louvain, 1954.

Marrou, H. I. "L'origine orientale des diaconies romaines." *Mélanges Archéologie* 57 (1940): 95–142.

Munier, H. *La scala copte 44 de la Bibliothèque nationale de Paris*, Vol. 1. Cairo, 1930.

Till, W. *Koptische Heiligen- und Märtyrerlegenden II*. Rome, 1936.

PETER GROSSMANN

Dome

A dome is an evenly curved vault (see below) over a circular base. It may be a complete hemisphere or only part of one or pointed. In traditional architecture it is made of rows of stone blocks or bricks. The Arabic term *qubbah* means both "dome" and the room beneath it. Thus it is applied to different areas of a church covered by a dome, such as the apse and *khūrus* (Ibn Sabbā', 1922, chap. 27) and the baldachinlike superstructure over the altar normally called a ciborium (Graf, 1954, p. 57). Finally the term applies to domed tomb constructions.

BIBLIOGRAPHY

Graf, G. *Verzeichnis arabischer kirchlicher Termini,* p. 87. Louvain, 1954.

Ibn Sabbā', Yūhannā ibn Abī Zakarīyyā. *La Perle précieuse,* ed. J. Péier. In PO 16. Paris, 1922.

PETER GROSSMANN

Gallery

In church architecture, a gallery is an upper story over an aisle or ambulatory. It is normally open onto the nave through rows of supporting columns, just as the aisles are on the ground floor. In the East, the gallery was reserved for women, as its Greek name (*hyperoon gnaikonitidos,* "women's gallery") implies. It is more common in Eastern churches than in Western churches, where women and men were separated by area but not by story. The Latin *matroneum* means only "place of the women." The Arabic word is *ustuwān.*

The gallery corresponds structurally to the upper story of a two-storied columned hall or a stoa (detached colonnade) such as those bordering public squares and gymnasia in ancient Greece and was called a *stoa diple.* It is found in secular Roman basilicas such as that in Fano (Vitruvius *De architectura,* 5.1.6) and in the forum of Leptis Magna, North Africa. The Great Basilica, the synagogue of Alexandria (destroyed in A.D. 116), was called a *diplostoon* and thus likely possessed galleries, which were reserved for women.

The gallery is not restricted to a specific type of church structure. It was taken over from the secular basilica and very likely spread chiefly from Constantinople and possibly also Alexandria. The relatively early examples of the gallery in Palestine are misleading, because they were commissioned by the emperor and were planned in Constantinople (Deichmann, 1959). The early local architecture of Palestine provides no examples of galleries. From the fifth and sixth centuries onward, the gallery was a regular feature of Eastern churches and synagogues.

Next to Asia Minor, Egypt was the area where galleries were most widespread. They are documented above all by the great Upper Egyptian monastery churches of Dayr Anbā Shinūdah and Dayr Anbā Bishoi, where they were, in fact, genuinely needed in order to accommodate the great number of nuns belonging to these monasteries (Leipoldt, 1903, pp. 93, 153–55). By contrast, the churches belonging to exclusively male monasteries, such as the large lauras of Scetis at Wādī al-Naṭrūn and Kellia, did not possess galleries. The gallery is, furthermore, a feature of town churches but apparently not of churches at the great pilgrim centers such as Abū Mīnā, where there is no sure evidence of the existence of a gallery.

The galleries were entered by means of stairs, which in important and carefully designed churches connected with the narthex or vestibule (see below). In Syrian churches, the side wings of the narthex were frequently developed into staircase towers. In churches in Constantinople the stairwells protruded from the body of the building on both sides of the narthex. As a rule, in Egypt there was only one staircase, which was often simply attached externally to one side of the church. Since only the gallery on that side could be reached, a footbridge was needed to link it to the gallery on the opposite side. This footbridge was normally placed over the return aisle. It subsequently became a canonical requirement, for it can be found from the fifth century onward, even in churches that have no galleries. Nevertheless, the presence of a staircase does not always imply the existence of a gallery. In most cases, the stairs led only to the roof, which can be assumed to have been flat over the side aisles.

The columns of the gallery are smaller than those of the nave and are, for obvious technical reasons, axially erected upon the nave columns. Some churches have piers (pillars or other supports) in place of columns. In the church of Dayr Anbā Bishoi, windows seem to have provided the only view of the interior from the gallery (Grossmann, 1969, pp. 158ff.). Windows may also have been used in small pier churches made from mud bricks. In churches with columns, cancelli were inserted between them as parapets. In the Church of Saint Mercurius in Dayr Abū Sayfayn the spaces between the columns are provided with a full-height grille.

After the introduction of the dome in Egypt, the gallery fell into disuse because it was technically difficult to construct in mud brick, especially because of the required height. In older churches where it was retained, the space was used to set up subsidiary altars, and the women were placed in a new area in the lower part of the church, the *bayt al-niṣā'* ("house of women").

BIBLIOGRAPHY

Butler, A. J. *The Ancient Coptic Churches of Egypt,* Vol. 1, 2nd ed. London, 1970.

Christern, J. "Emporerkirchen in Nordafrika." In *Akten des VII. internationalen Kongresses für christliche Archäologie.* Trier, 1965–1969.

Deichmann, F. W. "Empore." In *Reallexikon für Antike und Christentum,* Vol. 4, cols. 1255–63. Stuttgart, 1959.

Gordon, H. L. "The Basilica and the Stoa in Early Rabbinical Literature." *Art Bulletin* 13 (1931): 353–75.

Grossmann, P. "Die von Somers Clarke in Ober-Ansinā entdeckten Kirchenbanken." *Mitteilungen des Deutschen Archäologischen Instituts—Abteilung Kairo* 24 (1969):144–68.

Grossmann, P.; J. Kosčink; G. Severin. "Abū Mīna. Elfler vorläufiger Bericht. Kampagnen 1982 und 1983." *Mitteilungen des Deutschen Archäologischen Instituts—Abteilung Kairo* 40 (1984):123–51.

Leipoldt, J. *Schenute von Atripe.* Leipzig, 1903.

Orlandos, A. K. Βασιλική, pp. 196–202, 379–85. Athens, 1952.

Rave, P. O. *Der Emporenbau in romanischer und frühgotischer Zeit,* pp. 19–35. Bonn, 1924.

Sukenik, E. L. *Ancient Synagogues in Palestine and Greece.* London, 1934.

PETER GROSSMANN

Horseshoe Arch

A horseshoe arch is a circular arch that narrows at the base. It appears occasionally in imperial Roman architecture of the second century A.D., for example, at Villa degli Setti Bassi (Ashby, 1907, p. 99, pl. 7), but is otherwise very rare. There are a few early Christian examples from Asia Minor and Syria (Hauschild and Schlunk, 1978, pp. 92–93). It is found in the early Middle Ages in Umayyad architecture in North Africa and the Mozarabic architecture disseminated from it in Spain. The Church of al-Ḥayz in al-Baḥariyyah Oasis (Fakhry, 1950, pp. 55–60) is an example of an Egyptian church that contains several horseshoe arches.

BIBLIOGRAPHY

Ashby, T. "The Classical Topography of the Roman Campagna." *Papers of the British School at Rome* 4 (1907):3–153.

Fakhry, A. *Baharia Oasis.* Cairo, 1950.

Hauschild, T., and H. Schlunk. *Hispania Antiqua.* Mainz, 1978.

PETER GROSSMANN

Iconostasis

An iconostasis is the screen or wall in a church that separates the sanctuary, presbytery, or bema, restricted to the clergy, from the naos, or area of the laity. It developed in the fourteenth century in Byzantine areas, earlier in Egypt. The Arab word for it is *hijāb,* which literally means "curtains."

The spatial separation of clergy from laity began in the early church, where low cancelli (see above) shielded the sanctuary but did not hide it from view. In the sixth century in Byzantine areas the cancelli developed into the templon, a more ornate screen with curtains above it, which concealed the acts carried out at the altar from the view of worshipers. It is not known exactly when such concealment was considered necessary.

A similar effect was achieved when curtains were added above the cancelli in Western churches, first mentioned in the seventh century in *Liber pontificalis* (Duchesne and Vogel, 1955–1957, p. 375). About the same time, the western wall of the *khūrus,* a room between the naos and the sanctuary, was performing the function of concealment in Egyptian churches. The wall had a central opening, which might be narrow and provided with wooden doors, as in the churches of Dayr al-Suryān and Dayr al Baramūs in Wādī al-Naṭrūn, which have doors from the tenth century (Evelyn-White, 1972, pp. 187–90, 197–200). If the central opening was wide, as in the Church of Saint Mercurius in Dayr Abū Sayfayn, Cairo, columns were inserted in it and the space between them was provided with a wooden framework probably to hold a curtain.

During the Middle Ages the west wall of the *khūrus* became more solid and elaborate. Made of wood or stone, it was taller than a man and contained a main entrance that could be closed by a wooden door that was sometimes richly carved (see WOODWORK, COPTIC). There were also side entrances or windows. The stone *khūrus* was usually an undecorated wall surmounted by a simple cornice, but the wooden *khūrus* was frequently elaborately carved.

In the Fatimid period (tenth to twelfth centuries) a series of panels with figurative and ornamental carving, sometimes inlaid with ivory, were joined in a continuous framework. In the Mamluk period (thirteenth to sixteenth centuries) the *khūrus* wall was artfully constructed of different colored wood and ivory panels, as can still be seen in churches in Cairo. Meanwhile the *khūrus* room itself was opening into the sanctuary and gradually disappeared. The function of the west wall in hiding the sanctuary was then served by the iconostasis, a solid wall pierced by doors, which is covered with paintings of holy persons called icons. These are arranged according to a fixed pattern of subject matter and add greatly to the spiritual meaning and decorative effect of Coptic churches.

BIBLIOGRAPHY

Burmester, O. H. E. *The Egyptian or Coptic Church.* Cairo, 1967.

Chatzidakis, M. "Ikonostas." In *Reallexikon der byzantinischen Kunst,* Vol. 3, ed. K. Wessel and M. Restle. Stuttgart, 1978.

Duchesne, L., and C. Vogel, eds. *Liber pontificalis.* 2nd ed., Paris, 1955–1957.

Evelyn-White, H. G. *The Monasteries of the Wādī 'n Naṭrūn,* Pt. 3. New York, 1932; repr. 1972.

Graf, G. *Verzeichnis arabischer kirchlicher Termini.* CSCO 147. Louvain, 1954.

Leroy, J. *Les Peintures des couvents du désert d'Esna.* Mémoires publiés par les membres de l'Institut français d'Archéologie orientale 94. Cairo, 1972.

Pauty, E. *Bois sculptés d'églises coptes (époque fatimide).* Cairo, 1930.

PETER GROSSMANN

Khūrus

A *khūrus* (Greek, *choros*) is a room reserved for the clergy between the presbytery, or sanctuary, and the naos. It developed in the medieval Egyptian church in the late seventh and early eighth centuries. Its front (western) wall, which sets it off from the laity, fulfills a function similar to that of the templon (a type of cancelli) in Byzantine architecture. Both structures serve primarily to hide the liturgical actions carried out in the sanctuary from the view of the believers. Unlike the Byzantine templon, however, the *khūrus* is built as a massive wall reaching to the ceiling.

The *khūrus* presumably derived from a row of columns, unconnected to the ceiling, that was set up in front of the opening of the apse and whose purpose was purely aesthetic, to enrich the appearance of apsidal openings that in some churches appeared somewhat small. Among the earliest examples are the sanctuaries of the two monastic churches at Dayr Anbā Shinūdah and Dayr Anbā Bishoi (both fifth century) and the church in front of the pylon of the Luxor temple.

An intermediate link that illustrates the development of the *khūrus* is the small basilica, unfortunately not yet exactly dated, in front of the eastern gate of the temple of Madīnat Hābū. Here the columns placed in front of the apse have become a closed wall structure with only one opening in the middle. In this building, however, the presbytery clearly still extends beyond that wall into the nave, and consequently, at this stage there is no question of a change in use.

The *khūrus* also developed in Nubian churches. The wall block in front of the apse, containing an aperture in the middle, is in several instances adorned with two columns as at Adindān and Faras. There was no tradition for the *khūrus* in Nubia, however, and it was eventually rejected.

As the *khūrus* developed, the wall block, which previously stood unconnected, was replaced by a full dividing wall with separate entrances to the three rooms of the sanctuary. The *khūrus* itself, beyond this wall, first consisted only of a simple cross corridor as at Upper Ansinā and MANQABĀD. The depth of an actual room seems to have been acquired in the eighth century. From this time the possibility presented itself of merging the now broadly designed *khūrus* and the apse, which lay mostly open in its entire western breadth, into the greater shape of a triconch (a room with a semicircular extension on three sides, see below). This possibility was frequently exploited, particularly with older buildings, where the *khūrus* had been built in later.

The way of access to the *khūrus* is not uniform. In the al-'Adhrā' church of DAYR AL-SURYĀN, Wādī al-Naṭrūn, the *khūrus* has a single, broad opening in the middle. The two churches of Dayr Anbā Hadrā and DAYR AL-SHAYKHAH in Aswan possess, in addition to the middle aperture, a passage on the right-hand side, whereas a number of other edifices have a *khūrus* built with three openings.

The *khūrus* as an integrated component of the Egyptian church can be traced well into the Mamluk period (thirteenth to early sixteenth century). When, as a result of the increased frequency of masses during this period, it became customary to supply the churches with multiple altar rooms, the available side chambers of the apse of older churches were converted into additional altar rooms. At that time there was no reason to add a *khūrus,* so the practice was eventually abolished. In its stead, an iconostasis of bricks or wood was built immediately in front of the entrance to the sanctuary.

BIBLIOGRAPHY

Grossmann, P. "Zur christlichen Baukunst in Ägypten." *Enchoria* 8 (1978):89ff.

______. *Mittelalterliche Langhauskuppelkirchen und verwandte Typen in Oberägypten,* pp. 112ff. Glückstadt, 1982.

PETER GROSSMANN

Maqṣūrah

A *maqṣūrah* is a secondary side room off the sanctuary in some modern Coptic churches; it is frequently linked with the sanctuary by an opening like a window in the wall. Functionally it serves as a special prayer room for women and is therefore always adorned with a representation of the Virgin, in addition to numerous other icons. Furthermore, through the wall opening mentioned, the room can also be used for the receiving of communion. Genetically the *maqṣūrah* is probably derived from the governor's box of the same name beside the *miḥrāb* in the mosque. It was introduced there at the beginning of the Umayyad period, as a precaution against attacks upon the governor. There are early examples from Cairo in the al-Azhar mosque, built in A.D. 971 (Maqrīzī, 1970, Vol. 1, p. 465), and in the Ibn Ṭulūn mosque (Maqrīzī, Vol. 1, p. 466). How far there are links with corresponding structures in Byzantine architecture is so far not clear.

BIBLIOGRAPHY

Diez, E. "Maqṣūra." In *Enzyklopedia des Islam,* Vol. 3, pp. 394–95. Leiden, 1936.

PETER GROSSMANN

Naos

A naos is the sanctuary, or inner room, of an ancient Greek temple or the shrine in that room in an Egyptian temple. The term is also used to refer to the area of a church in which the laity assembles. It does not include the sanctuary or the narthex. The naos can take very different forms according to the type of building. In Egypt down to the tenth century, the nave and two side aisles of a basilica with a return aisle at the western end was by far the most common form. In addition, the naos also occurred as a nave without aisles, as in the original building of the old church in DAYR ABŪ ḤINNIS, Mallawī. In the small chapels of the seventh and eighth centuries that are occasionally found annexed to the monks' dwellings in the great laura of Kellia (see hermitages 14, 16, and 20 of Quṣūr Izeila in Kasser, 1983), the naos has the form of two domed rooms, one behind the other. The substantially later old church of Dayr Anbā Anṭūniyus has the same form. In the great transept basilicas of al-Ashmūnayn, Abū Mīnā, and HAWWĀRIYYAH, the naos includes the transept. In churches built on a central plan, tetraconchs (see below), and four-column churches, the naos, of course, has a central plan. However, in the Church of Sitt Maryam in Dayr al-Suryān, the naos consists only of a single vaulted bay in front of the *khūrus.* A modern Arabic term for the naos is *ṣaḥn al-kanīsah* ("construction of the church," evidently a parallel to *ṣaḥn al-masjid,* or "court of the mosque"; Burmester, 1967, p. 20).

BIBLIOGRAPHY

Burmester, O. H. E. *The Egyptian or Coptic Church.* Cairo, 1967.

Kasser, R. *Survey archéologique des Kellia Campagne 1981.* Louvain, 1983.

Monneret de Villard, U. "La basilica cristiana in Egitto." In *Atti del IV congresso internationale di archeologia cristiana,* pp. 315–18. Rome, 1940.

Orlandos, A. K. *Βασιλική.* Athens, 1952.

PETER GROSSMANN

Narthex

A narthex is a vestibule of a church, corresponding to the pronaos (porch) of a classical temple. The Greek word means literally "a reedlike plant." In the sixth century, Procopius of Caesarea, evidently for the first time, described the antechamber of a church as a narthex because it was small (Procopius *De aedificiis* 1.4.7, 5.6.23). In the West the word "narthex" was not used in antiquity, but the late medieval term *ardica* (*artica*) evidently comes for the same root (Grossmann, 1973, p. 1). The Arabic word *narṭiks* is apparently used only by the Melchites (Graf, 1954, p. 112). The modern Arabic term for *narthex* is *mamārr al-mādkhal* ("vestibule").

The narthex, which was the place for penitents and others not admitted to the church itself, is usually on the western end of the church. In early Christian churches, including those in Egypt, it took two forms—an exterior porch and an interior hall. The exterior form, familiar in the West, was a colonnaded porch distinguished from a portico by corresponding exactly to the breadth of the building. Occasionally the designation *exonarthex* is also used for this form (Orlandos, 1952, Vol. 1, pp. 136–37). According to F. E. Brightman, it was called the *proaulion* and was the result of a reduced atrium that lacked the other three sides, an opinion with which one can scarcely agree (Brightmann, 1896, p. 571). An Egyptian example is the great basilica of Fāw al-Qiblī (Pbow). Presumably the stoa mentioned in "Apa Claudius and the Thieves" (Drescher, 1942, pp. 63ff.) was also an external narthex.

The interior form of the narthex, predominant in the East, is a more compact area inside the church. It opens to the outside through a door or a single arch and opens into the naos through several doors or occasionally a larger opening in connection with a tribelon (passage divided by two columns, see below). The designation *esonarthex* was introduced for this form, especially since Hagia Sophia seemed to have had two narthexes. In the most recent investigations, however, the outer narthex has been shown to be the eastern portico of the atrium (Strube, 1973, pp. 33ff.). As a result the church has only one narthex, which consequently does not require any separate designation. Most Egyptian narthexes are of this second form, consisting of a compact room entered from outside by an ordinary door and connected by a second, not very imposing door with the naos. Examples are to be found in the church of Dayr Anbā Shinūdah (Monneret de Villard, 1926, p. 111ff.) and the main church (second half of the seventh century) of Dayr Apa Jeremiah, where the narthex is connected by a tribelon with the naos (Grossmann, 1982b, pp. 159–62). In the latter church, the adjoining return aisle, which is connected along its entire width with the nave and aisles, belongs entirely to the naos and has nothing to do with the narthex. In the small aisleless church in the area of ruins west of Dayr Abū Ḥinnis, a western section is separated from the naos by a transverse row of columns (Grossmann, 1982, pp. 128ff., ill. 54), an instance not of a narthex but of a return aisle reduced to the width of the aisleless naos.

While the narthex continued to play a prominent role in middle and late Byzantine architecture, its importance in Egypt declined. Even in the early Christian period it was employed only in important buildings, such as at Dayr Abū Fānah and those at Kellia, and was altogether lacking in provincial churches. In the main church of Dayr al-Suryān it was misunderstood as an antechamber to the staircase and was originally accessible only from the interior of the church (Grossmann, 1982 a, p. 114, fig. 47). In the Middle Ages the narthex fell completely out of use. Instead, there was used, at least in some monastery churches, a kind of propylon, called *duksār* ("porch") in Arabic (see below), which corresponds at least remotely to the narthex. The entrance hall at the Mu'allāqah church in Babylon, Cairo, consisting of a portico stretched between two projecting stair towers, such as is common in Syrian architecture, is not historical (Simaykah, 1937, pp. 55ff.).

BIBLIOGRAPHY

Brightman, F. E., and C. E. Hammond, eds. *Liturgies Eastern and Western,* Vol. 1. Oxford, 1896. Repr. 1962.

Drescher, J., ed. "Apa Claudius and the Thieves." *Bulletin de la Société d'archéologie copte* 8 (1942):67–87.

Graf, G. *Verzeichnis arabischer kirchlicher Termini,* Vol. 2. Louvain, 1954.

Grossmann, P. *S. Michele in Africa.* Mainz, 1973.

———. *Mittelalterliche Langhauskuppelkirchen und verwandte Typen in Oberägypten,* pp. 103ff. Glückstadt, 1982.

Grossmann, P., and H.-G. Severin. "Reinigungsarbeiten im Jeremiaskloster bei Saqqāra. Vierter vorläufiger Bericht." *Mitteilungen des Deutschen Archäologischen Instituts—Abteilung Kairo* 38 (1982):159–62.

Leclercq, H. "Narthex." In *Dictionnaire d'archéologie chrétienne et de liturgie,* Vol. 12, cols. 888f. Paris, 1935.

Monneret de Villard, U. *Les Couvents près de Sohag,* Vol. 2, pp. 111ff. Milan, 1926.

———. "La basilica cristiana in Egitto." In *Atti del IV congresso internazionale di archeologia cristiana,* Vol. 1, pp. 302ff. Rome, 1940.

Orlandos, A. K. *Βασιλική.* Athens, 1952.

Simaykah, M. *Guide sommaire du Musée copte.* Cairo, 1937.

Strube, C. *Die westliche Eingangsseite der Kirchen von Konstantinopel in justinianischer Zeit.* Wiesbaden, 1973.

Völkl, L. "Archäologische Funde und Forschungen in Rom-Montecassino-Syracus-Vaticano." *Römische Quartelschrift für christliche Altertumskunde und Kirchengeschichte* 48 (1953):237ff.

PETER GROSSMANN

Nave

A nave is the main area of a basilica church lying between two or more side aisles usually separated from it by rows of columns. It is higher than the aisles, the part of its walls above the aisle roof forming the clerestory. The nave extends from the west wall (the return aisle in Egyptian churches) to the transept (transverse arms) or, if there is no transept, to the triumphal arch that forms the opening to the sanctuary or apse. The east end of the nave, in front of the sanctuary, is occupied by the presbytery surrounded by cancelli. Until the eighth century, the altar stood in the presbytery, but when the *khūrus* was interposed between the apse and the nave, the altar disappeared from the nave.

In Egyptian basilica churches the nave usually has a saddleback (pitched) roof (see below). In early Christian times some village churches with relatively narrow naves had a barrel-vault roof (see "vault" below). But vaulting was not in general use until the late Middle Ages, in churches such as those at Dayr al-Suryān and Dayr Anbā Bishoi.

BIBLIOGRAPHY

Monneret de Villard, U. "La basilica cristiana in Egitto." In *Atti del IV congresso internationale di archeologia cristiana*, Vol. 1. Rome, 1940.

Orlandos, A. K. Βασιλική, pp. 154ff. Athens, 1952.

PETER GROSSMANN

Niche

A niche is a recess in a wall. It may hold useful objects or decorative objects, such as statues, or may itself be a decorative element.

Practical niches inside buildings serve as cupboards. Intended to store objects that might be lost or broken if left on the floor, they are usually at a convenient height. They may be divided into several compartments by the insertion of horizontal boards and provided with doors so that they can be closed. Some may have a high parapet in front to hold loose goods. Sometimes a large main niche will be flanked by two smaller, shallower side niches, as in ancient Roman houses in the Fayyūm, a symmetrical arrangement for the display of images of gods and ancestors. Similar arrangements can be found in several hermitages at Kellia. There are also very small niches, usually beside a staircase, to hold an oil lamp.

When cupboard niches are built into the wall during the construction of a building, they are rectangular and usually topped by a small arch or, less commonly, a lintel. When they are cut into a wall after it is built, possible in principle only with crude brick constructions, they are generally shapeless and have a rounded interior. Not infrequently they even go around the corner of a room. In rooms that have frequently been altered, such niches result in very irregular wall structure.

Niches constructed for decorative reasons or religious purposes are more elaborate. Since the deep, shadowed area of a niche forms a strong visual contrast with the otherwise flat wall, niches were used as decorative elements. In Roman temples and other public buildings, alternating rectangular and semicircular niches, holding statues of the gods or emperors, occur in regular sequence. Since churches in the Nile Valley generally had few other decorative elements, they were often provided, especially in Upper Egypt, with a close succession of niches in the side walls and the apse. In most examples, these probably had only a decorative significance. While in the early monastery churches in Wādī al-Naṭrūn only simple rectangular niches occur in sequence (Grossmann, 1982, figs. 47, 51), the churches of Dayr Anbā Shinūdah and Dayr Anbā Bishoi present in the naos and especially in the apse an alternation of rectangular and semicircular niches strongly reminiscent of those in Roman buildings. In the church of Dayr Abū Fānah, deep and shallow niches alternate with one another in the apse (Grossmann, 1982, p. 78, fig. 25). Wide but relatively shallow niches are employed in the altar

Niche with conch decoration. Cairo, Coptic Museum (Inv. 8137).

chambers of some Upper Egyptian churches. Further, there are several symmetrically arranged small niches in the apses of the churches in the area of Akhmīm, for the most part deriving from the Ottoman period (after the fifteenth century).

A special role is played by the niche in the east wall of rectangular altar chambers of Egyptian churches (*shaqq al-haykal* or *sharqīyyah,* "the eastern"). These niches apparently represent the apse and are copied from the prayer niches in anchorite cells. Although they were known since the early Middle Ages, it was only in the Mamluk period that they took on any significance.

BIBLIOGRAPHY

Grossmann, P. *Mittelalterliche Langhauskuppelkirchen und verwandte Typen in Oberägypten.* Glückstadt, 1982.

Hornborstel-Hüttner, G. *Studien zur römischen Nischenarchitektur.* Leiden, 1979.

Husson, G. "Un Sens méconnu de θυρίς et de fenestra." *Proceedings of the 15th International Congress of Papyrologists.* Oxford, 1974.

Monneret de Villard, U. *Les Couvents près de Sohag,* 2 vols. Milan, 1925–1926.

PETER GROSSMANN

Pastophorium

A pastophorium is a small side room of an ancient temple or Eastern church.

According to W. Otto (1905, Vol. 1, p. 96), the term in Egypt originally referred to the official room for the *pastophoroi,* bearers of the *pastos,* the small, cabinetlike chapels in which the Egyptians placed the statues of the gods when they carried them in processions (Hopfner, 1949, cols. 2107ff.). Pastophoria are also mentioned as dwelling places of the priests appointed to the temple. Elsewhere, according to ancient authorities, the term meant a sleeping chamber or even a bridal chamber (Lucian of Samo-sata *Dialogi Mortuorum, De Morte Peregrini* 23.3; Nonnus of Panopolis *Dionysiaca* 5.213) or a room in the Temple in Jerusalem (Josephus *Bellum Judaicum* 4.9.12, and several places in the Septuagint).

In early Christian church architecture, according to the *Apostolic Constitutions,* composed in fourth-century Syria, the pastophoria are two rooms, one on either side of the apse (2.57.1) and serve, among other purposes, to store the unused portion of the Eucharist (8.13). Such rooms are found in Syrian churches, beginning in the late fourth century. They assumed a distinctive form in the fifth century and became characteristic of Eastern churches. Unfortunately, archaeologists have used the designation "prothesis" for one pastophorium (traditionally on the north side of the sanctuary), which was thought to serve for the preparation of the Eucharist, and "diaconicon" for the other pastophorium (on the south side) or for both rooms. At that time, however, neither of the two rooms could have served eucharistic purposes because the special rite of preparation, which is also called prothesis, did not exist until the late eleventh century. Before that time, the preparations were made at the entrance of the church or even outside it in a room called the *scevophilacion* (Descoeudres, 1983, pp. 130–32). The room called the diaconicon was not assigned a function. In Syrian churches it usually has a larger entrance and is often filled with shrines of martyrs, so it may reasonably be called a martyrium.

Rooms corresponding to the pastophoria suitable for the functions mentioned are found in the oldest Egyptian churches, as early as the fourth century, but the designation "pastophoria" is not so far attested. It is therefore advisable to call them apse side rooms. Nevertheless, there is early mention of a diaconicon (*Apophthegmata Patrum* 178; *Gelasius* 3), which may refer to one of the apse side rooms. From the context it is clear that this was a separate room accessible from inside the church. Probably in Egypt also the term "diaconicon" was used for both rooms, disregarding their individual functions. In these early Egyptian examples, there were not just two but a large number of rooms, as in the transept basilica of al-Ashmūnayn at Hermopolis Magna and Dayr Anbā Shinūdah at Suhāj, one of which also served as a baptistery. Therefore, it may probably be concluded that the use of apse side rooms in Egypt was an independent development, not introduced under Syrian influence. They also appeared in Syria in the late fourth century (Schneider, 1949, p. 59).

BIBLIOGRAPHY

Descoeudres, J. *Die Pastophorien im syro-byzantinischen Osten.* Wiesbaden, 1983.

Hopfner, T. "Pastophoroi." In *Real-encyclopädie der classischen Altertumswissenschaft,* Vol. 18, pt. 3, cols. 2107–2109. Stuttgart, 1949.

Monneret de Villard, U. "La basilica cristiana in Egitto." In *Atti del IV congresso internationale di archeologia cristiana. Città del Vaticano, 1938,* Vol. 1, pp. 308–318. Rome, 1940.

Otto, W. *Priester und Tempel im hellenistischen Ägypten,* 2 vols. Rome, 1905–1908.
Passoni dell'Acqua, A. "Ricerche sulla versione dei LXX e i papiri I Pastophorion." *Aegyptus* 61 (1981):171–211.
Schneider, A. M. "Liturgie und Kirchenbau in Syrien." *Nachrichten der Akademie der Wissenschaften in Göttingen* (1949):45–68.

PETER GROSSMANN

Pillar

A pillar, like a column (see above), is a vertical architectural support, but it is usually rectangular in plan. Occasionally it may be octagonal, cruciform, or T-shaped. In traditional architecture, pillars are built of individual stones or bricks, not drums or an entire shaft. Because a pillar is heavier than a column (shorter in proportion to its cross-section), it can carry loads with a diagonal thrust. It is thus a support for wide, heavy arches. Particularly stout pillars, such as those under bridges, are called piers.

A pillar may have a base, shaft, and impost capital, but as a rule these elements are more simply shaped than those of a column, and the base or impost capital may be missing in purely utilitarian pillars, such as those of a cistern.

Pillars that have been adorned at the corners with engaged half- or three-quarter columns are called cantoned pillars. They were freely employed in the hermitages of Kellia in particular, since such corner columns could very easily be carved out of the corners of the brick pillars.

BIBLIOGRAPHY

Orlandos, A. K. Βασιλική, pp. 356–58. Athens, 1952.

PETER GROSSMANN

Porch

A porch is a covered entrance to a temple, church, or other building. Greek and Roman buildings had a pronaos (porch) in the form of a portico (with columns and a pediment). The narthex of some early Christian churches was a portico. A porch consisting of a bay and, generally, a large entrance opening appeared for the first time in Egyptian monastic churches in the Fatimid period (Horner, 1902, fol. 390; Evelyn-White, 1926–1933). The Greek word for this style of porch, *doxarion* (meaning "glory and honor") and the Arabic word for it, *dukṣār,* suggests that it was a sort of triumphal arch. It corresponded functionally to a narthex and indeed was described by Mattā al-Miskīn in his book on monasteries as *mamārr al-madkhal* ("vestibule"). In its single bay it may be compared to a propylaeum, an important temple or other entrance, especially between two pylons (truncated pyramidal towers) (Vitruvius 6.7.5), or a prothyron (a two-columned porch, see below). The *dukṣār* is where modern churchgoers remove their shoes. The oldest examples of the *dukṣār* are in front of the two original east entrances of the church of Dayr Anbā Hadrā. Similar examples in front of the churches of Dayr al-Suryān and Dayr Anbā Bishoi date from the Mamluk period. The porch in the al-ʿAdhrā church of Dayr al-Suryān originally had the shape of a tetrapylon (a porch with four pylons); the lateral arched openings were later blocked off.

BIBLIOGRAPHY

Burmester, O. H. E. *The Egyptian or Coptic Church,* p. 21. Cairo, 1967.
Evelyn-White, H. G. *The Monasteries of the Wadi 'n Natrun,* Vol. 3, *The Architecture and Archaeology.* New York, 1926–1933.
Horner, G. *The Service for the Consecration of a Church and Altar.* London, 1902.
Mattā al-Miskīn. *Al-Rahbanah al-Qibṭiyah,* Cairo, 1972.

PETER GROSSMANN

Presbytery

A presbytery (Greek, *presbyterion,* from *presbyteros,* meaning "elder") is the area of the church reserved for the clergy to carry out their liturgical functions. It is identical with the sanctuary. In early Christian basilicas the presbytery was usually a rectangular area at the east end of the nave in front of the apse. It was raised above the floor by several steps—it is sometimes called a bema (the Greek word for "raised platform")—and was shut off by cancelli from the area of the church for laity on the west and frequently also from the apse on the east. The altar stood at the western end facing the area for the laity. The reading of scripture also took place at that end. The presbytery could be entered from both sides and from the western end. In special situations a prostasis (an area of varying length closed at the sides by cancelli) was placed in front of it, as in several churches in Abū Mīnā. In several large Egyptian churches the presbytery was itself subdivided by inner screens in two sections. In early monastic churches at Kellia the presbytery was simpler—a rectangular altar chamber closed off from the laity by a screen between the jambs of the triumphal arch that formed its front opening.

The presbytery continued in use in medieval English cathedrals, where it often occupied the space between the choir and the high altar. In Egypt, however, it lost its significance, as the *khūrus* (see above) developed in the late seventh and eighth century as a room for the clergy carved out of the naos.

BIBLIOGRAPHY

Delvoye, C. "Bema." In *Reallexikon für Antike und Christentum,* Vol. 1, pp. 583–99. Stuttgart, 1966.

Nussbaum, O. *Der Standort des Liturgen am christlichen Altar vor dem Jahre 1000,* Vols. 1–2. Bonn, 1965.

Orlandos, A. K. *Βασιλική,* pp. 509–535. Athens, 1952.

PETER GROSSMANN

Prothesis

The term "prothesis" refers both to a small room in a church where the elements of the Eucharist are prepared and stored and the rite of preparation. In Greek antiquity *prothesis* meant, among other things, the ceremonial lying in state of the dead inside the house. Later in Christian usage the term referred to the ceremony, also called *proskomide,* dating from the late eleventh century, in which the bread and wine are laid out for the celebration of the Eucharist. It also meant the small room on the north side of the sanctuary (see pastophorium, above) in which the ceremony takes place and the table that is used. The Arabic term for the room is *haykal al-taqdimah* (Graf, 1954, p. 89).

BIBLIOGRAPHY

Descoeudres, G. *Die Pastophorien im syro-byzantinischen Osten.* Wiesbaden, 1983.

Graf, G. *Verzeichnis arabischer kirchlicher Termini,* p. 89. Louvain, 1954.

PETER GROSSMANN

Prothyron

A prothyron is an open porch supported by two columns in front of the outer doors of a church or other building. It is thus a diminutive propylaeum or a portico reduced to a single bay (see "porch," above). The roof, which is fixed to the building wall, may be a small dome or a saddleback, and the columns are connected to each other and the wall by architraves or arches. The prothyron is generally raised at least one step from the ground.

The prothyron was often used in classical times (Vitruvius 6.7) but was more commonly used in Byzantine churches. Examples in Egypt are rare and occur almost solely along the coast, especially in the vicinity of Alexandria. The Great Basilica at Abū Mīnā has prothyra placed inside (Schläger, 1965, ill. 1), but these lead to side rooms and chapels that can only be entered from the church. The prothyron also found its way into Islamic architecture and occurs repeatedly, in particular in the buildings of the sixteenth-century Turkish architect Mi'mar Sinan (Egli, 1976). In modern Coptic architecture the porch corresponds to it.

BIBLIOGRAPHY

Egli, E. *Sinan, der Baumeister osmanischer Glanzzeit.* Stuttgart, 1976.

Kaufmann, C. M. *Handbuch der christlichen Archäologie,* p. 183. Paderborn, 1913.

Schläger, H. "Abu Mena Zweiter Vorläufiger Bericut." *Mitteilungen des Deutschen Archäologischen Instituts—Abteilung Kairo* (1965):122–25.

PETER GROSSMANN

Return Aisle

A return aisle is a passage at the western end of a church that is a unique feature of the early Christian basilica in Egypt. It is spatially related to the nave in the same way that the long north and south aisles are (although its width may vary) and is connected to them without restriction by lateral buttresses or engaged pillars and columns. It is therefore fundamentally different from the internal narthex, which faces the inside of the church and is usually separated from the nave area by lateral buttresses.

The return aisle probably owes its origin to the need to find room for a bridge passage to connect the galleries over the long aisles. In this regard, a single staircase was sufficient. Thus, the return aisle is first of all an element in churches with galleries. Typologically, however, it seems to have been anticipated in some subterranean tomb complexes by an ambulatory, deriving from pagan times.

In Egyptian church building it became a requirement in the first half of the fifth century at the latest, for from this period on, it can be found even in churches that certainly never had a gallery. In the medieval Egyptian basilica it gradually fell out of use, but it is still found in several eighth-century churches.

BIBLIOGRAPHY

Grossmann, P. "Zur christlichen Baukunst in Ägypten." *Enchoria* Suppl. 8 (1978):89f.

Monneret de Villard, U. *Les Couvents près de Sohâg,* Vol. 2, p. 95. Milan, 1926.

______. "La basilica cristiana in Egitto." In *Atti del IV congresso internazionale di archeologia cristiana,* Vol. 1, p. 313. Vatican City, 1940.

PETER GROSSMANN

Roof

A roof is the top covering of a building and its supporting frame. It may be flat, saddleback (pitched), or vaulted. In Egypt since earliest times, the flat roof was preferred. Probably from the Hellenistic period, saddleback roofs were used only for buildings that had an unusually wide span, such as classical temple complexes, market buildings, and especially churches. Stone vaults were rare and were used only in areas where wood for roof beams and frames was not available. Even the earliest sepulchers, however, were built of lasting materials. Churches from the Fatimid period on used vaulting because it was less liable to be damaged by worms or fire, a change specifically mentioned in the sources.

The construction of a flat roof was essentially that of a ceiling (see above). It required additional precautions, however, to ensure the trouble-free draining of rainfall. The surface was strengthened with a layer of stones or bricks that were then completely covered by a coat of plaster, in order to seal all openings. To make it more solid, the plaster was often enriched with chips of burnt brick, producing a weatherproof mortar akin to *opus signium* developed in the Roman period. Roof tiles were not known in Egypt. Since the upper edges of a building can be easily damaged by wind and rain, the edges of the roof were always provided with at least a low wall. Higher buildings required a parapet. The surface of the roof was given either a slope or separate water channels, which let rain water flow into gutters at the edge of the roof.

Two drainage systems were in use in the pharaonic period. In large, high buildings, waterspouts projecting clear of the wall surfaces were employed, as at Dayr Anbā Shinūdah, which prevented the wind from splashing the water against the walls. In smaller buildings, including such pharaonic temples as that of Ramses II at Abydos, a somewhat simpler system involved water channels built into the wall itself. Buildings of mud brick had to be plastered with a lime mortar and required a device at the foot of the wall to keep the water away from it, since otherwise there was a danger that the foundations would wash away. Sometimes the water was led into cisterns to be used as drinking water (Grossmann, 1967, pp. 463ff.). That was particularly true of the hermits' houses in the lauras of Kellia and Abū Mīnā.

BIBLIOGRAPHY

Clarke, S., and R. Engelbach. *Ancient Egyptian Masonry,* pp. 155ff. Oxford, 1930.

Deichmann, F. W. "Untersuchungen zu Dach und Decke der Basilika." *Charities* (1952):249–64.

Durm, J. *Baukunst der Etrusker und Römer,* pp. 316ff. Stuttgart, 1905.

Grossmann, P. "Die siedlung im Kômring A." In *Archäologischer Anzeiger,* pp. 463–73. Berlin, 1967.

Haeny, G. "Decken- und Dachkonstruktion." In *Lexikon der Ägyptologie,* Vol. 1. Wiesbaden, 1975.

PETER GROSSMANN

Sacristy

A sacristy is a side room in a church for sacred vessels and vestments and for the vesting of the clergy. It is also called a vestry. Because vessels and vestments are often valuable, the room usually contains wall niches or cupboards that can be closed or locked.

One room with wall niches in an Egyptian church, on the north side of the sanctuary of the small north church of Quṣūr ʿIsa South I in Kellia, has been identified as a sacristy. Other side rooms with lockable wall niches, however, have not been identified as sacristies because a single such niche is not enough to determine the room's use. In the early Christian and Eastern churches, the functions of the sacristy are performed by the diaconicon and the prothesis (room for preparing the elements for the Eucharist). Since the care of valuables fell within the jurisdiction of the OIKONOMOS ("administrator"), the sacristy is the same as the *qunūmiyyah* ("room of the administrator").

BIBLIOGRAPHY

Burmester, O. H. E. *The Egyptian or Coptic Church.* Cairo, 1967.

Descoeudres, G. *Die Pastophorien im syro-byzantinischen Osten,* pp. 13–14. Wiesbaden, 1983.

PETER GROSSMANN

Saddleback Roof

A saddleback roof (Arabic, *jamalūn*) is a pitched roof that slopes on two sides from a ridgepole to the top of a wall. It has been used since antiquity, especially in rainy areas, to cover buildings with a broad span. In Egypt, saddleback roofs were constructed over basilicas until the Fatimid period, when they were replaced by vaults. A sixth-century example is the Church of the Holy Virgin (*Panagia*) in the MOUNT SINAI MONASTERY OF SAINT CATHERINE.

The framework of a saddleback roof is a truss, a series of triangular frames formed by a horizontal tie beam resting on two opposite walls and two rafters sloping from the ends of the beam to the ridgepole. A king-post runs from the center of the beam to the ridgepole, and struts attached to the king-post support the rafters. For wide spans two queen-posts joined by a collar beam replace the king-post. The sloping angle of the rafters facilitates the discharge of rainwater from the surface of the roof, and the rafters prevent any sagging of the tie beams, which are usually very long. For the latter reason, saddleback roofs are found also in areas with low rainfall. As a rule these tie beams are relatively close together and are rigidly braced by numerous stable horizontal battens to prevent any lateral movement. In Egypt roof trusses were generally made of cedar imported from Lebanon. Native palm was not strong enough and could be used only over a short span where no stress was involved.

The surface of the roof, which could consist of straw, wooden shingles, bricks, or even lead, was fixed over the rafters. Roof tiles of fired clay have so far not been identified in Egypt but appear—at least in the Roman period—to have been not entirely unknown (cf. Steinmeyer-Schareika, 1978, p. 88 and pls. 41, 45, where the structure of roofing plates can be clearly seen on the sloping roof of the small temple). As a rule, the surface of the roof—at least in large buildings—probably consisted of a layer of boards and then a layer of ordinary bricks or limestone slabs, the whole finally being spread with mortar. Only large buildings had further protection by lead plates, such as many Byzantine churches in Constantinople have and such as Eusebius expressly mentioned for the Church of the Holy Sepulcher in Jerusalem (Eusebuius *Vita Constantini* 3.36). For the decoration of the inside of the roof, coffering could be applied between the rafters or on a horizontal ceiling. The beams may have been painted, but in most cases they were visible from inside the church even if there was a ceiling. From the tenth century on, the saddleback roof was increasingly replaced by stone vaulting, which was less susceptible to damage from worms and fire (Grossmann, 1982, p. 161, n. 707).

BIBLIOGRAPHY

Butler, Howard Crosby. *Early Churches in Syria,* pp. 198ff. Princeton, 1929; repr., Amsterdam, 1969.

Choisy, A. *L'Art de bâtir chez les romains,* 2nd ed., pp. 143ff. Bologna, 1969.

Forsyth, G. H., and K. Wetzmann. *The Monastery of Saint Catherine at Mount Sinai: The Church and Fortress of Justinian.* Ann Arbor, Mich., 1973.

Grossmann, P. *Mittelalterliche Langhauskuppelkirchen und verwandte Typen in Oberägypten,* p. 161, n. 707. Glückstadt, 1982.

Lane, E. W. *Arabic-English Lexicon.* New York, 1955–1956.

Steinmeyer-Schareika, A. *Das Nilmosaik von Palestrina.* Bonn, 1978.

PETER GROSSMANN

Sanctuary

The sanctuary (Arabic, *haykal*) is the area around the altar. The term derives from the Hebrew *hēkal,* the main hall in the Temple in Jerusalem, which lay in front of the inaccessible Holy of Holies. The Arabic term is first used in the HISTORY OF THE PATRIARCHS by Sawīrus Ibn al-Muqaffa'. Older synonyms are *askina* (Greek, *skene*) and *irādiyūn* (Greek, *hierateion*). The term has a functional rather than an architectural significance.

In the fifth and sixth centuries the development of the altar area—at least in Egyptian parish churches—was in accordance with practice outside Egypt. It was an area at the eastern end of the church not in the apse but in front of it, projecting into the nave. It was surrounded at first only by low cancelli and was elevated by one or two steps. It was called, as has been noted, the *prestyterium* or *bema.* In Upper Egyptian churches with a triconch sanctuary, the altar seems to have stood not in the east (central) conch but in the center field of the triconch. The cancelli were brought forward as far as the arch at the front of the apse. The apse itself —in triconch churches, the eastern main conch—was adorned with several decorative niches. In the urban bishop's churches the apse contained a synthronon, or seating for the bishops and presbyters (see below).

Some early monastery churches, particularly in Kellia, show a somewhat simpler plan. They had a rectangular altar area, which contained the altar roughly in the middle and was connected with the naos through an arched opening that was fairly large but relatively small in proportion to its width. The cancelli were fitted in between the jambs of this arch. There were at first no niches in the east wall of these altar areas. They first appeared in the later churches of this type in the late sixth century and in their formation are roughly reminiscent of the prayer niches in the simple hermitages of anchorites. Possibly this simple style was an older form of building preserved in these small monastery churches, which in the parish churches and in the great churches of the Upper Egyptian cenobite monasteries had already fallen out of use.

When the *khūrus* was introduced in front of the sanctuary in the second half of the seventh century, it did not lead to any immediate change in the altar area. The altar remained in one of two possible places: within a rectangular chamber equipped with a niche in the east wall or in the area in front of the apse. In the latter place, however, it was now within the *khūrus*. Because the *khūrus* was separated from the naos by a strong, high wall, the surrounding cancelli were unnecessary and were abolished. The term *haykal* was transferred to the *khūrus* containing the altar. The area developed as the apse is given the architectural term concha or *gunka* (Greek, *konche;* Graf, 1954, p. 93), meaning a semicircular, shell-like form, although it was only rarely used in Egypt.

Since the late Middle Ages the *haykal* has been a largely self-contained room in the middle of which the altar stands. It is closed off on the west from the naos by a high screen (*ḥijab*). In some cases, however, the room is open to neighboring *haykals* on the sides. The oldest example is the old church at Dayr Anbā Antūnyūs, from the early thirteenth century. Part of the fittings of the rectangular *haykal* is a small, generally semicircular niche in the east wall, which is called *shaqq al-haykal* or simply *sharqiyyah* ("the eastern"). Functionally, it represents the apse and accordingly has a significance similar to that of the small prayer niches in the early Christian anchorite cells. In fact, in the *haykal* developed in the shape of an apse, such as was usual in the area of Akhmīm down to the nineteenth century, there is no particularly prominent niche in the east wall. These first appeared in combination with an apse in quite modern buildings (except in the church in front of the pylon of the Luxor temple, the function of which is not yet determined) or have been inserted in older apses at a later date, which suggests that the relationships were no longer understood. Finally, a flight of steps (*daraj al-haykal*) is often built in front of the east wall of the main *haykal*. Very probably it led to the synthronon in the older bishops' churches. It is no longer used for seating.

BIBLIOGRAPHY

Burmester, O. H. E. *The Egyptian or Coptic Church.* Cairo, 1967.

Busink, T. A. *Der Tempel von Jerusalem,* Vol. 1. Leiden, 1970.

Butler, A. J. *The Ancient Coptic Churches of Egypt,* Vol. 1. Oxford, 1884; repr., 1970.

Graf, G. *Verzeichnis arabischer kirchlicher Termini.* Louvain, 1954.

Grossmann, P. *Mittelalterliche Langhauskuppelkirchen und verwandten Typen in Oberägypten,* pp. 213–15. Glückstadt, 1982.

Muyser, J. "Des Vases eucharistiques en verre." *Bulletin de la Société d'archéologie Copte* 3 (1937):9–28.

Orlandos, A. K. Βασιλική. pp. 509–535. Athens, 1952.

PETER GROSSMANN

Synthronon

A synthronon is the bench for the clergy against the east wall of the apse of a church. Since the apse is usually semicircular, it is usually semicircular. It is made up of an elevated bishop's throne in the center between subsellia (low seats) for other clergy. Thus it is the mark of a cathedral church or other church in which the bishop is regularly present at the liturgy. Since monastic churches that have a synthronon, for example, the main church of Dayr Anbā Maqār in Wādī al-Naṭrūn, have a rectangular plan, the synthronon on the rear wall of the sanctuary is not curved but straight. A curved synthronon was usual in Coptic churches until the high Middle Ages. As a rule it consisted of a stone or wood construction several steps high, of which the topmost step, usually built somewhat higher and broader, served as a bench for sitting. The bishop's throne at the apex of the curve was provided with a back and arm rests. In some very rich communities, as in Cairo, the synthronon was adorned with a marble incrustation or sometimes polychrome paint. It is, however, unusual that in several Cairo churches the synthronon is set into a wall niche; it appears that here two different traditions have been blended. The synthronon in the Great Basilica of Abū Mīnā, built in at a later date, is unique. Since the space on the inside of the apse had been claimed by subterranean grave structures, the synthronon was erected not in but in front of the apse, and in addition, it had only a shallow curve. The steps on the rear wall of the sanctuaries of many modern Coptic churches are a degenerate form of the synthronon belonging only to modern times. A sequence of steps no longer suitable for sitting, they frequently serve for the display of icons.

BIBLIOGRAPHY

Burmester, O. H. E. *The Egyptian or Coptic Church,* p. 20. Cairo, 1967.

Butler, A. J. *The Ancient Coptic Churches of Egypt,* Vol. 1, pp. 35–37. Oxford, 1884; repr. 1970.

Graf, G. *Verzeichnis arabischer kirchlicher Termini,* p. 58. Louvain, 1954.

Orlandos, A. K. *Βασιλική,* pp. 489–501. Athens, 1952.

PETER GROSSMANN

Tetraconch

A tetraconch is a square or oblong room expanded on all four sides by semicircular rooms formed by a portico or open recess (conchas, or exedrae). The origin of the tetraconch is a matter of debate. Numerous examples suggest Syria or Asia Minor, but the Church of San Lorenzo is a fourth-century example from Milan. It is not native to Egypt, although there are a few tetraconch churches there, for example, at Abū Mīnā.

The tetraconch provides a church building with a particularly rich interior structure. The inner rectangular room has numerous columns and usually a wooden roof. The exedrae are formed by the erection of columns. The eastern one serves as an apse. The external shape of the church varies. Most frequently it has a wall of concentric design, shaped so that an ambulatory is created between it and the internal columns, as in the East Church at Abū Mīnā. Areas of the external wall may be utilized to accommodate the side rooms required by the liturgy. The Martyr Church (Justinian phase) at Abū Mīnā, however, has a rectangular external wall.

BIBLIOGRAPHY

Balty, J. C. "Le Groupe épiscopal d'Apameé, dit Cathédrale de l'est." In *Colloque Apamée de Syrie.* Brussels, 1972.

Grossmann, P. "Die zweischaligen spätantiken Vierkonchenbauten in Ägypten und ihre Beziehung zu den gleichartigen Bauten in Europa und Kleinasien." In *Das römisch-byzantinische Ägypten.* Aegyptiaca Treverensia 2. Mainz, 1983.

Kleinbauer, W. E. "Zvart'nots and the Origins of Christian Architecture." *Art Bulletin* 54 (1972):245ff.

PETER GROSSMANN

Tribelon

A tribelon, meaning "three curtains," is a passage divided by two columns, whose resulting three openings can be closed by three curtains. The central opening is, as a rule, slightly larger than the two side ones. The tribelon occurs sporadically in some pharaonic tomb entrances, for example, in several rock tombs at Banī Ḥasan and in the Sixth-Dynasty mastaba of Seshemnefer at Giza (Junker, 1953, pp. 92–109), but otherwise it must be considered as essentially a Greek structural element. Because of its inherent symmetry, it was readily employed in early Christian and medieval churches as a half-open linking of adjoining rooms (Orlandos, 1952). In several early Christian churches in Egypt, the narthex is connected with the naos by a tribelon, for example the main church of Dayr Apa Jeremiah and the Great Basilica of Abū Mīnā.

BIBLIOGRAPHY

Junker, H. *Giza,* Vol. 11, *Der Friedhof südlich der Cheopspyramide Ostteil.* Vienna, 1953.

Orlandos, A. K. *Βασιλική,* pp. 139, 148–50. Athens, 1952.

PETER GROSSMANN

Triconch

A triconch is a square, oblong, or circular room expanded on three sides by semicircular exedrae, most frequently covered by a semidome. In the oldest examples, the central room is unroofed, as in the Well of Herodes Atticus in Corinth (second century A.D.). Later it usually had a wooden saddleback or barrel-vaulted roof. Very few central rooms were domed.

The triconch was first developed in the Roman Empire. Because of its impressive spatial effect, it was used principally in palace architecture for banquet and entertainment halls. The three exedrae were well suited to hold triclinia (three-part couches for dining). Such triconchs were usually situated on one side of a peristyle. Examples of such triconchs are known from the fourth to the seventh century. Examples in Egypt are the main halls of the two monastery complexes in Hilwān.

In some late-Roman palaces of the western part of the empire, the triconch is pushed back right to the edge of the edifice, where it presumably functioned as a private dining room. The hypothesis that only members of the imperial family were entitled to the use of a triconch (Lavin, 1962) has so far not been confirmed.

In Palestine, Asia Minor, and Egypt in the Roman period, the triconch was also used for ecclesiastical structures—for the sanctuary at the eastern end of the Christian basilica. According to the significance given to the liturgical side rooms, the triconch occupied the full breadth of the church or only the nave. The altar stood at its center. In Egypt—where such supplementary rooms were needed, one on each side of the central niche—the triconch was narrower than the breadth of the church. If it was much narrower than the nave, an additional row of columns was set up in front of the sanctuary.

In principle, the triconch need not be composed of functionally homogeneous parts. Thus, in Ṭūr 'Abdīn the naos, ordinarily shaped like a broad, shallow room and covered by a transverse, barrel-vaulted roof, was combined with the normally semicircular apse in the middle of the eastern wall into a triconch. A similar merging of heterogeneous rooms into a triconch is exhibited in the design of the sanctuary in the medieval Egyptian churches. Here the *khūrus* was conjoined with the central niche into a triconch. Moreover, the ground plan in both cases is often rectangular. The conch shape, which in itself is based on the idea of a semicircular space, is then articulated only by the vault. Nevertheless, a triconch is not present if the broad room before the apse itself only forms part of a greater architectural form, as in the transept of the basilica of al-Ashmūnayn and that at Hawwāriyyah.

The triconch is also found in Byzantine churches. There, however, the individual conchs that form the rooms of the sanctuary are variously articulated. While the side conchas are for the most part shallow, the eastern concha is frequently stilted. There are also some examples from the high Middle Ages and later where the entire church is laid out as a triconch, as at Mount Athos. A similar situation obtains, moreover, in numerous churches in the West.

BIBLIOGRAPHY

Grossmann, P. "Die von Somers Clarke in Ober-Anṣinā entdeckten Kirchenbauten." *Mitteilungen des deutschen archäologischen Instituts—Abteilung Kairo* 24 (1969):144, 153–60.

Harrison, R. M. "Churches and Chapels of Central Lycia." *Anatolian Studies* 13 (1963):117ff.

Lavin, I. "The House of the Lord." *Art Bulletin* 44 (1962):1ff.

Monneret de Villard, U. *Les Couvents près de Sohâg,* 2 vols. Milan, 1925–1926.

______. *Le chiese della Mesopotamia.* Orientalia Cristiana Analecta 128. Rome, 1940.

Settis, S. "Per l'interpretazione di Piazza Armenia." *Mélanges d'archéologie et de l'histoire de l'Ecole française de Rome* 87 (1975):873–994.

PETER GROSSMANN

Triumphal Arch

A triumphal arch is a freestanding structure in Roman architecture and the arch at the entrance to the apse in church architecture.

From the second century A.D., the Romans built arches to commemorate some extraordinary political event or the outstanding achievements of some exalted personage. Such arches frequently stood astride a road and had either one or three passages through them. They were adorned with pilasters or engaged columns and with inscriptions or reliefs relating to the events that led to their erection. Arches in the provinces had the secondary aim of demonstrating Roman supremacy, to which their usually prominent position on main roads out of the city or at crossroads made a material contribution. Examples in Egypt are the arch at al-Qaṣr in al-Baḥriyyah Oasis (Fakhry, 1974, Vol. 2, pp. 89ff.) and the one at Philae, very probably erected under Diocletian (Lyons, 1896, p. 33 and pl. 25; Monneret de Villard, 1941, pp. 5ff.). Another arch was still standing in Antinoopolis down to the nineteenth century, while two more in Alexandria are known from designs on coins.

In Christian church building, the arch of the apse opening to the naos was described as a triumphal arch from the early ninth century (Duchesne, 1886–1892, Vol. 2, pp. 54–79). The Arabic *qawṣarah* is first found in late sources (*History of the Patriarchs*). The church's use of the secular term from Roman architecture suggested not only a certain structural similarity but also the status of the church as the church triumphant. It was usual to have a picture of the cross, the *crux triumphalis,* suspended from the arch. In the early transept basilicas in Rome, the arch separating the naos and the transept is called the triumphal arch. Consequently, in the triconch churches in Egypt at Suhāj and Dandarah, for example, the arch opening to the naos resting on two columns in front of the apse must be considered a triumphal arch as well, so these churches are actually furnished with two triumphal arches. It is better to speak of front and rear, or first and second, triumphal arches. From the sixth century on, the same feature occurs in several Egyptian churches with a simple apse.

From an architectural point of view, the triumphal arch forms the structural conclusion of the naos and, to some extent, the facade of the sanctuary. It is accordingly the most richly developed and ornamented structural element in the church. In early churches in Italy it was frequently provided with rich mosaic ornament (Deichmann, 1948; 1958). Generally, however, the predominant structural formulation consists of engaged pilasters or half-columns. In larger buildings the jambs of the arch are not infrequently developed as pilasters, as at Suhāj and al-Ashmūnayn. The main display side of these pilasters, however, is turned not toward the naos but to the opposite jamb. Only the voussoirs (wedge-shaped stones of the arch), which in Egypt are usually provided with a formal cornice, are fully turned toward the naos. In other cases, the arch was adorned with complete columns. These stand either below the arch itself or immediately in front of the jambs or are inserted into a vacant corner of the abutments as in the North Basilica at Abū Mīnā.

During the late Middle Ages the importance of the triumphal arch declined. The introduction in Orthodox churches of the templon, closed off by curtains, and of the iconostasis rendered important elements of the arch invisible. In its place, mosaics or paintings in the soaring half-dome of the apse emerged as a new feature to catch the eye. In Egyptian churches, where the view into the sanctuary was completely blocked by the introduction of the partition wall of the *khūrus,* the great door in the middle had of necessity to become the structural conclusion of the naos. Still, there are a few examples even in the buildings of the Fatimid period, in which this opening is framed with engaged pilasters and half-columns. It does not appear to have had any special designation. In texts in which it is mentioned, it is simply called *bāb* ("door").

BIBLIOGRAPHY

Deichmann, F. W. *Frühchristliche Kirchen in Rom.* Basel, 1948.

______. *Frühchristliche Bauten und Mosaiken von Ravenna.* Wiesbaden, 1958.

Dozy, R. *Supplément au dictionnaires arabes,* 2 vols. Leiden, 1881; repr. Beirut, 1981.

Duchesne, L. M. O. *Le Liber pontificalis,* 3 vols. Paris, 1886–1892.

Fakhry, A. *The Oases of Egypt,* Vol. 2, *Bahriyah and Farafra Oases.* Cairo, 1974.

Lyons, H. G. *A Report on the Island and Temples of Philae.* London, 1896.

Monneret de Villard, U. *La Nubia romana.* Rome, 1941.

Orlandos, A. K. *Βασιλική,* Vol. 1, pp. 206ff. Athens, 1952.

PETER GROSSMANN

Vault

A vault is a ceiling or roof, traditionally of stone or brick, that depends on the principle of the arch. It may be executed in various geometrical shapes depending, to some extent, on the shape of the area to be covered. The arrangement of the blocks (bond) is determined by whether the vault is to be built with the aid of a temporary wooden support (centering) or without it. Since the timber necessary for centering is not readily available everywhere (it was scarce, for example, in Eastern regions but not in the West), the bond used in the East was different from that used in the West.

The simplest form of vault is the barrel vault, known in Egypt from the architecture of the Old Kingdom. In shape, it is similar to a horizontally placed cylinder sectioned along its axis. It may be executed with or without centering. The longitudinal barrel bond built up of horizontal courses (layers) of blocks laid parallel with the imposts (top of the wall) is very stable but requires centering. The bond of vertical or, preferably, slightly *canted* (tilted) ring courses, which arch from one wall to the other, does not need centering. It is this method that was used most frequently in Egyptian vault constructions (Clarke, 1912, pp. 26–27).

Because constructing a barrel vault around a corner is possible only with centering, this type of vault was avoided as far as possible in Eastern architecture. If it was unavoidable, however, intermediate arches were introduced, or the vaulting surfaces were set at different heights. In one of the corridors in the big keep of Dayr Anbā Hadrā, the external corner of the corridor bend was covered with diagonally spanned ring courses, forming a kind of squinch (diagonal arch). On its frontal side leaned rampant ring courses springing from the inner corner of the corridor (Grossmann, 1982, pp. 245–46, pl. 36).

The most important derivations of the barrel vault are the groin vault (or cross vault) and the cloister vault (or domical vault). These forms are created by the intersection of two barrel vaults at right angles. In the groin vault the sections of the generating barrel vault that lie outside the edges of intersection are retained, so that the sharp edges (groins) appear from the underside. In the cloister vault only sections of the barrel vault within the edges of intersection are retained, so the edges appear as valleys. These types of vault can be executed only with the help of centering. Since both types of vault consist of surfaces that are curved only in one plane, the centering is simply made of straight wooden boards. Because these vault types need centering, they must both be considered typically Western construction types. In the East they have been constructed only in special cases. The cloister vault executed in ring courses without centering gained a certain currency in the East. In this construction, squinchlike structures executed in vertical ring courses were built diagonally over all four corners and joined together in a dovetail over the middle of the walls. In this way, a bellylike curvature was created over the corners instead of the sharp edges of the valleys. This type of vault is best designated a pseudo-cloister vault. (The formerly more common name, squinch vault, does not do justice to the peculiarities of the construction; Grossmann, 1982, pp. 246–50.) Such vaults were first archaeologically documented in Iran; they existed, however, in Egypt as well, from the late Roman period.

The sail vault consists of a truly spherical dome shell whose diameter equals more or less the diagonal of the area to be covered and which, in a sense, is suspended between the supporting vertical side walls. The sail vault may be executed either in horizontal ring courses (most frequently used in wide spans) or in vertical ring courses and dovetail joints over the corners. It does not require centering. In order to achieve a flawless spherical curvature for the dome shell, a rotating template fixed to the center of the curvature is used to indicate the position of each stone or brick (Clarke, 1912, pp. 29–31; Grossmann, 1982, pp. 250–57). Once a ring course has been closed, the construction is self-supporting. In the West, especially during the Roman imperial period, the dome was most frequently executed not of stone or brick but of a different, usually cruder material, a sort of concrete made of rubble and waste materials. This material required centering, but since only straight wooden boards were available to make it, it difficult to achieve a flawless spherical curvature. Consequently, domes were often imperfect in the West.

The dome whose radius of curvature equals half the distance between facing supporting walls can just as easily be executed in a free bond without centering. The dome shell itself is produced, like the sail vault, with the help of a rotating template. Only the center of curvature must be set higher. Nevertheless, difficulties are posed by the corners of the square area that the dome is to cover, since the circular base of the dome does not extend to the corners. In order to solve this problem, two fundamentally different structural designs have been developed. The simpler and older method is to bridge the corners with beams or squinches (ring courses of increasing radius) creating four more points of support, in addition to those at the middle of the walls. Many domed churches in the Nile Valley are built with squinches.

The other solution is the pendentive, a cantilevered construction with a spherically curved surface and a triangular shape. A pendentive requires construction materials with load-carrying capacity such as stone blocks or Roman concrete, but not the mud brick used in the East. It is, therefore, no coincidence that the pendentive dome was developed and almost exclusively used in Byzantine areas of the East. In Egypt such domes are quite rare and occur only over small areas.

BIBLIOGRAPHY

Clarke, S. *Christian Antiquities in the Nile Valley.* Oxford, 1912.

Fink, J. *Die Kuppel über dem Viereck.* Munich, 1958.

Grossmann, P. *Mittelalterliche Langhauskuppelkirchen und verwandte Typen in Oberägypten,* pp. 236–73. Glückstadt, 1982.

Reuther, O. "Sāsānian Architecture: History." In *A Survey of Persian Art,* ed. A. U. Pope, Vol. 1, pp. 493–578. London, 1938; repr. London and New York, 1964.

PETER GROSSMANN

ARCHIVES. There were already archives in Egypt in the pre-Christian period, according to Helck (1975). In Christian times, too, there were official and semiofficial Greek archives: those of soldiers, priests, manual workers, and other private individuals. An attempt to reassemble such archives was announced by Heichelheim in 1932. In these archives documents were preserved, in contrast with the libraries, where literary manuscripts were gathered together (see PAPYRI, COPTIC LITERARY). However, it is often not possible to make a clear distinction between archives and libraries, since in many both documents and literary papyri were discovered together. Occasionally documents were written on the back of literary manuscripts, or documents withdrawn from archives were used as writing material for literary works (Clarysse, 1984).

Various names were employed for archives (Gross, col. 614). The archive of the Phoibammom monastery at DAYR AL-BAḤRĪ is often described as βιβλιοϑήκη (*bibliotheke*), which, according to Liddell and Scott (1958), can mean "record office" or "registry" as well as "library."

Archives have been recovered through systematic excavation or through chance discovery, especially through the work of the *sabbākhīn* (manure diggers). In the latter case, archives that belong together were often divided into lots by the finders and/or the antiquities dealers and, like literary manuscripts, were acquired by different museums (see PAPYRUS COLLECTIONS). It has been, and still is, the task of the scholar to examine the documents to ascertain whether they belong to an archive, in order to reconstruct the original archive.

A single archive can contain documents in several languages. In the latest archives, Greek, Coptic, and Arabic documents were found (for instance, in Aphrodito). In archives from the fourth century on Greek and Coptic documents are united, while archives from the period prior to the fourth century consist only of Greek documents. In addition there were bilingual and sporadically even trilingual documents.

A few characteristic examples may be singled out from the multitude of archives known. The largest extant archive of the early Arab period is that of Basilios, pagarch of Aphrodito (see BASILIOS, ARCHIVE OF), found about 1901. Roughly contemporary is the archive of Papas, pagarch of Idfū. Five further archives of pagarchs and other officials of the seventh and eighth centuries are named by K. A. Worp (1984).

From Aphrodito comes the archive of the jurist and poet Dioscorus, who lived in the sixth century and composed literary works of his own in addition to Greek and Coptic documents.

For the Coptic documents of the sixth to eleventh centuries, Steinwenter holds (1955, pp. 15f.) that there were no public archives but only private, family, and monastery archives.

One private archive is that of the notary Shenute, who officiated in Hermopolis in the seventh century. It consists of fifty-six business letters, which have been published by Till (1958) but have not yet been examined as components of an archive.

Among the family archives is the one of the eighth century from Djeme described by Schiller. It contains fifteen papyrus documents and deals with family property over four generations (see the genealogical chart in Schiller, p. 374). Schiller believes that these documents, which came from the antiquities trade and are now in various museums, were found in the house of Comes in Djeme (Schiller, p. 370). These are documents relating to sales and settlements, and also wills.

A second family archive was purchased in 1964 by the Antiquities Museum in Leiden, and published by Green in 1983. It comprises eleven documents written, on parchment or paper, within a period of thirty-five years in the eleventh century. To these also belongs an Arabic text, so far unpublished. The documents deal with the property of a man named Rafael from Teshlot near Bāwīṭ, and with the division of his property among his family (survey in Green, p. 64).

The largest group is that of the extant monastery archives, the oldest of which comes from the fourth century. Its documents, written in Coptic and Greek, relate to a monk named Nepheros of the Melitian Phathor monastery. Further documents have now been added to these archival papyri (P. London 1913, 1920) bought more than half a century ago and published by Bell and Crum (1924, pp. 45ff.); they were bought by the universities of Trier and Heidelberg and were published in 1987 by B. Kramer and others.

In contrast, the documents of the Apollo monastery at Bāwīṭ and the Phoibammon monastery at Dayr al-Baḥrī come from the archives of orthodox Coptic monasteries.

On a lintel beam of the seventh or eighth century in the Apollo monastery (Krause, 1988) the names of three archivists (Athanasius, George, and Phoibammon) appear after the abbot and his deputy. This large number of archivists, which matches the size of the monastery, indicates a large archive. During the partial excavation of the monastery in 1901–1904 and 1913, papyri from this archive were found, but they have not been published. Even before the scientific excavation, the *sabbākhīn* had discovered the ruins of the monastery, and evidently found papyri from the archive as well as monuments; through the antiquities trade these were dispersed among different museums, and only some of the papyri have been published. Since there were at least five monasteries named for Apollo, we have to investigate in individual cases from which of these monastery archives the several papyri derive. The most important of the documents so far known are five sales documents bought by Budge in 1903 for the British Museum in London. They date from between 833 and 850, and deal with the purchase of parts of the monastery (Krause, 1985, pp. 126ff.).

The Phoibammon monastery built into the temple of Hatshepsut at Dayr al-Baḥrī must also have possessed a large archive. Since it was for a time, about 600, the seat of the bishop ABRAHAM of Hermonthis, who was at the same time abbot of this monastery, there would be the bishop's archives as well as those of the monastery. These two archives were not brought to light through systematic excavation of the monastery. Clandestine diggings in the last half of the nineteenth century unearthed the papyri, which were acquired by different museums. The excavation of the temple of Hatshepsut, carried out in 1894/1895, also yielded a quantity of Coptic ostraca (see: OSTRACON) published by Crum in 1902. The place of their discovery is not specified by E. Naville. More than five hundred other ostraca were carelessly thrown on dumps and were found in 1927/1928 by the Metropolitan Museum of Art in its inspection of the dumps, but are still unpublished. Other ostraca, likewise so far unpublished, came to light in the excavation of the temple of Mentuhotep in 1904–1911. Godlewski's list of the two archives, so far as it is published, comprises 379 items. To these may be added seventy-four papyri and ostraca relating to the monastery. Including the unpublished pieces, more than 1,000 texts from the two archives have survived.

To the monastery archives belong the testaments of the abbots, in which they appoint their successors (Krause, 1969); the child donation documents, in which children were presented to the monastery (Steinwenter, 1921); deeds of gifts of plots of land, palms, goats and sheep, and various other items; and contracts for work. The bishop's archive contained some 200 ostraca.

The extant remains of the archive of Bishop PISENTIUS OF COPTOS (569–632) are not so extensive. Individual writings have survived from the archives of other bishops, for instance, of Hermopolis or from the Fayyūm. A reconstruction of these archives is yet to be done.

Texts from state and church archives also have been found in Nubia, above all in QAṢR IBRĪM, but so far these are accessible only in preliminary reports (Plumley, 1975, 1978, 1982). The installation document of the bishop of Qaṣr Ibrim, of 16 November 1371, has been published (see ORDINATION, CLERICAL).

BIBLIOGRAPHY

Bell, H. I., and W. E. Crum. *Jews and Christians in Egypt*. London, 1924.

Clarysse, W. "Literary Papyri in Documentary Archives." In *Egypt and the Hellenistic World. Proceedings of the International Colloquium, Leuven 24–26 May 1982*, ed. E. van't Dack, P. van Dessel, and W. van Gucht, pp. 43–61. Louvain, 1984.

Crum, W. E. *Coptic Ostraca*. London, 1902.

Godlewski, W. *Der el Bahari V. Le monastère de St. Phoibammon*. Warsaw, 1986.

Green, M. "A Private Archive of Coptic Letters and Documents from Teshlot." *Oudheidkundige Mededeelingen uit het Rijksmuseum van Oudheden te Leiden* 64 (1983):61–122.

Gross, K. "Archiv." In *Reallexikon für Antike und Christentum*, Vol. 1, cols. 614–31. Stuttgart, 1950.

Heichelheim, F. "Bericht über ein Papyrusverzeichnis nach Gauen, Archiven und Jahrhunderten geordnet." *Chronique d'Egypte* 7 (1932):137–50.

Helck, W. "Archive." *Lexikon der Ägyptologie*, Vol. 1, cols. 422–24. Wiesbaden, 1975.

Kramer, B. *Das Archiv des Nepheros und verwandte Texte*, 2 vols. in 1. Aegyptiaca Treverensia 4. Mainz, 1987.

Krause, M. "Die Testamente der Äbte des Phoibammon Klosters in Theben." In *Mitteilungen des Deutschen Archäologischen Instituts, Abteilung Kairo*, pp. 57–67. Wiesbaden, 1969.

______. "Die Beziehungen zwischen den beiden Phoibammon-Klöstern auf dem thebanischen Westufer." *Bulletin de la Société d'archéologie copte* 27 (1985):31–44.

______. "Zur Edition koptischer nichtliterarischer Texte. P. Würzburg 43 neu bearbeitet." *Zeitschrift für ägyptische Sprache und Altertumskunde* 112 (1985):143–53.

———. Zur Möglichkeit von Besitz im apotaktischen Mönchtum Ägyptens. In *Acts of the Second International Congress of Coptic Studies. Rome, 22–26 September 1980*, ed. T. Orlandi and F. Wisse, pp. 121–33. Rome, 1985.

———. "Die Inschriften auf den Türsturzbalken des Apa-Apollon-Klosters von Bawit." In *Mélanges offerts à A Guillaumont*. Cahiers d'orientalisme 20, pp. 111–20. Geneva, 1988.

Liddell, H. G., and R. Scott. *A Greek-English Lexicon*. 9th ed. Oxford, 1958.

Naville, E. *The Temple of Deir el-Bahari*, Vols. 1–6. London, 1895–1908.

Plumley, J. M. "The Christian Period at Qasr Ibrim. Some Notes on the MSS Finds." In *Nubia. Récentes recherches. Actes du Colloque nubiologique international au Musée national de Varsovie 19–22 juin 1972*, ed. K. Michalowski, pp. 101–107. Warsaw, 1975.

———. "New Light on the Kingdom of Dotawo." In *Etudes nubiennes. Colloque de Chantilly 2–6 juillet 1975*, pp. 231–41 and pls. LV, LVI. Bibliothèque d'étude 77. Cairo, 1978.

———. "Preliminary Remarks on Four 5th Century MSS. from Qasr Ibrim." *Meroitica* 6 (1982):218–21.

Schiller, A. A. "A Family Archive from Jeme." In *Studi in onore di Vincenzo Arangio-Ruiz*, Vol. 4, pp. 327–75. Naples, 1952.

Shelton, J. "The Archive of Nepheros." In *Atti del XVII Congresso internazionale di papirologia*, Vol. 3, p. 917. Naples, 1984.

Steinwenter, A. "Kinderschenkungen an koptische Klöster." *Zeitschrift der Savigny-Stiftung* 42, kanonistische Abteilung 11 (1921):175–207.

———. "Zu den koptischen Kinderoblationen." *Zeitschrift der Savigny-Stiftung* 43, kanonistische Abteilung 12 (1922):385–86.

———. *Das Recht der koptischen Urkunden. Handbuch der Altertumswissenschaften*, Vol. 10, pt. 4, no. 2. Munich, 1955.

Till, W. C. *Die koptischen Rechtsurkunden der Papyrussammlung der Österreichischen Nationalbibliothek*. Corpus Papyrorum Raineri 4. Vienna, 1958.

Worp, K. A. "Studien zu spätgriechischen, koptischen und arabischen Papyri." *Bulletin de la Société d'archéologie copte* 26 (1984):99–107.

MARTIN KRAUSE

ARCHIVES OF PAPAS. Papas, son of Liberius, was pagarch of Apollōnos Anō (Idfū) from 703 to 714. The dossier of the correspondence sent to him, consisting of more than 100 Greek and a smaller number of Coptic (but no Arabic) documents, was found in 1921–1922 in a jar west of the southwest pylon of the temple at Idfū, where Papas evidently lived and had his office. While pagarch he was, as was frequently the case, owner of large estates.

As pagarch, Papas was directly subordinate to the amir of the Thebaid, or of the united provinces of the Thebaid and Arcadia; this was in contrast with Basilius, pagarch of Aphrodito, who communicated directly with the governor of Egypt at al-Fusṭāṭ without the intervention of intermediaries. The amir, often absent from his post on other duties or residing at al-Fusṭāṭ, was represented by a *topotērētēs* stationed at Antinoopolis; the latter, the chief intermediary with all the pagarchs of the Thebaid, was assisted by his *notarios*, Helladios, and others. Within the pagarchy Papas had complete authority in dealing with the local officials. The papyri, many in poor condition and extremely difficult to interpret, were excellently edited by R. Rémondon (1953).

The correspondence in the dossier covers a wide range of subjects. Some of the documents are requisition demands in the name of the amir, who played the financial role previously enjoyed by the Byzantine *dux* (as he is sometimes called); others are demands for payments in kind or cash to be advanced by the pagarch to the central treasury for the payment of salaries of persons serving with the fleet and elsewhere, or demands for direct contributions of raw materials. In one letter the amir instructs Papas to set out for al-Fusṭāṭ, as he had already been ordered twice to do, in order to submit the accounts of his pagarchy (cf. the instructions issued repeatedly by Qurrah ibn Sharīk to Basilius of Aphrodito). In another letter (no. 9; cf. 13) the *notarios* Helladios sends Papas a circular issued to all pagarchs of the Thebaid by the amir Jordanes regarding caulkers (*kalaphatai*) and others, domiciled at Apollonopolis and elsewhere, who were regularly requisitioned for naval service and had deserted their posts at the dockyards at Babylon. In another, written by Papas, a demand for the provision of 2,500 *knidia* of wine comes at a time when, as Papas points out to the *topotērētēs*, economic conditions are difficult.

Among the most interesting pieces in the dossier are a letter from Helladios to Papas concerning the exaction of taxes from the Blemmyes (see BEJA)—the last reference to these people in a Greek papyrus—and an instruction from the *notarios* that Papas send the legal adversaries (*antidikoi*) of a certain Sabinus to the *topotērētēs* while their womenfolk are kept in prison in Apollonopolis. This, while indicating that Papas had failed (as not infrequently) to carry out orders issued to him, sheds considerable light on the policing powers of the various officials of the provincial hierarchy from the amir down.

Other communications, sent by another *notarios,* Elias, to Papas, deal with the lasting problem of the supervision of canals, in this case, those of the neighboring pagarchy of Latopolis, which could not cope with the labor requirements of the crew. Platon, the pagarch of Latopolis, collaborated closely with Papas in such administrative matters, and also in the requisition and payment of labor for the fleet, another lasting problem of the early Arab period, which, in spite of continual efforts, the Umayyad authorities were unable to solve satisfactorily. Lack of trained manpower and reluctance to serve so far from home in unknown conditions led to the increase in fugitives, which also is reflected in this dossier, as in that of Basilius.

A less familiar aspect of life in the pagarchy, well represented in the dossier, is the role of the bishop as magistrate and justice. This is a survival of the wide financial and judicial powers that dignitary had received by virtue of the jurisdiction of Justinian, alongside the *defensor civitatis* (*ekdikos*), who presided over so many aspects of the life of the provincial city in the later sixth century, and who here exercises the same office in the Umayyad period. Other papyri show a *notarios,* Kollouthos, having difficulties in responding to the demands of his Muslim masters to provide prayer rugs as revenue in kind.

The dossier also includes a number of private documents, letters (among which is an invitation to a wedding), contracts, cadastral lists, tax registers (mostly fragmentary and of very uncertain interpretation), and lists of goods and natural products for registration and for private expenditure. Among the most elaborate is number 97, a daily list of all allocations, apparently of wine, for various persons during the month of Hātūr. The beneficiaries include (apparently) sick Nubian slaves, a cleric from Syene, the pagarch himself, and the cloakroom attendant at the local baths. Probably some of the wine was sacramental. Another document is a similar list of allocations of cereals for five of Papas' private estates.

Taken as a whole, the dossier of the pagarch Papas is of less general historical significance than that of Basilius of Aphrodito, mainly because the level of official administration that it illustrates is lower. This is, however, in itself a matter of some interest as showing the varieties of administrative practice in Umayyad Egypt, as well as the survival, in certain respects more clearly established by this dossier than by that of Basilius, of the old Byzantine institutions, both governmental and social. The dossier also includes a number of documents of more than passing human and personal interest.

BIBLIOGRAPHY

Butler, A. J. *The Arab Conquest of Egypt,* 2nd ed., ed. and enl. by P. M. Fraser. Oxford, 1977.

Rémondon, R. *Papyrus grecs d'Apollonos Ano.* Documents de Fouilles de l'Institut français d'Archéologie orientale du Caire 19. Cairo, 1953.

P. M. FRASER

ARCHON (from Greek ἄρχω, arkhō, meaning to lead, rule, or be first), a lay member of the Coptic church who through long years of experience and dedication to the church has earned honored status as a leading member of the Coptic community.

RANDALL STEWART

ARI, SAINT, or Ūrí, a priest of Shaṭanūf who was martyred under Diocletian (feastday: 9 Misrah). The text of his Passion has survived in only one Bohairic codex (Vatican Library, 61f., 69–89, ed. Hyvernat, 1886–1887). It begins with mention of the edict of Diocletian, brought by a dispatch bearer to the dux Armenius in Alexandria and then to Governor Culcianus of Pshati, who commands that it should be read out in public. Culcianus instructs soldiers to bring the priest Ari of the nearby town of Shaṭanūf (Shetnufe) to him, because word of Ari's fame has reached his ears. This is followed by an argument in court, imprisonment, and torture. The archangel MICHAEL appears to the saint in a vision. Then Culcianus sends Ari and others to Alexandria. There are the usual scenes of argument and torture, followed by miracles of healing performed by Ari. After nine months, Ari is again brought into court, where there are further arguments, miracles, and torture, followed by miraculous recovery. Finally there is the definitive sentence, and death, witnessed by Julius of Aqfahṣ.

This text has no particularly noteworthy features apart from the fact that it belongs to the Cycle of Julius of Aqfahṣ. It can be dated to the period of fictitious texts, that is, about the seventh century.

BIBLIOGRAPHY

Baumeister, T. *Martyr Invictus, Der Märtyrer als Sinnbild der Erlösung in der Legende und im Kult der frühen koptischen Kirche.* Münster, 1972.

Hyvernat, H., ed. *Les Actes des martyrs de l'Egypte tirés des manuscrits coptes de la Bibliothèque vaticane et du Musée Borgia.* Paris, 1886–1887.

TITO ORLANDI

ARIADNE. *See* Mythological Subjects in Coptic Art.

ARIANISM, a doctrine derived originally from a priest of the church of Alexandria named ARIUS (c. 270–336). It concentrated mainly on the status of the Son within the godhead, and held that he had originated at some point by the creative act of the Father's will. Arius at first held that the Son had been made "out of nothing," but he and his followers soon dropped this idea. Though eternal and enjoying the attributes of divinity, the Son was inferior in every respect to the Father.

Little of what Arius wrote survives, and there is no reason to think that he wrote much beyond a collection of verse setting forth his views, called the *Thaleia* (Banquet). Arius himself was of no great significance, but his doctrine sufficed to spark the Arian controversy, which convulsed the church from 318 to 381, when the creed of the Council of CONSTANTINOPLE is generally regarded as having brought the dispute to an end.

The principles of Arianism can be deduced not only from the writings of its bitter opponents but also from some recently recovered writings by Arians themselves, such as the scholia on the Council of Aquileia, fragments originally discovered by Angelo Mai (prefect of the Vatican Library, 1819–1854), the homilies of Asterius, and various other sermons and biblical commentaries. Arius' doctrine of the Son, though radical, would not have been regarded as completely unacceptable by many in his day. EUSEBIUS OF CAESAREA, though he joined in the condemnation of Arius at the Council of NICAEA in 325, in some respects sympathized with him, and later Arianism was much influenced by Eusebius' thought. There is much to be said for the theory that though we hear of almost no reference to the Incarnation by Arius himself, Arianism was, in fact, a theology devised to allow for a God who could suffer. One of the consistent themes of Arianism was that the incarnate Word had no human mind or soul; the divine nature thus was exposed to suffering, though not injured by it. The Arians assumed that only a lower God, representative of the higher, impassible God, could suffer. When they spoke of the Holy Spirit, they regarded Him as a being created by the Father through the Son, inferior to the Son, not divine, and only above angels in the hierarchy of being.

A variant of Arianism, usefully dubbed "Neo-Arianism" by Kopecek, appeared between 360 and 390, championed by Aetius and Eunomius of Cyzicus. It was rationalist, virtually unitarian, and relied upon a somewhat arbitrary choice of contemporary philosophy, especially Aristotelian logic. Opposition to it occupied the pens of the Cappadocian theologians, but it was not of lasting significance.

During the years it enjoyed imperial support (355–378), Arianism made significant headway in missionary work among various Gothic peoples, and this ensured its continuation among the Visigoths and Vandals in the fifth and following centuries. In Egypt it had little following outside Alexandria, and there its representative, George of Cappadocia, who had come into the see in 356 upon Athanasius' flight from the city, was lynched by a mob on 24 December 361. Arianism never threatened Athanasius again.

BIBLIOGRAPHY

Boularand, E. *L'Hérésie d'Arius et la "foi" de Nicée.* Paris, 1972.
Gregg, R. C., ed. *Arianism.* Oxford, 1985.
Hanson, R. P. C. *The Search for the Christian Doctrine of God.* Edinburgh, 1988.
Kopecek, T. *History of Neo-Arianism.* Cambridge, Mass., 1979.
Simonetti, M. *La crisi ariana nel IV secolo.* Rome, 1975.
Stead, C. *Divine Substance.* Oxford, 1977.
Williams, R. D. "The Logic of Arianism." *Journal of Theological Studies,* n.s. 34 (1983):56–81.

R. P. C. HANSON

ARIANUS, SAINT (feast day: 8 Baramhāt), fourth-century prefect of the Thebaid and portrayed in many Egyptian martyr legends as a bitter persecutor of the Christians, who later converted and became a martyr himself. In view of the novel character of these texts, one might think that Arianus, too, was an invention of their authors. However, the papyrus P. Grenf. II 78 of February–March 307 shows that Arianus is a historical personality (relevant passages in Vandersleyen, 1962, pp. 86–90). The activity of Arianus was thus known in later times, even if the passion story of a martyr was in other respects freely invented according to a popular pattern.

Other historical figures who likewise appear in novel contexts are the persecutors Culciannus and Hierokles. Such historical relics do not mean that we may uncritically regard other features of a legend as genuine reminiscences. In a legendary cycle probably deriving from Antinoopolis, Arianus is even presented as a Christian and a martyr.

The Greek Passion (*Bibliotheca hagiographica graeca* 1514) first relates the martyrdom of Saints APOLLONIUS AND PHILEMON, in which Arianus is the persecutor. A miracle serves as the connecting link to Arianus' subsequent martyrdom. Arianus has archers take aim at Philemon, but the arrows remain suspended in the air. When Arianus looks upward, he is struck in the right eye by an arrow. Philemon, however, promises that Arianus will be healed after Philemon's death if he applies to the blinded eye earth taken from the place to which Philemon's corpse is brought. The prefect does so, is healed, and thereupon becomes converted to the Christian faith. DIOCLETIAN learns of his conversion and sends for him. Arianus is buried alive but is miraculously delivered. Finally he is drowned in the sea along with the soldiers of his bodyguard, who also confess the Christian faith. In marvelous fashion the corpses are brought to Antinoopolis, and there laid to rest beside Philemon and Apollonius.

This account should make it clear that the text is an imaginative invention, probably composed in Antinoopolis in the fifth century. The Sahidic revision of this cycle, which F. Rossi published with an Italian translation (*Atti della R. accademia dei Lincei*, ser. 5, 1 [1893]:3–136, 307), includes major changes in the martyrdom of Arianus, which is conformed to the type of martyr legend predominant in Coptic hagiography.

Arianus is commemorated in both the Copto-Arabic SYNAXARION and the Ethiopian Synaxarion.

BIBLIOGRAPHY

Baumeister, T. *Martyr invictus*, pp. 92, 105–08, 172. Münster, 1972.

______. "Der Märtyrer Philemon." In *Pietas. Festschrift für Bernhard Kotting*, ed. E. Dassmann and K. S. Frank. Münster, 1980.

Delehaye, H. "Les martyrs d'Egypte." *Analecta Bollandiana* 40 (1922):5–154, 299–364.

Vandersleyen, C. *Chronologie des préfets d'Egypte de 284 à 395*, pp. 86–90. Brussels, 1962.

THEOFRIED BAUMEISTER

ARIUS (c. 270–336), controversial church figure. Probably born in Libya, he was named deacon by Patriarch PETER I. Eventually Peter had to excommunicate Arius after he had attached himself to the separatist church of the Melitians. Peter's successor, ACHILLAS (311–312), ordained Arius presbyter and entrusted him with one of the principal churches in the city, that of Baucalis. It was here that Arius attracted attention through his rhetorical talents and his pragmatic teaching, as well as his asceticism and his pastoral dynamism.

About 318, under Achillas' successor, ALEXANDER I, Arius' innovative ideas gained wider dissemination, first during a meeting of the Alexandrian presbyters at the patriarchal palace and subsequently in preaching at his own church, a departure from the traditional ways of Alexandrian pastoral orthodoxy. At Alexandria there was an institution known as Didaskaleion, a Christian cultural center where ecclesiastical education was provided mainly to a limited group of scholars, a kind of intellectual elite. There certain elements of Hellenistic thought were presented along with Christian teachings, a confusion that was more or less tolerated. It should not be forgotten that the church of Alexandria grew in an atmosphere of Greek philosophy, and consequently was prone to Greek influence in the course of its development. Under these conditions Christian theological thinking was in full process of elaboration, with all the risks that entailed.

Arius found his place at this critical point in the development of Christian thought. His preaching taught a kind of SUBORDINATIONISM with regard to Christ, the second Person of the Trinity, in maintaining the unity of God. He combated all heresies of his day, including SABELLIANISM. But he ultimately became a victim of his own logic, which was more philosophical than theological.

Finding himself in difficulty with the church hierarchy in Alexandria, Arius sought support in the anti-Alexandrian polemic of what has come to be known as the school of Antioch, then represented by LUCIAN OF ANTIOCH, who was under suspicion of heresy. Among the disciples of Lucian (the Collucianists) the most active and intriguing was Eusebius of Nicomedia, a very curious person whose intentions were not solely religious. The situation worsened to such an extent that in 320 Alexander I had to summon a synod at Alexandria to excommunicate Arius (which it did in 321). The polemic became more bitter. The Christians of Alexandria were divided between Arius, who was highly respected for his asceticism and his pragmatic teaching, and the church hierarchy.

Shortly after his arrival in the East in 324, Emperor CONSTANTINE I, anxious for the peace and unity of his empire, sent Bishop Ossius of Cordova to Alexandria with a view to finding a private compromise between Arius and Alexander. This mission was doomed to failure. The emperor, whose concern was political rather than doctrinal, decided, no doubt on the advice of Ossius, to summon an ecumenical council to settle these differences and all other ecclesiastical conflicts that threatened the peace of his empire. The meeting was first planned for Ancyra (Ankara), then for practical reasons it was decided to hold the council at the town of NICAEA (near Iznik, Turkey). At the beginning of the summer of 325, under the influence of the fiery deacon ATHANASIUS, who accompanied Alexander I, Arius was condemned and banished from Alexandria into Illyria. His friend Eusebius, bishop of Nicomedia, later used his influence at the imperial court to have Arius recalled from his exile (c. 334). Arius returned to Alexandria, where Athanasius had succeeded to the throne of Saint MARK. Athanasius refused to accept him, and Arius had to leave again. He died suddenly (possibly from poisoning) at Constantinople in 336.

Arius was more an eloquent orator than author. He seems to have written very little, and even less has survived, consisting almost entirely of quotations and paraphrases in the writings of his opponents. He spread his doctrines primarily through popular songs, known under the name of *Thaleia* (Banquet), of which only a few fragments have survived. Of his correspondence one letter has survived in which he asks the support of EUSEBIUS OF CAESAREA. Another letter, to Bishop Alexander, includes his profession of faith. At the end of 327 a final letter was submitted to Emperor Constantine; in it he records a credo intended to prove his orthodoxy.

Was Arius a heretic? Without entering into the details of his teaching, one may say that he represents a crucial moment in the cultural heritage of Alexandria and other regions, and that his shrewd, logical spirit, philosophical as well as polemical, made him a "typical case" in the history of theological "modernism." In fact, Arius was an adherent of the literal exegetical method of the school of Antioch; he had even been to Antioch to complete his education. The advanced dialectic of his logical mind drove him to consider Christ as subordinate to the Father (with biblical texts and philology, as well as logic and philosophy, to support him), a view with the purpose of preserving the unity of God in a "rational" manner. This outlook was already present in the school of Alexandria in the third century—for example, ORIGEN spoke of a *deuteros theos* (second God) with reference to Christ. Arius, then, did no more than push to extreme limits certain dialectical elements already present in Alexandrian speculations. He ought to have confined himself to private research. To display all this to a wider audience of the "uninitiated" was not a pastoral act, and the pope of Alexandria, in his capacity as shepherd of the flock, had to intervene. The polemic of Athanasius (despite the fact that it is not always objective) grasped the pastoral danger of such speculations. Later tradition made Arius the heretic par excellence.

The case of Arius, from the point of view of the development of Alexandrian thought and of the history of theology (with a Greek philosophical character), reveals a restless and active mind in search of new "rational" interpretations, a mind more concerned with philosophical rationality than with traditional orthodoxy. Origen had subordinationist ideas but in a context profoundly anchored to the ecclesiastical tradition (he was a philosopher despite himself). Arius burned all the bridges and, though proclaiming his orthodoxy, did not succeed in achieving a happy and harmonious union between Greek philosophy and ecclesiastical tradition (he was a theologian despite himself).

To clarify the case of Arius, here, in brief, are the basic positions: In Alexandrian orthodoxy the Logos, identified with Christ, is not the work of a decision, of an act of the divine will, as is the case with created beings. The Logos of God is the expression of God's eternal Being, and exists in God by nature, from all eternity. According to the speculation of Arius, the Logos, or Son, is the work of a decision, and came into existence by an act of the divine will. Arius associates generation and creation (philosophically and rationally). If the Logos, or Son, is the work of an act of the divine will, then in effect, before he was engendered or created, there was a time when he did not exist. Hence he is related to the created order: "In the beginning the Logos was and the Logos was with God . . ." (J. 1:1ff.).

BIBLIOGRAPHY

Bardy, G. *Recherches sur saint Lucien d'Antioche et son école*, pp. 216–78. Paris, 1926. The best col-

lection of Arius' extant literary arguments.
Boularand, E. "Les Débuts d'Arius." *Bulletin de Littérature ecclésiastique* 65 (1964):175-203.
Roncaglia, M. P. "Essai d'une typologie de l'Arianisme dans l'histoire des 'modernismes' théologiques: Hier et aujourd'hui." *Zeitschrift der deutschen morgenländischen Gesellschaft* supp. 3, 1 (1977):231-53.
Ruggiero, G. de. *La filosofia del cristianesimo,* Vol. 1, pp. 251-253. Bari, 1967.
Tresmontant, C. *La Métaphysique du christianisme et la naissance de la philosophie chrétienne,* pp. 198-208. Paris, 1961.
______. *Introduction à la théologie chrétienne,* pp. 358-78. Paris, 1974.

MARTINIANO P. RONCAGLIA

ARK. *See* Eucharistic Vessels and Instruments.

ARMANT. [*This entry consists of two articles:* History *and* Buildings.]

History

Armant is a city located in Upper Egypt on the west bank of the Nile about 8 miles (13 km) southwest of Luxor in the province of Qinā. The city was known in Greek as Hermonthis.

Coptic tradition dates the inception of Christianity in Hermonthis/Armant to the time of Jesus himself. The SYNAXARION relates that when Joseph, Mary, and their child were staying in al-Ashmūnayn during their FLIGHT INTO EGYPT, Eudaimon, an inhabitant of Hermonthis, was told that children of kings were in the nearby city. Upon arriving in al-Ashmūnayn, Eudaimon worshiped Jesus, who in turn promised Eudaimon that his house would always be a home for Mary and Jesus, that Eudaimon would be the first martyr of Upper Egypt, and that he would have a place next to Jesus in heaven. When Eudaimon returned to al-Ashmūnayn, his fellow citizens persecuted him and he was eventually martyred in his house because of his Christian beliefs. Later, a church was raised at the site of his house.

Hermonthis/Armant was a bishopric by the early fourth century when Bishop Plenes, a contemporary of ATHANASIUS I (326—373), administered in the city (Le Quien, 1958, Vol. 2, cols. 609—610).

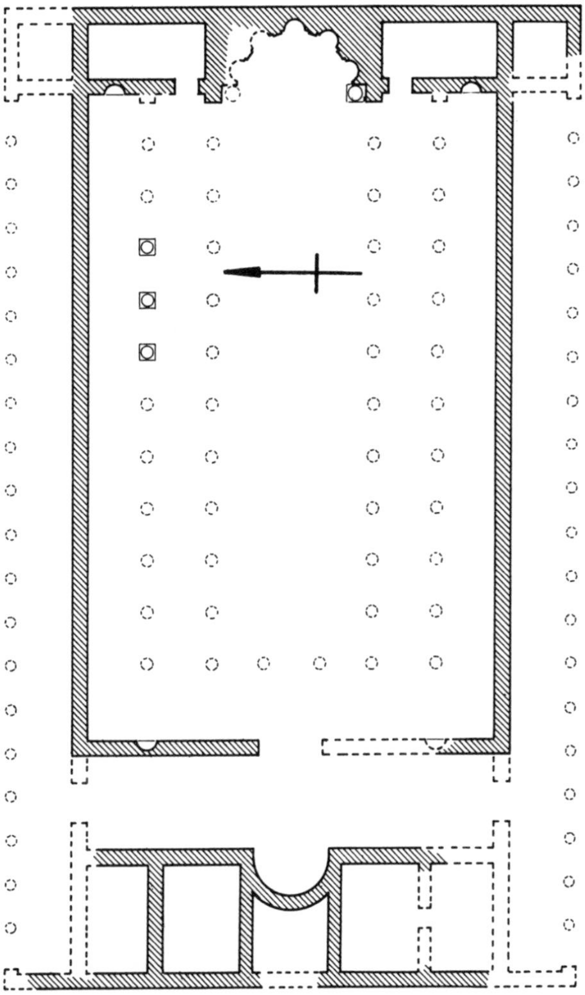

Plan of the large church at Armant. *Courtesy Peter Grossmann.*

BIBLIOGRAPHY

Amélineau, E. *La Géographie de l'Egypte à l'époque copte,* pp. 165—67. Paris, 1893.
Le Quien, M. *Oriens Christianus,* 3 vols. Graz, 1958. Reprint of Paris, 1740.
Timm, S. *Das christlich-koptische Ägypten in arabischer Zeit,* pt. 1, pp. 152—82. Wiesbaden, 1984.

RANDALL STEWART

Buildings

Of the late antique city, only a few meager house plans have been located in the area of the Bucheum temple. And almost nothing is left of the large church, probably the cathedral (to the south of the temple of Month), several sections of which were still standing at the time of the Napoleonic expedition. It might be identical with the "holy church of Hermonthis" as it is mentioned in Greek papyri (Antonini, 1940, No. XV, 1). To judge from drawings of this church, it was a five-aisled basilica with a multiroomed sanctuary and a sumptuous narthex section. Two columned outer porticoes run adjacent to both sides of the church. The granite column shafts that lie about the site and that obviously once belonged to this church as well as some bases, are spoils from the Roman period.

BIBLIOGRAPHY

Antonini, L. "Le chiese cristiane nell' Egitto del IV al IX secolo secondo i documenti de papiri greci." *Aegyptus* 20 (1940):129–208.

Eggebrecht, A. *Lexikon der Ägyptologie* I (1975): 435–41.

Jomard, E., ed. *Description de l'Egypte*, Vol. 1. Paris, 1821.

Mond, R., and O. H. Myers. *Temples of Armant*, Vol. 1. London, 1940.

PETER GROSSMANN

ARMENIANS AND THE COPTS. Copts and Armenians are regarded as making up the non-Chalcedonian Oriental Orthodox churches. How early they came into contact with one another is rather difficult to surmise. For various reasons (military, political, trade, slavery), Armenians have lived in Egypt since the time of the ancient Persian rule (sixth century B.C.). Through the centuries and in successive stages Egypt witnessed several influxes of Armenian families. However, aside from a few exceptions, Armenians did not assimilate with the native people of Egypt, but strenuously preserved their identity by retaining their social and racial characteristics, their language, and their religion.

In the fourth and fifth centuries A.D., during the Byzantine rule, several Armenian monks came to Egypt from Armenia and Jerusalem to join the ascetic Coptic fathers in their solitary desert life at the famed monastic center of NITRIA. Later, when numerous settlements of anchorites and monasteries developed around the dwelling caves of holy men in the Egyptian wilderness, there also developed one such Armenian settlement (see Aghavnuni, 1929). In the eleventh century, an Armenian bishop, Krikoris Vegayasayr, who later became the first Armenian prelate to Egypt, visited "the desert of Thebes to commune with the hermits there, to understand their lifestyle, to be informed about their rules and disciplines, and to collect data in order to introduce the same (rule) among the Armenian clergy" (Ormanian, 1912–1927, p. 1283).

The Coptic-Armenian relationship of the desert life is somewhat different from that of the established church. "It is misleading," says K. Sarkissian, "to try to find relations between the Armenian Church and Alexandria. Given the circumstances in which Christianity was introduced and spread in Armenia one cannot expect to see any regular or constant contact with Alexandria itself. Later, after the Council of Ephesus and, more particularly, after the Council of Chalcedon, relations were established for understandable reasons. At this early stage, Armenians could know the Alexandrian tradition only through their contacts with Cappadocian Christianity and with Constantinople" (Sarkissian, 1965, p. 110).

Indeed, the Armenians were not present at the two councils: EPHESUS (431) and CHALCEDON (451). The reason was the extremely unsettled state of their country under the Persian rulers. However, some fifty years after the Council of Chalcedon, Armenians became concerned with the Nestorian-Monophysite quarrels. In 506, the Armenian Synod under the leadership of Patriarch Bapken officially proclaimed the profession of Faith of the Council of Ephesus and rejected everything that was Nestorian, including the acts of the Council of Chalcedon. Consequently, the Christological teaching of CYRIL I (412–444) as embodied in his *Twelve Anathemas* was upheld and Zeno's HENOTICON was accepted.

During following centuries, especially when various Muslim dynasties ruled Egypt, Copts and Armenians learned to survive the hazards of a tumultuous life, as minority groups do. However, the religious history in Egypt for both the Copts and the Armenians is one of mixed nature—persecution or toleration, depending on the temperament of the period and the mood of the ruler.

Consequently, churches were built and destroyed according to the adopted policy of the rulers. This situation forced the Copts, rather than the Armenians, to either appropriate Armenian churches and monasteries or to claim ownership of these properties for one reason or another. That this is the case may be evidenced by visiting the existing as well as the various ruined Coptic churches in Egypt (e.g., DAYR AL-ABYAḌ monastery; see also the documents of certain writers, such as al-MAQRĪZĪ; Kushagian, 1937; and Kardashian, 1943). It must be stated that Armenians were allowed at various periods in history to conduct their own worship in Coptic churches or monasteries (Alboyadjian, 1941–1961).

For the first time since the fifth century, the Armenian and the Coptic churches, together with the Ethiopian, the Syrian, and the Syro-Indian churches met together at a conference in Addis Ababa, in 1965, under the auspices of HAILE SELASSIE I. Several important and far-reaching decisions were adopted at this meeting, including a new collective term of identification: Oriental Orthodox Churches (see *Report of the Oriental Orthodox Churches—Addis Ababa Conference, January 1965*).

One of the major difficulties in this area is the basic issue of sources. There are three interrelated obstacles to overcome: accessibility, relevance, and linguistic competence. The problem of accessibility of sources becomes most acute when tackling the Armenian materials. Because Armenians are dispersed throughout the world, many of their important manuscripts and documents are found in various established Armenian libraries: Soviet Armenia (Yerevan), Turkey (Istanbul), Lebanon (Antelias), Israel (Jerusalem), Egypt (Cairo, Alexandria), Italy (Venice), Austria (Vienna), and France (Paris). In addition, collections of a miscellaneous nature are also housed in certain North American libraries.

Second, the problem of determining the relevant material (both primary and secondary) is a major issue. The inherent difficulties in examining and sorting out the relevant Armenian materials that are scattered in the numerous libraries are too obvious to need any elucidation. One additional point must be borne in mind. Not all Armenian libraries have been able to catalog their material. As for the Coptic material, the problem is, in a sense, less critical, although not totally free from difficulties. Another source to be utilized is the "foreign" materials that allude to the topic under study. There is a tremendous task to perform in amassing all the relevant issues recorded in the writings of Roman, Byzantine, and Muslim Arab authors.

Third, the problem of linguistic competence is obvious. One must be capable of at least understanding the following languages: Coptic (last phase of ancient Egyptian language), Armenian (classical and modern in eastern and western dialect), Arabic (classical and modern), Latin, and Greek. Though many of the Greek and the Latin works are available in modern European languages, the Armenian, Coptic, and Arabic materials are, by and large, still in their original languages.

BIBLIOGRAPHY

Aghavnuni, A. "Desert Life in Egypt" (in Armenian). *Datev* (1929):39–50.

Alboyadjian, A. *History of Armenian Migrations* (in Armenian), 3 vols. Cairo, 1941, 1955, 1961.

______. *United Arab Republic of Egypt and the Armenians.* Cairo, 1960.

Kardashian, A. *Issues in the History of Armenians in Egypt* (in Armenian). Cairo, 1943.

Kushagian, T. *Ancient and Modern Armenian Churches in Egypt, and History of the Construction of the New St. Krikor Lousavoritch Church in Cairo* (in Armenian). Cairo, 1937.

Mahé, J. P. "Les Arméniens et l'Egypte." *Le Monde Copte* 9 (1980):23–27.

Ormanian, M. *History of the Armenian Nation* (in Armenian), 3 vols. Constantinople, 1912, 1914; Jerusalem, 1927.

______. *The Church of Armenia,* rev. ed., trans. G. M. Gregory. London, 1955.

Report of the Oriental Orthodox Churches—Addis Ababa Conference, January 1965. Addis Ababa, 1965.

Sarkissian, K. *The Council of Chalcedon and the Armenian Church.* London, 1965.

Thopouzian, H. K. *History of the Armenians in Egypt (1802–1952)* (in Armenian). Erevan, 1978.

SOLOMON A. NIGOSIAN

ARMY, ROMAN. Roman troops were already present in Egypt when the country was still ruled by the Ptolemaic dynasty. Ptolemy XII Auletes, who had been driven from his throne by the Alexandrian opposition, would hardly have been able to reenter Egypt without the military aid of the Roman legate Aulus Gabinius (55 B.C.). Since that time, Roman soldiers, partly in close connection with the remnants of the Ptolemaic army, were stationed at Alexandria and in the chora. After the end of the Alexandrian War (48–47 B.C.), this Roman presence was reaffirmed and regularized by Julius Caesar when he left three legions in Egypt under the command of Rufio (?), the son of one of his freedmen.

In the aftermath of the conquest of Egypt by Octavian (Augustus from 27 B.C.) in 30 B.C., Roman troops were distributed about Egypt in order both to control the conquered population and to seal off the borders of the country against foreign inroads. Legionary camps were established at Nikopolis, immediately east of Alexandria; at Babylon, at the southern point of the Delta, and at Thebes (the latter two to be reduced during the early principate). Lesser garrisons were stationed in various key places, such as frontiers (Pelusium, Syene), mines and quarries in the Eastern Desert, important road junctions (Coptos), and grain depots. The Roman army in Egypt was composed of three (later two) legions of Roman citizens and of various auxiliary units of provincials serving under Roman officers. These auxiliary units included infantry, cavalry, and a naval squadron based at Alexandria (*classis Alexandrina*). The Roman army in Egypt must have totaled 15,000–20,000 men until the end of the third century, allowing for alterations due to the overall military situation of the empire and especially to the requirements of Rome's eastern frontier.

Service in the legions, lasting normally for twenty-five years, was restricted to Roman citizens. Citizens of the Greek poleis of Egypt also were eligible to serve in the legions, becoming *cives Romani* immediately upon enlistment. As a rule, the Egyptian population had access only to the auxiliary troops, whose members became Roman citizens upon honorable discharge (*honesta missio*) after having served for twenty-six years. These auxiliary units were increasingly, but never exclusively, recruited in Egypt proper, above all from the gentry of the nome capitals, most of whom were descended from the Greek or Hellenized population. But until the second century, many non-Egyptians served not only in the legions but also in the auxiliary forces. These foreigners often stayed in Egypt after discharge. As veterans they enjoyed a privileged status, exempted from many of the taxes and services imposed upon the mass of the population. The papyri show the veterans as men of substance, active in the everyday life and commercial transactions of Egypt; they concentrated especially in the nome capitals and in the larger villages. The basic needs for the maintenance of the army (food, fodder, and fuel) were provided by taxes levied in Egypt. But the military were authorized to requisition additional supplies and services, such as billets and means of transport, a source of much friction and the raison d'être of many papyri.

There is no continuous record of the army of Byzantine Egypt, but we have at our disposal a variety of sources covering different aspects of the military situation in Egypt: the *Notitia dignitatum*, a survey of the Roman troops, their designations, and their garrisons in the fourth century (Berger, 1974), occasional notices in literary texts, legal sources, and many papyri giving a detailed but fragmentary insight into various activities of soldiers (such as the Abinnaeus Archive). While Diocletian maintained the frontier troops, from the middle of the third century on, we can observe the growing importance of the mobile field armies, the *comitatenses*, who accompanied the emperors on their journeys and expeditions. This development led to the system of Constantine the Great (306–337), characterized by the military masters (*magistri militum*) as commanders of the army and by the predominance of the *comitatus*, whereas the frontier army (*limitanei, ripenses*) was reduced in strength and prestige. The *Notitia dignitatum* reflects the military organization at about the time of Theodosius the Great (379–395) and as it continued to exist without substantial changes down to the time of Justinian I (527–565). The frontier army in Egypt was commanded by a *comes rei militaris* and by two *duces*, respectively of the Thebaid and of Libya. Compared with the third century, the army of the fourth century was split into a larger number of smaller units more evenly spread about Egypt.

We cannot discuss the details of the lesser units, but the creation and dislocation of new legions under Diocletian deserves at least a short mention. *Legio II Traiana fortis*, keeping its traditional garrison at Parembolē-Nikopolis near Alexandria, received (in 297 or 301/302) a sister unit, *legio III Diocletiana* stationed at Andropolis in the western Delta (near modern Hirbitā, province of Beheirah). From then on, these two legions formed the permanent occupation force of the province Aegyptus Iovia, but they also contributed detachments to the troops in Upper Egypt. In addition, the Thebaid received two legions of its own: *legio I Maximiana* at PHILAE (south of Aswan) and *legio II Flavia Constantia* at Cusae (al-Qūsiyyah). The newly created province of Aegyptus Herculia was occupied by detachments of *legio XIII Gemina* and *legio V Macedonica*. Notwithstanding their permanent garrison towns, these legions belonged to the mobile field army and contributed to it, at least in the fourth century, by detaching units to the *comitatus* (Hoffmann, 1969, Vol. 1, pp. 233–34; and, more generally, Bowman, 1978). The *Notitia dignitatum* records under the heading *Dux Thebaidos* a number of auxiliary units (*alae, cohortes, cunei*) in Upper Egypt and also the legions of the Thebaid proper, detachments of legions whose headquarters were in Lower Egypt. Thus, detachments of *legio III Diocletiana* are attested in Omboi and Thebes.

The bulk of our information on the military reforms of Diocletian in Egypt derives from written sources, but in some cases archaeology provides additional information. One particularly illuminating example is furnished by the camp of a detachment of *legio III Diocletiana* at Thebes. The foundations of that camp were built into the temple of Amon at Luxor (the name Luxor actually derives from *castra quṣūr* [plural of *qaṣr*] *al-Uqṣur*), obviously a good choice, since Amon was identified, following the pattern of *interpretatio Romana*, with Jupiter, the tutelary deity of the Diocletianic tetrarchy. At Luxor, the *dromos* of the pharaonic temple leads to the sanctuary of the *insignia* and of the ruler cult. In the apsis, the remains of wall paintings reveal the *adventus* and the *adlocutio* of an emperor. The assumption is justified that one of the outstanding features of this room was a throne standing under a baldachin. This highly ceremonial decoration probably bears testimony to a visit by Diocletian. The tetrarchic inscriptions of Luxor suggest the period 301–302 as the date of that visit and of the installation of that part of the *castra*. The camp of Luxor is attested until the Persian occupation of 619–629 and may have been destroyed during the Persian retreat. Not much later, the Christians began to erect churches in what had once been an Egyptian temple and a Roman camp.

In addition to the regular troops of the legions and *auxilia*, the army included federate formations, recruited from tribes beyond the frontiers of the empire and serving under their own tribal leaders. In Egypt, such contingents were furnished by the Blemmyes and Nobadae, by now well outside Egypt since Diocletian had abandoned Lower Nubia and established the new frontier at Philae, on the First Cataract. The maintenance of the army was assured by the *annona militaris*, taxes providing for payments in money and in kind. The papyri give ample information on the collection, transportation, and distribution of rations for the troops. They also illustrate in detail the conditions of military service, particularly the texts of the archive of Flavius Abinnaeus, an Egyptian (or perhaps a Syrian) who rose from the ranks to the command of the camp of Dionysius (Qaṣr Qarūn in the Fayyūm) in the time of Emperor Constantius II (337–361). Having served in the detachment of the *Parthosagittarii*, stationed at Diospolis in the Thebaid, he was ordered to escort envoys of the Blemmyes to the palace in Constantinople. This brought him promotion to the rank of *protector* (*ducenarius*) in 336 or 337. After having conducted the Blemmyes back to their country, Abinnaeus led recruits from the Thebaid to Hierapolis near the Euphrates, whereupon he was promoted to prefect (*eparchos*) of the *ala quinta praelectorum* at Dionysias about 340. What these papers also show is the important role of a military unit and its commander in the life of an Egyptian village.

It would be unwise to generalize on the living conditions of soldiers in Byzantine Egypt. Differences of rank and the changing state of general affairs during such a protracted period forbid any sweeping comment. But many soldiers, especially those who joined the *comitatus*, seem to have been far better off than most of their fellow Egyptians who were toiling in the rural areas. Different conditions applied to the *limitanei*, who were still a fighting force in the fourth century but degenerated into a hereditary, less professional peasant militia from the fifth century on. The scarcity of sources for the fifth century does not permit us to follow closely the development of the military organization in Egypt, but there surely was much continuity until Justinian.

Justinian, however, introduced an important reform in the command structure of the army in Egypt. Henceforward, the traditional separation of the military command from the civil administration was abandoned in the five provinces of Egypt (*Aegyptus, Augustamnica, Arcadia, Thebais, Libya*) and the direction of both civil and military affairs was unified under the control of one official designated as *dux Augustalis*. Jones (1964, Vol. 1, pp. 656–57) offers the following explanation for this reform:

> In Egypt there were three problems. The south was constantly troubled by razzias of the desert tribes, the Blemmyes and the Nobadae. Throughout the country the great landlords with their bands of *bucellarii* defied the administration. Above all, the attempts of the government to impose Chalcedonian patriarchs and clergy on the rabidly monophysite population provoked frequent civil disturbances, especially in Alexandria. To cope with the first problem the *dux* of the Thebaid had already in the fifth century been given administrative powers in the extreme south. To deal with the last, the offices of Augustal prefect and dux of Egypt had from time to time been vested in one person. Justinian made both these changes permanent, and seems to have extended the principle of a united civil and military command to all the provinces of Egypt.

Justinian's edict XIII, regulating above all the administrative competences with regard to the taxation of Egypt, sharply insists on the duty of the army to help tax collectors, if necessary, *militari manu*.

In the fifth century there already existed a tendency to assign regiments of the theoretically mobile field army to permanent garrisons, a feature that can be well observed in Egypt. Of course, the *limitanei* still constituted the bulk of the military effectives in Egypt. Beside these regular units, other formations were on the rise, such as the *bucellarii* (military retainees employed by private individuals). Great territorial magnates, often simultaneously high officials (for instance, the Apion family in fifth-century Egypt), were able to maintain private armies of *bucellarii* notwithstanding the efforts of the central government to curb this development. This traditional view of the *bucellarii* has been challenged by Gascou. In his opinion, the *bucellarii* were not private soldiers, but troops performing a public obligation (*munus*) and organized as an officially recognized corporation whose sustenance was provided by the "houses" (*oikoi*) of big landowners in fulfillment of a public duty. In a number of cases, the *bucellarii* were integrated into the imperial troops and fought in conjunction with regular units.

Another important change, perhaps well under way in the fifth century and attested by the time of Justinian, concerns the method of recruitment. Military service, still being largely hereditary in practice, had become entirely voluntary. Recruitment was predominantly local for the *limitanei* and even for the static units of the *comitatenses,* who, having lost their mobility, had become an Egyptian infantry force. The pool of the mobile troops adequate for rapid intervention thus further shrinking, one had, in case of an emergency (such as the wars against the Blemmyes), to call on *bucellarii* and on special *numeri,* chiefly composed of soldiers from the less civilized areas of the empire. As a consequence, the terms "soldier" and "barbarian" came to acquire the same meaning in the papyri of Byzantine Egypt. But these "barbarians" were slowly Egyptianized and lost much of their mobility (Rémondon, 1961, has admirably retraced this evolution in a remarkable contribution on the military situation in sixth-century Egypt).

The number of soldiers stationed in Byzantine Egypt is very difficult to estimate. It increased during the fourth century and may have reached about 64,000 *limitanei* at the end of that century in the provinces of Egypt, Thebaid, and Libya (Jones, Vol. 1, pp. 682–83). There is no guide to estimate even the approximate number of soldiers during Justinian's reign, at least for the *limitanei* in Egypt. In any case, their number and value had decreased since the fourth century.

[*See also:* CASTRUM.]

BIBLIOGRAPHY

Abinnaeus Archive. Papers of a Roman Officer in the Reign of Constantius II, ed. H. I. Bell et al. Oxford, 1962.

Barnes, T. D. "The Career of Abinnaeus." *Phoenix* 39 (1985):368–74.

Berger, P. *The Notitia dignitatum.* Ann Arbor, Mich., 1974.

Bowman, A. K. "The Military Occupation of Upper Egypt in the Reign of Diocletian." *Bulletin of the American Society of Papyrologists* 15 (1978):25–38.

Carrié, J.-M. "Le rôle économique de l'armée dans l'Egypte romaine." In *Armées et fiscalité dans le monde antique. Paris 14–16 octobre 1976.* Colloques nationaux du Centre national de la Recherche scientifique 936. Paris, 1977.

Cavenaile, R. "Prosopographie de l'armée romaine d'Egypte d'Auguste à Dioclétien." *Aegyptus* 50 (1970):213–320. Supplemented by N. Criniti in *Aegyptus* 53 (1973):93–158; 59 (1979):190–261.

Daris, S. *Documenti per la storia dell'esercito romano in Egitto.* Pubblicazioni dell'Università Cattolica del Sacro Cuore, Contributi, ser. 3, Scienze Storiche 9. Milan, 1964.

Devijver, H. "The Roman Army in Egypt (with Special Reference to the Militiae Equestres." In *Aufstieg und Niedergang der römischen Welt,* ed. H. Temporini, Vol. 2, pt. 1. Berlin and New York, 1974.

———. *De Aegypto et exercitu Romano sive Prosopographia militarium equestrium quae ab Augusto ad Gallienum sue statione seu origine ad Aegyptum pertinebant.* Studia Hellenistica 22. Louvain, 1975.

Diethart, J. M., and P. Dintsis. "Die Leontoklibanarier. Versuch einer archäologisch-papyrologischen Zusammenschau." In *Byzantios. Festschrift für Herbert Hunger zum 70. Geburtstag,* ed. W. Hörander et al. Vienna, 1984.

Drew-Bear, T. "Les voyages d'Aurélius Gaius, soldat de Dioclétien." In *La géographie administrative et politique d'Alexandre à Mahomet. Actes du Colloque de Strasbourg 14–16 juin 1979.* Université des Sciences humaines de Strasbourg, Travaux du Centre de Recherche sur le Proche-Orient et la Grèce antique 6. Leiden, 1981.

El-Saghir, M., et al., eds. *Le camp romain de Louqsor. Avec une étude des graffites gréco-romains du temple d'Amon.* Mémoires . . . Institut français d'Archéologie orientale du Caire 83. Cairo, 1986.

Fichman, I. F. "Egipetskij archiv serediny IV v. n. e." *Vizantijskij vremennik* 27 (1967):295–305. Deals with the Abinnaeus Archive.

Fink, R. O. *Roman Military Records on Papyrus.* Philological Monographs of the American Philo-

logical Association 26. Cleveland, 1971.
Gascou, J. "L'institution des bucellaires." *Bulletin de l'Institut français d'Archéologie orientale du Caire* 76 (1976):143–56.
Hoffmann, D. *Das spätrömische Bewegungsheer und die Notitia dignitatum,* 2 vols. Epigraphische Studien 7. Düsseldorf, 1969–1970.
Johnson, A. C., and L. C. West. *Byzantine Egypt: Economic Studies,* pp. 215–29. Princeton, N.J., 1949.
Jones, A. H. M. *The Later Roman Empire 284–602. A Social, Economic, and Administrative Survey,* 2 vols. Cambridge, 1964.
Lesquier, J. *L'armée romaine d'Egypte d'Auguste à Dioclétien.* Mémoires . . . Institut français d'Archéologie orientale du Caire 41. Cairo, 1918.
Maspero, J. *Organisation militaire de l'Egypte byzantine.* Bibliothèque de l'Ecole des Hautes Etudes 201. Paris, 1912.
Rémondon, R. "Problèmes militaires en Egypte et dans l'Empire à la fin du IVe siècle." *Revue historique* 213 (1955):21–38.
______. "Soldats de Byzance d'après un papyrus trouvé à Edfou." *Recherches de papyrologie* 1 (1961):41–93.
Speidel, M. P. *Roman Army Studies,* Vol. 1. Amsterdam, 1984. A number of contributions concern Egypt.
Van't Dack, E. "L'armée romaine d'Egypte de 55 à 30 av. J.-C." In *Das römisch-byzantinische Ägypten. Akten des internationalen Symposions 26.–30. September 1978 in Trier.* Aegyptiaca Treverensia 2. Mainz, 1983.

HEINZ HEINEN

ARSĀNĪ AL-MIṢRĪ, a monk at the monastery of Saint Catherine on Mount Sinai in 1396. On Thursday, 7 June 1396, he finished copying a liturgical manuscript (Sinai Arabic 220) of 215 folios, commissioned by another monk, Anbā Niqūlā al-Jaljūlī. Folios 106 to 201 were replaced and recopied at a later date by another hand.

This manuscript contains: a collection of troparia (fols. 1r–105r); a series of prayers (fols. 106r–45r); a long canon of praise to the Virgin (fols. 146r–68r); another series of prayers (fols. 168v–83v); part of a lectionary, with Epistles and Gospels (fols. 186r–200v); and more prayers (fols. 202r–207r). Here we find the colophon, dated 1396 (fo. 207r–207v).

Arsānī was a Melchite from Cairo. He was a good mathematician. In 1402 he composed computation tables giving the dates for the feast of Easter and the beginning of Lent, from the year 6910 of Adam to 6991/A.D. 1402–1483. He added these tables to the manuscript he had copied, on fols. 208r–15v.

Arsānī al-Miṣrī should not be confused with another Arsānī, monk of Sinai, who copied Sinai Arabic 117. The latter Arsānī was a priest and hermit (*ḥabīs*), who completed his manuscript on 31 December 1203.

BIBLIOGRAPHY

Atiya, A. S., and J. N. Youssef. *Catalogue Raisonné of the Mount Sinai Arabic Manuscripts* (in Arabic), pp. 229–30, 409. Alexandria, 1970.

KHALIL SAMIR, S.J.

ARSENAL OF TUNIS. Soon after Ḥasan ibn Nuʿmān, the Umayyad governor of Ifrīqiyyah (modern Tunisia), captured Carthage (A.D. 698), he began to build a city at the head of Lake Tunis in what was an ideal location for a marine arsenal. By approximately 700 the Umayyad caliph ʿAbd al-Malik ibn Marwān had ordered Ḥasan to build an Arab arsenal at Tunis.

At the same time ʿAbd al-Malik ordered his brother, who was the governor of Egypt, to send one thousand Copts and their families to Tunis in order to participate in the construction of a fleet. Instructions specified that ʿAbd al-ʿAzīz, the governor, should supply all necessary provisions (al-Bakrī, 1965, pp. 83–84), that the Berbers should supply the lumber, and that the Copts should construct and outfit the ships.

Existing studies indicate that Coptic artisans inhabited other ports in North Africa (al-Tijānī, 1958, pp. 6–7). Al-Bakrī reports that Copts inhabited the suburbs of Tripoli and that they composed most of the population of Ajdābiyyah (pp. 17, 20).

For a time the patriarch of Alexandria sent bishops to serve the Coptic communities in North Africa (Ibn Abī Dīnār, 1967, p. 15). At present the fate of these communities is not known.

BIBLIOGRAPHY

Bakrī, al-. *Description de l'Afrique septentrionale.* Arabic text and trans. Mac Guckin de Slane. Rev. ed., Paris, 1965.
Ibn Abī Dīnār. *Al-Muʾnis fī Akhbār Ifrīqīyah wa Tūnis,* ed. M. Shamām. Tunis, 1967.
Sebag, P. "Les Travaux maritimes de Ḥasan Ibn Nuʿmān." *Revue de l'Institut des Belles Lettres arabes* 33 (1970):41–56.
Tijānī, al-. *Riḥlat al-Tijānī,* ed. H. H. ʿAbd al-Wahhāb. Tunis, 1958.

LEONARD C. CHIARELLI

ARSENIUS OF SCETIS AND ṬURAH, SAINT, one of the most famous of the DESERT FATHERS, although not of Egyptian origin. In the alphabetical collection of the APOPHTHEGMATA PATRUM (Cotelier, 1864) he comes immediately after Saint ANTONY, and tradition gives him, as it gives the latter, the title of "the Great." He was probably born to a senatorial family at Rome in the middle of the fourth century. He received an excellent education and held high office at the court of the emperor Theodosius. On the basis of a poorly interpreted sentence in one apothegm (Cotelier, 1864, Arsenius 42; cf. PL 73, col. 955 C), he has even been held to be the tutor or the godfather of the sons of Theodosius.

Concerned about his salvation, he prayed one day and heard a voice say to him, "Arsenius, flee mankind and you will be saved" (Arsenius 1). The fame of the monks of Egypt was by then solidly established. Arsenius made haste to join them at SCETIS. This must be placed around 390. It is understandable that such a person's vocation would have seemed suspect to the aged Copts, who thought it necessary to submit the matter to the test at the hands of the wise abbot JOHN COLOBOS.

Training was rough, ready and swift. The new solitary soon had his cell in a remote spot 32 miles (48 km) from the monastic center (Arsenius 21), where he led the most austere of lives. He moved from there only after the Maziks had devastated the region. This was after Rome had been taken by Alaric, for Arsenius wept and said, "The world has lost Rome and the monks have lost Scetis" (Arsenius 21). The remainder of his life was passed either at Canopus, near Alexandria, or at Troa (modern-day Ṭurah), some 10 miles (15 km) southeast of Cairo; he died in Troa. A monastery of some size remained there until the fifteenth century, composed partly of cells and churches hollowed out of the rock. From this monastery came the papyri that were discovered in 1942 in a neighboring grotto and that contained works of ORIGEN and DIDYMUS.

Saint Arsenius seems always and everywhere to have been held in great honor in the Coptic church, following the fashion of the most eminent of the Egyptian fathers. He is mentioned on 13 Bashans in the various recensions of the Copto-Arabic SYNAXARION. He is commemorated on 8 May in the Greek Synaxarion and in the Georgian calendar. He also has his place in the Latin martyrologies on 19 July.

The apothegms tell us especially of the austerity with which Saint Arsenius always remained faithful to his initial vocation to forsake mankind. The divine voice drove him to it (Arsenius 2), and he encouraged himself to do it by ceaselessly repeating these words: "Arsenius, why have you gone forth [from the world]?" (Arsenius 40). Whether it was the patriarch, visitors of note, or people introducing themselves to him on the prelate's recommendation, the old man would hide (Arsenius 7–8, 28). Even the brethren could not easily obtain an interview with him, and they were astonished at the fact (Arsenius 26, 34, 37, 38). When asked by the abbot Mark why he was fleeing from them, Arsenius replied, "God knows I love you but I cannot be both with God and with men" (Arsenius 13). The saint was in fact united with God to the point of seeming to be literally on fire when one of the brethren cast an indiscreet glance through his cell window (Arsenius 27). Above all, he was horrified at the esteem and consideration given him by men (Arsenius 31). He concealed his practices so well that it was said that nobody could lay hold of the secret behind them (Nau, 1907, p. 54). However, it is known that he lived in extreme destitution (Arsenius 20) and that in church he used to stand hidden behind a pillar (Arsenius 42) clad in the worst of garments (Arsenius 4). His diet was most frugal. Once a year his supply of bread was renewed and some fresh fruit was brought to him, which he ate giving thanks to God (Arsenius 16, 17, 19). He slept for hardly an hour each night (Arsenius 14) and wove rope all morning (Arsenius 18). Every Saturday night he would remain standing in prayer, with hands uplifted, facing east (Arsenius 30). It was above all his spiritual life, which remained concealed in those invisible activities, about which he said, "Struggle with all your might so that your inward acts may be according to God's will, and you will conquer your outward passions" (Arsenius 9).

He did perhaps betray himself a little when he said, "If we seek God, he will appear to us; and if we hold on to him, he will abide with us" (Arsenius 10). One day, too, some of the brethren heard him crying to God, "O God, do not abandon me. I have done nothing good in thy presence; but in thy goodness put it in my power to begin" (Arsenius 3). On the approach of death, he kept the fear that had been with him throughout his life as a monk (Arsenius 40)—an indubitable sign of his perfection (cf. Sisoes 14), "filled with the Holy Spirit and with faith."

Despite the rather surly way in which he defended his solitude, Saint Arsenius did have a few disciples. We know of Alexander, Zoilus, and Daniel. But his contacts with them were intermittent (Arsenius 32) and he must have lived customarily alone in the desert. Some writings are attributed to him (Arsenius, 1864, cols. 1617–26). The most important is a letter preserved in Georgian and published by G. Garitte (1955). Its authenticity is acknowledged as probable by M. Van Parys (1981), a good judge, who stressed the points of convergence with the apothegms: attachment to his cell and to silence, perseverance in his cell, abstinence from food and sleep, and constant prayer. This letter completes the spiritual physiognomy of the saint and singularly enriches our knowledge of his teaching, which was wholly scriptural in its inspiration.

It is said that Arsenius "never wanted to speak about a question taken from Scripture, though capable of doing so, nor did he easily write a letter" (Arsenius 42). This text does not wholly exclude his having sometimes given directives to his disciples in writing or even scriptural explanations. In the *Catenae* (Chains) there are still some fragments attributed to him, the authenticity of which should not be rejected a priori. We know that Arsenius had contacts with Evagrius (*Vitae Patrum,* PL 73, cols. 912–13). With Van Parys, we may ask whether the great solitary would not be attached to the same spiritual current that was Origenist in inspiration.

BIBLIOGRAPHY

Acta sanctorum julii, Vol. 4, pp. 605–631. Antwerp, 1725.

Arsenius Eremita. *Doctrina et exhortatio.* In PG 66, cols. 1617–26. Paris, 1864.

Chitty, D. J. *The Desert a City,* pp. 53, 56, 61–64, 68, 70, 78. Oxford, 1966.

Cotelier, J. B., ed. *Apophthegmata Patrum.* In PG 65, cols. 88–108. Paris, 1864.

David, J. "Arsène." In *Dictionnaire d'histoire et de géographie ecclésiastique,* Vol. 4, col. 746. Paris, 1912.

Delehaye, H. *Propyl. ad Acta SS. Novembris,* cols. 664–66. Brussels, 1902.

______. *Propyl. ad Acta SS. Novembris,* p. 296, no. 8. Brussels, 1940.

Evelyn-White, H. G. *The Monasteries of the Wadi'n Natrūn,* pt. 2, *The History of the Monasteries of Nitria and Scetis.* New York, 1932.

Freire, J. G., ed. *Commonitiones sanctorum patrum* 6, pp. 393–98. Coimbra, 1974.

Garitte, G. "Une lettre de S. Arsène en géorgien." *Le Muséon* 68 (1955):259–78.

Geerard, M., ed. *Clavis Patrum Graecorum,* Vol. 3, pp. 57–58. Turnhout, 1979.

Meinardus, O. F. A. *Christian Egypt Ancient and Modern,* pp. 144, 350–53. Cairo, 1977.

Nau, F. N. "Histoire des solitaires égyptiens." *Revue de l'Orient chrétien* 15 (1907):54.

Schwartz, E., ed. *Kyrillos von Skythopolis: Leben des Euthymios,* p. 34. Texte und Untersuchungen zur Geschichte der altchristlichen Literatur 49, 1. Leipzig, 1939.

Theodorus Studita. *Laudatio S. Arsenii.* In PG 99, pp. 849–81. Paris, 1903.

Tillemont, L. de. *Mémoires pour servir à l'histoire ecclésiastique,* Vol. 14, pp. 676–702, 795–97. Paris, 1709.

Van Parys, M. "La Lettre de saint Arsène." *Irenikon* 54 (1981):62–86.

LUCIEN REGNAULT

ARSINOË. *See* Fayyūm, City of.

ART, BYZANTINE INFLUENCES ON COPTIC. It would be astonishing if Byzantine art had not exercised an influence on Coptic art, which was the art of a region included in the Byzantine empire. Byzantine art was at an advantage over Coptic art, since it was an imperial art, as dominant as it was rich and having all the splendor of brilliant luxury, whereas the values of Coptic art were modest and could only find models in Byzantium.

Thus Byzantine specialists naturally tend to see Coptic art as a department of Byzantine art to the extent of classifying among the techniques of Byzantine art the best works of Coptic art in painting, sculpture, and tapestry. This claim is made by scholars as well informed as A. Grabar (1966, pp. 173–89, 245–46, 264–69, 323–32), and it is carried to extremes by K. Wessel (1964). It is, however, rejected by E. Coche de la Ferté (1981, p. 29).

The claim loses substance when the facts are considered. Coptic art was already well established when Byzantine art came into being at the end of the fifth century. The possibility of direct and constant links between the two is limited to two centuries because of the conquest of Egypt by the Arabs. These were the years when the Byzantine authorities provoked Coptic hostility. These circumstances, then, make an influence of Byzantine art more plausible because of its dominant position, rather than that Coptic art should have been part of the Byzantine: not the style—which is the very life blood of art—but the iconography, a supporting feature, was affected.

If Byzantine influence occurred between the middle of the fifth and the middle of the seventh century, it could be revived only with some indulgence from the ninth to the twelfth century, when Tulunid and Fatimid Egypt gradually opened its gates to the Byzantine empire.

The first of these periods, then, is one of coexistence of these two art traditions, while Egypt was occupied by the Byzantine authorities.

In Egypt the basilicas of the crypt of ABŪ MĪNĀ, one erected by Constantine in the paleo-Christian period and the other added by Arcadius in the fifth century—each a part of an imperial program and constructed with rich materials—do not appear to have had a decisive influence. Rather, it seems that the Coptic basilica derives from the Roman Christian basilica, with some native modifications. This is apparent particularly in the side entrance, sometimes with a baffle, reentrant colonnades, and a tripling of the apse, which is itself also reentrant and a product of the vertical lines of the walls.

The decorative sculpture of Coptic churches may have borrowed certain motifs from Byzantine art, among them the foliated scrolls of the friezes. Nevertheless, the scrolls, as in the South Church of Bāwīṭ, may equally well have derived from those evident in Roman mosaics scattered around the periphery of the Mediterranean from Libya to Syria. Scrolls elsewhere developed according to a Coptic style characterized by the flat disposition of the whole and an extremely elaborate stylization. This transformation is particularly true of the corbeled capitals such as those in the South Church of Bāwīṭ. The corbeled capital, too, was of Libyan origin, from Sabratha and Leptis Magna, and earlier than Byzantine art. The imagination displayed here and the clear-cut right-angled contrast of surface and recess that throws it into relief are typically Coptic.

The pictorial decoration of the Chapel of Peace at al-Bagawāt was plainly Byzantine and not Coptic. It remained isolated at that oasis from all other Coptic productions, none of which included any of its features. Some liturgical attributes, such as the garments of the saints or the monks in the church of the monastery of (DAYR) APA JEREMIAH at Saqqara or in the devotional chapels of Bāwīṭ, matched those of the sacred figures of the sanctuaries of Ravenna. But there the form had lost the elegance of its drapery, and the figures were grouped side by side instead of gathered together, as if in an interpretation of movement, as is usual in the art of Ravenna and in Byzantine art as a whole. Another liturgical symbol, the sacred book adorned with precious stones and carried by a Christ shown with the Abbot Mena, painted on wood, clearly indicated the influence of Byzantine art in the stereotyped way it portrayed the Savior. Otherwise Byzantine influence was subsidiary; the subject matter, the style of the characters, and the language of the inscription that names them were entirely Coptic.

Various subjects in fabrics and tapestries are of Byzantine origin. Some of these are the fantastic animals that face each other in some groups of fabrics, the medallion showing Alexander on horseback (Museum of Textile, Washington), and certain pieces of silk from Antinoopolis (Louvre). But these are isolated examples and distinct from the major productions of Coptic fabrics. The subject of the tapestry hangings in the Cleveland Museum of Art, which show the Virgin seated in state with the Infant Jesus and busts of the Apostles and saints around the edges, is Byzantine, but the presentation has broken with the original style to become Coptic oriented.

The links between Constantinople and Egypt, which were interrupted by the Arab conquest of Egypt, resumed in the ninth and accelerated in the tenth to the twelfth centuries. But they were episodic and superficial among the Christians of Egypt, who were from that time a minority without influence. The church of the monastery of Abū Fānah in western Middle Egypt, which is uniformly decorated with Byzantine crosses, suggests that in that region Byzantine iconoclasm was in the ascendant; but this is an isolated case. The saints on horseback decorating the rear of the church of the Monastery of Saint Antony (DAYR ANBĀ ANṬŪNIYŪS) in the desert near the Red Sea are marked by Byzantine influence either by their postures or by the placing of a church under the horses' bellies; the faces of the horsemen, however, show Coptic features. The themes of shoulder bands and the cuffs of tunics contrast with everything Coptic though at the same time are part of it. These are characterized by the garments or details of garments (e.g., the *thorakion* [baldric] of the persons there represented) and are often accompanied on the edges by animals facing each other. But the whole is treated in crowded and angular fashion, typical of the Coptic style.

Thus the Byzantine presence was felt in Egypt as it influenced Coptic art. Sometimes the Byzantine characteristics were strong and isolated; sometimes they were slightly modified by Coptic features; sometimes their traces appeared in art that was completely Coptic in style. As with other art styles, especially Greco-Roman art, the Byzantine may have provided subjects that were entirely reworked in Coptic style in such a manner as to lose the marks of origin.

This assimilation and, *ipso facto*, difference had two causes. One was theological, particularly the cult of images, which set the Coptic expression of the common Christian faith at odds with that developed at Constantinople. The other was a less intellectual and spiritual perspective in an Egypt under foreign occupation. The genius of the invaders was to simplify and transform subjects from the pharaonic heritage into elaborate decoration.

BIBLIOGRAPHY

Bourguet, P. du. *Peintures chrétiennes; couleurs paléo-chrétiennes, coptes et byzantines*, pp. 200–201. Geneva, 1980.

Coche de la Ferté, E. *L'Art de Byzance*. Paris, 1981.

Grabar, E. *L'Age d'or de Justinien* Collection L'univers des formes. Paris, 1966.

Wessel, K. *L'Art copte*. Brussels, 1964.

PIERRE DU BOURGUET, S.J.

ART, COPTIC INFLUENCE ON EUROPEAN. Of all the imports from the East to the West, Coptic monasticism is one of the most important. The spread of the monastic phenomenon (its institution and spirituality) is evident from clear landmarks. Several Christian monuments in the West have led to the notion that this expansion spread into the domain of Christian iconography. However, the supporting data are unreliable, if not even imprecise. One might try to state the true relationship by limiting oneself to the themes most frequently mentioned in connection with a Coptic influence: the *Virgo lactans* (the Virgin suckling her child), the Devil, Saint George and Saint Michael, and the Triumph of Christ and the Ascension. The possible relations between Irish and Coptic art form a more general subject that is treated separately (see ART, COPTIC AND IRISH).

The Virgo Lactans

It is generally said that the iconography of Mary suckling the infant Jesus was established in Egypt, having derived from the ancient theme of Isis nursing Horus (Saitic epoch). However, it does not appear that the Copts inordinately represented the *Virgo lactans* despite the prototype found in the *Isis lactans*, which was doubtlessly known to the anchorites and monks of Egypt.

Near the end of the sixth century, this iconography appeared on a stela from the Fayyūm; then in the eighth century, it was painted on the walls of the apses of Bāwīṭ and Saqqara. Coptic art offers one of the most beautiful examples of the *Virgo lactans* on the wall of cell 1725 at Saqqara.

This caused numerous historians to state that Isis suckling Horus was the model that inspired the Coptic artists (Zuntz, 1929, pp. 32–35; Kondakov, 1914–1915, Vol. 1, pp. 255–258; Wessel, 1964, p. 17; Benigni, 1900, pp. 499ff.; Lasareff, 1938, pp. 26–65; and many others). But the very identification of certain statuettes is sometimes impossible to determine. Regarding a statuette from Beth Shean (Palestine), for example, Weitzmann entitles it "Figurine of Isis or *Virgo Lactans*?" (1978, p. 189). Two things prevent giving a purely Isiac origin to the iconography of the *Virgo lactans* in the East as well as in the West, apart from the fact that the Saitic Horus never takes his mother's breast. The Copts depicted the *Virgo lactans* only during the eighth century, and then rarely, and it was almost unknown in the West before the fourteenth century.

Virgo Lactans (Virgin mother nursing her child). Fresco. Saqqara, Dayr Apa Jeremiah, cell 1725. Seventh century. *Courtesy Mithilde Huybers.*

Nevertheless, it is indisputable that the cult of Mary began in Egypt during the first centuries A.D. at Alexandria; the doctrine of divine maternity was brilliantly defended by Cyril of Alexandria at the Ecumenical Council of Ephesus (summer of 431). The council not only condemned but also deposed Nestorius, as he proclaimed the Virgin as the Mother of God. It is also true that the tradition of *Isis lactans* was perpetuated and developed, from both the typological and the ideological points of view, under the Ptolemies and Roman emperors on the very soil of Egypt. Moreover, the spread of the cult of Isis into the entire Mediterranean basin has been demonstrated by Tran Tam Tinh (1973). However, all the ancient civilizations dedicated a cult to the mother and child and in all of them, the mother's milk had a role of equal importance. This stems from high antiquity, as is witnessed by the Cypriotic mothers nursing a child, which date from the third millennium B.C. (Louvre). With the Greeks as well, the mother nursing her child existed. This was distinct from the Isis cycle and dated from even before the Hellenistic era. The *Galactotrophousa* (nursing lady) of Santa Maria Vetere (Campania, third century B.C.; the nursing Hera (sixth century B.C.; Archaeological Museum, Athens), the *Mater Matuta* of Capua (second century B.C.), and many others attest to this.

The Copts, sensitive to the tender and natural gesture of the mother giving the breast to her child, which inspired sculptors and painters, were receptive to the Hellenized *Isis lactans*. Thus, the passing of the Greeks was necessary in order to establish this iconography with the Copts.

In the West, from among the best known examples, one may cite the fresco of Petit-Quevilly at Rouen (twelfth century), where Mary is nursing Jesus in a representation of the flight into Egypt. It is also found on the lintel of Anzy-le-Duc, on a round ivory relief from Metz (twelfth century), and in a few rare manuscripts. On the other hand, from the beginning of the fourteenth century, in the full light of humanism, Mary tenderly nursing the Infant Jesus appears everywhere, in the most diverse materials, on countless statues preserved today in the museums of Europe.

Why should one be obliged to associate Mary with Isis or one of the *kourotrophoi* (nursing mothers)? The artists at the end of the Gothic age simply wished to emphasize the purely maternal ties that unite a mother to her son. It was more a matter of making the hieratic image of the enthroned Virgin holding the Infant Jesus upon her lap less austere. (The meaning of the nursing scene on the walls of the apses of Bāwīṭ is discussed below in the section on the iconography of the Triumph of Christ.)

The Ascension and the Triumph of Christ

The liturgy of the Ascension is based on the reports of Luke (24:50–53), Acts (1:9–11), and Mark (16:19). Although references to the Ascension as a holiday—either independent of or as a part of Pentecost—came into existence rather late, it holds an extremely important place in the history of Christian iconography. However, the iconographical complexity of the Ascension has sometimes led historians to label as an Ascension what is, in fact, a Triumph of Christ.

The famous lintel of al-Mu'allaqah (Coptic Museum, Cairo), dating in all probability from the fourth century (Sacopoulo, 1957, pp. 96–116; Jouguet, 1957, p. 100; Christe, 1969, pp. 77f.), would be the first known scene of the Ascension. A central motif depicts Christ beardless and enthroned in a mandorla, which is supported by two angels with wings outspread, suspended in the air. In his left hand, Jesus holds the book of judgment decorated with a cross, and he lifts his right hand in a gesture reminiscent of the benediction (mutilated fragment).

Below the mandorla, the symbols of two evangelists can be distinguished: the lion and the ox (the other two, man and the eagle, do not appear on this lintel, probably due to lack of space). To the left of the central motif stands a woman clothed in a *maphorion* (cloak), her eyes fixed on the celestial vision; at each side are twelve figures holding either a cross with a long lance or a book engraved with a cross. Finally, two curtains, symbolizing the separation between heaven and earth, enclose and frame the scene.

If one accepts the limit of A.D. 430 set by M. Sacopoulo for the creation of the lintel, the introduction of the vision of Ezekiel and Mary into the iconography of the Ascension belongs to Egypt rather than to Syria, as Dewald maintains (1915, pp. 287–91), since the Gospel illuminated by the monk Rabula was executed in 586, as the colophon attests as to both date and origin. The Palestinian formula of the Ascension as illustrated by the Syriac illuminated Gospel and the AMPULLAE of Mouza takes its origin from the mosaics of the church erected on the Mount of Olives (Mâle, 1922, p. 88). This, however, does not indicate a sole Syrio-Palestinian origin for the Western iconography of the Triumph of Christ so common in the twelfth century on the

Ascension of Christ. Wood-sculptured lintel from the Church of al-Mu'allaqah (Old Cairo). Central panel. Fourth century. Height: 36 m; length: 2.74 m. *Courtesy Coptic Museum, Cairo.*

tympana of Western churches, for the Coptic lintel precedes by at least one century the productions of the ampullae and the Gospel of Rabula.

One finds repeated at Bāwīṭ the two principal ideas already expressed on the lintel of al-Mu'allaqah: the figure of Mary, recalling the mystery of the Incarnation, and the vision of Ezekiel relating to the themes of the Apocalypse. As Y. Christe explains (1969, p. 76), the extreme iconographical complexity of this lintel resides in the fact that it depicts, at once: (1) an Ascension-Parousia [second coming of Christ: "this Jesus, who was taken up from you into heaven, will come in the same way as you saw him go into heaven" (Acts 1:11)]; (2) a vision of Saint John; and (3) a reminder of the prophet Isaiah's theophany. Christ enthroned presents an element that, in effect, does not relate directly to the Ascension but rather to the vision of Isaiah: "I saw the Lord sitting upon a throne, high and lifted up" (Is. 6:1). The figures of Bāwīṭ are, in sum, a synthesis of several symbols that recall the Incarnation, the Ascension as a prelude to the Parousia, and the final glory of Christ, which is suggested by the four figures of the vision of Ezekiel.

Moreover, the Copts seem to establish a close relationship between the eucharistic prayer and a reminder of the vision of Ezekiel. In Egypt, the Virgin is represented as the *Theotokos* (Mother of God), who, having conceived by the grace of the Holy Ghost, gave birth to God incarnate; she recalls the sacrifice of Christ. In the apses of several chapels of Bāwīṭ (chapels 6, 17, 42, 45, and 46), Mary always appears in the lower register, flanked by the apostles or local saints, or both, while praying and nursing the Infant Jesus. She may be hieratic and frontal as the Hodighitria Virgin, or gesturing like the Syrian Virgins of the Ascension, her face turned upward toward Christ (Bāwīṭ, chapel 46). The figure of Mary on the frescoes of Bāwīṭ and Saqqara makes it in some sense improbable that the Copts wished to depict an Ascension. According to C. Ihm (1960), the presence of the Infant in the Coptic iconography conserves the memory of the close relation made in the primitive church between the Ascension and the Incarnation, events celebrated in a single holiday at Jerusalem. The *Virgo lactans* of chapel 42 at Bāwīṭ illustrates a passage from the book of Isaiah (7:14–15).

A pharaonic origin came to be ascribed to the four evangelical symbols, and this was seen as a Christian continuation of the four sons of Horus placed at the four corners of the sarcophagus of Osiris on Judgment Day (Ellis, 1930, p. 116). But their placement is unknown. Were they looking at Osiris or at the horizon? An answer could enlighten us as to the particular way in which the Copts depicted the four figures turning away from Christ. In any event, the four figures were a favorite subject of the Copts, who depicted them everywhere in Egypt: at Bāwīṭ, at Saqqara, at Saint Simeon of Aswan, at DAYR AL-SHUHADĀ, at DAYR AL-ABYAḌ, and in the central cupola of DAYR AL-AḤMAR of Suhāj, as well as in a chapel entirely devoted to the animals of the Apocalypse at the Monastery of Saint Anthony in the Thebaid.

According to Gabriel Millet (1945, pp. 55f.), the

Triumph of Christ. Painting. Bāwīṭ. Seventh century. Height: 100 cm; width: 100 cm. *Coptic Museum, Cairo. Courtesy André Held.*

figure of Christ associated with the four figures of the vision of Ezekiel was first transmitted to the East, specifically into Armenia, and then to the West, specifically into Italy. Jean Ebersolt has explained very well the relations that existed throughout the Mediterranean long before the Crusades: "At that time the Jews shared the traffic of Oriental trade with the Syrians . . . Papyrus, that precious conveyor of ideas, came from Egypt to Marseilles, where the ships had just unloaded their cargos of oil and other liquids . . . From Syria there came wine . . ." (after the *Historia Francorum* of Saint Gregory of Tours; Ebersolt, 1954, p. 24). In a paper presented at the thirteenth Congress of Orientalists at Hamburg (1903, pp. 1–39), Ebersolt stated: "It is in Italy, especially at Rome, that we find the most important colonies. From antiquity, satirists already complained about the invasion of Rome by the Syrians" (p. 3). Today it is thought that the transmission of the principal Middle Eastern themes to the West was effected progressively and almost naturally, as the Middle East attracted Gaul and vice versa. What is more controversial is the direct relationship between the Copts and the West that has been too easily established.

J. Hubert (1967, p. 74) was the first to invoke Coptic influences for the Abbey of Jouarre, founded around 630 thanks to the monastic apostolate of Saint Columban. The sepulcher of Agilbert, a great man of the seventh century, situated in the north crypt of Jouarre, relates to our subject. The most interesting part of that tomb is the panel depicting the head of Christ in majesty surrounded by the four evangelical symbols. The most striking detail of Jouarre's iconography is the position of the four figures in relation to Christ, as they are turned in the opposite direction. According to Hubert, the style and iconography of this tomb go back to Coptic Egypt: "The artist of Jouarre must have been a student at a Coptic atelier, having fled upon the invasion of Egypt by the Arabs" (p. 77). Unfortunately, the absence of any text about the installation of a Coptic atelier in France does not permit us to confirm this hypothesis. There is no mention whatever in the most ancient texts recounting the founding of the monastery of Jouarre, as, for example, in the Life of Saint Columban, edited by the hagiographer Jonas de Bobbio.

The position of the four figures of Jouarre, no matter how impregnated they may be by Coptic art, still remains an isolated case in Western iconography. Is this alone sufficient to imagine the displacement of a Coptic atelier into the West after the Arab invasion?

B. Brenk also notes a very strong Coptic influence at Jouarre (1964, pp. 99–100): "The form and the theme are intermingled with Coptic elements. . . ." But he admits the impossibility of explaining it, and concludes that the "how" remains unknown: ". . . but the sculptor of Jouarre saw Coptic sculptures or iconographs." This is a hypothesis difficult to contest, but who is to say that there was not a European monk among the team of artists at Jouarre who had undertaken the long trip to the Holy Land and Egypt? The Gallic bishop Arculfe was in Egypt around 670 (Ebersolt, 1954, p. 32), as were many others coming by ship from Narbonne or Marseilles, such as the friend of Sulpicius Severus, Postumianus (Sulpicius Severus, pp. 7–163).

Ascensions from the Orient were not accepted by the West before the twelfth century. Beginning with the eleventh century, iconography received a new Byzantine contribution. Christ in His majesty surrounded by the four figures, at Saint-Jacques-des-Guérets, recalls in many respects the Ascension-Parousia of the fresco of the Church of Saint Sophia of Ochrid (Coche de la Ferté, 1981, p. 212). But from the twelfth century onward, the intimate relationship of the two themes of the Ascension-Parousia is fully developed on the façades of churches throughout Burgundy and Languedoc, including Charlieu, Chartres, Bourges, Saint Trophime at Arles, Cahors, Carrenac, and many others. The tympanum of Charlieu and the fresco in the Abbey of Lavaudieu were related to the compositions at Bāwīṭ by E. Mâle (1922, pp. 34f.): "This great composition which appears to us as a creation of the twelfth century was already 700 years old when it was discovered painted in fresco on the wall of one of the chapels of Bāwīṭ in Upper Egypt" (p. 34). The composition of the fresco of Lavaudieu is divided into two registers: above, Christ enthroned, surrounded by the vision of Ezekiel; below, Mary, among the apostles, which certainly reminds us of Coptic Egypt. But one must try to discover the sources of inspiration for the painter and sculptors of Lavaudieu. The hypothesis of a Byzantine influence is difficult to maintain, for the vision of the Son of Man enthroned among the four symbolic animals is practically absent from Byzantine decoration, with the exception of the Hosios David (sixth century, Thessalonica). On the other hand, the visions of Ezekiel and Saint John depicted in the most ancient churches of Cappadocia might have served as an intermediary between the paintings of Bāwīṭ and our Roman tympana if the lower register depicting Mary and the apostles were not absent in the Cappadocian churches. That being said, in no other place, neither in France nor Italy nor elsewhere, is the complexity of the Coptic model to be found, a complexity in form as well as in meaning.

Christ in a mandorla surrounded by the four evangelical symbols. Stone sculpture. Main panel of the Tomb of Agilbert at Jouarre, France. Seventh Century. © *Gallimard-L'Univers des Formes.*

In the West, the interlaced and flaming wheels, the seraphim of Isaiah, Ezekiel in person substituted for Mary (as in chapel 45 of Bāwīṭ) are iconographical elements that are never seen elsewhere; nor does Mary accompanied by the Infant Jesus appear, and this detail brings Coptic influence into question. The fresco artists of Bāwīṭ and Saqqara invariably depicted Mary and her Son in the iconography of the Triumph of Christ, which was not the case in either Syria or Palestine. The hypothesis of a Middle Eastern prototype thus remains certain, whereas the direct influence of a Coptic model is less so.

Moreover, it is surprising that the title "Ascension" is no longer applied to the frescoes of Charlieu and Lavaudieu since they are closer to the Bāwīṭ compositions (persistently labeled as Ascensions) than they are to the Syrian miniatures or the ampullae of Monza.

The Devil

Even before E. Mâle wrote his *L'Art Religieux au XIIème siècle*, an Egyptian origin was given to certain representations of the devil in Christian iconography. In the twelfth century, Western iconography of the devil became definitively fixed. He keeps a human aspect even though certain parts of his body are deformed. The skin, sometimes covered with hair, is most often dark in color, usually black.

One must not look for an origin to this black skin in the texts of the Old Testament where Satan appears as a servant of God admitted to the heavenly courts (e.g., Jb. 1:6–12). Nor is this origin to be found in the New Testament, where the devil is considered as a power of darkness, which would not suffice to explain the color black that is generally attributed to him in Byzantine and Western iconography. P. du Bourguet (1972, pp. 271–72) offers an explanation for the word *négrillon* (little black boy) conferred upon the devil in the monastic accounts from Egypt: "The reason for this is furnished by the history of the last pharaonic dynasties and the traditional Egyptian beliefs. According to these latter, any enemy of Egypt, as an enemy of Pharaoh, is a personification of evil. Psamtik II/Psammetichus, who conquered the preceding dynasty—known as 'Ethiopian,' but in fact Nubian—made every effort to have the descendants of this dynasty labeled as 'the enemies of Egypt.' The Copts inherited this tradition, and thereby associated the spirit of evil with 'Ethiopian'" (du Bourguet, 1972).

The influence of the *Vita Antonii (Life of Anthony),* translated by Evagrius of Antioch (c. 390), was a determining factor in the diffusion of the theme of the fight against the devil, who appeared to the saint as a black child falling upon him. Indeed, it is in the literature of the desert that the devil appears in the form of a hideous black man and dragon. In the *Acts of the Martyrs of Egypt,* taken from Coptic manuscripts of the Vatican Library and translated by H. Hyvernat in 1886 (Vol. 1, fasc. 3, p. 187), one reads: "At this time Quintilian was ruler; he had a daughter. As she was sleeping, a black dragon crept inside her and lodged in her belly." The color black attributed to the devil is found in numerous Coptic monastic accounts. In the *Apophthegmata* it is related that when Abba Mūsa became a cleric and was clothed with the ephod, the archbishop wished to try him: "You have now become completely white, Abba Mūsa." Whereupon the old man replied: "My Lord and Pope, is it true outwardly, or inwardly as well?" Continuing the test, the archbishop directed the clerics: "When Abba Mūsa enters the sanctuary, follow him and listen to what he says." The old man then went in, and they reviled him and chased him, saying: "Out, Ethiopian." Upon leaving, he said to himself: "They acted well in your regard, you, who have skin black as cinders. Not being a man, why do you go among men?" (1976, pp. 104–105). This same feature is found in the texts of SHENUTE in the *Historia Monachorum* transmitted to the West by Rufinus Aquilae (Festugière, 1971), and in the *Collationes* of John CASSIAN (*Sources chrétiennes,* no. 64), where Satan is described as a black-skinned Ethiopian.

Few Coptic representations of this type of devil have reached us. Nevertheless, a twelfth-century miniature of the Coptic Manuscript 13 in the National Library in Paris offers a good example in a scene of the Temptation, in which the seraphim appear on the right, while the devil, on the left and depicted as a black seraphim, is rejected. The West adopted the Eastern tradition, and the most illustrious saints saw the devil appearing to them as black, such as Saint Luke of Thessaly, a hermit on Mount Joannitsa in Corinth, who in 946 saw the devil in the form of a small black man.

Saint George

The iconography of Saint George, who appears both in the East and West as the champion in the fight against the devil, also deserves mention in relation to Egypt.

In pharaonic symbolism, Horus trampling the crocodiles signifies the triumph of good over evil. The stela of Mīt Rahīnah in the Cairo Museum offers a good example of this iconography, which is very reminiscent of the iconography of Christ depicted on a Coptic textile deriving from Akhmīm and now found in the Forrer Collection at the Victoria and Albert Museum, London.

The transition of the image of Horus victorious over malevolent powers to that of Saint George trampling the dragon could have happened in two ways. The first hypothesis suggests that the transition coincides with the arrival of the Romans, who depicted Horus as a knight in armor. However, the Horus-cavalier was rarely portrayed, the only known example being in the Louvre. According to du Bourguet, the second, more complex hypothesis relates to the Christians exiled to the oasis of Khārjah by the emperor Diocletian. Under Theodosius, this oasis continued to serve as a place of exile, and the Nestorians, as well as all those contesting the official doctrines, were sent there. Du Bourguet has noted that a temple of the Twenty-eighth Dynasty, named al-Hibah, is located in this oasis. On the western wall of the north hypostyle of this temple,

Temptation of Christ in the desert. Illumination from a Copto-Arabic *Tetraevangelium* (the Four Gospels) (Miniature copte 13 fol. v°). Twelfth century. *Courtesy Bibliothèque Nationale, Paris.*

Horus on horseback. Sandstone. Sixth century. Height: 49.1 cm; width: 32 cm; thickness: 7.8 cm. *Courtesy Louvre Museum, Paris. Photo by Max Seidel.*

Horus appears on the lower register; he is standing, accompanied by a lion, and is piercing the malevolent serpent with his lance. Would those exiled to the oasis of Khārjah have remembered this figure piercing the Hydra, which they had before their eyes in the temple of al-Hibah, and subsequently brought it back to Constantinople? The image of good crushing evil would thus have been adopted by the Christians, first the Copts, and then the Byzantines, who introduced it to the West. Even the name of the oasis, Khārjah, may perhaps be related to the Coptic name Jirjis, meaning George. However, the simple relationship of the names Jirjis-George cannot serve as a basis for argument; such an argument would remain very hazardous since no ancient Coptic texts yet discovered make mention of the Jirjis-George relationship. Doubtless, one should also evoke the myth of Bellerophon lifted into the air by the horse Pegasus in order to kill the Chimera. This iconographical source for Saint George killing the dragon, though apparently more removed, merits some attention since Bellerophon is depicted on a Coptic textile of the sixth century, mounted on his winged horse and piercing the Chimera with his lance (du Bourguet, 1968, p. 150).

However, if Saint George, as a type, was created in Egypt, the Copts neither sculpted nor painted it. For a time it was thought that the cavalier-saint of Bāwīṭ was Saint George, but there is no doubt today that it is properly identified as Saint Sisinios.

Saint Michael

The iconography of Saint Michael is almost absent from Coptic art. It seem surprising that the doctrine of the weighing of souls, so strong in ancient Egypt, did not strike the mystical imagination of the Copts in one way or another. Yet there is no evidence of this. A long oral tradition, transmitted to the traveling monks in the deserts of Wādī al-Naṭrūn and Upper Egypt, might be postulated, but to our knowledge, there was no direct iconographical influence.

Conclusion

May it be concluded that there was no influence from Coptic art upon Western medieval art? In the present state of knowledge, it is, in fact, not so simple to support the theses or hypotheses that propose the displacement of Coptic artisans to the West (at Jouarre, for example; Hubert, 1967, p. 77) fleeing from the Persians or Arabs, as an explanation for certain iconographical or stylistic influences upon Merovingian sculpture. It must be recognized that the Copts were, and still are, a Christian disinherited minority within a Muslim country. Their destiny was to remain resolutely attached to their homeland. Their artistic production, reflecting this destiny, was modest, private, and conceived for places far removed in the hot deserts of Egypt. Neither in the Chronicle of John of Nikiou nor in the history of Egypt by the Arab historian al-Maqrīzī—where nonetheless the history of the Copts occupies a large place—is there any question of a flight before the invader, which anyway would have been a liberty denied them, given their status in a Muslim country.

Though uncertainty remains about the passage of Coptic iconography into the West, there is reason to believe that certain details could have been transmitted thanks to Coptic writings and monastic way of life, which was to become the source of Christian monasticism and its manifestations in the West.

Saint Sisinios on horseback. Limestone. Seventh century. Bāwīṭ, south church, above the side entry. *Courtesy Louvre Museum, Paris.*

BIBLIOGRAPHY

Benigni, U. "La Madona Allatante è un motivo bizantino?" *Bessarione* 7 (1899–1900):499ff.

Bourguet, P. du. "Chenouté: Diatribe contre le démon." *Bulletin de la Société archéologique du Caire,* Vol. 16, pp. 17 and 72. Cairo, 1962.

______. *L'Art copte* (Collection L'Art dans le monde). Paris, 1968.

______. *Actas del VIII Congresso di Argueologie Cristiana.* Barcelona, 1972.

Bréhier, L. "Les Colonies d'orientaux en occident au commencement du moyen-âge." Mémoire présenté au XIIIème congrès des orientalistes à Hambourg, 8ème section. *Byzantinische Zeitschrift* 12 (1903):1–39.

Brenk, B. "Marginalien zum Soggenmauten Sarkophag des Agilbert in Jouarre." *Cahiers archéologiques* 14 (1964).

Christe, Y. *Les Grands portails romans, études sur l'iconographie des théophanies romanes.* Geneva, 1969.

Coche de la Ferté, E. *L'art de Byzance.* Paris, 1981.

Dewald, J. E. "The Iconography of the Ascension." *American Journal of Archeology* (1915):287ff.

Ebersolt, J. *Orient occident,* ed. E. de Boccard. Paris, 1954.

Ellis, L. B. *The Animal Symbols of the Evangelists in Ancient Egypt.* London, 1930.

Festugière, A. J. *Historia Monachorum in Aegypto* (*Subsidia Hagiographica* 53). Brussels, 1971.

Gabory, D. *Les Ivoires du moyen âge.* Fribourg, 1978.

Guy, J. C. *Paroles des anciens apophtègmes des pères du désert.* Paris, 1976.

Hubert, J.; J. Porcher; and W. F. Volbach. *L'Europe des invasions.* Paris, 1976.

Hyvernat, H. *Les Actes des martyrs,* Vol. 1, fasc. 3.

Paris, 1886.
Ihm, C. *Die Programme der christlichen Apis Malerei, vom IV. Jahrhundert bis zur Mitte des VIII. Jahrhunderts.* Wiesbaden, 1960.
Kondakov, N. P. *Iconographie de la mère Dieu,* 2 vols. St. Petersburg, 1914–1915.
Lasareff, V. "Studies in the Iconography of the Virgin." *The Art Bulletin* 20 (1938):26–65.
Mâle, E. *L'Art religieux du XIIème siècle en France.* Paris, 1922.
Millet, G. *La Dalmatique du Vatican.* Paris, 1945.
Osborne, H. *Lychnos et Lucerna,* pp. 17ff. Alexandria, 1924.
Sacopoulo, M. "Le Linteau copte de al-Moàllaqà." *Cahiers archéologiques* 9–10 (1957):7ff.
Sulpicius Severus. *Dialogues.* Translation and notes by M. Herbert. Bibliothèque latine française. Paris, 1849.
Tram Tan Tinh, J. *Isis Lactans. Corpus des monuments gréco-romains d'Isis allaitant Harpocrate.* Etudes préliminaires aux religions orientales dans l'Empire romain 37. Leiden, 1973.
Weitzmann, K. *Age of Spirituality: Late Antique and Early Christian Art.* Catalogue of the Exhibit 19 November 1977–12 February 1978. New York, Metropolitan Museum.
Wessel, K. *L'Art copte.* Brussels, 1964.
Zuntz, D. *Eine Vorstufe der Madona Lactans.* Berliner Museum 50. Berlin, 1929.

MONIQUE BLANC-ORTOLAN

ART, COPTIC AND IRISH. It has been asserted that Irish art is derived from Coptic art. The only precise affirmations that resurface most often concern illuminated books, suggesting a need for concentrated research on this subject. C. Nordenfalk (1977, p. 13) formulated a prudent opinion on the subject.

> Towards the middle of the seventh century, a new advance was made when a kind of ornamentation previously unknown was found in Ireland: interlacings. The hypothesis is often proposed that this decorative motif was imported directly from Egypt. However, the fact that certain of these most evolved forms have been discovered in Coptic art does not constitute a decisive argument. Similar tendencies existed in Byzantine and Italian art.

Nordenfalk's brief list could be completed by adding the art of the Mesopotamians, Hittites, and Chaldeans, all of which accorded interlacings a privileged place, if one believes the objects discovered at Susa dating from 3000–2500 B.C. Nevertheless, it is indisputable that the Copts were very inventive in the field of decoration, notably in breaking monotony with interlacings. On the stringcourse at the base of the southern church at BĀWĪṬ, two braided stalks enclose animals, while squares and circles are interlaced. But one wonders whether this is sufficient reason to maintain that the interlacing motif or that of the fully illuminated page indicate Coptic influences in Ireland.

Interlacings

J. Baltrusaitis believes that between the Hittite and Coptic eras, interlacings were preserved by the barbarians, in particular the Scythian populations of the southeastern steppes of Europe and the shores of the Black Sea (1929, p. 38). This opinion is especially interesting if placed in a Celtic context.

Since the third century, the interlacing motif appeared on Coptic textiles conserved by the tens of thousands (du Bourguet, 1964, p. 17), and is later found on Coptic manuscripts, along with many other motifs that the Celts also held in high esteem at a very ancient epoch. The stylization of geometric lines—both rectilinear and curvilinear—which was pushed to the extreme, did not belong solely to Coptic civilization. Disks, wheels, crescents, spirals, interlacings and scrolls, chevrons, triangles, squares and rectangles—these were not born in Celtic Europe. Rather, they came from Eritrea, Greece, and the plateaus of Iran, and thus were borrowed forms to which the Celts gave a completely original plastic art and sacred meaning. In 1927 a pair of Celtic *oinokhoai* (cans for ladling wine) was discovered near Metz, France (fourth century B.C., bronze, British Museum). They offer not only an interesting synthesis of Greek art with that of Asia Minor but also attest to the Celts' knowledge of decorative interlacing. These *oinokhoai* formed the subject of an in-depth study in an unpublished paper by J. V. S. Megaw. It is thought-provoking to see how and when the Celts came into contact with the Mediterranean civilization, even to the point of abandoning the purely geometric style that animated their first works.

From the end of the Hallstatian period (c. 530 B.C.), Celtic art was influenced by figurative Mediterranean art, as is attested by P. M. Duval and V. Kruta (1982, p. 25). Later, in contact with the Etruscans—alongside whom they lived for nearly thirty years (480–450 B.C.) (Duval and Kruta, 1982, p. 28)—they transformed the human figure by stylizing it to the ultimate of the fantastic and monstrous, as may be seen on the ornamentation of the handles of the two *oinokhoai* from Basse-Yutz (Moselle) (Smith, 1929, pp. 1–12; Jacobsthal, 1969, no. 381, pls. 178–83; Duval, 1977, pp. 54 and 310). The repertoire of Celtic ornamental motifs was further enriched as a result of new Italian and Balkan conquests. O. Klindt-Jensen (1982, p. 83) asserts that "the Celtic style was influenced by the Orient from the beginning . . . it was not a question of direct contacts, but rather of spiritual affinities. . . ." According to him, Thrace was the liaison that—because of its geographic location—was in constant contact with both the Balkans and Asia Minor. Klindt-Jensen also states that the eastern art of the Balkans influenced the Scythians, as is evidenced by the objects discovered during the excavations of Kelermos and Melguenov: "One should not ignore the role played by the Scythian artisans around the Celts as intermediaries with the Oriental elements," an opinion confirming that of Baltrusaitis. It is evident that the interlacings at the base of the *oinokhoai* in the British Museum, which are of a similar date, can only have an eastern, but non-Coptic, inspiration. At Waldalgesheim (Germany) around 250 B.C., the interlacing motif appears on numerous objects. Spirals interlace: "no separate spiral is visible; one sees only one tendril" (Duval and Kruta, 1982, Fig. 11). According to Klindt-Jensen, intellectual affinities without direct contact could well have existed between Coptic Egypt and Ireland. However, the essentially spiritual nature of these affinities must be emphasized.

Ireland

Ireland—that veritable "conservatory of Celticism" spared by the Roman conquest—had a destiny very different from that of the other countries of Europe at the beginning of the Christian era. This distant country, enclosed within itself, was to develop an art that mixed all the influences received by the Celts during their formidable period of expansion, an expansion definitively interrupted in the first century of the Christian era when the Romans put an end to the Celtic powers, except the kingdoms of Ireland.

If one wishes to admit the very simple hypothesis of a strong and unique Celtic influence on Irish illuminated books, one must cite the influence that Gaul exercised on Ireland; this would have come only through the Druids who took refuge in Ireland, and later through monasticism (see below). In Gaul, Roman pavings with interlacing decoration flourished from the beginning of the Christian era everywhere in the South, in the provinces of Narbonensis, Lugdunensis, and Aquitania (Stern and Glay, 1975, Vol. 3, pl. 3 and 72).

Closer still to Ireland, Great Britain adopted the interlacing motif as seen on the marvelous treasure of Sutton Hoo (seventh century A.D.). Thus the different motifs exploited by the English silversmiths on the objects of the royal cenotaph of Sutton Hoo appear also on the Book of Durrow: checkerboards, spirals, interlacings, and Greek key patterns.

The Fully Illuminated Page

The same may be said for the fully illuminated page that the Copts supposedly passed to the Irish monks.

To take the oft-cited example of the great aniconical crosses painted at the head of manuscripts and across the full page, which is rather significant, "The oldest depiction of these aniconical crosses that we possess appears to be that conserved at the Leningrad Library, folio 2 of a manuscript dated 462" (Leroy, 1964, p. 2, pl. 4). The fully illuminated pages seem to have appeared in Syria before they appeared in Egypt. The examples of ornamental crosses given by J. Leroy (1964, Syr. 30, fol. 62; Syr. 70, fol. 1; Syr. 40, fol. 10v, p. 4, pls. 1, 2, and 3), dating from the end of the tenth century to the beginning of the twelfth and kept in the National Library in Paris, precede the great Coptic crosses that appear on the Bohairic-Arabic manuscript of A.D. 1319, the Pentateuch of A.D. 1398, and the Bohairic-Arabic manuscript of A.D. 1547 cited by M. Cramer (1969, pp. 46 and 47), though these are very similar to the Syrian crosses decorated with interlacings.

It is true that on Irish manuscripts, the intersecting foliated branch and the intersected cross (or the two scepters) are often held by the Evangelists in the traditional pose of Osiris, and a Coptic origin is often suggested for this. But the Copts did not adopt the Osirian poses in their own iconography for the Evangelists, and thus they cannot be at the origin of this Irish iconography.

"Illuminations—of clear Pharaonic tradition—do not seem to have appealed to Coptic scribes" (du Bourguet, 1967, p. 104) before the ninth century. However, the influence of Coptic Egypt on Ireland seems evident to one great specialist of Irish art, F. Henry, who believes that it was because of the circulation of Oriental textiles that the Irish were inspired by forms and motifs belonging to the repertoire of the Orient: "The Occidental world was filled with Oriental textiles used for hangings or to enwrap the relics, just as the heavy and stylized personages that the Copts had the habit of drawing must have inspired the Irish artists" (Henry, p. 51). True, the distribution of Middle Eastern textiles in Western Europe was accomplished by merchants, but one wonders if they were specifically Coptic. These textiles convey an overall decoration of great richness and variety whose influence is undeniable, but this decoration is found throughout the entire Mediterranean basin at the same period. However, tradition maintains that Coptic influence spread through Ireland thanks to the monks who copied in the scriptoria. This powerful monastic phenomenon that developed in Ireland during the fifth century owed, as did Gallic monasticism, the essence of its spirituality to Egypt. Everyone agrees on this, but the role played by Gaul itself in the spread of Egyptian monasticism is not cited often enough. Saint Martin of Tours founded Ligugé in 360 after the Egyptian model. According to L. Bouyer (1950, p. 15), the *Vita Antonii* began to circulate in Gaul from 370, after the arrival of Saint Athanasius in Trier. But it was not until the return of John CASSIAN and Jerome from Egypt, that is, the first years of the fifth century, that Ireland (like Great Britain and Spain) became aware of this *Vita*. Nonetheless, this suffices for many scholars to establish a relationship between Coptic and Irish art. This common point of relationship between the two countries has too easily served as a basis for affirming—without proof—that the Irish art of illumination found its source in Egypt.

Coptic Monks in Ireland

One trail, however, may lead from Egypt to Ireland. An Irish saint of the eighth century named Oengus the Culdée accorded a place in his writings to the foreign fathers, abbots and monks, buried in Ireland.

Saint Oengus or Aengus, called "le Culdée" (anchorite) because of the mortifications he inflicted upon himself as a young man, was born near the monastery founded by Saint Fintan at Clonegah in Ireland. His mysticism and profound devotion made him a remarkable poet. He left a considerable work known in Irish as *Feílire* (in Latin; *Festilogium de Sancti Aengus*). This work was not compiled in one place alone. According to E. O'Curry (Leabhar breac), Saint Aengus began his long poem at Cuil Bennchair in County Offaly, continued it at Cluain Eidhnech, and completed it during his priesthood at Tallagh. O'Curry, who spent years studying the manuscript of Aengus, thinks that it was written before, or at the very latest, in 798, as no saint who died after this date is named (Stokes, 1907, pp. 176f.).

Saint Aengus seems to have literally venerated the saints of his country. In his First Book he lists 345 bishops and 229 priests and abbots of Ireland, about whom he gives valuable information. The Second Book is known by the name of *Homonymi*, and refers to all the saints having the same name. It is divided into two parts, the first fifty chapters devoted to the holy men and the last twelve to the holy women of Ireland. The Third Book is devoted to the genealogy of the saints, while the Fourth Book treats the maternal ancestry of 210 saints. The Fifth Book, comprising part of the *Martyrology of Tallagh* and entitled *Book of Litanies* (cf. bibliography for Tallagh), is of particular interest. Here, in the form of an invocation, Saint Aengus enumerates the names of the principal saints and their disciples and introduces the names of several foreigners, among whom are some Copts who lived as hermits on the island and were buried there. In principle, this litany refers to the Oriental abbots, fathers, monks, and ecclesiastics who, attracted by Irish monasticism, lived in Ireland in the second half of the eighth century.

G. T. Stokes, the eminent specialist of Irish literature, explains that, during the iconoclastic crisis, the monks violently defied the Byzantine emperor and the iconoclasts made war against the monasteries, forcing the monks to seek refuge in the West. However, at this time, the Copts, who were under the Muslim yoke, had no relations with the iconoclastic Byzantine rulers. Thus this "exodus" cannot be connected to the iconoclastic crisis.

Conclusion

The testimony of Aengus actually offers little information about the Copts buried in Ireland during the eighth century, and it is questionable whether it explains a Coptic influence on Irish manuscripts or on the tomb of Agilbert of Jouarre (Hubert, 1967, p. 77). All these mysterious resemblances, which supposedly connect Bāwīṭ to Jouarre, or Coptic illuminations to those of Ireland, may be rather the common fruit of an awakening medieval art. Likewise, it cannot be confirmed that the Copts mentioned by Saint Aengus brought with them to Ireland any famous Coptic textiles or manuscripts that could have transmitted the idea to Irish illuminators for the decoration or iconography of their manuscripts.

Moreover, we do not know what books might have existed at the end of the eighth or beginning of the ninth century in such great Irish centers as Iona, Clonmacnoise, and Echternach, or what pictures might have inspired their painters. However, it seems logical to assume that the Celtic illuminators working in the scriptoria of Ireland profited from the experience acquired over the centuries by bronzesmiths, silversmiths, and goldsmiths, on the one hand, and by the Oriental scriptoria on the other. In fact, the influence of Syrian manuscripts might possibly be explained by the presence of the Irish in Rome (where they went in order to ascertain how the date of Easter was set) during the end of the seventh century. It is true that there must have been some exchange between Syria and Egypt in all artistic domains, including illumination. Certain elements of Coptic decoration could have slipped into Syrian illuminations and then been lost in the mass of motifs that made the Oriental manuscripts great. But this would have been very late, and in any case not before the twelfth century.

In summary, the source of a motif upon which are based nearly all the relations proposed between Irish and Coptic art—that of interlacing—is to be sought some three centuries before the Christian era. During the first centuries, interlacing and the fully illuminated page were reinforced in Europe itself by influences from Syria and Constantinople. Consequently, there is nothing to indicate any connection, in either the arrangement of the motifs or the style, to the Copts. The arrival in Ireland of an isolated group of a few Coptic monks who were buried there cannot suffice as evidence that they brought Coptic decorated textiles; direct proof is necessary, which no tomb or manuscript has yet revealed. Coptic illumination began only in the twelfth century, and there is no indication that it crossed the Mediterranean or English Channel at that time. Further, the sole knowledge of Coptic monasticism and its founders cannot furnish any kind of argument for the introduction of Coptic motifs into Ireland.

BIBLIOGRAPHY

Baltrusaitis, J. *Etudes sur l'art médieval en Géorgie et en Arménie.* Paris, 1929.

Bourguet, P. du. *Catalogue des étoffes coptes.* Musée national du Louvre. Paris, 1964.

______. *L'Art copte.* Paris, 1967.

Bouyer, L. *La Vie de saint Antoine.* Abbaye de Bellefontaine, 1950.

Cramer, M. *Koptische Buchmalerei.* Recklinghausen, 1964.

Duval, P. M. *Les Celtes.* Paris, 1977.

Duval, P. M., and V. Kruta. *L'Art celtique de la période d'expansion—IVème et IIIème siècle avant notre ère.* Geneva, 1982.

Henry, F. *Irish Art in the Early Christian Period.* London, 1940; 1947; 1965; Ithaca, N.Y., 1965.

Hubert, J. *L'Europe des invasions.* Paris, 1967; New York, 1969.

Jacobsthal, P. *Early Celtic Art,* Vols. 1 and 2. Oxford, 1944, 1969.

Klindt-Jensen, O. "Motifs orientalisants." In *L'Art celtique de la période d'expansion IVème et IIIème Siècles.* Paris, 1982.

Leroy, J. *Les Manuscrits syriaques.* Institut français d'Archéologie de Beyrouth, 1964.

Nordenfolk, C. *L'Enluminure moyen-age,* trans. Henri Stierlin and Pontus Grate. Geneva, 1988.

O'Curry, E. *Lectures on the Manuscript Materials of Ancient Irish History.* Dublin, 1861. Repr. Dublin and London, 1873; Dublin, 1878; 2 vols., New York, 1965.

Smith, R. A. "On the Basse Yutz Flagons." *Archaeologia* 79 (1929):1–12.

Stern, H. and M. Glay. *La Mosaïque gréco-romaine,* Vols. 1 and 2. Deuxième colloque international pour l'étude de la mosaïque antique. Vienna, 30 August to 4 September 1971. Paris, 1975.

Stokes, G. T. *Ireland and the Celtic Church.* London, 1907.

Tallagh. The oldest copy of the *Martyrology of Tallagh* is found in the book of Leinster. A Brussels manuscript (very incomplete), which is a copy of the *Martyrology,* was probably copied from the book of Leinster, conserved in the Franciscan monastery of Dublin. The Book of Litanies, the fifth book of the *Martyrology of Tallagh,* was translated and published in its entirety, with notes and explanations at the foot of the page, in the *Irish Ecclesiastic Record,* Vol. 8, no. 32, May-June, 1867.

MONIQUE BLANC-ORTOLAN
PIERRE DU BOURGUET, S.J.

ART, HISTORIOGRAPHY OF COPTIC.

The notion of "Coptic Art" is relatively recent. It became established only slowly, and not surprisingly it is still used with some quite diverse meanings.

In the nineteenth century, when the archaeology of the ancient civilizations was being established, it could hardly have been foreseen that a Christian minority merely tolerated in prosperous Muslim Egypt would deserve a period of its own in art history. True, outside of art, the Copts were credited with certain merits: the surge of Christian monasticism in the third and fourth centuries, which spread into the West and the Middle East; a few renowned churches and monasteries; and the preservation in some of these places of precious scriptural and patristic manuscripts. But given the history of this minority, it was unclear what works of art it could have produced. The Copts were a people who, since the fourth century B.C., had been kept down by the Ptolemaic, Roman, and Byzantine occupations, and who under the Muslim domination had been reduced from 7 million to scarcely 1 million people. They had survived only by clinging to their traditions and Christian practices, all the while devoting themselves either to menial labor or, in a few exceptional cases, to professional work of a subordinate rank. The interlude between pharaonic art and the art that began to take shape under the Muslim aegis seemed to deserve nothing more than the modest title "Coptic period," with no pretentions to being art.

A New Concept

Nevertheless, toward the end of the nineteenth century, numerous pieces of art and decorative articles, unearthed from the upper strata or environs of ancient sites, were verified by their position as being later than the principal object of the excavation, but they were not Hellenistic, Roman, or Byzantine. They could not be ignored, though some scholars, influenced by their emotions, did so. Moved by these discoveries, other art historians began to reevaluate what they could not classify as either pharaonic, Roman, Byzantine, or Muslim art.

The new concept of what may be described as Coptic art became evident in Alfred J. Butler's important inventory of Coptic churches (in 1884).

Gaston MASPERO also advanced this new concept. He opened a hall of Coptic objects in both the first and the second Egyptian Museums in Cairo, where he grouped principally decorative sculpture in relief, but he also included small pieces of all kinds that had been accumulating through the years in storage.

The identification "Coptic" made headway. In the last quarter of the nineteenth century, several collections of decorative textiles were assembled in various museums and by amateur collectors. These textiles were mostly fragments, but some were complete or almost complete; they were easy to transport and acquire; and they came from official or clandestine digs. Various DATINGS were proposed for these items: at first, the eighth and ninth centuries, and later, due to discoveries of objects in a more classical style, the Byzantine period. It was thought that the ARAB CONQUEST OF EGYPT in the middle of the seventh century had dealt the deathblow to all production of Coptic decorated textiles. Edouard Gerspach, of the Gobelins Museum in Paris, furnished the first technical studies of this weaving in 1887 and 1890, concentrating principally on tapestry.

Owing to the attention thus accorded them, acquisitions of these textiles became the object of avid research both by Alfred Gayet at Antinoopolis, at the urging of Emile Guimet, and by the Egyptian Museum in Berlin in the vicinity of Asyūṭ. Various capitals and other principal centers of scholarship in Europe eagerly sought to acquire them. The quantity discovered was so great that Emile Guimet exhibited a significant number from his museum at the Paris International Exposition of 1900, where this exhibit was one of the main attractions. Thus the value of Coptic decorative textile art was established and enhanced by exhibits, sometimes raising controversies at the Musée Guimet.

Nevertheless, if the title "Coptic" had become accepted, establishing the existence of a Coptic technique, the name was limited to one isolated genre despite the many pieces in other genres unearthed and exhibited.

The term "Coptic" doubtless attained a higher status with the appearance in the first quarter of the twentieth century of two catalogs: one from the Victoria and Albert Museum in London by Albert Franck Kendrick (1924), and the other from the Louvre in Paris by Rodolphe Pfister (1932). Both catalogs were based on solid historical criteria; the Louvre catalog included chemical analyses of the colors. A first step forward had been taken, but the tapestries and other Coptic decorated textiles continued to occupy the foremost rank in Coptic art as if nothing else existed.

Coptic architecture and its background were almost entirely ignored. In fact, as late as 1963, the Byzantine scholar Kurt Wessel, in a well-illustrated volume on Coptic art, remained supremely ignorant of this important art form, even having written in 1962 that Coptic architecture as such did not exist. Concurrently, official scholarly circles scarcely considered the relations between the genre of the Coptic textiles and that of Coptic architectural decoration, not to mention other objects in other techniques, such as CERAMICS, METALWORKS, GLASS (decorated or plain), ornamented leather, WOOD, and PAINTING (mural or panel). It was not that discoveries in these domains were lacking, for the excavations had furnished abundant items. But the museums and collectors invariably restricted themselves to decorated textiles, and every reference to Coptic art meant, even among the best informed, nothing other than Coptic textiles. This limited view is still frequently met. Even today, when speaking of Coptic art, beginners scarcely think of anything beyond decorated textiles.

Four Endeavors

However, there were four endeavors (one already noted above), guided by a larger vision, that were to be decisive in expanding the notion of Coptic art. These were based on a complete reclassification—built around the success of the classification of Coptic decorated textiles—of other genres heretofore left in isolation or treated with a disdain hardly compatible with a healthy notion of archaeology.

The first endeavor, Maspero's initiative, has already been mentioned. Taking a lesson from the facts, he had proceeded to group decorative items in stone that he considered to be Coptic in an exhibition hall and also in the storerooms of the Egyptian Museum in Cairo; with these articles he exhibited other, smaller objects that he thought could be related to this collection. Thereby he proved to be a precursor. The substantial catalog of these items prepared in 1904 by Josef Strzygowski recorded the results in a masterful fashion. By setting these architectural elements—sculpted or painted—in juxtaposition, Maspero revealed the ties of Coptic architecture to Coptic decorative art.

Following closely upon Maspero's initiative, was the second endeavor. The French Institute of Oriental Archaeology in Cairo excavated from 1901–1903 at BĀWĪṬ in Middle Egypt and published its findings about the monuments it discovered and their decoration. The institute was able to send to the Egyptian Museum in Cairo, and to donate to the Louvre, a substantial group of architectural decorations from a single site. The excavations resumed by Jean Maspero in 1912 added to this group. Beginning in 1907, Georges Bénédite, conservator of the Egyptian Section of the Louvre, operating from the same premise as the institute and Maspero, but applying it to other genres, increased the number and variety of objects in the Coptic collection by massive and repeated purchases made during nearly twenty years in Egypt.

In 1908 occurred the third endeavor, when the Coptic collector MURQUS SIMAYKAH began to assemble and constantly increase examples of every Coptic genre. In 1920 he founded the privately owned Coptic Museum, which he opened to the public.

The fourth endeavor was that of the Egyptian Museum in Berlin, which, either by purchases or excavations, notably in the region of Asyūṭ, assembled a varied collection of Coptic articles. These were described in the imposing catalog of Coptic and Byzantine objects that appeared in 1914, edited by O. K. Wulff.

Classification and Acquisition

In the history of the notion of Coptic art, the following period, from 1910 until the 1960s, was a time of reflection and classification. Meanwhile, acquisitions continued, mainly in the principal official collections already in existence.

A clear debate about Coptic textiles produced the first attempts at classification. Representations of persons and decorative motifs based on plants and/or animals were, for the most part, considered to be of Greek, Roman, Hellenistic, or sometimes Byzantine origin. This was a period when archaeological excavations still pursued prestigious and picturesque discovery at the expense of studying the site and its environs. Purchases of objects from clandestine diggings—the by-products of a search for organic or calcareous sediments useful for fertilizer—offered no firmer scientific certainty. As yet, the dating of an object could be based only on style and its evolution. In this regard, comparisons with classical art and its own modifications over the centuries could offer approximate dating. It is on such information that Wulff and W. F. Volbach in Berlin, A. F. Kendrick in London, and R. Pfister in Paris based their thinking; Pfister confirmed his data with analyses of the colors and their respective origins. Three periods came to be distinguished: an almost classical and Roman period (third to fifth centuries), a Byzantine and Christian period (six to seventh centuries), and an antique Muslim period (seventh to eighth centuries). The substitution of lac (a dye made from an insect imported from India) for madder to make the red color needed to obtain purple notably supported Pfister's hypothesis about the antique Muslim period.

In Cairo, important progress was made in assembling and enlarging the collections by the transfer of the Coptic collection in the Egyptian Museum to the Coptic Museum, which, by royal decree, had become a national museum in 1931 and henceforth eligible to receive and catalog all Coptic items deriving from excavations, official purchases, and gifts.

In 1928 the Louvre opened two Greco-Roman halls—one of which was called the Bāwīṭ Hall—exhibiting articles from Egypt that could be considered Coptic, that is, Egyptian-Byzantine. The majority consisted of a series of decorative mural reliefs from excavations of the churches of Bāwīṭ, as well as several dozen items purchased by G. Bénédite. This remained only the embryo of a separate collection, but it publicly demonstrated an advance toward developing such a collection. This assemblage of objects, which represented the essential art forms of a people, if not of a civilization, finally brought a recognition of the Copts' distinctive way of life.

However, the question arose of whether Coptic collections concerned art—with all that this implies as to depth, variety, and sound originality creating a unique aesthetic—or an ensemble of customs borrowed from the great civilizations that had successively dominated, first, Coptic Egypt, and then the Coptic community to which it was reduced.

As has been noted, INSCRIPTIONS in the Coptic language—and traceable to the Coptic people—and the manner of treating subjects in art permitted (and continue to permit) a far greater number of monuments and objects to be grouped together than history would have indicated; this number would include tens of thousands of still surviving ancient monuments and objects, as well as equal numbers that have been destroyed, as documents keep revealing. By virtue of size alone, Coptic productions from the third to the thirteenth centuries are as considerable as they are varied, far exceeding those of other regions under Roman, Byzantine, and later Muslim domination. Indeed, this is the only group of artistic objects to constitute a patrimony distinguished by its traits as well as by its continuity.

But a problem crucial to archaeology arose. As the number and variety of objects grew, it proved increasingly necessary to make dating more precise—insofar as possible and in a general way—and first of all, to establish the actual continuity of this patrimony.

As early as 1887 Edouard Gerspach had regarded the production of Coptic textiles at Antinoopolis as lasting from the fifth to the twelfth centuries. Common opinion soon afterward decided, perhaps arbitrarily, that this production ceased in the seventh to eighth centuries. However, in 1954, an analysis of a collection by Pierre du Bourguet confirmed Gerspach's hypothesis and assigned a number of important pieces—until then relegated to the seventh to eighth centuries—to the centuries following, up to and including the thirteenth. In 1959, John Beckwith, beginning with some significant pieces, reviewed the entire chronology of Coptic textiles, adding other arguments to these new data. Thus, as far as textiles were concerned, the Coptic patrimony proved to extend from the third to the twelfth centuries.

The most extensive display of this legacy was in Cairo in the Coptic Museum. All the important genres were represented there, some in unequaled number. These included (1) sculptures in relief obtained from transfer of objects from the Egyptian Museum and augmented notably in 1943 by items from the Nilometer in Rodah; (2) a ceramic collection of decorated vases, of all sizes and in considerable quantity; (3) wooden furniture and chests, of which many were encrusted with ivory or mother-of-pearl; (4) the usual objects in ivory and bone; (5) mural paintings of Christian subjects; (6) painted panels depicting saints or religious themes; and (7) illuminated manuscripts. In sum, there was in Cairo a veritable microcosm of Coptic art, which, owing to the enlightened administration of succeeding directors, has become an increasingly important tourist attraction.

Exhibitions Outside Egypt

A new understanding of Coptic art had emerged, but it was difficult to grasp in the scattered collections. Then, in 1960, at the urging of Volbach, the idea was born to present the reality of Coptic art at several places in Europe in a large collection. Volbach succeeded in interesting the Cultural Center of the Villa Hügel at Essen, which, in turn, made agreements with three other museums: the Kunsthaus of Zurich, the Academy of Fine Arts of Vienna, and the Louvre (Section of Christian Antiquities). Four exhibitions were arranged, with items assembled from the majority of the existing collections. These exhibitions lasted from April 1963 to October 1964 and were held at Essen—where the catalog was prefaced with a series of articles written by various specialists in the categories represented—Zurich, Vienna, and finally Paris. The first three exhibitions followed the same organization, while at Paris, in the Petit Palais, most of the items of these three exhibitions were combined with a large number of valuable pieces from the collections of the Louvre. Awareness of the ancient Coptic reality was no longer confined to Egypt, and from Europe awareness spread to the rest of the world, including Japan. The initiative of Volbach and the Villa Hügel had made history.

Since that time, there have been countless visiting exhibitions of Coptic objects in Europe and North America, with the emphasis on textiles. In addition, many museums on these two continents brought their Coptic textiles out of storage and, after restoration and mounting, accorded them special showcases in their permanent exhibition halls.

The question of the dating of Coptic textiles, only approximated to this time, now became acute; the 1964 exhibition at the Petit Palais had, in particular, rekindled interest in the problem. Articles from collections all over the world lent to the Villa Hügel at Essen had been grouped according to genre, with the date for each piece being that indicated by the lender. In nearly every case, there was no date later than the eighth century, and often the dates varied somewhat for similar items of the same style but coming from a different lender. This same method of grouping was followed in the succeeding exhibitions in Zurich and Vienna. The division by category was maintained in Paris, but duplicates badly dated by such division and of little interest were eliminated; the addition of other, significant articles from the collection of the Louvre increased the artistic value of the presentation and brought valuable pieces into the limelight, arousing the curiosity of the viewers. A substantial preface to the catalog by Pfister, du Bourguet, and Beckwith called attention to the Louvre contributions and included a summary of the Copts' history, traced the principal lines of Coptic art and presented a well-marked chronology clearly and articulately. As a result, dates were indicated on the notices accompanying each object or on larger panels. There were differences of opinion on particular points, but the coherence of such a complete and continuous display became itself an argument for the notion of Coptic art and was striking because of its rigor as well as its novelty.

The Paris exhibition had benefited from the analyses and conclusions by du Bourguet and Beckwith regarding the extension of Coptic decorated textile production beyond the eighth century, a limit then commonly accepted for Coptic works as a whole. The exhibition expanded this limit to the thirteenth century. This was a minor revolution and returned to the position previously advanced by Gerspach and other early analysts of Coptic objects. After Gerspach, simplistic conclusions based on the Arab conquest of Egypt in 641 had swept away his original idea, based as it was on good sense, as if the established customs and mentality, indeed the very life of a populous country with traditions thousands of years old, could be overthrown by a single, or almost single, blow.

In 1963, Beckwith confirmed for sculpture the brief chronology that he had formerly proposed for decorated textiles; this he presented in a large and well-chosen panorama of Coptic sculpture.

In 1964, du Bourguet, in turn, published the catalog of half of the Coptic textile collection of the Louvre, in which 1,500 pieces—complete or fragmentary, each with a commentary and photo on the facing page—were classified century by century, according to then known criteria. After a short account of the entry of various groups of pieces into the Louvre, his introduction added other data furnished by the most extensive study of Coptic weaving up to that date. The principles of the classification preceded the catalog itself.

These two authoritative publications marked a new step forward by pushing the terminal date of Coptic art five centuries forward, from the eighth to the thirteenth century. No longer could Coptic art be considered as ending with the Arab conquest. Already considerable in space by its production, it became considerable in time as well.

The variety of genres produced by the Copts could no longer be denied; they were comparable by their multiplicity to those of any other civilization. Nor could the duration of Coptic art to the thirteenth century be ignored.

The Question of an Original Totality

But one last problem surfaced: To what degree did an original totality emerge from the traits displayed in this collection of works, a totality whose aesthetic—if it existed—could allow the products of Coptic civilization to claim the prerogatives of an art in the proper sense of the term? In order to understand the question fully, a brief review of the periods of Coptic art is necessary.

Greco-Roman themes—dating from early in the eighth century B.C. and then increasing during the Ptolemaic period (332–31 B.C.)—became predominant, if not exclusive, after the Roman conquest of the Nile Valley. This transformation was facilitated by the detachment of the population from the pharaonic religion starting in the first millennium B.C. and their attraction to a newer religion more closely related to the changes and realities of the moment. Nor was this shift, in fact, an isolated movement. It followed the expansion of the Greeks, then the Macedonians, and finally the Romans in the Mediterranean world. Egypt, as much because of its territorial importance as its 7 million inhabitants or its civilization many thousands of years old, changed its course more slowly than other Mediterranean countries. This change was completed when the first Coptic productions appeared in the third century.

Thus, an almost total Greco-Roman, or even Hellenistic, influence was both natural and undeniable, though it is essential to note that the Greco-Roman ascendancy affected the themes of art only. These were reworked and inwardly transformed. The Greek gods had begun to overtake the pharaonic gods, for example, in large and small statues. But behind the forms of Dionysus and Aphrodite, the Egyptians, while adopting some attributes of these gods, continued to see Osiris and Isis. Moreover, Aphrodite was also persistently confused with Mut and Hathor.

Alongside the official art, whose modifications were evident in the great sanctuaries and principal cities, similar programs and coarser features appeared in the rural centers; these were to be seen in the smaller temples (which would become more numerous in the countryside) and in the objects and representations belonging to a given cult. Herein lay the beginnings of Coptic productions, still expressive of an artisan order, perpetuating a craft descended from a very long popular tradition and expressed in numerous objects. This was the work of pagan Egyptians, but they could qualify as Copts because, since the second century B.C., hieroglyphs had progressively given way to the Greek alphabet (though some signs derived from pharaonic demotic writing were kept for certain sounds), and the language, while maintaining its pharaonic structure, was loaded with a small group of Greek terms borrowed first from the administrative vocabulary and then bit by bit from the religious vocabulary of Christians—words derived mostly from koine Greek. It was therefore natural to see in these Coptic productions a secondary branch of Hellenistic art, above all in the pagan works, for Christian works became preponderant only in the middle of the fifth century A.D.

This was the position held by a number of scholars. It may be explained by what preceded and is even corroborated by tendencies that are almost similar, though due to different causes, in other Mediterranean countries. For example, in North Africa, a dependency on the Hellenistic style is clear. But Roman influences modified the classic workmanship by stylizing it into a sort of abstraction at the expense of the Hellenistic harmony. As emperors from the senatorial ranks were replaced by emperors from the equestrian and provincial classes (for example, Heliogabalus in the early third century was of Syrian origin), the old aesthetic requirements weakened, and a simplification and stiffness of form resulted. In fact, one could scarcely continue to speak of style and even less of uniform style.

In Egypt, still largely pagan in the first century A.D., Greco-Roman themes became more marked by Alexandrian elegance. The human figure, whether sculpted or painted, was altered not so much by the stiffness noted above as by modifications in proportion. These modifications, small at first, were not made at the expense of elegance but rather reinforced it. They kept increasing in size in order to emphasize a part of the body or some of its lines or even only the direction of the gaze. In decoration based on animal or plant motifs, stylization mechanized the forms by sacrificing the concrete—which was reduced to a mere pretext—to decorative invention of an astonishing quality. Very early, from the fourth century onward, a special feature often characterized sculpture in relief. The two surfaces were forcibly opposed by being cut at right angles. This opposition boldly altered the model, and by contrasting the two levels—of which the outer one was itself flattened—produced a striking effect of projecting, by means of shadow, the essential elements of the subject into the light. Very soon, an analogous procedure was adapted to artworks using color, notably in painting and decorated textiles. Here the surfaces of different colors were juxtaposed abruptly and directly, with the darker colors being suppressed to give a trompe l'oeil effect, and thereby accentuating the harmony or differentiation of the forms and other components. The result was a vigor unequaled elsewhere.

This double tendency—one toward creative disproportion to achieve emphasis, the other toward a decorative fantasy—may appear here and there in other provincial or official arts of this period around the Mediterranean. But in Egypt, this tendency was systematic and followed its own evolution. Thus, after the Arab conquest, the human figure was only vaguely suggested by a series of parallel lines, leaving no more than the indication of a pose or fixed look. This tendency also led to decorative fantasy in plant and animal forms, which soon became indistinguishable from one another.

This movement was intrinsic and not related to the Hellenistic style. Whereas Hellenistic art lost its strength in the seventh century due to neglect of execution of forms (such as appears, for example, in the ivories of the pulpit at Aix-la-Chapelle), Coptic art was distinguished from Hellenistic art in its vigor and inventive fecundity, all the while continuing its thrust many centuries beyond the seventh, which marked the end of Alexandrian art.

Because architecture is treated elsewhere (see ARCHITECTUAL ELEMENTS OF CHURCHES), let it suffice here to note that the Coptic borrowing of the BASILICA from Greco-Roman art was made with profound modifications of the model. Borrowing is not copying when it modifies; it is, rather, an assimilation and contributes to a new art. This preponderance of the idea in relation to the forms and this zeal for decoration tempt one to propose a resurgence in Coptic art of the fundamental tendencies inherited from pharaonic art but in a more moderate degree and via Greco-Roman themes.

One other influence, the Byzantine, has been proposed as having affected Coptic work and as being at the source of some of its successes. This notion has been accepted to such a degree that certain Byzantine specialists—and not the least among them—relegate these Egyptian works, when some merits are found in them, to the Byzantine patrimony.

The allegation, already too widespread, that everything Mediterranean dating from the first centuries A.D. must be attributed entirely to early Latin art is no more than an idea; Mediterranean here includes paleo-Christian art, which however, was already clearly distinct in the third and fourth centuries. The claim that locates Coptic art in the realm of Byzantine art—while naturally rejecting everything that lacks the stamp of harmony—has no support. The only fact that one might try to advance in favor of this idea is that the Byzantine occupation of Egypt from the middle of the fourth century to the middle of the seventh century would have determined the quality of works of art. It is true that Egypt was occupied by the Byzantines before the middle of the fifth century. However, the art that was to become Byzantine had not yet left Constantinople. Coptic genres, from architecture to sculpture and painting, and including the minor arts, notably the decorated textiles with their distinctive tendencies (some of value), had already been implanted on Egyptian soil in all their authenticity. During the period of the Byzantine occupation, Coptic art successfully maintained its driving force, while Justinian's art was just beginning to establish itself, gloriously to be sure, but with its own particular tendencies. The only borrowing that Coptic art could have made from Constantinople is the basket-capital; this is not impossible, but the basket-capital itself originated in the Libyan art of the third and fourth centuries and thus influenced Byzantine art. Moreover, Egypt lies adjacent to Libya and could have adopted its themes and genres directly. The relations between Christian Egypt and the Byzantine Empire, and therefore with Byzantine art, were never restored (even until recent centuries), except by the Syrians in the eleventh century, and this concerned only rare works of a secondary order. Furthermore, the Christian outlooks of Egypt and Byzantium, differed so much that Byzantine specialists do not claim as Byzantine any Coptic works after the seventh century.

Once these prejudices can be set aside, the notion of Coptic art becomes self-evident. It is then necessary, in effect, to recognize its authenticity and its quality, both of which are based upon the variety of its genres in an imposing mass of artworks, and upon the marked and autonomous tendencies whose refinement and decorative invention cannot be denied. Given these facts, the output of Coptic art—even if it has not attained the level of the greatest art—must be recognized as an authentic art with all its prerogatives and—in spite of its weaknesses, which the most prestigious art has—all its value.

Some people still have reservations. However, the more than precarious situation of the Egyptians during this long period of Roman and Byzantine and Muslim domination did not prevent them from showing their originality in language and literature; nor did it keep them from triumph in founding monasticism and in aesthetic thought. In fact, it was precisely under the aegis of the church—in itself a stifling circumstance—that they were about to establish their own elite: monks and ecclesiastics, artisans of all kinds, sculptors and painters, architects and masons (to whom the Muslims turned, even outside Egypt), small landowners, and even village notables.

Copts have succeeded in imposing themselves even in other domains. Thus it is not surprising to find that they constituted their own art. Even Byzantine art historians have not hesitated—despite the improbabilities—to place Coptic works among the best examples of Byzantine production. The fundamental objection to this is that they judge all the art of this period according to classical norms. By now, if considered from a broader perspective, Coptic art could be viewed as a precursor to modern art. The conclusion is that Coptic art—modest in proportions but with full rights—merits recognition as an art worthy of the name.

BIBLIOGRAPHY

Beckwith, J. "Les Tissus coptes." *Cahiers Ciba,* 7, no. 83 (1959).

______. *Coptic Sculpture.* London, 1963.

Bourguet, P. du "La Fabrication des tissus coptes a-t-elle largement survécu à la conquête arabe?" *Bulletin de la Société archéologique d'Alexandrie* 40 (1953):1-31.

______. "Die koptische Kunst als mögliche Erbin der pharaonischen Kunst." *Koptische Kunst, Christentum am Nil.* Catalogue of the Exhibition at the Villa Hügel. Essen, 1963, pp. 122-30.

______. *L'Art copte.* Paris, 1964.

______. *Catalogue des étoffes coptes.* Musée du Louvre, Paris, 1964.

______. *L'Art paléochrétien.* Amsterdam, 1970.

______. *Peintures chrétiennes: Couleurs paléochrétiennes, coptes et byzantines.* Histoire universelle de la peinture. Geneva, 1980.

Butler, A. J. *The Ancient Churches of Egypt.* Oxford, 1884.

Chassinat, E. *Fouilles à Baouit.* Mémoirs de l'Institut français d'Archéologie orientale 13. Cairo, 1911.

Clédat, J. *Le Monastère et la nécropole de Baouit.* Mémoires de l'Institut français d'Archéologie orientale 12 and 39. Cairo, 1904 and 1916.

Gayet, A. *Notice relative aux objets recueillis à Antinoé pendant les fouilles exécutées en 1899-1900.* Paris, 1902-1907.

Gerspach, E. "Les tapisseries coptes du Musée des Gobelins." *Gazette des Beaux-Arts* no. 362 (1887).

______. *Les tapisseries coptes.* Paris, 1890.

Ghali, M.B. "Marcus Simaika Pacha (1864-1944)." *Bulletin de la Société d'archéologie copte* 10 (1944):267-69.

Kendrick, A. F. *Catalogue of Textiles from Burying-grounds in Egypt.* London, 1920-1922.

Koptische Kunst. Christentum am Nil. Catalog of the exhibition at the Villa Hügel. Essen, 1963.

Maspero, J. *Fouilles exécutées à Baouit.* Mémoires de l'Institut français d'Archéologie orientale 59. Cairo, 1932.

Munier, H. "Gaston Maspéro et les études coptes." *Bulletin de la Société d'archéologie copte* 1 (1935):27-36.

Munier, H., and G. Wiet. "L'Egypte byzantine et musulmane." *Précis de l'histoire d'Egypte par divers historiens et archéologues,* Vol. 11. Cairo, 1932-1935.

Pfister, R. "Teinture et alchimie dans l'Orient hellénistique." *Seminarium Kondakovianum* 7 (1935):1-59.

Strzygowski, J. *Koptische Kunst.* Catalogue général des antiquités égyptiennes du Musée du Caire. Vienna, 1904.

Wessel, K. *Kunst der Kopten.* Sammlung des Ikonenmuseums Recklinghausen. Recklinghausen, 1962.

______. *Koptische Kunst, Die Spätantike in Ägypten.* Recklinghausen, 1963.

Wulff, O. K. *Altchristliche und byzantinische Athenaion,* 2 vols. Berlin-Neubabelsberg, 1914.

PIERRE DU BOURGUET, S. J.

ART AND ARCHITECTURE, COPTIC.

Coptic art and architecture span no less than ten centuries, from the third century to the thirteenth. This is a remarkable length of time, inasmuch as the conditions in which they were born and developed would seem to have worked against a consistent development over so long a period. This article surveys the sculpture, painting, architecture, ceramics, and textiles of Coptic Egypt. See also ARCHITECTURAL ELEMENTS OF CHURCHES; BONE AND IVORY CARVING, COPTIC; BOOK DECORATION, COPTIC; CERAMICS, COPTIC; GLASS, COPTIC; METALWORK, COPTIC; PAINTING, COPTIC; PORTRAITURE, COPTIC; TEXTILES, COPTIC; WOODWORK, COPTIC. For the art and architecture of cities and monasteries see under the name of the city or fo the monastery, which is listed as DAYR. . . .

Historical Origins

In the first century B.C. the 7 million Copts were by far the largest population of the time and of the area, but three centuries of Ptolemaic rule (332 to 31 B.C.) had dispossessed them of their lands as well as most of their rights. The elite had been unseated and the ancient pharaonic pantheon had been submerged beneath new Greek gods. The Egyptians received but a few crumbs from the table of those in command: small pieces of land with their humble farms, the crafts of rural artisans, and certain subordinate positions in the administration. Only the pagan clergy, whose duties and culture most nearly approached those of the Macedonian ruling class, was able to maintain its position. The population as a whole was composed mostly of fellahin (farm laborers) and small craftsmen, destined to

Corinthian capital. Dayr Apa Jeremiah (Saqqara). *Courtesy Coptic Museum, Cairo.*

nourish and serve the occupying forces and pay taxes to them.

This state of affairs both worsened and improved slightly under the Roman occupation (30 B.C.–340 A.D.). After his victory over Mark Antony's and Cleopatra's rebellion, Octavian denied Egypt the status of a Roman province and reserved the country's production of grain for Rome, for which it became the imperial granary. He established the tax of the *annona* (grain), which placed in his hands the essentials for nourishing and maintaining the people of Rome, the source of his imperial power. Egypt was thus bled white. In comparison to the other Roman provinces, the Egyptians were governed by a separate statute, and for a long time they could not attain the rank of Roman citizens.

Nonetheless, certain advantages left from the preceding Ptolemaic rule remained intact: the small landholdings as well as the activities of the ateliers in the villages and small towns. Such ateliers were located near one or several temples of a size proportionate to that of the community and still served by the priests of the pharaonic religion. For the most part, representations of the Greco-Roman gods replaced those of the Egyptian gods, but behind these figures bearing foreign names and even new attributes, the Egyptians continued to honor in their minds and hearts the divinities from pharaonic times. Further, the subordinate duties of the administration were increasingly confided to the Egyptians, with resulting possibilities for their advancement. Thereby, the traditions of millennia were perpetuated in the techniques of the craftsmen and the agricultural civilization so firmly anchored near the Nile, and the priest, who was always more or less a scribe, found it easier to write his language (a language inherited from pharaonic times with some administrative terms added) in Greek characters rather than in demotic Egyptian. In the third century A.D. the anomaly of the Egyptians' position began to disappear. Among those Egyptians recruited as auxiliaries of the Roman legions, veterans gained Roman citizenship on personal grounds and thereby received the right to own and transmit property and acquire high positions in the village.

At the end of the third century, Christianity, which had probably been established at Alexandria during the first century and had spread gradually westward and southward, brought a new and vigorous possibility for religious buildings and representations. This occurred not only in its churches, still few in number, but also through the development of monasticism. Christianity continued to expand during the fourth century, as it achieved official acceptance, and contributed in an important way to the elevation not so much of the standard of living as of a civilizing spirit.

Therefore, in a milieu where material misery reigned more acutely than anywhere else, a small elite never ceased to keep its head above water, and thanks to the new and ardent élan of Christianity, this group did not hesitate to enrich its productions with architectural and decorative value.

Period of Diverse Tendencies (First to Late Third Century)

The Greeks, and later the Romans, were attracted by the still numerous manifestations of pharaonic art. In religious architecture, the political rulers encouraged the building of temples to Egyptian divinities by presenting themselves as, if not successors, at least the representatives of the god Horus, from whom the Egyptian dynasties were said to descend. Hence, along with the temples, a *mammisi* (birthplace) of the god Horus was erected, which perpetuated his divine power through the new rulers. They kept the general plan of the pharaonic temples and modified mainly the façades by constructing walls of intercolumniation with engraved scenes; this in effect overburdened the front of the building. But the introduction of the three-zoned Corinthian capital, in which the acanthus leaf was replaced by the palm and various other plants of

Egypt, was an artistic success; the only success among these transformations, it was much more an Egyptian assimilation than it was a borrowing.

The exterior and interior walls of temples were laden with scenes and hieroglyphic inscriptions, valuable for the knowledge of the liturgy but serious obstacles to the soberness of the work. The poses of the figures sculpted in relief suffered from the attempt to inject into a two-dimensional art substitutes for the third dimension: foreshortenings that resulted in discordance and a turgidity of forms that acted as a trompe l'oeil. The spectator is constantly shocked while perusing the walls of the great temples of Dandarah, Idfū, and Philae. This hybrid style, which may employ the Greek tunic even to clothe subjects from the pharaonic tradition (as in vintage scenes, for example), is also found in tomb decorations (as in the tomb of Petosiris at Tūnah al-Jabal in Middle Egypt).

Sculpture inherited these turgid forms from the Ptolemaic period, but during the Roman era, it turned toward the robust realism of the time in both religious and civil statues.

The same may be said of painting as in the Rape of Proserpine found in a funerary chapel from the Roman period at Tūnah al-Jabal.

A certain number of funerary objects—treated in a harmonious fashion in the best examples, but more often rather awkward and coarse—bear witness to an attraction, particularly for the Romans, of the rites of Egyptian antiquity. These items may be grouped into two typical categories. The first comprises the linens of mummies; a linen in the Louvre shows a Roman full-face, clothed in a toga, on a boat connecting the two worlds. He is juxtaposed to his own mummy, which is wrapped in bandages, standing, and being introduced into the underworld by Anubis, who places his right arm around the mummy's shoulders in a protective gesture. The second category comprises Romano-Egyptian portraits painted on wood and placed above the head of the mummy but still visible under the bandages covering the rest of the body. The style is "Pompeian," dating from various periods from the second to the fourth centuries, but the rite—even the carved head of the sarcophagus being replaced by a painted portrait—is generally a borrowing by the veterans of the Roman legions. The sources of their models thus were drawn from Egypt and Rome. This is also the case on a large scale in a Roman funerary chapel at Tūnah al-Jabal, where a lady is pictured almost full-face, wearing Roman clothes and with curly hair falling upon her shoulders, upon whom Horus and Toth (their names in hieroglyphics) pour the purifying ritual lustration.

The Ptolemies and the Romans also introduced into Egypt architectural programs and artisans' techniques that were adopted by the Copts. The basilica has its antecedents at the pilgrimage center of ABŪ MĪNĀ in the northwest desert, as well as at

Orpheus and Eurydice. Limestone sculpture. Ahnāsyah. Third century. *Courtesy Coptic Museum, Cairo.*

Orpheus with lyre. Ahnāsyah. Third century. *Courtesy Coptic Museum, Cairo.*

Hermopolis Magna (see al-ASHMŪNAYN). The arcade work has its origins in Rome and must have passed from there into Egypt, thanks to the direct relations created by the expansion of the grain tax. Terracotta was introduced from Rome, as was the building of walls by stacking rows of bricks layer by layer upon wooden beams. Encaustic painting on wood may have had a Roman origin, as might be indicated by the Latin custom of depicting images representing the dead in procession.

The Ptolemies were responsible for the importation of sheep and the use of wool, which tended to replace the linen that had been exclusively used under the pharaohs, when clothing woven from animal fiber was considered impure and hence prohibited. Such a change was permitted by the weakening of the pharaonic religious requirements. Tapestry decoration and its technical processes seem to have come from Syria, notably from Palmyra, as may be seen from the bands of decorative plant motifs on the clothing of funerary statues dating from the second century A.D.; this was perhaps due to the exchanges of Roman occupation troops within the two countries.

These diverse contributions increased the Egyptians' possibilities for decoration inherited from their ancestors in various techniques such as ceramics and glass (with or without decoration), mural paintings (as well as painting and sculpture on plaster or wood), embossed metals, and carved ivory. Nevertheless, the Egyptians of this period did not produce mosaic. Apparently it was held in honor only in Roman circles in Alexandria or the great provincial cities. The reason probably lies in the high cost and great amount of time required by this craft, a luxury beyond the means of the Egyptians at that period, who were limited to less expensive techniques (as were the Byzantines themselves during times of difficulty).

In summary, this was a period of transition and contrast between the two civilizations that successively settled in Egypt; transition and contrast also marked the concepts, as well as the artisans' techniques, still in existence and widespread on Egyptian soil. This circumstance suggests several observations.

In architecture, only the basilica was introduced, and it was reserved at first for Roman civil edifices (Hermopolis Magna) and later (fourth century) for imperial religious constructions. It seems that the pagan temples in the great centers and small towns kept their traditional forms. Some churches existed in Egypt before 260—as is attested by the edict of Gallenus, which returned the churches to the Christians—but their plan is not known.

Greek or Roman figures and architectural elements were justaposed with those of Egypt in rather large numbers, but many did not go much further. Actually, and this is important, the majority of these

Bust of a man with palmyran beard. *Courtesy Coptic Museum, Cairo.*

juxtapositions are to be imputed to the Greeks (for example, a cult of Isis supplied in Greek fashion with "initiation mysteries") and to the Romans (for example, elements of funerary rites or even the adoption of representations of Egyptian gods, which might be deformed in a most disgraceful way). There was no reciprocation from the Egyptians, except, as has been noted, for the Corinthian capital, which a Greek, not seeing any acanthus leaves, may not have recognized.

"Egyptomania" flowed once again north of the Mediterranean, where the Isis cult flourished in numerous sanctuaries. The Nile god was to become the central figure, for example, in a fourth-century mosaic at Palestrina, Italy. Much earlier the portrayal of this great divinity had tempted Alexandrian artists, one of whom depicted a bust of him in a tapestry medallion dating from the end of the second century (Pushkin Museum, Moscow). This piece, by its very delicate shadings, is a good illustration of the close dependence during this preliminary period upon Hellenistic art by the Egyptian artists, who were quite able to adapt themselves to it. The Nile was not only a god; its waters were inhabited with fish frolicking and participating in its divine life. The heavy shadows underlining the lower part of their bodies are imitated in a Pompeian manner and betray a Greco-Roman naturalism.

But in return, during this period in Egypt, the Greek and Roman divinities were, via Alexandria and the provincial centers, gradually supplanting their Egyptian counterparts except for Isis, but this was true only in the Greco-Roman milieus. Once again the Egyptians made their choices, but it was not a question of one pantheon replacing another. Artemis, Daphne, the Three Graces, Hercules, Mithra, Orpheus, Pan, Serapis, the Phoenix, Leda with the Swan—all appear from time to time. Here and there one finds subjects borrowed from Hellenistic mythology: pastoral figures, the Seasons, the Victories supporting an *imago* (a Roman bust) in its crown of laurel, the Parthian horseman or hunter, and the gladiator. However, the subjects that most often recur are (1) Dionysus, Aphrodite with Cupid, the birth of Aphrodite (Aphrodite anadyomene), with or without their respective entourages of bacchantes or Nereids and Tritons; (2) dancers, alone or in pairs; and (3) a Nereid, alone or joined with another, all frequently placed in a continuous decorative scheme of plants and animals. Such a preponderance of Dionysus and Aphrodite was certainly the result of a choice, and beneath the traits of these two gods, or in the evocation of one or the other by some figure from their retinues, it is respectively Osiris and Isis who are evoked. Certain distinctive traits identifying Dionysus or Aphrodite in Greek mythology occasionally enrich that of Egypt, but undeniably behind the Greek masks, it is the Egyptian religion and reflexes that are perpetuated. The pharaonic conceptions, not to mention the artisans' techniques and professions, continued to underlie the ideology of the Egyptians at this time, just as the basic structure and vocabulary of the pharaonic language are to be found behind the letters of the Greek alphabet. The Egyptians surrendered, but they abandoned nothing of their ancestral mentality. (See MYTHOLOGICAL SUBJECTS IN COPTIC ART.)

The First Glimmers of Coptic Art (from the End of the Third Century to the First Half of the Fifth Century). Except for the plans and decorations of the great temples and the structure of temples in the small cities, pharaonic art had been completely submerged, to the point of disappearing, by the subjects and forms of another civilization. However, in these new forms, an Egyptian art was discovering itself. It issued from levels of society that, though not always rooted in the masses, were subjected no less to the power of the occupiers. The majority of these forces were pagan; consequently, the figures and decorations came to be borrowed (within an ambiance that still was and would long remain sacred) from the predominant religion of the Mediterranean, that of the Roman empire. Although a Christian minority had surely existed from the second century and very likely from the first century, especially in the north of Egypt, at the beginning of this period the Christians were still subjected to a regime of persecution from which they were not to be liberated until the first quarter of the fourth century. They were not yet capable of inventing their own figurative or decorative motifs; there were scarcely any Christian subjects to be found. The mass of themes and decorations continued for the most part to be borrowed from Greco-Roman mythology, although some were marked with the Christian cross. This predominance of Greco-Roman mythological subjects was common to both Christian and pagan Egyptians of this period, for except in religion, they had a common outlook. This can be seen by an appellation given them much later by the conquering Arabs: "Copt," a word that in modern times has become a convenient label to distinguish them first from the occupying Romans and then from the Byzantines. This name is all the more appropriate for both Christian and pagan Egyptians because they spoke the language of pharaonic times (taking into account its evolution to that moment), but with the Greek alphabet substituted for demotic. One may ask if this was the result of the religious freedom, without economic improvement, introduced by Constantine.

Greco-Roman elegance and often picturesque grace were hardly perpetuated in Hellenistic art except in Alexandria; the works excavated in the rest of the country—and thereby produced by Copts, who were for the most part pagan—display pronounced and significant distortions. A sort of detachment emerged in Egypt in relation to the classical imperatives, and one can see therein the first signs of a new perspective. Because it first and most evidently appeared in sculpture, this medium may serve as a guide for analyzing the others.

Sculpture. With the exception of some magic dolls and a multitude of figurines of mixed mythology (such as Aphrodite-Isis-Hathor, Eros or Hercules, and many others), statuary was extremely rare; there were only a few pieces among the Coptic productions. This was common throughout the Mediterranean. Though statuary had taken root earlier in Egypt than elsewhere and was to continue for centuries, three-dimensional representation gradually went out of style. Nonetheless, one may cite a limestone statuette of an auxiliary of a Roman legion in the Louvre, Paris: he was a typically Egyptian face, but the necessary short Roman haircut characteristic of the later third or beginning of the fourth century.

Statuary was replaced by relief in Coptic sculpture in very clear stages; each stage was marked by exemplary items in limestone, a unique situation in the productions of this period. It will suffice to outline the succession.

The birth of Aphrodite in an archivolt from AHNAS AL-MADĪNAH (Coptic Museum, Cairo) breaks from the Hellenistic norms regarding the grace of the goddess. Her body leans without stress against the background of the veil she holds in her hands; the veil falls in folds with supplely arranged lines, all of which might create an illusion as to the style. The face is not emphasized, but the waist, scarcely curved above legs bent in a seated position, is of a length that, while creating an elegant effect, contradicts all art known of the Alexandrian epoch and elsewhere.

A further development is evident in the Dionysiac piece (Louvre) perhaps originating from Shaykh Abādah (ANTINOOPOLIS), also in Middle Egypt. The remnants of Hellenistic grace have disappeared. In the slightly concave surface surmounted by a fragment of broken pediment, a Dionysiac figure shown full-face disengages himself violently from a vine-branch. His nudity exaggerates the movement, which is translated by a sort of disappearance of the legs and the increased proportions given to the upper part of the body and head with its fixed and insistent look. This is an astonishing illustration of vigor as strong as that of the juice of the grape.

The first evolutionary cycle ends and at the same

Birth of Aphrodite. Stone. Ahnāsyah. Fourth century. Length: 78 cm. *Coptic Museum, Cairo. Courtesy André Held.*

Nereids in high relief. Limestone. Ahnāsyah. Fourth–fifth century. Height: 60 cm; width: 52 cm. *Courtesy Civic Museum of History and Art, Trieste.*

time initiates another with an Eros on a dolphin, waving his torch between two Nereids in the mythic waves under a pediment broken by a mask, now located at the Civic Museum of History and Art in Trieste. The natural proportions are more respected except for—as is often the case—those of the medallion necklaces and earrings of the Nereids. Their conventional faces enhance the somewhat sly smile of the Eros. But if their forms and poses are nearly acceptable, only two delicate ribbons attach them to the flat background. Herein one finds an opposition of the surface to the background, to the advantage of high relief, at which the Copts stopped for the moment, and which prepares, as will be seen, for a new direction in Coptic relief.

These three examples of figures were chosen from among many others representing these same developmental stages. They are numerous and often of good quality in the Coptic Museum at Cairo, more isolated in other museums.

A veritable proliferation occurred in the ornamental decorations of the temples, which were still largely pagan at this time. Those coming from excavations of Oxyrhynchus in Middle Egypt have been grouped in the Greco-Roman Museum in Alexandria. For the greater part, they are vegetal or geometric motifs, which, though simplified, are still close to the Alexandrian models. Most often they are found in the friezes and capitals. A chronology established by E. Kitzinger (1938, pp. 181–215), who made comparisons with a capital dating from 390 from Gethsemane (now at Jerusalem), allows us to date the ensemble of the decorations from the Egyptian site by their analogy to similar elements from regions nearby and of like spirit. Several modifications to the Corinthian capital are found both in the Gethsemane capital and in the Egyptian pieces, such as the tendency for the leaves of the second zone to cover those of the higher zone, the stylizing of the foliage to the point of abandoning naturalism, the elongation of the acanthus leaves, and the termination of the acanthus leaves in a point. This last characteristic was transferred to the decorative friezes of acanthus leaves, whose angular aspect was transferred, in an analogous way, to the geometric motifs (such as meanders or Greek key patterns) that enlarged the artists' repertoire.

This slight departure from naturalism occurred as well in the softer materials such as ivory, bone, and wood, for objects routinely used in both liturgical (representations of Nereids and Erōtēs, garlands and boughs) and secular (unguent boxes, decoration on spindle-whorls) situations.

Painting and Pottery. The Coptic penchant for colors also deserves some discussion. Unfortunately, neither the walls of the pagan temples nor Christian monuments furnish as many examples of painting as might be desired. Almost nothing of colored decoration has remained from the pagan tombs and nothing from the temples. Nor can the Egyptian Christians be credited with the decoration of a tomb at Antinoopolis, or of the catacomb of Karmūz near Alexandria (known only by a recent sketch), or of a third tomb discovered in 1964 in the Wardyān quarter of Alexandria; all three are examples of Alexandrian Christian art. This scarcity is not surprising, since Christianity was not yet widespread in Egypt. Moreover, first evidences of mural paintings have rarely survived.

The omission of another genre of painting, manuscript illumination, is somewhat surprising. It is known that in Alexandria at the end of the third century, Origen used scribes and tachygraphers to disseminate scriptural or catechetical texts. One manuscript of the Gospel of John, almost complete in Sahadic Coptic and dating from the middle of the fourth century, has been conserved in the library of the British School of Archaeology in Egypt at London. Like the Gospel fragments dating from the second century and the volumes of Gnostic and Manichaean texts from the fourth century, this item

Tunic decoration. Tapestry. Fifth century. Detail: Bust of a woman representing "Spring." Diameter of medallion: 8 cm. *Courtesy Louvre Museum, Paris.*

contains no illuminations of any kind. The pagans at the time accompanied their magic writings with rude drawings at least, but nothing of the sort is to be found among Christian and Gnostic books. One must conclude that, as in other countries, there was a rupture, caused not by a religious interdict—since the carved figure still persisted—but rather by the loss of a craft that, although ancestral, was no longer in fashion.

There is, however, more information about two other domains that employ color: painted pottery and, above all, decorative textiles.

Painted pottery perpetuated a technique inherited from ancient times for everyday objects and manifested a search for elegance and variety, along with a desire for embellishment by means of colored decoration. Here, the themes have become frankly Greco-Roman; they transpose plants and animated beings of nature into a colored design, which may or may not have been conserved in the vases. The style closely approaches the Alexandrian harmony and brilliance. The terra-cotta figurines have already been mentioned in relation to the statuary.

Textiles. Coptic textiles are rich in decorative elements, used mainly to adorn the frame around predominantly mythological scenes. To these may be added pastoral subjects. Alexandrian subjects were still used; their forms were rough but pleasant. Only one piece among tens of thousands of recorded Coptic textiles can be dated with near certainty, thanks to a coin from the fourth century found close to it, and it marks a turning point. It is a tapestry medallion on a purple background in which squares with geometric motifs around a rosette are connected to each other at angles with white thread. This medallion, and others of similar interlaced floral motifs that decorate the front of vestments, seem to have inaugurated in Egypt the use of the flying shuttle, but as yet only in a purely decorative manner. The flying shuttle, perhaps borrowed from Syria, is a shuttle independent of the weft threads forming the background through the warp. It allows a new thread of weft to skip, shot by shot, over one or more consecutive threads of normal weft during the weaving, so as to cast straight or curved lines and outline the traits of the face, the contours of limbs and muscles of a figure, or the detail of an object. It thereby makes the introduction of color easier eliminates the process of "shading"—that is, trompe l'oeil to indicate the modeling—and opts for the return to two dimensions on a flat background. Its use continues to suggest, but prevents imposing, the illusion of depth, projection, or shadow. In this, it departs clearly from Greco-Roman art and frankly renews its ties to the painting of the pharaonic era.

During this period, the two procedures—flying shuttle and shading—continued to coexist so that color gradually became more important. Such color may be seen in numerous mythological scenes. For example, it is found in a square depicting a Parthian horseman framed by a border of *canthari* (jugs with handles) and medallions, a piece in the Louvre Museum dating from the fourth century, in which yellow and white lines enhance the figurations against a purple background. At the end of the fourth century, color, including purple, clearly predominated. The square portraits of Dionysus and Ariadne in the Louvre are good illustrations of this use of color, though they still remain faithful to shadings in color to render the nuances and shadows.

Metal work. Finally, it must be noted that metal was little used during this period, with the exception of small jewels in silver (earrings, rings, and bracelets), some rare liturgical objects (such as a censer decorated in high relief with the four symbols of the evangelists, now in the Louvre), and some bronze lamps, of which certain ones are of symbolic animal figures such as the dolphin and the dove.

Architecture. In this overview of media, meeting places—notably religious—must be mentioned, for they represent a form appropriate to religious communities. It has been established that in this period, the pagan temples (which at first were still numerous in the villages) were abandoned for the churches, whose style was apparently not yet fixed. The historian JOHN OF NIKIOU mentions a circular martyry erected in honor of Saint MARK, the presumed founder of Christianity in Egypt, during the second century near the eastern shores of Alexandria; another martyry was dedicated to Saint Metra in the same city. This circular plan must have remained an isolated instance. Given Alexandria's close connections to Rome and judging by what followed, the basilical plan must have gained a very early foothold in Egypt for Christian gatherings, both in the villages and in the cities. At this stage, even in its simplest form, the Egyptian basilica must not have departed from the Roman model. It is still found in reduced dimensions in the crypts of the churches of Abū Sarjah and Abū Sayfayn in Cairo. Perhaps one original trait of this plan may be seen in the Church of Mār (Saint) Mīnā, located not far from Cairo; that is, the back has three apses that prolong the nave and two aisles, in possible imitation of the pagan Ptolemaic temples.

Overview. From the foregoing discussion, many observations follow.

In the mixture of three religions—pharaonic, Greco-Roman, and Christian—the first two predominated throughout this period. However, there is one striking peculiarity: if the pharaonic themes disappeared, their significance was still perpetuated in the Greco-Roman representations. In craftsmanship, Hellenistic harmony and picturesque elegance—already stylized at Alexandria—were freed in the productions of the Egyptian population (pagan or Christian) under the effect of a vigor that departed from the usual forms in order to emphasize an idea or movement. In sculpture, relief predominated as elsewhere in the Mediterranean, but with a more striking contrast of the surface to the background. In textiles, a new technique, the flying shuttle, came to confirm the renunciation of an illusory three-dimensional rendering of forms and allowed the rediscovery of the ancestral Egyptian tradition of two-dimensional figures.

If certain genres are not, or are hardly, represented in Coptic productions—such as mosaic, statuary, and illuminated manuscripts—the Copts cannot be reproached for following the styles of the time, nor for renouncing certain techniques, either beyond their means or of no use to them. But the mass of their production manifests a strong concern with the visible interpretation of reality and shows changes powerful enough to hint at a new and positive vision.

Mastery (Mid-Fifth to Late Seventh Century)

In the middle of the fifth century, when the majority of the Egyptian people had become Christian, the Council of CHALCEDON, which condemned monophysite doctrine, separated Egypt from the rest of the Christian world. The church of Egypt lost both its upper-class audience and its possibilities for relations beyond the country's frontiers. But from a national point of view, it profited from a sense of Egyptian self-consciousness, and even though buffeted by diverse currents, the church affirmed its own traits with a great vigor that also affected the domain of art. This art, save for certain exceptions destined for extinction, was to evolve for two centuries in its own, practically Christian, country while accentuating even more its distance from the occupying Byzantine power and knowing that it could depend only upon itself.

The church became increasingly organized as the number of its faithful grew and adopted the basilica as the architectural plan of its religious edifices, although the general plan and a few details were inconsistent with some pharaonic and Ptolemaic characteristics.

During this period, new tendencies appeared in several genres. For the sake of clarity, the discussion below will present general themes first; it will proceed with a description of the plastic arts and conclude with a description of arts employing line and color.

Coptic Themes. In this period Christian themes made their appearance, clearly but in a limited way. Christ was almost always depicted as an infant in His mother's arms. His role as the Savior was not emphasized until the seventh century, and this was done in a special manner. One may ask if other interpretations of Christ existed; but this can hardly be true, for even with limited examples of other interpretations, some would have had to survive. We deduce this from the relatively numerous portrayals of the Virgin, who is always depicted with her Son. Activity in Egypt had prepared for and accompanied the definition of the divine maternity

Niche showing Christ in Glory, in mandorla surrounded by the four evangelical figures, below which is Mary holding the Christ child and flanked by the Twelve Apostles. *Courtesy Coptic Museum, Cairo.*

of Mary, which was proclaimed at the Council of EPHESUS (431) and promoted by the head of the Coptic church, CYRIL I, patriarch of Alexandria. The ardent devotion to this aspect of Christian doctrine was not affected by the condemnation of monophysitism twenty years later, nor by the resultant separation of Chalcedonian Christianity from Monophysite Egypt. It is not impossible that this veneration of the Virgin constituted the transformation, sincerely Christianized, of the ancestral veneration given Isis, mother of the god Horus-Ra, and this in a country where the family is deeply rooted. It is no less significant that episodes from the childhood of Christ survived until recently in the murals of the stone monasteries of DAYR ABŪ ḤINNIS and Dayr Apa Apollo at Bāwīṭ. Several depictions of the baptism of Christ rightly insist on the role of the Savior sent by the Father. In the seventh and eighth centuries, in contrast, Christ in glory appears several times above the Virgin and the apostles in the devotion cells at Bāwīṭ in Middle Egypt; in one panel portrait, He stands, protecting the abbot of the monastery. The back of the choir in the South Church at Bāwīṭ portrays Him presiding at the Last Judgment in the middle of His apostles. The absence of any representations of the Good Shepherd is understandable in a country with so little grassy land for sheep to graze upon. Except for the apostles in this painting of Christ in glory, martyrs, whether Western or Eastern, other than Saint Menas or Saint Thecla, scarcely attracted the Copts' devotion. The Copts directed their veneration rather to Coptic monks, and especially to the great founders of the monasteries: Saints ANTONY, Apollo of Bāwīt, PACHOMIUS, of Tabennēsē, MACARIUS THE EGYPTIAN, JEREMIAH, and a host of others. The angels and the archangel MICHAEL, for their part, are constantly present. One may discern here a piety for which speculation had little attraction, but which, rather, permeated everyday existence with a sacred and protective ambiance.

Some rare subjects from the Old Testament were held in high esteem. They probably derived from the influence of the Roman catacombs: Abraham's sacrifice, Jonah and the whale, the angel with the Three Hebrews in the Furnace. (See BIBLICAL SUBJECTS IN COPTIC ART.) Certain Christian symbols enjoyed more favor: the Greek cross, the *crux ansata* (cross in the form of an ANKH), the Alpha and Omega, and the phoenix. (See SYMBOLISM IN COPTIC ART.) Nevertheless, some objects of a magical nature may have appeared as protectors against demonic attacks, as happened in a chapel of Dayr Apa

Apollo. The devil was not portrayed, though his personage was frequently mentioned in the texts, notably monastic ones.

One quite unexpected aspect of iconography is that the motifs decorating vestments, furniture, and utensils continued to be borrowed from mythology, and so it remained until the eighth century. Only a few gods were held in honor—Dionysus, Aphrodite, Daphne, Artemis, Hercules, the Nile god (above all the first three), or the allegorical figure of the orant (praying person)—but these reappear frequently. The same may be said for their respective retinues of bacchantes, dancers (male and female), Nereids, or simply *erotes* (cupids). The figures of these retinues may appear in groups or alone and may accompany the gods or be isolated from them. No doubt one might suppose that there was a pagan survival and syncretism of the two religions, but this was not the case. Just as Dionysus served as a mask for Osiris, and Aphrodite as a mask for Isis during the Ptolemaic period, for the Christians, Dionysus and Aphrodite evoked respectively the vine of the Last Supper and the soul being reborn from the waters of baptism. Their retinues or companions may act as substitutes in the same role. Thus, pagan symbolism became Christian symbolism, occasionally identified by a Christian emblem such as the cross, but most often in need of none.

Sculpture. During the preceding period (the late third to the early fifth century), sculpture departed from the classical tradition; this was suggested in the decoration of a capital of the Church of Gethsemane, dated from 390 by E. Kitzinger, who recognized it among the fragments of capitals from Oxyrhynchus displayed at the Greco-Roman Museum at Alexandria. This is a very important landmark because, on the one hand, it signifies a revolutionary tendency emerging in the Mediterranean world, and on the other, it shows that this tendency, though relatively isolated in the Middle East, was adopted on a grand scale in a relatively important sanctuary of pagan Coptic Egypt. The tendency was further reinforced in Egypt in two arts that employ color decoration, ceramics and textiles, by a progressive replacement of the illusion of modeling by the use of lines that merely suggest it.

From the mid-fifth to the late seventh century, this abandonment of the classical, ideal harmony was further accentuated in the Middle East. Kitzinger has uncovered two precise examples showing the development of this tendency, once again on two Corinthian capitals: one from the Church of the Golden Gate in Istanbul dating from 425–430, and the other from the Church of Saint John the Baptist in Jerusalem dating from 450–460. Here the volutes of the superior zone are continuously absorbed by the leaves of the second zone; the points of the acanthus leaves are reduced in number and placed laterally instead of vertically; and the foliage has lost its naturalism. These traits, which also characterize the numerous fragments of the temples of Ahnās al-Madīnah in Egypt, constitute yet one more step in the total separation of Middle Eastern art from academicism and picturesque affectation. A coarseness resulted that was sometimes restrained, sometimes extreme. However, whereas this style appeared episodically in the Byzantine countries and in many cases did not abandon the traditional forms, it became characteristic of Coptic sculpture, both pagan and Christian, where it was restricted to sculpture in relief and then rather quickly adopted to a flat surface.

It is not that the Copts disdained borrowing Byzantine themes, but they used them almost uniquely in architectural ornaments and in very limited numbers of which only the basket capital was truly distinctive. Moreover, the Copts did not hesitate to treat the basket capital in their own fashion. This consisted in many cases of flattening the surface in relation to the ground from which it was carved at a right angle, emphasizing the subject in a striking way.

Furthermore, the tendency that had already appeared in the preceding period of taking liberties with proportions in order to emphasize a pose, a movement, or a trait became predominant. Works

Basket capital. *Courtesy Coptic Museum, Cairo.*

of quality emerged, some of them masterpieces.

In the architectural ornamentation of the church at Bāwīṭ the high friezes with foliated scrolls, the basket capitals, a particular broken pediment sheltering a seashell—all are striking in their perfection. The rhythm of the friezes, the lace effect of the capitals, and the triumphal aspect of the decoration of the shell are the marks of a self-assured craft and inspiration. This self-assurance is also found on the pilaster of a portal from the same site, whose two sides are decorated in relief in ascending rhythm, one side with balanced geometric decorations, the other with delicate, "inhabited" stems that rise from a vase and interlace. One element of decoration rises toward Christ and the other toward an angel with flowing robes. It is a successful marriage of a return to classical forms and new tendencies, with the latter, however, destined to prevail.

These new tendencies operated in figurative art and sculpture (henceforth in bas-relief) as well as in architectural ornament. First, they can be seen in pieces now in the Louvre, once again deriving from the South Church of Bāwīṭ, where protective panels depicting a passing lion or the whale disgorging Jonah employ deep carving to detach the subjects from the surface, which remains flat elsewhere. An entire fishing scene, of another provenance (also in the Louvre), maintains the same detachment in the carving of the subjects, with the figures projected from a flat background without using deep carving, keeping the level of the outer surface flat as well.

Dolphin surmounted by a cross. Limestone relief. Armant, near Luxor. Height: 25.5 cm; width: 34.3 cm. *Courtesy Louvre Museum, Paris.*

Without doubt, the greatest masterpiece of all, as proven by its great popularity, is the panel from the now destroyed church of Armant near Luxor (also in the Louvre) in which the design of a dolphin covers a short, wide rectangle. The fish, diving from the right and carrying the cross raised upright upon its mouth, touches the borders of the supporting piece. A greater impression of relief is produced because all the elements are cut at right angles from the background and are even with the outer surface of the panel. One should also mention a wooden fragment of an Annunciation scene that shows the Virgin seated and spinning in front of the archangel, whose foot alone has survived. Her pose, full-face with her body in profile, recalls the conventions of pharaonic murals in relief and painting.

Painting. This general return to two dimensions was no less esteemed in the arts using color. Depth was suggested by grouping and contrasting dominant colored surfaces, over which fine lines were traced, either by brush in painting or by the flying shuttle in tapestry. It even reached the point that the shading meant to indicate shadows was often misplaced. This development marked a total abandonment of the three-dimensional style of the Byzantine mosaic and relief. This is suggested by the badly deteriorated scenes of Christ's childhood, dated from the sixth century, found in the chapel carved from stone at Dayr Abū Ḥinnis or in a chapel at Bāwīṭ.

Bāwīṭ offers a large demonstration of this return to two dimensions in numerous devotional chapels, but examples have survived only in black-and-white photographs and some painted reproductions. A baptism of Christ may date from the sixth century, judging by the simplicity of lines and the proportion of the forms. The elongation of the body in a scene of the Three Hebrews in the Furnace and in portrayals of various monks in liturgical groupings, as well as in some scenes of guardian saints against magic, denotes a great sureness of the artist's sight and brush control. However, several triumphs of Christ from various chapels, of which there is an example in the Coptic Museum at Cairo, opt for heavier forms. This is also the case of a first-rate work, also dating from the seventh century, probably originating from Bāwīṭ (now in the Louvre), a wooden panel depicting the Savior protecting the monk Menas. The two figures stand side by side, and their bodies, clothed in robes that ascend in curves, direct the spectator's eye toward the protective gesture of Christ, giving supreme importance both to this pose and to the rounded heads of Christ

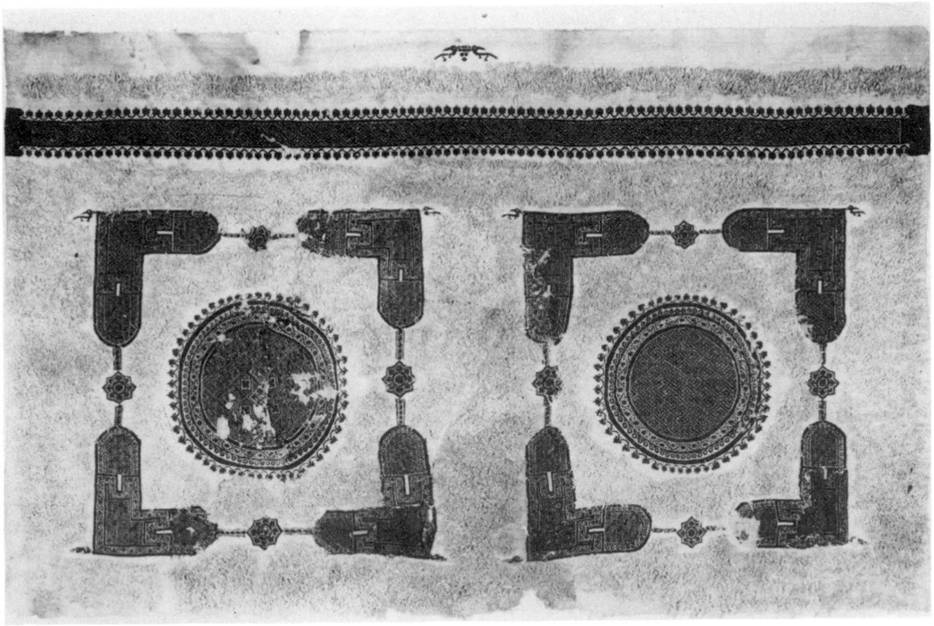

Decorative wall hanging. Loop-woven fabric. Seventh century. *Courtesy Collection Ch. Grand, Zurich, and Holle Publishing Company, Paris.*

and Menas. This is far removed from the Byzantine style and represents another spirituality not inferior to the Byzantine and very modern.

These liberties taken with proportions are especially well realized, particularly in the decoration of ceramics, as can be seen in a bowl in the Louvre bearing a design of stylized deer and birds that traverse interlacings of ocher tones, all highlighted against a yellow background.

Textiles. Tapestries with geometric patterns, such as those in purple, vividly detached from a surrounding loopwoven background, or tapestries of Nilotic scenes and portraits bordered by geometric patterns, display great self-assurance. A departure from this pronounced detachment is found only in a few highly colored pieces treating mythological subjects. Examples are Dionysus with a follower (in the Louvre) and a Nereid holding a bowl (in the Cleveland Museum of Art), both of which use misplaced shadings, and a group of Pan and Dionysus (in the Boston Museum of Fine Arts).

In return, the seventh-century hanging (in the Cleveland Museum) of an enthroned Virgin surrounded by superimposed busts of apostles shows a resumption of the Byzantine style, but in a different interpretation and with different features, which places it among valuable autochthonous works.

Other Genres. A great number of funerary stelae are generally of a stereotyped art, but some of them, though relatively flat and at first glance quite simple, are to be recommended by the nature of the portrait or symbol they contain.

Alongside these works, there are other very inferior works, which are mentioned only for the sake of information. In their accentuated disproportion they occasionally achieve boorishness through a gross deformation of Hellenistic art.

These disgraceful, sometimes brutal, works are actually rare and appear chiefly in pagan temples in a rural setting. They are limited to stone, bronze, and ivory. The fact that many of them may lack grace in no way detracts from the value of those works mentioned above—the best examples of Coptic art—that are sufficient for evaluating Coptic art and appraising its fundamental tendencies. It still is a flagrant injustice that certain scholars have seized upon the exceptions, an indistinguishable lot of largescale productions and attempts at reproducing reality, to describe Coptic art as barbaric (Wessel, 1963), and then in a rather astounding transfer classify as Byzantine certain Coptic works of value, though they employ a visual vocabulary totally contrary to that of Byzantium. This attitude must be denounced as inadmissible.

Coptic art reached a summit that in certain examples is on a level with the best, above all for those eyes that modern art had led to an appreciation of a two-dimensional restriction for representations on flat surfaces. Perhaps this art might have risen even higher. The Arab conquest put a stop to its vigor

Nereid holding a bowl. Tapestry. Seventh century. Length: 65.7 cm; width: 64.8 cm. *Courtesy Cleveland Museum of Art.*

but could not prevent its energetic forces from operating for many years thereafter in new and meritorious directions.

One cannot guess what other heights Coptic art might have attained under different circumstances. At first sight an archivolt in the Louvre is occasionally considered to be Romanesque. Beneath the outer border—itself ornamented with garlands—is a rather wide arcade decorated with undulating stems, surmounted in the middle by a triple knot of stalks. The archivolt terminates with angel-musicians in high relief against the rest of the decoration. The flatness of the vegetal motifs leaves no doubt about the Coptic appurtenances of the piece, while the triple folioles of the arcade work place it in the eighth century. Such a striking and original work stands as a beacon on a road unfortunately barred.

New Directions (Eighth to Thirteenth Century)

The Muslim domination did in effect close many promising avenues. The decoration of churches as well as the construction of new ones became sluggish. In any event, pressures on the Copts brought conversions to Islam that within 200 years affected progressively almost the total population and reduced the Copts to a minority community by the end of the ninth century. Little by little the Copts' means became no more than those of an artisan class assigned to weaving and woodwork, as the Persian traveler Nasiri Khosrow noted in the eleventh century. It is nonetheless significant that the *Kabati* (Copts) quickly dominated the production of decorated Egyptian textiles, a dominance that continued for a long time in the considerable territory controlled by Islam. Wood and ebony carving have remained the Copts' domain up to the present day. As for architecture and construction in stone, the Copts shared these specialties with the Syrians even while in the service of the Muslims, as is attested by many witnesses such as Leonce of Neapolis in the seventh century and Balādhurī, Samhūdī, and the papyri of Aphrodito of Egypt in the eighth century. There can be no further doubt about this when one realizes that, under the Tulunids and Fatimids, all the decorative work in wood, whether on doors, furniture, or all kinds of ornamentation, was taken over by the Copts. This is true to the extent that the style is commonly called "Copto-Muslim" whether it concerns Christian or Muslim furnishings.

The Coptic artisan class, formed by millennia of craftsmanship and representing Egypt's autochthonous population, whether Christian or converted to Islam, lasted for five centuries more, perpetuating the tradition of the preceding four centuries and thereby assuring the survival of the mass of the laborers' productivity in all genres. Some artisans worked primarily in construction, furniture, certain luxury fabrics, glass, and metals, serving the Muslim governors for their religious pageantry, for their administration in part, and for their army as a whole, as well as for their families. Other workers cared for the needs of the rest of the population, needs that, even with the religious differences within the Egyptian people, were to remain homogenous for a long time.

Influences emanating from foreign regions ruled by the central Islamic government made themselves felt even in works produced by Christians; these influences contributed to the evolution of the decorative themes of their works, as well as to the evolution of the Coptic style, which pursued its own unique tendencies and prevailed even in works produced for the Muslims.

This same observation can be verified for each epoch in the sequence of Coptic art until the thirteenth century, if we restrict ourselves to works attributable to Christians. Such works comprise a considerable collection in any event, since they come from the ornamentation of Coptic edifices or from items—notably textiles—found on the dead in their tombs (Muslims were buried in a simple white shroud).

Architectural Decoration. In Coptic architectural ornamentation, there were certain new traits held in common with the art of Samarra, the Abbasid capital established in 836 north of Baghdad, which Ibn Ṭūlūn ruled before becoming governor of Egypt. Copts were employed at Samarra, and one may ask if they instigated the common traits.

This is doubtful in regard to certain traits that in Egypt were confined to one site. This is true for reliefs on stucco ornamented with palmettes contained in interconnecting octagons. Such reliefs decorate the windows and doors of the *haykal* (sanctuary) at DAYR ANBĀ MAQĀR, as well as those in the church of al-'Adhrā' at Dayr al-Suryān in Wādī al-Naṭrūn.

In this same Dayr Anbā Maqār, there is a series of niches from the Fatimid period (tenth to twelfth century) in which the two branches of the arcade ascend vertically and curve inward obliquely, one toward the other halfway up so as to meet in a pointed summit. Such niches are also found in Muslim art, for example, at the Mosque al-Azhar, but nowhere else in Coptic art.

Finally, a decorative motif in mosaic in the cupola of the Dome of the Rock at Jerusalem, not necessarily of Muslim inspiration and even less so in the eighth century, appears to have reached the Copts, probably through Muslim intermediaries. This motif consists of a vertical series of open flowers that continuously alternate with a pair of half-flowers cut by the border on either side of the design. It passed from the Palestinian mosaic into Coptic tapestries, notably vestments, during the ninth and tenth centuries.

This motif marks the end of the influence exercised or transmitted by the Muslims to the Copts. It was in the opposite direction that the current flowed in other Mediterranean arts, with Islam creating in its turn and according to its own tendencies, but not hesitating to borrow, principally from the Copts.

For five more centuries, despite their progressively reduced numbers, the Copts continued to produce art in order to accommodate the needs of their still considerable population: on the one hand, in architecture and architectural decoration, and on the other, in routinely used decorative pieces (most often in the liturgy) as well as in textiles and in ceramics.

Architecture. Architecture, in fact, was not at first hindered by the new rulers. The construction and even the maintenance of the churches were guaranteed in principle by the surrender treaty of 641. It was only in 850 that a decree of the Abbasid caliph al-Mutawakkil ordered the destruction of sanctuaries no longer in use as a result of the progressive conversion of Copts to Islam. However, except under the persecutor-caliph al-ḤĀKIM in the eleventh century, construction only slowed but did not stop, even in the elaboration of great projects, notably the monasteries. The cupola was held in high honor and remained so.

Sculpture and Painting. This slowing may also be observed in painting and sculpture. But there were some commendable works, such as a cycle of the story of David painted at Bāwīṭ in the eighth century and the pictoral decoration of the Church of Saint Antony in the DAYR ANBĀ ANṬŪNIYŪS, from the Fatimid period. Certain reliefs, striking by their vigorous lines, include a Christ mounted between two angels dating from the ninth century in the Egyptian Museum, Berlin. Two pieces stand out: the Virgin of Tenderness in ivory from the ninth century (in the Walters Art Gallery, Baltimore), an ancestor, strikingly vivid in its somewhat coarse style, of the Russian Virgins of Tenderness; and the Martyrdom of Saint Thecla in stone, of a simple and concentrated flatness (in the Brooklyn Museum).

Cupolas. A monastery in Wādī al-Naṭrūn. *Courtesy Pierre du Bourguet.*

Christ mounted between two angels. Stone. Suhāj. Ninth century. Height: 42 cm; length: 61 cm. *Courtesy State Museum of Berlin.*

Later, even under the Fatimids, the decoration of doors with panels depicting a person or animal in relief produced an ornamental effect imitated by the Muslims.

Textiles and Other Genres. There are other abundantly represented categories that remain to be mentioned: ceramics of various forms (sometimes animal) and with often naïve decoration; metals, whether crosses (often engraved with inscriptions of personages), censers of surprising forms, or paterae with the stem in the form of a female dancer carrying a cross; glasses of all kinds, of which some are decorated (e.g., one with a horseman, in the Louvre); and above all, textiles, such as tunics, cloaks, and wall hangings, better conserved because they are more recent, all displaying a most involved ornamentation.

In most of these works, the lines of the already stylized face became less and less important, and the same may be said for the portrayal of both human and animal figures. Everything became a pretext for the invention of new forms that discarded reality to follow nothing but fantasy—sometimes of the wildest order—and succumbed to an acute sense of decoration for decoration's sake. Since this tendency was characteristic of Coptic art, the first attempts can be seen from the very beginning. The decorations in sculptured stone in the churches (at Bāwīṭ, for example) surrendered to this tendency in a rather astonishing fashion. One example marking this final stage is in the form of a scroll with swirling foliage, whose central fruit is nothing more than the hub of a wheel, the natural subject having become the pretext for abstract invention. In decorated textiles, it appears just as often in a profusion of fine works. In its own way, this sense for decoration joined with a fundamental tendency of pharaonic art.

In keeping with this general movement, the value of which is striking, some pieces stand out, particularly wall hangings. One of these, dating from the ninth century (in the Abegg Stiftung at Riggisberg, Switzerland) depicts in full-face a family standing side by side in a rigid orant position beneath two arcades, one sheltering an eagle and the other a peacock, both stylized. Another piece from the ninth century (in the Louvre) is a triumph of the cross, with the cross in the form of an *ankh* placed between two panels, one depicting the ass of Balaam (Nm. 22:21–30) and the other showing Jonah praying as he is disgorged by the whale (Jon. 2:10). These are portrayed above lions and sheep together, which are symbolic of the Christian peace announced by Isaiah. Dating from the ninth century as well is a tapestry portrait of an evangelist (in the Detroit Institute of Art) made by juxtaposing colored surfaces almost at right angles or in wide curves.

Virgin enthroned between two angels. Ivory. Ninth century. Height: 26 cm; width: 11.6 cm; thickness: 5 cm. *Courtesy The Walters Art Gallery, Baltimore.*

Illuminated Manuscripts. Two series of illuminated manuscripts, of which certain traits are still typically Coptic, while others have already plunged into an art that is largely Arabicized, complete this general account of Coptic art. These works decorate two Copto-Arabic books of Gospels, both in Paris. In the first series, from the twelfth century, in the National Library, the illuminations are inserted into the Coptic text and occupy the greater part of numerous pages, with the Arabic text at one side. The pictures are remarkable for the vividness of the personages, although they are a bit cramped. In the second series, in the Catholic Institute, the illuminations are grouped in pairs in three succeeding registers on the same leaf, so as to occupy about twenty pages scattered throughout the work, with the texts distributed on the same model as the Gospel Book in the National Library. The figures and colors are more finely drawn, in a manner that would suggest a Syrian influence.

At this point Coptic art came to a halt. It succumbed because it was abandoned by both the elite and the majority of Copts, who could no longer resist social pressures for conversion to Islam. Never again did it completely achieve its particular visual characteristics. But it had made its mark,

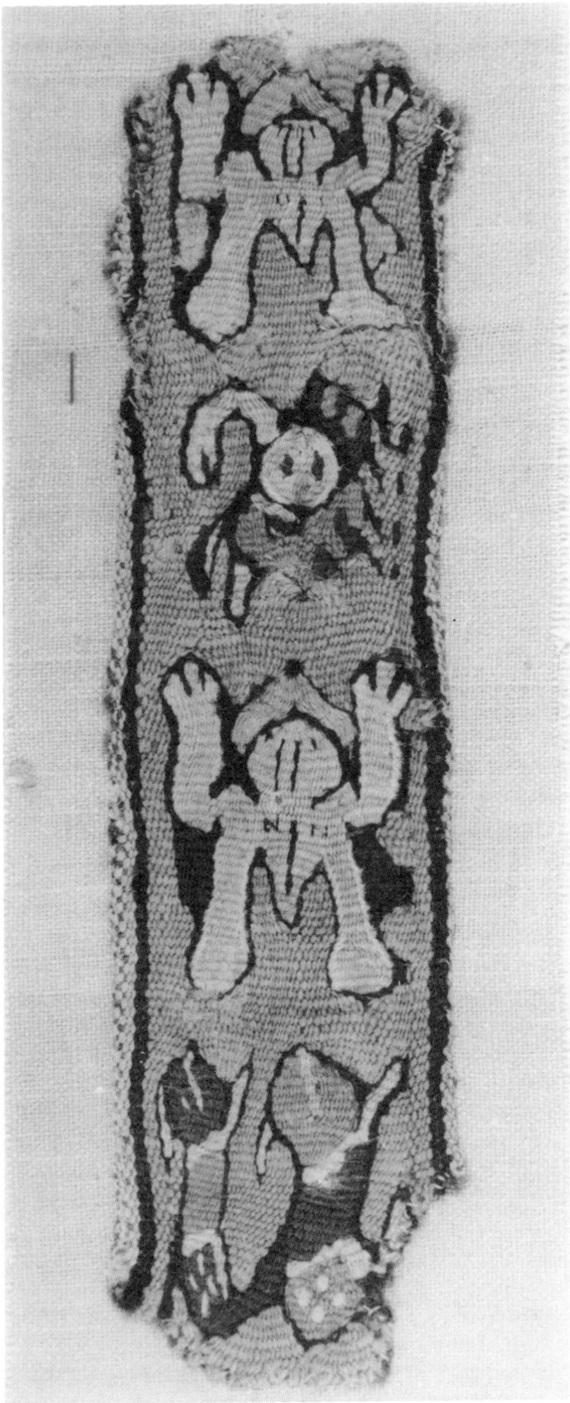

Fragment of a tapestried shoulder-band decorated with stylized dancers in *orans* pose and a *putto* holding an animal. Tenth century. Length: 17 cm; width: 4 cm. *Courtesy Louvre Museum, Paris.*

Wall hanging depicting family in *orans* pose. Loop-woven fabric. Akhmīm. Seventh century. Length: 163 cm; width: 123 cm. *Courtesy Abegg Foundation, Bern. Photo by A. Javor.*

which cannot be erased. It established itself by its autonomy, by an evolution ever faithful to its imperatives, and by soaring works that exhibit a power of decorative invention which allies Coptic art to the best of modern art.

BIBLIOGRAPHY

Bourguet, P. du. *L'Art copte. Petit Palais.* Exhibition catalogue. Paris, 1964.

______. *L'Art copte* (collection L'Art dans le monde). Paris, 1968.

______. *Une Assimilation abusive: Actes du XXIXe Congrès international des Orientalistes (Paris, juillet 1973).* Paris, 1975.

Cresswell, K. A. C. *Early Muslim Architecture.* Harmondsworth, 1958.

Effenberger, A. *Koptische Kunst.* Leipzig, 1973.

Kitzinger, E. "Notes on Early Coptic Sculpture." *Archaeologia* 87, 2nd ser. 37 (1938):181.

Koefoed-Petersen, O. *Koptisk Kunst.* Copenhagen, 1944.

Krause, M. "Ägypten." *Reallexikon zur byzantinischen Kunst.* Stuttgart, 1963.

Munier, H., and G. Wiet. "L'Egypte byzantine et musulmane." *Précis de l'Histoire d'Egypte,* Vol. 2. Cairo, 1932–1935.

Wessel, K. *Koptische Kunst. Die Spätantike in Ägypten.* Recklinghausen, 1963.

Zaloscer, H. *Die Kunst im christlichen Ägypten.* Vienna/Munich, 1974.

PIERRE DU BOURGUET, S. J.

ARTOPHORION. *See* Eucharistic Vessels.

ART PRESERVATION. Coptic art found expression through materials as diverse as earthenware, stone, metals, and textiles.

Individual pieces of art have been subjected to the ravages of time. Their preservation today poses problems specific to the materials of which the objects are composed, and to the milieu to which they belong, such as ancient collections and recent excavations. Under good conditions, meticulous cleaning and temporary repair preserve the object until it can be restored by a specialist.

Terra-Cotta

The Copts used terra-cotta and unbaked clay for the manufacture of numerous utilitarian or liturgical objects. Their preservation requires a preliminary desalination, for the Egyptian subsoil in which they were covered contains a marked salinity.

For terra-cottas that are strong enough, with or without decoration, the operation consists of simple steeping in frequently renewed distilled water until all the soluble salts are removed. Very often it is necessary to strengthen porous ceramics by impregnating them with synthetic resin, or to protect a fragile decoration with a coat of soluble nylon.

For objects in unbaked clay the use of water is absolutely out of the question; the object must be consolidated. Soluble salts are extracted by using damp pads after applying a layer of soluble nylon, permeable to the salts but not to water.

On terra-cotta and unbaked clay, accretions insoluble to water are removed mechanically or chemically depending on their nature. For the assembling of fragments belonging to the same piece of pottery, it is advisable to use gums of a temporary nature. After the piece has been put together again, the gaps left by vanished fragments may be filled with other temporary materials such as plaster.

Textiles

The beauty, diversity, and significant number of Coptic textiles have contributed in large measure to our knowledge of Coptic art. The fibers that make up these textiles are essentially linen, linen and wool, wool, and gradually silk at a later date. Careful examination of the fabric allows us to determine the nature of any stains and the tenacity of the dyes. Cleaning can be done in several ways: with distilled water or in softened water without iron and using a nonacidic soap (Lissapol), or, when the dyes are soluble in water or when there are fatty stains, by dry cleaning with the aid of solvents. The presence of mold requires sterilization by thymol vapor. It is sometimes necessary to treat for the removal of insects.

The Coptic fabric thus treated often requires mounting on acid-free backing, by sewing, or by thermocollage (for very brittle silks). For good conservation, the fabric should be screened from light between leaves of nonacidic paper, either flat or rolled, according to its dimensions.

Wood

The numerous Coptic objects made of wood or formed from various vegetable fibers often present similar problems of conservation. Wood and fibers are attacked by insects and by mold. The insects must be dealt with by fumigation in a vacuum with methyl bromide or by gamma rays, and the mold is removed by sterilization with thymol vapor. Fragile objects can be provisionally reinforced by impregnation with vinyl resin; final consolidation will be obtained through thermoplastic treatment by polymerization in a vacuum.

In the case of stuccoed wood, the layer of stucco, often crumbling, should be restored before treating the painted or decorated surface. The use of reinforcement on a polychrome Coptic wooden object need not entail any alteration in the colors.

Papyrus

The Copts inherited from ancient Egypt the use of papyrus as their main writing material. For a long time the major problem posed by this extremely fragile material was the unrolling of the precious manuscripts. Today, however, some museums prefer to keep the rolls intact; hence the most common work is the smoothing away of folds and creases in the papyrus so that the texts may be more clearly read.

There are several methods that allow a gradual and limited moistening of the fibers while preserving the ink and the colors. The papyrus that has recovered its elasticity can then be carefully flattened out and dried. The use of a fungicide preserves the document from mold. The different fragments of the same papyrus may be assembled by strips of rice paper glued to ordinary paper treated with fungicide. The cleaning and bleaching, when they are necessary, must be carried out by specialists. The preservation of papyrus requires that it be screened from ultraviolet rays.

Parchment

The Copts also used parchment as a writing material. Methanol gives good results for removing folds and creases in parchment while preserving the ink. More specific treatment, such as cleaning, should be entrusted to specialists. The gum in parchment allows the different fragments of a single leaf to be pasted together. It is sometimes necessary to reinforce the page with rice paper when the parchment is very fragile.

Ostraca

Splinters of stone or pottery that served as writing material suffer above all from the presence of soluble salts. These salts can be removed either by the repeated immersion in distilled water or by the application of damp pads regularly renewed until all the salts have been extracted, care being taken beforehand to protect the ink with a layer of soluble nylon. Final reinforcement is achieved by the application of, or impregnation with, a synthetic resin appropriate to the material which does not alter the appearance of the ostracon.

Coptic Sculptures, Reliefs, and Architectural Fragments

When these are made of materials such as sedimentary rock (limestone), siliceous rock (sandstone), or carboniferous rock (bitumen), they often suffer chemical disintegration. Here again, preservation requires desalination, care being taken to protect by resins any colors and any surfaces that are too crumbly. According to the porosity of the rock, the final consolidation is achieved by impregnation with acrylic, polyester, or epoxide resin incorporating a fungicidal agent. In the case of a stone with several colors, the medium employed must not change the colors.

Metals

Work in metals and their alloys has enriched Coptic art with numerous objects and trinkets, but these are generally materials sensitive to chemical transformation due to the milieu in which they are or have been preserved. These items often show evidence of numerous alterations. Accretions covering an object may be removed either mechanically (by scraping or pricking) or chemically; in the latter case it is essential to determine the chemical constituents of the impurities.

After any treatment, the object, whose surface is highly reactive, should be protected from contact with the surrounding air by a screen of wax, paraffin, acrylic resin, or epoxide resin, depending on its porosity.

Glass

Numerous objects of clear glass and opaque glass suffer essentially from chemical changes. These changes are often accompanied by a disintegration caused by soluble salts. In fact, glass may become soluble in water through an excess of soda, and its decomposition may be furthered by excess of lime. Chemical treatment carried out by specialists can halt the process of disintegration and stabilize the glass. Thereafter the fragments of a single Coptic object in glass may be fitted together either by using a cyanoacrylate glue or an epoxy-type optic glue.

Hides and Skins

The Copts used hides and skins for clothes, footwear, and various objects. Skin disintegrates in humidity and it is equally sensitive to alkaline and acidic solutions; certain marine salts, alum, and tannin are favorable to its preservation. Lanoline, ox foot oil, or castor oil may be used to restore the elasticity of hides. Acetone fungicide may be used to remove organic deposits such as fungus and mold. Fumigation in a vacuum with methyl bromide or ethylene oxide will remove insects. Temporary reinforcement is ensured by impregnation with polyvinyl alcohol, while final consolidation requires a vinylic resin mixed with a fungicidal agent.

Bone and Ivory

Bone and ivory, from which the Copts manufactured numerous small objects, present different problems of preservation and conservation.

Fossilization of bone and ivory is frequent, through the association of the chalky matter they contain with the quartz and silica contained in the soil.

These materials are subject to great deformation in a humid milieu. In an acid environment, on the other hand, the osteine, which is an organic constituent, is attacked, reducing bone and ivory to a sponge.

Excellent results are obtained by mechanical or chemical treatments. Because of their fragility, the objects thus cleaned and treated must often be reinforced by resins.

MARIE-FRANÇOISE BOUILLET DE ROZIÈRES

ART SURVIVALS FROM ANCIENT EGYPT. In Egypt in the first century A.D., pharaonic themes became rare; Coptic art in its beginnings contained practically none. Such themes yielded to Greek iconography, which was already in competition with them under the Ptolemies. Later, subjects of Roman origin were added. In the pre-Coptic period, the artistic style itself included a mixture of pharaonic names and attitudes with figures and forms inspired by Alexandrian art, juxtaposing them rather than combining them to emphasize the subject. Conversely, Greco-Roman iconography underwent a double transformation from the beginnings of Coptic art, for which it provided the great majority of themes. First, it perpetuated the divine personages of ancient Egypt under the names and semblances of Greek divinities. Second, its style gradually abandoned the classical manner to obey in greater or lesser degree the dictates of native and ancestral tradition. Pharaonic survival should thus be looked for not so much on a superficial and external level as in the depths of the Coptic soul and its surface expression.

Coptic art, even in its beginnings, preserved no pharaonic theme or motif. The only themes that recall ancient times are themselves exceptional. From the Louvre Museum, for example, one can cite only a seventh-century stone relief of Horus as a Roman horseman lancing a crocodile. The Christianized motif of the *ankh* sign, which became the *crux ansata,* appears in various media, especially decorated textiles. An eighth-century tapestry in the Louvre may also be included; its *Udjat* (sacred eye of Ra) in the form of an eye given to a stalk with its husk must have been inspired by motifs that the artist no doubt saw in surviving temples.

A typical pose of Isis seated with her left arm holding her son Horus on her knees may have been the iconographic prototype of the seated Mary holding the infant Jesus. The large number of Isiac sanctuaries, among them one in Rome in the time of Tiberius, suggests this hypothesis, although representations of mother and child are also found in Greek sacred monuments. One cannot go further, even admitting the predilection of the Copts for the theme of the Virgin as evidenced by numerous Madonnas (See VIRGIN ENTHRONED) in painting or in relief, notably from the monastery of Saint Jeremiah at Saqqara (Coptic Museum, Cairo). We can detect a Roman influence through the classical and pre-Byzantine style of an enthroned Virgin Mary incised in stone from the Fayyūm (Berlin Museum). The preference for this subject can thus be attributed not so much to the iconographic prototype of Isis as to a Christian continuation of Isiac myths which could be integrated and transformed into devotion to the Mother of Christ. The survival would then be due more to atavistic Egyptian attachment to the maternal sentiment than to any precise iconographic prototypes, whether native or foreign.

A survival of a symbolic kind that is, nevertheless, widespread in Coptic art finds expression through Greco-Roman themes by seeing the Egyptian gods inherited from pharaonic times in the Greek gods introduced by the Ptolemies or in the Roman gods added to them and preserving their original names. The subjects were gods as important in the late pharaonic era as Osiris and Isis. The process occurred in two successive stages: the first began under the pharaohs, when, for example, representations of Queen Nefertari at Abu Simbel took on the attributes of the goddesses Isis, Hathor, and Mut; the second followed, for example, in the first centuries A.D. in the terra-cottas representing Aphrodite in the pharaonic hieratic pose with the combined attributes of the same Egyptian goddesses.

The Egyptian attitudes and attributes may have disappeared in the fourth century, but their significance remained. Despite the goddess's name, it is not so much Aphrodite who is represented in terracottas as are the Egyptian goddesses, although in composite form. It is the same with Dionysus as a representative of Osiris. The line thus chosen was to be continued in the Coptic Christian period by the substitution of Christian significance for that of Egyptian gods in the semblance of Greek or Roman deities. This substitution is analogous to the practice of the Christian artists of the catacombs in Rome, who used themes of pagan origin, such as Cupid and Psyche, the Elysian fields, Orpheus, or the seasons. In place of Isis-Hathor-Mut, the birth of Aphrodite (Aphroditē anadyomenē), for example, became the symbol of the soul reborn from the waters of baptism.

One survival, which though subtle is nonetheless clear, appears in style. It is certain that under the influence of various factors—Neoplatonism and the accession of Roman knights and provincial Latins, and even Orientals, to the imperial throne and to the senatorial order and court functions—simplification and abstraction tended to supplant the classical elegance of form from the beginning of our era. This transformation was brought about through a lessening of the sense of perspective. The proof lies in the decadence of Hellenistic works, when they are seen in the perspective of this decline. The Alexandrian ivories in the throne of Aix-la-Chapelle are flagrant examples, particularly in the faces and in the extremities of the limbs of the figures. When an authentic inspiration governed by new factors rises from the roots, one of two things may happen. Either the style grows stronger while abandoning some primitive traits, as was the case with Byzantine art; or it modifies features hitherto characteristic of the ancient motifs (in this case the Alexandrian) to the point of choosing gradually and finally the exact reverse, as was the case with Coptic art.

It is true that Coptic art like contemporary forms of Mediterranean art, followed the same movement toward abstraction and stiffening of classical forms. But in contrast to other forms, which, apart from

Byzantine art, abandoned themselves in a kind of mechanical automatism, Coptic art adopted for the better whatever classical forms it could. If in its beginnings, it preserved something of Hellenistic elegance, it destroyed Hellenistic proportions in order to emphasize important elements of the subject. In short, it developed toward signifying some typical feature, sacrificing an external harmony for an internal and striking one. A choice example is the Dionysian figure spouting from the vine like juice from the grape in a stone sculpture in the Louvre. The objective was attained in sculpture by sacrificing plasticity; it was attained in painting with an illusion of relief, as well as by insisting on an opposition to or correspondence with neighboring volumes or surfaces. Coptic art even produced chiaroscuro effects by contrasting two flat surfaces in stone reliefs and in looped textiles, as well as by contrasting somber and bright colors in paintings and in tapestries. There is here a unity of concept, the constant element that touches all techniques, including architecture, to the point of making mystery triumph over any conventional or apparent harmony of forms. If some works allowed even noticeable deformities to break through, that is the inevitable price of any artistic quest and the fate of any art, even a prestigious one. Art is judged by works of quality, and Coptic art is sufficiently provided with these. Even if the processes became different with time and circumstances, these works show the same quest for symbolic effect that animated the artists of pharaonic times.

In addition, the decorative element became a characteristic, one that developed even more in the Muslim period. Abstraction and even mechanization became processes of improvement, and their use redeemed, to a large extent, the damage done to classical harmony. In decoration on stone, cloth, or pottery, the Coptic artist became enchanted with his work, which was marked by an entirely original fantasy. For example, the basket capitals at Bāwīṭ are one of the remarkable successes of Coptic art.

This vigorous tendency cut across all contemporary arts. In it one may legitimately see a heritage from the pharaonic style, profoundly marked by a symbolic conception opposed to the naturalistic arts. Curiously and as a kind of confirmation, a fragmentary Annunciation in relief on painted wood (in the Louvre) adopts in its own way one of the major conventions of the art of ancient Egypt. In a flat-surface technique, the seated Virgin appears full-face with her body in profile; this posture stands in an inverse but nonetheless striking relationship to the ancient showing of faces in profile and torsos full-face.

BIBLIOGRAPHY

Bourguet, P. du. "Die koptische Kunst als mögliche Erbin der pharaonischen Kunst." *Koptische Kunst: Christentum am Nil.* Catalogue of the Exhibition at Villa Hügel, Essen, 1963, pp. 122–30.

______. *L'Art copte* (collection *L'Art dans le monde*); pp. 1–54. Paris, 1968.

______. "L'Art Paléochrétien." *Meulenhoff et Lausanne formes et couleurs,* p. 209, n.33. Amsterdam, 1970.

PIERRE DU BOURGUET, S.J.

AS'AD ABŪ AL-FARAJ HIBAT ALLĀH IBN AL-'ASSĀL, AL-, one of three brothers, members of the same family generally known as AWLĀD AL-'ASSĀL, who lived in the thirteenth century, all being notable writers on religious subjects, jurisdiction, canon law, theology, philosophy, and Coptic philology.

Al-As'ad's full name is Abū al-Faraj Hibat-Allāh ibn Abī al-Faḍl As'ad ibn Abī Isḥāq Ibrāhīm ibn Abī Sahl Jirjis ibn Abī al-Bishr Yuhannā ibn al-'Assāl. He enjoyed the title of *Fakhr al-Dawlah* (pride of the state), signifying that he occupied an important position in the administration of the Ayyubid government of Egypt. No precise date can be assigned to his life, but it is certain that he lived in the first half of the thirteenth century (Mallon, 1905, p. 518), moving between Damascus and Cairo.

Al-As'ad's major and enduring contribution to the field of Christian religious studies was his new translation of the Gospels into Arabic. Before his time, there were sundry Arabic versions that were uncanonical and in need of critical study to render them true to the accepted original texts in Greek, Syriac, and Coptic, which al-As'ad collected for the purpose of rendering his recension. Copies of his translation dated between 1259 and 1280 are to be found in manuscript in London, Milan, Rome, the Vatican, Leiden, Oxford, and other places (Mallon, 1905, p. 523).

Parallel to this work, he composed an introduction to the epistles of Saint Paul consisting of eight sections subdivided into various chapters and preceded by a historical life of Saint Paul.

Beyond the field of religious studies, he composed a grammar of the Coptic language in Arabic, of which copies in manuscript are in Paris, London, Oxford, Rome, the Vatican, and the Patriarchal Library in Cairo.

The following Arabic titles are enumerated under al-As'ad's name in the dictionary of Arab authors compiled by 'Umar Riḍā Kaḥḥalah. They are all in the field of Christian religious studies, and all are derived from Cheikho's catalog of Arabic manuscripts: (1) *Majmū' Uṣūl al-Dīn wa-Masmū' Maḥṣūl al-Yaqīn;* (2) *Tafsīr Mār Būlus al-Rasūl;* (3) *Tafsīr al-Amānah al-Muqaddasah;* (4) *Al-Tabṣirah al-Mukhtaṣarah fī al-Aqā'id al-Naṣraniyyah;* and (5) *Tafsīr mā warada fī al-Injīl 'an Alām al-Masīh.*

BIBLIOGRAPHY

Mallon, A. "Ibn al-'Assāl, Les trois écrivains de ce nom." *Journal Asiatique,* 10, 6 (1905).

AZIZ S. ATIYA

ASCENSION, FEAST OF THE. *See* Feasts, Major.

ASCENSION OF CHRIST. *See* Christ, Triumph of.

ASCLA, SAINT, martyr in the persecutions under DIOCLETIAN (feast day: 21 Ṭūbah). His Passion has survived in Coptic in only one codex, in Sahidic dialect (Turin, Museum Egizio, 63000.XV, ed. F. Rossi, 1892, pp. 65–69), but it is also known in Greek and Latin (Bibliotheca hagiographica Graeca 1514, Bibliotheca hagiographica Latina 722).

It begins with Ascla's capture and his appearance before ARIANUS, prefect of the Thebaid. Arianus orders him to make sacrifice, and Ascla refuses. This is followed by the usual exchange of words, and then Arianus decides to leave Antinoopolis with Ascla and travel to Shmūn. Ascla miraculously stops the ship in mid-river and forces Arianus to abjure in order for the ship to be able to lay anchor. However, once he has landed, Arianus goes back on his words, tortures Ascla, and orders that he be drowned in the river near Antinoopolis.

This text is one of the basic ones of the Cycle of Arianus.

BIBLIOGRAPHY

Baumeister, T. *Martyr Invictus. Der Märtyrer als Sinnbild der Erlösung in der Legende und im Kult der frühen koptischen Kirche.* Münster, 1972.
Rossi, F. *Un nuovo codice copto del Museo Egizio di Torino." Atti Accademia dei Lincei* series 5, 1 (1892):3–136.

TITO ORLANDI

ASCLEPIADES, an Alexandrian Neoplatonic philosopher of the late fifth century, from an Egyptian family that owned an ancestral estate at Phenebythis in the nome of Panopolis. He is mentioned in three primary sources: Damascius' *Life of Isidorus,* composed in the early sixth century, offers information about his role as a pagan religious figure; the Syriac *Life of Severus,* written by Zachariah of Mitylene, numbers him as one of six Neoplatonists connected with an outbreak of religious violence near Alexandria in 485; a papyrus letter composed in Greek by Flavius Horapollon and found at Kom Ishqāw. The letter has been translated and studied by J. Maspero, who demonstrated that Asclepiades was the father of HORAPOLLON, the author of the letter. In it, he was praised by his son as a famous professor who spent a lifetime teaching at the Alexandrian Museum.

Asclepiades was both a Neoplatonic philosopher and an Egyptian priest. Damascius' commentary *On First Principles* (ed. Ruelle, chap. 125) states that he and his brother Heraiscus were Egyptians who employed Egyptian mythology as a medium for philosophical speculation. A few fragments from the *Life of Isidorus* allude to Asclepiades' priestly activity. He is said to have been more learned in Egyptian wisdom than his brother. He was constantly surrounded by Egypt's sacred books and wrote hymns on Egypt's gods, a book on Egypt's history, and a treatise on the harmony of all theological matters. He was devoted to the "care of the gods," a phrase that Damascius uses for priestly temple ritual. One fragment says that on Heraiscus' death, Asclepiades tended to his brother's funeral rites and prepared to hand over to the priests the customary funeral objects, including the bandages of Osiris in which the body was to be wrapped, a notation indicating that ancient Egyptian rites of burial were still being approximated as late as the fifth century.

BIBLIOGRAPHY

Asmus, R. "Zur Rekonstruktion von Damascius' Leben des Isidoros." *Byzantinische Zeitschrift* 18 (1909):424–80; 19 (1910):265–84.
———. *Das Leben des Philosophen Isidoros von Damaskios aus Damaskos.* Leipzig, 1911.

Cumont, F. "Le Culte égyptien et le mysticisme de Plotin." *Monuments et mémoires publiés par l'Académie des inscriptions et belles-lettres* 24 (1921):77–92.

Damascius. *Damascii successoris dubitationes et solutiones de primis principiis in Platonis Parmenidem*, C. A. Ruelle, 2 vols. Paris, 1889.

———. *Damascii Vitae Isidori reliquiae*, ed. C. Zintsen. Hildesheim, 1967.

Kaegi, W. "The Fifth Century Twilight of Byzantine Paganism." *Classica et Mediaevalia* 27 (1966):243–75.

Maspero, J. "Horapollon et la fin du paganisme égyptien." *Bulletin de l'Institut français d'Archéologie orientale* 2 (1914):163–95.

Otto, W. *Priester und Tempel im hellenistischen Ägypten*, 2 vols. Leipzig, 1905.

Remendon, R. "L'Egypte et la suprème résistance au christianisme, (Vᵉ–VIIᵉ siècles)." *Bulletin de l'Institut français d'Archéologie orientale* 51 (1952):63–78.

STEWART L. KARREN

ASCLEPIUS 21–29. The Coptic version of *Asclepius 21–29* is the eighth tractate from Codex VI of the NAG HAMMADI LIBRARY, and occurs immediately after a scribal note (VI, 65.8–14) concerning the selection and copying of Hermetic discourses. Although it is untitled in the Coptic manuscript, *Asclepius 21–29* is assigned its present title because it is an excerpt from the long Hermetic treatise *Asclepius* (or, *Perfect Discourse*) previously known in Latin translation and brief quotations in Greek. This Coptic translation functions as the concluding tractate in a codex that contains three such Hermetic texts: the DISCOURSE ON THE EIGHTH AND NINTH (VI, 6), THE PRAYER OF THANKSGIVING (VI, 7), and *Asclepius*.

Asclepius assumes the typical form for a Hermetic tractate by presenting a dialogue between a teacher or mystagogue, Hermes Trismegistus ("Thrice-greatest" Hermes), and his pupil or initiate, Asclepius. The Coptic tractate opens with Trismegistus drawing a comparison between the Hermetic mystery and sexual intercourse. In both cases the persons involved strengthen each other by utilizing words and actions in secret. Most people, Trismegistus continues, do not understand these profound realities, since the masses are impious, wicked, and ignorant. Those of the pious minority, however, embrace the learning (*episteme*) and knowledge (*gnosis*) that have been sent by God (66.24–26), and thus such mortal humans become good and immortal—that is, they become divine. In fact, says Trismegistus, "Humans become better than the gods, since (the) gods are immortal, but humans alone are both immortal and mortal" (68.1–6).

After a query from Asclepius about idols, there follows an apocalypse (70.3–74.7) with Egyptian and Jewish affinities: Trismegistus focuses the discussion upon Egypt, which he characterizes as the "image of heaven" (70.4–5), the "temple of the world" (70.9–10), the "school of religion" (71.33). Nevertheless, he declares to Asclepius and two additional initiates (cf. 72.30–31: "O Tat [from "Thoth"], Asclepius, and Ammon"), this "divine Egypt" (71.29) will be forsaken by the gods; the gods will flee from Egypt and foreigners will lord it over Egypt instead, so that "the country which was more pious than all countries will become impious" (70.30–33). With vivid apocalyptic imagery Trismegistus describes the horrors and evils that will befall Egypt and the whole world, until at last God the creator will culminate his opposition to disorder and error by bringing about the restoration of the cosmos, "the birth of the world" (74.6–7). The tractate concludes with Trismegistus depicting the final fate of the individual: the soul will separate from the body, face the Great Daimon designated as "overseer (*episkopos*) and judge (*dikastes*) over the souls of humans" (76.24–26), and go to its appropriate reward or punishment.

Asclepius 21–29 can be classified as a fourth-century Coptic translation of an earlier Greek text. Although the Greek text of *Asclepius* presumably had a fairly complex redactional history, apparently it was known (cf. Lactantius, *Divinae institutiones* 7.18.3–5) in roughly its present form by about A.D. 300, and hence may be dated prior to that time.

BIBLIOGRAPHY

Dirkse, P. A., and D. M. Parrott. "Asclepius 21–29 (VI, 8)," 300–307. In *The Nag Hammadi Library in English*. San Francisco, 1977.

———. "VI, 8: Asclepius 21–29." In *Nag Hammadi Codices V, 2–5, and VI with Papyrus Berolinensis 8502, 1 and 4*, ed. D. M. Parrott. Nag Hammadi Studies 11. Leiden, 1979.

Facsimile Edition of the Nag Hammadi Codices: Codex VI. Leiden, 1972.

Krause, M. "Ägyptisches Gedankengut in der Apokalypse des Asclepius." *Zeitschrift der deutschen morgenländischen Gesellschaft*, Supplement 1 (1969):48–57.

Krause, M., and P. Labib. *Gnostische und hermetische Schriften aus Codex II und Codex VI*, pp.

59–62;187–206. Abhandlungen des Deutschen Archäologischen Instituts Kairo, Coptic Series 2. Glückstadt, 1971.

Mahé, J. *Hermès en Haute-Égypte: Les textes hermétiques de Nag Hammadi et leurs parallèles grecs et latins,* 2 vols. Bibliothèque copte de Nag Hammadi, section Textes 3. Quebec, 1978.

Tröger, K. "Die hermetische Gnosis." In *Gnosis und Neues Testament,* ed. K.-W. Tröger. Berlin, 1973.

MARVIN W. MEYER

ASHMŪN, a city in the Nile Delta in the Minūfiyyah Province 23 miles (about 37 km) northwest of Cairo. It appears in Coptic documents with the name ϭⲙⲟⲩⲙⲓ (Gjmoumi). In older Arabic sources it is known as Ashmūn al-Juraysāt.

In his encomium of MACROBIUS (who preceded him as bishop of NIKIOU) Bishop Mena of Nikiou mentions that Macrobius was from the village of Gjmoumi in the eparchy of the city Psati. After his martyrdom in Alexandria, Macrobius' body was brought back to Gjmoumi, where the Christian inhabitants built a church as a memorial for him (Zoega, 1810, pp. 133–34). The SYNAXARION gives a similar account of Macrobius for 2 Baramūdah, the day of his commemoration. These sources make it evident that in the early fourth century there were not only Christians in Gjmoumi/Ashmūn but a church as well.

The colophon in a Coptic manuscript in the Vatican Library (no. 59, fol. 29) suggests that at the end of the ninth century there may have been a church or a monastery in Gjmoumi/Ashmūn where manuscripts were being copied. The colophon, dated to the year A.M. 600 (A.D. 884) contains the subscriptions of a lector named Isaak and a deacon known as Kiriani, son of the deacon Stauros from Gjmoumi (Hebbelynck and Lantschoot, 1937, no. 59).

Beyond this colophon, definite attestations of Christianity in Gjmoumi/Ashmūn during the Arabic period are wanting. Nonetheless, there is still a church in Ashmūn. This building, probably of more recent construction, is dedicated to Takla Haymanot (see ETHIOPIAN SAINTS).

BIBLIOGRAPHY

Amélineau, E. *La Géographie de l'Egypte à l'époque copte,* p. 182. Paris, 1893.

Hebbelynck, A., and A. van Lantschoot. *Codices Coptici Vaticani, Barberiniani, Borgiani, Rossiani,* Vol. 1. Vatican City, 1937.

Timm, S. *Christliche Stätten in Ägypten.* Wiesbaden, 1979.

______. *Das christlich-koptische Ägypten in arabischer Zeit,* pt. 1, pp. 192–94. Wiesbaden, 1984.

Zoega, G. *Catalogus codicum copticorum manuscriptorum qui in Museo Borgiano Velitris adservantur.* Rome, 1810.

RANDALL STEWART

ASHMŪNAYN, AL- (Hermopolis Magna). [*This entry consists of two articles:* History and Architecture *and* Sculpture.]

History and Architecture

In the pharaonic period al-Ashmūnayn was the capital of the fifteenth Upper Egyptian nome of the Hare and of the Greek Hermopolite nome. Known as an episcopal see since the second half of the third century, the city sheltered the chief shrine of Thoth, god of the art of writing and of science, who was represented as a dog-headed baboon (*cynocephalus*) or as an ibis. For this reason there exist extensive cemeteries for each animal in the necropolis of al-Ashmūnayn, the present-day Tūnah al-Jabal.

The late Roman settlement expanded principally in the area of the temple of Thoth, which after its desecration lay open for civilian Christian rehabitation. Numerous papyrus finds that date to the beginnings of the Mamluk period offer information about life in al-Ashmūnayn. Regarding the architecture of the city, however, less is known. Remains of early Christian churches were discovered at the propylaeum of the temple of Thoth in the area of the temple of Amon, which was located in the same region of the city, and more recently in the neighborhood of the temple of Ramses II. Apart from this, seven churches and a monastery dedicated to Saint Severus are known by name and partly by location. The great cathedral, which was probably founded in the first half of the fifth century, lies outside the area of the Thoth temple, however; it was erected on the remains of a Ptolemaic shrine belonging to the Greek garrison once stationed there. It constitutes an independent complex enclosed by porticoes, and is entered by two monumental and richly decorated gateways at the north and west sides. From the northern gate one enters the church immediately, after crossing a couple of minor vestibules. The western gate, however, leads

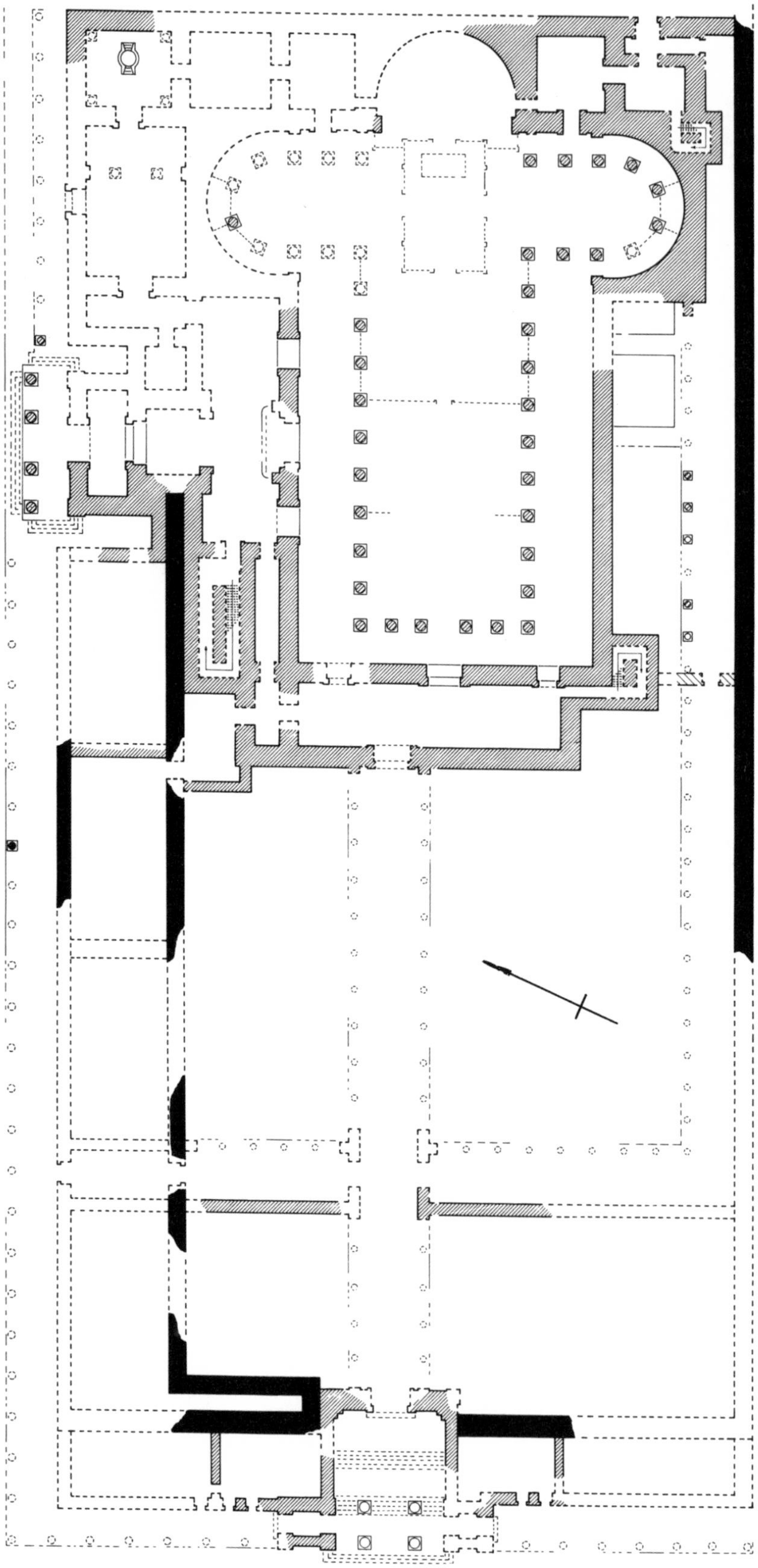

Corinthian columns of the transept basilica, al-Ashmūnayn. *Courtesy Maurice Martin, S.J., College of the Holy Family, Cairo.*

at first into a vast atrium, which is divided into four square sections by a portico erected along the entrance axis and open on both sides, with a transverse passage crossing it at right angles. The church proper, which was one of the largest and richest churches in Egypt, is set off a little to the south within the complex. Architecturally, it belongs to the type of transept basilica of which the three-aisled transept ends on both sides in a semicircle. Otherwise the church is traditional in form, with a return aisle and a separate narthex, which is slightly staggered to the side. The sanctuary is subdivided into several rooms and includes the baptistery at the far north end. For the division between the nave and the aisles, a series of tall Roman granite columns were reused. In all probability these originated from the Roman agora of al-Ashmūnayn. Several staircases introduced at various points indicate the existence of a gallery.

A second very large church is situated in front of the temple of Ramses II. It also has a very broad nave (it spans 13 yards, or 12 meters), but it is less well preserved than the transept basilica. However, the two stylobates with some column bases and the southern side of the apse are almost visible. Beside the southeast corner of the church, a fairly well preserved underground tomb was found with a staircase and two rooms separated from each other by a flattened archway. Both rooms are equipped with niches. The ceiling (probably a sailing vault) is missing. West of the tomb, remains of some installations are visible. They have been erroneously taken for a wine press (Bailey, 1982, pp. 15–18). More likely the whole installation belongs to the former baptistery tank situated on this side of the church while the small channel apparently served for leading away the used water when the ceremony of baptism came to an end.

Facing page: Plan of the great transept basilica at al-Ashmūnayn. *Courtesy Peter Grossmann.*

PETER GROSSMANN

Sculpture

The architectural decoration of the great church of Hermopolis Magna is by no means chronologically homogeneous, as reported in a 1959 monograph (Wace et al., 1959). Most of the decorated building segments were reused, as, for example, the majority of the column bases and shafts and the series of Corinthian capitals, which may have been taken from older buildings of the second to the third centuries. Certainly prepared for the church were individual Corinthian capitals and some pieces of work at special positions, including corner pilaster capitals; sheath-leaves, helices, and volutes were here merged into a single motif. A dating to the first half of the fifth century yields an important fixed point for the typological classification of Middle Egyptian capitals.

Fragments of the heads of niches and of cornices that were found in or near the building may come from the same period, but cannot yet be indisputably assigned to definite positions in the history of church architecture.

Beside a basilica situated in the south, which was not recognized as a church building by the authors of a recent report (Bailey et al., 1982), a two-chambered subterranean tomb structure was excavated (also not recognized there as a tomb). The construction had most probably a homogeneous decoration (especially Corinthian full-leaf pilaster capitals and bases) and is to be dated to the fifth century.

BIBLIOGRAPHY

Bailey, D. M. "A Late Roman Building and a Wine Press." British Museum Occasional Paper 32, pp. 11–18. London, 1982.

Bailey, D. M.; W. V. Davies; and A. J. Spencer. *Ashmunein (1980).* British Museum Occasional Paper 37, pp. 11–19. London, 1982.

Deichmann, F. W. *Die Spolien in der spätantiken Architektur,* pp. 60–62. Munich, 1975.

Grossmann, P. *Propyläen Kunstgeschichte,* Supplement 1. Berlin, 1977.

______. "Neu frühchristliche Funde aus Ägypten." *Actes du XIe Congrès international d'archéologie chrétienne.* Lyons, 1986.

Hoepfner, W. *Zwei Ptolemaierbauten,* pp. 81–87. Berlin, 1971.

Kessler, D. *Lexicon der Ägyptologie.* Wiesbaden, 1977.

Le Quien, M. *Oriens Christianus,* 3 vols. Paris, 1740.

Mähler, H. *Papyri aus Hermopolis.* Berlin, 1974.

Roeder, G. *Hermopolis 1929–1931.* Hildesheim, 1959.

Wace, A. J. B.; A. H. S. Megaw; and T. C. Skeat. *Hermopolis Magna Ashmunein: The Ptolemaic Sanctuary and the Basilica.* Alexandria, 1959.

HANS-GEORG SEVERIN

ASHMUNEN. *See* Ashmūnayn, al-.

ASHMŪN ṬANĀH, the ancient name of an Egyptian town now known as Ashmūn al-Rummān in the province of Daqahliyyah. It is located in the eastern Delta in the district of Dikirnis, about 2.5 miles (4 km) east of Dikirnis and about 25 miles (40 km) southwest of Dumyāṭ (Damietta). In Coptic documents the name of the town appears as ϣⲙⲟⲩⲛ ϭⲣⲙⲁⲛ (Schmoun Erman). Despite the fact that the town existed as early as the Byzantine period and was even the seat of a bishop, its Greek name is not known.

A story in the SYNAXARION for 10 Misrā about Bishop Apa Colluthos (Anbā Kalūj), Apa Philippus (Anbā Filibbus), and Johannes, residents of Ashmūn Tanāḥ who were apprehended and martyred for their profession of the Christian faith, attests to the presence of a Christian congregation in Ashmūn Tanāḥ at least as early as the great persecution of DIOCLETIAN.

Ancient sources indicate that Ashmūn Ṭanāḥ became a Coptic bishopric no later than the end of the thirteenth century. Bishop Mark from Ashmūn and Dumyāṭ was present at the election of the patriarch JOHN VIII in 1300 (Lantschoot, 1932, p. 229). Mark's successor as bishop was named Peter (Munier, 1943, p. 39).

BIBLIOGRAPHY

Amélineau, E. *La Géographie de l'Egypte à l'époque copte,* pp. 170–71. Paris, 1893.

Lantschoot, A. van. "Le Ms. Vatican copte 44 et le Livre du Chrême (Ms. Paris arabe 100)." *Le Muséon* 45 (1932):181–234.

Munier, H. *Recueil des listes épiscopales de l'église copte.* Cairo, 1943.

Timm, S. *Das christlich-koptische Ägypten in arabischer Zeit,* pt. 1, pp. 195–98. Wiesbaden, 1984.

RANDALL STEWART

ASKINAH (more rarely *iskīnah*), the normal designation in older texts for sanctuary and used almost exclusively, for example, in the HISTORY OF THE PATRIARCHS of SĀWĪRUS IBN AL-MUQAFFAʿ, up to the Fatimid period. After this period, in the process of a conscious reversion within Coptic Christianity to its religious origins in Judaism, the term was gradually superseded by the expression *haykal (sanctuary),* which derives from the Hebrew *hēkal* (Holy of Holies).

BIBLIOGRAPHY

Graf, G. *Verzeichnis arabischer kirchlicher Termini*, CSCO 147, p. 9, item 15. Louvain, 1954.

Muyser, J. "Des vases eucharistiques en verre." *Bulletin de la société d'archéologie copte* 3 (1937):9–28.

PETER GROSSMANN

ASQIT. *See* Scetis.

ASSEMANI, the Latinized form of the Arabic al-Sim'ānī and surname of four Maronite members of a Syrian family of noted Orientalists who lived from the late seventeenth to the early nineteenth century. They are Joseph Simeonis (Arabic, Yūsuf Sim'ān; 1687–1768), Stephen (Arabic, Istafān) Evodius (1709–1782), Joseph (Arabic, Yūsuf) Aloysius (1710–1782), and Simon (Arabic, Sim'ān; 1752?–1821). All of them graduated from the Maronite College at Rome, and all became attached to the Vatican Library in various capacities while contributing greatly to its publication series and the cataloging of accumulated Oriental manuscripts.

Joseph Simeonis Assemani was an active collector of manuscripts on behalf of the Vatican, especially those in Syriac, Coptic, and Arabic from Middle Eastern sources, including the Coptic monasteries of Wādī al-Naṭrūn (see SCETIS). He was twice commissioned by Pope Clement XI, in 1715 and 1735, to travel in the countries of the Middle East for that purpose. In 1736, Clement XII nominated him to preside over a national Maronite council at Dayr Luwayzah near Beirut, where Joseph Simeonis was instrumental in bringing his native church into closer relationship with Rome. Subsequently he became titular archbishop of Tyre and prefect of the Vatican Library until his death on 13 January 1768.

His major contributions include *Bibliotheca Orientalis* (4 vols., Rome, 1719–1728); *Chronicon Orientale Petri Rahebi Aegyptii* . . . (Venice, 1729); "Kalendaria Ecclesiae Universae," in A. Mai, *Scriptorum Veterum Nova Collectio*, Vol. 5 (Rome, 1731); *Ephraemi Syri Opera Omnia* (6 vols., Rome, 1732–1746); *Bibliotheca Juris Orientalis Canonici et Civili* (5 vols., 1762–1766), and many subsidiary works.

Stephen Evodius, nephew of Joseph Simeonis, under whom he received his training while studying at the Maronite College in Rome, traveled widely as a missionary for the Sacred Congregation for the Propagation of the Faith in the Middle East. He returned to Europe and there resumed his extensive travels. In the end, he settled in Rome and was nominated by the Vatican as titular archbishop of Apamea and succeeded his uncle as prefect of the Vatican Library. He is credited with the publication of the *Bibliotheca Mediceae-Laurentianae et Palatinae Codicum MSS. Orientalium Catalogus* (2 vols., Florence, 1742) and *Acta Sanctorum Martyrum Orientalium et Occidentalium* (2 vols., Rome, 1748). He also published *Catalogus Bibliothecae Vaticanae Codicum MSS.* (3 vols., Rome, 1756–1759), an ambitious project originally planned in twenty volumes but interrupted by the fire of 1768.

A second nephew, Joseph Aloysius, became professor at the Pontifical Academy. He produced a number of relatively minor publications and his major work, entitled *Codex liturgicus ecclesiae universae in quo continentur libri ritualis, officia, dypticha . . . ecclesiarum occidentalis et orientalis* . . . (13 vols., 1749–1766, repr., 1902).

Simon, a descendant of the same family, was born in Tripoli in 1749 or 1752, received his education at Rome, and then became a missionary for twelve years in Syria. Ultimately he returned to Italy, where he became professor of Oriental languages at the University of Padua. He was the Arabist of the family. His publications included *Saggis sull'origine, culto, literatura e costumi degli Arabi avanti il pseudoprofeta Maometto* (Padua, 1787). He also published *Catalogi de' codice manoscritti orientali della Biblioteca Naniana* (Padua, 1787). He died in Padua.

Although most of the Assemani publications lack the technique of modern scholarship, they have proved to be of enduring value to succeeding generations of scholars.

BIBLIOGRAPHY

Debs, Elias Yūsuf. *Kitāb Tārīkh Sūriyā*, Vol. 8. Beirut, 1903.

Petit, L. "Assemani." In *Dictionnaire d'archéologie chrétienne et liturgie*, Vol. 1. Paris, 1907.

Vida, G. L. della. *Richerche sulla formazione del più antico fondo dei manoscritti orientali della Biblioteca Vaticana*. Studi e testi 92. Vatican City, 1939.

AZIZ S. ATIYA

ASSUMPTION, the taking up of Mary into heaven. The calendar of feasts of the Coptic church celebrates the death of the Virgin Mother of God and the ascension of her soul into heaven on 21 Ṭūbah. The metamorphosis or conveyance of her body into heaven is placed on 16 Misrā. There is thus a 206-day interval between these two complementary feasts. None of the Eastern churches has preserved this state of affairs, apart from the daughter church of Ethiopia.

The Coptic Tradition

The Copts have an abundant literature on the Assumption, which was in part described by A. van Lantschoot in 1946. The Ethiopian texts were published by V. Arras in 1973 and 1974. To understand the strangeness of the 206 days that separate the process of the Assumption into two phases, it is necessary to give a general survey of the tradition.

Nicephorus Callistus Xanthopoulos in the fourteenth century attributes to the emperor Maurice (582–602) the fixing of the feast to 15 August (PG 147, col. 292). This date corresponds to the construction by the emperor of a new church at Gethsemane, the dedication of which took place on 23 October but in which the celebration of the Virgin is placed on 15 August (Garitte, 1958, pp. 302–303, 365).

The Georgian tradition has further preserved the memory of a congregation on 17 August at the Nea, the new Saint Mary's built by Justinian in 543. In addition, the Georgian Menaia, or hymnic calendar, retains on 16 August a commemoration of the deposition of the Virgin "from Sion to Gethsemane." Finally, a Georgian Transitus attributed to Basil mentions apostolic "prescriptions" creating a kind of *quatriduum* from 14 to 17 August. Since the Nea was destroyed in 614, as was also the Church of Maurice, and only Saint Sion was rebuilt with Gethsemane, it follows that the cycles of which traces remain in Georgian are from the period of Justinian, before the date of 15 August was fixed upon. The development of the liturgy there implies a "holy" week of the Virgin, imitating that of Christ and running from 9/10 August to 16/17 August (van Esbroeck, 1981, pp. 284–85).

In all probability this is the origin of the date of 7 August among the Copts, who separated from the usage of Jerusalem before the fixing of the feast on 15 August. The occasion is made clear in the panegyric of MACARIUS OF TKOW by pseudo-Dioscorus, a Coptic pseudepigraph. When Juvenal of Jerusalem came back from the Council of CHALCEDON, this text relates, the dissidents assembled at the church in the valley of Jehoshaphat on 21 Tobe, the feast of the death of Mary among the Copts. However fictitious may be the sequel to the story, which has Peter the Fuller's formula intoned by the assembled crowd, the information remains significant. From the beginning, the sanctuary of Gethsemane became the symbol of opposition to Chalcedon. Nor is the date of 29 January any more fortuitous. It falls in the octave of the Epiphany (see FEASTS, MAJOR), which at the beginning of MONOPHYSITISM was identified with the Nativity by literal exegesis of Luke 3:23, Jesus being thirty years old at his baptism and having been born in divine and human natures simultaneously.

There was already a movable feast of Mary shortly before 25 December at the end of the fourth century, before the introduction of Christmas on that day. Among the Greek Orthodox the feast was transferred by the emperor JUSTINIAN, as the Annunciation, to 25 March. Before that, it remained on 26 December or later, the Sunday in the octave of Christmas or, by substitution after the Epiphany, in Monophysite circles. From 7 to 16 January we have thus a week parallel to that of 10 to 17 August. That of 29 January lent itself to the celebration of the death of the Virgin at the time when the distinction of the two natures at Chalcedon was understood as detrimental to the title *Theotokos*. It is known that after Juvenal's return a certain Theodore or Theodosius became a counterbishop for the opposing faction. The latter's activity is certainly expressed in the liturgy. Furthermore, the structure of the legends of the Dormition justifies an initial association of the December festival with the death of Mary. The Latins are witness to this state of affairs: Gregory of Tours at the end of the sixth century knew a feast "in the middle of the month of January" for the death of the Virgin. For its part, the Virgin's *natalis dies* occurs on 15 August for the first time among the Latins in a Wurzburg capitulary going back to about 675, although traces of 18 January appear concurrently (Morin, 1911, p. 313). The variation from 16 to 18 January is explained by the third day on which, among the Copts, the apostles hear the promise of the assumption of the body for 16 Misrā.

The numerous legends of the Assumption may be divided into two groups. The first describes the unique destiny of Mary, marked by the descent of an angel who hands over the palm of immortality. The apostles assemble close to Mary only in Jerusalem. The attempt by the Jews to destroy her body is presided over by the high priest Jephonias. The second group is characterized by a preliminary gathering of the apostles at Bethlehem, by continual censings, by the replacing of the palm by a dry stick, and by the reduction of Jephonias to an ordinary Jew of exceptional stature, the leader of the adversaries. Reserving the question of a theological concept that the body of the Virgin is a real temple, we may consider that the story in the Syriac letter of CYRIL OF JERUSALEM on the destruction of the Temple has influenced an episode in the second legend (Brock, 1977, p. 283), and that it is thus a little later than the beginning of the fifth century, when these ideas were still matters of some interest. The other legend is earlier. All the texts preserved in Coptic belong to the first form of the legend. It seems probable that the Marial feast near 25 December had been linked with the death of Mary, according to the most ancient representations.

On the contrary, the second type, which includes Bethlehem, would in origin be linked with the celebration of the Nativity in the month of August. There is indeed for 13 August a Synaxis preserved in Georgian at the church of the Kathisma three miles from Jerusalem on the road to Bethlehem. This church was in fact the foundation of a woman whose name was Ikelia and was consecrated by Juvenal around 450 on 2 December (Garitte, 1958, p. 301). It seems almost certain that this was not the first church there, as B. Capelle thinks (1943, pp. 21–22). Juvenal, who was trying to introduce the date of 25 December to Jerusalem, had reason to establish there an advance post to promote the celebration of Christmas on 25 December.

The transplanting of the Virgin's death to the month of August entailed the second cycle of legends. At that point when Maurice fixed the feast at 15 August, the text that seems trustworthy is the Greek legend (*Bibliotheca Hagiographica Graeca* 1055), attributed without hesitation to John the Evangelist. This is an epitome of the second form, the developed types of which attempt with powerful argument to attribute it to John. Fortunately, the diligence of John of Thessalonica has preserved for us a double reconstruction of the first legend (*Bibliotheca Hagiographica Graeca* 1144d and 1144), and A. Wenger has recovered a form of the ancient legend (*Bibliotheca Hagiographica Graeca* 105bd). Thanks to the parallel versions of Ethiopic, Georgian, and Irish, these permit a glimpse of the earliest state of this first type, of which there is also a Syriac fragment of the fifth century. To this type belong all the following Coptic derivatives (cf. van Esbroeck, 1981, p. 267):

C.1 The *Transitus* published by Révillout (1907), pp. 174–83.

C.2 *Cyril of Jerusalem*, ed. Forbes Robinson (1896), pp. 24–41, to which corresponds the Pierpont Morgan M 597, fols. 46–74 (*Bibliotheca Hagiographica Orientalis* 671b). A related version is found in W. Budge (1915), pp. 49–73, which corresponds to the Pierpont Morgan M 583, pp. 139–57, recently published by A. Campagnano (1980), pp. 152–94.

C.3 *Evodius of Rome*, fragment ed. W. Spiegelberg (1903), pp. 2–4, and Pierpont Morgan M 596, pp. 20–25, and M 598, pp. 1–9 (*Bibliotheca Hagiographica Orientalis* 667).

C.4 *Evodius of Rome*, Bohairic version, ed. P. A. de Lagarde (1883), pp. 38–63, and Sahidic version, ed. F. Robinson (1896), pp. 162–84 (*Bibliotheca Hagiographica Orientalis* 666).

C.5 *Theodosius of Alexandria*, Vatican 61, Bohairic version, ed. F. Robinson (1896), pp. 90–126, and M. Chaine (1934), pp. 272–314 (*Bibliotheca Hagiographica Orientalis* 671).

C.6 *Theophilus of Alexandria*, ed. W. H. Worrell, (1923), pp. 249–321.

C.7 Bohairic fragments, ed. H. G. Evelyn-White (1926), pp. 55–58.

The text C.2 is unfortunately fragmentary. All its elements form part of the first group. The interest of these pages lies in the fact that the announcement of the Assumption of the body on 16 Misrā may have been made without passing by the tomb at Gethsemane. But the fragmentary state of paragraph 129,23 leaves the door open for a good many improvements. The texts attributed to Cyril of Jerusalem (C.2) replace the Dormition in the more general framework of the Life of the Virgin, which is evoked to counter Ebionite and Harpocratian heretics. The point is to oppose ideas of mere "fantasy"; it has to be shown that there really is a tomb, and that the Virgin is not a phantom. The witnesses to the Dormition adduced by C.2 belong to the Johannine cycle of Prochorus: John, Peter, Verus, and James. The Ethiopic version of C.2 published by V. Arras in 1974 (pp. 1–33) is a development in the same line as C.2 in connecting the witnesses with the cycle of Prochorus. The doctrinal attacks seem to be aimed at the disappearance of the body according to the complete witnesses of C.1.

C.3 and C.4 base their accounts of the facts on another group of witnesses: Evodius, the successor of Peter at Antioch before Ignatius; Peter; Alexander; and Rufus. The presentation of the facts corroborates the doctrinal attacks of C.2. The role of John is reduced to very small dimensions. It is probable that the two presentations and the two groups of witnesses correspond to the respective traditions of the aphthartodocetic Gaianites and those of the Severians, who formed a majority in the Coptic church. We may gain some idea of the antiquity of these representations by noting that the cycle of Dionysius the Areopagite, born toward the beginning of the sixth or the end of the fifth century, is a rejoinder from Juvenal. Dionysius, Titus, Timothy, and Hierotheus are present at the Dormition. PULCHERIA, the wife of the "impious" Marcian, demands the body of Mary from Juvenal, for she has learned of the existence of the tomb. Juvenal explains that the body disappeared from the tomb at the moment when the apostle Thomas, at first absent, came back and asked for the tomb to be opened (*Historia euthymiaca, Bibliotheca Hagiographica Graeca* 1056e). This defense *pro domo* is intended to cast a shadow upon the erroneous presentations of the Chalcedonian Marcian. Dionysius the Areopagite speaks of the body that received God, *theodokhon soma* (PG 3, col. 681), transferring the Nestorian adjective to the inanimate body of Mary alone. Conversely, C.5, the discourse of Theodosius, was obliged to show that the body of Mary was the object of an assumption different from those of the bodies of Enoch and Elijah. The two Coptic types, C.2 and C.4, thus have their source in developments prior to 500. This is not the case with the blossoming of the second group, but the latter is transmitted practically only in Arabic.

The Arabic Tradition

The Arabic tradition on the Assumption touches the Coptic world very closely. Almost all the attributions come back to Egyptian bishops. But the body of the legend belongs almost always to the second group. The following is a preliminary description of the Arabic corpus:

A. 1 The *Transitus* in six books. Edited from a recent manuscript by M. Enger in 1864 (*Bibliotheca Hagiographica Orientalis* 633–38), this text exists in a tenth-century manuscript pointed out by G. Graf (1915), p. 340, and today at Bryn Mawr College.

A. 2 Under the name of CYRIL OF ALEXANDRIA, a homily for 21 Ṭūbah has been published (1927), pp. 210–48.

A. 3 Under the name of Cyril of Alexandria, a homily for 16 Misrā (1927), pp. 248–60.

A. 4 Theodosius of Alexandria, Vatican Arabic 698, fols. 85–102. Translation of C.5.

A. 5 Transitus, in Paris Arabic 150, translated by J. Leroy (1910), pp. 162–72.

A. 6 Theophilus of "Landra," Vatican 698, fols. 41–48, translation of the Greek homily of Theoteknos of Livias, *Bibliotheca Hagiographica Graeca* 1083u.

A. 7 Vatican Arabic 170, fols. 317–39, homily of Cyriacus of Bahnasā.

A. 8 A variant of the *Historia euthymiaca* published by M. van Esbroeck (1975–1976), pp. 485–88.

A. 9 Transitus of John the Evangelist, in Vatican Arabic 698, fols. 51–84.

A.10 Coptic Museum in Cairo 105 (Hist. 477), fols. 145–54.

The legend in six books, based on Syriac models, goes back to copies of the sixth century. The very artificial construction of the six books is based on the story of the finding of the book written by the apostle John. This discovery was made at Ephesus by three monks from Sinai at the invitation of Cyril of Jerusalem. The cycle of the finding of the Cross and of JUDAS CYRIACUS is included in the report of the Dormition. The end of the text alludes to apostolic canons appointing three Marial feasts for 24 December, 15 May, and 13 August. The inclusion of Bethlehem in the story of the Dormition is central. In theory, each of the six books was composed by two apostles, but one can scarcely see how this principle could be applied in the course of the narration.

Forms A.2, A.3, and A.5 combine this legend with elements from the cycle of Prochorus (C.2). A.7 contaminates the two groups even further. A.8 is particularly interesting, because it is a witness to the *Historia euthymiaca*, relating how the apostle Thomas arrived too late and prompted the authentication of the disappearance of the Virgin's body. But in A.8 it is Eudocia or EUDOXIA who makes the request for the relic, not Pulcheria. A.10 develops the episode of Thomas. Coming from India, Thomas, traversing the region on the clouds, meets with the Virgin carried up into heaven. She leaves him her veil as a relic, and Thomas lets it fall in Egypt at the Monastery of the Fountain, west of Akhmīm. There are parallels to these legends in a Latin form (Bibliotheca Hagiographica Latina 5348–50). The Virgin's two linen robes are collected by Verus (in Coptic, Bibros) in C.2, which also relates the building by Constantine and his sons of the church for the feast of the disappearance of the Virgin on the night of 20 Tobe. Gregory of Tours in his work *In gloria martyrum* at the end of the sixth century also speaks of the basilica built by Constantine.

The Coptic traditions, as we see, have collected

their elements at all the stages of the development of the legends about the Dormition of Mary. We may add that MICHAEL and GABRIEL play considerable roles in the first group of legends, and that the book of the enthronement of each archangel, peculiar to the Copts, derives from the tradition about the Assumption of the Virgin, in type C.2, which gives a large place to the disciples of John, Verus, and Prochorus.

BIBLIOGRAPHY

Arras, V., ed. *De Transitu Mariae Apocrypha Aethiopice* 1. In CSCO 342, Scriptores Aethiopici 66. Louvain, 1973.

______, ed. *De Transitu Mariae Apocrypha aethiopice* 2. CSCO 352, Scriptores Aethiopici 69, pp. 72–74. Louvain, 1974. Supplies an excellent bibliography.

Brock, S. P. "A Letter Attributed to Cyril of Jerusalem on the Rebuilding of the Temple." *Bulletin of the School of Oriental & African Studies* 40 (1977):267–86.

Budge, E. A. W. *Miscellaneous Coptic Texts in the Dialect of Upper Egypt.* London, 1915.

Campagno, A. *Omilie copte sulla Passione el la crocee e sulla Vergine.* Milan, 1980.

Capelle, B. "La Fête de la vierge à Jérusalem." *Le Muséon* 56 (1943):1–33.

Chaine, M. In *Revue de l'Orient Chrétien* (1934): 272–314.

______. *Apocrypha de B. Maria Virgine.* Rome, 1909. Repr. 1955.

Enger, M., ed. *Joannis Apostolis de transitu B. Mariae Virginis liber.* Eberfeld, 1854.

Esbroeck, M. van. "Historia Euthymiaca." *Parole de l'Orient* 6–7 (1975–1976):485–88.

______. "Les Textes littéraires sur l'assomption avant le Xe siècle." In *Les Actes Apocryphes des Apôtres. Christianisme et le monde païen,* ed. F. Bovon. Geneva, 1981.

Evelyn-White, H. G. *The Monasteries of the Wadi 'n Natrūn,* Vol. 1. *New Coptic Texts from the Monastery of Saint Macarius.* New York, 1926.

Garitte, G. *Le Calendrier palestino-géorgien du Sinaīticus* 34. Brussels, 1958.

Graf, G. "Forschungen und Funde." *Oriens Christianus* n.s. 4 (1915):338–40.

Gregory of Tours. *De gloria beatorum martyrum.* In PL 71. Paris, 1879.

Lagarde, P. A. de. *Aegyptiaca.* Göttingen, 1883.

Lantschoot, A. van. "L'Assomption de la sainte vierge chez les Coptes." *Gregorianum* 27 (1946):439–526.

Leroy, J. "Transitus." In *Revue de l'Orient chrétien* 15 (1910):162–72.

Malalas, John. *Ioannis Malalae Chronographia,* ed. Ludwig A. Dindorf. Bonn, 1831.

Morin, G. "Liturgie et basiliques romaines du VIIe siècle d'après les listes d'évangiles de Wurzbourg." *Revue bénédictine* 28 (1911):296–330.

Revillout, E., ed. *Les apocryphes coptes.* In PO 2, pt. 2; 9, pt. 2. Paris, 1907.

Robinson, Forbes. *N. T. Apocryphal Books. Gospels. Coptic.* Cambridge, Eng., 1896.

Spiegelberg, Wilhelm. *Geschichte der ägyptischen Kunst bis zum Hellenismus im abriss dargestellt.* Leipzig, 1903.

Wenger, A. *L'Assomption de la très sainte Vierge dans la tradition byzantine du VIe au Xe siècle.* Paris, 1955.

Worrell, W. H., ed. *The Coptic Manuscripts in the Freer Collection.* New York, 1923.

MICHEL VAN ESBROECK

ASSUMPTION OF THE THEOTOKOS, FAST OF THE. *See* Fasts.

ASSUMPTION OF THE VIRGIN'S BODY, FEAST OF THE. *See* Theotokos, Feast of the.

ASṬĀSĪ AL-RŪMĪ, or Eustathius the Greek, one of the most productive painters of Coptic icons in the latter part of the nineteenth century. An Arabic-speaking Greek iconographer from Jerusalem, he worked in Egypt for a period of approximately thirty-five years, from 1836 to 1871. Most of his many icons, which were commissioned either by Coptic priests or by Coptic notables, were painted in Cairo, where he lived in the ḤĀRIT AL-RŪM. Many of his icons were produced during the iconoclastic controversy within the Coptic church, when the Patriarch CYRIL IV ordered the destruction of many icons, particularly in Upper Egypt. There is not evidence that Asṭāsī was familiar with the Greek, Coptic, or Latin script, and his errors on inscriptions indicate that he was unfamiliar with the Greek and the Latin alphabets. He painted all his icons on wood, a noteworthy fact because during the nineteenth century most Coptic icons were painted on canvas. In addition, he adorned numerous chalice arks with his paintings. In all instances he added to the bottom of his paintings an Arabic text in the form of a votive inscription including his name and the date. In most cases he used the Coptic calendar and in some instances the Islamic calendar.

His subjects can be divided into three groups: the Holy Virgin and Child, the feasts of the church, and the saints of the church. Asṭāsī's icons are found in the Coptic churches of Old Cairo, the Ḥārit al-Rūm, the ḤĀRIT ZUWAYLAH, the churches of the monasteries of the Wādī al-Natrūn, the Monastery of the Holy Virgin (DAYR AL-MUḤARRAQ), the Church of the Holy Virgin, JABAL AL-ṬAYR, and ASYŪṬ.

BIBLIOGRAPHY

Meinardus, O. "The Iconography of Astasi al-Rumi." *Studia Orientalia Christiana Aegyptiaca, Collectanea* 14 (1970–1971):377–97.

OTTO MEINARDUS

ASTERISK. *See* Eucharistic Vessels and Instruments.

ASWAN (Syene), a town on the east bank of the Nile, at the position of the First Cataract, which in pharaonic times marked the borders of Egypt on the south. In the imperial period it was an administrative center and garrison town (Strabo *Geographica* 17.1.12), and from an early date (since A.D. 325; cf. Timm, 1984, p. 222) the seat of a bishop, to whose dioceses ELEPHANTINE and Contra-Syene also belonged (Wilcken, 1901, p. 399).

The fortification wall of the town, evidently going back to late Roman origins, could be followed almost throughout its course down to the Napoleonic expedition, but today, apart from a few sections, it has disappeared. Similarly, no early or even medieval church remains have been preserved in Aswan. The Ptolemaic temple of Isis does show clear traces of Christianization, allowing us to deduce its conversion into a three-aisled church with remains of paintings on both pronaos pillars and a few Coptic graffiti, but this church was certainly not the chief church of the town. Another Ptolemaic temple transformed into a church in the Christian period is mentioned by an unknown author in *Proceedings of the Society of Biblical Archaeology* (1908, pp. 73–74; see also Bresciani and Pernigotti, 1978). A group of granite columns, some still standing in the southwest of the temple of Domitian (Jomard, 1820, Vol. 1, pl. 38, 9; on the layout, pl. 31) presumably belongs to a loggia-type building of the late third century at the Roman forum of Aswan.

However, in 1896, during excavations for *sabakh* (fertilizer) in the southwest of the town, remains of a basilica with several granite columns were discov-

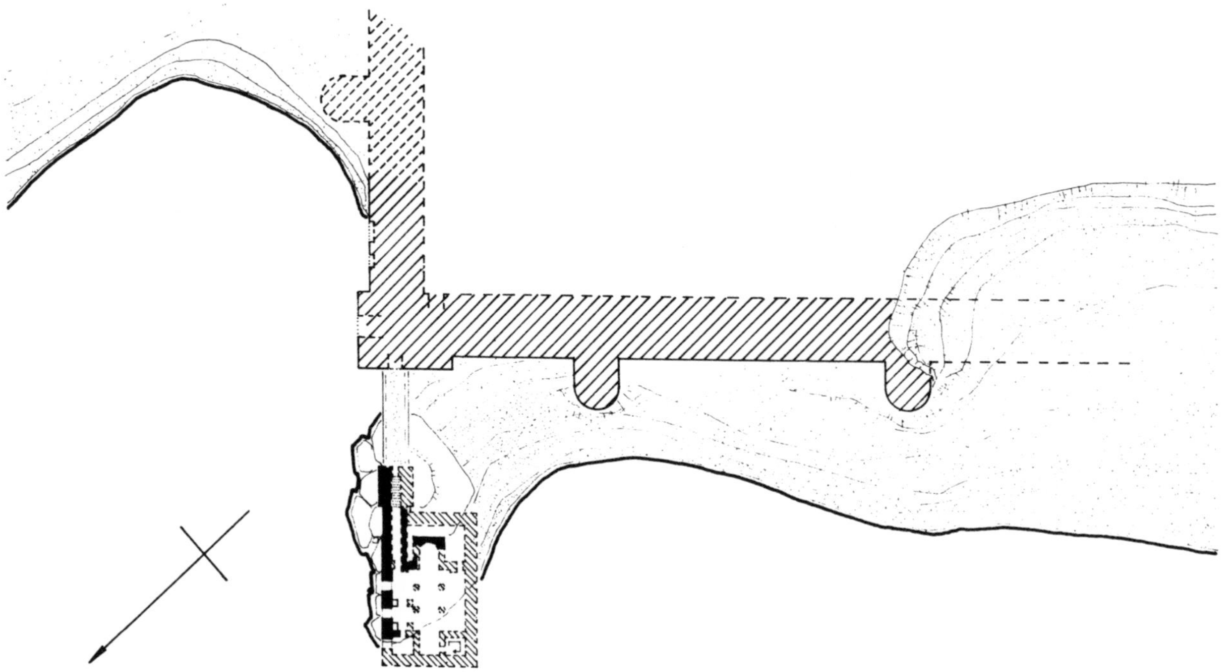

Map showing the exact location of the church of Saint Psote before the Nile bank was straightened. *Courtesy Peter Grossmann.*

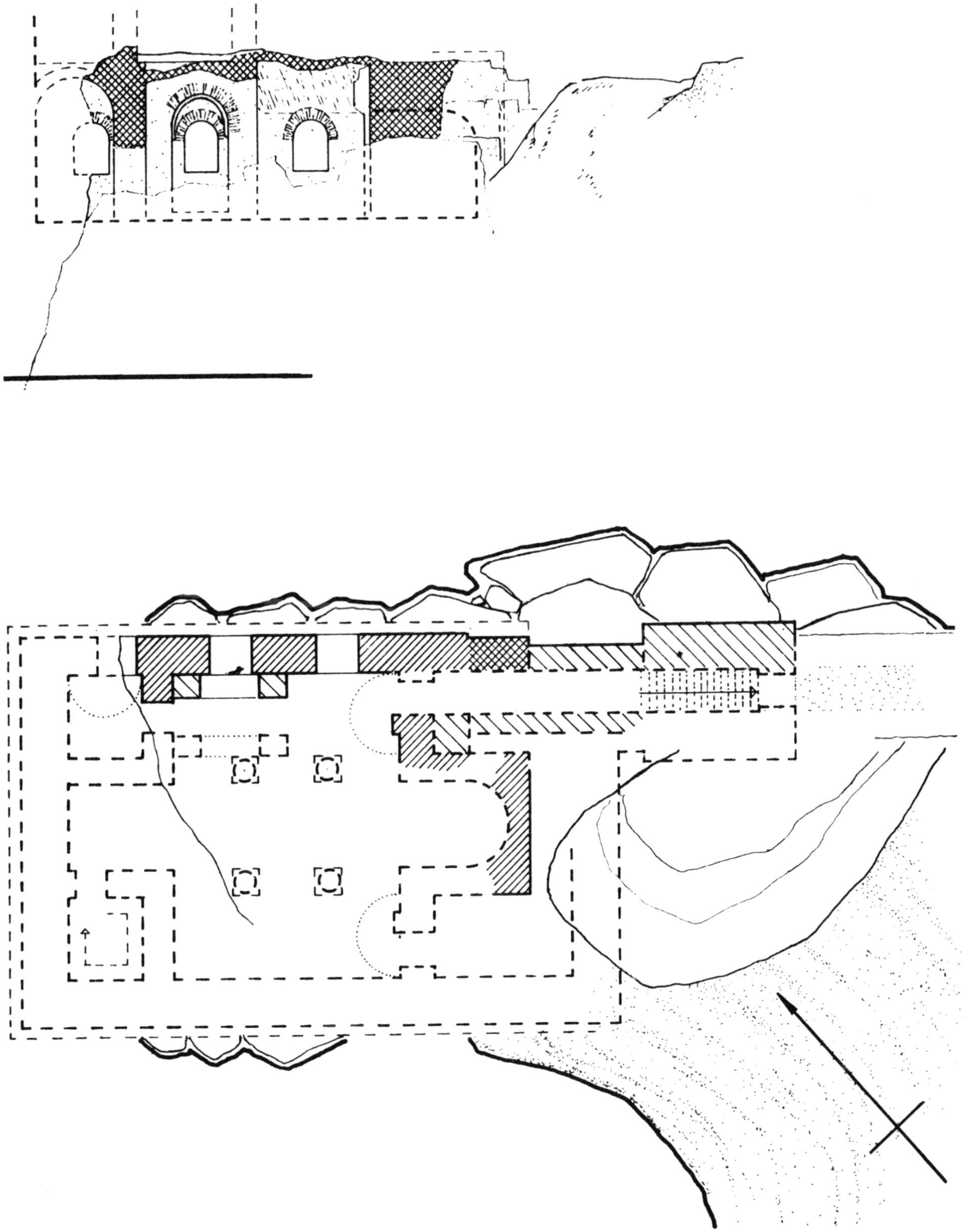

Elevation and plan of the medieval church of Saint Psote, at one time located at Aswan. *Courtesy Peter Grossmann.*

ered, as well as a baptistery belonging to it (Jouguet, 1896, pp. 37ff.; on the columns and capitals, cf. Monneret de Villard, 1927, p. 152). A scientific examination of these remains was not, however, carried out at the time. Today the exact location of this site can no longer be determined.

In addition, part of the medieval church of Saint PSOTE (presumably the basement floor), mentioned by ABŪ AL-MAKĀRIM (*The Churches* . . ., 1895 fols. 101b–102a, pp. 276–77), survived down to 1965. It was built on a spit of land in front of the northwest corner tower of the late Roman castrum lying directly on the riverbank, and in later times was submerged during high Nile floods. Typologically this church was related to the Nubian four-column buildings, but in contrast to these it was built in stone instead of mud bricks. It was demolished in 1966 in the course of straightening the Nile bank. With the aid of some old photographs, it was reconstructed (Jaritz, 1985) as a building with four internal columns and a three-partite sanctuary.

BIBLIOGRAPHY

Bresciani, E., and Pernigotti, S. *Assuan, Il tempio tolemaico di Isi,* pp. 38–41, 146, pls. 37 and 38. Pisa, 1978. Reconstruction of the church was not attempted.

Jaritz, H. "Die Kirche des Hl. Psōti vor der Stadtmauer von Assuan." In *Mélanges Gamal Eddin Mokhtar.* Bibliothèque d'Etude 97, Vol. 2. Cairo, 1985.

Jomard, E. F., ed. *Description de l'Egypte.* Vol. 1, *Antiquités.* Paris, 1820.

Jouguet, P. *Comptes rendus de l'Académie des Inscriptions et Belles-Lettres.* Paris, 1896.

Monneret de Villard, U. "Il monastero di S. Simeone presso Aswan." In *Descrizione Archeologica.* Milan, 1927.

Timm, S. *Das christlich-koptische Ägypten in arabischer Zeit,* Vol. 1, pp. 222–35. Wiesbaden, 1984.

Wilcken, U. "Heidnisches und Christliches aus Ägypten." *Archeological Papyrus* 1 (1901):396ff.

PETER GROSSMANN

ASYŪṬ, a city on the west bank of the Nile in middle Egypt. The Greeks called the city Λύκων πόλις, Lúkōn pólis (Lycopolis, "wolf city") because of the citizens' reverence for Wepwawet, the wolf god. Asyūṭ, the city's modern Arabic name, is derived from the Coptic ⲥⲓⲟⲟⲩⲧ.

Lycopolis, home of a Christian community since at least as early as the great persecution of DIOCLETIAN at the beginning of the fourth century, became one of the most important centers of Christianity in Egypt during the Roman and Byzantine periods. The SYNAXARION for 1 Amshīr relates that Bishop Apadion from Antinoë (ANTINOOPOLIS) found a group of Christians in Lycopolis when he visited the city at the beginning of the fourth century. The persecutions themselves reached the city in the person of ARIANUS, who condemned and martyred many Christians in Lycopolis, among them Saint Thecla (Till, 1935–1936, Vol. 1, p. 116; Vol. 2, p. 131). The martyr Phoibammon was also killed in Lycopolis, and later a church was raised there as a memorial to him.

Saint VICTOR OF SHŪ was born in Asyūṭ, and Saint Claudius of Antioch was buried not far from the city. The most celebrated ascetic associated with the city was JOHN OF LYCOPOLIS, who lived in the fourth century in a cave some five miles from Lycopolis (*Historia Monachorum* 1.6). In the fourteenth century, when the Arabic Synaxarion was written, there were two churches in the vicinity of John's cave, a church of John himself and a church of the archangel Michael.

Among the early bishops of Lycopolis were ALEXANDER, Apollonius, and MELITIUS. Alexander was a Neoplatonist philosopher who converted to Christianity and was said by Photius of Constantinople to have become bishop of Lycopolis (*Contra Manichaeos* 1.11). Apollonius apostatized in the persecutions of 304–305, and Melitius became well known as the leader of a schismatic group that ordained its own bishops in many cities and towns in Egypt. In 325 Bishop Plusanius of Lycopolis attended the Council of NICAEA. Eudaimon succeeded him in the office sometime around 347 (Munier, 1943, pp. 5, 10). One of the most important bishops of Lycopolis was CONSTANTINE, who was ordained by Patriarch DAMIAN (569–605). Constantine was an author of Coptic panegyrics, some of which are also preserved in Arabic translation (for a list of his works, see Garitte, 1950, pp. 278–304).

For several centuries after the ARAB CONQUEST OF EGYPT in 641 there are no records of bishops in Lycopolis/Asyūṭ. Then a colophon in a manuscript from DAYR ANBĀ SĀWĪRUS in Jabal Rifā dated 1003 mentions a bishop Gregory of Asyūṭ (Crum, 1915, pp. 47, 104–105). The HISTORY OF THE PATRIARCHS relates that some time later Patriarch SHENUTE II (1032–1046) ordained the archpriest Apater (Badīr) as bishop of Asyūṭ, but Apater was not accepted by the people for three years because he had paid Shenute to perform the ordination. Bishop Antony of Asyūṭ attended the synod in Cairo in 1086 (Munier, 1943, p. 29). An inscription in DAYR ANBĀ SHINŪDAH near Suhāj indicates that Christodoulus was bishop in Asyūṭ around 1237 (Crum, 1904, p. 558). According to Munier (1943, p. 31), in 1240 Christodoulus signed the canons of Patriarch CYRIL III IBN LAQLAQ (1235–1243). At the consecration of the holy chrism in 1308 Bishop Severus of Asyūṭ was present, and Bishop Philotheus of Asyūṭ attended the same event around 1330 (Munier, 1943, pp. 38, 40). Philotheus was bishop until at least 1362, at which time he signed a document of appointment (Crum, 1909, no. 909). When J. VANSLEB visited Egypt in 1672 he met with John, who was bishop of ASYŪṬ, NAQĀDAH, JIRJĀ, and ABŪ TĪJ (Vansleb, 1678, pp. 218–219, 227). This John was present at the preparation of the chrism in 1703 as the bishop of Asyūṭ and Manfalūṭ (Munier, 1943, p. 42). In 1794 a manuscript was dedicated to Bishop Michael of Asyūṭ (Graf, 1934, no. 387). Through their writings we know also of Paul, who was bishop of Asyūṭ, Abū Tīj, and Manfalūṭ, and of YUHANNIS, BISHOP OF ASYŪṬ, though there is no record of when they were in office. Paul was the author of martyrdoms (Graf, 1944–1953, Vol. 1, p. 532; Vol. 2, pp. 505–6) and Yuhannis is known as the compiler of the accounts of Saint Dilagi and the martyrs of Isnā (Graf, 1944–1953, Vol. 1, p. 536).

As one would expect in a place with a long and rich tradition of Christianity, there are a number of churches and monasteries in and around Asyūṭ. For detailed information about these sites, see the articles on DAYR ABŪ BIFĀM (Asyūṭ), DAYR ABŪ ISḤĀQ (Abnūb-Asyūṭ), DAYR ABŪ MAQRŪFAH, DAYR ABŪ MŪSHĀ, DAYR AL-'ADHRA' (Abnūb-Asyūṭ), DAYR AL-'AWANAH, DAYR AL-BALĀYZAH, DAYR AL-'IẒĀM, DAYR AL-JABRĀWĪ, DAYR AL-MALĀK MĪKHĀ'ĪL (Rayramum Asyūṭ), Dayr al-Muḥarraq, DAYR AL-MUṬṬIN, DAYR AL-NAṢĀRĀ (southeast of Asyūṭ), DAYR BUQṬUR OF SHŪ, DAYR DURŪNKAH, DAYR HARMĪNĀ, DAYR RĪFAH, DAYR TĀSĀ, and MONASTERIES OF THE MIDDLE ṢA'ĪD.

BIBLIOGRAPHY

Amélineau, E. *La Géographie de l'Egypt à l'époque copte*, pp. 464–66. Paris, 1893.

Crum, W. E. "Inscriptions from Shenoute's Monastery." *Journal of Theological Studies* 5 (1904):552–68.

______. *Catalogue of the Coptic Manuscripts in the Collection of the John Rylands Library, Manchester.* Manchester, 1909.

______. *Der Papyruscodex saec. VI–VII der Phillippsbibliothek in Cheltenham.* Strasbourg, 1915.

Garitte, G. "Constantin, évêque d'Assiout." In *Coptic Studies in Honor of Walter Ewing Crum*, pp. 287–304. Boston, 1950.

Graf, G. *Catalogue de manuscrits Arabes chrétiens conservés au Caire.* Vatican City, 1934.

Munier, H. *Recueil des listes épiscopales de l'église copte.* Cairo, 1943.

Reymond, E. A. E., and J. W. B. Barns. *Four Martyrdoms from the Pierpont Morgan Coptic Codices.* Oxford, 1973.

Till, W. *Koptische Heiligen- und Märtyrer-Legenden*, 2 vols. Rome, 1935–1936.

Timm, S. *Das christlich-koptische Ägypten in arabischer Zeit*, pt. 1, pp. 235–51. Wiesbaden, 1984.

Vansleb, J. M. *Present State of Egypt.* London, 1678.

RANDALL STEWART

ATHANĀSĪ AL-MISRĪ, monk, most probably of the Melchite monastery on Mount Sinai, known solely from an incomplete manuscript of 360 folios transcribed probably in the thirteenth century (Sinai Arabic 245). It contains Byzantine liturgical texts in Arabic.

As his name implies, Athanāsī came from Cairo. He may have been the copyist of the manuscript. In any case, a note on folio 360b records that he translated the text from Greek into Arabic, which indicates he had a good knowledge of these two languages.

Two questions are unresolved: whether Athanāsī was the first translator of the text into Arabic, and whether there is more than one medieval Arabic translation. The answer will involve a comparison of the various collections containing liturgical texts. As far as the Sinai Arabic manuscripts are concerned, there are nine of these, apart from *Sinai Arabic 245.* Comparison with the only twelfth-century manuscript will be particularly important, as it could give information concerning the period in which the translator lived.

BIBLIOGRAPHY

Atiya, A. S., and J. N. Youssef. *Catalogue Raisonné of the Mount Sinai Arabic Manuscripts* (in Arabic). Alexandria, 1970.

Clugnet, L. *Dictionnaire grec-français des noms liturgiques en usage dans l'église grecque.* Paris, 1895.

KHALIL SAMIR, S. J.

ATHANASIAN CREED, a profession of faith widely used in the West down to recent times, wrongly attributed to Athanasius. Its statements opposing Apollinarianism suggest the period 380–430 as the time of compilation; its Latin language, Gaul or north Italy as its place of origin.

BIBLIOGRAPHY

Kelly, J. N. D. *The Athanasian Creed.* London, 1964.

W. H. C. FREND

ATHANASIUS I, the Apostolic Saint, twentieth patriarch of the See of Saint Mark (326–373). Athanasius' life has been treated in detail by numerous authors. These sources can be categorized as follows: (1) the writings of Athanasius himself, which should be considered the most authentic of the sources. These include his historical tracts, encyclicals, an apology to Constantine, another apology against the Arians, his letters to Serapion and to the monks, and his festal letters; (2) the works of contemporary church fathers, including Hilary of Poitiers, BASIL THE GREAT, GREGORY OF NAZIANZUS, and Epiphanius; and (3) chronicles of older historians such as RUFINUS, SOCRATES, Sulpicius Severus, THEODORET, and SOZOMEN, whose authority on details must be taken with some caution. To these may be added the Arabic life rendered by E. RENAUDOT but originally prepared for the pious Copts, which is simply a legendary account of little historical import. Of course, the official record of the church is represented in the Copto-Arabic SYNAXARION and cannot be overlooked.

The secondary literature on the great saint is profuse, and only a selection of the most prominent biographers may here be mentioned by way of introduction: B. Montfaucon, L. S. de Tillemont, J. A. Moehler, S. Cave, H. G. Opitz, E. Schwartz, L. Atzberger, H. M. Gwatkin, F. L. Cross, and G. Mueller.

Early Life

Athanasius was probably born in Alexandria around the year 296, although, according to an Arabic document found in DAYR ANBĀ MAQĀR, it is said that his parents originally came from the city of al-Balyanā in Upper Egypt. It is possible that his early education took place in the CATECHETICAL SCHOOL OF ALEXANDRIA; it is also possible that he could have attended classes in the Museon where he became conversant with Neoplatonism. As a young man, he must have witnessed the later period of the age of persecutions, though he would have been far too young to recollect incidents related to Maximian's persecution of 303. After Constantine declared Christianity to be the religion of the state, in the Edict of Milan in 312, his family must have suffered through the nascent Arian heresy, a movement destined to be the focal point of his struggle throughout his life. Rufinus and subsequent historians relate a story about Athanasius' boyhood. It is said that Patriarch ALEXANDER I, watching the seashore from his window, saw a group of children playing at Christian baptism; one of the boys played the bishop. Intrigued by this sight, the patriarch summoned the children to his presence and recognized the authenticity of the baptism thus performed. He kept at his court the boy-bishop, Athanasius, who ultimately became his secretary and his closest companion.

The Council of NICAEA in 325 marked the inauguration of the ecumenical movement. The young Athanasius, as Alexander's secretary, was the power behind the throne, and his influence was felt in the composition of the Nicene Creed. Athanasius succeeded Alexander in 326. The new archbishop now faced alone the spreading doctrine of Arianism.

Arius was probably of Libyan origin and a pupil of Lucian of Antioch. He was first ordained by Achillas (d. 311) as presbyter of the important church of Bucalis in Alexandria. An eloquent speaker and a pragmatic thinker, Arius captivated a large congregation in Alexandria with his ideas. He denied the coequality and coeternity of Jesus with the Father and held that the Father created the Son from nothing, only in turn to create the world. Thus the consubstantiality of the Father and the Son was denied by Arius, whose position was supported by Eusebius, bishop of Nicomedia. The idea was rejected by Alexander, and its vehement opponent was Athanasius, who defended his view at the Council of Nicaea using the famous term HOMOOUSION to describe the consubstantiality of the Father and the Son. The defeat of the Arians at that council did not end the controversy nor did it eliminate the Arian party, whose teachings continued to spread. This inaugurated a period of theological strife between Arius and Athanasius. The situation was aggravated by the infiltration of Arianism into the imperial court and its increasing popularity among the populace, whose thinking was more amenable to the simple and pragmatic ideas of Arius. In addition, Arius expressed his ideas in a series of popular poetic hymns called *Thalia* (banquet), setting them to music adapted from old, familiar tunes of the ancient Egyptians. These could be heard in the shipyards and all over Alexandria.

Emperor CONSTANTINE I, eager to preserve the unity of his empire, first accepted the verdict of Nicaea, but later wavered in his judgment. He was probably influenced by his Arian sister Constantia and Eusebius of Nicomedia, as well as by the expanding number of Arian followers. At this point Arius seemed to soften his attitude toward the Nicene decision, and the emperor consequently wanted Athanasius to be reconciled with his enemies and to reinstate Arius in church communion. A synod of 335 formally confirmed the reconciliation movement, but Arius died mysteriously in the following year, while the suspicious Athanasius continued to refuse a dubious reconciliation. In the meantime, in 335 the emperor commanded Athanasius to go into exile at Trier in Germany. This proved to be only the first of a series of five exiles of this staunch archbishop, who stood fast by his theology against a movement that survived its author and kept expanding.

The Five Exiles

Athanasius remained in Trier a little more than two years, a period during which he must have composed and developed some of his theological works. With the death of Constantine I in 337, Athanasius and some of the banished Nicene bishops were free to return to their dioceses. Though the people of Alexandria hailed him, Athanasius' return was beset by intrigues from outside. Eusebius of Nicomedia was moved to Constantinople where, as a staunch supporter of Arianism, he had direct access to the imperial court and could influence the emperor against Athanasius. The Arians hoped to depose Athanasius, and in 340, they installed Gregory of Cappadocia in the archiepiscopal throne of Alexandria. Athanasius decided to go into hiding, while his new antagonist reveled in orgies and committed heinous crimes such as causing Philagrius to scourge thirty-four women at church and masterminding the incarceration of other pious Christians. In the midst of such Arian atrocities, Athanasius decided to flee at Easter of the year 340 from Alexandria to Rome.

Thus began his second exile, which lasted three years at the curia of Pope Julius I (337–352) in Rome. Apparently this time the exile was a voluntary one. He was accompanied by a number of Egyptian monks, and perhaps the most significant outcome of that exile was the introduction of the monastic system, which had originated in the Egyptian deserts, to the western Latins. The acceptance of the Egyptian monastic order by the Roman papacy must be regarded as a vital step in the development of Christianity in Europe and the preservation of the Roman heritage in the Middle Ages. On this occasion, too, Athanasius established friendly relations with the Roman see, which recognized his position as archbishop and offered him support throughout his reign. Finally, through the influence of Constantius II (337–361), he was restored to his diocese in Alexandria, now vacated from Arian vestiges by the murder of its Arian occupant, Gregory of Cappadocia, in February 345.

Athanasius' return proved to be an honorable one. He was given imperial letters of congratulations at Aquileia, from where he started the long journey home via Constance, Trier, with its memories of the first exile, and Rome, where Pope Julius offered him an eloquent letter of support. He passed through Hadrianopolis on his journey to Antioch, where he had another opportunity to see the eastern emperor Constantius, who received him with honor. Athanasius refrained from vilifying his opponents to the emperor, but took leave to confront his detractors carrying Constantius' letters to the clergy of Egypt pleading for a unified church. From Antioch Athanasius went to Jerusalem, where he attended a council held in his honor. Athanasius arrived in Alexandria on 24 Bābah. Gregory of Nazianzus described the tumultuous welcome by the people, who streamed forth "like the river Nile." Even the dissenting Arian element of the population seemed, for the time being, to have faced the prelate's restoration with charitable clemency.

After these festivities, peace appeared to have reigned for a few years, and as many as 400 bishops, including those substituting for Arians, showered letters of support on Athanasius. Emperor Valens (364–378), it would seem, anathematized Arianism. Nevertheless, it would also seem that the Arians were only procrastinating in the face of irresistible support for Athanasius. Although the western emperor Constans (337–350) lent his support to the great prelate, the eastern emperor Constantius II, being greatly influenced by Eusebius in particular and the Arians in general, turned against him. Constantius condoned and even incited the persecution of Athanasius.

As the restoration festivities began to calm down, the pro-Arian military power started to maneuver against the reestablished orthodoxy. One story is told of a certain General Sebastian, a Manichaean, who came with a batallion of 3,000 soldiers to a cemetery where a company of virgins remained in prayer after the rest of the congregation had dispersed. Sebastian asked the virgins to embrace Arianism. When they refused, he had them stripped and they were thrashed so heavily that some of them died. Such incidents were reputed to have occurred around the churches of Alexandria where the Orthodox bishops were relentlessly pursued, and dozens of them fled. Athanasius stood firm against his opponents, who were led by a certain George the Cappadocian, who intended to replace him on the throne of Alexandria. Athanasius resisted until he could place his case before Constantius, but to his disappointment the emperor issued an imperial missive in which he described the orthodox prelate as a criminal fugitive. Constantius also advised the Ethiopian sovereign to send Frumentius (see ETHIOPIAN PRELATES) founder of the Ethiopian church, back to receive his new ordination, not from Athanasius, but from the Cappodocian George. Frumentius had been consecrated as bishop of Axum by Athanasius prior to 368. Cornered, Athanasius exiled himself from Alexandria again. He joined the increasing number of Coptic monks in the desert. During this exile, which lasted more than six years, he wrote most of his theological works. While keeping contact with his Alexandrian flock through letters of encouragement, he moved from the Nitrian Desert to the Thebaid and lived for a while in the Eastern Desert. He must have spent some time with Saint ANTONY THE GREAT before his death. And it was then that he was able to compose his classic work, the *Life of Saint Antony*.

With the death of Constantius II in 361, JULIAN THE APOSTATE (361–363) acceded to the imperial throne. Julian had long been contemptuous of the arguments of the Christians, whether orthodox or Arian. The immediate result of Julian's accession was the emergence of the pagan population, who were determined to avenge themselves on George the Cappadocian, who had been determined to exterminate them. The Arian bishop was murdered, and his body was then circulated through the city on a camel. Finally, he was cremated and his remains were thrown into the sea. Although Julian did not favor this gesture at the beginning of his reign, he issued an edict allowing all fugitive bishops to return peacefully to their dioceses. Seizing this opportunity, Athanasius returned to Alexandria on 22 February 362, where he was again met with tumultuous glee by his Orthodox followers.

On his return, Athanasius held a council to resolve all outstanding problems, whether in Alexandria or in Antioch. One of the decisions of that council provided that all who had forfeited their communion with the church could regain it by simply declaring their allegiance to the terms of Nicaea. Those who spoke of three hypostases were found to mean three persons, whereas the Nicene formula prescribed one HYPOSTASIS, the actual Incarnation of the Logos, or assumption of manhood by the Son. Athanasius issued a synodal epistle or tome to the Antiochians about the findings of the council in the hope of achieving church unity. He was unsuccessful because Paulinus, a dissenter, had already been elevated to the episcopate of Antioch, thus starting a schism.

In the midst of these internal difficulties, Julian the Apostate denounced all Christian teachings, as well as the right of Athanasius to his episcopal throne. Julian issued a special edict for the expulsion of Athanasius, which was communicated to him by Pythiodorus, a pagan philosopher, on 23 October 362. Thus began the fourth exile of the great prelate. Athanasius left for Memphis and the Thebaid in the year 363. After Julian's death in 363 Athanasius returned to his episcopal throne.

After his arrival at Alexandria via Hermopolis, where he was hailed by throngs of monks, he received an encouraging letter from the new emperor Jovian (363–364) instructing him to exercise the duties of his episcopal office and prepare a formal statement delineating the Orthodox elements of the faith. Athanasius at once summoned a council, which, under his leadership, framed a synodal epistle that affirmed the Nicene Creed and condemned Arianism and Semi-Arianism, while it denounced the triple definition of the hypostasis and maintained the coequality of the Holy Spirit with the Father and the Son—positions that anticipated the terms of the creed of Constantinople (381).

Armed with these decisions, Athanasius sailed to Antioch, where he was enthusiastically received and where his principles were accepted. The church was consequently united, and even in the West, Pope Liberius (352–355 and 365–366) is known to have made a full declaration of orthodoxy in Rome. In 364, after writing another festal letter at Antioch, Athanasius safely returned to Alexandria shortly before Jovian's death. He was succeeded by Valens (364–378), who was confided the administration of the eastern empire by his brother Valentinian II (375–392). In 365, Valens ordered the expulsion of the bishops that had been allowed to return by Julian. The newly adopted Arian policy caused trouble for the orthodox population and in particular for Athanasius, who stood on the defensive, while the prefect of Alexandria mustered his forces to act against the prelate. Athanasius quietly made his escape through the Church of Saint Dionysius and took refuge for the next four months in a house outside the city. This short period might be considered a fifth and self-inflicted exile. It was terminated by the advent of an imperial notary named Barasides, who came forth with another imperial order for the release of the prelate and his return to his episcopal throne.

From the time of his return to Alexandria until his death in May 373, Athanasius was occupied by disputations against the Arians, by the building of new churches, and in writing some of his final works. He occupied the See of Saint Mark for a total of forty-six years during which he was subjected to persecution that bordered on martyrdom, but his faith in the Nicene Creed was never shaken. According to the Copto-Arabic Synaxarion, his commemoration date occurs on 30 Tūt.

In his later years, Athanasius completed his triumph over Arianism, whose exponents were silenced in the Byzantine empire. With the extermination of their teachings from the empire, the splinter of their remaining representatives crossed the Byzantine borders to the realm of the barbarians where they could preach their Arian doctrines in peace to the Goths. Their apostle was ULPHILAS (c. 311–383), originally a Cappadocian, who was consecrated bishop by Eusebius, the Arian bishop of Nicomedia. The Goths remained faithful to Arian precepts even until they descended on the western Roman empire. Their conversion to orthodoxy was a lengthy process in subsequent centuries.

Together with the discomfiture of Arianism and the firm establishment of the Nicene Creed, Athanasius, through his relations with the Pachomian monks and Serapion, was able to give monasticism and ascetic life in Egypt tremendous encouragement and support. Moreover, he was directly responsible for the introduction of monastic rule in the West. As a biographer of Saint Antony, he dedicated his life of the great saint to the people of Gaul and Italy. His theology remained the solid rock on which future generations of theologians continued to build. He was canonized, and the next generation described him as the Apostolic and the Great.

Writings

Athanasius is known to have written most of his works in Greek and has been described in *A Select Library of the Nicene and Post-Nicene Fathers* (1953, p. ixvi) as a Greek father. In fact, the Greek fathers did not know Coptic, and Athanasius, like many educated Copts, was proficient in both Greek and Coptic. Antony and Athanasius must have communicated in Coptic, for Antony did not know Greek.

While Athanasius was still in his twenties, around the year 318, he wrote two short treatises: *Against the Gentiles* and *De Incarnatione Verbi Dei*, which became an authoritative theological classic. His thesis in the latter treatise is that by the union of God the Logos with manhood in the person of the Son, Jesus restored to fallen humanity the image of God in which it had been created (Gn. 1:27). By his death and resurrection, Jesus overcame death, which was the consequence of sin. Both treatises predated the outbreak of the Arian controversy in 319. Most of his subsequent work concentrated on the opposition to Arianism beginning with Nicaea.

It is not easy to present a complete bibliography of Athanasius, which has been progressively enriched by new discoveries. Attempts at a compilation of his works have been made by scholars since 1482 when, for the first time, a Latin version of some of his works appeared. Subsequently, two of his genuine works together with a group of spurious ones appeared in Paris in 1520. While rejecting the authenticity of the letters to Serapion, Erasmus edited another collection in 1527; an edition combining the collections of 1520 and 1527 appeared at Lyons in 1532. A more developed Latin edition of all his known works was published by Nannius in 1556, while the first Greek edition by P. Felckmann appeared at Heidelberg in 1608–1612. The Greek text with a Latin version published in Paris in 1627 seems to have superseded all others and may have been supplemented by the one dated 1681 in Leipzig. However, all were overshadowed by the Benedictine edition of 1698 to which B. Montfaucon juxtaposed the Life of the saint. Additional remnants by Montfaucon were compiled in 1707 within the series known as *Nova patrum et scriptorum Graecorum collectio*. Athanasius' work on the Psalms was edited by N. Antonelli at Rome in 1746 and republished in four folio volumes, which incorporated most of his previous works. Published in English at Oxford in 1842–1844 are the *Historical Tracts of St. Athanasius* as well as two volumes of *Treatises in Controversy with the Arians*. His works include the festal letters; his encyclicals; and his special letters to the monks, to Serapion, to the Egyptians and the Libyans, as well as: *Apology to Constantius, Apology for His Flight, Apology Against the Arians, History of the Arians, Against the Gentiles, On the Incarnation, Orations and Discourses Against the Arians, Exposition of the Psalms,* and *Life of Saint Antony.*

BIBLIOGRAPHY

For early publications of the works of Athanasius, see above section on his writings. Early editions, rather incomplete, are superseded by the B. Montfaucon edition in 3 volumes, Paris, 1698. Another edition, with further additions compiled by the Bishop of Padua, N. A. Guistiniani, is in 4 volumes, Padua, 1777. See also PG, Vols. 25–28. The most recent edition, still in progress, is edited by M. G. Opitz for the Berlin Academy, Berlin, 1934, et seq.

Altaner, B. *Patrology,* Eng. trans. H. C. Graef. Freiburg, Edinburgh, and London, 1960.

Atzberger, L. *Die Logoslehre des Athanasius, ihre Gegner und Vorläufer.* Munich, 1880.

Bardenhewer, O. *Patrology,* trans. Thomas J. Shahan. Freiburg in Breisgau and St. Louis, Mo., 1908.

Bardy, G. *Les Saints.* Paris, 1914.

Bernard, R. *L'Image de Dieu d'après St. Athanase.* Paris, 1952.

Bright, W. *The Orations of St. Athanasius Against the Arians.* Oxford, 1873.

———. *Historical Writings of St. Athanasius According to the Benedictine Text.* Oxford, 1881.

Cross, F. L. *Study of St. Athanasius.* New York, 1945.

Cureton, W. *Festal Epistles.* London, 1848.

Daniélou, J., and H. Marou. *The Christian Centuries,* Vol. 1. New York, 1964.

Gwatkin, H. M. *Studies in Arianism.* Cambridge and London, 1882, 2nd ed., Cambridge, 1900. Repr. New York, 1978.

———. *The Arian Controversy.* 1903. Repr. New York.

Lauchert, P. *Die Lehre des heiligen Athanasius.* Leipzig, 1895.

Lebon, J. *Lettres a Sérapion sur la divinité du Saint-Esprit Athanase d'Alexandrie.* Sources chrétiennes 15. Paris, 1947.

Meyer, R. T. *Athanasius: The Life of St. Antony.* Ancient Christian Writers 10. Westminster, Md., 1950.

Moehler, J. A. *Athanasius der Grosse und die Kirche seiner Zeit,* 2 vols. Mainz, 1827, 1844.

Mueller, G. *Lexicon Athanasianum.* Berlin, 1944–1952.

Musurillo, H. *The Fathers of the Primitive Church.* New York, 1966.

Opitz, H. G. *Untersuchungen zur Überlieferung der Schriften des Athanasius.* Berlin and Leipzig, 1935.

Prestige, G. L. *God in Patristic Thought.* London, 1952.

Quasten, J. *Patrology,* 3 vols. 5th edition. Utrecht and Antwerp, 1975.

Robertson, A. *De Incarnatione.* London, 1882.

Schwartz, E. *Zur Geschichte des Athanasius.* In *Nachrichten von der königlichen Gesellschaft der Wissenschaften zu Göttingen.* Göttingen, 1894–1924.

Select Library of the Nicene and Post-Nicene Fathers of the Christian Church. 1st series, 14 vols., ed. Philip Schaff. Buffalo, 1886–1889. Vols. 5–14 published in New York. 2nd series, ed. Philip Scheff and Henry Wace. Grand Rapids, Mich. 1976.

Shepland, C. R. B. *The Letters of St. Athanasius Concerning the Holy Spirit.* London, 1951.

Stücken, A. *Athanasiana.* Texte und Untersuchungen zur Geschichte der christlichen Literatur 19.4. Leipzig, 1899.

Szymusiak, J. M. *Two Apologies.* Sources chrétiennes 56. Paris, 1947.

Tillemont, L. S. Le Mainde *Mémoires pour servir à l'histoire ecclésiastique des six premiers siècles, justifiéz par les citations des auteurs originaux,* 10 vols. in 5. Brussels, 1732.

AZIZ S. ATIYA

ATHANASIUS II, SAINT, twenty-eighth patriarch of the See of Saint Mark (488–494). Athanasius succeeded PETER III MONGUS to the archiepiscopal throne of Alexandria. His reign was uneventful, and all that is known about him is derived from the HISTORY OF THE PATRIARCHS by SĀWĪRUS IBN AL-MUQAFFA', bishop of al-ASHMŪNAYN. B. T. A. Evetts' translation of the Arabic text follows: "When the holy Father Peter went to his rest, Athanasius was appointed. He had been priest in charge of the church of Alexandria, and now he was made patriarch over it. He was a good man, full of faith and the Holy Ghost; and he accomplished that with which he was entrusted; and in his days there was no disorder or persecution in the holy church. He remained seven years, and went to his rest on the twentieth of Tūt." Apparently the confusion created by the Council of CHALCEDON (451) during the reign of DIOSCORUS I had subsided by his time.

AZIZ S. ATIYA

ATHANASIUS III, seventy-sixth patriarch of the See of Saint Mark (1250–1261). Athanasius was peacefully selected to the throne of Saint Mark after an interregnum of seven years, during which the patriarchal seat remained vacant. The reasons are hard to explain beyond the lack of unanimity on any candidate and the general unrest that accompanied the transfer of power in Egypt from the Ayyubid to the Baḥrī Mamluk dynasty.

The son of Makārim or Abū al-Makārim ibn Kalīl, the priest of Our Lady's Church of al-Muʿallaqah, Athanasius III was born in Cairo (though the date of his birth is unknown), and he became a deacon in the same church at the time of taking the monastic vow at the Monastery of Saint Antony (DAYR ANBĀ ANṬŪNIYŪS) in the Eastern Desert. The date of his monasticism is also unknown. He had no rivals, and his selection and consecration at Alexandria were unopposed.

His biography in the HISTORY OF THE PATRIARCHS is succinct and appears in a few lines only, and we must look for any events of his reign in the Islamic sources. One significant event during his reign was the appointment of a Copt as vizier for the first time in the Mamluk state. His name was al-Asʿad Sharaf al-Dīn Hibat Allāh ibn Sāʿīd al-Fā'izī, and he was famous for the reorganization of the tax system, which earned for him Muslim discontent; the Copts were penalized by the doubling of the poll tax or JIZYAH.

Athanasius was a contemporary of a number of Baḥrī Mamluk sultans, beginning with the famous Shajarat al-Durr (1250–1252), and including ʿIzz al-Din ʿAybak (1252–1257), al-Manṣūr Nūr al-Dīn ʿAlī ibn Aybak (1257–1259), and al-Muẓaffar Sayf al-Dīn Quṭuz (1259–1260). The most prominent event of his time was the Seventh Crusade, which Saint Louis, king of France (1226–1270), directed against Egypt. After landing at Damietta in 1249, he penetrated the Delta as far as al-Manṣūrah, where the Mamluks opened the dikes of the Nile, and the invaders found themselves paralyzed in water. Louis and his nobles were consequently defeated by the batallions of Shajarat al-Durr in 1250, and all were seized as prisoners. The story of these stirring events has been poignantly related by an eyewitness, the French chronicler Joinville. Negotiations concerning the liberation of the king and the French nobility were opened at once. In addition to the evacuation of Damietta, the terms included the payment of a ransom amounting to half a million *livres tournois* or the equivalent of approximately 1 million dinars. Afterward the French contingent set sail to ʿAkkā, which was still the seat of the shadowy Frankish kingdom of Jerusalem.

Within the Mamluk realm in Syria, however, sad events were reported about the position of the Jacobite Christians in the city of Damascus. Mob riots of the Islamic population resulted in the burning of the Church of Our Lady as well as a number of houses belonging to Christians. Their property was pillaged, and many of them died in the fray. About the same time, in 1265, the battle of ʿAyn Jālūṭ was fought between Mongols and the Muslims. Syrian Christians were accused of clandestine support to the Mongols. Finally Sayf al-Dīn Quṭuz (1259–1260) quelled the rebels and imposed a penalty of 150,000 dirhems on the Christians. The sum was raised and surrendered to a Mamluk emir who was the atabeg of the army, Fāris al-Dīn Aqaṭāy.

Evidently the accumulation of penalties from the French and the Syrian Christians, as well as the taxes and capitation previously levied in Egypt, enriched the Mamluks, and we hear of no additional imposts on Athanasius and his congregation. Nevertheless, there is no evidence of church building or restoration during his patriarchate. He died in the opening year of the sultanate of al-Ẓāhir Baybars (1260–1277), after remaining in office for a period of eleven years and fifty-six days.

BIBLIOGRAPHY

Atiya, A. S. *Crusade, Commerce and Culture.* Bloomington, Ind., 1962.

Lane-Poole, S. *The Mohammadan Dynasties.* London, 1894.

Runciman, S. *History of the Crusaders*, 3 vols. Cambridge, 1951–1954.

SUBHI Y. LABIB

ATHANASIUS, bishop of Qūs of the eleventh or fourteenth century, who wrote books on the Coptic language. According to G. Graf and G. Bauer, the title of his grammar, *Qilādat al-Taḥrīr fī ʿIlm al-Tafsīr* (Necklace of Writing for the Science of Translation) gives the only known information on his life. It says he was born as the son of a priest named Ṣalīb in the region west of QAMŪLAH, which is on the west bank of the Nile between QŪS and Luxor, and became a monk in the nearby monastery of Mār Buqṭur, also known as Dayr al-Kūlah. He became bishop of Qūs, which is about 12 miles (19 km) north of Luxor, on the east bank of the Nile. He is not mentioned by the known writers of grammars and dictionaries of the thirteenth century, and he does not appear in IBN KABAR's author index. His manual on the Coptic language treats only nouns, verbs, and particles, but has been transmitted in both Sahidic and Bohairic versions. Concerning the date of his life, this has been given as the eleventh century, but according to Bauer (1972) the Berlin manuscript of the grammar of Athanasius contains the preface to another grammatical work, likely by Athanasius, which mentions Yuḥannā al-Samannūdī's *al-Sullam al-Kanā'isī* (The Ecclesiastical Ladder) and other philological material, which argues that he lived at the earliest in the second half of the thirteenth century, and perhaps in the fourteenth century since there was an Athanasius of Qūs who composed poetry in the period of 1365–1378 and a history of the chrism consecration under the patriarch GABRIEL IV (see the German translation of the Berlin manuscript in Bauer, 1972, pp. 303–306; and Graf, 1947, Vol. 2, pp. 445).

Graf lists other anonymous grammatical works and dictionaries in manuscript, and an anonymous work that has been called the swan song of Coptic literature, named the *Triadon* for its triplet rhyme. It is a voluminous didactic poem in the Sahidic dialect with a rhyme pattern of three rhyming lines in four-line stanzas, with the fourth line ending in "on" or "an." The writer, a monk from Upper Egypt who emigrated to Lower Egypt, says he used the old language of his homeland to obtain its reintroduction and to demonstrate its use. It is important because an Arabic translation, probably not by the author, accompanies the text. The text and translation are from the first half of the fourteenth century, and the single manuscript is at the National Library in Naples (von Lemm, 1903).

BIBLIOGRAPHY

Bauer, G. *Athanasius von Qūs, Qilādat al-Taḥrīr fī 'Ilm al-Tafsīr. Eine koptische Grammatik in arabischer Sprache aus dem 13./14. Jahrhundert.* Islamkundliche Untersuchungen 17. Freiburg im Breisgau, 1972.

Leipoldt, J. "Triadon." In *Geschichte der christlichen Literatur des Orients,* 2nd ed. Die Literaturen des Ostens 7. Leipzig, 1909.

Lemm, O. von. *Das Triadon, ein sahidisches Gedicht mit arabischer Übersetzung. St. Petersburg, 1903.*

VINCENT FREDERICK

ATHANASIUS OF ANTIOCH,

the Jacobite patriarch of Antioch from 595 to 630. Around 615, he personally visited Alexandria to reestablish the union of the two sees after the misunderstandings that had arisen during the period of the tritheist controversy (see DAMIAN). Maybe on account of this merit, the Copts translated his biography of SEVERUS OF ANTIOCH rather than the more famous ones by Zechariah the Scholastic and John of Beth Aphthonia.

Fragments exist in Sahidic from two codices of the White Monastery (DAYR ANBĀ SHINŪDAH); a fragment from the Bohairic version (Athanasius, 1908); probably the Arabic version (cf. Graf, 1944, pp. 315 and 420), and the Ethiopic version. The text is more markedly hagiographical in character and more in tune with the taste of the period than the abovementioned biographies.

BIBLIOGRAPHY

Athanasius, Saint. *The Conflict of Severus, Patriarch of Antioch.* Ethiopic text ed. and trans E. J. Goodspeed with remains of Coptic versions by W. E. Crum. In PO 4, pt. 6, no. 20. Paris, 1908.

Baumstark, A. *Geschichte der syrischen Literatur.* Bonn, 1922.

Orlandi, T. "Un Codice copte del Monastero Bianco." *Le Muséon* 81 (1968):401–02.

TITO ORLANDI

ATHANASIUS OF CLYSMA,

third-century martyr and undoubtedly an Egyptian saint although probably not a Coptic saint. His Passion exists in Greek, Georgian, and Arabic. It may be considered to be a Greco-Palestinian document. The Greek text (Bibliotheca Hagiographica Graeca 193) was published by A. Papadopoulos Kerameus in 1898 from the still unique Paris manuscript (Coislin 303, tenth century). In the following year, H. Delehaye noted the close links between this text and that of Saints Sergius and Bacchus (Bibliotheca Hagiographica Graeca 1624). The Georgian text was published in 1962 by K. Kekelidze from three manuscripts, two of which were from the tenth century. But there are still other Georgian copies that he did not use. The Arabic version is in three manuscripts (Sinaiticus 440, 1251, fols. 99v–106; Sinai Arabic 535, thirteenth century, fols. 111–18; and British Museum, Or. Add. 26117, eleventh century, fols. 23–35, which is a manuscript also with a Sinai provenance).

There is nothing original about the Passion. It tells of the following events: under Diocletian and Maximian, persecution set in throughout the whole empire. Athanasius is a burning light because of his faith and holds an important post in the imperial household. His two brothers, Sergius and Bacchus, resemble him. Maximian sends Athanasius as a faithful servant and a relative to close all the churches in Egypt as far as the Thebaid and to open temples to the gods. Athanasius sheds tears as he takes leave of his brothers, Sergius and Bacchus, foreseeing the martyrdom to which they are all called. Arriving at Alexandria he treats Bishop Peter like a brother and shows contempt for idols. At once he is denounced to Maximian. The latter appoints a judge to interrogate Athanasius. The prefect of Egypt receives the letter and summons him.

The dialogue follows the most classical of patterns. Athanasius states that he is stopping at Clysma where his heart's desire will be fulfilled. Once at the town, Athanasius halts "not far from the spot where today there is a cross" and there makes a prayer. He enters the town just when Christ's nativity is being celebrated, participates in the rejoicings, and then announces the closure of the churches in accordance with the emperor's order. The judge then orders Athanasius to sacrifice to the gods, but the saint refuses and turns to God in his prayers. Confronting the judge, Athanasius quotes Saint Paul against the wisdom of the heathen. The judge argues to "render unto Caesar the things that are Caesar's" but the saint continues to save his soul, forcing the judge to demand the supreme sacrifice. In the final prayer before he is beheaded, Athanasius makes a strange and rare invocation; he calls on God to protect the Christian kings in the lands of the Romans and the Ethiopians. This phrase, which has disappeared in the Greek but remains in the Arabic and Georgian, is also found in the Ethiopian Synaxarion. In fact, Saint Athanasius of Clysma is one of the rare saints not in the Coptic-Arabic SYNAXARION but present in Ethiopian tradition. The Arabic text of the Passion adds an epilogue after the decapitation on 18 Tammuz. The population of Clysma went out to the judge with Julian, their bishop, and asked him for the body. They arranged for its burial at the church of Our Lady of Clysma, covering it with precious cloths and laying it in a marvelous coffin. From then on numerous cures took place at his tomb.

Among the foundations of Justinian in the Sinai area listed by Eutychius ibn Batrīq is a church dedicated to Saint Athanasius. The plenipotentiary sent to the governor of Egypt "gave the order to build a church at al-Qulzum, and to build the monastery of Rāyah, to build the monastery of Mount Sinai and to fortify it to the extent that there was none better fortified in the world. When the legate arrived at al-Qulzum, he built in al-Qulzum the church of Mār Athanasius, and built the convent of Rayah and went to Mount Sinai and found the Bush there" (Eutychius, ed. E. Chiekho, 1906, pp. 202–03).

ABŪ ṢĀLIḤ THE ARMENIAN writes about a century after Eutychius: "Al-Qulzum was the king's fortress, on the frontier with the Hijāz, named after the weaving loom cord and known as Qulzum. A Church of Athanasius existed there, so did the convent within the bounds of Rāyah founded by Justinian" (Evetts, 1895, p. 73). Rāyah, says Yāqūt, is also the name of a village in Egypt opposite al-Qulzum (Yāqūt, 1846, p. 199). Procopius in *De Aedificiis* (1906, pp. 167–68), knows that Justinian founded Phoinikon, the Greek equivalent of Rāyah. This place-name was famous because tracks were shown there of the chariots of the pharaoh who went down into the Red Sea, according to COSMAS INDICOPLEUSTES (1968, and Peter the Deacon in the twelfth century; Geyer, 1898, pp. 115–17).

Thus the cult of Saint Athanasius was linked with Justinian's policy for defense against invasions from the south, within the framework of an alliance with Ethiopia, where the cult of Saint Arethas of Najrān appears to be a further warrant. In fact, the expansion of the cult of Saint Athanasius was strictly linked with Justinian's Chalcedonian policy. A complete liturgical canon has been preserved in Georgian (Mount Sinai manuscripts 1 and 56; Garitte, 1958, p. 283). But the Greek Passion expediently dropped the prayer for the Ethiopian sovereigns after it had become clear that the church there was developing in a direction different from Chalcedonianism. In the Life of JOHN COLOBOS, the saint withdraws to Clysma and is finally buried there: "He was laid beside other saints such as Saint Athanasius the martyr, abbā Djidjoi, and abbā Djimi, and the grace of God effected marvels by means of the bodies of these saints excessively, and above all through that of our holy father John [Colobos], for the healing and salvation of anyone, until there took place the Devil's Synod at Chalcedon and polluted the earth with a perverse and abominable doctrine like a prostitute" (Amélineau, 1894, pp. 405, 406). It is not impossible that Justinian had looked for the body of the martyr of Clysma at the spot where the consecrations stopped at the time of the Council of CHALCEDON. In every way the Passion of the martyr and its relationship with the record of Sergius and Bacchus make the account of the martyrdom itself extremely artificial. According to the Arabic supplement there would only be the slenderest data on a Bishop Julian to make it possible to extract commonplaces. This name is not elsewhere attested.

BIBLIOGRAPHY

Amélineau, E. *Histoire des monastères de la Basse-Egypte.* Paris, 1894.

Cosmas Indicopleustes. *Topographie chrétienne,* ed. Wanda Wolska-Conus. Paris, 1968–.

Delehaye, H. "Les martyrs d'Egypte." *Analecta Bollandiana* 40 (1922):5–154; 299–363.

Esbroeck, M. van. "L'Ethiopie à l'époque de Justinien: Saint Arethas de Negran et saint Athanase de Clysma." *IV Congresso Internazionale di Studi Etiopici (Rome, 10–15 April 1972),* Vol. 1, pp. 117–39. Rome, 1974.

Eutychius. *Annales,* ed. L. Chiekho. Beirut and Paris, 1906.

Garitte, G. *Le Calendrier palestino-georgien du sinaiticus 34.* Brussels, 1958.

Geyer, P., comp. *Itinera Hierosolymitana Saecvli IIII-VIII.* CJEL 39. Vienna, 1898.

Kekehdze, K. "Mart'viloba Atanase K'ulizmelisa." *Et'iudebi zveli Kartuli lit'erat'u is ist'ori* (1962):56–70.

Procopius. *De Aedificiis,* ed. J. Haury. Leipzig, 1906.

Yāqūt. *Kitāb al-mushtarak,* ed. F. Wüstenfeld. Göttingen, 1846.

MICHEL VAN ESBROECK

ATHRIBIS. *See* Atrīb.

ATNATEWOS. *See* Ethiopian Prelates.

ATONEMENT, the basic doctrine of the reconciliation of fallen man to God through the sacrificial death of Christ, who, by shedding His blood for humanity, satisfied both divine justice and mercy. "They are justified by his grace as a gift, through the redemption which is in Christ Jesus, whom God put forward as an expiation by his blood, to be received by faith. This was to show God's righteousness, because in his divine forbearance he had passed over former sins" (Rom. 3:24–25).

According to ancient Jewish practice, the tenth day of the seventh month (Tishrin) was kept as an annual day of expiation. The Day of Atonement was one of strict fasting, total abstinence from manual labor, business transactions, and physical indulgence. The laws of purification and atonement were commanded by God to Moses (Lv. 16:1–34) and meticulously followed by Aaron, the high priest, to make expiation for himself and for others. These laws included the choice of a he-goat to be the scapegoat of the year. It had all the sins of the people laid upon its head by the symbolic imposition of the high priest's hands and was then released into the wilderness to carry away the burden of guilt. The ritual also included the sprinkling of the blood of two sin offerings, a bull and a goat, over the altars in order to obliterate the stain of guilt adhering to them.

The concept and application as specified in the Old Testament were in fact a symbolic prelude to the all-powerful and efficacious atonement of the Lord Jesus Christ. Two major differences, however, must be noted.

First, Aaron and the subsequent high priests who followed him were ordinary human beings who had to atone for their own weaknesses as well as those of other people; whereas the Incarnate Son of God offered Himself for all humanity. "Indeed, the law appoints men in their weaknesses as high priests, but the word of the oath, which came later than the law, appoints a Son who has been made perfect for ever" (Heb. 7:28).

Second, in the Old Testament atonement was a recurrent annual event, restricted in terms of time, medium, and objective. By contrast, Christ's atonement transcended all limitations, boundaries, and restrictions. It was unique; it effected the required reconciliation once and for all. "Nor was it to offer himself repeatedly, as the high priest enters the Holy Place yearly with blood not his own" (Heb. 9:25). It was unworldly; it was independent of an earthly medium; ". . . when Christ appeared as a high priest of the good things that have come, then through the greater and more perfect tent (not made with hands . . .)" (Heb. 9:11). It was universal, embracing all nations; ". . . he is the expiation for our sins, and not for ours only but also for the sins of the whole world" (1 Jn. 2:2).

There are three parallels between the two types of atonement. First, just as the high priest would not be admitted into the Holy of Holies without sprinkling the blood of the sacrifices, man would not be admitted to the glories of heaven without atonement for his sins, an atonement effected in full by Jesus Christ. Second, none but the high priest could accomplish the atonement. Likewise, Christ alone atoned for mankind. "And there is salvation in no one else, for there is no other name under heaven given among men by which we must be saved" (Acts 4:12). Third, "without the shedding of blood there is no forgiveness of sins" (Heb. 9:22). In the Old Testament it was the blood of animals, which had no free will of their own to accept to offer themselves for sacrifice. This symbolic relationship is clearly expressed in Hebrews (9:12–14): "he entered once for all into the Holy Place, taking not the blood of goats and calves but his own blood, thus securing an eternal redemption. For if the sprinkling of defiled persons with the blood of goats and bulls and with the ashes of a heifer sanctifies for the purification of the flesh, how much more shall the blood of Christ, who through the eternal Spirit offered himself without blemish to God, purify your conscience from the dead works to serve the living God."

BIBLIOGRAPHY

Franks, R. S. *A History of the Doctrine of the Work of Christ in Its Ecclesiastical Development.* London, 1918.

Grenste, L. W. *A Short History of the Doctrine of Atonement.* London, 1920.

Mīkhā'īl Mīnā. *'Ilm al-Lāhūt,* Vol. 3, pp. 118–25. Cairo, 1938.

Mozley, J. K. *The Doctrine of Atonement.* London, 1915.

Rivière, J. *Le Dogme de la rédemption chez Saint Augustine.* Paris, 1928.

Turner, H. E. W. *The Patristic Doctrine of Redemption.* London, 1952.

ARCHBISHOP BASILIOS

ATRĪB, one of the best known cities in the Nile Delta in the Greco-Roman and Christian periods. It is mentioned often in classical authors and papyri (cf. Pietschmann, 1896, cols. 2070–71) as well as in Coptic and Arabic-Christian literature. The ruins of the city, which in Greek was called 'Αθρίβις and in Coptic ⲁⲑⲗⲏⲃⲉ or ⲁⲑⲗⲏⲃⲏ, are to be found in TALL ATRĪB, located some thirty miles north of Cairo, next to Banhā in the Qalyūbiyyah Province.

Atrīb was a bishopric even before 325, as attested by the Passion of SHENUFE, which mentions a Bishop Plasse of Athribis/Atripe (Reymond and Barns, 1973, p. 86 [Coptic text]; p. 188 [English translation]). The city still had a bishop at the end of the sixteenth century (Muyser, p. 163).

Atrīb figures prominently in Coptic martyrologies, such as the martyrdom of Julius of Aqfahs, whose confession of faith and subsequent martyrdom in Atrīb inspired the governor of the city to convert to Christianity. The martyr ANUB was from Atrīb and the miracles attendant on his persecution and martyrdom prompted many pagans in the city to adopt Christianity.

There was a monastery and a church of the Virgin in Atrīb. Bedouins destroyed the monastery around 866, and the church was ruined in the thirteenth century.

BIBLIOGRAPHY

Acta Martyrum, ed. and trans. I. Balestri and H. Hyvernat. CSCO 43, *Scriptores Coptici* 3. Louvain, 1955. Latin translation in CSCO 44, *Scriptores Coptici* 4. Louvain, 1955.

Amélineau, E. *La Géographie de l'Egypte à l'époque copte,* pp. 66–69. Paris, 1893.

Muyser, J. "Contribution à l'étude des listes épiscopales de l'église copte." *Bulletin de la Société d'archéologie copte* 10 (1944):115–76.

Pietschmann, R. "Athribis." In *Real-encyclopädie der classischen Altertumswissenschaft,* Vol. 4, cols. 2070–71. Stuttgart, 1896.

Reymond, E. A. E., and J. W. B. Barns, eds. *Four Martyrdoms from the Pierpont Morgan Coptic Codices.* Oxford, 1973.

Timm, S. *Das christlich-koptische Ägypten in arabischer Zeit,* pt. 1, pp. 257–65. Wiesbaden, 1984.

RANDALL STEWART

ATRĪS, village on the left bank of the Rosetta branch of the Nile, in the *markaz* (district) of Imbābah, Minufiyyah, not far from Banī Salāmah, 45 miles (73 km) northwest of Cairo. The existence of a monastery in or near this village is attested by the *Chronicle* of JOHN OF NIKIOU (second half of the seventh century): "And the three chief men of Manūf, Isidore, John and Julian, and those who had concealed themselves in the convent of Atrīs" (Charles, 1916, p. 172).

Today there are in this area, less than a mile apart, two dependencies of the monasteries of Wādī al-Naṭrūn, one of Saint Macarius, DAYR ANBĀ MAQĀR, and the other that of the Syrians. The first seems very old, but the second dates only from around 1830. The church of the village is dedicated to Saint Macarius (Clarke, 1912, p. 205, n. 1).

In 1657, Thévenot indicated, on the basis of hearsay, that to go to the Monastery of Saint Macarius one passes by Drīs (Atrīs), where the monastery has a hospice (Evelyn-White, 1921, p. 418). Sicard, who made the journey himself in 1712, came to "Etris, a village half a league from Oüardan. There we found a hospice for the solitaries of the desert which is nearby" (Sicard, 1982, Vol. 2, p. 10; see also pp. 11, 12, 27).

U. Monneret de Villard (1929, pp. 149–52) suggested that the tomb of Saint Macarius may have been there in the fourteenth century. Unfortunately the documents relating to the translations of the body of Macarius invalidate this hypothesis: at some time before 480 his remains were carried to Shabshir (east bank of the Rosetta branch, near Minūf), where they remained until 784, and were then removed to Ilmāy (to the east of Shibīn al-Kom). The remains of Macarius were brought back to his monastery under the patriarch JOHN IV (776–799 A.D.), (Evelyn-White, 1926, pp. 131–34, 1932, pp. 292–4).

BIBLIOGRAPHY

Amélineau, E. *La Géographie de l'Egypte à l'époque copte,* pp. 70–71. Paris, 1893.

Charles, R. H. *The Chronicle of John, Coptic Bishop of Nikiu.* London, 1916.

Clarke, S. *Christian Antiquities in the Nile Valley.* Oxford, 1912.

Evelyn-White, H. G. *The Monasteries of the Wadi'n Natrūn,* Pt. 1, *New Coptic Texts from the Monastery of Saint Macarius.* New York, 1926. Pt. 2, *The History of the Monasteries of Nitria and Scetis.* New York, 1932.

Meinardus, O. *Christian Egypt, Ancient and Modern,* pp. 178–79. Cairo, 1965. 2nd ed., pp. 265–66. Cairo, 1977.

Monneret de Villard, U. "La tomba di St. Macario." *Aegyptus* 10 (1929).

Sicard, C. *Oeuvres,* 3 vols., ed. M. Martin. Cairo, 1982.

RENÉ-GEORGES COQUIN
MAURICE MARTIN, S.J.

ATRIUM. *See* Architectural Elements of Churches.

AUDIENTIA EPISCOPALIS, the adjudication by a bishop of civil matters in dispute (see Codex Justinianus 1.4), as well as of disciplinary matters among the clergy. On the basis of 1 Corinthians 6:1 the Christians—like the Jews—were not to conduct lawsuits before the judges of the pagan state. Disputes were, rather, to be settled within the community. The jurisdiction of such cases therefore passed into the hands of the bishop. After the recognition of Christianity as *religio licita,* Constantine the Great conferred the civil *audientia episcopalis* on the bishop. Thereby the bishop judged not only in virtue of his spiritual authority but also on the strength of imperial authority.

If proceedings were to be taken before the bishop, the agreement of both sides was requisite (see Codex Justinianus 1.4.7 from the year 398 and Codex Theodosianus 1.27.2 from the year 408). By *Novellae* 79 and 83, Emperor Justinian placed the clergy and monks under episcopal jurisdiction in civil affairs. According to *Novella* 86.2, the bishop, upon rejection of the state judge, was to decide the case in conjunction with the rejected judge.

This administrative activity of the bishop in civil law as a justice of the peace can be distinguished only with difficulty from his purely ecclesiastical disciplinary function. This is shown by the Coptic legal documents, particularly the writings preserved in the correspondence of bishop ABRAHAM of Hermonthis from the period around 600. They often portray the entire proceedings of the *audientia episcopalis.* In all of the documented cases, people turned to the bishop to redress the injustice done to them by other persons. Among the disputes known from the ostraca are a case concerning forceful appropriation of a share in a paternal estate (Crum, 1902, 184) and a case of indictment before a secular court because of a pledge (British Museum no. 24,948).

In most cases, the bishop commissioned clergy to investigate the facts and wrote as *defensor civitatis* to the persons who had committed the injustice, commanding them to rectify the wrong immediately. In addition, he often imposed an ecclesiastical punishment (PENALIZATION, EXCOMMUNICATION, DEFROCKING OF PRIESTS, INTERDICT). In one case (Crum, 1939, no. 37), the bishop sent two men (one of them a priest) to arrest a man and hand him over to the lictors (*lashane*), so they could inflict corporal punishment upon him.

Other writings dealt with disputes over questions of private law, which were decided by the bishop—for instance, a nephew sued his uncle because of a dining room. Both parties (Crum, 1902, nos. 42 and 155) pledged that they would accept the verdict, no matter in whose favor. If they did not accept the verdict, they would be required to pay the penalty and acknowledge the judgment before the bishop.

BIBLIOGRAPHY

Crum, W. E., ed. *Coptic Ostraca from the Collections of the Egypt Exploration Fund, the Cairo Museum and Others.* London, 1902.

———. *Varia Coptica.* Aberdeen, 1939.
Krause, M. "Apa Abraham von Hermonthis. Ein oberägyptischer Bischof um 600," 2 vols. Doctoral diss., Berlin, 1956.
Steinwenter, A. "Zur Lehre der Episcopalis audientia." *Byzantinische Zeitschrift* 30 (1929–1930): 660–68.
———. "Episcopalis audientia." In *Reallexikon für Antike und Christentum,* Vol. 1, cols. 915–17. Stuttgart, 1950.

MARTIN KRAUSE

AUTHENTIKOS LOGOS. The *Authentikos Logos* is an account, didactic in character, of the history of the soul. It forms the third tractate of Codex VI of the NAG HAMMADI LIBRARY. According to the tractate, "When the spiritual soul was cast into the body, it became a brother to lust and hatred and envy, and it became a material soul" (23.13ff). In this way the soul's misadventures began. She bore, without a partner, children who are called adoptive, for they had no father. She sank into prostitution, for she chose for herself a spirit of prostitution who dragged her into a brothel. This spirit of prostitution (24.8–10) brought her vice, and the soul abandoned all modesty. She also gave herself up to drunkenness (24.14–16), and she forgot her heavenly brothers and her father, for she was deceived by pleasure. Renouncing knowledge, she fell into bestiality (24.20–22). But because of her divine origin the soul was not entirely separated from the world above. The dwellers in the Pleroma (22.20–22) saw her; she gazed at them in the invisible *Logos.* Her heavenly bridegroom, seeing her in distress, secretly brought her food and a balm with saving power. This food and this balm were the Logos. Through this, the soul saw and recognized "her kinsman and learned about her root in order that she might cling to her branch from which she first came forth, in order that she might receive what was hers and renounce matter" (22.29–34). Once the soul perceived the vanity of worldly things, she launched out in the search for God, although this search was exhausting (35.3–5). She abandoned the passions, having understood their evil (31.19–28). She freed herself from them, adopting a new mode of conduct (31.29–30). Thus, wearing her true clothing, she adorned herself in a bridal robe and hastened to her bridegroom. In the nuptial chamber, located in the East, she joined the bridegroom and fed herself at a banquet with immortal food (35.8–24).

The *Authentikos Logos* is more didactic than philosophical (Ménard, 1977). Taking as his starting point the story of the soul, the author communicates several teachings. The Gnostics, like the soul, will have to renounce passions and devote themselves to the search for God. This search will be difficult because of many hidden traps which the enemy puts in their way: "For this reason, then, we do not sleep nor do we forget the nets that are spread out in hiding, lying in wait for us to catch us. For if we are caught in a single net, it will suck us down into its mouth while the water flows over us, striking our face. And we will be taken down into the dragnet, and we will not be able to come up from it. . . . The adversary spies on us, lying in wait for us like a fisherman, wishing to seize us, rejoicing that he might swallow us. For he places many foods before our eyes, [things] which belong to this world so that he may seize us with his hidden poison and bring us out of freedom and take us in slavery" (29.3–30.20). The metaphors with which the Gnostic author enriches his writing all belong to the syncretistic world of the Hellenistic period (Ménard, 1977, p. 3); the fisherman, wine, drunkenness, the good shepherd, chaff, and wheat are some examples.

The Valentinian myth of the fall of the Sophia (wisdom) recurs, in simplified form, in the *Authentikos Logos* in the history of the spiritual soul, prostituting herself in the lower world before joining her heavenly bridegroom. The themes of the bridegroom, the bridal chamber, true clothing, and rest in the nuptial chamber justify comparison of the *Authentikos Logos* with the EXEGESIS ON THE SOUL and the GOSPEL OF PHILIP from the Nag Hammadi Library.

BIBLIOGRAPHY

MacRae, G. W. "The Authoritative Teaching." In *Nag Hammadi Codices V, 2–5 and VI,* ed. D. M. Parrott. Nag Hammadi Studies 11. Leiden, 1979.
Ménard, J.-E. *L'Authentikos Logos.* Bibliothèque copte de Nag Hammadi, section Textes 2. Quebec, 1977.
Scopello, M. "Un Rituel idéal d'intronisation dans trois textes gnostiques de Nag Hammadi." In *Nag Hammadi and Gnosis,* ed. R. McL. Wilson. Nag Hammadi Studies 14. Leiden, 1978.

MADELEINE SCOPELLO

AWLĀD AL-ʿASSĀL. This Coptic family came originally from the village of Sadamant in the province of Banī Suef in Middle Egypt at an unknown date and settled in Cairo, where its members rose to wealth and high station at the court of the Ayyubid dynasty (A.H. 565–648/A.D. 1169–1250). They owned a residence in the capital and occupied a position of leadership in the Coptic community. Though their private history is somewhat obscure, what remains of their literary, philosophical, and theological heritage shows them to have been among the most learned Copts in medieval times.

Early modern historiographers of Egypt appear to have recognized the name of Ibn al-ʿAssāl only as a single personality in medieval Christian Arabic literature until in 1713 E. Renaudot (pp. 585–86) revealed that two different brothers had written independently under that common surname. While classifying some of their manuscripts in the British Museum in 1894, C. Rieu (1894, p. 18) was able to establish the fact that there were three brothers instead of two. Then, in 1905, from different sources (especially the National Library in Paris), A. Mallon (1905, pp. 509–529) confirmed Rieu's thesis and proved that the three brothers had attained great literary eminence under the collective name of Awlād al-ʿAssāl, that is, the sons of the honey producer or merchant, presumably the title and vocation of the founder of that family. Coptic historians, however, including Yaʿqūb Nakhlah Rufaylah (1889, p. 185) and the Commission of Coptic History (*Lajnat al-Tārīkh al-Qibṭī*, 1925, pp. 148–52) increased the number of Awlād al-ʿAssāls by two more—the father and a fourth brother—who also were high dignitaries in the Ayyubid bureaucracy, though their rich literary heritage could only be ascribed to the other three. In 1943, A. J. B. Higgins labored to establish a new thesis that two sets of Awlād al-ʿAssāls had lived—one at the beginning of the eleventh century and another in the thirteenth century. Since this argument is based on a dubious date (500/1107) by an unknown scribe in the colophon of a single British Museum manuscript (Arabic e 163, fol. 288r), we must for the present maintain that thirteenth-century group is the only one convincingly established.

The full names of the Awlād al-ʿAssāl are as follows: (1) Abū al-Faḍl ibn Abī Isḥāq Ibrāhīm ibn Abī Sahl Jirjis ibn Abī al-Yusr Yūḥannā ibn al-ʿAssāl, the father, known as al-Kātib al-Miṣrī, who bore the title *fakhr al-dawlah*, "the Egyptian scribe" or "secretary"; (2) AL-ṢAFĪ ABŪ AL-FAḌĀ'IL IBN AL-ʿASSĀL with the title *ṣafī al-dawlah;* (3) al-Asʿad Abū al-Faraj Hibat-Allāh ibn al-ʿAssāl; (4) al-Mu'taman Abū Isḥāq Ibrāhim ibn al-ʿAssāl, with the title *mu'taman al-dawlah;* (5) al-Amjad Abū al-Majd ibn al-ʿAssāl, who was secretary of the important *Diwan* (office) of the army. The last two were stepbrothers of the preceding two, who were described as full brothers.

The three literary figures in the list were al-Ṣafī, al-Asʿad, and al-Mu'taman. In spite of their apparent importance, knowledge of their lives will remain meager until further data are gleaned from their numerous works, the chief source for any study on Awlād/alʿAssāl. All lived approximately in the tumultuous first half of the thirteenth century, when Egypt resisted successive crusading attacks on its shores, culminating in the fall of Dumyāṭ (Damietta) in 1248 and the ultimate discomfiture and imprisonment of King Louis IX of France at the famous battle of Manṣūrah in 1250. The firm position of the Awlād al-ʿAssāl in the Ayyubid administration during those years reveals the loyalty of the Copts to the reigning dynasty and their hostility to the Crusades—a movement that aimed at their humiliation as being schismatics, and thus worse than heretics.

From a citation by their third stepbrother, both al-Ṣafī and al-Asʿad are known to have died before 1260. The major works of the three are believed to have been written approximately in the decade 1230–1240. All were men of great learning in both the humanities and the sciences. All were masters of Arabic style and, in addition, were well acquainted with Coptic, Greek, and Syriac.

Until Ayyubid times, Coptic was still in use as a national language throughout Egypt, though Arabic was becoming a serious menace to its survival. This situation resulted in the rise of a new class of scholars who concentrated on writing Coptic grammars in Arabic and compiled Copto-Arabic dictionaries to ensure the preservation of their ancestral tongue. The Awlād al-ʿAssāl distinguished themselves in this school, as may be witnessed from the enumeration of their works below. In addition to their excellence in Coptic philology, they made outstanding contributions to Coptic canon law, theology, philosophy, Christian polemics, homiletics, biblical studies, exegesis, and all manner of inquiry into their own religion.

The church must have meant a great deal to them, since, as archons or secular leaders of their community, they carried high the torch of reform at a moment when the partriarchate itself fell into the hands of the ungodly. The infamous CYRIL III (ibn Laqlaq) (1235–1243) occupied the throne of Saint Mark by treachery and flourished on simony, while buying royal support by bribery. Finally in

1239 the prelates of the church forced Cyril to convene a synod, probably at the Muʿallaqah, the Church of Our Lady in Old Cairo, which reviewed all ecclesiastical evils and prescribed a program of total reform. It is noteworthy that al-Ṣafī was the secretary of that synod and its moving spirit. The bishops commissioned him to compile what became the greatest and most enduring digest of Coptic canon law and tradition from all the ancient sources available. This tome was named after him as *al-Majmūʿ al-Ṣafawī*, which remains the most authoritative work in the field of canonical jurisprudence to this day.

The Awlād al-ʿAssāl's monumental contributions may be appraised from the number and nature of their known manuscripts. The Coptic Museum alone has forty-nine, besides many more that are found in European collections, including the Vatican, Florence, the Bodleian, the British Museum, the National Library in Paris, and numerous others, public and private, the most elaborate survey of which was compiled by G. Graf (1947).

In addition to their numerous religious and philological works they also wrote some good Arabic poetry, and the formulation of legal rules of inheritance. It may be deducted from the above that al-Ṣafī was the canonist and philosopher, al-As'ad the exegete and grammarian, and al-Mu'taman the theologian and philologist. Their legacy appears to represent the consummation of the Coptic culture in the Islamic Middle Ages, though our comprehension of the depth and breadth of their endeavor is still in its infancy.

BIBLIOGRAPHY

Graf G. "Die koptische Gelehrtenfamilie der Aulād al-ʿAssāl und ihr Schrifttum." *Orientalia* n.w. 1 (1932):34–56, 129–48, 193–204.

Higgins, A. J. B. *Ibn al-ʿAssāl." Journal of Theological Studies* 44 (1943):73–75.

Jirjis Philūthā'us ʿAwaḍ. *Al-Majmūʿ al-Ṣafawī*. Cairo, 1908.

Ladjnat al-Tarīkh al-Qibṭī Tarīkh al-Ummah al-Q ibtiyyah, 2nd ser., pp. 148–52. Cairo, 1925.

Mallon, A. "Ibn al-ʿAssāl, Les trois écrivains de ce nom." *Journal Asiatique* 10th ser. 6 (1905):509–29.

———. "Une Ecole de savants égyptiens au moyen âge." *Beyrouth Mélanges* 1 (1906):122ff.

Mikhā'īl al-Shiblanjī. *Khuṭab al-Shaykh al-Ṣafī ibn al-ʿAssal*. Cairo, 1878.

Renaudot, E. *Historia patriarcharum alexandrinorum*, pp. 585ff. Paris, 1713.

Rieu, C. *Supplement to the Catalogue of Arabic Manuscripts in the British Museum*, p. 18. London, 1894.

Vansleb, J. M. *Histoire de l'église copte d'Alexandrie*, pp. 335ff. Paris, 1677.

Yaʿqūb Nakhlah Rufaylah. *Tarīkh al-Ummah al-Qibṭiyyah*, p. 185. Cairo, 1889.

AZIZ S. ATIYA

AWSHIM. *See* Karanis.

AWSHIYAH, an ecclesiastical Arabic term sometimes pronounced *awkīyah* or *okiyah* (pl. *awāshī* or *awākī*') from the Greek *ευ'χή* meaning "recited prayer." These include a number of examples first from the evening and morning service of the raising of incense, recited inaudibly while the priest makes three circuits around the altar. These are the three small *awāshi* for the peace of the church, for the church fathers and the patriarch, and for the congregation. Other *awāshī* consist of what is known as the seven small and great *awāshī* after the Epiclesis in which additional prayers are made for the land and the waters, the seeds and the heavenly winds, the sick, the travelers, the king, the deceased faithful, and the catechumens. These prayers are to be reiterated in the services of holy baptism, of sanctification of the waters on the feast of Epiphany, of the foot washing on Maundy Thursday, and on the feast of Saints Peter and Paul.

BIBLIOGRAPHY

Burmester, O. H. E. *The Egyptian or Coptic Church*, pp. 320–41. Cairo, 1967.

Maher, E. *Kitāb al-Khūlāji al-Muqaddas* (in Coptic and Arabic). Cairo, 1902. (Many other editions.)

EMILE MAHER ISHAQ

AWSHIYAH, MELODIES OF. *See* Music, Coptic: Description of the Corpus and Present Musical Practice.

AWSĪM, a town located about 7.5 miles (12 km) northwest of Cairo in the Giza province. Ancient Egyptians knew the town as Khem. In Greek it was called Letopolis and in Coptic it was known as ⲃⲟⲩϣⲏⲙ (Boushem).

The town has a long Christian tradition. The martyr Phoibammon (see MARTYRS, COPTIC), who was killed in the early fourth century, hailed from Awsīm (O'Leary, 1974, pp. 229–31). By the eighth century Awsīm was a bishopric, as evidenced by a reference to a Bishop Jamūl (Shamul) Shamul of the town in the life of ALEXANDER II (705–730) recorded in the HISTORY OF THE PATRIARCHS.

BIBLIOGRAPHY

Amélineau, E. *La Géographie de l'Egypte à l'époque copte*, pp. 51–54. Paris, 1893.

Maspero, J., and G. Wiet. *Matériaux pour servir à la géographie de l'Egypte*, p. 231. Cairo, 1919.

O'Leary, de L. *The Saints of Egypt*. London and New York, 1937. Repr. Amsterdam, 1974.

RANDALL STEWART

AXUM. This small town in the Eritrean highlands (also spelled Aksum) was the earliest imperial capital of Ethiopia. Later it became, and it remains to this day, the most important center of Christian worship in the country.

The first historical mention of Axum is in the *Periplus of the Erythraean Sea*, a Greek navigator's guide to the Red Sea written in the first century A.D. The author describes the Red Sea port of Adulis (near modern Massawa), and states that "eight days' journey inland lay the metropolis of the Axumites" (sec. 4). The Axumite king, named Zoscales, was reported to be "noble and imbued with Greek education" (sec. 5). There was indeed a good deal of Greek influence in the early kingdom of Axum, as seen in its Greek-style coinage and in the Greek inscriptions left by some of its rulers. In the third and fourth centuries A.D., Axum extended its dominion over most of what is today Ethiopia and across the Red Sea into South Arabia.

One of the most active of Axumite rulers, Aezana, left commemorative stelae in three languages: Greek, the Sabaean language of South Arabia, and the native Ge'ez of Ethiopia. In his earlier stelae, Aezana attributes his military victories to the intervention of the Ethiopian god Mahrem (equivalent to Ares), but the last of the stelae begins and ends with Christian invocations. The latest coins of Aezana also have a cross on the reverse face, in place of the crescent and disk found on earlier Axumite coinage. From these facts one may infer that the Axumite ruler, and presumably his subjects, were converted to Christianity shortly before the year 350.

The story of Ethiopia's conversion is confirmed in most of its details by the Roman historian RUFINUS. He tells how two educated Greek youths, Aedesius and Frumentius, were kidnapped and taken to Axum, where in time they became great favorites of the reigning king. When the king died, they were made guardians and tutors of his infant son, Aezana, and in this role they began spreading the Christian faith within the country. When Aezana reached manhood, he allowed the brothers to go their ways, but Frumentius went to the patriarch of Alexandria with the request that he be allowed to return to Ethiopia as bishop-missionary. This was granted by the newly installed patriarch, ATHANASIUS I, and upon his return to Axum, Frumentius effected the official conversion of Aezana and of his subjects. Ethiopia was thus brought under the wing of the Alexandrian church, where it was to remain until 1958. Frumentius has come to be known in Ethiopian tradition as Abbā Salāmah (father of peace). (See SALAMA I, ABUNA.)

The power of Axum gradually weakened after the fifth century, in part because of continual involvement in the wars of South Arabia. However, one of the seventh-century rulers, Armah, gave sanctuary to some of the earliest followers of Muḥammad when they were temporarily driven from Arabia, and this was remembered with gratitude by the early Muslims. For a time Axum was exempted from the *dār al-harb*, the list of sanctioned military targets for Islamic conquest. Later, however, the nomadic BEJA TRIBES of the Red Sea littoral were converted to Islam, and it was these local enemies and erstwhile subjects of Axum who played a major role in the final weakening of the kingdom. The Axumite monarchy vanished into oblivion near the end of the tenth century, and power passed to another Ethiopian people, the Agau. "Encompassed on all sides by the enemies of their religion, the Aethiopians slept near a thousand years, forgetful of the world by which they were forgotten," as Edward Gibbon put it.

It was inevitable that Axum should become, after the conversion of Aezana, the most important center of Christian worship in Ethiopia. A tradition that must date from this time claims that Menelik I, the legendary son of Solomon and Sheba and founder of the Ethiopian empire, carried away the Tables of the Law when he left Jerusalem, and that they ultimately came to rest at Axum. Another tradition, possibly more historically accurate, tells how in the fifth century Axum became a place of asylum for the Nine Saints, learned Monophysite scholars who had been expelled from the Byzantine domains in

Syria. Supposedly it was they who brought the monastic tradition to Ethiopia and who translated the Greek scriptures into the native Ge'ez language. The names of the Nine Saints figure prominently in Ethiopian hagiography, and many monasteries are named for them.

The traditions of the Twelve Tables and of the Nine Saints were sufficient to assure that Axum would retain its religious importance long after its political eclipse. The Church of Saint Mary of Zion, built according to tradition in the year of Aezana's conversion, had the status of a kind of national cathedral. It was seen and described by the Portuguese missionary Alvares in the sixteenth century, but soon afterward was destroyed by the Muslim invader Aḥmad Gran. The present Church of Saint Mary, which occupies the same spot, was first built around 1665. It continues to enjoy the special status of its predecessor, and until the twentieth century nearly every Ethiopian emperor was crowned there. The ceremony was performed in the courtyard immediately in front of the cathedral, where a monolithic coronation throne can still be seen.

Although the original church has vanished, other antiquities of the Axumite period are numerous in and around the town. The most spectacular remains are the enormous stelae, sometimes called obelisks, that were erected by Axumite rulers and nobles of the pre-Christian era. At one time there were more than fifty of these, but many have fallen down and been partially destroyed. The great royal stelae are elaborately carved in the form of imitation "sky-scrapers," with a false door at ground level and lines of false windows at successively higher levels, culminating in a crescent-shaped capital at the top. The largest of them, now fallen, stood 110 feet (33 m) high and had thirteen stories. The tallest stela that is still standing is 70 feet (21 m) high, with ten stories. Recent excavation has disclosed very extensive tomb chambers beneath the stelae, though most of their contents have long since been removed by plunderers.

In a field near the town of Axum are the scattered blocks of a large stone monument. According to tradition it marked the tomb of Menelik I and his mother, the queen of Sheba, but its actual time of origin is unknown. Elsewhere is a large rock-cut cistern, presumably for irrigation, which has come to be known as the "bath of the queen of Sheba." Somewhat farther away in the hills behind Axum are the rock-cut tombs of the historically attested emperors Kaleb and Gabre Maskal, from the sixth century.

Excavations by a German expedition in 1906 uncovered the remains of three sumptuous palaces from the Axumite era. In 1958 a French expedition found the remains of a pre-Christian temple and of two very early churches, one in fifth-century Syrian style. The most recent excavations at Axum beneath the royal stelae were carried out by a British team in 1973 and 1974.

BIBLIOGRAPHY

Buxton, D. *The Abyssinians*, pp. 37–46, 89–97. New York, 1970.

Doresse, J. *Ethiopia*, pp. 26–89, 205–208. London, 1959.

Jäger, O. A. *Antiquities of North Ethiopia*, pp. 82–95. Stuttgart, 1965.

Jones, A. H. M., and E. Monroe. *A History of Ethiopia*, pp. 22–43. Oxford, 1955.

Littmann, E.; D. Krencker; and T. von Lüpke. *Deutsche Aksum-Expedition*, 5 vols. Berlin, 1913.

Monneret de Villard, U. *Aksum, ricerche di topografia generale*. Rome, 1938.

Ullendorff, E. *The Ethiopians*, pp. 47–57. London, 1960.

WILLIAM Y. ADAMS

'AYIN. *See Appendix.*

'AYN 'AMŪR. On the ancient track between the oasis of Kharjah and that of Dakhlah farther to the west, at the summit of an *'aqabah* (a rough and difficult ascent) that opens on to the plateau dominating the Kharjah depression, are the ruins of a Roman fortress and a pharaonic temple. They seem to have been occupied by hermits when they were abandoned, for one sees there some inscriptions and a cross. These were noted by the archaeologist who specialized in the oases (Fakhry, 1940, pp. 763–65; repr. 1942, pp. 192–93).

BIBLIOGRAPHY

Fakhry, A. "A Roman Temple Between Kharga and Dakhla." *Annales du Service des Antiquités de l''Egypte* 40 (1940):763–65 (the Coptic graffiti are edited by E. Driotan).

______. *Recent Explorations in the Oases of the Western Desert*. Cairo, 1942. Reprints of articles from *Annales du Service des antiquités de l'Egypte*, including the one above.

RENÉ-GEORGES COQUIN
MAURICE MARTIN, S.J.

ʿAYN BARDAH. *See* Monasteries of the Eastern Desert.

ʿAYN MURRAH. The site of ʿAyn Murrah, which means "bitter spring," is not marked on any map, and is known only from references in books. It is to the northeast of Barīs, halfway from the summit of the plateau, and hence in the region of the hermitages of the JABAL TAFNĪS, with which, however, it must not be confused. South of the spring are many walls in ruins. These were obviously hermitages, as is confirmed by Greco-Coptic inscriptions painted in red, and in particular a long list of fathers, among whom we may recognize Apa Moses, Apa Johannes, Apa John of Pake, Apa Hor, Apa Pimen, and others.

BIBLIOGRAPHY

Winkler, H. A. *Rock Drawings of Southern Upper Egypt,* p. 117, pl. 7. London, 1938–1939.

GUY WAGNER

ʿAYN NISIMAH. *See* Qasr Nisīmah.

AYYUBID DYNASTY AND THE COPTS.

The situation of the Coptic community in Egypt under the rule of the Ayyubid dynasty (1171–1250) was controlled by the progress of the Crusades and the Muslim reaction. With the death of the last Fatimid caliph, al-ʿĀḍid, on 25 September 1171, and the termination of Fatimid rule in Egypt, Saladin, a young Kurdish soldier who had gone to Egypt in the train of his uncle Shirkuh, was invested with the power of the state in Cairo, under the titular control of the Abbasid caliphate in Baghdad. On 15 May 1174, Nūr al-Dīn died in Syria, and Saladin was able to seize his throne. Saladin consequently became sultan of the whole area extending from Mosul to Aleppo in the north and Egypt in the south. In this way, Saladin extended his borders around the Latin Kingdom of Jerusalem, and confrontation with its forces became inevitable.

In Jerusalem, the Latin occupants, who were lenient with most of the Eastern Christian communities, took a rather different position with regard to the Orthodox Copts in Egypt, whom they considered heretics, and kept them away from the holy places. Thus, the Copts were forbidden the performance of pilgrimage to the Holy Sepulcher in Jerusalem, which they regarded as the fulfillment of their religious duties. Consequently, they looked forward to the liberation of the Holy City from Catholic occupation and watched the following events with the greatest of interest.

On 1 May 1187, Saladin defeated the Templars outside Nazareth and proceeded to lay siege to the important city of Tiberias. This proved to be the beginning of the end, since it led to the battle of Hittin, in which on 4 July 1187 he destroyed the crusading hosts beyond repair. With his triumph, the way to Jerusalem became clear. After a short siege of twelve days, on 2 October the Holy City surrendered. The chivalrous behavior of the sultan in his benevolent treatment of the departing Latin population contrasted with the massacre that attended the conquest of the city in 1099. This proved to be a welcome event for the Copts, who were allowed to resume their interrupted pilgrimage to the Holy Sepulcher.

Of course, Saladin's attitude toward the Copts was different from that of the majority of the tolerant Fatimid caliphs. In fact, his dismissal of Copts from his government on his accession could only be explained as a movement to rid the state of the vestiges of Fatimid influence in the administration rather than outright hatred for Coptic functionaries, who were replaced by other members of the same community. Furthermore, Saladin suppressed a number of subsidiary taxes that he had inherited from the Fatimids, and this must have pleased his subjects.

During reigns subsequent to that of Saladin, the Crusades were directed toward Egypt, as the key to the submission of the Holy Land. Consequently, two expeditions took place; one reached Damietta, and the other, al-Manṣūrah. The first was conducted by Jean de Brienne in the year 1218, and the other by Louis IX of France in 1249. Apparently Damietta had a considerable Coptic population that was strongly Melchite. This explains why they had ties with the Crusaders and spied for them. The result of this situation was a wave of hostility against the Copts that made no distinction between the Melchites and the Jacobites, and within Damietta and outside it massacres were carried out by both Christians and Muslims. That situation also provided the administrative authorities with a pretext for the levy of financial imposts on the Copts to help in the defense of the country. This movement extended to Alexandria, where the Ayyubid sultans decided to raze the Cathedral of Saint Mark, which overlooked the harbor and could furnish an invader with a fortified position in the city. This project was carried out in spite of the objections of the Copts, who to no avail offered a handsome ransom for saving it. The situation of the Copts in that decade became so precarious that word reached the Ethiopian emperor, Lalibella, who expressed his willingness to receive ten thousand refugees from the Coptic community in Egypt.

In 1249–1250, toward the end of Ayyubid rule, the Crusade of Saint Louis of France, aimed at the occupation of Damietta, which presented no problem, and the French forces penetrated the eastern Delta to the city of al-Manṣūrah. Here their progress was arrested, for the Egyptians opened the dikes of the Nile at a time of flood, and the French were marooned in an impassable pool of water. The king and his nobles virtually became prisoners and could gain freedom to leave Egypt only by payment of a heavy ransom. In the circumstances of the discomfiture of the Crusaders, it is doubtful whether the Copts fared as badly as in other situations, more especially as the administration of the sultanate was in a state of confusion and transition to Mamluk rule.

The idea that the Copts provided the Crusaders with a network of spies is not easy to confirm from the contemporary Arabic sources. It is true that such informants existed, but these were probably Melchites and Catholics. One name, however, is quoted by the author of *Aqbāṭ wa-Muslimūn*. This is Abū al-Faḍā'il ibn Dūkhan, whose surname appears to be foreign to the native Jacobite Copts.

BIBLIOGRAPHY

Atiya, A. S. *Crusade, Commerce and Culture.* Bloomington, Ind., and Oxford, 1962.

Lane-Poole, S. *A History of Egypt in the Middle Ages.* London, 1901.

Runciman, S. *A History of the Crusades,* 3 vols. Cambridge, 1951–1954.

Tajir, J. *Aqbāṭ wa-Muslimūn Mundhu al-Fatḥ al-Arabi ilā ʿām.* Cairo, 1951.

Wiet, G. "L'Egypte arabe." In *History de la nation egyptienne,* Vol. 4, ed. G. Hanotaun. Paris, 1931–1940.

AZIZ S. ATIYA

AZARĪ, medieval town in the province of Gharbiyyah. Administrative documents of the time situate it in an area called at that time Jazīrat Banī Naṣr, stretching eastward from the Rosetta branch of the Nile, slightly southwest of Minūf, and from Niqiyūs in the south as far as Qulayb Ibyār in the north. It was called "the island of the Banī Naṣr" because of a canal, al-Bājūriyyah, which bounded its territory to the east and made it, as it were, an island (Guest, 1912, p. 959 and map). M. Ramzī (1953–1963, Vol. 1, p. 19) thinks that this small town has disappeared but that its site is today occupied by the village called Kafr al-Bājah in the *markaz* (district) of Kafr al-Zayyāt. Azarī was not, therefore, very far from Ibyār.

The life of the patriarch CHRISTODOULOS states that toward the end of his life he wrote to the new patriarch of Antioch, John XI (1075–c. 1095). John replied through the intermediary of a native of Jerusalem, a Syrian priest called Samuel, who became a recluse in a hermitage at Azarī, although some manuscripts have Ararī (Sāwīrus ibn al-Muqaffaʿ, Vol. 2, pt. 3, pp. 206 [text], 319 [trans.]). Later, some bishops proposed this same recluse Samuel, who was living in the hermitage of Azarī, as successor to CYRIL II in 1093, but he was set aside because of his unorthodox opinions (ibid., pp. 234 [text], 372 [trans.]).

It does seem that this Samuel may be the Samuel bar Cyriacus who was copyist of five Syriac manuscripts, written between 1081 and 1102, that came from the DAYR AL-SURYĀN and are today preserved in the British Museum in London (Wright, 1870–1872, Vol. 1, pp. 52, 160–61, 181; Vol. 2, pp. 606, 913–14, 1021). In the colophons he presents himself as a native of the eastern town of Maʿdan and describes himself sometimes as a priest and Stylite and sometimes as a priest and recluse "in the island which is in the region of Alexandria and Miṣr" and once "in the island of Niqiyūs." Evelyn-White had understood *begazarta* to be a place near Alexandria, but it is much more likely that it must be understood as *bi-jazīrat* (the island—i.e., of Banī Naṣr), where indeed Niqiyūs was situated.

Slightly later, the patriarch MACARIUS II resided in this place "Azarī, in the Jazīrat Banī Naṣr" (Sāwīrus ibn al-Muqaffaʿ, Vol. 3, pt. 1, pp. 7 [text], 12 [trans.]). With the evidence of this last witness, it is certainly necessary to correct the strange opinion of Evelyn-White: "The 'Cell at Adari' [Azarī] . . . is perhaps the Syrian Monastery itself" (1932, p. 363).

After the just-cited mention of Azarī in the *History*

of the Patriarchs, no other is to be read, and it is noticeable that the twelfth-century chronicler Abū al-Makārim makes no allusion to it.

BIBLIOGRAPHY

Evelyn-White, H. G. *The History of the Monasteries of Nitria and Scetis.* New York, 1932.
Guest, R. "The Delta in the Middle Ages." *Journal of the Royal and Asiatic Society,* n.s. 42 (1912):941–80.
Meinardus, O. F. A. *Christian Egypt, Ancient and Modern,* 2nd ed., pp. 235–37. Cairo, 1977. (Several details are incorrect.)
Ramzī, M. *Al-Qāmūs al-Jughrāfī lil-Bilād al-Miṣrīyyah,* 2 vols. in 5 pts. Cairo, 1953–1963.
Wright, W. *Catalogue of the Syriac Manuscripts in the British Museum.* London, 1870–1872.

René-Georges Coquin
Maurice Martin, S.J.